Categorization by Humans and Machines

Categorization by Humans and Machines

Edited by **Glenn V. Nakamura** and **Douglas L. Medin**

Roman Taraban

Department of Psychology
Texas Tech University
Lubbock, Texas

Department of Psychology
Northwestern University
Evanston, Illinois

THE PSYCHOLOGY OF
LEARNING AND MOTIVATION, VOLUME 29
Advances in Research and Theory

ACADEMIC PRESS, INC.
A Division of Harcourt Brace & Company

San Diego   New York   Boston   London
Sydney   Tokyo   Toronto

This book is printed on acid-free paper. ∞

Academic Press, Inc.
1250 Sixth Avenue, San Diego, California 92101-4311

United Kingdom Edition published by
Academic Press Limited
24–28 Oval Road, London NW1 7DX

International Standard Serial Number: 0079-7421

International Standard Book Number: 0-12-543329-8

PRINTED IN THE UNITED STATES OF AMERICA
93 94 95 96 97 98 BC 9 8 7 6 5 4 3 2 1

CONTENTS

INTRODUCTION: A COUPLING OF DISCIPLINES IN CATEGORIZATION RESEARCH

Roman Taraban

PART I

MODELS OF DATA-DRIVEN CATEGORY LEARNING AND PROCESSING

MODELS OF CATEGORIZATION AND CATEGORY LEARNING

W. K. Estes

THREE PRINCIPLES FOR MODELS OF CATEGORY LEARNING

John K. Kruschke

EXEMPLAR MODELS AND WEIGHTED CUE MODELS IN CATEGORY LEARNING

Roman Taraban and Joaquin Marcos Palacios

THE ACQUISITION OF CATEGORIES MARKED BY MULTIPLE PROBABILISTIC CUES

Janet L. McDonald

PART II

DATA-DRIVEN AND THEORY-DRIVEN PROCESSING AND PROCESSING MODELS

PROCESSING BIASES, KNOWLEDGE, AND CONTEXT IN CATEGORY FORMATION

Thomas B. Ward

CATEGORIZATION AND RULE INDUCTION IN CLINICAL DIAGNOSIS AND ASSESSMENT

Gregory H. Mumma

A RATIONAL THEORY OF CONCEPTS

Gregory L. Murphy

PART III

CONCEPTS, CATEGORY BOUNDARIES, AND CONCEPTUAL COMBINATION

CONCEPT STRUCTURE AND CATEGORY BOUNDARIES

Barbara C. Malt

NON-PREDICATING CONCEPTUAL COMBINATIONS

Edward J. Shoben

EXPLORING INFORMATION ABOUT CONCEPTS BY ASKING QUESTIONS

Arthur C. Graesser, Mark C. Langston, and
William B. Baggett

HIDDEN KIND CLASSIFICATIONS

Edward Wilson Averill

IS COGNITION CATEGORIZATION?

Timothy J. van Gelder

WHAT ARE CONCEPTS? ISSUES OF REPRESENTATION AND ONTOLOGY

William F. Brewer

CONTRIBUTORS

Numbers in parentheses indicate the pages on which the authors' contributions begin.

Edward Wilson Averill, Department of Philosophy, Texas Tech University, Lubbock, Texas 79409 (437)

William B. Baggett, Departments of Psychology and Mathematical Sciences and Institute for Intelligent Systems, Memphis State University, Memphis, Tennessee 38152 (411)

Ray Bareiss, The Institute for the Learning Sciences, Northwestern University, Evanston, Illinois 60201 (157)

William F. Brewer, Department of Psychology, University of Illinois at Urbana-Champaign, Champaign, Illinois 61820 (495)

W. K. Estes, Department of Psychology, Harvard University, Cambridge, Massachusetts 02138 (15)

Douglas Fisher, Department of Computer Science, Vanderbilt University, Nashville, Tennessee 37235 (219)

Arthur C. Graesser, Departments of Psychology and Mathematical Sciences and Institute for Intelligent Systems, Memphis State University, Memphis, Tennessee 38152 (411)

John K. Kruschke, Department of Psychology and Cognitive Science Program, Indiana University, Bloomington, Indiana 47405 (57)

Mark C. Langston, Department of Psychology, Memphis State University, Memphis, Tennessee 38152 (411)

Barbara C. Malt, Department of Psychology, Lehigh University, Bethlehem, Pennsylvania 18015 (363)

Janet L. McDonald, Department of Psychology, Louisiana State University, Baton Rouge, Louisiana 70803 (129)

Raymond J. Mooney, Department of Computer Sciences, University of Texas at Austin, Austin, Texas 78712 (189)

Gregory H. Mumma, Department of Psychology, Texas Tech University, Lubbock, Texas 79409 (283)

Gregory L. Murphy, Beckman Institute, University of Illinois at Urbana-Champaign, Urbana, Illinois 61801 (327)

Joaquin Marcos Palacios, Department of Computer Science, Texas Tech University, Lubbock, Texas 79409 (91)

Edward J. Shoben, Department of Psychology, University of Illinois at Urbana-Champaign, Champaign, Illinois 61820 (391)

Brian M. Slator, The Institute for the Learning Sciences, Northwestern University, Evanston, Illinois 60201 (157)

Roman Taraban, Department of Psychology, Texas Tech University, Lubbock, Texas 79409 (1, 91)

Timothy J. van Gelder, Department of Philosophy, Indiana University, Bloomington, Indiana 47405 (469)

Thomas B. Ward, Department of Psychology, Texas A&M University, College Station, Texas 77843 (257)

Jungsoon Park Yoo, Department of Computer Science, Middle Tennessee State University, Murfreesboro, Tennessee 37132 (219)

PREFACE

Earlier work on category structure and categorization emphasized the notion of characteristic features. That work called into question the "classical view," in which categories were defined by necessary and sufficient features, and replaced it with a view in which features had only a probabilistic relationship to concepts and categories. In some models, categories were defined by prototypes that abstracted and summarized independent featural information from instances. Category membership was determined by considering how similar an item was to category prototypes. According to other models, abstraction was not necessary, nor were prototypes. Rather, memory for instances was considered essential, and mathematical approaches were developed for expressing category membership as a function of the similarity of an item to stored instances of a category. While these findings were important, questions in many areas were still unanswered. First, these models were not process models. Issues surrounding the details of processing, representation, and learning needed further development and refinement in terms of working mechanisms. Second, it was not evident why concepts and categories included the features that they did: By definition, category members are similar in some way, but this says little about how a person (or machine) might select the features on which to base those similarity/equivalence relations.

Current experimental and theoretical work on concepts and categories has led to discoveries that help to answer questions in both areas. First, the development of machine learning models in psychology and in computer science has provided detailed learning mechanisms. These include versions of neural-style "connectionist" models (see articles by Estes, Kruschke, Taraban & Palacios, and McDonald) as well as more traditional symbol-based AI models (see articles by Bareiss & Slator, Mooney, and Fisher & Yoo). Issues in the second area have been addressed by work that has emphasized the role of background knowledge in category formation. According to this view, the selection of category features is guided by relevant background knowledge available to the learner (human or machine) (see articles by Mooney, Fisher & Yoo, Ward, Mumma, and Murphy). In the present volume there is an emphasis on learning and processing mechanisms and the role of background knowledge, as already indicated. Additionally, there is a theoretical and experimental examination of the contents of concepts and categories (see articles by Malt; Shoben; Graesser, Langston, & Baggett; Averill; van Gelder; and Brewer).

In this special volume in *The Psychology of Learning and Motivation* series we provide a forum for the presentation of new developments in machine learning and experimental psychology on the topics of categories and concepts. The prospect of a productive convergence of ideas from computer science and psychology gave us much of the incentive to produce this book. It is noteworthy that many of the authors strive to uncover details of the cognitive representations underlying concepts and categories, and they endeavor to specify details of the mechanisms that could account for concept and category formation and processing. Although we admit that it is still too early to say what a complete and sufficient mechanism would look like, we suggest that the articles make a significant contribution in the right direction.

This work was supported by the Army Research Institute for Behavioral and Social Sciences under the auspices of the U.S. Army Research Office Scientific Services Program administered by Battelle (Delivery Order 2690, Contract DAAL03-86-D-0001). The views, opinions, and/or findings contained in this volume are those of the authors and should not be construed as official Department of the Army positions, policies, or decisions. Additional support was provided by the College of Arts and Sciences, the

Department of Psychology, and the John Harvey endowment of Texas Tech University.

We gratefully acknowledge the assistance of Dr. Michael Drillings and Dr. George Lawton, of the Army Research Institute, and of Dr. Philip H. Marshall of the Department of Psychology at Texas Tech. They provided the basic support and direction that made this book a reality. Dr. William Brewer, Dr. Douglas Fisher, Dr. Arthur Graesser, and Dr. Douglas Medin provided early comments on our ideas for a book and for its organization and content. We heartily thank Dr. Medin for his tireless efforts in helping us, as guest editors of this series, to produce a volume of the highest quality. There are many others who deserve our thanks. Among them are Dr. Kathleen Harris and the Office of Research Services of Texas Tech University and Nikki Fine and Jean Mayer of Academic Press. Graduate students in our psychology program who helped with various facets of this project are Gregory Liddell, Sandra Pennington, Bret Roark, Sharon Robinson, and James Worthen. A number of our colleagues helped also: Dr. Robert Bell, Dr. Dennis Cogan, Dr. Patricia DeLucia, Dr. Jeffrey Elias, Dr. Susan Hendrick, Dr. C. Steven Richards, and Dr. Jane Winer.

Roman Taraban
Glenn V. Nakamura

INTRODUCTION: A COUPLING OF DISCIPLINES IN CATEGORIZATION RESEARCH

Roman Taraban

I. Introduction

Theoretical and experimental work on concepts and categories is progressing quickly in a number of related disciplines, particularly in experimental psychology and within that area of computer science research dealing with machine learning. Admittedly, the goals of these two disciplines generally differ in basic ways, regardless of the topic. Machine learning models often set out to accomplish a practical engineering purpose, like evolving an expert system (see ORCA in Bareiss & Slator, this volume). Experimental psychology, on the other hand, is committed to revealing aspects of human cognition and behavior. Computer simulation models developed within this discipline typically test a set of ideas (a theory) that is meant to explain human performance. In spite of this apparent discrepancy between these disciplines, historically both have influenced each other in a positive way. Work in machine learning has produced as a by-product models or components of models that have been useful to cognitive/experimental psychology. Work in cognitive/experimental psychology has set problems (goals) for machine learning research and has suggested new approaches (as in the area of early vision and speech recognition). In this volume we seek the common ground—the issues and ideas—currently shared by both machine learning and experimental psychology on the topics of categories and concepts. Our purpose

1

is to provide an informed presentation of timely issues and discoveries in both areas, to bring out the commonalities and differences in ongoing work, and to set the stage for further productive interaction between these disciplines.

Three topics play a central role in the book. The first two reflect recent developments that are likely to have a continuing impact on current and forthcoming work on concepts and categories in both psychology and machine learning: the development and testing of connectionist categorization models, and a growing interest in how two factors—background knowledge and exposure to instances—contribute to category learning and processing. The third topic has to do with more basic questions about the contents of concepts, conceptual combinations, and categories. In the next section, I provide a more detailed presentation of these topics. Following that, I point out some of the insights and challenges that emerge from these chapters and also note some promising directions for the future.

II. Overview of the Chapters

A. DATA-DRIVEN MODELS

In this volume, *data-driven* refers to models that construct their internal representation of a category either from stored instances (exemplars) of the category or from stored features or clusters of features, derived from instances, that are associated with the category. In order to provide a high degree of experimental control, data-driven models have often been tested using artificial categories (see Estes, this volume; Kruschke, this volume; McDonald, this volume; Taraban & Palacios, this volume). These controlled tests have led to a concise understanding of category learning and generalization to new instances. Insights from experiments with this class of models have extended beyond the experimental laboratory to real-world domains, like medical diagnosis (Bareiss & Slator, this volume), clinical diagnosis and assessment (Mumma, this volume), and natural language processing (McDonald, this volume).

Connectionist models are a type of data-driven model. These models consist of neural-style computational mechanisms that dynamically change their internal representations through experience. Research with these models has often emphasized human learning, in contrast to the approach of much past work in categorization research that included a learning phase but focused on the analysis of test and transfer items, ignoring the dynamic changes in the underlying representations that were being learned. In shifts away from the view that there are necessary and sufficient features that determine category membership (Smith & Medin, 1981; Estes, this volume; Malt, this volume; McDonald, this volume), connectionist models have gained prominence. This is because they have been able to show how category membership might be learned when the features of the category members do not allow for clearcut classification rules.

Within a connectionist model, processing units are linked to each other using adjustable weights and are organized into layers (or clusters). We can refer to the overall organization of the layers of units as the "architecture" of the network. Each chapter on connectionist models addresses roughly four basic questions and answers the questions somewhat differently. The questions are: (1) What does a unit in the network represent? (2) How are units activated? (3) What is the architecture of the network? and (4) How are weights changed within the particular architecture? Kruschke's ALCOVE model encodes *exemplars* in an *n*-dimensional psychological space. Exemplar representations in an internal layer of the network are activated through *attentional weights* associated with features of the input. One of Taraban and Palacios's models stores representations of exemplars in an internal layer and activates them using a fuzzy conjunctive (AND) operation. In a "standard" back propagation model with three layers of units (input, hidden, output), contiguous layers are fully interconnected and the internal units are allowed to set up their own representations of the inputs. In all three of these models, the weights connecting the input to the internal representations and the weights connecting the internal representations to category labels are modified as learning proceeds. Estes' hybrid model (SimNet) uses a *memory array* representation to store exemplars and connects these representations to category labels through weights that are adjusted with learning. McDonald describes a *dominance hierarchy* that prioritizes input "cues" to reflect their relative importance in category decisions. All of these models include some version of a learning rule that changes weights in order to reduce the error in the network. The error is computed from a feedback signal that is provided to the network.

Part of the motivation for much of the connectionist research in this volume has come from an interest in the implications of influential mathematical formulations for categorization, particularly those of Medin and Schaffer (1978) and Nosofsky (1984, 1986). The articles in this volume show that connectionist network models provide a tractable environment in which to implement, explore, and extend these mathematical models, which are in themselves static, not dynamic like the networks that incorporate them. In general, this research is in its early stages but has nonetheless yielded important insights into the properties of these networks, as discussed in detail in Part I.

B. DATA-DRIVEN AND KNOWLEDGE-DRIVEN MODELS

Category research in psychology has tended to focus on the relationship between perceptible features of objects and category membership. This includes work with connectionist models (e.g., MacWhinney, Leinbach, Taraban, & McDonald, 1989; McClelland & Rumelhart, 1985), as well as research with other models, like cue validity models, distance models, and prototype models (e.g. Beach, 1964; Posner & Keele, 1968; Reed, 1972; Rosch, 1978; Rosch & Mervis, 1975). As Mooney (this volume) points out, a nearly exclusive emphasis on empirical, data-driven models also describes much of the work that has been done in machine learning. While continued work on data-driven models remains important, the focus of many researchers is shifting away from simple data-driven processing.

Under the emerging view, there are two sources of influence on concept formation and categorization. One of these is the background knowledge already in the system (human or machine). The other source consists of features of the instances or descriptions presented to the system as examples of a concept or category. I refer to these instances here, as I did in the previous section, as the *data*. Neisser (1987) has encapsulated this development in the assertion that "categories are never defined by objective similarity alone" and the further qualification that the perceptual similarity of objects nevertheless plays a critical role in categorization. This position has been discussed in a number of places, particularly by Murphy and Medin (Medin, 1989; Murphy, 1992; Murphy & Medin, 1985). Put simply, it means that there is a connection between perceptual features and members of cognitive categories, as has been assumed all along by psychologists working on data-driven categorization and by (at least some) philosophers and computer scientists. But this can only be part of the story. The features that end up being important are at least partly selected through the influence of background knowledge of various degrees of sophistication. There is rarely a case of pure data-driven categorization in the real world, according to this view. Contributors to this section explore the ways in which data and background knowledge interact, in cognitive models (Mumma, this volume; Murphy, this volume; Ward, this volume), and in machine models (Fisher & Yoo, this volume; Mooney, this volume).

Ward (this volume) looks carefully at preschoolers' reliance on *shape* information in learning about categories. Overall, his results suggest that preschoolers rely no less on background knowledge than adults do (cf.

Nakamura, 1985; Wattenmaker, Nakamura, & Medin, 1987; Wisniewski & Medin, 1991). First, children and adults let background knowledge direct and constrain the processing of instances. Their knowledge focuses their attention either toward or away from particular attributes of the stimuli and thus guides their formation of categories. Part of what background knowledge does (in machines and in humans) is to provide *explanations* for why certain features are important for category membership and others are not. Second, preschoolers are not rigid in applying their knowledge. When they learn about substances, for instance, they focus on attributes other than shape, recognizing that shape is not particularly relevant. This is important, since children do have a shape bias but are flexible in how shape information is used. When functional considerations are relevant, as when objects have wheels, children naturally exploit those characteristics of the stimuli, again demonstrating the knowledge-driven nature of their categorizations.

Many of the arguments emphasizing the importance of background knowledge have been based on experimental data. Ward's article is one example. Although these arguments have been convincing, there have been few proposals for mechanisms that could coordinate background knowledge and new data. Mooney (this volume) and Fisher and Yoo (this volume) make distinctive contributions on this topic. These authors are computer scientists who provide machine models for the interaction of background knowledge and data. The major topics of psychological interest that are developed and modeled in Fisher and Yoo are problem-solving and the development of expertise. They use empirical work from psychology (e.g Chi, Feltovich, & Glaser, 1981; Larkin, 1981; Koedinger & Anderson, 1990) to ground their models on plausible psychological processes. Mooney presents two machine models for integrating background knowledge and instances, and he accounts for a body of experimental data collected in independent experiments with adults (Ahn & Brewer, 1988; Wisniewski, 1989; Wisniewski & Medin, 1991) with a notable degree of qualitative success.

C. Concepts, Category Boundaries, and Conceptual Combination

What sort of information is contained in concepts? This question gets asked in a number of different ways. Malt (this volume) considers artifacts, like boats, and natural kinds, like water, and asks whether these concepts contain a core property or essence that determine concept boundaries. She concludes that cognitive representations of these have neither. While it is true that a boat, for instance, has the function of carrying one or more people over a body of water for purposes of work or recreation, this is not a core property of a "boat." Neither do natural kinds, like "water," have an essence—such as containing H_2O. Instead, Malt emphasizes the "fuzzy" nature of category boundaries and the *flexibility* with which factors external to the concept itself can influence categorization. Two such external factors are manufacturers' labeling of products and historical connections. As an example of the former, *soda water* is more likely to be considered a type of "water" than *club soda,* even though they contain the same ingredients. Regarding historical connections, people are more willing to accept an unusual example of a category if the example is placed in a future time period. The notion of flexibility presented here is related to Ward's claim of flexibility in preschoolers, specifically in that both derive from the application of background factors to the task of finding the boundaries of a concept or category. In neither case can category boundaries be easily predicted directly from the available features of the objects themselves.

Averill (this volume), who is a philosopher, argues for a particular variant of "psychological essentialism," specifically, for a view that allows for essential properties for natural kinds (like water), biological kinds (like dogs), and functional kinds (like hammers), and that also insists on the importance of these essences to cognitive representation. The gist of his argument is that in spite of what psychological studies (like Malt's) may indicate, the goals and behaviors of a lot of people would be hard to explain unless, for instance, gold had an atomic number of 79 and either a person knew what that meant in the context of a coherent scientific theory (the expert) or at least knew but could not explain that fact (the non-expert). What Averill's analysis suggests is that there may be scientific theories that people hold in common. For certain categories, like natural kinds, there may be defining features for category members. To the extent that this is true, Malt's results, in my view, suggest that any necessary and defining features that may be present are in competition with other features that may in fact appear more important to a subject (cf. MacWhinney, 1989). Thus, Malt's subjects judged *drinking water* to be a more typical example of "water" than *purified water* even though the latter is closer to pure H_2O based on subjects' own accounts.

Graesser, Langston, and Baggett (this volume) examine concept formation and concept boundaries using an information search task. They show that the questions a person asks in order to gain information depends on the specific goals in the task. To use their examples, if the goal is to assemble a band for a party, the questions one asks about musical instruments will be different than if one has the task of designing a new musical instrument. Shoben (this volume) considers another aspect of concept formation which has to do with how simpler concepts combine to form more complex concepts, like "horse rash." His results show that conceptual combination is a flexible process. One clear effect in his findings that supports this conclusion is the influence of prior context on the interpretation that is selected for an ambiguous phrase like *horse rash*. Part III of the book also includes a historical summary of concept representations within psychology as well as in other disciplines (Brewer) and a consideration of how much of cognition one could reasonably expect to explain with processes like pattern matching and categorization (van Gelder).

III. A Uniform Basis for Model Development

The authors in this volume communicate a sense of the high level of research activity on categorization in their respective areas of interest. This comes through partly in the iterative refinement of models. Estes considers memory array models as well as connectionist models for category learning and tentatively settles on a hybrid solution. Taraban and Palacios demonstrate the viability of "standard" back propagation learning for accounting for human category learning but then extend the back propagation method to a distinctively different exemplar-based architecture. Bareiss and Slator begin by presenting an expert system (Protos) that operates effectively on well-specified problems but then extend this model to deal with ill-structured problems (ORCA). Mooney describes a learning model, IOU, that uses background knowledge to bias the construction of a category definition and then extends this approach in EITHER to allow for the revision of background knowledge when that knowledge is incomplete or imperfect. Fisher and Yoo present COBWEB, which is a data-driven model, and then significantly extend the processing approach in COBWEB in a new model, EXOR, that integrates background knowledge and data. Is this very active work in model development within psychology and machine learning, as well as related experimental work, coming together? I think that it is, as evidenced in the way researchers are paying attention to activity in related disciplines and working in tandem with developments in relevant areas. I can suggest two ways in which this interchange might be increased: (1) establishing a common set of model-theoretic principles, and (2) finding a common language for both approaches. These suggestions are largely speculative but seem to me to be useful for understanding and advancing beyond the current studies.

A. SEARCHING FOR COMMON PRINCIPLES

One goal of model development is to account for data that earlier models could not account for. But are there constraints on models beyond those provided by a set of data? I suggest that one set of constraints may come in the form of model-theoretic principles. Kruschke (this volume) makes the most explicit case for this possibility. As he suggests, on the surface, models that look different may turn out to be equivalent. The conditions of equivalence are specified by a set of underlying processing principles. Kruschke's analysis of the relevant principles for categorization models is borne out in research that he has conducted as well as in work reported in Estes (this volume), Taraban & Palacios (this volume), and (partly) McDonald (this volume). While these principles work for data-driven models, one would want to ask how they fare with models that incorporate data and background knowledge. Here we are left with an open question— to my mind a very interesting open question. Fisher and Yoo (this volume), for instance, implement a measure of *category utility* (cf. Corter & Gluck, 1992) which balances the within-category similarity of category members against their between-category similarity. This seems consonant with Kruschke's principles but is not identical to anything that he claims. Mooney (this volume) implements yet other methods of computing item similarity in the inductive (data-based) phase of category learning. Should the same principles apply here as in other data-driven models?

Beyond these clear cases where principles may carry over from data-driven models to aspects of models that incorporate data and background knowledge, it is not evident at this stage what additional principles might be required in order to accommodate the interactive effects in this latter class of models. Working these out would help to inform the continuing development of data-driven models and models incorporating data and background knowledge and to more fully engage the insights from both lines of work.

B. SEARCHING FOR A COMMON LANGUAGE FOR CONNECTIONISM AND TRADITIONAL ARTIFICIAL INTELLIGENCE

The development of connectionist principles in data-driven models has advanced independently of the development of models that incorporate background knowledge and data. A comparison of representations in the two types of models—those in Parts I and II of the book—shows that they are characteristically different. Representations in connectionist models exhibit continuous levels of activation, and the current state of the model is represented by patterns of activation in various parts of the network. In contrast, the models in Part II (i.e., Fisher & Yoo; Mooney) have discrete, symbolic representations. Fisher and Yoo's EXOR model, for instance, searches a *problem space* for a solution. The representation of states in this problem space consists of partial schemas (concepts), and the space itself is organized as an *abstraction hierarchy*. Mooney's models either derive a specialized rule or modify background knowledge, both of which are represented using general propositions. The concept "cup," for example, is represented as: "has-bottom & flat-bottom & lightweight & . . . → cup."

One way to bring these two approaches into closer communication might be by combining the two types of representation into a model in which the activation patterns from distributed connectionist networks project their outputs to a symbolic *representation plane* (Estes, 1988). Another possibility is to find a representation that could more directly exploit the "fuzziness" embodied in the activation of processing units in a connectionist model but that could be operated on logically at the level of symbols. In the work of Oden (1988, 1992) on *fuzzy propositions* in connectionist networks and in the work of Williams (1986) on fuzzy Boolean functions, we find possible candidates for such an intermediate representation.[1] Adopting either one of these combined connectionist/symbolic schemes could produce a number of tangible benefits. It might, for example, allow the application of principles of parallel activation and competition inherent in connectionist networks to machine models that incorporate data and background knowledge. Further, the principles being tested in data-driven models could more easily be considered in data- and knowledge-driven models. In general, it could allow researchers to exploit the advantages of both types of representation. Although the outcome cannot be known in advance, it seems that examining models with connectionist/symbolic representations could pay off.

IV. A Coupling of Disciplines

Our goal in this volume was to focus on current issues in research on concepts and categories, to present the methods being applied to these issues in psychology and machine learning, and to allow the reader to glean from these papers a sense of where the field currently stands and what issues seem especially promising for ongoing research. I believe that all the contributors have made a laudable contribution toward those goals and, particularly, to the exchange of ideas across disciplines.

---

[1] For an extensive bibliography of connectionist models with symbolic processing, see Appendix A in Sun and Bookman (1993).

In surveying developments in psychology and machine learning, one gets a real sense of the emerging interest in background knowledge. From one perspective, this might be viewed as just an interest in "top-down" processing effects. Currently, though, this label would not be all that satisfying or informative. There is a determination among current researchers to build and test models that spell out the "top-down" and "bottom-up" factors and the ways in which they interact.

Part of the importance of the work of Fisher and Yoo and of Mooney (this volume) is that it incorporates a cross-disciplinary focus. Indeed, it is Fisher and Yoo's view that the relationship between psychology and artificial intelligence (AI) should go beyond a "loose coupling of disciplines" in which psychology provides a specification of various intelligent behaviors and AI provides the means of implementing those specifications. Rather, AI models of intelligence need to make predictions about unexplored or poorly understood phenomena and to suggest areas for further psychological research. Fisher and Yoo and Mooney do succeed in both of the suggested ways, modeling some rough specifications provided in the psychological literature but also suggesting new ways in which to extend and further test insights into psychological processes and representations. This stands in my mind as a promising exemplar of forthcoming work that crosses disciplinary lines.

ACKNOWLEDGMENTS

This chapter is based in part on work supported by the Texas Advanced Research Program under Grant No. 0216-44-5829. I would like to especially thank Bill Estes and Doug Medin for comments on earlier versions of this article. I also thank Bill Brewer, Philip H. Marshall, Janet McDonald, and Greg Murphy.

REFERENCES

Ahn, W., & Brewer, W. (1988). Similarity-based and explanation-based learning of explanatory and nonexplanatory information. In *Proceedings of the Tenth Annual Conference of the Cognitive Science Society* (pp. 524–530). Hillsdale, NJ: Erlbaum.

Beach, L. (1964). Cue probabilism and inference behavior. *Psychological Monographs, 78,* 21–37.

Chi, M., Feltovich, P., & Glaser, R. (1981). Categorization and the representation of physics problems by experts and novices. *Cognitive Science, 5,* 121–152.

Corter, J., & Gluck, M. (1992). Explaining basic categories: feature predictability and information. *Psychological Bulletin, 111,* 291–303.

Estes, W. K. (1988). Toward a framework for combining connectionist and symbol-processing models. *Journal of Memory and Language, 27,* 196–212.

Koedinger, K., & Anderson, J. R. (1990). Abstract planning and perceptual chunks: Elements of expertise in geometry. *Cognitive Science, 14,* 511–550.

Larkin, J. (1981). Enriching formal knowledge: A model for learning to solve textbook physics problems. In J. R. Anderson (Ed.), *Cognitive skills and their acquisition* (pp. 311–334). Hillsdale, NJ: Erlbaum.

MacWhinney, B. (1989). Competition and lexical categorization. In R. Corrigan, F. Eckman, & M. Noonan (Eds.), *Linguistic categorization* (pp. 195–242). Philadelphia: Benjamins.

MacWhinney, B., Leinbach, J., Taraban, R., & McDonald, J. (1989). Language learning: Cues or rules? *Journal of Memory and Language, 28*, 255–277.

McClelland, J., & Rumelhart, D. (1985). Distributed memory and the representation of general and specific information. *Journal of Experimental Psychology: General, 114*, 159–188.

Medin, D. (1989). Concepts and conceptual structure. *American Psychologist, 44*, 1469–1481.

Medin, D., & Schaffer, M. (1978). Context theory of classification learning. *Psychological Review, 85*, 207–238.

Murphy, G. (1992). Theories and concept formation. In I. Van Mechelen, J. Hampton, R. Michalski, & P. Theuns (Eds.), *Categories and concepts: Theoretical views and inductive data analysis* (pp. 173–200). London: Academic Press.

Murphy, G., & Medin, D. (1985). The role of theories in conceptual coherence. *Psychological Review, 92*, 289–316.

Nakamura, G. (1985). Knowledge-based classification of ill-defined categories. *Memory & Cognition, 13*, 377–384.

Neisser, U. (1987). Preface. In U. Neisser (Ed.), *Concepts and conceptual development: Ecological and intellectual factors in categorization* (pp. vii–ix). New York: Cambridge University Press.

Nosofsky, R. (1984). Choice, similarity, and the context theory of classification. *Journal of Experimental Psychology: Learning, Memory, and Cognition, 10*, 104–114.

Nosofsky, R. (1986). Attention, similarity, and the identification–categorization relationship. *Journal of Experimental Psychology: General, 115*, 39–57.

Oden, G. (1988). FuzzyProp: A symbolic superstrate for connectionist models. In *Proceedings of the IEEE International Conference on Neural Networks: Vol. 1* (pp. 293–300).

Oden, G. (1992). Direct, incremental learning of fuzzy propositions. In *Proceedings of the Fourteenth Annual Conference of the Cognitive Science Society* (pp. 48–53). Hillsdale, NJ: Erlbaum.

Posner, M., & Keele, S. (1968). On the genesis of abstract ideas. *Journal of Experimental Psychology, 77*, 353–363.

Reed, S. (1972). Pattern recognition and categorization. *Cognitive Psychology, 4*, 382–407.

Rosch, E. (1978). Principles of categorization. In E. Rosch and B. B. Lloyd (Eds.), *Cognition and categorization* (pp. 28–48). Hillsdale, NJ: Erlbaum.

Rosch, E., & Mervis, C. (1975). Family resemblance studies in the internal structure of categories. *Cognitive Psychology, 7*, 573–605.

Smith, E., & Medin, D. (1981). *Categories and concepts.* Cambridge, MA: Harvard University Press.

Sun, R., & Bookman, L. (Eds.). (1993). *Computational architectures integrating neural and symbolic processes.* Boston: Kluwer.

Wattenmaker, W., Nakamura, G., & Medin, D. (1987). Relationships between similarity-based and explanation-based categorization. In D. Hilton (Ed.), *Contemporary science and natural explanation: Common sense conception of causality* (pp. 204–240). Sussex: Harvester Press.

Williams, R. (1986). The logic of activation functions. In D. Rumelhart, J. McClelland, & the PDP Research Group (Eds.), *Parallel distributed processing: Explorations in the microstructure of cognition: Vol. 1. Foundations* (pp. 423–443). Cambridge, MA: MIT Press.

Wisniewski, E. (1989). Learning from examples: The effect of different conceptual roles. In *Proceedings of the Eleventh Annual Conference of the Cognitive Science Society* (pp. 980–986). Hillsdale, NJ: Erlbaum.

Wisniewski, E., & Medin, D. (1991). Harpoons and long sticks: The interaction of theory and similarity in rule induction. In D. Fisher, M. Pazzani, & P. Langley (Eds.), *Concept formation: Knowledge and experience in unsupervised learning* (pp. 237–278). San Mateo, CA: Morgan Kaufmann.

PART I
MODELS OF DATA-DRIVEN CATEGORY LEARNING AND PROCESSING

MODELS OF CATEGORIZATION AND
CATEGORY LEARNING

W. K. Estes

I. Introduction

Why should categorization, a topic that can scarcely be found in the literature of psychology before the mid-1970s, now be the subject of a major conference?[1] The answer is not hard to come by if we look at the variety of research and theory represented in the conference, all bearing on the common theme of how we bring the results of past experience to bear on new situations in domains ranging from everyday life to artificial intelligence. The theme is by no means a new one, and in fact has been central to the study of "higher mental processes" since the beginnings of experimental psychology. What has changed most conspicuously is the label—from *concept formation* in the earlier literature to the currently more popular *categorization.*[2] More importantly, however, the change in label has paralleled a major shift in research emphasis and theoretical outlook, from an approach grounded in a view of concept formation as a form of problem solving to one in which concept formation is treated as a product of the interplay of processes of learning and memory. I review this

---

[1] Reference is to the Conference on Categorization and Category Learning in Humans and Machines, Texas Tech University, Lubbock, Texas, October 11–13, 1991.

[2] Like Smith and Medin (1981), I use these terms interchangeably except when there is reason to take cognizance of the broader scope of concept formation, which in common usage includes knowledge processes, e.g., those pertaining to propositional networks (Anderson, 1976, 1983), as well as those customarily subsumed under categorization.

background briefly before homing in on a few of the issues that seem most influential in current research.

A. CATEGORIZATION AS PROBLEM-SOLVING

In the problem-solving approach, the concepts studied experimentally are based on formal categories similar to many commonly met in school—for example, soluble/insoluble, noun/verb, animate/inanimate—always definable in terms of critical features or properties common to all members of a category and both necessary and sufficient for category membership. The problem for the learner in such studies is viewed as one of formulating hypotheses about the critical features and testing the hypotheses against observations of a sequence of category exemplars until an adequate hypothesis is discovered. This approach dominated research on concept formation from its early explication by Heidbreder (1924) to its last major summarization by Bourne (1970). By the end of this period, our understanding of the cognitive processes in hypothesis testing had been materially advanced by the innovative studies of Bruner, Goodnow, and Austin (1956) and Levine (1967), among others. The large body of research done in this tradition had given rise to a commensurate body of theory, much of it taking the form of mathematical or computer-simulation models (Bourne & Restle, 1959; Hunt, Marin, & Stone, 1966; Trabasso & Bower, 1968).

Why, then, should the zeitgeist have changed? To my mind, two events set the stage for the transition. The first event was Bourne's (1970) review, which recognized the progress that had been made in the hypothesis-testing tradition but at the same time pointed out why the theory that had developed might be limited in applicability to a special class of situations. The reason is that, prior to encountering a task calling for concept formation, the learner must have enough relevant experience to come equipped with a set of hypotheses that need only be heuristically searched to yield the one defining the needed concept.

Solution of categorization problems by trial-and-error hypothesis testing may be quite characteristic of the kind of experience one has in chemistry laboratory courses, but it does not typify the more common varieties of concept formation in school learning, where rules for categorization are usually communicated verbally or by example rather than being left to be discovered by the student. Still less are hypothesis-testing models applicable to the learning of linguistic or natural categories in ordinary environments. The problem for a child learning to classify objects such as plants, animal species, or substances, or for an adult learning to respond categorically to the phonological units of a new language, is not to test a set of hypotheses known a priori, but to develop memorial representations of category structures.

B. FUZZY CONCEPTS AND NATURAL CATEGORIES

The second event contributing to a shift of zeitgeist was a new flourishing of interest in the learning and functions of natural categories. In the early 1970s, several investigators, most notably Eleanor Rosch and her colleagues, marshalled insights from anthropological as well as psychological sources to make a convincing case that most of the categories that enter into concept formation during a child's cognitive development, and that predominate in ordinary life even for adults, are of a different character from those assumed in hypothesis-testing theory. Rather than being defined in terms of strict rules, natural categories are "fuzzy" or "ill-defined," in the sense of being better characterized in terms of family resemblance than by sets of necessary and sufficient features (Rosch, 1973; Rosch & Mervis, 1975). The term *fuzzy* refers to the fact that exemplars of a natural category are more similar, on the average, to other members of the category than to the exemplars of alternative categories, so that categorization is possible on the basis of differential similarities even though no individual feature may belong exclusively to a particular category.

Rosch and her associates recognized that, in their natural environments, people find it adaptive to learn to categorize objects—for example, animals, plants, tools—because of the usefulness of classifying together things that have significant properties in common. For the most part this learning occurs without any trial-by-trial feedback from a teacher and eventuates not in rules for classification, but in mental representations of categories. Proceeding from these observations, investigators of categorization and concept formation from the mid-1970s to the present have been predominantly engaged in developing models for category representations, for cognitive operations on these memory structures, and for the learning that gives rise to them.

II. Categorization Models Deriving from Memory Theory

A. OVERVIEW

The type of model needed to enable categorization theory to capitalize on the insights concerning fuzzy categories and family resemblance clearly must draw on resources in the more general body of research and theory on memory. It was essential to find a tractable yet fruitful way of formalizing the vague notion of memory representations of categories and the cognitive operations by which the memory structures could be accessed and utilized in computations leading to categorization judgments. A solution to the problem of representation was in fact at hand in the conceptions of multidimensional memory trace (Bower, 1967; Spear, 1976; Underwood, 1969) and episodic memory (Tulving, 1972). And, possibly adventitiously, during the period when the new view of categorization was taking shape, a solution to the problem of access was emerging from the seemingly distant domain of discrimination learning theory (Medin, 1975) in the form of an algorithm for the computation of similarities between perceived and remembered stimulus patterns.

These constituents were combined by Medin and Schaffer (1978) into a model that has been of central importance in the flourishing of categorization theory during the ensuing period down to the present. I refer to their formulation as an *exemplar model,* because the basic learning mechanism is conceived to be the storage of featural representations of perceived category exemplars. Others prefer the term *context model* because of the way in which each feature of a stimulus pattern is assumed to act as context for others (Medin & Schaffer, 1978; Nosofsky, 1984, 1986). The importance of the model stemmed from its parsimony, tractability, and adaptability to a variety of roles in categorization research. Among the theoretical approaches of the 1970s, the exemplar model was notable in depending solely on assumptions that had independent support from existing theories of learning and memory. With a minimum of postulation, it yielded quantitative accounts of category learning and transfer but was simple enough in form to be easily applied. And it has proved to be useful both as a stand-alone model for the interpretation of simple experiments and as a module in the construction of models for more complex phenomena. Since understanding the exemplar model is a prerequisite to following much of the current work in categorization theory, I present a compact tutorial on the model in the next section. Lest I seem to be going overboard with praise for this model, however, I will mention that the review discloses some limitations and sets the stage for introducing the other main branch of theoretical development in the domain of categorization and category learning.

B.   The Exemplar-Similarity Framework

In broadest qualitative terms, the view of categorization in the framework of the exemplar model is as follows. On a series of learning experiences, an individual perceives stimuli that are labeled as belonging to one or another of a set of alternative categories and forms a record of these experiences in memory, each stimulus and its category tag encoded in terms of their attributes, or features. When called on, either during or following the learning series, to categorize a stimulus pattern, the learner compares the perceived pattern to the array stored in memory and tends to assign the test stimulus to the category whose stored members are, overall or on the average, most similar to it. During the hypothesis-testing period, a number of experimenters looked for evidence of such storage of memory for instances and reported negative results (e. g., Bourne & O'Banion, 1969; Coltheart, 1971; Dominowski, 1965; Trabasso & Bower, 1964). However, following the early work of Reber (1967, 1969) on implicit concept learning, it began to be realized that stored memory representations of a kind suitable to provide a basis for categorization need not be available to recall or recognition on direct memory tests. Brooks (1978) presented a carefully reasoned case that instance memory may actually mediate concept formation and categorization but stopped short of formulating a model for the way in which the process might be accomplished. That final step was taken by Medin and Schaffer (1978).

Not surprisingly, the various investigators who have revised and extended the exemplar model since its initial presentation differ somewhat with respect to details of their treatments. Medin and his associates have investigated many qualitative implications of the model but have remained noncommittal regarding the specific processes of memory search and retrieval that underly categorization performance (Medin, Altom, Edelson, & Freko, 1982; Medin, Dewey, & Murphy, 1983). Nosofsky (1984, 1986, 1988a, 1988b) has formalized the model and elucidated its relationships to others in the domain of measurement and scaling theory. I have been concerned primarily with learning and information processing mechanisms (Estes, 1986a, 1986b, in press; Estes, Campbell, Hatsopoulis, & Hurwitz, 1989). The version I sketch here is a core model, incorporating the assumptions common to these variants, essentially as described in Estes (1986b), but fleshed out with more specific processing assumptions.

1. The Core Exemplar Model

In a typical category learning experiment, subjects have the task of assigning members of a set of stimulus patterns to alternative categories (for example, images on a radar screen to types of aircraft or symptom patterns to alternative diseases). On each of a sequence of trials, a subject is shown a pattern (a category exemplar), chooses a category, and receives informative feedback, usually the display of the correct category label. We assume that at the end of each trial, a representation of the exemplar in terms of its attributes is stored in the memory array, together with the correct category label (e.g., a list of symptoms characterizing a patient together with a disease category). At the beginning of each trial after the first, the subject computes the similarity of the exemplar presented to each member of the current memory array, sums its similarity to all the members associated with each category, computes the probability of each category, and generates a response based on these probabilities.[3] It is not assumed that the individual consciously carries out these calculations as a computer would do—only that the processing system in some way generates the same response probabilities as those produced by a computer programmed to simulate the model.

The processes of coding memory representations of category exemplars, computing similarities between them and newly perceived patterns, and generating categorization probabilities can be conveniently illustrated in terms of the minimal problem illustrated in Fig. 1. The stimuli are light and dark triangles and squares, assigned to categories in such a way that dark triangles and squares occur only in Category A and light triangles and squares occur only in Category B. The subjects see these stimuli singly in a random sequence with a display of the correct category label following the subject's response on each trial. For convenience in representing tasks of this kind, I follow a standard practice of coding the attribute values as shown in Table I. The entries 1 and 2 in the column headed "Coded representation" denote the attribute values dark and light respectively, and 1 and 2 in the second column denote triangle and square.

Now we are ready to consider the memory array we would expect to be formed after a subject has seen each of the four exemplar patterns once. The patterns are listed at the left in Table I, and the entries 1 and 0 under Category indicate that patterns 11 and 12 have been stored in the A column and patterns 21 and 22 in the B column. The tabular arrangement with columns corresponding to categories is just an expository convenience, of course; we assume only that the memory record of the sequence of learning trials includes a feature pattern together with a category tag for each trial.

As the basis for predicting categorization probabilities on tests given at this point in learning, I start by computing the similarity of the first pattern, pattern 11, to both of the items stored in Category A. The algorithm for computing similarity between two patterns, termed the *product rule,* is to compare them feature by feature, entering a 1 into a product when there is a match and a quantity s (a similarity parameter having a value in the range 0–1) when there is a mismatch. When we compare Pattern 11 to itself, we

---

[3] Elsewhere (Estes, in press), I have assembled evidence that supports the conception of a global comparison between a test stimulus and the contents of the memory array when categorization is based on relatively long term memory, but suggests a sequential search process eventuating in retrieval of a single stored representation when categorization is based on short-term memory.

Training   Category
pattern

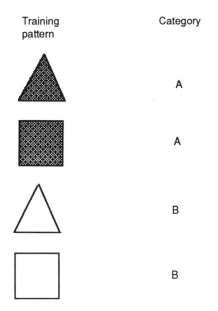

Fig. 1. Stimulus figures, with category assignments, for a simple categorization task.

obtain $1 \times 1 = 1$, and when we compare it to 12, we obtain $1 \times s = s$. Thus the summed similarity of test pattern 11 to the current memory array for Category A is $1 + s$. Comparing the same test pattern to the representations stored for Category B yields $s \times 1 = s$ and $s \times s = s^2$ for the comparisons to patterns 21 and 22 and a summed similarity, henceforth termed SimCat, of $s + s^2$. Our prediction of the probability of a correct

TABLE I

FEATURE CODING AND CATEGORY SIMILARITIES (PRODUCT RULE) FOR MINIMAL CATEGORIZATION PROBLEM

Coded representations	Category		Sim A	Sim B
	A	B		
1 1	1	0	$1 + s$	$s + s^2$
1 2	1	0	$1 + s$	$s + s^2$
2 1	0	1	$s + s^2$	$1 + s$
2 2	0	1	$s + s^2$	$1 + s$

$$\text{Correct response probability} = (1 + s)/((1 + s) + (s + s^2))$$
$$= 1/(1 + s)$$

response (that is, a Category A response) to pattern 11 is given by the ratio of SimCatA to the sum of SimCatA and SimCatB, that is,

$$P_{11}(A) = \text{SimCatA}/(\text{SimCatA} + \text{SimCatB})$$
$$= (1 + s)/(1 + 2s + s^2) = 1/(1 + s)$$

which can easily be shown to be the probability of a correct response to each of the other patterns in this simple case. Thus, my prediction is that, unless s is equal to unity, the probability of a correct response will be greater than $\frac{1}{2}$, and if s is equal to zero the probability correct will be unity.

2. A Research Application of the Core Model

It is clear that the minimal categorization model based on the product rule can exhibit learning of simple problems, but does it learn them in the way people do? Can we, for example, predict anything in advance about the relative difficulty of different categorization problems, given only the minimal model defined above with no parameters evaluated from data? To obtain a preliminary answer, I will apply the model to a pioneering study of categorization in relation to problem difficulty reported 30 years ago by Shepard, Hovland, and Jenkins (1961).[4] Those investigators had subjects learn six different categorization problems, constructed to represent several levels of complexity in the logical structure of the categories. Several different sets of stimulus materials were used in different problems, but the formal structures were the same and can be conveniently illustrated in terms of a case in which the stimuli were constructed by combining two types of form with two levels of brightness and two levels of size. The assignments of stimuli to categories are illlustrated for three of the problems in Fig. 2. The simplest logical structure is that of Problem I, in which all dark figures are to be assigned to Category A and all light figures to Category B. The structure of Problem II involves logical conjunctions, dark triangles and light squares belonging to Category A, light triangles and dark squares to Category B. Problem VI, intended to be the most difficult, defies any simple characterization in terms of logical structure.

The designs of all six of the Shepard et al. (1961) problems are presented in Table II in the standard binary coding, the entries 1 and 2 in the first, second, and third positions of each exemplar representation (i.e., the three members of each feature triad) representing the attributes dark/light, large/small, and triangle/square on the brightness, size, and form dimensions, respectively. The average number of errors per problem during learning in

---

[4] In this application, I am following the lead of Nosofsky (1984), who showed that the study is well suited to this purpose.

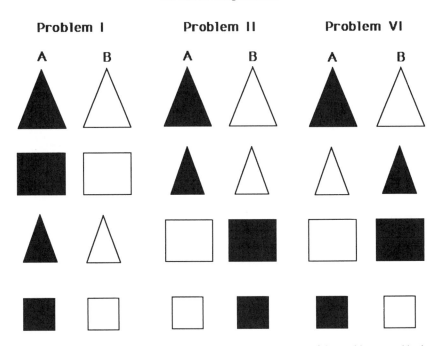

Fig. 2. Stimulus figures, with category assignments, for three of the problems used in the study of Shepard, Hovland, & Jenkins (1961).

the Shepard et al. (1961) study, rescaled by a linear transform to make them visually comparable to the error probabilities that will be derived from the exemplar model, are shown as the hatched bars in Fig. 3. It may be seen that the error scores vary widely, reflecting rapid learning for the problems of simplest structure but slow and incomplete learning for the problems of most complex structure.

One of the purposes of Shepard et al. (1961) was to determine whether a principle of stimulus generalization, combined with assumptions drawn from associative learning theory, could account for the relationship between difficulty of a categorization problem and its logical structure. Their conclusion was that the answer is negative. In the state of theory three decades later, however, we may arrive at a different answer. I will illustrate the analysis of this study in terms of the exemplar model, starting from the premise that learning of the categorizations that are describable in terms of simple rules (like Problems I and II in Fig. 2) and that those that are not (Problem VI) can be interpreted in terms of the same basic model.

In order to apply the exemplar model, we have to choose a value for the similarity parameter s, and since we are not trying actually to fit the data, I have simply set s equal to the intermediate value .5. To generate the

TABLE II

CATEGORIZATION PROBLEMS WITH PROTOTYPES: SHEPARD, HOVLAND, & JENKINS (1961) STUDY

	Problem					
	I		II		III	
	A	B	A	B	A	B
	1 1 1	2 1 1	1 1 1	1 1 2	1 1 1	2 1 1
	1 1 2	2 1 2	1 2 1	2 1 1	1 1 2	1 2 2
	1 2 1	2 2 1	2 1 2	1 2 2	1 2 1	2 1 2
	1 2 2	2 2 2	2 2 2	2 2 1	2 2 1	2 2 2
Focal exemplars					1 1 1	2 1 2
					1 2 1	2 2 2
Average prototype	1.0 1.5 1.5	2.0 1.5 1.5	1.5 1.5 1.5	1.5 1.5 1.5	1.25 1.5 1.25	1.75 1.5 1.75

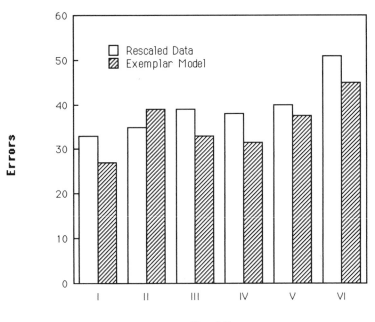

Fig. 3. Error data from the Shepard, Hovland, & Jenkins (1961) study (rescaled for expository purposes) and predictions from the exemplar model (with no free parameters estimated from the data).

	Problem					
	IV		V		VI	
A	B	A	B	A	B
1 1 1	1 2 2	1 1 1	2 1 1	1 1 1	1 1 2
1 1 2	2 1 2	1 1 2	1 2 2	1 2 2	1 2 1
1 2 1	2 2 1	1 2 1	2 1 2	2 1 2	2 1 1
2 1 1	2 2 2	2 2 2	2 2 1	2 2 1	2 2 2
		1 1 1	2 1 1		
1.25 1.25 1.25	1.75 1.75 1.75	1.25 1.5 1.5	1.75 1.5 1.5	1.5 1.5 1.5	1.5 1.5 1.5

desired predictions, we can, for each problem, compute the pairwise similarities for all eight stimuli and then the summed similarity of each stimulus to all four stored in the A category and to all four stored in the B category, and finally the probability of each category in the presence of each stimulus, just as was done for the illustrative example. Starting with the large dark triangle shown under Category A for Problem I in Fig. 2: Its similarity to itself is 1, to the large dark square is s, to the small dark triangle is s, to the small dark square is s^2, and its summed similarity to the members of the A category is $1 + 2s + s^2$; and so on for the other stimuli in each column.

Now, on the assumption that both categories and all stimuli within each category occurred equally often during learning, we can convert the correct response probabilities based on these similarities to error probabilities. For illustrative purposes, I have done these calculations for a point in learning at which each stimulus has been presented exactly once, and the values obtained are shown as the open bars in Fig. 3. It will be seen that the correlation between the predictions and observations is appreciably above chance, and, in fact, except for the aberration for Problem II, the model does an almost perfect job of ordering these problems of varying difficulty as they are ordered in the subjects' error data. The agreement between theoretical and observed values could be substantially improved by allowing the value of s to differ for different stimulus dimensions and choosing the best values by a model-fitting program (Nosofsky, 1984), but here I wish only to make the point that the simplest form of this exemplar-memory model can yield nontrivial, a priori predictions about some properties of the data on the basis of assumptions that contain no reference to the logical structure of the categories or to rules that might be used by the subjects.

Preparatory to other applications of the exemplar model, I discuss a number of technical points having to do with its implementation. The first of these is the format of the memory array. Suppose that in an experiment with the exemplars and categories shown in Table I, the first few trials ran as shown under "Chronological array" in Table III—pattern 1 1 on the first and second trials with Category A correct, pattern 2 1 on the third trial with Category B correct, and so on. For series of the length typical of actual experiments (from tens to hundreds of trials), it is not convenient to carry out similarity computations on a memory array of this form, so it is standard practice to convert it into the format shown under "Canonical array" in Table III, the cell entries being the frequencies of occurrence of each of the distinct exemplars that has occurred up to the given point. Similarity computations are then carried out as shown below the array. Rather than comparing pattern 11 to itself three times, we make the

TABLE III

SIMILARITY COMPUTATION IN THE EXEMPLAR MODEL

Chronological array			Canonical array			Limit (average) array		
Trial	A	B	Exemplar	A	B	Exemplar	A	B
1	1 1		1 1	3	0	1 1	.5	0
2	1 1		1 2	1	0	1 2	.5	0
3		2 1	2 1	0	2	2 1	0	.5
4		2 2	2 2	0	2	2 2	0	.5
5	1 2							
6	1 1							
7		2 1						
8		2 2						

Similarity computations

Similarity 11 to A	$3 + s$	$.5 + .5s$
Similarity 11 to B	$2s + 2s^2$	$.5s + .5s^2$

Probability computations

$$\text{Probability 11 (A)} = \frac{3 + s}{3 + s + 2s + 2s^2} \qquad \frac{.5 + .5s}{.5 + .5s + .5s + .5s^2}$$

$$= \frac{3 + s}{3 + 3s + 2s^2} \qquad \frac{1}{1 + s}$$

	If $s = 0$,	= 1	1
	If $s = .5$,	= .70	.67

comparison once and multiply the similarity by 3; rather than comparing it to pattern 21 twice, we make the comparison once and multiply the result by 2; and so on. Section V,A includes a discussion of some technical points concerning computation on the canonical array that I do not have occasion to refer to in this article.

When we know the design of an experiment in advance, we can make use of a *limit*, or average, array for purposes of deriving a priori predictions. Suppose that for an experiment using the category structure of Table I, we knew that over the learning series Categories A and B would occur with equal probabilities, that patterns 11 and 12 would occur equally often on Category A trials, and that patterns 21 and 22 would occur equally often on Category B trials. Then we could expect that, over a long series of trials, the essential properties of the memory array generated could be represented in the form shown under "Limit array" in Table III, the cell entries being the probabilities (and, therefore, long-term relative frequencies) of occurrence of the exemplar patterns in the two categories. As illustrated by the computations shown below this array in Table III, we can operate on the limit array just as on the canonical array, the result in this illustration being the predicted probability of assigning pattern 11 to Category A at the end of a long series of trials (technically, the expected asymptotic probability).

C.   TREATMENTS OF SOME CENTRAL ISSUES

The value of formal models resides not mainly in their quantitative accounts of data, impressive though these may be in some instances, but in their usefulness as conceptual tools that help us analyze and explain the phenomena that fuel major research efforts. In this section, I illustrate this role of the exemplar model in interpreting two types of phenomenon that have been central to a great deal of research on categorization, one having to do with generalization, or induction, the other with abstraction.

1.   Categorization and Induction

A prime source of interest in categorization for centuries has been its relevance to the problem of induction—how we derive generalized knowledge from specific past experiences. It seems that the most popular answer among many philosophers and psychologists is that, having observed a number of members of a category, a person forms a mental representation in the form of an abstract image, or prototype (Smith, 1989; Smith & Medin, 1981). The representation lacks the detail of a sensory image but contains enough information to serve as the basis for classifying new instances of a category. The conception of an abstract image was popularized by Sir Francis Galton (1878) in his studies of composite photographs, but was first subjected to experimental analysis nearly a century later in the work of Posner and Keele (1968, 1970), who showed that people can learn fuzzy categories defined by random variations on prototypic patterns.

Until recently, it may well have seemed inconceivable that generalization and induction could be explainable by any theory that did not assume the development of abstract representations of categories, the only question being whether these would prove to be verbal in form or more akin to sensory images. Advances in memory theory during the past two decades have, however, opened up the possibility that category judgments that seem to exhibit generalization or induction from past experience might depend, not on abstract representations of categories, but rather on computations performed, at the time of decision, on a store of memories for specific experiences.

For an illustration of the way in which this possibility may be realized in the framework of the context model, it will be convenient to refer again to the simplest categorization task in the Shepard et al. (1961) study , Problem I in Table II. Suppose that, on the first few trials of an experiment with this design, a learner saw the pattern–category combinations

$$1\ 1\ 1\ A\ 2\ 1\ 1\ B\ 2\ 2\ 1\ B\ 1\ 1\ 2\ A$$

then was tested with the previously unexperienced pattern 122. Referring to Table II, it is apparent that the categories can be defined in terms of a simple rule—patterns with the first feature having value 1 belong to Category A, those with the first feature having value 2 to Category B. A learner who had already induced this rule after the four learning trials would classify the new pattern 122 correctly. But what can we predict about an individual who learns in accord with the exemplar model? To determine the answer, we compute the similarity of pattern 122 to those stored with Category A tags and to those stored with Category B tags, obtaining $s + s^2$ and $s^2 + s^3$, respectively. The predicted probability of a Category A response to pattern 122 would, then, be

$$P(A) = (s + s^2)/(s + s^2 + s^2 + s^3)$$
$$= (1 + s^2)/(1 + s)^2$$

which is greater than .5 provided only that s is less than 1. For s equal, say, to .25, we would have $P(A) = .68$, for s equal to .05, $P(A) = .91$, and for s equal to 0, $P(A) = 1$. We see that performance based on a memory record of learning experiences, together with the kind of similarity computation assumed in the exemplar model, can yield generalization to new stimulus patterns of the same kind that could be produced by use of an induced rule.

From the more elaborate analyses of the Shepard et al. (1961) data reported by Nosofsky (1984), we know that this demonstration is not a fluke; generalization to new category exemplars in all the problems, regardless of logical complexity of the category structures, is well accounted for by an exemplar model that includes no special process of abstraction. The next question to be addressed is whether predictions for the Shepard et al. data could equally well have been derived from models based on conceptions of abstract mental representations of categories such as prototypes.

2. Average Prototypes and Focal Exemplars

It is interesting to note that prototype theory is by far the most visible variety in the literature (see reviews by Hunt, 1989; Rosch, 1978; Smith, 1990; Smith & Medin, 1981) although it can be credited with none of the close quantitative accounts of categorization data that have appeared during the last decade, the majority of which have been achieved by exemplar-similarity models (Estes, 1986b; Estes et al., 1989; Medin & Schaffer, 1978; Nosofsky, 1984, 1986, 1987, 1988a; Nosofsky, Clark, & Shin, 1989; Nosofsky, Kruschke, & McKinley, 1992). The popularity of prototype theory appears to derive from a combination of factors—its intuitive appeal, its long history, and some results of experiments employing categories of objects (typically irregular polygons or dot patterns) produced by means of variations on experimenter-defined prototypes (Attneave, 1957; Posner & Keele, 1968, 1970).

The term *prototype* has no unique definition with respect to categorization, and may refer either to objective properties of a category or to a hypothesized mental representation of a category formed during learning. Rosch (1978) has argued that only the former usage is well justified and that the notion of a prototype as a constituent of human information processing is problematic. The influential studies of Posner and Keele (1968, 1970) set the stage for the continuing practice of shifting between the two usages. Using haphazard dot patterns as stimuli, those investigators created categories by starting with particular dot patterns as prototypes and generating category exemplars by producing small perturbations in the positions of individual dots from their positions in the prototypes. They assumed that, during learning of a categorization, individuals form mental representations of the category prototypes (by some unspecified process of abstraction) and predicted that, following a sequence of learning trials on which the prototypes never occurred, the prototypes, when presented on tests, would be categorized more efficiently than exemplars that had actually occurred during learning. Confirmation of this and related predictions was taken as strong support for a prototype model. That implication was weakened, however, when it was shown some years later that the same predictions could be derived from exemplar-similarity models (Medin & Schaffer, 1978; Nosofsky, 1986).

In more recent research, the conception of a prototype has branched into two main variants, one defined in terms of the central tendency of a category and the other in terms of a prototype as a highly representative exemplar of a category. Reed (1972) formalized the idea that a prototype represents the central tendency of a category. Various measures of central tendency may be used, but the average is most common and I will use it for illustrative purposes. An average prototype has the form of a category exemplar but with feature values that are the averages of the values for all members of the category. Using this definition, I have computed the average prototypes for categories A and B in all six of the Shepard et al. (1961) problems, and these are included in Table II.

In a prototype model for categorization, it is assumed that when tested on any exemplar pattern, the learner mentally computes its similarity to the prototypes of the two categories for the given problem and assigns the pattern to the category with the closer prototype (Reed, 1972). Looking across the rows of category prototypes in Table II, we see immediately that a model based on central-tendency prototypes cannot predict better than chance performance on either Problem II or Problem VI, because the prototypes are the same for both categories, (whereas the data reported by Shepard et al., 1961, exhibit significant learning on both). More generally, an average prototype model cannot predict learning of any categorization in which individual features are invalid and better than chance performance depends on use of relational information (as in Estes, 1986b, Experiment 2). It now seems clear that even if central-tendency prototypes are formed in a learner's memory system, as some believe, they cannot provide the basis for categorization performance except under very special conditions.

The notion of a prototype as a representative or *focal* member of a category has not been embodied in any categorization learning model but nonetheless seems to be the favored version (Osherson & Smith, 1981; Rosch, 1978; Smith, 1990; Smith & Medin, 1981; Smith & Osherson, 1984). Within the framework of the exemplar model, it is natural to define a focal exemplar as the exemplar with highest summed similarity to the members of a category.[5] The focal exemplars, so defined, for each problem in the Shepard et al. (1961) study are shown in Table II. It turns out that only Problems IV and V have unique focal exemplars, whereas Problem III has two for each category, and Problems I, II, and VI are uninteresting cases with all members of each category having identical summed similarities. Analyses by Kruschke (1990) of an unpublished replication of the Shepard et al. study show that, as predicted by the exemplar model, the focal exemplars are the fastest learned, in accord with observations of Rosch and Mervis (1975) regarding natural categories.

Though more promising than the central-tendency prototype, the notion of a focal exemplar seems to have little place in the interpretation of category learning because it is a matter of happenstance when a focal exemplar might first appear during a learning series and thus come to be represented in the learner's memory system. Potentially more useful is a concept that might be termed the *configural prototype* of a category, defined as the exemplar pattern, among all those that can be constructed from the features defined for a task, having the highest summed similarity to the category. This concept differs from the concept of focal exemplar in that the configural prototype, like an average prototype, need not be a pattern that actually occurs during learning of a categorization. Two questions arise concerning this concept: (1) Will anything distinctive be learned about a configural prototype, regardless of whether it occurs as a category exemplar during learning? and (2) What useful function might a configural prototype serve in a categorization task?

To see how these questions can be addressed in the framework of the exemplar model, consider Problem IV in Table II, and imagine a learning experiment in which pattern 111 was never allowed to occur, but the other patterns all occurred with equal frequencies, as illustrated in Table IV. Entries 1 and 0 under either category signify that the row exemplar did or did not occur, respectively, in the category during learning; each entry under "Predicted typicality" is the summed similarity of the row exemplar to Category A, expressed as a percentage of the summed similarities in the column. Analyzing the situation in terms of the exemplar model, we note

---

[5] This definition needs an important qualification. Categorization performance would be based on focal representations in memory, which might not be the same as focal exemplars identified by looking only at the list of exemplars used in a task. In the Shepard et al. (1961) study, all exemplars of each category occurred equally often, so we can assume that focal memory representations would be the same as the focal exemplars identified in Table II. In other cases, the restriction to equal frequencies might not obtain; then it would be necessary to use frequency-weighted similarities in the computation of values of similarity-to-category, and different patterns might be identified as focal.

first of all that, so long as the similarity parameter is greater than zero, a memory representation of pattern 111 will develop during learning by virtue of its similarity to exemplar patterns that do occur. In fact, if the similarity parameter is much greater than .5, the summed similarity-to-category of pattern 111 at the end of a learning series of any length, so long as the stipulations about relative frequencies are met, will be the largest in its category. And in that event, we would predict that, at the end of the learning series, subjects asked to pick the pattern most typical of Category A would select pattern 111 with higher probability than any of the patterns that did occur during learning. If, however, the similarity parameter were appreciably smaller than .5, pattern 111 would not qualify as a configural prototype, and on a test it would not be selected as the most typical examplar of Category A. In a research situation, one would, of course, need to evaluate the similarity parameter, either from a previous experiment or from the learning data of the given experiment, in order to be in a position to predict test performance at the end of learning.

It is of interest also to consider another measure related to categorizability, which may be termed the relative typicality of an exemplar pattern with respect to two categories. In the analysis presented in Table IV, for example, we could compute the predicted typicality of each pattern in Category B just as was done for Category A, and then the relative typicality of the pattern for Category A, defined as the typicality to Category A divided by the sum of the typicalities for Categories A and B. Performing

TABLE IV

TYPICALITY OF AN UNPRESENTED CONFIGURAL
PROTOTYPE PREDICTED BY THE EXEMPLAR MODEL:
DESIGN FROM SHEPARD ET AL. (1961) PROBLEM IV

	Category		Predicted typicality[a] in Category A similarity (s)			
Pattern	A	B	.75	.50	.25	.15
1 1 1	0	0	14	15	13	10
1 1 2	1	0	13	15	19	23
1 2 1	1	0	13	15	19	23
2 1 1	1	0	13	15	19	23
1 2 2	0	1	12	11	9	7
2 1 2	0	1	12	11	9	7
2 2 1	0	1	12	11	9	7
2 2 2	0	1	10	7	3	2

[a] Summed similarity to the patterns appearing in Category A, expressed as a percentage.

this calculation, we find that, for all of the values of the similarity parameter s shown in Table IV the configural prototype, pattern 111, has the highest relative typicality for Category A. Therefore, we would predict that, on its first test at the end of the learning series, pattern 111, the configural prototype of its category, would be correctly categorized with higher probability than any of the exemplars that had actually occurred in Category A. It is important not to overgeneralize this result, however. It is easy to find categorization problems (including, e.g., Problem V of the Shepard et al., 1961, study) in which a configural prototype that did not occur during learning would not be predicted to be correctly categorized with the highest probability of the exemplars in its category. The general point is that, given the design of a categorization task, one can carry through an analysis like the one illustrated here and determine just what can be predicted about typicalities and ease of categorization.

I can see no obvious motivation for constructing special models incorporating the concepts of focal exemplars or configural prototypes, because within the framework of the exemplar model, it is the state of the memory array together with the process of similarity computation that mediates the generalization of learning to new instances. There might be some interest in formulating and testing a variation of the exemplar model in which we assume that, after sufficient experience with a task, learners begin to compare test patterns only to focal exemplars or configural prototypes of categories, rather than to the full memory array. I will be surprised if a model of that kind exhibits any superiority so long as attention is confined to situations in which learners acquire knowledge about categories by observing sequences of category exemplars with feedback. If, however, information about a categorization were conveyed to learners verbally or by demonstrations (as done in a study by Medin, Altom, & Murphy, 1984), then an implication of the exemplar model is that describing or presenting configural prototypes to subjects would facilitate categorization performance, and would generally do so more effectively than presenting average prototypes.

D.   On Category Structures and Conceptual Levels

Before proceeding to a discussion of the second main type of categorization model, I give one more illustration of how the exemplar model, even in its simplest form, can be used to aid in the interpretation of a problem of general interest. This application has to do with the conception of levels of categorization.

Observations of the way people form taxonomies in ordinary life show that the natural categories formed for domains like plants and animals are not all of a kind, but may be grouped into structures that correspond approximately to scientifically based taxonomies (D'Andrade, 1989). Proceeding from these observations, Rosch and her associates (Rosch, 1975; Rosch, Mervis, Gray, Johnson, & Boyes-Braem, 1976; Rosch, Simpson, & Miller, 1976) developed the idea that natural categories typically exhibit a hierarchical organization in terms of a particularly important basic level, corresponding approximately to the level of generic classes in biological taxonomies, plus superordinate and subordinate categories. An example of a basic level category is chair, with superordinate furniture and subordinates rocking chair, folding chair, and so on; another is dog with superordinate animal and subordinates spaniel, collie, and so on. Many empirical studies have found that objects are most rapidly categorized at the basic level (Jolicoeur, Gluck, & Kosslyn, 1984; Murphy & Smith, 1982; Rosch, Mervis, Gray, Johnson, & Boyes-Braem, 1976). Seeking a psychological basis for the ease of categorizing at the basic level, Rosch et al. obtained evidence that more people list the same features for basic level categories than for superordinates and that exemplars at the basic level are easier to image than those at the superordinate level, perhaps because of greater commonality in shape.

In natural environments, structural properties of categories are necessarily confounded with many other factors. Thus, in order to sort out the various contributors to categorization performance, it is important to have experimental studies that use simplified category structures and control such variables as stimulus salience and frequencies of occurrence of categories and exemplars. The first reported study of this kind (Murphy & Smith, 1982) used sets of pictorial stimuli constituting artificial examples of familiar classes of objects (e. g., tools that can serve as "pounders" and "cutters"), with class relationships intended to mirror some of the properties believed to characterize natural categories. Stimuli assigned to the basic level had relatively large numbers of features that were common to all members of a category but distinct from the features of alternative categories, whereas members of superordinate and subordinate categories had fewer of both common and differentiating features. Tests given following categorization training yielded shortest correct categorization reaction times for basic level, longer for subordinate level, and longest for superordinate level, in at least rough qualitative agreement with the pattern that had been observed for natural categories.

To illustrate how the exemplar model can be used to analyze the learning of categories at different levels, I use a slightly simplified rendition of the Murphy and Smith (1982) study. The category structure, with my interpretation of the featural composition of stimuli, is shown in Table V. The category exemplars in Murphy and Smith's study were drawings of common objects that could be classified into the superordinate categories

TABLE V

LEVELS OF CATEGORIZATION: MODIFIED FROM MURPHY AND
SMITH (1982)

Feature	Level	Category							
	Superordinate:	P				C			
	Basic:	H		B		K		P	
	Subordinate:	H1	H2	B1	B2	K1	K2	P1	P2
1		1	1	2	2	1	1	2	2
2		1	1	2	2	3	3	4	4
3		1	1	2	2	3	3	4	4
4		5	6	7	8	9	10	11	12

pounder (P) and cutter (C), each of which comprised two basic categories, hammer and brick, and knife and pizza cutter, respectively, and each of these, in turn, two subordinate categories. The feature structure was designed to mirror, at least to some degree, the structures that have been depicted for hierarchies of natural categories. Exemplars of a basic level category are quite similar, agreeing in three of the four features, but dissimilar to members of other categories at that level. Members of a subordinate category (type of hammer, brick, knife, or cutter) agree on the features 1–4 but differ on some idiosyncratic feature, not shown in Table V. Members of a superordinate category do not uniformly agree on any features, but the two superordinate categories are differentiated by a disjunctive relation on features 2 and 3 (a feature value of 1 or 2 signifying Category P and a 3 or 4 Category C).

For illustrative computations with the exemplar model, I will assume that tests are given after a series of training trials on which all categories were represented equally often, as was true in Murphy and Smith's (1982) study. Applying the simplest case of the model, with the same value of the similarity parameter used for all feature mismatches, we can compute the summed similarity of each exemplar to each of the categories it belongs to, and from these SimCat values the probability of a correct categorization at each level (as shown in Section V,B). With the value of the similarity parameter set equal to .5, the model predicts a basic level superiority of roughly the magnitude observed by Murphy and Smith.

I do not want to make too much of this result because, first, the assumptions I have made about feature coding and learning conditions are only a convenient idealization of the actual conditions of Murphy and Smith's (1982) study, and second, we have little information about how closely the conditions of the study mirror those of learning natural categories outside the laboratory. What we do see illustrated in this example is the usefulness and convenience of the simple exemplar model for analyzing stimulus similarity relationships and yielding a priori predictions, at least on an ordinal scale, about results to be expected in a novel experiment.

III. Categorization Models Deriving from Connectionist Theory

We might characterize the present status of the exemplar model by saying that it has a good claim to recognition as the model of choice for what might be termed the static aspects of categorization—generalization and transfer from learning to new situations, analysis of the structure of categories and category hierarchies, and the like. However, the model has some limitations for coping with the dynamics of learning. Under some conditions, the model yields satisfactory accounts of category learning once its parameters have been evaluated from the data, but it generally can tell us little in advance of an experiment about the probable course of learning or even about expected asymptotes.

By referring again to the minimal categorization problem illustrated in Table I, it is easy to point up the basis of this limitation. The design is, in essentials, shown in the following tabulation, in which the cell entries denote probabilities of occurrence of exemplars in categories.

	Category	
Exemplar	A	B
1 1	.5	0
1 2	.5	0
2 1	0	.5
2 2	0	.5

The expression derived from the exemplar model for probability of a correct response after each training pattern has occurred once (or at any point when all patterns have occurred equally often) takes the form $1/(1 + s)$. Surely, normal human learners would reach a level of 100% correct responding after even a moderate number of trials, and this result can be predicted from the model if the similarity parameter s is equal to zero. However, if we assume that s is equal to zero, we run into another difficulty. It is known that in the early stages of learning, errors of categorization are systematically related to similarities between exemplars, and the model can account for this fact only on the assumption that s is greater than zero. If, in a lengthy learning series, we fit the model to successive blocks of trials separately (as I have done for the data of Estes, 1986b), estimates of s from the data decline over blocks. However, there is no theoretical process in the exemplar model to produce changes in s over a learning series, and introducing some arbitrary function would, of course, have no explanatory value.

A. GLUCK AND BOWER'S ADAPTIVE NETWORK MODEL

I have investigated various ways of modifying the exemplar model to improve its capability for interpreting learning, but none has seemed very promising. It may be that a better strategy lies in the more radical approach of replacing the learning assumptions of the exemplar in toto with new ones drawn from a type of theory known to be well adapted to cope with the dynamics of learning. A promising source, perhaps, is the family of "connectionist" network models. A convenient starting point for discussing this approach is a model adapted from the discrimination theory of Rescorla and Wagner (1972) and applied to categorization by Gluck and Bower (1988b). In the form originally presented by Gluck and Bower, the model is based on a network of nodes and connecting paths, as illustrated in Fig. 4. A node is defined for each member of the set of features from which category exemplars are generated, and each is connected to the output nodes, which correspond to the categories available for choice. The path from any feature node i to category node j has an associated weight w_{ij} whose value measures the degree to which input from the feature node tends to activate the category node. The stimulus pattern presented on any occasion activates its feature nodes, and the output from these to the category nodes determines the probability of the corresponding categorization responses. The way the model works can be illustrated in terms of a learning trial on which the exemplar pattern presented comprises

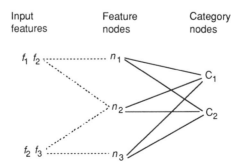

Fig. 4. Network assumed in the model of Gluck and Bower (1988b).

features f_1 and f_2, which activate feature nodes n_1 and n_2. The output of the network to category node C_1 is

$$o_{11} = w_{11} + w_{21} \tag{1}$$

and the output to C_2 is

$$o_{12} = w_{12} + w_{22} \tag{2}$$

The ratios of these outputs (transformed by an exponential function to avoid negative quantities, as described in the next section) determine the categorization probabilities. The probability of a Category 1 response, for example, is given by

$$P(1) = o'_{11}/(o'_{11} + o'_{12}) \tag{3}$$

where o'_{ij} signifies the transformed output. At the end of the trial, when the learner is informed of the correct category, the weights on the active paths are adjusted by a learning function with a form known in the connectionist literature as the *delta rule* (Gluck & Bower, 1988a, 1988b; Stone, 1986). In this case, the weight on the path from feature node n_1 to category node C_1 increases according to

$$w'_{11} = w_{11} + \beta(1 - w_{11} - w_{21}) \tag{4}$$

if Category 1 is correct and decreases according to

$$w'_{11} = w_{11} - \beta(w_{11} + w_{21}) \tag{5}$$

if Category 2 is correct. The w_{ij} terms on the right sides of these equations are the values at the beginning of the given trial and the w'_{ij} terms on the left the values at the end of the trial; β is a learning parameter with a value in the range 0–1.

In applications to a special type of categorization task in which features are uncorrelated within categories, this model proved to be at least equal, and in a few instances superior, to the exemplar model for describing the course of category learning (Estes et al., 1989; Gluck & Bower, 1988b). However, the scope of this model is severely limited, for it cannot account for learning in the very common situations where combinations of features have higher validities than the features individually. To overcome this limitation, Gluck and Bower (1988a) augmented the simple model with the assumption that the network includes not only nodes representing individual features but also nodes representing pairs of features (so that, for example, the network in Fig. 4 would also include nodes n_{12} and n_{23}). The resulting *configural cue* model, which in general may include nodes representing feature combinations of any size, remedies the deficiencies of the simple network quite well. Still, I find this approach somewhat unsatisfying in that the number of potential configural nodes becomes very large when the category exemplars are even moderately complex, and we lack any principled way of deciding in advance of an experiment which of the potential configural nodes should be included in a network.

B. The Simple Similarity-Network Model

A different way of augmenting the simple network model is suggested by the observation that its deficiencies are precisely of the kind that were overcome by the introduction of the product rule in the case of the exemplar model. Perhaps what we need is some combination of the exemplar and network approaches that could offer the advantages of both the learning mechanism of the network and the similarity algorithm of the exemplar model. A proposal that I put forward a few years ago (Estes, 1988) seems not to be entirely satisfactory in details, but by building on some recent work of Gluck (1991), I think it is possible to modify that proposal and assemble a combined model that can give us the best of both worlds. The approach I take closely parallels the independent development of basically similar, though more complex, models by Hurwitz (1990), Kruschke (1990, 1992), and Nosofsky et al. (1992).

The model is based on the stimulus representation of the exemplar model but combines it with the learning mechanism of the Gluck and Bower model. The memory structure in this model is a network of nodes and connecting pathways, but it differs from the network of the Gluck and Bower model in not having feature nodes. The basic representational assumption is that a node is entered in the network for each stimulus pattern perceived by the learner. Associated with each node is a featural description of the stimulus with the same properties as the representations in the exemplar model. A key assumption is that similarity between an input pattern and the featural description associated with a node is computed exactly as in the exemplar model, and the computed similarity determines the level of activation of the node (hence the designation *similarity-network* or, for brevity, SimNet model). The network also includes a node for each category defined in the given task, and a pathway connects each memory node with each category ("output") node. This structure is illustrated in Fig. 5 for the categorization task of Table I, but with only a few of the pathways shown, to reduce clutter in the diagram.

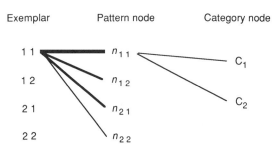

Fig. 5. Pattern and category nodes of similarity-network model. For simplicity only a few of the paths from input patterns to pattern nodes and from pattern to category nodes are shown.

The lines of varying thicknesses leading from input pattern 11 to the memory nodes reflect the assumption that each memory node will be activated in proportion to the similarity of its associated pattern to pattern 11 as computed by the product rule. Node n_{11} would be most strongly activated, since similarity of pattern 11 to itself is 1; activation of nodes n_{12} and n_{21} would be lower since each differs from 11 with respect to one feature; and activation of node n_{22} would be lowest, since pattern 22 differs from 11 with respect to two features. Weights on the paths from the memory nodes to the output nodes are defined exactly as for the Gluck and Bower model.

The general function for adjustment of weights on learning trials is described in Section V. To illustrate in terms of the simple categorization task, it will be convenient to refer to the four input patterns and their corresponding memory nodes in Fig. 5 by subscripts $i = 1,2,3,4$ and the categories by subscripts $j = 1,2$. On a trial when the exemplar presented is pattern 11 and Category 1 is correct, for example, the function for adjustment of the weight on the path from the pattern to the category node is

$$w'_{11} = w_{11} + \beta[1 - (w_{11} + sw_{21} + sw_{31} + s^2 w_{41})] \tag{6}$$

where, as in Eqs. (4) and (5), β is a learning rate parameter, and w_{11} on the right and w'_{11} on the left side of the equation denote the old and new values, respectively. The quantity inside the parentheses is the total output from all four pattern nodes to category node 1 on the trial, and, extending the notation of Eqs. (1) and (2), can be denoted by o_{11}; then the learning function can be written more compactly as

$$w'_{11} = w_{11} + \beta(1 - o_{11}) \tag{7}$$

The expression for probability of assigning the exemplar pattern to Category 1 takes the same form as Eq. (3).

An interesting and important property of the learning function is that learning is competitive in the sense that the magnitude of the adjustment to a weight on any trial depends on the weights on other concurrently active paths. Thus, in Eqs. (6) and (7), it is apparent that the increment to w_{11}, the weight on the path from stimulus node 1 to Category Node 1, is reduced as the output from other pattern nodes to the same category node (a joint function of their weights and the value of s) increases.

The way in which this model resolves the problem of predicting both similarity effects and asymptotes of learning functions, which could not be satisfactorily handled by the exemplar model, is illustrated in Fig. 6. The learning functions portrayed were computed trial-by-trial from Eq. (6) (and the corresponding equations for the other pattern-category combinations) with the learning parameter β set equal to .25 and the similarity parameter s to the values shown in the figure. In accord with well-known empirical results (Gynther, 1957; Robbins, 1970; Rudy & Wagner, 1975; Uhl, 1964), the difficulty of learning, indexed by the speed with which a curve approaches its final level, and therefore the number of errors that occur on early trials, is directly related to the magnitude of the similarity parameter s, but for the smaller values of s, both of the functions approach a final level of virtually perfect discrimination. The major advance over the exemplar model is that these predictions do not require any change in the similarity parameter over learning trials, so that if an estimate of s is available for a

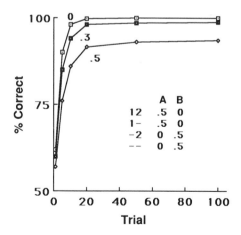

Fig. 6. Illustrative learning functions for the similarity-network model applied to the simple categorization task of Fig. 1 computed for three values of the similarity parameter s.

given situation from previously obtained data, the course of learning of a categorization can be predicted in advance.

Another limitation of the exemplar model, discussed in the Appendix (Section V,A) is its underestimate of the ability of learners to cope with changes in rules of categorization or shifts in the sampling probabilities of exemplar patterns in categories. Suppose, for example that on an individual's initial experiences with a drug, it produces sleepiness and therefore is categorized as a soporific. Then, unknown to the individual, the manufacturer changes the formula to make the drug act as a stimulant. According to the exemplar model (for reasons detailed in Section V,A), speed of learning the new categorization as a result of further experiences may be rapid if there were only a few experiences in the initial "preshift" condition but will be greatly retarded if there were many. Experimental simulation of this situation has shown, however, that speed of learning the new categorization is almost independent of the amount of preshift experience (Estes, 1989). The similarity-network model, without any added assumptions, yields the correct prediction (Estes, in press).

C. PREDICTING FEATURES FROM CATEGORIES

One of the main values of learning a categorization is that, once it has been accomplished, discovery of the category to which a new object or event belongs yields information about properties of the object or event that might not be directly perceptible. This function of categorization may be important even at a relatively primitive level. Animals or young children might, for example, learn to classify wild plants on the basis of visual properties into categories whose members do or do not have bitter tastes or produce illness and then be able to respond adaptively to new instances. Category-to-feature inference must be ubiquitous in human adults, who have learned many categorizations and can be given information verbally about the category memberships of objects or events whose perceptual properties are not immediately available.

On the basis of studies of natural categories (Rosch, Mervis, Gray, Johnson, & Boyes-Braem, 1976) and the cognitive processing of semantic categories (Smith, Shoben, & Rips, 1974), it seems reasonable to suppose that many categories encountered outside the laboratory are structured in the following fashion with respect to the types of features of which exemplars are composed. At the most superficial level are perceptual features that are normally available when an exemplar is encountered and that are useful, although not defining, for categorization (e.g., four legs and fur for the category mammal). At a deeper level (termed the *core* by Smith & Medin, 1981) are features (e.g., gives birth to live young) about which evidence may be gained by perception only on some occasions and is more often provided by verbal communications.

The adaptive, or functional, value of having learned a categorization lies in the fact that ascertaining the category membership of an object from its perceptual features or by being informed of the category label conveys information about features, such as flammable, poisonous, or nutritious, that may be critically important even though not immediately observable (Corter & Gluck, 1992). Further, as noted by Nakamura (1991), there are close theoretical connections between category structures and schemas. Consider the schemas people are presumed to have formed with respect to various types of buildings. These must be based on learned categorizations, each type of building being represented in memory by an array of stored feature patterns, possibly with subcategories at different levels. One's schema for an air terminal, for example, will include representations of ticket counters, security inspectors, baggage carts, and phone booths. All of these may not be immediately perceptible to one entering a terminal, but the category representation will contain information relative to the probabilities that the unobservable items are present and about probabilities of various feature values, such as those having to do with location in the terminal. Thus the ability to infer "missing features" of category exemplars must be a practically important, if not the most important, aspect of category learning.

In most laboratory studies of category learning, the only behavioral indicator of learning is categorization performance, that is, assigning exemplars to categories, and this orientation is reflected in the models that have been developed. It will be possible to show, however, that both the exemplar and the similarity-network model can yield testable predictions concerning the converse relation between categories and features. Just as is the case in ordinary life, we should expect that, in experiments conducted with the standard designs, appropriate interrogation of the learners might show that they are capable of reversing the usual task and producing estimates of the likelihoods that particular features will occur in exemplars of a category. I summarize one study (MacMillan, 1987) that has both investigated this possibility and yielded data suitable for analysis in terms of the models.

I first sketch the design of MacMillan's (1987) study, then develop theoretical predictions from the exemplar and similarity-network models before reviewing the results. Up to a point, MacMillan's experiment resembles others on category learning discussed in preceding sections. Stimulus materials were lists of symptoms characterizing hypothetical individuals (cases), and the task for the experimental subjects was to learn to assign cases to the categories Disease or No Disease. The design of

MacMillan's Experiment 1 (limited to the two conditions of immediate interest) is shown in Table VI in the usual format, with the labels actually used replaced by A and B for categories and f_i for feature (symptom) values. Different groups of subjects learned under the High Validity and Zero Validity conditions. In the former, it will be seen that one symptom pair occurs predominantly on Category A trials and the other three predominantly on Category B trials, so it is possible for a learner to reach a reasonable level of proficiency (78% correct categorizations on the average). In the Zero Validity condition, however, all symptom pairs occur equally often in both categories, so nothing can be learned about feature–category relationships that will contribute to correct performance; the maximum level of proficiency is 67%, attainable by making optimal use of information about the category base rates (the relative frequency of Categories A and B during learning being 33 : 67). Subjects in both groups were tested at the end of the 200-trial training series with questions asking them to estimate the percentage frequency of occurrence of each symptom value in the presence of the disease (i.e., in Category A).

The question of main interest for the present discussion is whether subjects in either or both conditions will learn something about the category structure that will enable them to produce veridical judgments about

TABLE VI

Design of Study on Category-to-Feature Frequency Estimates: MacMillan (1987), Experiment 1[a]

		Condition			
Exemplar		High Validity		Zero Validity	
f_1	f_2	A	B	A	B
1	1	55	10	55	55
1	2	15	30	15	15
2	1	15	30	15	15
2	2	15	30	15	15

[a] Categories A and B were labeled Disease and NonDisease; features f_1 and f_2 were labeled CSF Count and PKU Level, with the feature values 1 and 2 denoting high and low Counts or Levels. Category base rates were 33 and 67% for Categories A and B, respectively.

the relative frequencies of different symptoms within categories. As we will see, both models predict that such learning will occur, but they differ with regard to the effect of high versus low validity conditions. Let us examine the way in which predictions can be generated from each model.

Starting with the exemplar model, we can calculate from the relative frequencies in Table VI that at the end of the 200-trial learning series, the typical state of the memory array for High Validity subjects would be

	A	B
1 1	37	13
1 2	10	40
2 1	10	40
2 2	10	40

That is, on the average, about 37 instances of pattern 1 1 would be stored in the Category A and 13 in the Category B column, and so on. We do not know the value of the similarity parameter s of the model, but the level of performance reached indicates that it is small, so I assume $s = 0$ in making predictions. With this assumption, the predicted asymptotic probability of assigning pattern 1 1 to Category A is $37/(37 + 13)$, and the probabilities for the other patterns are $10/(10 + 40)$; from which we can compute an asymptotic percentage correct of approximately 78. However, our primary interest here is in what we can predict about performance when subjects are asked to estimate the relative frequency with which, say, value 1 of Feature 1 occurs on Category A trials. The answer, for the exemplar model, is given by a calculation exactly analogous to that used to predict categorization performance except that ratios of summed similarities are computed within columns of the memory array rather than across rows. We assume that the desired estimate is the expected relative frequency with which either of the patterns containing the given feature value, in this case patterns 1 1 and 1 2, occurs in Category A. Thus, referring again to the expected memory array for this group, the predicted relative frequency is $(37 + 10)/(37 + 10 + 10 + 10)$, or approximately .70. More generally, with the value of s unspecified, the result would be $(47 + 20s)/(67 + 67s)$, so we could predict in advance of the experiment that the observed mean estimate for this feature value in Category A, expressed as a percentage, should fall between 50 and 70.

For the novel condition of this experiment, that of the Zero Validity group, the expected memory array at the end of 200 learning trials would be

	A	B
1 1	37	73
1 2	10	20
2 1	10	20
2 2	10	20

and obviously the prediction for an estimate of relative frequency of Feature 1, value 1 in Category A is the same as for the High Validity condition. With the particular design used, this predicted estimate holds also for Feature 2, value 1 in Category A (and also for both feature values in Category B). In view of this equivalence, the observed symptom frequency estimates for this experiment shown in Table VII are averages over symptoms. Thus, prior to the experiment, we could have predicted that, for both groups, the symptom frequency estimates should fall between 50 and 70. The theoretical values given in Table VII narrow down this prediction, however, because the learning data were used to estimate the value of s. It will be observed that the prediction agrees quite well with the data for the High Validity group but is far off for the Zero Validity group, whose mean estimates deviate little from the chance value of 50.

Predictions from the the similarity-network model are derived in basically the same way except that the expected memory array at the end of the learning series has pattern–category weights rather than frequencies as the cell entries, i.e.,

	A	B
1 1	w_{11}	w_{12}
1 2	w_{21}	w_{22}
2 1	w_{31}	w_{32}
2 2	w_{41}	w_{42}

With the exemplar patterns numbered from 1 to 4 (as ordered from top to bottom in Table VI), w_{ij} is the weight for the connection of exemplar i to category j. To generate predictions about feature frequency estimates, the values of the w_{ij} were obtained by running the model through 200 learning trials and computing the weights at the point of the feature frequency test.

TABLE VII

Results on Estimation of Feature Frequencies in Category A (Disease Present): Data from Macmillan (1987), Experiment 1[a]

Symptom level	Condition							
	High Validity				Zero Validity			
	True freq.	Subj. ests.	Ex. mod.	Net. mod.	True freq.	Subj. ests.	Ex. mod.	Net. mod.
High	70	65	65	70	70	42	65	52
Low	30	30	35	30	30	54	35	48

[a] High and low symptom levels correspond to feature values 1 and 2 in Table VI. Cell entries are relative frequencies expressed as percentages. For the true frequencies and the model predictions, the percentages in each column must sum to 100; however, the experimental subjects estimated the frequencies of high and low symptom levels separately, so their estimates do not necessarily sum to 100.

These weights then replace the frequency values in the formula used to predict relative frequency estimates in the exemplar model.

The predictions so obtained are presented in Table VII, and it is apparent that the model correctly predicts the large observed difference between the High and Zero Validity conditions. This rather striking confirmation of the similarity-network model is impressive in that, so far as I know, no extant version of exemplar, feature-frequency, or prototype models (reviewed by Estes,1986a; Nosofsky,1986; Reed, 1972; Smith & Medin, 1981) can predict the observed result. On the other hand, within the network family, the prediction is not unique to the similarity-network model. It can, for example, be derived from the model of Gluck and Bower (1988b), which differs in being based on a network whose nodes represent feature values.

It is important to be clear as to just what is predicted by the network model for the Zero validity condition. It would not be correct to conclude that, according to the model, the subjects learn nothing about invalid features. The prediction is, rather, that subjects' estimates of the frequencies of these features should deviate from chance in the appropriate directions on tests given early in learning but then should decline to chance as learning trials continue (Estes, in press). This prediction was confirmed by another experiment in MacMillan's study (MacMillan, 1987, Experiment 3).

These results provide the clearest evidence available to date that, at least when categorization depends on relatively long-term memory, the nature of the category learning process is captured much better by an adaptive network model than by models that represent learning simply in terms of trial-by-trial storage of exemplar or feature representations.

IV. Summary

Over the history of research on concept formation and categorization from the early 1920s to the present, emphasis has shifted drastically from idealized, rule-defined concepts to natural and typically fuzzy categories. In parallel, the dominant type of theory has changed from models of hypothesis testing to models of memory representations and learning processes.

The most intensively developed body of theory in the new tradition is a class of information-processing models based on storage and retrieval of representations of instances of categories. The core model of this class, termed the exemplar model, combines these assumptions with a powerful algorithm, the product rule, for computing similarities between perceived and stored stimulus patterns. Applications of the exemplar model discussed in this article show it to be a sharp and convenient conceptual tool for analyzing problems and issues ranging from the nature of generalization and induction to the organization of natural categories. From these analyses together with related research, the conclusion has emerged that categorization performance generally results from on-line computations on a memory array rather than from reference to unitary, preformed mental representations such as abstract images or prototypes.

The observation that the exemplar model, even the enriched and extended version termed the *general context model* by Nosofsky (1988a, 1988b), has some limitations for interpreting the more dynamic aspects of category learning has led to interest in drawing on the resources of connectionist models. This possibility has been intensively explored during the last few years by Gluck and Bower (1988a, 1988b), Estes (1988), and Kruschke (1992), among others. One outcome, discussed in this article, is a relatively simple model that combines the exemplar model's assumptions about memory encoding and similarity computation with a network representation and an adaptive learning mechanism. This model overcomes the principal deficiencies of the exemplar model with respect to predictions about learning and has exhibited striking successes in the interpretation of category-to-feature inferences.

V. Appendixes

A. Refinements of the Exemplar Model

In nearly all applications of the exemplar model to category learning, the basic model described in the text is now augmented in two minor respects, one having to do with speed of learning following shifts in category assignments, the other with the effect of initial memory load on learning rates (Estes, in press; Nosofsky et al., 1992).

With regard to shift effects, imagine, for example, that an individual is learning to classify images of aircraft seen on a radar screen into two categories, C_1 and C_2. The result of the first few learning trials might be the memory array

Plane	C_1	C_2
1	2	0
2	0	1
3	1	3

where an image of Plane 1 occurred twice with C_1 indicated to be correct, and so on. Now we can predict from the exemplar model that on further tests of these displays, probability of correct categorizations would be high (assuming the similarity parameter s to be small). But suppose it is discovered at this point that the information given the learner on these trials was incorrect, Plane 1 actually belonging to category C_2 and Planes 2 and 3 to C_1. The incorrectly stored representations cannot be erased from memory, but after only a moderate number of additional learning trials with the correct feedback rules in effect, they would be outweighed by the new experiences. The new memory array after a dozen relearning trials might be

Plane	C_1	C_2
1	2	4
2	3	1
3	6	3

so the learner would be well on the way toward giving correct categorizations with high probability. Suppose, however, that the discovery about incorrect feedback did not occur till much later, when the memory array was, say,

Plane	C_1	C_2
1	20	40
2	30	10
3	60	30

Now the same dozen relearning trials would produce

Plane	C_1	C_2
1	20	44
2	33	10
3	65	30

on tests at this point, the learner would still be giving categorizations that would be correct by the original rules but incorrect by the new rules, and many more relearning trials would be needed to produce accurate performance under the new rules. It is easy to see that, in general, relearning after a shift in categorization rules will be slower the greater the number of learning trials prior to the shift.

This prediction has been sharply disconfirmed by an appropriately designed experiment (Estes, 1989), which showed that speed of relearning proceeded at virtually identical rates after early and late shifts. It is possible to reduce the excessive inertia of the exemplar model, and improve the account of shift effects, by adding a parameter representing the probability that any stored pattern suffers retention loss (i.e., becomes unavailable for comparisons with newly perceived patterns) during any trial following storage, so that memory does not build up as rapidly as in the basic model. The added "decay" process improves the exemplar model's account of relearning after shifts even though it does not bring the model fully in line with the data.

A related problem for the exemplar model is that if an individual begins a task with an empty memory array, that is, one containing no stored exemplars of the to-be-learned categories, then the model predicts an unrealistically high rate of learning. The remedy is to recognize that the initial memory array may always contain representations of previously encountered stimuli that have some similarity to those that will occur during learning in the new task and to define a parameter s_0 denoting the average similarity between that residual memory and exemplars of categories in the new task. Suppose, for example, that item I_1 is presented in Category A and item I_2 in category B on the first two trials of an experiment. With s denoting the similarity between I_1 and I_2, the similarity of I_1 to the contents of the Category A array would be $1 + s_0$ and the similarity to the contents of the category B array $s + s_0$. At this point, the predicted probability of assigning I_1 to Category A would be $(1 + s_0)/(1 + s + 2s_0)$. At the cost of one additional parameter to be estimated from the data, this modification radically improves the exemplar model's account of the detailed course of learning curves (Estes, in press; Nosofsky et al., 1992).

B. SIMILARITY COMPUTATIONS FOR TABLE V

The following computations are for the summed similarity (SimCat) of one of the exemplars of a subordinate category to categories at the superordinate, basic, and subordinate levels (P and C, H and B, and H_1 and H_2, respectively.

$$\text{SimP} = 1 + s + 2s^2 + 4s^5 \qquad \text{SimC} = 4s^4 + 4s^5$$
$$\text{SimH} = 1 + s + 2s^2 \qquad \text{SimB} = 4s^5$$
$$\text{SimH}_1 = 1 + s \qquad \text{SimH}_2 = 2s^2$$

It is assumed that each subordinate category includes two exemplars, denoted h_1 and h_1' in the case of Category H_1, differentiated by a single feature that is not listed in the table. Taking Exemplar h_1 for an illustration, we note that the similarity of h_1 to itself is 1 and to h_1' is s; hence its summed similarity to Category H_1 is $1 + s$. Exemplar h_1 differs from each of the exemplars of Category H_2 on two features (feature 4 and the unlisted feature), so its summed similarity to Category H_2 is $2s^2$ and thus to Category H is $1 + s + 2s^2$. Proceeding similarly, we obtain all the summed similarity expressions listed above. Setting s equal to .5 in these expressions for illustrative purposes, and entering these similarities in the usual formula for categorization probability,[6] we obtain probabilities of .85, .94, and .75 for choosing P over C, H over B, and H_1 over H_2, respectively.

C. LEARNING AND OUTPUT FUNCTIONS OF THE SIMILARITY-NETWORK MODEL

In general, the adjustment rule is as follows. On a trial when any pattern h is presented, the weight from any node i to category node j changes by

$$w_{ij}' = w_{ij} + \beta(z_j - o_j)a_{hi} \tag{8}$$

where the terms w_{ij}' oin the left and w_{ij} on the right side denote the weight at the end and beginning of the trial respectively, z_j denotes a "teaching signal," which is equal to 1 if category j is correct and equal to 0 otherwise, a_{hi} denotes activation level of node i when pattern h is presented, β is a learning rate parameter with a value between 0 and 1, and o_{hj} is the output of the network to category node j on that trial. The activation level a_{hi} is just the similarity between patterns h and i, and the output o_{hj} is given by

$$o_{hj} = \sum a_{hk}w_{kj} \tag{9}$$

the summation running over all memory nodes in the network.

As in the Gluck and Bower (1988b) model, the o_{hj} values are subjected to an exponential transformation, so for any two-category situation [with Categories A and B indexed by letting j in Eqs. (8) and (9) equal 1 or 2], the probability of assigning stimulus h to Category A is given by

---

[6] Referring to the third pair of similarities, for example, the probability of correctly assigning the given exemplar at the subordinate level is given by $(1 + s)/(1 + s + 2s^2)$.

$$P_h(A) = \frac{e^{co_{h1}}}{e^{co_{h1}} + e^{co_{h2}}}$$

$$= \frac{1}{1 + e^{-c(o_{h1}-o_{h2})}} \tag{10}$$

where c is a scaling parameter whose value is either chosen a priori on theoretical grounds or estimated from the data to which the model is being applied. It will be seen that response probability is an ogival function of the difference in outputs to the two category nodes, running from zero when o_{h2} is much larger than o_{h1} to unity when o_{h1} is much larger than o_{h2}.

ACKNOWLEDGMENTS

Preparation of this chapter was supported in part by Grants BNS 88–21029 and BNS 90–09001 from the National Science Foundation.

REFERENCES

Anderson, J. R. (1976). *Language, memory,* and *thought.* Hillsdale, NJ: Erlbaum.
Anderson, J. R. (1983). *The architecture of cognition.* Cambridge, MA: Harvard University Press.
Attneave, F. (1957). Transfer of experience with a class-schema to identification-learning of patterns and shapes. *Journal of Experimental Psychology, 54,* 81–88.
Bourne, L. E., Jr. (1970). Knowing and using concepts. *Psychological Review, 77,* 546–556.
Bourne, L. E., Jr., & O'Banion, K. (1969). Memory for individual events in concept identification. *Psychonomic Science, 16,* 101–103.
Bourne, L. E., Jr., & Restle, F. (1959). A mathematical theory of concept identification. *Psychological Review, 66,* 278–296.
Bower, G. H. (1967). A multicomponent theory of the memory trace. In K. W. Spence & J. T. Spence (Eds.), *The psychology of learning and motivation: Advances in research and theory:* Vol. 1 (pp. 230–327). New York: Academic Press.
Brooks, L. (1978). Nonanalytic concept formation and memory for instances. In E. Rosch & B. B. Lloyd (Eds.), *Cognition and categorization* (pp. 170–211). Hillsdale, NJ: Erlbaum.
Bruner, J. S., Goodnow, J. J., & Austin, G. A. (1956). *A study of thinking.* New York: Wiley.
Coltheart, V. (1971). Memory for stimuli and memory for hypotheses in concept identification. *Journal of Experimental Psychology, 89,* 102–108.
Corter, J. E., & Gluck, M. A. (1992). Explaining basic categories: Feature predictability and information. *Psychological Bulletin, 111,* 291–303.
D'Andrade, R. G. (1989). *Cultural cognition. In M. I. Posner (Ed.), Foundations of cognitive science* (pp. 795—830). Cambridge, MA: MIT Press.
Dominowski, R. L. (1965). The role of memory in concept learning. *Psychological Bulletin, 63,* 271–280.
Estes, W. K. (1986a). Array models for category learning. *Cognitive Psychology, 18,* 500–549.

Estes, W. K. (1986b). Storage and retrieval processes in category learning. *Journal of Experimental Psychology: General, 115,* 155–174.

Estes, W. K. (1988). Toward a framework for combining connectionist and symbol-processing models. *Journal of Memory and Language, 27,* 196–212.

Estes, W. K. (1989). Early and late memory processing in models for category learning. In C. Izawa (Ed.), *Current issues in cognitive processes: The Tulane Flowerree symposium on cognition* (pp. 11–24). Hillsdale, NJ: Erlbaum.

Estes, W. K. (in press). *Classification and cognition.* Oxford: Oxford University Press.

Estes, W. K., Campbell, J. A., Hatsopoulis, N., & Hurwitz, J. B. (1989). Base-rate effects in category learning: A comparison of parallel network and memory storage-retrieval models. *Journal of Experimental Psychology: Learning, Memory, and Cognition, 15,* 556–571.

Galton, F. (1878). Composite portraits. *Nature, 18,* 97–100.

Gluck, M. A. (1991). Stimulus generalization and representation in adaptive network models of category learning. *Psychological Science, 2,* 50–55.

Gluck, M. A., & Bower, G. H. (1988a). Evaluating an adaptive network model for human learning. *Journal of Memory and Language, 27,* 166–195.

Gluck, M. A., & Bower, G. H. (1988b). From conditioning to category learning: An adaptive network model. *Journal of Experimental Psychology: General, 117,* 225–244.

Gynther, M. D. (1957). Differential eyelid conditioning as a function of stimulus similarity and strength of response to the CS. *Journal of Experimental Psychology, 53,* 408–416.

Heidbreder, E. (1924). An experimental study of thinking. *Archives of Psychology, 11*(73).

Hunt, E. (1989). Cognitive science: Definition, status, and questions. *Annual Review of Psychology 40,* 603–629.

Hunt, E. B., Marin, J., & Stone, P. (1966). *Experiments in induction.* New York: Academic Press.

Hurwitz, J. B. (1990). *A hidden-pattern unit network model of category learning.* Ph.D. dissertation, Harvard University, Cambridge, MA.

Jolicoeur, P., Gluck, M., & Kosslyn, S. M. (1984). Pictures and names: Making the connection. *Cognitive Psychology, 16,* 243–275.

Kruschke, J. K. (1990). *A connectionist model of category learning.* Ph.D. dissertation, University of California, Berkeley.

Kruschke, J. K. (1992). ALCOVE: An exemplar-based connectionist model of category learning. *Psychological Review, 99,* 22–44.

Levine, M. (1967). The size of the hypothesis set during discrimination learning. *Psychological Review, 74,* 428–430.

MacMillan, J. (1987). *The role of frequency memory in category judgments.* Ph.D. dissertation, Harvard University, Cambridge, MA.

Medin, D. L. (1975). A theory of context in discrimination learning. In G. H. Bower (Ed.), *The psychology of learning and motivation: Advances in research and theory: Vol. 9* (pp. 263–314). New York: Academic Press.

Medin, D. L., Altom, M. W., Edelson, S. M., & Freko, D. (1982). Correlated symptoms and simulated medical classification. *Journal of Experimental Psychology: Learning, Memory, and Cognition, 8,* 37–50.

Medin, D. L., Altom, M. W., & Murphy, T. D. (1984). Given versus induced category representations: Use of prototype and exemplar information in classification. *Journal of Experimental Psychology: Learning, Memory, and Cognition, 3,* 333–352.

Medin, D. L., Dewey, G. I., & Murphy, T. D. (1983). Relationships between item and category learning: Evidence that abstraction is not automatic. *Journal of Experimental Psychology: Human Learning and Memory, 9,* 607–625.

Medin, D. L., & Schaffer, M. M. (1978). Context theory of classification learning. *Psychological Review, 85,* 207–238.

Murphy, G. L., & Smith, E. E. (1982). Basic-level superiority in picture categorization. *Journal of Verbal Learning and Verbal Behavior, 21,* 1–20.

Nakamura, G. V. (1991, October). *Relationships between categories and schemas.* Paper presented at the Conference on Categorization and Category Learning in Humans and Machines, Texas Tech University, Lubbock.

Nosofsky, R. M. (1984). Choice, similarity, and the context theory of classification. *Journal of Experimental Psychology: Learning, Memory, and Cognition, 10,* 104–114.

Nosofsky, R. M. (1986). Attention, similarity, and the identification–categorization relationship. *Journal of Experimental Psychology: General, 115,* 39–57.

Nosofsky, R. M. (1987). Attention and learning processes in the identification and categorization of integral stimuli. *Journal of Experimental Psychology: Learning, Memory, and Cognition, 13,* 87–108.

Nosofsky, R. M. (1988a). Exemplar-based accounts of relations between classification, recognition, and typicality. *Journal of Experimental Psychology: Learning, Memory, and Cognition, 14,* 700–708.

Nosofsky, R. M. (1988b). Similarity, frequency, and category representations. *Journal of Experimental Psychology: Learning, Memory, and Cognition, 14,* 54–65.

Nosofsky, R. M., Clark, S. E., & Shin, H. J. (1989). Rules and exemplars in categorization, identification, and recognition. *Journal of Experimental Psychology: Learning, Memory, and Cognition, 15,* 282–304.

Nosofsky, R. M., Kruschke, J. K., & McKinley, S. (1992). Comparisons between adaptive network and exemplar models of classification learning. *Journal of Experimental Psychology: Learning, Memory, and Cognition, 18,* 211–233.

Osherson, D. N., & Smith, E. E. (1981). On the adequacy of prototype theory as a theory of concepts. *Cognition, 9,* 35–58.

Posner, M. I., & Keele, S. W. (1968). On the genesis of abstract ideas. *Journal of Experimental Psychology, 77,* 353–363.

Posner, M. I., & Keele, S. W. (1970). Retention of abstract ideas. *Journal of Experimental Psychology, 83,* 304–408.

Reber, A. S. (1967). Implicit learning of artificial grammars. *Journal of Verbal Learning and Verbal Behavior, 6,* 855–863.

Reber, A. S. (1969). Transfer of syntactic structure in synthetic languages. *Journal of Experimental Psychology, 81,* 115–119.

Reed, S. K. (1972). Pattern recognition and classification. *Cognitive Psychology, 3,* 382–407.

Rescorla, R. A., & Wagner, A. R. (1972). A theory of Pavlovian conditioning: Variations in the effectiveness of reinforcement and non-reinforcement. In A. H. Black & W. F. Prokasy (Eds.), *Classical conditioning II: Current research and theory* (pp. 64–99). New York: Appleton-Century-Crofts.

Robbins, D. (1970). Stimulus selection in human discrimination learning and transfer. *Journal of Experimental Psychology, 84,* 282–290.

Rosch, E. (1973). On the internal structure of perceptual and semantic categories. In T. E. Moore (Ed.), *Cognitive development and the acquisition of language* (pp. 111–114). New York: Academic Press.

Rosch, E. (1975). Cognitive reference points. *Cognitive Psychology, 7,* 532–547.

Rosch, E. (1978). Principles of categorization. In E. Rosch & B. B. Lloyd (Eds.), *Cognition and categorization* (pp. 28–48). Hillsdale, NJ: Erlbaum.

Rosch, E., & Mervis, C. B. (1975). Family resemblance studies in the internal structure of categories. *Cognitive Psychology, 7,* 573–605.

Rosch, E., Mervis, C., Gray, D., Johnson, & Boyes-Braem, P. (1976). Basic objects in natural categories. *Cognitive Psychology, 8*, 382–439.

Rosch, E., Simpson, C., & Miller, R. S. (1976). Structural bases of typicality effects. *Journal of Experimental Psychology: Human Perception and Performance, 2*, 491–502.

Rudy, J. R., & Wagner, A. R. (1975). Stimulus selection. In W. K. Estes (Ed.), *Handbook of learning and cognitive Processes: Vol. 2. Conditioning and behavior theory* (pp. 269–303.) Hillsdale, NJ: Erlbaum.

Shepard, R. N., Hovland, C. I., & Jenkins, H. M. (1961). Learning and memorization of classifications. *Psychological Monographs, 75*, 1–41.

Smith, E. E. (1989). Concepts and induction. In M. I. Posner (Ed.), *Foundations of cognitive science* (pp. 501–526). Cambridge, MA: MIT Press.

Smith, E. E. (1990). Categorization. In D. N. Osherson & E. E. Smith (Eds.), *An invitation to cognitive science: Vol. 3. Thinking* (pp. 33–53). Cambridge, MA: MIT Press.

Smith, E. E., & Medin, D. L. (1981). *Categories and concepts.* Cambridge, MA: Harvard University Press.

Smith, E. E., & Osherson, D. N. (1984). Conceptual combination with prototype concepts. *Cognitive Science, 11*, 337–361.

Smith, E. E., Shoben, E. J., & Rips, L. J. (1974). Structure and process in semantic memory. *Psychological Review, 81*, 214–241.

Spear, N. (1976). Retrieval of memories: A psychobiological approach. In W. K. Estes (Ed.), *Handbook of learning and cognitive processes: Vol. 4. Attention and Memory* (pp. 17–90). Hillsdale, NJ: Erlbaum.

Stone, G. O. (1986). An analysis of the detla rule and the learning of statistical associations. In D. E. Rumelhart & J. L. McClelland (Eds.), *Parallel distributed processing: Vol. 1, Foundations* (pp. 444–459). Cambridge, MA: MIT Press.

Trabasso, T. & Bower, G. H. (1964). Memory in concept identification. *Psychonomic Science, 1*, 133–134.

Trabasso, T. & Bower, G. H. (1968). *Attention in learning.* New York: Wiley.

Tulving, E. (1972). Episodic and semantic memory. In E. Tulving & W. Donaldson (Eds.), *Organization of memory* (pp. 382–403). New York: Academic Press.

Uhl, C. N. (1964). Effect of overlapping cues upon discrimination learning. *Journal of Experimental Psychology, 67*, 91–97.

Underwood, B. J. (1969). Attributes of memory. *Psychological Review, 76*, 559–73.

THREE PRINCIPLES FOR MODELS OF
CATEGORY LEARNING

John K. Kruschke

I. A Connectionist Framework

As this volume attests, recent decades have produced a variety of models of category learning. In this article I show how three underlying principles of several models—including the (generalized) context model (Medin & Schaffer, 1978; Nosofsky, 1986) and standard back propagation networks (Rumelhart, Hinton, & Williams, 1986)—have been synthesized into the ALCOVE model (Kruschke, 1990, 1992). I illustrate the importance of each principle with data from human category-learning experiments. Whereas models that incorporate the three principles can fit the human data from various experiments reasonably well, several other models that lack one or more of the principles fail to capture human performance.

A paradigmatic task in category learning experiments is the prediction of some missing feature, such as a category label, on the basis of some given features, such as color, size, and shape. In many laboratory settings, the feature to be predicted is always an arbitrary category label prescribed by the experimenter. In principle, however, the feature to be predicted could be anything absent from the stimulus; for instance, prediction of color when given category label, size, and shape.

A connectionist framework for this general task is shown in Fig. 1. Information flows upward from the lowest level in the diagram. The framework assumes that the stimulus can be appropriately described in terms of

57

John K. Kruschke

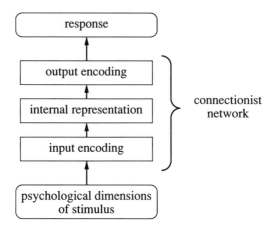

Fig. 1.   A framework for models of category learning.

its values on psychological dimensions, either nominally or continuously scaled. The psychological values are then *encoded* by the first layer of nodes in the network. The choice of encoding is not restricted by the framework; it only needs to be a well-defined mapping from psychological space to input node activations. For example, there could be one input node for each psychological dimension, with different activation levels representing different values, or instead there could be separate nodes for each value on each dimension, with presence of a value indicated by positive activation of the corresponding node. The former encoding scheme is sometimes called *amplitude coding,* and the latter *place coding* (cf. Ballard, 1987; Hancock, 1989; Walters, 1987).

Activation on the input layer then propagates to the "hidden" layer, which transforms the input encoding into some *internal representation.* For example, the nodes of the hidden layer might correspond to prototypes, and the activation of a prototype node would indicate the similarity of the input to the prototype. Alternatively, hidden nodes might represent small regions around individual exemplars, or vast regions bounded by a hyperplane through input space. In any case, the activation of the internal representation is spread to the output layer, which encodes the to-be-predicted psychological dimensions. The output layer can use the same encoding scheme as the input layer, but that is not necessary.

Finally, the activations at the output layer must be translated into some performance variable that can be directly compared with human behavior, such as proportion correct or response latency. Some models assume a quantitative function relating network output to response performance, whereas others assume only a monotonic relationship.

As will be shown, this framework accommodates a number of categorization models, but certainly not all. Despite its generality, it does not encompass network models with recurrent connections, such as J. A. Anderson's "brain state in a box" (Anderson, Silverstein, Ritz, & Jones, 1977; Knapp & Anderson, 1984) or McClelland and Rumelhart's (1981) interactive activation networks or McClelland's (1991a, 1991b) GRAIN networks. Moreover, models of theory construction, or other forms of reasoning, are not addressed by this framework. Nevertheless, by providing a common framework for several other models, the similarities and differences of those models are more easily discerned, and potential hybrid models are suggested.

II. Models Synthesized in ALCOVE

Figure 2 shows the intellectual genealogy of ALCOVE (Kruschke, 1990, 1992). The genealogy begins with three underlying principles formalized by different models and indicates the convergence of the principles in

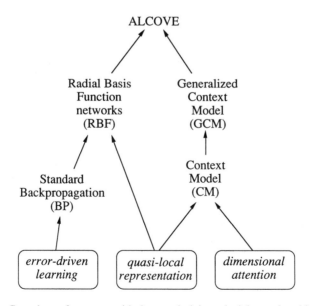

Fig. 2.   Genealogy of ALCOVE, with three underlying principles enclosed in boxes.

John K. Kruschke

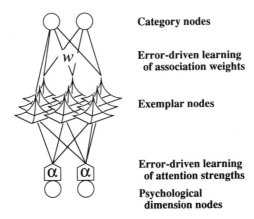

Category nodes

Error-driven learning
of association weights

Exemplar nodes

Error-driven learning
of attention strengths

Psychological
dimension nodes

Fig. 3.   The architecture of ALCOVE. From Kruschke (1992, Fig. 1). Copyright 1992 by the American Psychological Association. Reprinted by permission of the publisher.

successive models. Because the genealogy reflects the idiosyncratic development of ALCOVE in the mind of its inventor, the figure omits some models that also formalize some or all of the same underlying principles. In this section I describe the models, and in the next section I show how each of the three underlying principles is important in accounting for human learning behavior. All the models in the genealogy fit the framework in Fig. 1. Estes (this volume) gives an introduction to antecedents of ALCOVE from another perspective; in this article I emphasize ALCOVE's relations to connectionist models (see also Kruschke, 1992; Nosofsky & Kruschke, 1992).

A.   ALCOVE

The basic architecture of ALCOVE stems from the generalized context model (GCM; Nosofsky, 1986), and is shown in Fig. 3. Whereas the GCM was not originally described as a connectionist network, its formal structure allows it to be implemented as one. In ALCOVE, as in the GCM, stimulus dimensions are assumed to be continuous and interval-scaled, and each dimension is encoded by a separate input node using amplitude encoding. Thus, if ψ_i is the psychological scale value of the stimulus on dimension i, then the activation of input node i is

$$a_i^{\text{in}} = \psi_i \qquad (1)$$

There is one hidden node established for each training exemplar.[1] The activation of a hidden node corresponds to the *similarity* of the current stimulus to the exemplar represented by the node. Similarity drops off exponentially with distance in psychological space, as suggested by Shepard (1987), and distance is computed using a city-block metric for psychologically separable dimensions (Garner, 1974; Shepard, 1964). The profile of the hidden-node activation function is suggested by the "pyramids" in the middle layer of Fig. 3. The hidden node is significantly activated only by a localized region of input space; that is, its *receptive field* is small and bounded. It is this property that embodies the principle of *quasi-local representation*. Formally, the activation value is given by

$$a_j^{\text{hid}} = \exp\left(-c\sum_i \alpha_i |h_{ji} - a_i^{\text{in}}|\right) \tag{2}$$

where c is a constant called the *specificity* which determines the overall width of the receptive field, α_i is the *attention strength* on the ith dimension, and h_{ji} is the scale value of the jth exemplar on the ith dimension. Increasing the attention strength on a dimension has the effect of stretching that dimension, so that differences along that dimension have a larger influence on the similarity. This attentional flexibility is very useful for stretching dimensions that are highly relevant for distinguishing the categories and shrinking dimensions that are irrelevant to the category distinction, as is described later in more detail.

Each output node represents a category label, and the activation of the kth category node is determined by a linear combination of hidden-node activations:

$$a_k^{\text{out}} = \sum_{\substack{\text{hid} \\ j}} w_{kj} a_j^{\text{hid}} \tag{3}$$

where w_{kj} is the association weight to category node k from exemplar node j. Category node activations (exponentiated to make them non-negative)

---

[1] Alternatively, hidden nodes can be randomly scattered across the stimulus space, thereby forming a "covering map" of the space. This approach avoids the problem of having to know where to place hidden nodes before training begins and was also the original conceptualization of ALCOVE (Kruschke, 1990), giving ALCOVE the last four letters of its name: Attentional Learning COVEring map. It is not used here, however, because the exemplar-based approach is computationally less intensive and yields results very similar to the covering map approach (Kruschke, 1990).

are mapped to response probabilities using the Luce choice rule (Luce, 1963):

$$\Pr(K) = \exp(\phi a_K^{\text{out}}) \Big/ \sum_{\substack{\text{out} \\ k}} \exp(\phi a_k^{\text{out}}) \qquad (4)$$

where ϕ is a scaling constant. In other words, the probability of classifying the given stimulus into category K is determined by the magnitude of category K's activation relative to the sum of all category activations. Equations (3) and (4) are taken from the models of Estes, Campbell, Hatsopoulos, & Hurwitz (1989), Gluck & Bower (1988b), and Nosofsky (1986).

The three layers of nodes in ALCOVE correspond to the three layers of the general network in the framework of Fig. 1. Equations (1)–(4) correspond to the four arrows in Fig. 1.

The dimensional attention strengths α_i and the association weights w_{kj} are learned by gradient descent on sum-squared error, as used in standard backprop (Rumelhart et al., 1986). Each presentation of a training exemplar is followed by feedback indicating the correct response. The feedback is coded in ALCOVE as *teacher* values, t_k given to each category node. For a given training exemplar and feedback, the *error* generated by the model is defined as

$$E = \tfrac{1}{2} \sum_{\substack{\text{out} \\ k}} (t_k - a_k^{\text{out}})^2 \qquad (5)$$

where the teacher values are defined as

$$t_k = \begin{cases} \max(+1, a_k^{\text{out}}) & \text{if stimulus} \in k \\ \min(-1, a_k^{\text{out}}) & \text{if stimulus} \notin k \end{cases} \qquad (6)$$

These teacher values are defined so that activations "better than necessary" are not counted as errors. Thus, if a given stimulus should be classified as a member of the kth category, then the kth output node should have an activation of at least $+1$. If the activation is greater than $+1$, then the difference between the actual activation and $+1$ is not counted as error. Because these teacher values do not mind being outshone by their students, I call them *humble* teachers. The motivation for using humble teacher values is that the feedback given to subjects is nominal, indicating only which category the stimulus belongs to, and not the degree of membership. Hence the teacher used in the model should only require some minimal level of category-node activation and should not require all instances ultimately to produce the same activations. Humble teachers are discussed further by Kruschke (1990, 1992), and they do not play a central role here.

Upon presentation of a training exemplar to ALCOVE, the association weights and attention strengths are changed by a small amount so that the error decreases. Following Rumelhart et al., they are adjusted proportionally to the (negative of the) error gradient, which leads to the following learning rules (derived in Kruschke 1990, 1992):

$$\Delta w_{kj}^{\text{out}} = -\lambda_w \frac{\partial E}{\partial w_{kj}^{\text{out}}} = \lambda_w (t_k - a_k^{\text{out}}) a_j^{\text{hid}} \tag{7}$$

$$\Delta \alpha_i = -\lambda_\alpha \frac{\partial E}{\partial \alpha_i} = -\lambda_\alpha \sum_{\substack{\text{hid} \\ j}} \left[\sum_{\substack{\text{out} \\ k}} (t_k - a_k^{\text{out}}) w_{kj} \right] a_j^{\text{hid}} c \left| h_{ji} - a_i^{\text{in}} \right| \tag{8}$$

where the λ's are constants of proportionality ($\lambda > 0$) called *learning rates*. The same learning rate, λ_w, applies to all the output weights. Likewise, there is only one learning rate, λ_α, for all the attention strengths. If application of Eq. (8) gives an attention strength a negative value, then that strength is set to zero, because negative values have no psychologically meaningful interpretation.

Learning in ALCOVE proceeds as follows: For each presentation of a training exemplar, activation propagates to the category nodes, using Eqs. (1)–(4). Then the teacher values are presented and compared with the actual category node activations. The association weights and attention strengths are then adjusted according to Eqs. (7) and (8). In fitting ALCOVE to human learning data, there are four free parameters: the fixed specificity c in Eq. (2); the probability mapping constant ϕ in Eq. (4); the association weight learning rate λ_w in Eq. (7); and the attention strength learning rate λ_α in Eq. (8).

To summarize, ALCOVE formally instantiates all three of the underlying principles in Fig. 2. It uses error-driven learning to adjust association weights and attention strengths (and the same principle can also be used to adjust other parameters in the network). It uses a quasi-local representation in its hidden nodes, which are located at the positions of training exemplars and activated according to the similarity of the current stimulus to the exemplar represented by the node [Eq. (2)]. Finally, it uses dimensional attention strengths for differential use of relevant or irrelevant dimensions. The importance of each of those principles in accounting for human performance will be demonstrated after comparing ALCOVE with its predecessors.

B.   THE GENERALIZED CONTEXT MODEL

The GCM (Nosofsky, 1986; Medin & Schaffer, 1978) motivated the feed-
forward computations in ALCOVE and makes category choice predictions
using Eqs. (1)–(4). [The GCM also has response bias parameters not
shown in Eq. (4)]. However, the GCM does not have error-driven learning
of association weights, and has no learning mechanism at all for attention
strengths, as indicated in Fig. 4. Instead, learning of an association weight
consists of making a constant-sized increment whenever that exemplar is
presented as a member of that category. Formally,

$$\Delta w_{kj}^{out} = \begin{cases} 1 & \text{if exemplar } j \text{ has category label } k \\ 0 & \text{otherwise} \end{cases} \qquad (9)$$

[compare Eq. (9) with Eq. (7)]. Thus, on each trial one and only one weight
is changed, by a fixed amount that is independent of the actual performance of the system.[2]

The GCM has no learning mechanism at all for attention strengths.
Instead, they are free parameters, independently estimated for different
times in the course of learning. One of the contributions of ALCOVE is the
suggestion that the dimensional attention strengths can be learned by back
propagating error signals through the exemplars.

Figure 2 summarizes the facts that the GCM formalizes the principles of
quasi-local representation and dimensional attention, but not the principle
of error-driven learning.

C.   STANDARD BACK PROPAGATION

Standard back propagation (Rumelhart et al., 1986), or *backprop*, was
originally proposed as a learning mechanism for multi-layer, smoothed
perceptrons (Minsky & Papert, 1969; Rosenblatt, 1958) and was not pro-
moted as a model of human category learning. Nevertheless, many re-

---

[2] Learning in the GCM can be construed as a form of winner-take-all "Hebbian" learning
and formalized in terms of gradient ascent:

$$\Delta w_{kj}^{out} = \begin{cases} \partial(\Sigma_m t_m a_m^{out})/\partial w_{kj}^{out} & \text{if } a_j^{hid} = \max_h\{a_h^{hid}\} \\ 0 & \text{otherwise} \end{cases}$$

where the teacher value t_k is 1.0 if the exemplar is a member of category k and 0.0 (not -1.0)
otherwise. Thus, the learning mechanism in the GCM can be understood as a form of hill
climbing, but it is not error-driven.

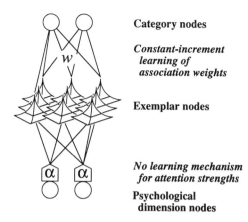

Category nodes

Constant-increment learning of association weights

Exemplar nodes

No learning mechanism for attention strengths

Psychological dimension nodes

Fig. 4.   The generalized context model (GCM).

searchers have used backprop in models of human learning at the molar level. Several reports have emphasized its success (Cohen, Dunbar, & McClelland, 1990; McClelland & Jenkins, 1991; Seidenberg & McClelland, 1989; Sejnowski & Rosenberg, 1988; Taraban, McDonald, & Mac-Whinney, 1989), and others have emphasized its failures (Gluck, 1991; McCloskey & Cohen, 1989; Pavel, Gluck, & Henkle, 1989; Ratcliff, 1990).

Unlike the GCM and ALCOVE, backprop makes no commitments to any particular stimulus or response encodings on its input and output nodes. For maximal comparability of models, I assume the same input and output encodings for backprop as are used in ALCOVE. (An alternative choice of representation is considered later.) The fact that this choice is not a committed property of backprop is indicated in Fig. 5 by the parentheses around the labels for the input and output nodes.

A key architectural property of standard backprop is that its hidden nodes have a *linear-sigmoid* activation function, given by

$$a_j^{\text{hid}} = 1 \bigg/ \left(1 + \exp\left[-\left(\sum_i^{\text{in}} w_{ji}^{\text{hid}} a_i^{\text{in}} - \theta_j \right) \right] \right) \tag{10}$$

where a_j^{hid} is the activation of the jth hidden node, w_{ji}^{hid} is the connection weight to the jth hidden node from the ith input node, a_i^{in} is the activation of the ith input node, and θ_j is a threshold for the jth hidden node. The activation profiles of some hidden nodes in backprop are shown in Fig. 5, and a direct comparison with ALCOVE's hidden nodes is shown in Fig. 6.

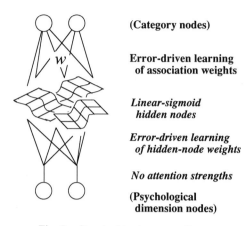

(Category nodes)

**Error-driven learning
of association weights**

*Linear-sigmoid
hidden nodes*

**Error-driven learning
of hidden-node weights**

No attention strengths

(Psychological
dimension nodes)

Fig. 5.   Standard back propagation.

These nodes are called "linear sigmoid" because their level contours ("horizontal" lines in Fig. 6) are linear and the heights of the level contours change according to a sigmoid. The weights w_{ji}^{hid} determine the orientation of the linear level contour, and the threshold θ_j determines the displacement of the sigmoidal "cliff" from the origin.

As can be seen in Fig. 6, the receptive field of a linear-sigmoid node is huge: an entire half-space of the input space. In other words, a linear-sigmoid node in standard backprop is not selectively sensitive to small regions in input space. Therefore the genealogy in Fig. 2 does not include "quasi-local representation" as an underlying principle in standard backprop. As is described in detail below, one consequence is the potential for catastrophic forgetting of previously learned associations when novel as-

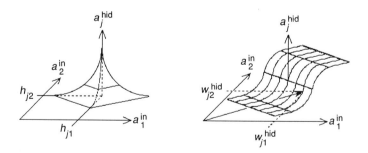

Fig. 6.   Left: Activation profile of a hidden node in ALCOVE and the GCM [Eq. (2)]. Right: Activation profile of a hidden node in standard back propagation [Eq. (10)]. From Kruschke (1992, Fig. 11). Copyright 1992 by the American Psychological Association. Reprinted by permission of the publisher.

sociations are trained (Kruschke, 1990, 1992; McCloskey & Cohen, 1989; Ratcliff, 1990).

A second key architectural property of backprop is that is does not have explicit dimensional attention strengths. Instead, each dimension has many independently adjustable weights leading from it. As described in detail below, this allows backprop to learn some category distinctions involving multiple dimensions much more easily than people can (Kruschke, 1990, 1992, 1993).

Backprop and ALCOVE also differ in their goals. Many applications of backprop have as one of their goals the development of new representations in the hidden layer which can mediate the mapping from input to output. Indeed, that was the goal emphasized in the title of Rumelhart et al.'s (1986) landmark paper: "Learning internal representations . . . ." The internal representation in ALCOVE is relatively fixed, however. The goal of ALCOVE is not to learn a new internal representation but to use the given exemplar representation for modeling category acquisition.

The essential idea from standard backprop that *is* incorporated into ALCOVE is error-driven learning. All the weights and thresholds in a backprop network are adjusted by gradient descent on error, analogous to Eqs. (5)–(8).

D.   RADIAL BASIS FUNCTION NETWORKS

The linear-sigmoid activation function used in backprop [Eq. (10)] was motivated as a smoothed, differentiable approximation to the discontinuous, discrete linear-threshold function used in perceptrons. If backprop is abstracted from its origins in perceptrons and instead considered as a case of fitting a continuous function (the network) to data points (the training cases), then other activation functions are suggested. In particular, interpolation using *radial basis functions* is possible (e.g., Powell, 1985). A radial basis function network has hidden nodes with activation function given by $d_j^{hid} = f(\|\mathbf{h}_j - \mathbf{a}^{in}\|)$ for some function f, where $\mathbf{h}_j$ is the vector of coordinates for the jth training exemplar. Networks using these hidden nodes are called *radial basis function networks* (RBFs) because the functions are radially symmetric and form a basis set of functions for describing the mapping from input to output. Robinson, Niranjan, and Fallside (1988) described a variant of that approach in which the hidden node activation functions are multivariate Gaussians, which Poggio and Girosi [1990, Eq. (6)] generalized as:

$$a_j^{hid} = \exp\left[-(\mathbf{h}_j - \mathbf{a}^{in})^T \mathbf{D}_j^T \mathbf{D}_j (\mathbf{h}_j - \mathbf{a}^{in})\right] \qquad (11)$$

where $\mathbf{D}_j$ is a matrix of dimension strengths for the jth node. Note that such a node has a localized receptive field and is maximally sensitive to a particular point $\mathbf{h}_j$ in input space. Because of that property, I have drawn an arrow in Fig. 2 from the principle of "quasi-local representation" to "RBF" (despite the fact that the receptive fields are not localized for other choices of the basis function f). Unlike standard RBFs, the variant in Eq. (11) has dimension strengths which make the receptive fields non-radial. For simplicity, I refer to both standard RBFs and Robinson et al.'s (1988) variant as RBFs. Additional theoretical and applied research on RBFs has been described by, among others, Broomhead and Lowe (1988), Moody and Darken (1989), and Niranjan and Fallside (1988).

When $\mathbf{D}_j$ is diagonal, then Eq. (11) can be rewritten as

$$a_j^{\text{hid}} = \exp\left(-\sum_i \mathbf{D}_{j(ii)}^2 |h_{ji} - a_i^{\text{in}}|^2\right) \qquad (12)$$

where $\mathbf{D}_{j(ii)}$ is the ith diagonal element of $\mathbf{D}j$. A comparison of Eqs. (12) and (2) reveals the close resemblance of ALCOVE to RBFs. Both networks use hidden nodes with localized receptive fields, both networks use error-driven learning, and both networks have a form of dimensional weighting. There are some important differences, however. First, unlike ALCOVE, RBFs can have fewer hidden nodes than training exemplars. Thus a hidden node in an RBF can act as a prototype for a cluster of nearby training exemplars. Second, unlike ALCOVE, the locations h_{ji} of hidden nodes in RBFs are not necessarily fixed and can be adjusted via error reduction. This is motivated by the fact that there are more training exemplars than hidden nodes, so the best locations for hidden nodes must be established by learning. Third, and most important, dimensional weightings in an RBF are far less constrained than in ALCOVE. The attention strengths in ALCOVE are "attached" to the input dimensions, with the same strengths applying to every hidden node. In an RBF, each hidden node has its own set of dimensional attention strengths. Moreover, an RBF allows non-zero off-diagonal elements in the matrix $\mathbf{D}_j$ [Eq. (11)] which correspond to co-variance terms in the multi-variate Gaussian. These covariance terms allow the hidden nodes to differentially accentuate diagonal directions in input space, unlike the attention strengths in ALCOVE. Because of those differences, I have not drawn an arrow from "dimensional attention" to "RBF" in Fig. 2.

The comparison of ALCOVE to RBFs is noteworthy for two reasons. First, in terms of its intellectual genealogy, ALCOVE was conceived when I noticed the obvious similarities of the GCM and RBFs. Second, the greater flexibility of RBFs suggests directions for variations of ALCOVE, such as exemplar-specific dimensional attention strengths and exemplar specificities that are individually adjusted to reduce error.

III.   Three Underlying Principles

In the previous section I described how ALCOVE formalizes three underlying principles: error-driven learning, quasi-local representation, and dimensional attention. In this section I demonstrate that each of those principles is important within the general framework of Fig. 1 and that none can be jettisoned without causing large qualitative discrepancies from human performance. There is no claim that these three principles are sufficient to account for all human category learning. Nor is there any claim that the three principles must be formalized as in ALCOVE. Other principles and formalizations are discussed later.

A.   DIMENSIONAL ATTENTION

Imagine a category-learning situation in which a single stimulus dimension is relevant. For example, suppose all large stimuli belong to category A, and all small stimuli to category B; that is, only size is relevant to the categorization. Such situations are called *filtration* tasks, because the irrelevant dimensions can be "filtered away" without loss of categorization accuracy. On the other hand, suppose that categorization depends on two or more dimensions, as when large and bright stimuli belong to category A, but large and dim stimuli, and small and bright stimuli, belong to category B. The latter situation is called a *condensation* task, because information from multiple dimensions must be condensed into a single response. It is intuitively plausible, and has been repeatedly empirically verified, that filtration tasks are easier to learn than condensation tasks (Gottwald & Garner, 1972, 1975; Posner, 1964). Filtration advantage is commonly attributed to selective attention: filtration is easier because we can selectively attend to the relevant dimension; conversely, condensation is more difficult because we cannot selectively attend to a combination of dimensions with the same ease as single dimensions. Filtration advantage is robust and fundamental and is an effect that models of category learning should address.

  To test the ability of the models to show filtration advantage, I gathered learning data from subjects in simple category learning tasks. The stimuli were single rectangles that had one of four possible heights, with an interior, vertical line segment that that had one of four possible lateral positions. Only 8 of the 16 possible combinations were used, and these were assigned to categories as shown in Fig. 7. Each dot is a point in the two-dimensional stimulus space and represents a particular training exemplar. The color of the dot (open or filled) represents the correct category label. There were four different category structures, learned by four different groups of subjects. Two structures were filtration tasks (one with height relevant, the other with position relevant), and two were condensation tasks. All subjects, in all four groups, were presented with the same sequence of training stimuli; all that varied between groups was the feedback. Full procedural details and statistical analyses are given in Kruschke (1993).

Results are shown in Fig. 8. There are four curves corresponding to the four groups of subjects. Each point plots the proportion of trials correct for the preceding "epoch" of 8 trials (one presentation of each distinct stimulus). As expected, the filtration conditions were learned much more quickly than the condensation conditions. (Presumably, subjects would be able to learn the condensation task to very high accuracy if they were trained longer; the point is that the speed of acquisition is much slower than in the filtration condition.) The purpose of obtaining these data is to provide trial-by-trial learning curves to which the models can be fit.

Fitting ALCOVE to these data requires knowing the psychological scale values of the stimuli. Therefore a similarity scaling study was conducted with naive subjects. Subjects were shown two stimuli in succession and

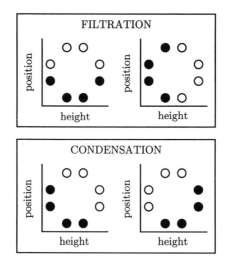

Fig. 7. Structure of the filtration and condensation categories. Open circles denote one category, filled circles the other. From Nosofsky and Kruschke (1992, Fig. 16, p. 239).

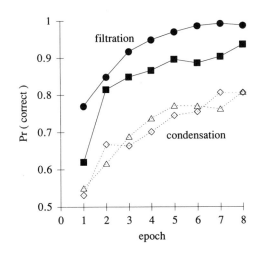

Fig. 8. Human learning data for the four category structures shown in Fig. 7. One "epoch" is one sweep through the eight different stimuli. Filled circles show the position-relevant filtration; filled squares show the height-relevant filtration. Open markers show results from the two condensation conditions. From Nosofsky and Kruschke (1992, Fig. 17, p. 240).

asked to rate their similarity. Then the psychological coordinates were derived that best accounted for the mean pairwise similarities. Details are supplied in Kruschke (1993). Most relevant for my purposes here are two facts. First, a city-block metric fit the similarity ratings notably better than a Euclidean metric. Therefore the use of a city-block metric in Eq. (2) is appropriate. Second, the psychological distance between the two intermediate positions was greater than the psychological distance between the two intermediate heights. Therefore the categories in the position-relevant filtration should be more discriminable, and easier to learn, than the categories in the height-relevant filtration. That predicted difference was in fact observed in the learning data, as can be seen in Fig. 8.

The best fits of ALCOVE and backprop are shown in Fig. 9. For these fits, ALCOVE had four free parameters, and backprop had five, as described in Kruschke (1993). The same parameter values were used to fit all four curves simultaneously, and the best fits had root mean square deviations (RMSD) of 0.116 and 0.152 respectively. Clearly, ALCOVE shows strong filtration advantage, whereas backprop shows none. ALCOVE also shows the advantage of the position-relevant filtration over the height-relevant filtration because the hidden nodes reflect the greater separation of the intermediate positions as compared to the intermediate heights. On the contrary, the best that backprop can do is approximate the mean of the

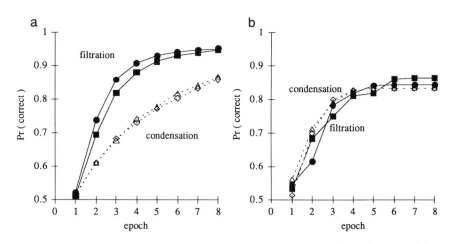

Fig. 9.   Best fits of (a) ALCOVE and (b) backprop to data in Fig. 8. Fig. 9a from Nosofsky and Kruschke (1992, Fig. 17, p. 240).

four conditions. (The inability of the models to capture the rapidity of learning in the early trials is discussed in the final section of this article.)

How does ALCOVE show filtration advantage, and why does backprop fail? Figure 10 shows that the attention learning mechanism in ALCOVE has the effect of stretching relevant dimensions and shrinking irrelevant ones. Such attentional learning benefits the filtration condition. By contrast, attentional learning cannot benefit the condensation condition because "diagonal" directions through stimulus space cannot be differentially stretched. (In the condensation condition, both dimensions are simultaneously stretched or shrunk by attentional learning, but that affects both diagonal directions equally, not differentially.) It seems that humans have an analogous constraint, in that they can differentially attend to psychological dimensions but find it much harder to combine dimensions. Backprop does not have such a constraint. Its linear-sigmoid hidden nodes can orient themselves in any direction in stimulus space, so that a "diagonal" category boundary, like that in the condensation tasks here, is just as easy to learn as a boundary orthogonal to one of the stimulus dimensions.

The point of this section has been to demonstrate the importance of dimensional attention learning in models of category learning. Standard backprop lacks this property and consequently fails to show filtration advantage.

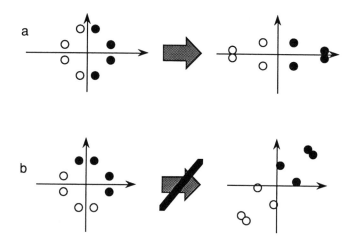

Fig. 10. (a) Increasing attention to the horizontal dimension and decreasing attention to the vertical dimension benefits a filtration situation. (b) ALCOVE cannot differentially attend to diagonal axes in a condensation situation.

B.   ERROR-DRIVEN LEARNING

A second principle embodied in ALCOVE is error-driven learning. The importance of error-driven learning can be illustrated by applying the model to a phenomenon discovered by Gluck and Bower (1988b). They studied category learning in a simulated medical diagnosis paradigm: Subjects were presented with lists of four symptoms (stimulus dimensions), denoted s1–s4, which had to be diagnosed as one of two diseases (categories). The two diseases had different base rates of presentation, one occurring 75% of the time, and the other occurring 25% of the time. The probabilities of each symptom, given the disease, are shown in the following tabulation.

	Disease	
Symptom	Rare	Common
s1	.6	.2
s2	.4	.3
s3	.3	.4
s4	.2	.6

For example, given the rare disease, the probability of symptom s1 occurring was 60%.

A key feature of the design is that the normative probability of the rare disease, given symptom s1, is 50%. Thus, if presented with symptom s1 alone, a Bayesian classifier would choose the rare disease 50% of the time. Human data showed reliably higher selection of the rare disease, however. This result has been replicated by Estes et al. (1989); Nosofsky, Kruschke, and McKinley (1992); and Shanks (1990). The Nosofsky et al. study used substitutive symptoms, such as "runny nose" versus "stuffy nose," denoted as s1 and s1* respectively. Subjects were trained for 240 trials on lists of four symptoms and then tested with lists that included just a single symptom, two symptoms, three symptoms, or no symptoms. Here I am concerned only with the single symptom conditions; the reader is referred to Nosofsky et al. for full details. As will later be seen in Fig. 12, when tested with symptom s1 alone, subjects chose the rare disease much more than 50% of the time.

How might we account for this apparent base rate neglect? Gluck and Bower (1988b) pointed out that certain exemplar-based models could not account for the effect. In those models, each exemplar is stored along with the category label. When a new stimulus is presented, all stored exemplars which match it on the given symptoms are polled for their category "votes." In the present design, of all exemplars containing symptom s1, the number that were assigned to the rare category equaled the number assigned to the common category, so the poll would result in a choice probability of 50%. Nosofsky et al. (1992) showed that the GCM, which includes non-linear similarities among exemplars, makes even worse predictions, favoring the common category. As ALCOVE is also an exemplar-based model, it faces a challenge from these results.

Gluck and Bower (1988b) proposed an alternative adaptive network model in which input nodes representing symptoms (or configurations of symptoms) were connected directly to output nodes representing categories. Figure 11 shows the configural-cue model for two binary-valued input dimensions. There are two *component-cue* input nodes for the two values on the first dimension, two more component-cue input nodes for the two values on the second dimension, and four *configural-cue* input nodes for the four pairwise combinations of values from the two dimensions. Dotted lines indicate correspondences from psychological dimensions to input nodes, but those dotted lines are not actual, weighted connections in the model. Connection weights are adjusted by gradient descent on error. Estes et al. (1989) used a version of that model in which output node activations were mapped to choice probabilities using Eq. (4), and that version is assumed here. Of key importance for us is the fact that their

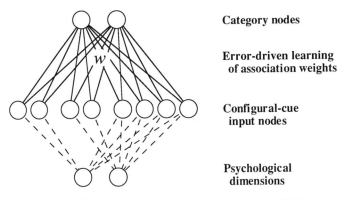

Category nodes

Error-driven learning
of association weights

Configural-cue
input nodes

Psychological
dimensions

Fig. 11.   Configural-cue model of Gluck and Bower (1988).

model is not exemplar-based: in the component-cue version, only single symptoms (cues) are included, and in the configural-cue version (Gluck and Bower, 1988a), full patterns of four symptoms are represented along with single symptoms, pairs, and triples, on separate input nodes. Gluck and Bower (1988b) showed that the component-cue model could indeed capture the apparent base-rate neglect, at least qualitatively.

ALCOVE, the component-cue model, and the configural-cue model were fitted to learning and test data from the experiment reported in Nosofsky et al. (1992). Details of procedures for these fits can be found in Kruschke (1992). The RMSDs of the models from the data are shown in the following tabulation, where it can be seen that ALCOVE did as well as the component-cue model and better than the configural-cue model.

		RMSD	
Model	Total	Learning	Test
ALCOVE	0.101	0.106	0.0955
Component-Cue	0.116	0.109	0.123
Configural-Cue	0.151	0.113	0.181

The predicted choice probabilities for single symptoms are shown in Fig. 12. (Predictions of the configural-cue model are not shown because they deviate badly from the data and show only very slight apparent base-rate neglect for symptom s1.) While the predictions of the models are not a stunning fit to the data, the point is that ALCOVE, an exemplar-based

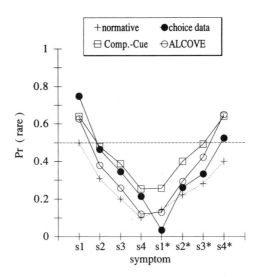

Fig. 12. Predicted and observed choice probabilities for transfer trials. Note that ALCOVE and the component-cue model show nearly the same "base-rate neglect" for symptom s1. From Kruschke (1992, Fig. 8). Copyright 1992 by the American Psychological Association. Reprinted by permission of the publisher.

model, predicts the tendency to choose the rare category for symptom s1 to the same extent as the component-cue model.

How does ALCOVE exhibit the apparent base-rate neglect? For sake of explication, consider a two-symptom situation, with symptoms **a** versus **a*** and **b** versus **b***. Figure 13 shows the frequencies with which each combination occurs, out of a total of 105 instances. For example, the symptom combination **ab** occurs a total of 11 times, and 10 of those times it is assigned to the rare category. Importantly, of the 30 instances in which symptom **a** occurs, it is assigned 15 times to the rare category and 15 times to the common category, so that a Bayesian classifier would choose the rare category just 50% of the time when presented with symptom **a** alone. The table in Fig. 13 acts as a geometric analogue of the two-dimensional stimulus space, and we can imagine that over each cell in the table is the diamond-shaped receptive field of the corresponding exemplar node in ALCOVE. Emanating from each exemplar node are association weights to the rare or common category nodes. The strengths of those weights are indicated by the widths of the arrows emanating from the cells of the table. Two facts are of crucial importance: First, the weight from the **a*****b*** exemplar (to the common category node) is only moderately large. The reason is that its neighboring exemplars, **a*****b** and **ab***, are also usually

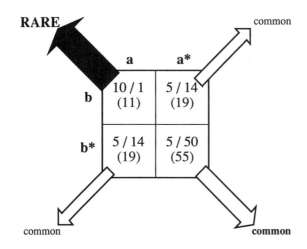

Fig. 13.   Each cell of the table shows frequency of rare disease, frequency of common disease, and total frequency (in parentheses). The strengths of association weights from each exemplar are indicated by the widths of the arrows emanating from the cells.

assigned to the common category, and they cooperate with a*b* to reach the desired output activation on the common category node. The weight stops growing larger because there is negligible error. Second, the weight from the **ab** exemplar (to the rare category node) is very large, because it must compete with its neighboring exemplars, **a*b** and **ab***. The weight grows large because there is error introduced by the influence of the neighboring exemplars. The result is that when symptom **a** is presented alone, the large weight from exemplar **ab** to the rare category is enough to overcome the moderate weights to the common category.

The point of this section has been to demonstrate the importance of error-driven learning. Exemplar-based models without error-driven learning were previously shown to be unable to account for apparent base-rate neglect, whereas ALCOVE accounts for it as well as the models proposed by Gluck and Bower (1988b). The source of this phenomenon in ALCOVE is the combination of error-driven learning along with similarity-based activations of exemplars, whereby neighboring exemplars can interact to facilitate error reduction or hinder it.

C.   QUASI-LOCAL REPRESENTATION

A third underlying principle formalized in ALCOVE is quasi-local representation of categories. The principle of quasi-local representation asserts that the internal representation of the stimuli (see Fig. 1) should consist of elements sensitive to localized regions of *psychological* space. For example, the hidden nodes in ALCOVE are quasi-local, whereas the hidden nodes in standard backprop are not (see Fig. 6). Quasi-local representation is not strictly "localist" in the sense that only one hidden node is activated for a given stimulus. Instead, several quasi-local nodes are partially activated, and the representation of the stimulus is distributed across many nodes. The distribution is less extreme, however, than that commonly observed in standard backprop networks using linear-sigmoid hidden nodes. The distinction between quasi-local and non–quasi-local representations is roughly (but not exactly) analogous to the distinction in the traditional psychological literature between exemplar or prototype-based representation, on the one hand, and rule-based representation, on the other (Smith & Medin, 1981). That is, only a relatively localized region of stimuli are very similar to an exemplar or prototype, but many stimuli, across vast regions of psychological space, can satisfy the conditions of a rule (depending on the particular conditions of the rule, of course). In this section I show that the non–quasi-local, linear-sigmoid hidden nodes in backprop cause a problem known as *catastrophic forgetting,* a problem which can be solved by using quasi-local representation.[3]

Consider the category structure shown in Fig. 14. The actual stimuli were rectangles that varied in height, with an interior segment that varied in lateral position, as used in the filtration/condensation experiment described earlier. Each exemplar was assigned to one of two categories, indicated by the X or O. Training consisted of two phases: In the first phase, exemplars in squares in Fig. 14 (inside the dotted boundary) received explicit category feedback, while exemplars in circles (outside the dotted boundary) were (usually) shown with only *?* as feedback. In the second phase of training, exemplars in squares received *?* feedback, while exemplars in circles were shown with explicit feedback. The transition between phases was unmarked and unannounced to the subjects. (Full procedural details can be found in Kruschke, 1993).

How will learning of the "square" exemplars in the first phase affect generalization to the ambiguous "circle" exemplars? And how will learning of the "circle" exemplars in the second phase affect memory for the "square" exemplars from the first phase? The answers are shown in

---

[3] The comparison of linear-sigmoid nodes with rules might make some connectionists uneasy; after all, isn't part of the radical connectionist agenda to prohibit rules? The unruly may temporarily rest at ease, for I argue that it is exactly the rule-like quality of linear-sigmoid nodes which causes the problem of catastrophic forgetting. Later in the chapter, however, the unruly might form lines against me, when I suggest a rule-based system is needed to account for some aspects of category learning.

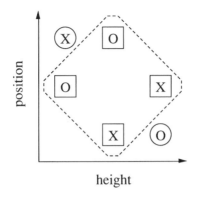

height

Fig. 14.   Category structure to demonstrate catastrophic forgetting in a backprop. Exemplars inside dotted boundary, in squares, had explicit feedback during the first phase of training but not during the second phase; the reverse was true of exemplars outside the dotted boundary (circles). Category assignment is indicated by X or O.

Fig. 15, which plots proportion correct as a function of learning trial. Circles and squares show the mean proportion correct for exemplars denoted by circles and squares (respectively) in Fig. 14. Filled markers denote trials on which there was explicit category feedback for those exemplars; open markers denote trials on which the feedback was *?*. One important result is that during the second phase, which begins with the 121st trial, memory for the initially trained exemplars (open squares) remains very strong despite the fact that newly trained exemplars (filled circles) are learned very well. Another important result is that during the first phase, generalization to the ambiguous exemplars (open circles) starts far below chance and improves to about chance level by the end of the first phase. The improvement in generalization occurs in jumps, giving the learning curve a scalloped appearance. The reason for the jumps is that ambiguous exemplars were actually given explicit category feedback (not just *?*) every fifth epoch during the first phase (as marked by the filled circles in Fig. 15). The jumps in performance occur on trials just after each presentation with explicit feedback; memory then decays somewhat until the next presentation with explicit feedback. Explicit feedback was supplied every fifth epoch merely to let the subject know that there really was a correct answer for those exemplars and that they should not just give up or ignore them.

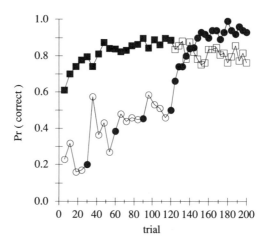

Fig. 15.   Human learning data for structure in Fig. 14. Circles and squares show the mean proportion correct for exemplars marked as circles and squares (respectively) in Fig. 14. Filled markers denote trials on which there was explicit category feedback for those exemplars; open markers denote trials on which the feedback was ?.

Best fits of ALCOVE and backprop[4] are shown in Fig. 16. ALCOVE fits the data well (RMSD = 0.0727), showing the scalloped generalization curve in the first phase and the lack of forgetting in the second phase. By contrast, backprop fails to generalize appropriately in the first phase and shows "catastrophic forgetting" in the second phase, with proportion correct dropping nearly to chance (RMSD = 0.208). Previous authors have noted catastrophic forgetting in backprop (McCloskey & Cohen, 1989; Ratcliff, 1990); what is new here is the quantitative fit to actual trial-by-trial learning data.

The quasi-local hidden nodes in ALCOVE allow it to fit the data so well. There is only slight forgetting in the second phase, and not catastrophic forgetting, because hidden nodes representing the exemplars from the two phases have only slightly overlapping receptive fields. On the other hand,

---

[4] The version of backprop used here was actually an extended version that included dimensional attention strengths α_i, so that

$$a_j^{\text{hid}} = 1 \Big/ \left(1 + \exp\left[-g\left(\sum_{\substack{\text{in} \\ i}} w_{ji}^{\text{hid}} \alpha_i a_i^{\text{in}} - \theta_j \right) \right] \right)$$

In this extended model, we trade hidden weight learning for attention strength learning. The extended model can show filtration advantage, with a best fit RMSD of 0.125 to the data in Fig. 8; for details see Kruschke (1993).

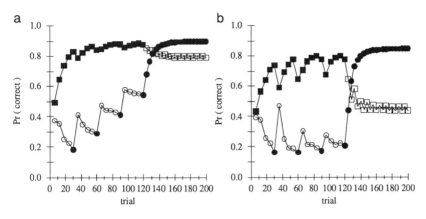

Fig. 16.   Best fits of ALCOVE (a) and (extended) backprop (b) to learning data in Fig. 15.

the overlap of receptive fields is enough to account for the worse-than-chance generalization data in the first phase. Thus, the quasi-local representation allows the exemplars to remain distinguishable enough to avoid catastrophic forgetting, yet interactive enough to exhibit generalization (in this experiment) and apparent base-rate neglect (reported in the previous section).

The linear-sigmoid hidden nodes in backprop cause it great difficulty with these data. In Fig. 14, the first phase exemplars (squares) can be correctly discriminated by a line running along the right diagonal, with all exemplars below the line assigned to X and all exemplars above the line assigned to O. A hidden node in backprop tends to align its linear receptive-field boundary along that linear category boundary. Unfortunately, that assignment directly conflicts with the second phase exemplars, which can also be discriminated by the same boundary, but with the opposite assignment to categories. Because of their huge receptive fields, the same hidden nodes that respond to and learn the square exemplars also respond strongly to the circle exemplars. Hence generalization in the first phase is poor, and learning the second phase exemplars causes the first phase exemplars to be unlearned.

D.   MODELS WITHOUT THESE PRINCIPLES

Other models that fit into the framework of Fig. 1 but do not incorporate the three underlying principles in Fig. 2 tend to fail in one or more of the situations described above. I demonstrated that standard backprop fails to show filtration advantage because it does not have dimensional attention learning, and it suffers catastrophic forgetting because it does not use quasi-local representation. The GCM cannot exhibit the apparent base-rate neglect reported by Gluck and Bower (1988b) because it does not use error-driven learning. The component-cue and configural-cue models of Gluck and Bower (1988a) cannot account for filtration advantage (Kruschke, 1991) because they have no dimensional attention mechanism. The component-cue model also suffers catastrophic forgetting in the situation presented by Fig. 14 because it does not use quasi-local representation, whereas the configural-cue model might be spared from catastrophic forgetting because it includes exemplar nodes in its input representation.

Another model that has recently attracted interest is the *rational model* (J. R. Anderson, 1990, 1991). The rational model fits into the general framework presented in Fig. 1 (cf. J. R. Anderson, 1990, Fig. 3–8, p. 135) and is closely related to the context model (Nosofsky, 1991a), but the rational model does not incorporate all three underlying principles in Fig. 2. One principle the rational model does embody is quasi-local representation. But rather than representing a category by its exemplars, the .ational model uses multiple *prototypes,* one for each cluster of exemplars (the clusters need not correspond to category labels). The rational model does not use the principle of error-driven learning, however. When a stimulus is presented, learning consists of first determining which existing cluster prototype is most similar (i.e., most probable given the stimulus), and then adjusting the prototype of the winning cluster and adjusting the association weights between the winning cluster and the feature (label) nodes, to reflect inclusion of the stimulus in that cluster. A new cluster prototype is created when an exemplar is encountered that is sufficiently different from all previously constructed prototypes.

The rational model lacks error-driven learning and instead uses a Bayesian (rational) increment rule, which causes the model to be unable to account for the apparent base-rate neglect observed by Gluck and Bower (1988b). J. R. Anderson (1990, pp. 123–125) dismissed the effect as an artifact of Gluck and Bower's experimental procedure, but the effect has since been replicated using improved procedures (Estes et al., 1989; Nosofsky et al., 1992; Shanks, 1990).

The rational model also lacks dimensional attention learning, which makes it unlikely to be able to account for filtration advantage, in general. The rational model might be able to mimic filtration advantage in some filtration/condensation comparisons because of a confounding factor in the stimulus structures, because in many such structures the within-category variances along each dimension differ between the filtration and condensation conditions. In Fig. 7, for example, the within-category variances along each dimension are larger for the condensation categories than for the relevant dimension in the filtration categories. Because the rational model has parameters which learn the variance of each cluster along each dimension, it can learn these particular filtration categories faster than the condensation categories. A more challenging situation for the rational model is shown in Fig. 17. Here the within-category variances are the same for both conditions, and so it is doubtful that the rational model could show filtration advantage. On the contrary, it is highly probable that humans would show filtration advantage in this situation. (A lengthier critique of the rational model is given by Murphy, this volume.)

There are several other models which fit the framework of Fig. 1 and, like the rational model, use quasi-local representation but lack error-driven learning and dimensional attention. Among these are Estes' (1986) array-exemplar model (cf. Estes, this volume), Kanerva's (1988) sparse distributed memory (cf. Keeler, 1988), and many others. No doubt they too would fail to show apparent base-rate neglect and filtration advantage, in general.

E.   ALTERNATIVE FORMALIZATIONS

I argued that the three underlying principles in Fig. 2 are essential for accounting for human learning performance, and I showed that the particular formalization of those principles in ALCOVE does a reasonably good job of accounting for a variety of empirical learning curves. The emphasis is on the principles, however, rather than on the formalization. Alternative formalizations are possible, and only concrete simulations and fits to data will allow ranking their relative veracity.

As an example of an alternative formalization, I construct an approximation to ALCOVE using linear-sigmoid hidden nodes and place coding of

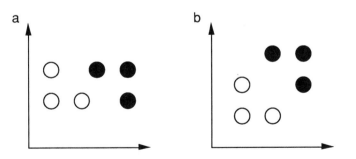

Fig. 17.   Candidate filtration (a)/condensation (b) comparison for testing the rational model.

input dimensions instead of the distance-similarity hidden nodes and amplitude encoding of input dimensions used in ALCOVE. For ease of reference, I call this model APPLE (for APProximately Alcove); it is shown in Fig. 18. The input dimensions are each place-coded by an array of quasi-local nodes, positioned at all values that occur in the training set. For example, consider the exemplars from the catastrophic learning experiment (Fig. 14). They take on three different heights and three different positions, so APPLE's implementation has three input nodes on each dimension, as illustrated in Fig. 18. Formally, the activation of an input node, centered on scale value h_i of dimension i, is given by

$$a_{hi}^{in}(\psi_i) = \exp(-\alpha_i|h_i - \psi_i|) \tag{13}$$

where ψ_i is the psychological scale value of the stimulus.

Hidden nodes in APPLE correspond to training exemplars, as in ALCOVE. Each hidden node is linked to one (and only one) input node in each input dimension. Figure 18 shows four hidden nodes, corresponding to the four exemplars from the catastrophic learning experiment inside the dotted boundary in Fig. 14. Note that each hidden node has only two incoming connections, one from each input dimension. Figure 18 shows each hidden node with a sigmoidal curve in it, indicating the sigmoidal activation function. Formally, the activation of hidden node j, linked to value h_1 on dimension 1, h_2 on dimension 2, and so on, is given by

$$a_j^{hid} = 1 \left/ \left(1 + \exp\left[\sum_{h_i \in j} a_{h_i}^{in} - \theta_j\right]\right)\right. \tag{14}$$

where the sum is taken over all input nodes connected to hidden node j. It is convenient, though not essential, to set $\theta_j = N$, where N is the number of stimulus dimensions. In that case, the generalization gradient, as a function of distance in *psychological* space, closely resembles the exponential generalization gradient of a hidden node in ALCOVE. (Approximations to *gaussian* nodes using linear-sigmoid nodes have been previously noted by Hartman & Keeler, 1991, and Mel, 1990, Fig. 5.)

I have not yet simulated APPLE and fitted it to data because I do not expect it to be a dramatic improvement over ALCOVE (nor do I expect it to be dramatically worse than ALCOVE). The point is to show that the three underlying principles embodied in ALCOVE can also be formalized using linear-sigmoid hidden nodes, if the input dimensions are appropriately encoded. In particular, what matters about the principle of quasi-localized representation is localization in the *psychological* space, not localization in the *input node* space.

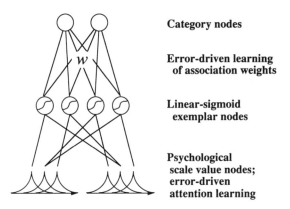

Category nodes

Error-driven learning
of association weights

Linear-sigmoid
exemplar nodes

Psychological
scale value nodes;
error-driven
attention learning

Fig. 18. ALCOVE can be approximated using linear-sigmoid hidden nodes and place coding of input dimensions.

Another alternative formalization of the three principles was proposed by Hurwitz (1990), who independently developed "hidden pattern unit model version 2" (HPU2) at the same time I developed ALCOVE. HPU2 uses the formalism of the context model (Medin & Shaffer, 1978) instead of the formalism of the generalized context model (Nosofsky, 1986). Both HPU2 and ALCOVE use gradient-descent on error as their error-driven learning mechanisms. Their implementations of the other two principles differ in their details, however. Whereas both models use exemplar-based (quasi-local) representations, HPU2 recruits new nodes for novel exemplars whereas the original version of ALCOVE assumes a covering map of the input space (see Kruschke, 1992, p. 39). And, whereas both models adjust dimensional attention strengths, ALCOVE assumes those strengths are primitives in the formalization, but HPU2 treats them as non-monotonic functions of underlying dimensional variables (see Footnote 4 of Kruschke, 1992).

The principle of error-driven learning has a long history in psychology and has been expressed in many different ways. For example, Kamin (1969) and Rescorla and Wagner (1972) argued that many phenomena in animal conditioning could be accounted for if the driving mechanism was surprise, that is, discrepancy of expectation from the actual state of the world. Levine (1975) showed that people tend to use a "win-stay–lose-shift" strategy for hypothesis testing in concept learning tasks, so that if the currently held hypothesis correctly predicts the outcome, the hypothesis is retained, but if there is error, the hypothesis is changed. More recently, McClelland and Jenkins (1991, p. 45) proposed a principle of error-driven learning as applying to long-term learning on a developmental time scale, across diverse domains such as language, ontological categories, and conservation tasks. Its formalization in backprop, as gradient descent on an error function, is just one possible expression of the general principle. The principle of error-driven learning suggests only that learning is motivated by discrepancies between predictions and actual outcomes. The principle stands opposed to methods which learn without using predictions; that is, without comparing system performance (prediction) to the real world.

F. OTHER PRINCIPLES

The three principles indicated in Fig. 2—error-driven learning, quasi-local representation, and dimensional attention—might be necessary to model human category learning, but they surely are not sufficient. For example, processing in ALCOVE assumes noise-free input and spreading activation, with probabilistic responding tacked on at the end of processing in the form of the Luce choice rule [Eq. (4)]. That approach was taken because of historical precedent, particularly in the GCM. An alternative approach is to use inherently stochastic spread of activation with a deterministic choice rule. This principle has been discussed by Ashby (Ashby & Gott, 1988; Ashby & Maddox, in press), McClelland (1991a, 1991b), and others. It remains for future research to demonstrate how this additional principle, or others, might benefit models like ALCOVE.

The connectionist framework in Fig. 1, while useful for comparing models, is surely incomplete. A more complete account of human category learning might posit additional representational capabilities and accompanying processes. For example, there are cases for which a rule-based representation can be a more accurate description of the processes underlying human categorization (Levine, 1975; Nosofsky, 1991b; Nosofsky, Clark, & Shin, 1989) than the quasi-local (exemplar-based) representation in ALCOVE. In particular, rule-based theories might account for the rapidity of early learning in the filtration task (Fig. 8). For such simple stimuli it is natural for subjects to quickly hypothesize and test rules such as, "If the rectangle is tall, it's in category *B;* otherwise it's in category *N.*" Such a strategy would solve the filtration task in the course of just a few trials. ALCOVE is not necessarily incompatible with rule-based accounts. I have suggested elsewhere (Kruschke, 1990, 1992) that the attention strengths in an ALCOVE-like system could help steer the generation of rules, by first testing rules using the dimensions with the highest attention strength. Of course, the rule system could also affect the associative learning system.

The influence of prior knowledge could also be (partially) expressed in ALCOVE. For example, (Pazzani, 1991) showed that subjects could learn a disjunctive rule faster than a conjunctive rule when prior knowledge suggested that the dimensions in the disjunction were relevant to the categorization but dimensions in the conjunction were irrelevant. Such biases from prior knowledge could be implemented in ALCOVE by setting the initial attention strengths appropriately. Thus, a dimension thought by prior knowledge to be highly relevant could have its initial attention strength set to a larger value than the others.

A desideratum for future research is a grander synthesis of these additional principles in a single, coherent, formalized model. In general, if a model matches human behavior reasonably well, we have confirmatory evidence that both its underlying principles and their particular formalization might be accurate descriptions of human cognition. In this case the model is an *explanation* of the human behaviors it captures, to the extent that its formalizations are understandable and its underlying principles are acceptable as axioms (rather than properties which themselves require explanation). On the other hand, if a model fails, then either its underlying principles, or their formalization, or both, are incomplete. In this case we are left to decide whether an alternative formalization of the same explanatory principles can satisfy the data, or whether alternative underlying principles must be considered.

ACKNOWLEDGMENTS

Some of the research reported here was supported by Biomedical Research Support Grant RR7031-25 from the National Institutes of Health, and by a Summer Faculty Fellowship from Indiana University.

REFERENCES

Anderson, J. A., Silverstein, J. W., Ritz, S. A., & Jones, R. S. (1977). Distinctive features, categorical perception, and probability learning: Some applications of a neural model. *Psychological Review, 84*, 413–451.

Anderson, J. R. (1990). *The Adaptive character of thought*. Hillsdale, NJ: Erlbaum.

Anderson, J. R. (1991). The adaptive nature of human categorization. *Psychological Review, 98*, 409–429.

Ashby, F. G., & Gott, R. E. (1988). Decision rules in the perception and categorization of multidimensional stimuli. *Journal of Experimental Psychology: Learning, Memory, and Cognition, 14*, 33–53.

Ashby, F. G., & Maddox, W. T. (in press). Relations between prototype, exemplar and decision bound models of categorization. *Journal of Mathematical Psychology*.

Ballard, D. H. (1987). Interpolation coding: A representation for numbers in neural models. *Biological Cybernetics, 57*, 389–402.

Broomhead, D. S., & Lowe, D. (1988). Multivariable functional interpolation and adaptive networks. *Complex Systems, 2*, 321–355.

Cohen, J. D., Dunbar, K., & McClelland, J. L. (1990). On the control of automatic processes: A parallel distributed processing account of the Stroop effect. *Psychological Review, 97,* 332–361.

Estes, W. K. (1986). Array models for category learning. *Cognitive Psychology, 18,* 500–549.

Estes, W. K., Campbell, J. A., Hatsopoulos, N., & Hurwitz, J. B. (1989). Base-rate effects in category learning: A comparison of parallel network and memory storage-retrieval models. *Journal of Experimental Psychology: Learning, Memory and Cognition, 15,* 556–576.

Garner, W. R. (1974). *The processing of information and structure.* Hillsdale, NJ: Erlbaum.

Gluck, M. A. (1991). Stimulus generalization and representation in adaptive network models of category learning. *Psychological Science, 2,* 50–55.

Gluck, M. A., & Bower, G. H. (1988a). Evaluating an adaptive network model of human learning. *Journal of Memory and Language, 27,* 166–195.

Gluck, M. A., & Bower, G. H. (1988b). From conditioning to category learning: An adaptive network model. *Journal of Experimental Psychology: General, 117,* 227–247.

Gottwald, R. L., & Garner, W. R. (1972). Effects of focusing strategy on speeded classification with grouping, filtering and condensation tasks. *Perception & Psychophysics, 11,* 179–182.

Gottwald, R. L., & Garner, W. R. (1975). Filtering and condensation tasks with integral and separable dimensions. *Perception & Psychophysics, 18,* 26–28.

Hancock, P. J. B. (1989). Data representation in neural nets: An empirical study. In D. Touretzky, G. Hinton, & T. Sejnowski (Eds.), *Proceedings of the 1988 Connectionist Models Summer School,* (pp. 11–20). San Mateo, CA: Morgan Kaufmann.

Hartman, E. & Keeler, J. D. (1991). Predicting the future: Advantages of semilocal units. *Neural Computation, 3,* 566–578.

Hurwitz, J. B. (1990). *A hidden-pattern unit network model of category learning.* Doctoral dissertation, Harvard University, Cambridge, MA.

Kamin, L. J. (1969). Predictability, surprise, attention, and conditioning. In B. A. Campbell & R. M. Church (Eds.), *Punishment* (pp. 279–296). New York: Appleton-Century-Crofts.

Kanerva, P. (1988). *Sparse Distributed Memory.* Cambridge, MA: MIT Press.

Keeler, J. D. (1988). Comparison between Kanerva's SDM and Hopfield-type neural networks. *Cognitive Science, 12,* 299–329.

Knapp, A. G., & Anderson, J. A. (1984). Theory of categorization based on distributed memory storage. *Journal of Experimental Psychology: Learning, Memory and Language, 10,* 616–637.

Kruschke, J. K. (1990). *A connectionist model of category learning.* Doctoral dissertation, University of California, Berkeley.

Kruschke, J. K. (1991). Dimensional attention learning in models of human categorization. In *Proceedings of the Thirteenth Annual Conference of the Cognitive Science Society* (pp. 281–286). Hillsdale, NJ: Erlbaum.

Kruschke, J. K. (1992). ALCOVE: An exemplar-based connectionist model of category learning. *Psychological Review, 99,* 22–44.

Kruschke, J. K. (1993). Human category learning: Implications for backpropagation models. *Connection Science, 5,* 3–36.

Levine, M. (1975). *A cognitive theory of learning: Research on hypothesis testing.* Hillsdale, NJ: Erlbaum.

Luce, R. D. (1963). Detection and recognition. In R. D. Luce, R. R. Bush, & E. Galanter (Eds.), *Handbook of mathematical psychology* (pp. 103–189). New York: Wiley.

McClelland, J. L. (1991a). Stochastic interactive processes and the effect of context on perception. *Cognitive Psychology, 23,* 1–44.

McClelland, J. L. (1991b). *Toward a theory of information processing in graded, random, interactive networks* (Technical Report PDP.CNS.91.1). Pittsburgh, PA: Carnegie Mellon University.

McClelland, J. L., & Jenkins, E. (1991). Nature, nurture and connections: Implications of connectionist models for cognitive development. In K. VanLehn (Ed.), *Architectures for intelligence*. Hillsdale, NJ: Erlbaum.

McClelland, J. L., & Rumelhart, D. E. (1981). An interactive activation model of context effects in letter perception: Part 1. An account of basic findings. *Psychological Review, 88*, 375–407.

McCloskey, M., & Cohen, N. J. (1989). Catastrophic interference in connectionist networks: The sequential learning problem. In G. Bower (Ed.), *The Psychology of Learning and Motivation: Vol. 24* (pp. 109–165), New York: Academic Press.

Medin, D. L., & Schaffer, M. M. (1978). Context theory of classification learning. *Psychological Review, 85*, 207–238.

Mel, B. W. (1990). The sigma-pi column: *A model of associative learning in cerebral neocortex* (CNS Memo 6). Pasadena, CA: California Institute of Technology.

Minsky, M. L., & Papert, S. A. (1969). *Perceptrons*. Cambridge, MA: MIT Press. 1988 expanded edition.

Moody, J., & Darken, C. J. (1989). Fast learning in networks of locally-tuned processing units. *Neural Computation, 1*, 281–294.

Niranjan, M., & Fallside, F. (1988). *Neural networks and radial basis functions in classifying static speech patterns* (Technical Report CUES/F-INFENG/TR.22). Cambridge, England: Cambridge University, Engineering Department.

Nosofsky, R. M. (1986). Attention, similarity and the identification–categorization relationship. *Journal of Experimental Psychology: General, 115*, 39–57.

Nosofsky, R. M. (1991a). Relation between the rational model and the context model of categorization. *Psychological Science, 2*, 416–421.

Nosofsky, R. M. (1991b). Typicality in logically defined categories: exemplar-similarity versus rule instantiation. *Memory & Cognition, 19*, 131–150.

Nosofsky, R. M., Clark, S. E., & Shin, H. J. (1989). Rules and exemplars in categorization, identification and recognition. *Journal of Experimental Psychology: Learning, Memory, and Cognition, 15*, 282–304.

Nosofsky, R. M. & Kruschke, J. K. (1992). Investigations of an exemplar-based connectionist model of category learning. In D. L. Medin (Ed.), *The Psychology of Learning and Motivation: Vol. 28* (pp. 207–250). New York: Academic Press.

Nosofsky, R. M., Kruschke, J. K., & McKinley, S. (1992). Combining exemplar-based category representations and connectionist learning rules. *Journal of Experimental Psychology: Learning, Memory and Cognition, 18*, 211–233.

Pavel, M., Gluck, M. A., & Henkle, V. (1989). Constraints on adaptive networks for modeling human generalization. In D. S. Touretzky (Ed.), *Advances in Neural Information Processing Systems 1* (pp. 2–10). San Mateo, CA: Morgan Kaufmann.

Pazzani, M. J. (1991). Influence of prior knowledge on concept acquisition: Experimental and computational results. *Journal of Experimental Psychology: Learning, Memory and Cognition, 17*, 416—432.

Poggio, T., & Girosi, F. (1990). Regularization algorithms for learning that are equivalent to multilayer networks. *Science, 247*, 978–982.

Posner, M. I. (1964). Information reduction in the analysis of sequential tasks. *Psychological Review, 71*, 491–504.

Powell, M. J. D. (1985). Radial basis functions for multivariable interpolation: A review (Technical Report DAMTP 1985/NA12). Cambridge, England: Cambridge University, Department of Applied Mathematics and Theoretical Physics.

Ratcliff, R. (1990). Connectionist models of recognition memory: Constraints imposed by learning and forgetting functions. *Psychological Review, 97,* 285–308.

Rescorla, R. A., & Wagner, A. R. (1972). A theory of Pavlovian conditioning: Variations in the effectiveness of reinforcement and non-reinforcement. In A. H. Black & W. F. Prokasy (Eds.), *Classical Conditioning: II. Current Research and Theory* (pp. 64–99). New York: Appleton-Century-Crofts.

Robinson,. A. J., Niranjan, M., & Fallside, F. (1988). Generalising the nodes of the error propagation network (Technical Report CUES/F-INFENG/TR.25). Cambridge, England: Cambridge University, Engineering Department.

Rosenblatt, F. (1958). The perceptron: A probabilistic model for information storage and organization in the brain. *Psychological Review, 65,* 386–408.

Rumelhart, D. E., Hinton, G. E., & Williams, R. J. (1986). Learning internal representations by error propagation. In J. L. McClelland & D. E. Rumelhart (Eds.), *Parallel distributed processing: Vol. 1. Foundations* (pp. 318–362). Cambridge, MA: MIT Press.

Seidenberg, M. S., & McClelland, J. L. (1989). A distributed, developmental model of word recognition and naming. *Psychological Review, 96,* 523–568.

Sejnowski, T. J., & Rosenberg, C. R. (1988). Learning and representation in connectionist networks. In M. S. Gazzaniga (Ed.), *Perspectives in memory research* (pp. 135–178). Cambridge, MA: MIT Press.

Shanks, D. R. (1990). Connectionism and the learning of probabilistic concepts. *Quarterly Journal of Experimental Psychology, 42A,* 209–237.

Shepard, R. N. (1964). Attention and the metric structure of the stimulus space. *Journal of Mathematical Psychology, 1,* 54–87.

Shepard, R. N. (1987). Toward a universal law of generalization for psychological science. *Science, 237,* 1317–1323.

Smith, E. E., & Medin, D. (1981). *Categories and concepts.* Cambridge, MA: Harvard U. Press.

Taraban, R., McDonald, J. L., & MacWhinney, B. (1989). Category learning in a connectionist model: Learning to decline the German definite article. In R. Corrigan, F. Eckman, & M. Noonan (Eds.), *Linguistic categorization* (pp. 163–193). Philadelphia: Benjamins.

Walters, D. (1987). Properties of connectionist variable representations. In *Program of the Ninth Annual Conference of the Cognitive Science Society* (pp. 265–273). Hillsdale, NJ: Erlbaum.

EXEMPLAR MODELS AND WEIGHTED CUE MODELS IN CATEGORY LEARNING

Roman Taraban
Joaquin Marcos Palacios

I. Categorization Models

When cognitive psychologists study category learning, they want to understand the mental representations and processes that are responsible for the learning behavior that they observe. Models of categorization learning certainly must agree with data that are collected through experiments or observation. To check that agreement, standard statistical methods are typically applied. However, it is not the goodness of the statistical fit that is of primary importance. Rather it is the clarity, precision, and completeness with which the model explains judgments and decisions about categories: "Is the bird I am looking at a dove or a hawk?" "Is the mood on Wall Street bullish or bearish?" In order to provide an explanation, models posit underlying cognitive representations and the cognitive operations that encode, store, retrieve, and process those representations. These questions are the main focus of this article.

In order to make the issues apparent from the outset and to set the stage for the remainder of this essay, consider the following hypothetical category learning problem. A person is presented with descriptions of homes from two towns and must learn the town associated with each home. We refer to each home (e.g., Home 1) as an *exemplar* and to each descriptor or feature of a home (e.g., stucco) as a *cue value*.

	Town A		Town B
Home 1	2-story brown stucco	Home 5	1-story brown stucco
Home 2	2-story brown brick	Home 6	1-story brown brick
Home 3	2-story white stucco	Home 7	1-story white stucco
Home 4	1-story white brick	Home 8	2-story white brick

An examination of individual cues makes it clear that neither the color of the home nor the material that it is constructed from is predictive of the town it comes from. In fact, if one ignores the first cue, the homes in Town A are identical to those in Town B. The only predictive cue is the first one (1- vs. 2-story). A person might learn that in Town A one should expect 2-story homes and in Town B 1-story homes, but the person would also have to learn the 2 exceptions (Home 4 and Home 8).

The earliest models of category learning (Beach, 1964; Reed, 1972; Rosch & Mervis, 1975), which belong to a class of models we refer to as *weighted cue* models, would predict that the exceptions would be the most difficult cases to learn and that Homes 1, 2, and 3 in Town A and Homes 5, 6, and 7 in Town B would be equally easy to learn. These predictions would be based on emphasizing ("weighting") the first cue and ignoring the other cues. One way to quantify the typicality (and ease of learning) of the instances is through a "family resemblance" analysis (Rosch & Mervis, 1975) in which each feature is weighted in accordance with the number of items in the category possessing that feature. These weights can then be added to derive a family resemblance score. This within-category sum, balanced against the overlap of the features in the competing category, reflects how well an instance fits its category—that is, its typicality. (As in Rosch & Mervis, 1975, the overlap score represents the number of features in an instance that occur in the competing category.) In Table I, where we provide the family resemblance and overlap scores, it is clear that Homes 1, 2, 3, 5, 6, and 7 are equally typical and thus, consistent with the earlier suggestion, should be equally easy to learn. Homes 4 and 8 are atypical and should be difficult to learn. If we calculate a cue validity measure for each instance, we come to the same conclusion. The cue validities shown in Table I are identical to the conditional probability of the associated feature (cf. Beach, 1964; Reed, 1972; Rosch & Mervis, 1975). Indeed, examining the set, it may be difficult to imagine how one could make any other prediction or to intuit why a weighted cue or family resemblance model could be wrong in this case. As we shall show shortly

TABLE I

FAMILY RESEMBLANCE, OVERLAP SCORES, AND CUE
VALIDITIES FOR EACH CATEGORY MEMBER

Category	Family resemblance score	Overlap score	Cue validity		
			Cue 1	Cue 2	Cue 3
Home 1	7	3	.75	.50	.50
Home 2	7	3	.75	.50	.50
Home 3	7	3	.75	.50	.50
Home 4	5	3	.25	.50	.50
Home 5	7	3	.75	.50	.50
Home 6	7	3	.75	.50	.50
Home 7	7	3	.75	.50	.50
Home 8	5	3	.25	.50	.50

using an isomorph of the town problem (i.e., a problem with the identical structure), these predictions would only be half correct. The exceptions (Homes 4 and 8) are the most difficult to learn, but Homes 1 and 5 are also the easiest.

A. EXEMPLAR SIMILARITY

First, let us consider why Homes 1 and 5 are the easiest. The answer lies in the *similarity* of these exemplars to members of their own category and to the competing category. To make this description usable, there are two requirements: (1) a way of quantifying the similarity of one member of a category to another member, and (2) a way of combining these computed similarities. Part of the answer to (1) is provided in Shepard's (1987) Universal Law of Generalization, which was proposed as a natural law of cognitive systems. Applying this law to the town problem, we would expect that the perceived similarity between two exemplars should drop off exponentially, not linearly, with mismatches in their features. Exemplars that differ in one versus two versus three cues (e.g., Home 1 vs. 2, 7, and 4) do not differ in similarity by a constant amount (a linear relation); rather, similarity drops off quickly as the number of mismatches goes up. In order to fulfill the first requirement, we can compute the similarity of an item t to a member x of category X, as in Eq. (1) (Medin & Schaffer, 1978):

$$\text{Similarity}(t, x) = \prod s_i \tag{1}$$

where $s_i = 1$ if the values of feature i in x and in t match, and $0 \leq s_i \leq 1$ if they mismatch. With regard to the town problem, a match or mismatch is determined by whether the two cues being compared are the same or different. For the second requirement, the similarities from Eq. (1) can be combined to predict the probability of choosing a particular category X for an item t, as summarized in Eq. (2) (Medin & Schaffer, 1978):

$$P(X|t) = \frac{\sum_{x \in X} \text{Similarity}(t, x)}{\sum_{x \in X} \text{Similarity}(t, x) + \sum_{y \in Y} \text{Similarity}(t, y)} \tag{2}$$

where the values of the s_i's are parameters that must be estimated from data and Y is the competing category. (The town problem would have three s values to estimate: one for story, one for color, and one for material.) The discussion in this article focuses on these two equations from Medin and Schaffer (1978). Other formalizations of exemplar similarity that derive from the Medin and Schaffer (1978) equations have been implemented in Nosofsky's Generalized Context Model (GCM) and Kruschke's ALCOVE. (See Kruschke, this volume, for a summary.)[1]

B. NON-LINEAR SEPARABILITY

As we have already pointed out, weighted cue models predict the difficulty in learning Homes 4 and 8. The goal of these models is to find a weight for each individual cue such that when the weighted cues of an exemplar are added together, each exemplar falls in the right category. When a set of weights that can do this does not exist, the set of items is *non-linearly separable*. In the town problem, the 2-story cue value must be strongly weighted to Town A and the 1-story cue value to Town B; the remaining cues (color and material) are not helpful. Using independent weighted cues, this is the only way to get any of the items right. But this will mean that Homes 4 and 8 will always get misclassified. Thus, if they are learned at all, they will be learned with difficulty (using some additional method like rote memorization, say).

Medin and Schwanenflugel (1981), in explaining the advantage for cases like Homes 1 and 5, also argued that linear separability failed to explain

---

[1] In order to see why Home 1, for instance, has a higher similarity (and is more prototypical of the category) than Home 2, note the following difference. Home 1 has two close "neighbors" within its own category. These are Homes 2 and 3, which mismatch on one feature. Home 1 also has 1 "distant" neighbor—Home 4, which mismatches on three features. In comparison, Home 2 has one close neighbor, Home 1, and two "middling" neighbors, Homes 3 and 4. Due to the nature of the exponential similarity function described in Eq. (1), it is better to have a close and a distant neighbor than it is to have two middling neighbors.

category learning. They were correct in two ways. First, the principles underlying models in which linear separability is important are inadequate (viz., Shepard's law). Second, the non-linearly separable effects that independent cue models predict can also be predicted by the exemplar similarity functions in Eqs. (1) and (2), as amplified later in this article.[2]

C. Exemplar Similarity and Learning

The exemplar similarity relations just reviewed are fundamental to the work presented here. There is a body of research in categorization that has focused on the end product of learning. Parameters for Eqs. (1) and (2), or some other model, would be fitted to test data collected after a learning phase. Our primary interest was learning, though, and the detailed course that learning would follow for a problem like the town problem. Equations (1) and (2) fail in two ways. First, finding the best-fitting values for the s_i's at one point in learning tells you nothing about how the s_i's might change at a later stage of learning. Second, even if the equations were adopted to learning, they would not provide the type of cognitive model described in Section I, that is, a model with cognitive representations and related processes. We deal with these in turn.

As a first step, we reinterpreted Eq. (1) to be more consonant, in our minds, with the learning process. To understand our rationale, consider first a learning experiment with the town problem. Things will be clearest if we think of each trial in the experiment as adding a record of the exemplar and its category to memory (cf. exemplar-memory models in Estes, 1986). Any number of blocks of exposure to the items would build up multiple memory representations for the items, but for any given item the computed probability, using Eq. (2), would be identical, since the buildup of memory records would maintain the same proportional relation from block to block. On this view, if learning is to take place, the s_i's must change.[3]

Another question concerns how we want to fit the s_i's. The manner in which s_i's change should reflect two separate parameter adjustments—those for a match and those for a mismatch. In order to see this best, it helps to view s_i as if it were an associative strength that was weak early on but was strengthened through learning. From this perspective (which is close to the one we develop later), it would not make sense to have

[2] We do not currently know whether the exemplar similarity functions would always predict the non-linearly separable items.

[3] Estes (1986) also considers the relation of s to learning and suggests that changes in s might be understood within signal detection theory as related to a changing decision criterion. The models that we successfully test and extend in this chapter take a different approach. This does not preclude the possibility that equally good explanations could be worked out that were consonant with Estes' suggestion.

unchanging associations for roughly half the learning processes (those for matches). We note that in normally fitting Eq. (2) to a set of data, the outcome of the fit is not affected by setting one set of parameters—namely, those for matches—to a constant value, as is usually done, nor is the outcome of the analysis improved by estimating parameters for matches and mismatches in Eq. (1). However, we think that this approach makes the learning process more understandable. With this in mind, we set s for cue i equal to m when there was a match and to $1 - m$ when there was a mismatch at any given stage in learning $(0.5 \leq m \leq 1.0)$.[4]

Our reformulation of Eqs. (1) and (2) allows us to plot out the range of processing differences we would expect to find over the course of learning for a set stimuli, as we will show shortly in Fig. 1, but these equations still do not provide a cognitive model of the sort we seek. First, although we posit that the m parameter changes with learning, there is still a question of what the learning curve itself should look like. Second, there is a need to relate (1) and (2) more carefully to cognitive representations and processes.

D. OVERVIEW

In the remainder of this article, we use Eqs. (1) and (2) as the theoretical foundation for examining cognitive models. We begin by establishing the exemplar similarity effects predicted by (1) and (2) using a simple experimental paradigm in which subjects learn an isomorph of the town problem. We then turn to cognitive models which are all connectionist in nature. Models in this class are in principle capable of behaving like weighted cue models as well as like exemplar similarity models and so do not limit a priori the types of solutions that we might observe. We examine the course of learning in these models at each step by setting just a single parameter at the beginning of each simulation, which is the *rate* at which a model learns.[5] The town problem is important here, since the models that we test make different predictions for what will get learned.

The connectionist models that we consider can be divided into those that use the more powerful *back propagation* learning method and those that use the simpler *delta rule*. Both are learning-on-error methods (cf. Kruschke, this volume; McDonald, this volume). Our results show that delta rule models either fail to model the human data or require conjunctive cues (i.e., combinations of cues acting as a unit, like brown-stucco).

---

[4] Medin and Edelson (1988) also considered treating matches as a variable with graded effects: specifically, letting matches increase similarity.

[5] This is just roughly true. See McClelland and Rumelhart (1988) for more details.

Conjunctive cue representations are not learned by the network. They are externally specified prior to the learning simulation. From this, we conclude that delta rule networks may have significant limitations.

We then focus on the back propagation method. In order to relate our discussion more clearly to Kruschke (this volume), we refer to the original formulation of back propagation by Rumelhart, Hinton, and Williams (1986) as *standard* back propagation. In our first set of simulation results we show that standard back propagation produces the similarity effects predicted by Eqs. (1) and (2). This is important, since back propagation networks have demonstrated the capacity to solve very difficult category learning problems. One class, of particular interest to the first author, requires the network to extract implicit linguistic categories (like gender and case) and the paradigms (''tables'') that organize them (MacWhinney, Leinbach, Taraban, & McDonald, 1989; Taraban, McDonald, & MacWhinney, 1989). There is evidence for back propagation networks' capacity to do this and to generalize their knowledge to novel items, but it had not been determined whether they would also extract the similarity effects predicted by Eqs. (1) and (2) and observed in the human category learning data reported in this article. We show that standard back propagation extracts these similarity relations.

Finally, we look closely at network architectures (i.e., the organization and linking of network units). In recent arguments for alternatives to back propagation, like ALCOVE, Kruschke (1992, this volume) has suggested that standard back propagation learning cannot replicate the ''condensation'' and ''filtration'' effects found in human category learning. Filtration problems can be solved by weighting the cue values from a single dimension of the stimuli (like their size); condensation problems require the coordination of cue values from more than one dimension. Since this points to a substantive limitation to back propagation, it was important for us to first show that with *pooled* internal units, back propagation easily produces condensation and filtration effects. Second, we test a radically different organization of internal units, which functions in a manner generally consonant with exemplar memory models. We show that this new type of architecture and the back propagation learning procedure extract the exemplar similarity relations and categorization behavior predicted by Eqs. (1) and (2). We conclude by relating our exemplar-based back propagation model to the principles for category learning models and ALCOVE outlined by Kruschke (this volume), and we consider ways in which the model can be tested further and extended in interesting ways. In summary, we consider: (1) similarity effects in human category learning, (2) the ability of connectionist networks to capture these effects, and (3) extensions of the back propagation method to exemplar-based architectures.

II. A Test for Similarity Effects in Human Learning

The design of this experiment was meant to tap subjects' representations of the items in a learning set at each step in learning. Rather than using Eqs. (1) and (2) to predict the probability that a subject would select a particular category in response to a test item, as has usually been done, we collected category membership ratings and used the equations to fit the ratings. The stimuli were based on the Type V set in the classic monograph by Shepard, Hovland, and Jenkins (1961) (see Table II). Type V stimuli were chosen because of the rich differences between the members, which produce three levels of similarity (high, medium, low), with one of these levels corresponding to the non-linearly separable items of weighted cue models (the low similarity level).[6]

We chose to use pseudowords as our stimuli because our primary interest derives from the manner in which children and second-language learners use the morphology (loosely, spelling or pronunciation) of words to extract the implicit linguistic categories of their language. Experiments with pseudowords and other non-verbal stimuli can provide insight into language learning (see McDonald, this volume; McDonald & MacWhinney, 1991). With regard to language acquisition and language processing, exemplar similarity has turned out to be completely ignored. The Competition Model of Bates and MacWhinney (1982, 1987, 1989) is one model that could benefit from attention to exemplar similarity (see Taraban & Palacios, 1992) because it is one of the very few current models that (correctly, we think) has a strong learning component.

Consider how the ratings for an item's own and its competing category would change as a function of strengthening the match variable in the range of 0.5–1.0, as shown in Fig. 1 for the Type V stimuli. When the match parameter is weak (i.e., equal to 0.5) and equal to the mismatch value (1.0 *minus* 0.5 also equals 0.5), any given item is rated as belonging equally to either of the two competing categories. Similarly, when the match parameter is strong (i.e., equal to 1.0) an item is rated as belonging to its own correct category with a 1 and to the competing category with a 0. The differences between the *high-similarity* (*zub, vub*), *medium-similarity* (*zob, zud, vob, vud*), and *low-similarity* (*vod, zod*) subclasses reflect differences in computed similarity, using Eqs. (1) and (2) and our translation of s into m and $1 - m$. The result would have been the same if we had used s as defined at (1) above.

There are two striking aspects to this plot. First, except at the bounding

---

[6] Interested readers may want to consult Kruschke (1990) for a related examination of these stimuli.

TABLE II

PSEUDOWORDS, ASSIGNED
CATEGORIES, AND DERIVED
SIMILARITY LEVELS

Pseudoword	Category label	Similarity level
zub	Jets	High
zud	Jets	Medium
zob	Jets	Medium
vod	Jets	Low
vub	Sharks	High
vud	Sharks	Medium
vob	Sharks	Medium
zod	Sharks	Low

values of 0.5 and 1.0, subjects should be subject to the effects of exemplar similarity, even when very little learning has taken place. Second, within the low range of m values, the non-linear separability that would be predicted by weighted-cue models is apparent but disappears as m is strengthened. Our primary interest in this experiment was in determining if

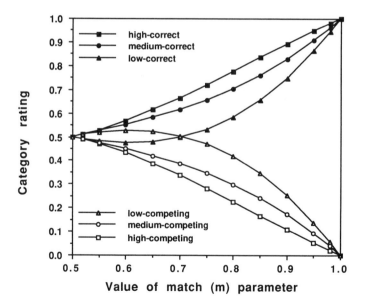

Fig. 1. Category ratings for Type V stimuli. Note: "high-correct" means "a high similarity item's category rating for the correct category," and so on for the others.

and when subjects who were learning artificial categories would show the plotted similarity effects.

A. METHOD

Twenty-four undergraduates participated in this experiment for course credit. The stimuli are shown in Table II. Each category consisted of 4 three-letter pseudowords, which were presented to subjects as code names for gang members in the Jets and the Sharks. (To relate these stimuli to the Town problem example, each letter position should be interpreted as a two-valued cue.)

Each subject was presented with 40 blocks of trials on an IBM AT clone, with the pseudowords appearing one at a time in random order within each block. One block consisted of one presentation of the eight pseudowords. Subjects used a rating scale of 0–9 and made two ratings on each trial. One rating was for the item's membership in one gang and the second rating was for membership in the other gang. The order of ratings was random. Feedback was provided after each trial to indicate the correct gang. Subjects were warned that early on in the experiment they would know little about the gang membership, so they should avoid extreme ratings. Subjects responded using the computer keyboard and all responses were recorded automatically.

B. RESULTS AND DISCUSSION

Since subjects were instructed to use whole number ratings, a middle rating (4.5), important in the early trials, was not available to them, and subjects tended to begin with ratings of 5. In order to convert the ratings to the range 0–1, in order to fit Eq. (2), to correct for the artifact of the rating scale, and to assure that the sum of residuals in the analyses was 0, each rating was divided by 9 and then a derived correction factor of 0.069 was subtracted.

As shown in Fig. 1, high-similarity items should receive the highest ratings for their own category and the lowest ratings for the competing category; for low-similarity items, this is reversed. This is precisely the pattern obtained. An examination of Table III reveals higher ratings for high- versus medium- versus low-similarity items for the items correct category; similarly, lower ratings for high- versus medium- versus low-similarity items for the items competing category. An ANOVA using Similarity (high, medium, low), Rating Type (for items' correct category or for the competing category), and Block (1–40) showed a significant effect for the crucial 2-way interaction in these data: Similarity $\times$ Rating Type $[F(2, 46) = 6.58, p < .004,$ by subjects; $F(2, 5) = 6.69, p < .04,$ by items].

TABLE III

Mean Ratings[a]

	Correct category			Competing category		
	High	Medium	Low	High	Medium	Low
Overall (40 blocks)	.70	.66	.62	.29	.33	.37
Block 1	.55	.50	.41	.47	.47	.59
Block 2	.63	.47	.46	.37	.53	.52
Block 3	.59	.53	.50	.41	.46	.49
Block 4	.55	.54	.48	.48	.47	.54
Block 5	.65	.52	.56	.38	.48	.48
Block 6	.60	.63	.56	.42	.38	.46

[a] High, medium, and low subclasses are based on the computed similarity shown in Fig. 1.

The effect of the 3-way interaction was non-significant [$F(78, 1794) = 0.63$, ns, by subjects; $F(78, 195) = 0.70$, ns, by items], which suggests that there was a significant difference between the high, medium, and low items and that the effect did not vary significantly across the blocks of trials. We performed F tests using one degree of freedom to verify that there was an overall significant difference between the mean high and mean medium ratings for items' correct category [.70 vs. .66: $F(1, 23) = 13.94, p < .002$, by subjects; $F(1, 4) = 9.14, p < .04$, by items], and between the mean high and mean medium ratings for items' competing category [.29 vs. .33: $F(1, 23) = 7.61, p < .02$, by subjects; $F(1, 4) = 6.03$, $p < .07$, by items]. As is evident in Table III, which shows the earliest performance patterns, differences between ratings for high- and medium-similarity items emerge in Block 1, at least for items' correct category.

We were particularly interested in the crossover effect for low-similarity items indicated in the plot in Fig. 1. When the values of the m parameter are low, the items are misclassified—that is, the rating for the competing category is higher than for the correct category. This misclassification is just what a weighted-cue model would predict for these items, but for different reasons. As pointed out earlier, the effect disappears as m is strengthened.

Examining the early blocks of human ratings, we find evidence of misclassification and eventual recovery, as predicted. In order to statistically examine this result more closely, we analyzed just the low-similarity items and looked for a Rating Type × Block interaction. Since subjects clearly recover from their misclassification after about 6 blocks of trials, we chose to examine the effect in just the first six blocks. We found a significant Rating Type × Block effect by items [$F(5, 5) = 7.97, p < .02$] but not by subjects [$F(5, 115) = 1.29$, $p < .25$], suggesting significant variability in the performance of subjects but providing some support for the effect nonetheless. In the same block of 6 trials we looked for evidence that the high versus medium similarity items were producing an effect. One-df F-tests were again used and showed a significant difference between the mean high and mean medium ratings for items' correct category [.60 vs. .53: $F(1, 23) = 10.72$, $p < .003$, by subjects; $F(1, 4) = 26.65$, $p < .007$, by items], and between the mean high and mean medium ratings for items' competing category [.42 vs. .47: $F(1, 23) = 5.64$, $p < .03$, by subjects; $F(1, 4) = 9.68$, $p < .04$, by items], showing that the similarity effects do indeed develop early on.

Figure 1 shows how category ratings should change with changes in the match parameter m but not how m will change over the course of learning trials. Since we wanted to fit the learning curves in this study, we searched for an expression for m in terms of learning *block*. We found that the logarithmic function

$$m = 0.5 + \text{lrate} \times \ln(\text{block}) \tag{3}$$

provided a good fit, where lrate controls how quickly m changes. Specifically, each of the 640 means (16 ratings × 40 blocks) was coded according to the formula in Eq. (2) and the best-fitting lrate_i was found for each letter position.[7] This analysis provided an excellent fit, with total residual error equal to 2.54, and $R^2 = 0.89$. The mean human ratings and mean fitted ratings are shown in Fig. 2 using ten 4-block segments (we grouped the data for visual ease).

Considering the results overall, we showed that by using the formulas in Eqs. (1) and (2) and fitting m as a parameter changing with learning, we could reasonably fit the human learning curves. This was important to demonstrate. The specific predictions that this approach made were also verified. First, the human learning curves show a clear separation of the high, medium, and low subclasses in the expected relationship to one another. Second, there is evidence for these effects when very little learning has taken place (i.e. when the ratings are low). Third, there is a visible tendency to prefer the competing category as the correct category for low-similarity items in the early trials.

---

[7] In this analysis there are 3 parameters to fit, as there would be using Eq. (2) for a set of test data; thus there is no increase in the number of parameters in order to fit the learning data. These parameters were fitted using the iterative method of Gill, Murray, Saunders, and Wright (1984), which is implemented in SPSSX, Version 4.0. In our experience this algorithm produces fits nearly identical to those using the Levenberg–Marquardt algorithm.

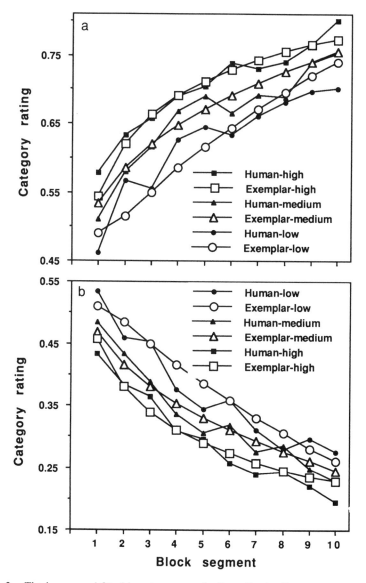

Fig. 2. The human and fitted learning curves for Type V stimuli. (a), Mean ratings for items' correct category; (b), mean ratings for items' competing category. Note: "Exemplar-high" is the fitted model's prediction for high-similarity items, and so on.

III. Exemplars, Weighted Cues, and Hidden Units

At this point we were ready to provide a rough test of the ability of connectionist networks to produce the basic effects that we found in the human data. The models are summarized in Table IV. *Weighted cue* models are all similar in that they iteratively arrive at a Least Mean Squares (LMS) solution. An LMS solution reflects one answer to the question of what gets learned over the course of learning. Gluck and collaborators (Gluck, 1991; Gluck & Bower, 1988; Gluck, Bower & Hee, 1989) have argued for the broad explanatory power of this solution. One way of reaching an LMS solution iteratively—that is, through multiple learning trials—is by changing weights in a network of inputs and outputs using the *delta rule* for learning on error (Gluck & Bower, 1988; Rumelhart et al., 1986; Stone, 1986). The network for the *simple cue* model is shown in Fig. 3a. A change in weight w_{ji} for an input–output pattern (i.e., a learning trial) is equal to:

$$\Delta w_{ji} = \eta \delta i_i \tag{4}$$

In words, the change in the weight connecting an input and output unit for a learning trial is equal to the difference δ between the desired and actual output values for the output unit on that particular learning trial multiplied by η, which controls the rate of learning and is a parameter that must be set, and the activation of the unit on the input side of the weight i_i. The "desired" output referred to above is the learning feedback that the net-

TABLE IV

Characteristics of Models

Models	Type of input	Inputs for example pseudoword *vub*
Weighted cue: Simple	Single cues	*v-u-b*
Configural	Single cues & cue conjunctions	*v-u-b* *vu-vb-ub*
Cue + rote	Single cues & exemplars	*v-u-b* *vub*
Back propagation	Single cues	*v-u-b*

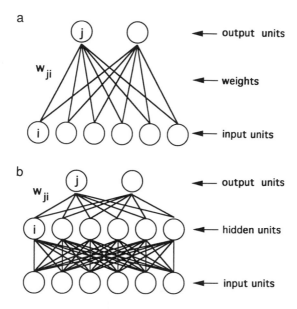

Fig. 3.   Connectionist networks: (a), without hidden units; (b), with hidden units.

work is provided with, which is either 1.0 if the output unit should be active ("on") or 0.0 if it should be "off."

The *back propagation* model is based on a generalization of the delta rule by Rumelhart et al. (1986) that allows one or more layers of "hidden" units (i.e., one or more layers of units between the input and output layers) as shown in Fig. 3b, to form internal representations of the inputs before passing them on to the output units. Because the activation of a unit (i.e., its output) is usually based on a logistic transformation of the net input to the unit, and because one needs to be able to compute the δ for internal units for which there is no set *desired output value,* computing Δw_{ji} is somewhat more complicated; however, the basic description provided for the delta rule above applies. (A more complete derivation of the delta rule and generalized delta rule, based on Rumelhart et al., 1986, is provided in Section VI; see also Estes, this volume).

The simple cue model is the original LMS model tested by Gluck & Bower (1988) and continues, with various extensions, to show promise. Gluck (1991; Gluck & Bower, 1988) has speculated that a configural cue model with cue conjunctions no more complicated than "doublets" may be adequate; thus the configural cue model in Table IV uses simple cues and doublets. The *cue + rote* model is a version of a configural cue model that uses input units for simple cues and for each exemplar. This model should help to show the role of exemplars when they are treated as weighted rote associations to category labels. The possibility that rote associations may be important when simple cues are insufficient was considered by MacWhinney et al., 1989. The model is also related to the treatment of item-level inputs in Medin and Schaffer (1978), where those authors found in a number of their analyses that a weighted-cue model that included item-level information did as well as their exemplar model, expressed in Eqs. (1) and (2). Finally, the Back propagation model uses only simple cues as its inputs. As already suggested, the model has been very successful in modeling human learning of linguistic categories (MacWhinney et al., 1989; Taraban et al., 1989), but it was not known whether the model is sensitive to the similarity relations in Eqs. (1) and (2). Observing the performance of the other three models and comparing it to the Back propagation model will allow us to determine whether the Back propagation model acts like either of those models, or whether it acts differently.

In order to plot the learning curves for the three weighted cue models, we set the initial weights to 0 and chose a learning rate that would bring the network near its asymptotic performance level within 100 epochs. An epoch is one complete pass through the learning set, similar to a block of trials; the Δw's are collected during the epoch and weight changes are made at the end. Changing weights after each pattern would produce nearly identical results. The learning rates for the simple cue, configural cue, and cue + rote models were .01, .01, and .05, respectively. Out of convenience we used the routines in McClelland & Rumelhart (1988) for back propagation, with the network configuration shown in Fig. 3b and with the network initialized with small random weights.[8] Figure 4 shows the mean performance of each network. The weighted cue models were initialized with weights 0 so there was no need to do multiple tests.[9] The results for the back propagation model for 5 consecutive simulations, using a new set of random weights each time and a learning rate of .25, showed the same distinction between the high, medium, and low similarity subclasses as shown in Fig. 4d, which plots the mean performance for the 5 simulations.[10] The category response (category rating) in all the networks

[8] The network in Fig. 3b does not show bias units, so we note that each of the hidden units and output units had an associated bias unit. See McClelland and Rumelhart (1988) for the operation of these units.

[9] Random weights here would allow for a slightly noisy result each time; with hidden units they are important to the solution.

[10] In our discussion here and in Section VI we gloss over another parameter in this model termed *momentum*, which stabilizes the error correction process—this parameter remained at its default value of 0.9.

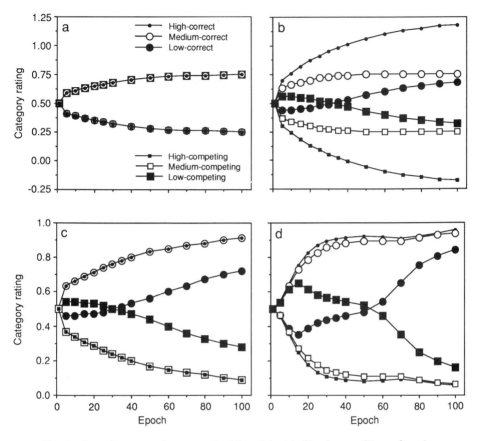

Fig. 4. Learning curves for connectionist models. (a), Simple cue; (b), configural cue; (c), cue + rote; (d), back propagation. Note: "High-correct" are ratings for the correct category for high-similarity items, and so on.

in this article was computed by using the ratio of the category activation to the sum of activations of both categories. For example, a Jets rating would be computed as the ratio Jets/(Jets + Sharks). This ratio is based on Luce (1963) and will be seen to be embedded in Eq. (2), upon close examination (see Nosofsky, 1984). Since the networks (and subjects) provided activation (rating) values for both categories on each trial, Fig. 4 (and the human data in Fig. 2) include two sets of learning curves. These are separated into ratings for the items' correct category and those for the items' competing category. Early in learning the rating for an item's correct category and for the competing category are near 0.5; as learning progresses, the ratings for the item's correct category approach 1.0 and those for the item's competing category approach 0.0 (except in the simple cue model).

A. BACK PROPAGATION: A PROMISING SOLUTION

Based on our simulations, in which basically a single parameter was fitted (i.e., *learning rate*), we argue that the back propagation model provides the best solution, based on four considerations that we apply to all the models:

1. Evidence of early "non-linear separability" effects (more correctly, low-similarity effects) that are ultimately overcome;
2. Evidence of a sensitivity to the other similarity differences, specifically, between the "high" and "medium" similarity subclasses;
3. The ability to achieve complete learning—that is, asymptotic performance levels of 0 and 1;
4. The ability to learn, rather than be provided with, the relevant representations of the input.

The simple cue model in Fig. 4a reflects a classic case of non-linear separability. At each point in learning, the low-similarity items produce incorrect ratings for both the correct category and the competing category. As is evident in the figure, these ratings are as wrong as the remaining ratings are right. Thus, for example, "Low-competing" (i.e., ratings of low-similarity items for the competing class) overlaps perfectly with "High-correct" in Fig. 4. This model is rejected without further discussion. The remaining models show similar but far weaker effects for the low-similarity items early on and recover from these effects with further learning.

The cue + rote model in Fig. 4c similarly has a problem with low items, but eventually recovers and reaches asymptotic levels very near 1.0 and 0.0 (not evident in the figure) for the correct and competing categories. Crucially, though, it fails at every point to show any sensitivity to the similarity relations that hold between high- and medium-similarity items in the human data, so it must be rejected as well.

As is evident in Fig. 4b, the configural cue model produces all the similarity effects predicted by Eqs. (1) and (2) and found in the human data. The model is near its asymptotic performance levels by the final epoch shown. These are 0.75 (-0.75), for medium- and low-similarity items, and 1.25 (-1.25) for high-similarity items, instead of the desired value of 1.0 (0.0). This problem is easily handled by passing the activations of the network through a logistic transformation:

$$\frac{1}{1 + e^{-c(\text{net input})}}$$

with an appropriate value for the scaling parameter c. Thus, this model passes the learnability test. However, as a process model, it leaves a substantive portion of the learning unspecified. The model cannot abstract on its own the cue configurations (e.g., *vu, zu, vo, zo*) that would be useful. Rather, these are "placed" on the input layer before learning begins. Thus, it has limited appeal as a complete learning model.

The back propagation model in Fig. 4d fulfills all the requirements set out above, including producing the full range of similarity effects. Therefore, relative to the criteria above, it provides the best solution. A major question that we had was whether this model would act like one of the other models or differently. First, although its inputs consist of single letters, just as in the simple cue model, it clearly outperforms that model. Second, if the network were simply extracting representations of the "cue validities" of the inputs in order to improve performance and additionally creating item-level codes in order to counter the "non-linear separability" factor, we would expect it to perform like the cue + rote model in Fig. 4c, but it does not. It overcomes the "non-linear separability" forces and additionally appears to automatically extract the cue conjunctions that produce the similarity relations between high- and medium-similarity inputs. Finally, in contrast to the configural cue model, the cue conjunctions are not specified on the input layer prior to the beginning of the learning simulation. Rather, through the dynamics of the back propagation method, the network extracts the necessary conjunctive representations on its own and represents these to itself on the hidden layer. In comparing back propagation to the configural cue model, we find no real qualitative difference in performance at the output layer, but a major difference in the "external" help that the configural cue network needs in order to adequately represent the input. In this regard, back propagation outperforms the configural cue model.

There is an interesting inconsistency in our finding that the back propagation model does appear to conform to predictions derived from Eqs. (1) and (2). On the one hand, Eqs. (1) and (2) were developed to model exemplar memory. On the other hand, exemplar representations were not forced on the model. A better way to put this is to say that the internal representations are *distributed*, that is, spread out across many hidden units; they are not *localist*, that is, a specific unit (or location in the network) is not assigned to represent an exemplar, as one would expect in an exemplar storage model. This suggests that the particular *internal* (hidden unit) coding of instances that are presented on the input layer is not crucial (assuming that the learning algorithm codes correct ones).

Do the hidden units fulfill the requirement of "quasi-local" representations as specified in one of Kruschke's (this volume) principles for category learning models? According to the principle, the degree of activation of the internal representations in a network should be based on their similarity to the exemplar on the input layer, not on independent cues in the input. Quasi-local activation should result in performance consistent with Eqs. (1) and (2); thus the notion is important to Kruschke, as well as to us and others (cf. Estes, this volume). Activation of the second sort is what Kruschke refers to as "rule-based" and should basically fail in modeling human performance. One way of guaranteeing that representations are quasi-local is by assuring that hidden units represent exemplars, as we do later on in our "exemplar-based" back propagation model and as Kruschke often (but not always) does in ALCOVE (1992, this volume). The results with this back propagation model suggest that distributed representations can produce the similarity effects of Eqs. (1) and (2) without requiring explicit exemplar representations on the hidden layer.

In summary, our results from these simulations show that weighted cue models fail to replicate the similarity effects observed in human performance unless the inputs to the network include cue combinations. The cue combinations must be set at the beginning of a simulation and the representations themselves remain outside the learning process throughout the course of learning. Standard back propagation produces the desired similarity effects when the inputs are simple cues and when the internal representation of individual exemplars is distributed across many hidden units. Developing a method that would allow networks to autonomously create distributed internal representations was, of course, a major goal in the initial formulation of backpropagation by Rumelhart, Hinton, and Williams. Designing back propagation to produce the similarity effects observed here was not their explicit goal, which points to the theoretical strength of back propagation.

B.   How Good Is the Fit?

Although the back propagation model evidences all the desirable characteristics that we set out above, we still need to consider the goodness of the fit. The main problems appear to be twofold. One is a problem that is common to these networks, which is slow initial learning. There are a number of "speedup" modifications to the learning rule that are being examined by others that may be helpful here (e.g., Jacobs, 1988; Kruschke & Movellan, 1991; see also Gluck, Glauthier, & Sutton, 1992).

Another problem seems to be over-weighting the single cue information, which results in "non-linear separability" effects that are larger than those predicted in Fig. 1 and also larger than those found in the human data. The reverse is true for the similarity effects for high- and medium-similarity items. One approach to this problem is to look carefully at the emergence of representations at the hidden layer to determine what additional constraints on the model might align it more closely to the human data. This is a viable approach that we plan to examine in the future. For now, we would like to consider another possibility, which is to tailor the model more closely to Eqs. (1) and (2), which we turn to next.

IV.   Architectures

Configuring a connectionist network is often a very open-ended matter. Indeed, the open-endedness has evoked some amount of criticism for lack of constraints on these systems (e.g., Massaro, 1988). One of the goals of connectionist modeling should be to identify cognitive principles that constrain networks. Kruschke provides a set of such principles in this volume. More work of this type is required.

In the case of standard back propagation architectures, Taraban et al. (1989) found that the nature of the connectivity of input units to the first (or only) layer of hidden units mattered. In those particular simulations, we were interested in training a network to process German case and gender distinctions, which are an integral part of German grammar. In our experience, extracting the case and gender paradigm ("table") and generalizing it to novel instances depended on limiting the connections of gender cues to one pool, or collection, of hidden units and the connections of case cues to another pool of hidden units. MacWhinney et al. (1989), in a theoretically refined approach to the same learning problem, pooled hidden units too, with good success. In a somewhat different domain, McClelland & Jenkins (1991) configured separate pools of hidden units connected to *weight* and *distance* input cues. By their admission, the separation was crucial. The consensus of all the above researchers is that the underlying reason for the differences that arise from pooling hidden units is still not well understood; however, it is nonetheless an important consideration.

A.   Filtration and Condensation

Since our results for back propagation were so encouraging with regard to similarity effects, we were curious to know whether it was indeed incapable of modeling the relative differences humans show in learning filtration versus condensation category learning problems (see Kruschke, 1992, this

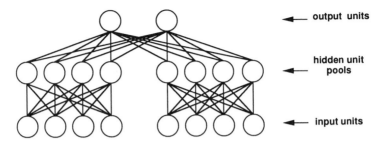

Fig. 5.   A network with pools of hidden units.

volume). If it were, then that would seriously limit its utility as a modeling tool. The basic finding in the human data is that people find the filtration problem easier to learn.

In this simulation, as in the others, we fitted just a single parameter with the goal of obtaining a reasonable qualitative fit to ALCOVE (see Kruschke, this volume, Fig. 9). Since *height* and *position* seemed much like the quantitative cues of *weight* and *distance* in the McClelland and Jenkins (1991) simulation, we configured a network, as shown in Fig. 5. The input layer was constructed by specifying a node for each value for each dimension (four height values and four position values). Stimuli were coded as shown in Table V. We ran 5 consecutive simulations for both problems, using a new set of small random startup weights for each pair of filtration and condensation simulations, and a learning rate of 0.1.

The mean results for the simulations are plotted in Fig. 6, with each individual simulation showing the same advantage of filtration over condensation. In similar simulations that did not pool units, we were unable to produce these effects, so the pooling of hidden units appears to be important for this problem. In explaining the filtration advantage in humans, Kruschke (this volume) points out that it is easier for humans to base category decisions on a single dimension (filtration) than on a combination of dimensions (condensation). An effect of pooling hidden units as we did is to make the combination of cues from two dimensions more difficult than learning cues from a single dimension. At this stage, it seems reasonable to speculate that establishing these pools through planned patterns of connections may be one way of introducing dimensional attention into standard back propagation networks.[11] If we combine our result here with the first author's experience with linguistic case and gender, the general result

---

[11] See Kruschke (this volume) for alternative ways of introducing dimensional attention.

TABLE V

Input–Output Patterns for Filtration–Condensation Simulation

	Height				Position				Filtration outputs		Condensation outputs	
	h_1	h_2	h_3	h_4	p_1	p_2	p_3	p_4				
Pattern 1	1	0	0	0	0	1	0	0	1	0	1	0
Pattern 2	0	1	0	0	1	0	0	0	1	0	1	0
Pattern 3	0	0	1	0	1	0	0	0	1	0	1	0
Pattern 4	0	0	0	1	0	1	0	0	1	0	0	1
Pattern 5	1	0	0	0	0	0	1	0	0	1	1	0
Pattern 6	0	1	0	0	0	0	0	1	0	1	0	1
Pattern 7	0	0	1	0	0	0	0	1	0	1	0	1
Pattern 8	0	0	0	1	0	0	1	0	0	1	0	1

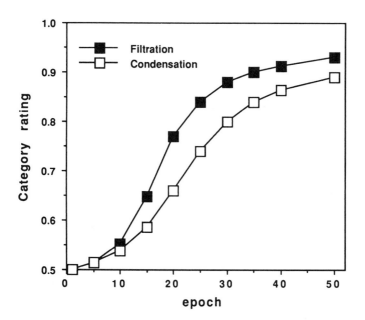

Fig. 6.   Learning curves for the filtration and condensation problems.

would appear to be that qualitative differences between cues must be reflected in pools of units at the hidden level. We will confess, though, that the conditions under which units should be pooled is still not clear to us. There may indeed be cases when pooling may not make a difference. These questions require further work.

Given the multiple findings reported so far, it would be useful to generally summarize our simulation results and to indicate the direction for the remainder of the article. We have focused on weighted cue models and have found them lacking in various ways. In testing standard back propagation on our human data and additionally testing it on the filtration–condensation task, we found that it produced good qualitative fits to human data. Importantly, although standard back propagation differs vastly from ALCOVE, it does not necessarily diverge from the principles underlying ALCOVE, outlined by Kruschke in this volume, that derive in large measure from the Medin and Schaffer formulas in Eqs. (1) and (2). The "exemplar-based" back propagation model, which we develop next, is also consistent with these principles and with the back propagation method. Our purpose in developing a new model was to provide an interesting and tractable environment for further development of a learning model. Before going on, we will mention that one problem associated with back propagation has been catastrophic forgetting (see Kruschke, 1992, this volume). This has not been an issue in this article, important though it is. We refer the interested reader to Hetherington and Seidenberg (1989) and Murre (1992) for ideas on ways to overcome catastrophic forgetting in back propagation.

B.   AN EXEMPLAR-BASED BACK PROPAGATION MODEL

Since the back propagation method had worked well in the tests above, we were interested in examining extensions of the method to other architectures, particularly one that would more closely approximate exemplar-memory storage and Eqs. (1) and (2), using ideas from Williams (1986) on Boolean activation functions. Figure 7 shows part of the network. The hidden layer consists of units that store information about specific exemplars. Each exemplar is connected to letter detectors that check for the presence and absence of the letters making up just that exemplar, and each exemplar is connected only to the category label for which it receives feedback. By connecting exemplars only to their own category labels, we deviate from the usual practice of fully connecting the hidden layer to the output layer. The theoretical benefit is that we more closely approximate exemplar-memory storage, in which a person would store a representation

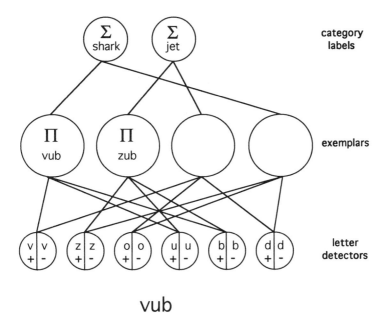

vub

Fig. 7. A portion of the exemplar-based network.

for an exemplar and the category label associated with the exemplar. The model also allows us to observe the effects of sparse connectivity, in the connections from the input to the hidden layer and from the hidden layer to the output layer. The sparse connections are motivated by the fuzzy logic described next. The connections in the figure are weights, as usual.

In order to implement Eqs. (1) and (2), we proceeded as follows. First, the similarity between a probe item and stored item was computed earlier as:

$$\prod s_i \qquad (5)$$

where $s_i = m$ for a match and $s_i = (1 - m)$ for a mismatch $(0.5 \leq m \leq 1.0)$. If we let the strength of m reflect the "fuzzy truth" that the associated feature is present, then match $= 1 =$ True and mismatch $= 0 =$ False, when $m = 1$. Further, when $m = 1$, then Eq. (5) can be viewed as a Boolean AND, and for values of $m < 1$, Eq. (5) is Boolean-like. Since we needed a differentiable function for back propagation, we adopted the logistic function with a "temperature" (cf McClelland &

Rumelhart, 1988) of 0.19.[12] The logistic function shown in Eq. (6) determined the "truth value" of matches and mismatches:

$$t_h = \frac{1}{1 + e^{-[(d_iw_i)/0.19]}} \tag{6}$$

For the ith feature, $d_i * w_i = +w_i$ (i.e., the product of the output of the letter detector d_i, which is either $+$ or $-$, and the weight w_i leading to the exemplar) when the input and hidden unit match, and $-w_i$ when they mismatch. The truth value of $w = 0.5$ is close to 1.0, and the truth value of $-w$ is close to 0. The activation of the AND-like function produced by the product of the truth values is simply:

$$o_h = \prod_{i=1}^{3} t_{hi} \tag{7}$$

where o_h is the activation of an exemplar unit. Each exemplar unit "checks" the input for the presence of the symbols that make up the representation stored at that unit. Since each exemplar unit is composed of three symbols, there are three weights leading from the letter detectors to each exemplar unit, as shown in Fig. 7. For our simulation, Eq. (7) computes the product of three "truth values" for each exemplar unit. A depiction of the activation function for the exemplar units is provided in Fig. 8, for 2 dimensions. At the output layer, where the activation of the category label is computed, the activations of the exemplar units connected to the category units are combined linearly:

$$o_j = \sum_{h \in X} (w_{jh}o_h) \tag{8}$$

where o_j is the activation of the output unit for Category X, o_h is the activation of an exemplar unit, and w_{jh} is the weight between a hidden unit and an output unit. Since exemplars are only connected to their correct category label, the summation in Eq. (8) is over the four exemplar units associated with the output unit for the exemplar's category. The complete forward activation pass is multiplicative in its activation of exemplars and additive in combining those activations.

---

[12] The "temperature" simply changes the slope of the logistic function, which is the standard activation function in back propagation networks, as stated earlier. A temperature of 0.19 was selected because it provides the closest fit to a symmetric linear function with a range of 1 for the activation/truth value as well as for the net input (-0.5 to $+0.5$).

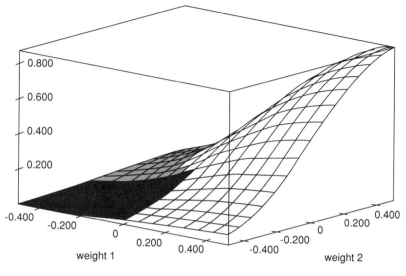

Fig. 8.   Depiction of the AND activation function.

Since we develop this model as a "back propagation" model, we apply the same principles as those shown for the generalized delta rule above and in Section VI. In our model, we use a linear activation function for the output units, so the δ_j for these units is $(t_j - o_j)$ and $\Delta w_{jh} = \eta(t_j - o_j)o_h$, where the subscript h refers to a hidden unit. The error signal is back propagated from the output layer to the exemplar units and the Δw_{hi} for the weights connecting letter detectors to the exemplars is:

$$\Delta w_{hi} = \eta(\Sigma\delta_j w_{jh})\frac{\delta o_h}{\delta w_{hi}} \qquad (9)$$

which consists of the δ_h, or error, for the hidden unit that is back propagated from the output units to which it is connected ($\Sigma\delta_j \ w_{jh}$) and a specification of how to change the weights connected to the hidden unit given its activation. We expand Eq. (9) for the interested reader in Section VI.

In our preliminary tests, we used "linked" weights for the letter detectors (See McClelland and Rumelhart, 1988, for a discussion of linked weights.) This amounted to summing the weight changes calculated for all the patterns for any given epoch of learning trials and setting each of the weights for a specific position to the same value. Specifically, all the links from input letters v and z were updated to the same value, all the links from o and u were updated to the same value, and all the links from b and d were updated to the same value.

The mean result of 5 consecutive simulations is graphed in Fig. 9. For each of our simulations, we used a different set of small random startup weights, a learning rate of 0.35 for the exemplar-to-category weights, and one-eighth of this learning rate for the lower weights.[13] Each individual simulation produced learning curves that varied little from those displayed. As in all the previous simulations, the category response (rating) was computed as the Luce ratio, so for "Jets" it was Jets/(Jets + Sharks). Subsequent simulations have shown that neither linked weights nor two learning rates are necessary in order to produce the results shown in Fig. 9.

First, the simulation shows the early crossover for low items from the incorrect category into the correct category. Second, during the remaining trials the differences between high-, medium-, and low-similarity items are comparable and decreasing. Both of these effects are present in Fig. 1 as well as in the human data. These particular fits can be contrasted to the earlier back propagation model which tended to over-weight the "nonlinear separability" effect and under-weight the remaining similarity effects. Thus, this model does appear to provide a possible improvement.

Our preliminary success with an exemplar-based model suggests that equations (1) and (2) from Medin and Schaffer (1978) and some rough assumptions about exemplar memory (Estes, 1986) together provide very workable guidelines for building a mechanism for category learning (see Kruschke, 1992, this volume; Nosofsky, 1984, for related views). In order to capture the nature of this model more completely, we first discuss it in relation to the three principles for category learning models formulated by Kruschke (this volume). We then focus on what we perceive to be interesting extensions of the current model.

The exemplar-based model is consistent with Kruschke's three principles. First, it uses error-driven learning (see also McDonald, this volume). Weight changes are made throughout the network in response to deviations on the output layer from the correct response. Second, representations at the hidden layer have localized receptive fields—that is, they are quasi-local representations. In our model, this means that the activation of any given exemplar unit on the hidden layer is directly based on its

---

[13] A proportion of one-eighth was derived from the number of weight changes that were summed as part of "linking" the weights; the net result was to set the input-to-exemplar weights to the average weight change for the epoch.

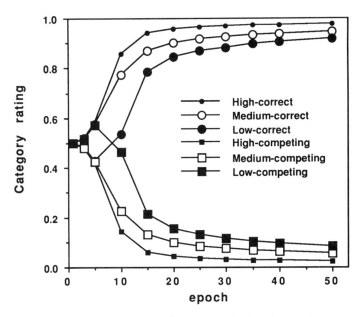

Fig. 9.   Learning curves for the exemplar-based network.

similarity to the input. Finally, the model has dimensional attention strengths. This is achieved by limiting the sensitivity of an exemplar unit to one signal for each of its dimensions and by linking the weights from the input to the hidden units.[14] As we have subsequently discovered, the weights do not need to be linked. With unlinked weights, each exemplar unit would develop a distinct set of weights. In that case we would say that the network has "exemplar-specific" dimensional attention (cf. Kruschke, this volume).

A number of reasonable (but not necessarily correct) assumptions were posited in constructing this network. One major assumption was that memory storage is "localist," with one unit for each exemplar in contrast to the alternative "distributed" representations possible for connectionist models. In this respect, the organization of letter detectors and exemplar units in our model is similar to the McClelland and Rumelhart (1981) interactive activation model, which represented letters at one level and words at another, the latter being part of the bottom-up word activation. These localist representations are also consistent with exemplar-memory

---

[14] We thank John Kruschke for emphasizing these points to us.

models (see Estes, 1986). A category label is associated with each exemplar by simply linking each exemplar unit to its correct category unit. The storage of a category tag with an exemplar is also consistent with exemplar-storage models, but the reduction in competitive learning and the associated reduction in network connections also diverge from standard connectionist practice. These assumptions, as implemented in the complete model, had no apparent negative consequences. One is still inclined to ask what additional benefit we hope to achieve through this approach.

Of current interest to us is the process in the model, which is a type of fuzzy logic. In conjunction with the learning component, it may provide the means for a closer examination of the emergence of simple representations, expressed as fuzzy propositions; of the encoding and learning of complex propositions; and of the interaction of the two. A model with an expanded ability to deal with complex representations will be useful in the first author's interest in linguistic categories and their combinations in complex structures (cf. Gupta and MacWhinney, 1992, for an alternative connectionist approach that constructs and uses instance-based traces for remembering the complex linguistic structures to which it has been exposed).

The exemplar-based approach could also be useful in modeling the interaction of prototype and exemplar representations in a learning context (e.g., Nakamura, 1985). It might also be of use in examining the integration of theory and data over the course of learning (cf. Fisher & Yoo, this volume; Mooney, this volume). The localist representations would appear to be useful in all these cases for implementing the fuzzy logic. We are encouraged by other work using fuzzy propositions in a connectionist network currently being conducted by Oden (1992). One current challenge that we perceive in the further development of this model is in providing the network with autonomous means for creating new exemplar representations. In the current implementation the network cannot modify itself to accomodate new exemplars.

V. Conclusion

In this article we have looked at human performance in a simple category learning experiment and we have considered a number of connectionist possibilities for modeling that performance. In our simple test, we identified three very different models that all seem to possess the necessary characteristics for responsiveness to the similarity differences in the stimuli. These are the configural cue model, standard back propagation, and the exemplar-based back propagation model. Of these, we view models implementing back propagation as the most interesting for future development.

Within our results, there are a number of noteworthy findings. First, back propagation finds the cue configurations that result in activation that is sensitive to exemplar similarity. Nobody told the network which cue combinations to represent internally based on the single letter inputs, nor how to weight these representations. This is truly a plus for back propagation, since the method was presumably not formulated with this specific result in mind, and the fact is that on the feedback side the network is simply told "right" or "wrong"—that is, the feedback is not geared toward producing similarity effects.

Back propagation as a general computational method also seems to work for a variety of "hidden unit" configurations and activation functions. The exemplar-based back propagation model that we present encodes the exemplar representations through weights that must be learned, although we do make prior assumptions about how the weights are set up, more in accord with an exemplar-memory model than a "distributed" connectionist model. In future work we need to work out in detail how the network might add new exemplar nodes in response to new stimuli.

Second, one is inclined to probe networks to determine what makes them work: in this case, to shed some light on what the relevant cue weightings and combinations are. It might be most accurate to state that the best *predictor* of human performance, and in a sense the grand-daddy of our exemplar-based model and other models like ALCOVE and GCM (cf. Kruschke, this volume; Nosofsky, 1984), are the similarity-based equations of Medin and Schaffer (1978), expressed in Eqs. (1) and (2). These equations predicted levels of performance consonant with stimulus similarity and made the somewhat unintuitive prediction that similarity effects would emerge before much learning had taken place. As a tool for the examination of learning sets in order to gain an understanding of how they are constituted, these equations seem quite useful. This is important to appreciate, since our simulations indicate that the generalization factors may abide more closely in the nature of the objects to be learned than in the specifics of a large group of models capable of extracting that nature, each in its own manner.

Finally, our entire endeavor here has rested largely on examining what would happen if the mismatch parameter in Eq. (1) were related to learning. We showed that this approach seems to work in at least three separate ways. First, it let us fit learning curves to data over many blocks of trials. Second, it helps one to understand what is driving the "hidden" weight configuring of the back propagation model. Third, in the exemplar-based back propagation model, the weights leading from the inputs to the exemplars had to change in order to improve performance. These weights in a definite sense defined the exemplar at any stage of learning and were explicitly configured to mirror the match parameter. We look forward to our future work with the various tools that we have honed somewhat in the studies described here—a computational formula with good predictive power and two types of computational environments, one in which the burden for discovery falls on the system and another which allows more explicit control of what gets encoded.

As a postscript we will note that it may appear as though we have constructed our argument on the basis of a single set of data. In order to avoid such a misperception, we point out that we have tested our approach with other Types in the Shepard et al. (1961) set, and, importantly, with larger sets of 20 category instances. It was actually from these data with ordinary undergraduate subjects and second-language learners (Taraban & Roark, 1993) that we became convinced of the utility of the exemplar similarity formulation. It is somewhat difficult, though, to develop a set of stimuli that provide a sharp contrast between weighted-cue predictions and exemplar similarity predictions. The predictions of both models would be identical, for example, for Type I stimuli. We use Type V stimuli here simply because they pit similarity-based predictions against weighted-cue predictions with a clarity that no other set that we have yet discovered does. The set also produces equally clear results.

The strong theoretical underpinning of the mathematical formulation in Eqs. (1) and (2) (see Estes, this volume; Kruschke, 1992, this volume; Luce, 1963; Medin & Schaffer, 1978; Nosofsky, 1984; Shepard, 1987) and our recent results lead us to expect that our learning approach should be generalizable to any learning situation where similarity relations hold between the encoded instances. In further work we hope to link the back propagation learning method more closely to fuzzy propositional representations, with the expectation that this will greatly increase the expressive power of this type of connectionist model and our ability to observe and understand its behavior.

The similarity-based formulation of the relations that hold between cognitive representations defies intuition, as we hoped we demonstrated with the Town example. Often students' response to the presentation of psychological findings is, "My grandmother could have told me that," that is, the finding appears to require nothing more than common sense. We submit that most if not all grandmothers would fall for the weighted-cue trap.

VI. Appendixes

A. THE DELTA RULE

Given an interconnected network of inputs and outputs, as shown in Fig. 3a, the delta rule will iteratively arrive at an LMS solution to the input–output mapping (i.e., one that minimizes the sum of squared residuals between the desired and obtained output values) by changing the weights connecting inputs and outputs, from trial to trial. The model operates in a forward "activation" pass and a backward "error correction" pass. Upon presentation of an input/output pattern, which specifies how to activate each of the i_i input units and the *desired* activation values t_j for the o_j output units, the net input to o_j is equal to:

$$o_j = \sum_i w_{ji} i_i \qquad (10)$$

where w_{ji} is the weight connecting input unit i_i to output unit o_j. In order to provide a consistent account of error correction for the delta rule and for the generalized delta rule, Rumelhart et al. (1986) set the error E on a pattern to be equal to:

$$E = \tfrac{1}{2} \sum_j (t_j - o_j)^2 \qquad (11)$$

the error δ for a given input pattern and an output unit o_j to be equal to:

$$\delta_j = -\frac{\partial E_p}{\partial o_j} = t_j - o_j \qquad (12)$$

and the change in weight w_{ji} to be equal to:

$$\Delta w_{ji} = -\frac{\partial E_p}{\partial o_j} \frac{\partial o_j}{\partial w_{ji}} = \eta \delta_j i_i \qquad (13)$$

where η controls the rate of learning and is a parameter that must be set.

B. The Generalized Delta Rule

A major reason for generalizing the delta rule was to allow networks with "hidden" units to learn non–linearly separable problems, that is, those problems that could not be solved using a weighted sum of inputs. The general idea is to compute δ as in Eq. (12) and then propagate the error signal down through the layers of weights, adjusting each weight in proportion to its contribution to the error at the output units. Since in Rumelhart et al. the net input to a unit is transformed through a logistic activation function to produce the output o_j,

$$o_j = \frac{1}{1 + e^{-\text{net input}}} \tag{14}$$

the δ_j for output units is equal to:

$$\delta_j = -\frac{\partial E_p}{\partial o_j} \frac{\partial o_j}{\partial \text{net input}_j} = (t_j - o_j)o_j(1 - o_j) \tag{15}$$

and for hidden unit i, δ_i equals:

$$\left(\sum_j \delta_j w_{ji} \right) o_i(1 - o_i) \tag{16}$$

Since the δ for any unit in the network can be computed, the calculation for Δw in the preceding section still holds, where i_i (o_i) is the unit sending activation along w.

C. Extension of the Generalized Delta Rule to "Exemplar" Units

$$\Delta w_{hi} = \eta \left(\sum \delta_j w_{jh} \right) \frac{\partial o_h}{\partial w_{hi}} = \eta \left(\sum \delta_j w_{jh} \right) \frac{1}{\text{temp}} d_i t_{hi} o_h e^{-(d_i w_i)/\text{temp}} \tag{17}$$

where temp $= 0.19$, d_i is the output of the letter detector ($+$ or $-$), and t_{hi} is the incoming activation to exemplar$_h$ on the w_{hi} link.

ACKNOWLEDGMENTS

This article is based in part on work supported by the Texas Advanced Research Program under Grant 0216-44-5829 to the first author. We would like to thank Steve Dopkins, Evan Heit, John Kruschke, Phil Marshall, Brian MacWhinney, Janet McDonald, Doug Medin, Glenn Nakamura, and Vir Phoha for comments on an earlier draft of this article. We would also like to thank Bob Bell, Tom English, Jerry Myers, Mukesh Rohatgi, and Yiannis Vourtsanis for helpful comments and suggestions related to this research. Finally, we would like to thank Sandra Douglas, Chris McGee, and Mark Stephan for help in running the experiment and in analyzing the data.

REFERENCES

Bates, E., & MacWhinney, B. (1982). Functionalist approaches to grammar. In E. Wanner & L. Gleitman (Eds.), *Language acquisition: The state of the art* (pp. 173–218). Cambridge, England: Cambridge University Press.

Bates, E., & MacWhinney, B. (1987). Competition, variation, and language learning. In B. MacWhinney (Ed.), *Mechanisms of language acquisition* (pp. 157–193). Hillsdale, NJ: Erlbaum.

Bates, E., & MacWhinney, B. (1989). Functionalism and the competition model. In B. MacWhinney & E. Bates (Eds.), *The crosslinguistic study of sentence processing* (pp. 3–73). New York: Cambridge University Press.

Beach, L. (1964). Cue probabilism and inference behavior. *Psychological Monographs, 78,* 21–37.

Estes, W. (1986). Array models for category learning. *Cognitive Psychology, 18,* 500–549.

Gill, P. E., Murray, E. W., Saunders, M. A., & Wright, M. H. (1984). Procedures for optimization problems with a mixture of bounds and general linear constraints. *ACM Transactions on Mathematical Software, 10,* 282–296.

Gluck, M. (1991). Stimulus generalization and representation in adaptive network models of category learning. *Psychological Science, 2,* 50–55.

Gluck, M., & Bower, G. (1988). Evaluating an adaptive network model of human learning. *Journal of Memory and Language, 27,* 166–195.

Gluck, M., Bower, G., & Hee, M. (1989). A configural-cue network model of animal and human associative learning. In *Proceedings of the Eleventh Annual Conference of the Cognitive Science Society* (pp. 323–332). Hillsdale, NJ: Erlbaum.

Gluck, M., Glauthier, P., & Sutton, R. (1992). Adaptation of cue-specific learning rates in network models of human category learning. In *Proceedings of the Fourteenth Annual Meeting of the Cognitive Science Society* (pp. 540–545). Hillsdale, NJ: Erlbaum.

Gupta, P. & MacWhinney, B. (1992). Integrating category acquisition with inflectional marking: A model of the German nominal system. In *Proceedings of the Fourteenth Annual Meeting of the Cognitive Science Society* (pp. 253–258). Hillsdale, NJ: Erlbaum.

Hetherington, P., & Seidenberg, M. (1989). Is there "catastrophic interference" in connectionist networks? In *Proceedings of the Eleventh Annual Conference of the Cognitive Science Society* (pp. 26–33). Hillsdale, NJ: Erlbaum.

Jacobs, R. (1988). Increased rates of convergence through learning rate adaptation. *Neural Networks, 1,* 295–307.

Kruschke, J. (1990). A connectionist model of category learning. Doctoral dissertation, University of California, Berkeley.

Kruschke, J. (1992). ALCOVE: An exemplar-based connectionist model of category learning. *Psychological Review, 99*, 22–44.

Kruschke, J., & Movellan, J. (1991). Benefits of gain: Speeded learning and minimal hidden layers in back-propagation networks. *IEEE Transactions on Systems, Man, and Cybernetics, 21*, 273–280.

Luce, R. (1963). Detection and recognition. In R. Luce, R. Bush, & E. Galanter (Eds.), *Handbook of mathematical psychology* (pp. 103–189). New York: Wiley.

MacWhinney, B., Leinbach, J., Taraban, R., & McDonald, J. (1989). Language learning: Cues or rules? *Journal of Memory and Language, 28*, 255–277.

Massaro, D. (1988). Some criticisms of connectionist models of human performance. *Journal of Memory and Language, 27*, 213–234.

McClelland, J., & Jenkins, E. (1991). Nature, nurture, and connections: Implications of connectionist models for cognitive development. In K. VanLehn (Ed.), *Architectures for intelligence* (pp. 41–73). Hillsdale, NJ: Erlbaum.

McClelland, J., & Rumelhart, D. (1981). An interactive activation model of context effects in letter perception: Part 1. An account of basic findings. *Psychological Review, 88*, 375–407.

McClelland, J., & Rumelhart, D. (1988). *Explorations in parallel distributed processing: A handbook of models, programs, and exercises*. Cambridge, MA: MIT Press.

McDonald, J., & MacWhinney, B. (1991). Levels of learning: A comparison of concept formation and language acquisition. *Journal of Memory and Language, 30*, 407–430.

Medin, D., & Edelson, S. (1988). Problem structure and the use of base-rate information from experience. *Journal of Experimental Psychology: General, 117*, 68–85.

Medin, D., & Schaffer, M. (1978). Context theory of classification learning. *Psychological Review, 85*, 207–238.

Medin, D., & Schwanenflugel, P. (1981). Linear separability in classification learning. *Journal of Experimental Psychology: Human Learning and Memory, 7*, 355–368.

Murre, J. (1992). The effects of pattern presentation on interference in backpropagation networks. In *Proceedings of the Fourteenth Annual Meeting of the Cognitive Science Society* (pp. 54–59). Hillsdale, NJ: Erlbaum.

Nakamura, G. (1985). Knowledge-based classification of ill-defined categories. *Memory & Cognition, 13*, 377–384.

Nosofsky, R. (1984). Choice, similarity, and the context theory of classification. *Journal of Experimental Psychology: Learning, Memory, and Cognition, 10*, 104–114.

Oden, G. (1992). Direct, incremental learning of fuzzy propositions. In *Proceedings of the Fourteenth Annual Conference of the Cognitive Science Society* (pp. 48–53). Hillsdale, NJ: Erlbaum.

Reed, S. (1972). Pattern recognition and categorization. *Cognitive Psychology, 4*, 382–407.

Rosch, E., & Mervis, C. (1975). Family resemblance studies in the internal structure of categories. *Cognitive Psychology, 7*, 573–605.

Rumelhart, D., Hinton, G., & Williams, R. (1986). Learning internal representations by error propagation. In D. Rumelhart, J. McClelland, & the PDP Research Group (Eds.), *Parallel distributed processing: Explorations in the microstructure of cognition: Vol. 1. Foundations* (pp. 318–362). Cambridge, MA: MIT Press.

Shepard, R. (1987). Towards a universal law of generalization for psychological science. *Science, 237*, 1317–1323.

Shepard, R., Hovland, C., & Jenkins, H. (1961). Learning and memorization of classifications. *Psychological Monographs: General and Applied, 75* (Whole No. 517).

Stone, G. (1986). An analysis of the delta rule and the learning of statistical associations. In D. Rumelhart, J. McClelland, & The PDP Research Group (Eds.), *Parallel distributed processing: Explorations in the microstructure of cognition: Vol. 1. Foundations* (pp. 444–459). Cambridge, MA: MIT Press.

Taraban, R., McDonald, J., & MacWhinney, B. (1989). Category learning in a connectionist model: Learning to decline the German definite article. In R. Corrigan, F. Eckman, & M. Noonan (Eds.), *Linguistic categorization* (pp. 163–193). Philadelphia: Benjamins.

Taraban, R., & Palacios, J. (1992). Exemplar competition: A variation on category learning in the competition model. *Proceedings of the Fourteenth Annual Conference of the Cognitive Science Society* (1140–1145). Hillsdale, NJ: Erlbaum.

Taraban, R., & Roark, B. (1993). *Exemplar representations in linguistic category learning.* Unpublished manuscript, Texas Tech University, Department of Psychology, Lubbock.

Williams, R. (1986). The logic of activation functions. In D. Rumelhart, J. McClelland, & The PDP Research Group, *Parallel distributed processing: Explorations in the microstructure of cognition: Vol. 1. Foundations* (pp. 423–443). Cambridge, MA: MIT Press.

THE ACQUISITION OF CATEGORIES MARKED BY MULTIPLE PROBABILISTIC CUES

Janet L. McDonald

I. Introduction

Research in concept learning has gone through several historical changes (Smith & Medin, 1981), dealing first with well-defined categories based on the presence of individual features or logical combinations of features (Bruner, Goodnow, & Austin, 1956; Hunt, Marin, & Stone, 1966; Shepard, Hovland, & Jenkins, 1961), then shifting to more ill-defined categories with probabilistic features. Models developed to account for these latter types of categories include (1) *prototype models,* where a central category member is abstracted from the exemplars for each category and new items are then compared to these prototypes during classification (e.g., Posner & Keele, 1968; Rosch & Mervis, 1975); (2) *feature frequency models,* where exemplars are broken down into their individual features, frequency counts maintained for these features in the various categories, and the features of new items compared to these counts during classification (e.g., Neumann, 1974; Reitman & Bower, 1973); and (3) *exemplar-based processing models,* where the individual exemplars from each category are stored as units and compared to new items during classification (e.g., Medin & Schaffer, 1978).

In this article I deal with a special case of ill-defined categories. These particular categories are marked by probabilistic features; however, any particular combination of features always has the same categorization.

THE PSYCHOLOGY OF LEARNING
AND MOTIVATION, VOL. 29

129

Specifically, categorization of any exemplar is based on the relative strength or dominance of the features present, with the strongest feature indicating the correct categorization. Such categories turn out to be commonplace in language, and a variation of the feature frequency model, known as the *competition model* (Bates & MacWhinney, 1982, 1987, 1989), has been developed within the arena of psycholinguistics to account for the acquisition and use of such categories.

Specifically, the types of categories dealt with here are marked by multiple probabilistic cues. The probabilistic nature of these cues stems from two sources: First, a cue that marks the category may not be present on all category members. Second, a cue that marks the category may also be present on non-members. For example, although exemplars in the linguistic category of actor (who or what performs the action of the verb in a sentence) tend to be animate nouns (e.g., *The boy destroyed the anthill*), some actors are inanimate (e.g., *The rust destroyed the garden furniture*), and some non-actors are animate (e.g., *The scandal destroyed the politician*). Despite the probabilistic nature of the individual cues, categorization of any particular combination of cues contained on an exemplar is not probabilistic. Rather, the individual cues differ in their strength relative to one another, such that the information from some cues overrides or dominates information from other cues. Thus, for any particular combination of cues present on an exemplar, correct categorization is indicated by the most dominant cue present. This dominance relation is especially relevant when two or more cues are present on an exemplar and they disagree about the categorization. The correct categorization is given by the relatively most dominant cue.

II. The Competition Model

The competition model (Bates & MacWhinney, 1982; 1987; 1989) has fared well in accounting for the acquisition of categories of the above nature in the psycholinguistic domain. This model states that people will acquire and use cues in proportion to their utility in marking the category. It also specifies how these cue weights are combined in order to categorize an exemplar. Specifically, the weights of all cues present are distributed to the categorization they favor, and the one with the highest cumulative weight wins. When cues agree, their weights are simply combined, and categorization occurs quickly and correctly. When cues disagree, the weights are distributed over several alternatives, and categorization will tend to be slower and more error-prone. The use of mathematical formulas (such as Luce's 1959 choice rule) to capture this cue combination process allows for the prediction of error rates and relative reaction times over different types of exemplars (see McDonald & MacWhinney, 1991, for details).

While the competition model claims that cue weights are proportional to their utility in marking the category, there are several different ways of defining this utility (McDonald, 1989). One measure used by past categorization researchers has been that of *cue validity*, that is, the conditional probability of a category given a cue [i.e., P(category|cue)]. Given equal-sized categories, cue validity is equal to the frequency of a cue in a particular category divided by the total frequency of the cue over all categories (Beach, 1964; Reed, 1972; Rosch & Mervis, 1975). One of the measures of cue utility used in the competition model is a modification of this standard definition of cue validity, called *overall validity*. Overall validity is the product of the probability of a cue occurring over all exemplars (known as *availability* in the competition model) and the conditional probability of a category given a cue (this is the standard definition of cue validity; within the competition model it is called *reliability*). Thus,

$$\text{Overall validity} = P(\text{cue})P(\text{category}|\text{cue}) \tag{1}$$

and denotes the percentage of time over all exemplars, both category members and non-members, that the cue is present and indicates the correct categorization. Multiplying the old cue validity measure by cue frequency adds useful information to the overall validity measure. Consider, for example, two cues which have equal cue validity, but one of which occurs more frequently than the other. While the old measure of cue validity does not differentiate the usefulness of these cues, the overall validity measure does—it claims that the more frequently occurring cue will be more useful in the categorization task because it will correctly classify a larger number of exemplars.[1] Thus, a cue high in overall validity because it is frequently present and frequently correct will be a useful cue in categorization; a cue low in overall validity because it is either infrequently present but often correct, or frequently present but not often correct, will be less useful.

Frequency of cue occurrence may not have been included in initial attempts at defining cue utility because most early experiments tended to use cues of roughly equal frequency. However, the importance of cue frequency is highlighted in the psycholinguistic domain, where different cues marking the same category can have wildly different frequencies (see,

---

[1] It will also, of course, incorrectly classify more exemplars. However, if the goal is to maximize correct answers rather than minimize errors, the cue highest in overall validity will achieve this.

e.g., Sokolov, 1989, where the most frequent cue to the linguistic category of patient in Hebrew is 3200 times more available than the least frequent cue). More recent work on categorization has started to include the idea of cue frequency into other measures of utility (Corter & Gluck, 1992; Fisher & Langley, 1990; Fisher, this volume). Specifically, these researchers are trying to predict basic level category effects through the use of a measure known as *category utility* (that is, how useful a category is for predicting the cues present on individual exemplars). Category utility is essentially the sum over all cues of the product of cue frequency [P(cue)], cue validity [P(category|cue)], and category validity [P(cue|category)]. Thus, this measure integrates the concept of cue validity with category validity as well as cue frequency.

A second measure of cue utility used within the competition model is based on exemplars containing conflicts between the cues. For the categories considered in this paper, whenever two particular cues conflict, the same cue indicates the correct categorization. Examination of these conflict cases shows which of the cues is relatively stronger in the face of contradictory information from the other cue. Thus, cues can be placed into a *dominance hierarchy*, which captures the relative strength of the cues in conflict situations. While the dominance hierarchy may be treated as an ordinal notion, with cues simply listed in their order in the hierarchy, it is also possible to get numerical estimates of the relative strength of cues in conflict situations by computing how often cues are correct over all exemplars containing conflicts. This quantified version of the dominance hierarchy is known as *conflict validity* in the competition model (McDonald, 1986, 1987). In the discussion and experiments presented below it is assumed that the dominance hierarchy measure of utility affects performance consistent with its quantified rather than ordinal form.

It is important to note that the concepts of overall validity and dominance hierarchy are distinct. For example, a cue can have low overall validity while simultaneously being high in the dominance hierarchy. This situation can happen when a cue does not occur very frequently, but when it does occur, it always indicates the correct categorization, even if other cues contradict it.

According to the competition model, these two different measures of cue utility, overall validity and the dominance hierarchy, determine strength of cue usage at different points in the learning curve. While initial cue acquisition is predicted by overall validity, final strengths at mastery are predicted by the dominance hierarchy (McDonald, 1986, 1987, 1989; McDonald & MacWhinney, 1991). This change in cue strengths over the course of learning is predicted by a learning-on-error mechanism (McDonald, 1986, 1989), which adjusts cue weights over the course of

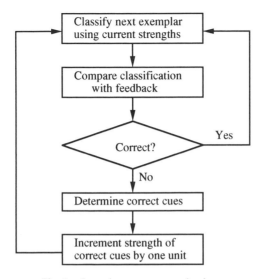

Fig. 1. Learning-on-error mechanism.

learning to yield maximum correct performance. This learning-on-error model, illustrated in Fig. 1, works as follows: Categorization of a particular exemplar occurs based on the current cue strengths. If the exemplar is correctly classified, no adjustments are made to the cue strengths. However, if the exemplar is incorrectly classified, the strength of the cues that would have yielded a correct classification are incremented one unit.[2] This incrementation mechanism is hypothesized to be automatic and similar to frequency counting mechanisms found in other psychological domains (Hasher & Zacks, 1984).

Consider how this learning-on-error model would function at the beginning stages of acquisition. At this point, there would be no or random weights between all potential cues and the category. Therefore initial attempts to categorize would be at chance levels, and learners would basically incorrectly classify a representative sample of all exemplars. Over this sampling, the strengths of the cues that would have given the correct classification would be increased. The single cue receiving the most strengthening over this sampling of all exemplars would be the one that was most often correct over all exemplars. This, by definition, is the cue with the highest overall validity. Thus, according to the learning-on-

[2] It is also possible that the strengths of the incorrect cues are simultaneously decremented; however, what is important is that the relative weights of the cues are adjusted in favor of the cue(s) indicating the correct categorization.

error model, the first cue to be significantly used during category learning should be the one with the highest overall validity. This makes sense, in that if one only has command over a single cue, the best one to acquire, or the one with the most utility, would be the one that gives the most total correct categorizations.

However, unless the first cue correctly classifies all exemplars, learners will continue to make errors in categorization. Specifically, they will incorrectly classify a sampling of exemplars that do not contain the first cue, and all exemplars where the first cue indicates the wrong categorization. Weights of the cues that would give correct classifications over this pool of incorrectly classified exemplars would therefore be incremented, until other relevant cues gain enough strength to significantly influence performance. The weights of all these relevant cues would then combine in classifying further exemplars. If certain exemplars are still being misclassified, the relative weights of these cues would be adjusted via the learning-on-error mechanism until all exemplars are correctly classified. Note that in order for totally correct classification to take place, these final cue weights must reflect the relative strength of the cues in conflict situations. That is, cue weights at mastery must reflect the dominance hierarchy.

To give a more concrete example of how this learning-on-error mechanism works, consider the simple categorization problem given in Table I. There are ten exemplars to be classified into one of two categories; each exemplar is marked by one or two cues. The first cue, called here the *overall cue,* is present on all exemplars, and indicates the correct categorization on the eight exemplars where it is the only cue present. Its overall validity is thus 80%. The second cue, called here the *conflict cue,* is only present on two exemplars, but when it is present it does indicate correct

TABLE I

SIMPLE CATEGORIZATION PROBLEM

Exemplar	Category favored by overall cue	Category favored by conflict cue	Correct category
1	1	—	1
2	1	—	1
3	1	—	1
4	1	—	1
5	2	—	2
6	2	—	2
7	2	—	2
8	2	—	2
9	1	2	2
10	2	1	1

categorization. Its overall validity is therefore 20%. If initial acquisition of the cues is tied to overall validity, we would expect earlier mastery and greater cue strength initially associated with the overall cue than the conflict cue. Note however, that on the two exemplars where the two cues conflict, it is always the second cue, the conflict cue, that indicates the correct categorization. Thus, the conflict cue dominates or is higher in the dominance hierarchy than the overall cue. If cue strengths at mastery correspond to the dominance hierarchy, we would predict final cue weights to show relatively greater cue strength associated with the conflict cue than the overall cue.

This simple categorization problem in Table I was submitted to a computer implementation of the learning-on-error mechanism. The initial strength of each cue was set to zero and then adjusted after each incorrect categorization decision. As predicted, early on in learning, before cue strengths overcame a noise threshold, errors were distributed randomly over all exemplars. This caused greater initial strength for the overall cue than the conflict cue. As exposure continued, errors became concentrated on the two conflict cases, causing relative increases to the cue strength of the conflict cue. With enough exposure to the training set, the relative strength of the conflict cue overcame that of the overall cue. At asymptote, or mastery, the conflict cue was clearly relatively stronger than the overall cue. The relative strengths of the overall and conflict cues as number of exposures to the learning set increased is shown in Fig. 2.

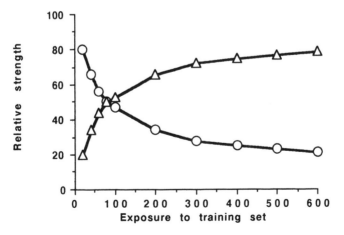

Fig. 2. Changes in relative cue strength with increasing number of exposures to the training set. as predicted by the learning-on-error mechanism. In this example, the overall cue (circles) has higher overall validity than the conflict cue (triangles), but in conflict situations the conflict cue dominates the overall cue.

To summarize, the competition model in conjunction with a learning-on-error mechanism predicts that for categories marked by multiple probabilistic cues arranged in a dominance hierarchy, initial acquisition will depend on the overall validity of the cues, while the final strength of the cues at mastery should reflect the dominance hierarchy of the cues. It should be noted that although the type of categories discussed here is governed by a dominance hierarchy, the competition model does not claim that people use these cues hierarchically in a strict IF–THEN–ELSE manner. That is, although correct categorization of an exemplar is achievable by simply consulting the single cue present that is highest in the dominance hierarchy, the competition model claims that people use information from all cues in making their categorization decision. Thus, even at mastery, the competition model predicts that people will be quickest and most accurate when the dominant cue is accompanied by other, less dominant cues favoring the same categorization, a bit slower if the dominant cue alone is present, and slowest and least accurate when the dominant cue is accompanied by less dominant cues favoring the opposite categorization. Although it is possible that at some late point in learning subjects will learn to ignore the irrelevant information from less dominant cues, to date there is no empirical evidence to support this stage of learning.

The competition model with its learning-on-error mechanism is a variation of a feature frequency model. Exemplars are broken down into their component features and counts maintained on these features. However, in standard feature frequency models, counts are updated on every exemplar; this would result in counts always reflecting overall validity. By changing counts only on error, the competition model is able to improve its performance with exposure by having weights shift from reflecting overall validity to reflecting the dominance hierarchy. Indeed, this learning-on-error mechanism is central to predicting the learning curve in the competition model. Other recent models, such as connectionist models of category learning, also appear to gain much of their power from a learning algorithm based on error correction (Estes, Campbell, Hatsopoulos, & Hurwitz, 1989; Kruschke, 1992).

III. Testing the Model in the Psycholinguistic Domain

As mentioned above, it turns out that many psycholinguistic categories have the structure of the categories discussed in this article—that is, the categories are marked by multiple probabilistic cues that are governed by a dominance hierarchy. Below I briefly review some of the past research on one such psycholinguistic category, that of the actor role, and then report an experiment on another psycholinguistic category, that of the recipient role.

A. CATEGORY OF ACTOR ROLE

The actor role[3]—that is, who or what performs the action of the verb—is marked by multiple probabilistic cues arranged in a dominance hierarchy. In English, the actor tends to be the preverbal noun, agrees in number with the verb, tends to be animate rather than inanimate, and if a pronoun is used, is in the nominative rather than the objective case. All these cues are present and point to *He* in the sentence *He hits the balls*. However, in any particular sentence, some of these cues may not be present or informative. For example, in *The bat hit the ball,* only the cue of preverbal position provides relevant information; it favors *the bat* as the actor. In addition, conflicts can occur between the cues—for example, in *The ball hit the boy,* animacy favors *the boy* as the actor, but preverbal position correctly favors *the ball* as the actor. The fact that word order correctly favors *the ball* indicates that it is higher in the dominance hierarchy for English than is animacy.

Interestingly, in English, the cue with the highest overall validity and the one highest in the dominance hierarchy is one and the same—preverbal position. Thus we see no shift between the cue that English speaking children first master, and the one used most strongly by English-speaking adults—the cue of word order fulfills both functions (McDonald, 1986). However, in other languages, the cue with the highest overall validity is different from the one highest in the dominance hierarchy. For example, in Dutch we see a clear developmental trend from initial mastery of the most overall valid cue, to adult ranking based on the dominance hierarchy (McDonald, 1986, 1987). Other languages such as Italian, French, Hungarian, Serbo-Croatian, and Walpiri, also show a shift between the cue most used by children and that most strongly used by adults (Bates & Mac-Whinney, 1989; Bates, MacWhinney, Caselli, Devescovi, Natale, & Venza, 1984; Bavin & Shopen, 1989; Kail, 1989; MacWhinney, Pleh, & Bates, 1985; Slobin & Bever, 1982). Some of these changes are clearly due to differences in cue ranking according to overall validity and the dominance hierarchy; others may also be influenced by other factors such as ease of processing and detectability.

---

[3] The concept of *actor* is meant to capture the simple notion of who or what present in the sentence performed the verbal action. It is not meant to be taken as the more technically defined case role of *agent*.

B. CATEGORY OF RECIPIENT ROLE

Another linguistic category marked by multiple probabilisitic cues arranged in a dominance hierarchy is that of the recipient role. The recipient is the person or thing that receives something as a result of the action of a dative verb; syntactically it is the indirect object. In English, this role is marked by the cues of noun animacy (a recipient tends to be an animate rather than an inanimate noun), dative preposition (the recipient may be preceded by *to* or *for*) and word order (the recipient tends to occupy the position immediately following the verb).

These cues can all be present and agree as to the recipient role, as in the sentence *The clothes lent to Mr. Brown an air of utter sophistication. Mr. Brown* is indicated as the recipient by its animate status, its occurrence after the preposition *to,* and its post-verbal position. However, in any particular sentence, some of these cues may not be present. For example, in the sentence *The broken windows lent the building an air of utter neglect*, only the post-verbal word order cue is present, and it indicates *the building* as the recipient. Conflicts between the cues can arise when two or more cues are present in the same sentence but favor different nouns as the recipient. For example, in the sentence *I assigned a janitor to the new building* animacy and word order favor *a janitor* as the recipient, while the preposition correctly favors *the building*. In this case, the preposition defeats the combination of animacy and word order, showing its relative dominance in such conflict situations.

The recipient category thus meets the criteria for a category marked by multiple probabilistic cues governed by a dominance hierarchy. The course of learning predicted for this category by the competition model would therefore be that the first cue acquired would be the one with the highest overall validity, while final cue weights would reflect the dominance hierarchy in conflict situations. In order to test these predictions, we must establish overall validity rankings and the dominance hierarchy for cues to this category.

In order to determine the overall validities of the cues of noun animacy, dative preposition, and word order in marking the recipient role in dative sentences in English, I examined parental utterances in the Jean Berko Gleason corpus (Gleason, Perlmann, & Greif, 1984; Masur & Gleason, 1980) donated to CHILDES (MacWhinney, 1991; MacWhinney & Snow, 1985, 1990). This corpus contains conversations between mothers and their child in a programmed play situation, between fathers and their child in the same play situation, and family conversation around the dinner table. The 24 white, middle-class children participating in the project ranged in age from 2;1 to 5;2. All parental dative utterances containing both direct and indirect objects after the dative verb *give*[4] were extracted from this corpus and analyzed for presence and correctness of the cues of noun animacy, preposition, and word order for the recipient role. A total of 266 qualifying utterances were found. The overwhelming number of these utterances (236) used both noun animacy and word order to indicate the recipient role (e.g., *Give your kid sister one*). Twenty-one of the utterances used noun animacy and a dative preposition to correctly indicate the recipient role; word order opposed these cues and indicated the incorrect noun as recipient (e.g., *I gave all of it to Lee*). Finally, nine of the utterances used word order alone to indicate the recipient (e.g., *Give it a hard turn*). Based on these 266 sentences, it is possible to compute the availability [how often each cue is present—P(cue)] the reliability [how often, when present, the cue is correct—P(category|cue)] and overall validity [the product of availability and reliability—P(cue)P(category|cue), or, in other words, how often the cue is correct over all 266 sentences] of each cue. The measures of availability, reliability, and overall validity for each of the three cues to the recipient role are shown in Table II.

The cue highest in overall validity in the Gleason sample is noun animacy. Indeed, all but 3% of the sentences can be correctly assigned a recipient by the use of this single cue. Close behind noun animacy with respect to overall validity is word order. This cue may therefore also show early acquisition, particularly as it correctly classifies those sentences where animacy is unavailable. However, since this cue also occurs in a larger number of sentences where it is incorrect (and animacy and the preposition are correct), its acquisition may be somewhat delayed.

In order to establish the dominance hierarchy among the cues of noun animacy, dative preposition, and word order, it is necessary to find all the types of grammatical English sentences involving conflicts between these cues. In the Gleason corpus, the only type of conflict sentence found involved the cues of animacy and preposition defeating that of word order. From this type of sentence we only know that either animacy, the preposition, or the combination of both dominates word order. To completely establish the hierarchy, let us consider the following additional possible types of grammatical conflict situations. The indirect object is in boldface in each example.

1. When the dative preposition is pitted against word order in the absence of an animacy contrast on the two post-verbal nouns, the preposition wins: *I awarded the architectural prize to **the new office building**.*

---

[4] Sentences with the verb *give* were counted because the experimental stimuli administered to children to test cue usage for the recipient role all involved this verb.

TABLE II

Availability, Reliability, and Overall Validity
of Cues to the Recipient Role

	Availability (%)	Reliability (%)	Overall validity (%)
Noun animacy	97	100	97
Dative preposition	8	100	8
Word order	100	92	92

2. When the dative preposition is pitted against word order and animacy, the preposition wins: *I assigned a janitor to* ***the new office building***.
3. When word order is pitted against animacy in the absence of a preposition, word order wins (this type of sentence is exceedingly rare): *I assigned* ***the new office building*** *a janitor*.

Thus, the dominance hierarchy illustrated in these example sentences shows that the dative preposition dominates word order, which in turn dominates noun animacy. Thus, if mature native speakers adjust their cue weights to reflect this dominance hierarchy, they should use the preposition more strongly than word order, which in turn should be used more strongly than noun animacy.

Given the difference between initial overall validity (noun animacy most overall valid cue to recipient role) and the dominance hierarchy (preposition over word order over noun animacy), we should see a developmental trend in cue usage in assigning the recipient role. Younger English speakers should make strong use of noun animacy. With continuing exposure to the language, this cue should gradually decline in relative strength, while the dative preposition and to some extent word order should increase in relative strength.

This prediction was tested in an experiment in which 42 native English speakers ranging from kindergarteners to adults were asked to name the recipient in dative sentences involving the cues of noun animacy, dative preposition and word order.[5] Example stimuli are shown in Fig. 3. For all sentences, the cue of word order was always present and favored the first post-verbal noun as the recipient. The second cue, noun animacy, could be uninformative (both post-verbal nouns animate), agree with the word order cue (first post-verbal noun animate, second inanimate), or disagree

---

[5] The current analysis collapses over an additional factor, that of the noun/pronoun status of the two post-verbal nouns.

	Noun animacy uninformative	Noun animacy favors first postverbal noun	Noun animacy favors second postverbal noun
	Cell 1	Cell 2	Cell 3
Preposition uninformative	I gave Dr. Adams Mr. Elliot	I gave the doctor the jar	I gave the toy the fisherman
	Cell 4	Cell 5	Cell 6
Preposition favors first postverbal noun	I gave to Mr. Barnes Dr. Black	I gave to the friend the bread	I gave to the table the painter
	Cell 7	Cell 8	Cell 9
Preposition favors second postverbal noun	I gave Dr. Michelson to Mrs. Stevenson	I gave the boy to the newspaper	I gave the present to the uncle

Fig. 3.   Stimuli used to test for the recipient role.

with it (first post-verbal noun inanimate, second animate). The levels of the third cue, dative preposition, were completely crossed with the levels of noun animacy. It could similarly be uninformative (no preposition present), agree with the word order cue (*to* placed in front of first post-verbal noun), or disagree with it (*to* placed in front of second post-verbal noun). For all subjects except the adults, all stimuli involved the verb *give;* for the adults, several other types of dative verbs were also used. Four examples of each of the nine types of sentence in Fig. 3 were given.

Subjects listened to the 36 dative sentences and after each one named who or what had gotten something as a result of the dative verb. By examining which noun subjects assigned to the recipient role over these sentences, it was possible to determine not only if a cue significantly influenced choice of recipient, but also the relative strengths of the various cues. This latter measure is indexed by the percent variance accounted for by each cue in an ANOVA.

For the youngest groups of children the only cue significantly used to assign the recipient was that of noun animacy [kindergartners/first graders: $F(2, 12) = 10.1$, $p < .005$; second graders: $F(2, 12) = 8.2$, $p < .01$]. Third and fourth graders continue strong use of the animacy cue [$F(2, 18) = 14.5$, $p < .001$] but begin to show marginal use of the prepositional cue [$F(2, 18) = 3.1$, $p < .07$). The older kids and adults show significant usage of all three cues [fifth to seventh graders—animacy: $F(2, 16) = 4.3$, $p < .05$; preposition, $F(2, 16) = 6.5$, $p < .01$; word order: $F(1, 8) = 5.9$, $p < .05$; adults—animacy: $F(2, 16) = 8.6$, $p < .005$; preposition: $F(2, 16) = 35.8$, $p < .001$; word order: $F(1, 8) = 26.2$, $p < .001$). Thus, it is clear that the first cue mastered for the assignment of the recipient role is, as predicted, that of noun animacy.

In order to examine the relative strength of the cues, the percent variance accounted for by each cue for each group is plotted in Fig. 4. At the youngest ages the only cue to account for any variance is noun animacy. However, as acquisition continues, learners gradually lessen the relative strength of the noun animacy cue, greatly strengthen that of the prep-

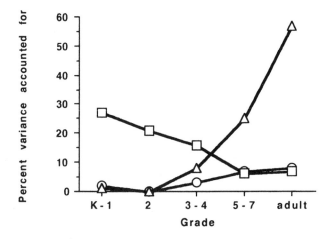

Fig. 4.   Relative strength of the cues (triangles, preposition; squares, noun animacy; circles, word order) for determining the dative-construction recipient role over the various age groups.

osition, and strengthen to a lesser extent that of word order. At adulthood, native English speakers have reordered the relative strengths of their cues for the assignment of the recipient role such that the preposition is by far the strongest cue, followed by word order, which is only slightly stronger than noun animacy. This final ordering directly reflects the dominance hierarchy of these cues for interpreting English dative sentences.

Thus the results of this experiment confirm the predictions of the learning-on-error mechanism within the competition model. The first cue acquired, that of noun animacy, is the one highest in overall validity. The final ranking of cue strengths, preposition over word order over animacy, matches the dominance hierarchy of the cues. It is important to point out that the initial reliance the younger learners show on noun animacy is *not* a general semantic strategy of interpretation. English speakers of this age and younger use word order and not animacy in other tasks, such as assigning the actor role, where word order is the more highly valid cue (Bates et al., 1984; McDonald, 1986).

IV. Testing the Model in the Concept Learning Domain

While the competition model was originally formulated to account for psycholinguistic categories, it has been tested in a variation of a standard laboratory concept-learning task (McDonald & MacWhinney, 1991). The relevant category in this task was marked by multiple probabilistic cues, and the cue highest in overall validity was lowest in the dominance hierarchy, so that shifts in relative cue weights should occur with learning. That is, over the course of learning, a shift from strongest use of the cue highest in overall validity to the cue highest in the dominance hierarchy should be apparent.

The category to be acquired in the concept learning task was that of *dominant figure*. Subjects were given pairs of geometric figures contrasting on one to three relevant dimensions and asked to pick the dominant or stronger one of the pair. Examples of relevant dimensions could be (1) interior (a blank interior dominating a cross-hatched one), (2) dottedness (a figure with corner dots dominating one with no dots), and (3) orientation (a horizontal figure dominating a vertical one). The dominance hierarchy established for these cues was cue 2 (dottedness) over cue 3 (orientation) over cue 1 (interior). Cues were probabilistic in that on any exemplar a particular cue could be present or absent, and when it was present, it could favor the wrong figure as dominant if it conflicted with a cue higher up in the dominance hierarchy.

Nine different types of exemplars were devised. Examples of these are shown in Fig. 5. As you examine this array, you will see that the first cue (interior contrast) was always present on all exemplars. The second cue (dottedness contrast) could either be uninformative (i.e., both figures dotted or both not dotted), agree with the first cue (i.e., the blank figure would also be dotted and the cross-hatched figure not), or disagree with the first cue (i.e., the blank figure would not be dotted and the cross-hatched figure would be dotted). The third cue (orientation contrast) was completely crossed with the second cue and similarly could be uninformative (i.e., both figures horizontal or both vertical), agree with the first cue (blank figure would be a horizontal, cross-hatched figure vertical), or disagree with the first cue (blank figure would be a vertical and cross-hatched one horizontal). The frequency with which the various cells in this design occurred was manipulated such that the first cue (interior) was by far the most overall valid cue—80% of the exemplars could be correctly judged by this cue alone, while cue 2 (dottedness) had an overall validity of 55% and cue 3 (orientation) one of 48%. Thus, cue 1 (interior) was the best single cue for the classification task and should therefore be the first cue acquired. However, as mentioned above, the dominance hierarchy established for this task was cue 2 (dottedness) over cue 3 (orientation) over cue 1 (interior). Thus, at mastery, the relative strengths of the cues should reflect this hierarchy. Over the course of learning, therefore, we should see a relative decrease in the original strength of cue 1 and an increase in strength for cue 2.

These predictions were tested by exposing subjects to a random ordering of the exemplars, with each of the nine types occurring with the frequency shown in Fig. 5. For each exemplar, subjects chose one of the figures as dominant and then were given feedback as to the correctness of their decision. After every set of 25 exemplars, subjects were tested as to their mastery by making judgments on each of the nine types of exemplars without feedback. These test data were then analyzed to determine the relative strength of the various cues over the course of learning. Figure 6 shows the changes in percent variance accounted for in an ANOVA by each of the cues over the course of learning. Note that early on in learning, the strongest cue is cue 1—the one with the highest overall validity. However, as exposure to the problem continues, this cue loses in relative strength and is ultimately replaced by cue 2—the cue highest in the dominance hierarchy—as the strongest cue. At the end of the experiment, the ranking is cue 2 over cue 1 over cue 3. This ranking does not perfectly reflect the dominance hierarchy of cue 2 over cue 3 over cue 1, because most subjects did not succeed in completely mastering the problem by the

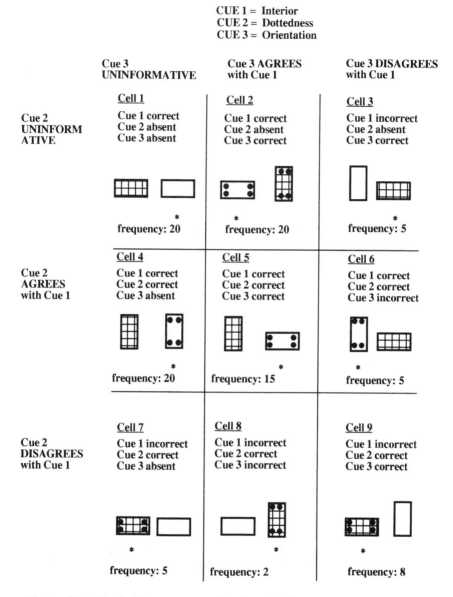

CUE 1 = Interior
CUE 2 = Dottedness
CUE 3 = Orientation

Fig. 5.   Stimuli for the laboratory concept learning task. The correct (i.e., dominant) figure of each pair is indicated by the asterisk.

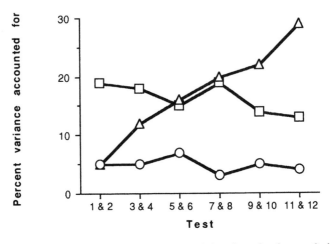

Fig. 6.   Relative strength of the cues (squares, cue 1: interior; triangles, cue 2: dottedness; circles, cue 3: orientation) in the concept learning task over the course of learning.

end of testing. Indeed, most were still making errors on the cell where cue 3 conflicted with cue 1 by continuing to follow the weaker cue 1.[6]

Thus, this laboratory concept-learning experiment validates the claims made by the competition model in conjunction with the learning-on-error mechanism. Initial learning is influenced by overall validity; at mastery, cue strengths reflect the dominance hierarchy.

V.   Other Possible Realms for the Competition Model

The predictions of the competition model have fared well in linguistic role assignment tasks and a laboratory concept-learning task. It should be possible to expand the realm of the competition model to include all categories marked by multiple probabilistic cues and governed by a dominance hierarchy. However, many categories marked by multiple probablistic cues, including some linguistic categories, have only partial or unclear dominance hierarchies. It remains to be seen how well the competition model can handle such cases, although the use of the model in a connectionist realization has shown promise (MacWhinney, Leinbach,

[6] Indeed, even subjects who were no longer making errors on this cell may have achieved this by simply memorizing exemplars of this cell, rather than correctly reordering the strengths of cue 3 and cue 1. Such exemplar memorization may be likely in cases where the number of distinct exemplars the subjects see is limited.

Taraban, & McDonald, 1989; Taraban, McDonald & MacWhinney, 1989). Below I briefly outline a few possible realms which may show the shift in cue strengths from overall validities to the dominance hierarchy predicted by the competition model.

A. GRAMMATICAL GENDER

Within the language arena, another type of category marked by multiple probabilistic cues is that of grammatical gender—in many languages, all nouns are classified according to formal gender subcategories, such as masculine and feminine. Cues such as natural gender and certain morphological or phonological forms probabilistically mark exemplars for grammatical gender. For some languages the relation between cues and gender category is stronger than others. For example, in Spanish the *-o* or *-a* endings on a noun are strongly although not perfectly indicative of masculine and feminine gender, respectively. In other languages, such as German, there is no single cue or even small set of cues that reliably indicates gender across all nouns, although there are correlations between numerous cues with limited scope and particular genders (Koepcke, 1982; Zubin & Koepcke, 1981). The probabilistic nature of these cues is easily illustrated in German. For example, although natural gender is correlated with grammatical gender (e.g., *die Frau* 'the woman' has feminine natural and grammatical gender), it is often not present (e.g., *der Tisch* 'the table' has no natural gender, but masculine grammatical gender), and even when present can indicate incorrect grammatical gender category (e.g., *das Mädchen* 'the girl' has femine natural gender, but neuter grammatical gender).

Research on the acquisition of cues to gender seems to show that the first to be mastered are those which occur on many words and are fairly reliable when present; because of its limited scope, natural gender is not usually one of the early cues acquired (French: Karmiloff-Smith, 1979; German: MacWhinney; 1978; Mills, 1986; Hebrew: Levy, 1983). The early acquisition of these broad-based cues with few exceptions fits in nicely with the predictions of the competition model—these are precisely the cues with high overall validity. There is also some evidence of developmental changes in relative cue strength with increasing exposure to the language that is congruent with learning the dominance hierarchy. For example, Karmiloff-Smith (1979) finds that while younger French-speaking children tend to use phonological cues more strongly than natural gender and formal grammatical cues in making gender assignments, older children display just the opposite pattern. Such a shift fits in with the greater dominance of these latter cues in conflict situations.

In many cases, however, there is not a clear dominance hierarchy of the cues to grammatical gender. For example, in German the phonological beginning of *s + consonant-* is correlated with masculine gender; the ending *-fricative + t* is correlated with femine gender. However, when these two cues conflict, sometimes the masculine cue wins (e.g., *der Stift* 'the pencil') and sometimes the feminine cue wins (e.g., *die Schrift* 'the writing'). Since no clear dominance hierarchy exists in these cases, adult speakers may use the cue that is most often correct in such conflict situations. However, it remains for empirical data on this question to be gathered. The only information currently available on this problem comes from a computer simulation in a connectionist framework in which a network was trained to make gender classifications on a set of German words coded for their cues (MacWhinney et al., 1989; Taraban et al., 1989). As performance within this model improved, it was found that connection weights changed from reflecting the validity of the various cues in general to reflecting the co-occurrence information among the cues, a part of which has to do with which cues dominate in conflict situations.

B.   DATIVE VERB SUBCLASSES

Another linguistic categorization problem marked by multiple probabilistic cues deals with subclasses of verbs. For example, some dative verbs, called alternating verbs, can be used in either a double object or a preposition frame (e.g., both *I gave the man the book* and *I gave the book to the man* are acceptable). Other dative verbs, however, can only be used in the preposition frame (e.g., *I donated the book to the library* is acceptable while *I donated the library the book* is not). Although it is not immediately obvious, it turns out that these subclasses of dative verbs are imperfectly marked by cues such as the origin of the word (alternating verbs tend to be native rather than Latinate), number of syllables (alternating verbs tend to be monosyllabic rather than polysyllabic), and the type of relationship (alternating verbs tend to deal with possession rather than non-possession) between the indirect and direct object (Gropen, Pinker, Hollander, Goldberg, & Wilson, 1989; Mazurkewich & White, 1984; Pinker, 1989). Native-speaking children show sensitivity to these correlations—for example, they are more likely to use double object forms with monosyllabic than polysyllabic nonce words (Gropen et al., 1989). From current data it is not clear which cue is first acquired for putting dative verbs into subclasses. However, all these cues to alternation seem to have high overall validity in adult input to children—most dative verbs in parental input are short, simple native verbs (Gropen et al., 1989). There may also be a dominance hierarchy among these cues. Some adult rating data gathered by Gropen et al. indicate that the semantic cue of change of possession may dominate that of number of syllables in allowing the dative verb to alternate. Such a ranking of cues fits in with polysyllabic verbs of transfer that do alternate (e.g., *award, assign*) and monosyllablic verbs not involving possession which do not alternate (e.g., *wash, solve*). However, this dominance hierarchy appears not to be absolute—Gropen et al. also point out that for some semantic subclasses of dative verbs morphophonological constraints are more important than meaning in determining whether verbs will alternate (e.g., *donate,* which does not alternate, while *give* does). The possible use of the competition model in an area with such an unclear and complex dominance pattern among the cues remains to be tested.

C.   WORD MEANING

One can conceive of concepts or word meanings as consisting of multiple, often probabilistic features. For example a *bird* is usually thought of as a smallish animal that has feathers, can fly, nests in trees, sings, and so on. Based on their probability of occurrence, these features can be broken down into two categories, *characteristic features* and *defining features* (Smith, Shoben, & Rips, 1974). Characteristic features are highly typical of most and the most frequent instances of a concept; they are probabilistic because they do not necessarily occur on all exemplars. For example, while most birds can fly, flying is a characterstic feature because some birds (e.g., penguins) cannot fly, and some non-birds (e.g., bats) can fly. Defining features are both necessary and jointly sufficient to insure an instance is an example of the concept; their probability of occurring on every exemplar is 100%. Egg-laying, for example, would be a defining feature of birds, as all bird species lay eggs.

   Keil (1989; Keil & Batterman, 1984) has investigated the acquisition of the meaning of concepts such as *island* or *uncle* that contain both characteristic and defining features. He finds that younger children consider the presence of characteristic features (e.g., an island has palm trees, the weather there is very warm) more important than the presence of defining features (e.g., an island is surrounded by water on all sides) in deciding whether an item is an example of the concept. However, older children show the opposite pattern, considering the presence of defining features more important than characteristic features.

   Although not the solution offered by Keil, one possible explanation of this characteristic-to-defining shift has to do with differences in the ranking of the features according to overall validity versus the dominance hierarchy. For example, if characteristic features occur more frequently than defining features in the examples seen by children, the characteristic features will have higher overall validity. This would lead to their earlier acquisition and stronger initial use. However, because defining features are necessary, and therefore 100% correct indicators of a category, they must necessarily be higher in the dominance hierarchy than characteristic features. Thus, at mastery, defining features should be used more strongly than characteristic features in making classifications. This is easily seen in cases where defining and characteristic features contradict each other. For example, a place that is barren and cold, but surrounded by water on all sides, is an island, even though it contains features opposite to the typical characteristic features of an island. And a place that is sunny and has palm trees, but has water on only three sides, is not island, because the defining feature is not present.

Support for the greater overall validity of characteristic features over defining features can be found in a study of the definitions parents give their children (Keil, 1989). While typically both types of features are given, when only one type is offered, it is three to four times more likely to be a characteristic than a defining feature. This higher frequency of characteristic features over defining features in the input gives higher overall validity to the former. Thus, children should and do acquire these characteristic cues early on. However, as the child uses these characteristic features to classify exemplars, errors will occur on conflict cases—that is, cases where use of characteristic features yields one classification, while use of defining features yields the opposite classification. After such errors, the relative weights of the various features would be adjusted, so that eventually the defining features would become stronger than the characteristic features.

This acquisitional pattern fits in perfectly with the pattern predicted by the learning-on-error mechanism in the competition model. That is, the first features that children use for understanding these concepts are those high in overall validity. Errors made on conflict cases force the readjustment of cue weights to reflect the relative dominance of the features, until at mastery defining features are considered more important than characteristic features.

D. Medical Diagnosis Task

A categorization task that has recently been investigated in several laboratory studies is that of medical diagnosis (Estes et al., 1989; Gluck & Bower, 1988a, 1988b; Medin & Edelson, 1988; Shanks, 1991). In this task people are shown a set of symptoms and asked to diagnose the patient's disease. There are multiple symptoms corresponding to a disease, and a symptom may not always be present in all instances of a particular disease, and when present, may not always indicate the correct diagnosis. Thus, there are multiple probabilistic cues to a category; however, there is no explicit dominance hierarchy. At mastery, however, people appear to have developed an implicit dominance hierarchy for the cues, which interestingly enough, sometimes contradicts base rate information.

To understand this problem better, let us look at an example from the work of Medin & Edelson (1988). During training, subjects saw pairs of symptoms associated with various diseases. Between some diseases there was an overlap of one of the symptoms. For example, while *earaches* and *dizziness* indicated disease 1, *earaches* and *back pain* indicated disease 2. Base rates of these diseases with an overlapping symptom were manipulated so that one disease (say disease 1) occurred three times as often as the other (disease 2). After training to a level of expertise, subjects were then tested on single symptoms and new combinations of symptoms. The interesting result came when two non-overlapping symptoms from disease 1 and disease 2 were paired. Rather than following base rate probabilities, which would favor a diagnosis of the more frequent disease 1, subjects judged that the combination of *dizziness* and *back pain* was more indicative of the less frequent disease, disease 2. That is, the less frequent symptom, *back pain,* is seen to dominate the more frequent symptom, *dizziness,* in making the diagnosis, although such a dominance relation is nowhere explicitly present in the task.

These results, although initially surprising, are probably explainable by a learning-on-error mechanism. One such mechanism that has proven particularly successful at capturing these base-rate violations in the medical diagnosis task is the delta rule implemented in connectionist networks (Estes et al., 1989; Gluck & Bower, 1988a, 1988b; Kruschke, 1992; Shanks, 1991). This learning algorithm takes into account the competition among cues and asymptotes to weights that reflect the relative predictiveness of the cues. For example, because the overlapping symptom *earaches* is more strongly associated with disease 1 than disease 2, the symptom marking disease 2, *back pain,* must gain relatively more strength to defeat the competition from *earaches,* while the symptom marking disease 1, *dizziness,* need not gain relatively in strength because it basically cooperates with *earaches* in favoring the diagnosis of disease 1 (see Kruschke, 1992, this volume, for a related discussion).

Connectionist models thus capture the fact that asymptomatic weights must reflect relative cue predictiveness—a fact also predicted by the competition model. Both predictions stem from learning algorithms that involve correction on error and competition among cues. In addition to predicting weights at mastery, however, the competition model also emphasizes that initial learning should be tied to the overall validity of the cues. However, most empirical research on the medical diagnosis task has concentrated on asymptotic weights, that is, performance at mastery (see Estes et al., 1989; Kruschke, 1992, for exceptions). It is important to test changes in cue strengths over the course of learning and see if cue weights at various points in acquisition reflect different statistical properties of the input.

VI.   Summary

The competition model, together with a learning-on-error mechanism, fares well in predicting the course of cue acquisition and cue strength at mastery for a special kind of ill-defined categorization problem. These categories are marked by multiple probabilistic cues governed by a dominance hierarchy. It was predicted that initial cue acquisition for these categorization problems would be related to overall validity, a measure that combines the standard definition of cue validity and cue frequency. Final cue strengths at mastery were predicted to reflect the dominance hierarchy—that is, the relative strength of the cues when they were in conflict with each other. Both of these predictions were supported in studies within the psycholinguistic and laboratory concept-learning domains. Thus, although the competition model was originally formulated to account for psycholinguistic data, it has been shown to successfully generalize to a non-linguistic domain with similar category structure. The final section of the chapter pointed out some other domains which may also show the shift in cue strengths from overall validities to the dominance hierarchy. Thus, there may be even more domains for fruitful application of the model.

While the competition model was formulated to account for categories marked by multiple probabilistic cues governed by a strict dominance hierarchy, it is interesting to see how far it can be pushed to account for performance on categorization tasks with other types of structure. As noted in the discussion of other domains which may show a shift from reliance on overall validity to reflecting the dominance hierarchy, it is not clear how well the competition model can handle categories that have less than strict dominance hierarchies. Probably the easiest case to handle would be a categorization problem that generally followed the dominance hierarchy but had a limited number of exceptions to the rule. The competition model could handle this variation by including more cues in the categorization decision process; these cues would have to allow the exceptions to be distinguished.

A more radical departure from the dominance hierarchy occurs in categories that are not linearly separable—for these types of categories there is no hyperplane through the space of exemplars that places them into the correct category. Although the cues in these types of problems are not governed by a dominance hierarchy, people are able to learn them (Medin & Schwanenflugel, 1981). In order for the competition model to handle such categories, types of cues considered relevant would have to be expanded to include combinations of cues, a solution offered by other modelers (Gluck, 1991; Gluck & Bower, 1988a; Gluck, Bower, & Hee, 1989) but criticized for its post-hoc nature and problem with the explosion in the number of cues that must then be considered (Kruschke, 1992). Thus, it is not clear how satisfactorily the current competition model would be able to handle gross violations of or total lack of a dominance hierarchy such as are found in non-linearly separable categories.

Another categorization problem that does not follow a dominance hierarchy is one that depends on the use of correlated cues to mark a category. Again, people are able to master this problem (Medin, Altom, Edelson, & Freko, 1982). Since the current competition model considers each cue independently, it could not capture this phenomenon unless cue combinations were included in the decision process.

Despite its current inability to easily acocunt for results on categories not governed by a dominance hierarchy, it is important to emphasize what the competition model does contribute. One of the strengths of the competition model is that it focuses on the course of learning, not just the end state. (Connectionist models also predict the course of learning; however only a few studies—Estes et al., 1989, and Kruschke, 1992—have examined it.) This encourages experiments where the course of learning itself is considered a crucial part of the data, rather than just reporting performance at mastery. The learning-on-error mechanism allows predictions about initial and final performance based on particular statistical properties of the input. By getting representative samples of input, such as what is available in language databases for psycholinguistic experiments, or using the stimulus set from a controlled laboratory concept-learning experiment, mathematical predictions about the course of learning can be made.

The mechanism that allows the prediction of the course of learning, the learning-on-error mechanism, has similar counterparts in other models of categorization, particularly connectionist models (Estes et al., 1989; Gluck & Bower, 1988a, 1988b; Kruschke, 1992; Shanks, 1991). The result of such learning procedures is that mastery weights reflect relative rather than absolute predictiveness of the cues. Connectionist studies have pointed out how this type of learning mechanism can account for associative learning phenomena (Shanks, 1991) and base rate neglect (Estes et al., 1989; Gluck & Bower, 1988a; Kruschke, 1992; Medin & Edelson, 1988).

The competition model adds to this list of effects the shift in cue weights from overall validities to the dominance hierarchy (McDonald, 1986; Mc-Donald & MacWhinney, 1991).

ACKNOWLEDGMENTS

I thank Roman Taraban, Glenn Nakamura, and Doug Medin for helpful comments on earlier drafts of this article.

REFERENCES

Bates, E., & MacWhinney, B. (1982). Functionalist approaches to grammar. In E. Wanner & L. Gleitman (Ed.), *Language acquisition: The state of the art* (pp. 173–218). Cambridge: Cambridge University Press.
Bates, E., & MacWhinney, B. (1987). Competition, variation, and language learning. In B. MacWhinney (Ed.), *Mechanisms of language acquisition* (pp. 157–193). Hillsdale, NJ: Erlbaum.
Bates, E., & MacWhinney, B. (1989). Functionalism and the Competition Model. In B. MacWhinney & E. Bates (Ed.), *The crosslinguistic study of sentence processing* (pp. 3–73). New York: Cambridge University Press.
Bates, E., MacWhinney, B., Caselli, C., Devescovi, A., Natale, F., & Venza, V. (1984). A cross-linguistic study of the development of sentence interpretation strategies. *Child Development, 55,* 341–354.
Bavin, E. L., & Shopen, T. (1989). Cues to sentence interpretation in Walpiri. In B. MacWhinney & E. Bates (Ed.), *The crosslinguistic study of sentence processing* (pp. 185–205). New York: Cambridge University Press.
Beach, L. (1964). Cue probabilism and inference behavior. *Psychological Monographs, 78*(5), 1–20.
Bruner, J., Goodnow, J., & Austin, G. (1956). *A study of thinking.* New York: Wiley.
Corter, J. E., & Gluck, M. A. (1992). Explaining basic categories: Feature predictability and information. *Psychological Bulletin, 111,* 291–303.
Estes, W. K., Campbell, J. A., Hatsopoulos, N., & Hurwitz, J. B. (1989). Base-rate effects in category learning: A comparison of parallel network and memory storage-retrieval models. *Journal of Experimental Psychology: Learning, Memory & Cognition, 15,* 556–571.
Fisher, D., & Langley, P. (1990). The structure and formation of natural categories. In G. Bower (Ed.), *The psychology of learning and motivation, Vol 26* (pp. 241–284). San Diego, CA: Academic Press.
Gleason, J. B., Perlmann, R. Y., & Greif, E. B. (1984). What's the magic word? Learning language through routines. *Discourse Processes, 6,* 493–502.
Gluck, M. A. (1991). Stimulus generalization and representation in adaptive network models of category learning. *Psychological Science, 2,* 50–55.
Gluck, M. A., & Bower, G. H. (1988a). Evaluating an adaptive network model of human learning. *Journal of Memory & Language, 27,* 166–195.
Gluck, M. A., & Bower, G. H. (1988b). From conditioning to category learning: An adaptive network model. *Journal of Experimental Psychology: General, 117,* 227–247.
Gluck, M. A., Bower, G. H., & Hee, M. R. (1989). A configural-cue network model of animal

and human associative learning. In *Proceedings of the eleventh annual conference of the Cognitive Science Society* (pp. 323–332). Hillsdale, NJ: Lawrence Erlbaum.

Gropen, J., Pinker, S., Hollander, M., Goldberg, R., & Wilson, R. (1989). The learnability and acquisition of the dative alternation in English. *Language, 65,* 203–257.

Hasher, L., & Zacks, R. T. (1984). Automatic processing of fundamental information: The case of frequency of occurrence. *American Psychologist, 39,* 1372–1388.

Hunt, E. B., Marin, J., & Stone, P. J. (1966). *Experiments in induction.* New York: Academic Press.

Kail, M. (1989). Cue validity, cue cost, and processing types in French sentence comprehension. In B. MacWhinney & E. Bates (Eds.), *The crosslinguistic study of language procesing* (pp. 77–117). New York: Cambridge University Press.

Karmiloff-Smith, A. (1979). *A functional approach to child language.* Cambridge: Cambridge University Press.

Keil, F. C. (1989). *Concepts, kinds and cognitive development.* Cambridge, MA: MIT Press.

Keil, F. C., & Batterman, N. (1984). A characteristic-to-defining shift in the development of word meaning. *Journal of Verbal Learning & Verbal Behavior, 23,* 221–236.

Koepcke, K. M. (1982). *Untersuchungen zum Genussystem der deutschen Gegenwartsprache.* Tübingen: Niemeyer.

Kruschke, J. K. (1992). ALCOVE: An exemplar-based connectionist model of category learning. *Psychological Review, 99,* 24–44.

Levy, Y. (1983). The acquisition of Hebrew plurals: The case of the missing gender category. *Journal of Child Language, 10,* 107–121.

Luce, R. D. (1959). *Individual choice behavior.* New York, Wiley.

MacWhinney, B. (1978). The acquisition of morphophonology. *Monographs of the Society for Research in Child Development, 43.*

MacWhinney, B. (1991). *The CHILDES project.* Hillsdale, NJ: Erlbaum.

MacWhinney, B., Leinbach, J., Taraban, R., & McDonald, J. (1989). Language learning: Cues or rules? *Journal of Memory & Language, 28,* 255–277.

MacWhinney, B., Pleh, C., & Bates, E. (1985). The development of sentence interpretation in Hungarian. *Cognitive Psychology, 17,* 178–209.

MacWhinney, B., & Snow, C. (1985). The child language data exchange system. *Journal of Child Language, 12,* 271–296.

MacWhinney, B., & Snow, C. (1990). The child language data exchange system: An update. *Journal of Child Language, 17,* 457–472.

Masur, E., & Gleason, J. B. (1980). Parent–child interaction and the acquisition of lexical information during play. *Developmental Psychology, 16,* 404–409.

Mazurkewich, I., & White, R. (1984). The acquisition of the dative alternation: Unlearning overgeneralizations. *Cognition, 16,* 261–283.

McDonald, J. L. (1986). The development of sentence comprehension strategies in English and Dutch. *Journal of Experimental Child Psychology, 41,* 317–335.

McDonald, J. L. (1987). Assigning linguistic roles: the influence of conflicting cues. *Journal of Memory and Language, 26,* 100–117.

McDonald, J. L. (1989). The acquisition of cue–category mappings. In B. MacWhinney & E. Bates (Eds.), *The crosslinguistic study of language processing* (pp. 375–396). New York: Cambridge University Press.

McDonald, J. L., & MacWhinney, B. (1991). Levels of learning: A comparison of concept formation and language acquisition. *Journal of Memory & Language, 30,* 407–430.

Medin, D. L., Altom, M. W., Edelson, S. M., & Freko, D. (1982). Correlated symptoms and simulated medical classification. *Journal of Experimental Psychology: Learning, Memory & Cognition, 8,* 37–50.

Medin, D. L., & Edelson, S. M. (1988). Problem structure and the use of base-rate information from experience. *Journal of Experimental Psychology: General, 117,* 68–85.

Medin, D. L., & Schaffer, M. M. (1978). Context theory of classification learning. *Psychological Review, 85,* 207–238.

Medin, D. L., & Schwanenflugel, P. J. (1981). Linear separability in classification learning. *Journal of Experimental Psychology; Human Learning & Memory, 7,* 355–368.

Mills, A. (1986). *The acquisition of gender.* Berlin: Springer-Verlag.

Neumann, P. G. (1974). An attribute frequency model for the abstraction of prototypes. *Memory & Cognition, 2,* 241–248.

Pinker, S. (1989). *Learnability and cognition.* Cambridge, MA: The MIT Press.

Posner, M., & Keele, S. (1968). On the genesis of abstract ideas. *Journal of Experimental Psychology, 77,* 353–363.

Reed, S. (1972). Pattern recognition and categorization. *Cognitive Psychology, 3,* 382–407.

Reitman, J. S., & Bower, G. H. (1973). Storage and later recognition of concepts. *Cognitive Psychology, 4,* 194–206.

Rosch, E., & Mervis, C. (1975). Family resemblances: Studies in the internal structure of categories. *Cognitive Psychology, 7,* 573–605.

Shanks, D. R. (1991). Categorization by a connectionist network. *Journal of Experimental Psychology: Learning, Memory & Cognition, 17,* 433–443.

Shepard, R. N., Hovland, C. S., & Jenkins, H. M. (1961). Learning and memorization of classifications. *Psychological Monographs, 75,* No. 13.

Slobin, D. I., & Bever, T. G. (1982). Children use canonical sentence schemas: A cross-linguistic study of word order and inflections. *Cognition, 12,* 229–265.

Smith, E. E., & Medin, D. L. (1981). *Categories and concepts.* Cambridge, MA: Harvard University Press.

Smith, E. E., Shoben, E. J., & Rips, L. (1974). Structure and process in semantic memory: A featural model for semantic decisions. *Psychological Review, 81,* 214–241.

Sokolov, J. L. (1989). The development of role assignment in Hebrew. In B. MacWhinney & E. Bates (Eds.), *The crosslinguistic study of language processing* (pp. 118–157). New York: Cambridge University Press.

Taraban, R., McDonald, J. L., & MacWhinney, B. (1989). Category learning in a connectionist model: Learning to decline the German definite article. In R. Corrigan, F. Eckman & M. Noonan (Eds.) *Linguistic categorization* (pp. 163–193). Philadelphia: John Benjamins.

Zubin, D. & Koepcke, K. M. (1981).Gender: A less than arbitrary grammatical category. In R. Hendrik, C. Masek, & M. Miller (eds.), *Papers from the seventeenth regional meeting of the Chicago Linguistic Society* (pp. 439–449). Chicago: Chicago Linguistic Society.

THE EVOLUTION OF A CASE-BASED COMPUTATIONAL APPROACH TO KNOWLEDGE REPRESENTATION, CLASSIFICATION, AND LEARNING

Ray Bareiss
Brian M. Slator

I. Introduction

Many real-world domains are characterized by a lack of reliable general principles. In these "weak-theory" domains (e.g., medicine, law, and business), knowledge is incomplete, uncertain, and even contradictory. Real-world learners and classifiers in such domains must operate under constraints that are inherent to the problems they are solving. These are constraints in (1) the representational demands of concepts in weak-theory domains, (2) the conditions under which classification is typically performed, and (3) the experience (i.e., training) that is actually available for learning.

Concepts in real world, weak-theory domains are inherently polymorphic—their instances vary greatly in observable features, and this variability is not explainable in terms of general domain knowledge (Rosch & Mervis, 1975; Smith & Medin, 1981; Wittgenstein, 1953). In order to be successful, a system for concept acquisition, machine or human, must not make representational assumptions inconsistent with the concepts that it must acquire. For example, the concept *furniture* includes *tables* and *lamps* as well as *chairs*. Such a concept is difficult (or perhaps impossible)

THE PSYCHOLOGY OF LEARNING
AND MOTIVATION, VOL. 29

to define in terms of features which are singly necessary and jointly sufficient for classification; a system's concept representation scheme must be
sufficiently flexible to describe all concept instances adequately and cannot make assumptions which preclude complete and accurate representation.

Classification in a weak-theory domain is neither a process of sound
deduction from definitions in terms of necessary and sufficient features,
nor is it a process of matching prototypical concept descriptions. Further,
classification is seldom "all or none" (Langley & Ohlsson, 1984). A system must be able to classify unusual instances as well as typical ones, and
the classification process must function with non-ideal input. The environment often provides noisy descriptions of cases, and concepts have atypical instances which lack many of the features of prototypical instances.
Spurious features may be present, and important features may be missing
or incorrectly observed. For example, a medical patient with an acute
bacterial infection may have a rash which is spurious to diagnosing that
infection, and his temperature may have been misread during the examination. As a result, classification imposes constraints on the architecture of a
system. A classification system must be able to impose a consistent interpretation on its inputs and to deal with uncertainty in reaching its conclusions.

Constraints on representation and classification are constraints on
learning as well, because learning is not a distinct task but is a process
which occurs within a larger problem-solving task (Bylander & Chandrasekaran, 1987). Learning must support the needs of classification by
acquiring an appropriate representation for use in the classification
process. If learning is integrated with performing classification, the system
can improve the robustness of its problem-solving in ways specific to its
experience. Furthermore, a learning system must be able to learn from the
types and amount of training available in its environment.

This article discusses research on artificial intelligence systems for performing classification in weak-theory domains. In particular, the research
focuses on expert problem-solving. The first system, *Protos,* is a general-
purpose knowledge acquisition and classification system which has been
extensively evaluated in the domain of clinical audiology. The second
system, ORCA, extends the Protos approach with strategies for incremental
data gathering and classification of very complex problem situations
(Bareiss & Slator, 1992; Slator & Bareiss, 1992). It is being applied in a
business consulting domain. Through discussion of these systems, we will
explicate the strong link between expert problem-solving and categorization, which is consistent with the view of many (e.g., Fisher, this
volume; Medin, 1989) that understanding categorization is a key to understanding expert problem-solving.

II.   The Protos System

The Protos automated knowledge acquisition and classification system was designed to embody a unified approach to satisfying the interrelated constraints of concept representation, classification, and learning in weak-theory domains. Protos learns an exemplar-based representation in the course of performing classification under the guidance of a human teacher. When a new case is presented, Protos attempts to recall a previous case and to explain its similarity to the new case. If it fails to do so appropriately, Protos interacts with the teacher to acquire a new exemplar, refine its indices, and extend its general domain knowledge.

A.   THE PROTOS KNOWLEDGE REPRESENTATION

Protos is able to capture the polymorphy of concepts because its representation is extensional. A category (the extension of a concept) is represented by a retained subset of its members. These exemplars are chosen by the system to represent the variability of relevant features found in the entire range of category members. For example, *birds* might be represented by retaining the descriptions of a *robin*, a *sparrow*, a *penguin*, et cetera.

Unlike most approaches to machine learning, no attempt is made to induce a summary definition of the category (cf. prototype learning models in psychology such as Posner & Keele, 1968). In contrast, Protos's category definition remains implicit in the collection of exemplars (cf. exemplar learning models in psychology such as Medin & Schaffer, 1978). Since no attempt is made to induce a category-wide definition, information which might prove useful in future classification is not abstracted away. This makes an atypical instance of a category easier to classify by comparison to a similar instance than by deductive reasoning from a general definition (see Medin, Altom, Edelson, & Freko, 1982, for an account of why this may occur in human classification). For example, a *platypus* might be difficult to classify by reasoning from a general definition of *mammal*.

Two important issues arise from the choice of an exemplar-based representation: representation of the cohesiveness of categories, and representation of indexing information to facilitate classification.

1.   Category Cohesiveness

A collection of exemplars does not adequately represent the intension of a category. Category cohesiveness requires that the underlying commonality of category members be explicit in the representation (Murphy & Medin, 1985). Therefore, a category in Protos is more than simply a collection of exemplars, described in featural terms. Each exemplar feature has associated domain knowledge which explains its relevance to category membership. For example, *legs* is relevant to *chairs* because *"legs* is a specialization of *seatSupport* which enables *holds(person)* which is the function of *chairs."*

In addition, Protos's representation includes domain knowledge which captures the equivalence of features. An explanation of featural equivalence is an explanation that, because of underlying domain knowledge, two features provide a similar type of evidence for a classification. This sort of domain knowledge contributes to category cohesiveness by explaining equivalences among the features of the exemplars of a category. For example, with respect to chairs, a *pedestalBase* is equivalent to *legs(4)* because both are *seatSupports.*

2. *Protos's Indices*

Four types of index enable efficient access to Protos's category structure: reminding links, censors, exemplar links with prototypicality ratings, and difference links. These indices contribute in different ways to Protos's choice of an appropriate exemplar with which to compare a new case.

1. *Reminding links* (cf. Rosch, 1978; Schank, 1982) associate features with categories or particular exemplars. Such associations provide Protos with hypotheses during classification, which restrict its search for a matching exemplar. For example, *feathers* reminds Protos of *birds*.

2. *Censors* (cf. Winston, 1986) are negative reminding links. They are negative associations between features and categories which note counter-evidence to certain hypotheses. For example, *cold-blooded* would be a censor for the category *mammal*.

3. *Exemplar links with prototypicality ratings* identify the exemplars of a category and provide a partial ordering based on family resemblance. Exemplars of a category which have the highest family resemblance (i.e., are most similar to other members of the category) are most prototypical (Rosch & Mervis, 1975; Wittgenstein, 1953) and hence most likely to match new category instances.

4. *Difference links* note near misses (*cf.* Winston, 1975) which occurred during previous problem solving episodes. They record important featural differences between exemplars, which may suggest alternate classifications and better exemplars for use during classification.

B. THE PROTOS CLASSIFICATION PROCEDURE

Protos classifies a new case by using a retrieved exemplar as a model for interpreting its features. This model-based approach allows Protos to deal with non-ideal cases by concentrating on important features while ignoring others. The exemplar model provides expectations of the features of the new case and suggests the importance of fulfilling them. For example, a chair of a particular type should have a *backrest,* a *seat, legs,* and *arm-rests*; it may also have *wheels,* but they are spurious to the classification. Because a category is generally represented by several exemplars, a range of models is available to classify atypical as well as prototypical cases.

Classification is a two-step process: (1) the classification of a new case is hypothesized, and (2) the hypothesis is confirmed by selecting an exemplar and using domain knowledge to construct an explanation of the equivalence of the new case with the selected exemplar.

The features of the new case remind Protos of categories which form its set of hypotheses. These categories are likely to contain similar exemplars that can be used to confirm the hypothesis. This process employs two of the types of index introduced above: reminding links and censors. The features of a new case typically provide many remindings, which are combined to yield a few hypothesized classifications for the case. Multiple remindings to the same category are used to increase the system's belief in its relevance. Censors may offer a degree of disconfirmation ranging from mild to absolute. If a censor suggests absolute disconfirmation, the hypothesized category is excluded from further consideration. However, if a censor provides weaker disconfirmation, its negative strength serves only to weaken the hypothesis. Weakening affects the order in which hypotheses will be tried but does not preclude their consideration.

After Protos has hypothesized a classification, an exemplar is selected for use in confirming the classification. The exemplar serves as a model for interpreting the new case (cf. Nii, Feigenbaum, Anton, & Rockmore, 1982; Weiss, Casimir, & Amarel, 1978), providing expectations about the features a case should possess.

If Protos is not reminded of a particular exemplar of the hypothesized category, it uses prototypicality ratings to choose an exemplar based on expectations of similarity. A prototypical exemplar is a priori more likely to be similar to a new category member. The similarity between the new case and the exemplar model is gauged by using a search-based process to construct explanations of the equivalence of their features.

The similarity between a new case and an exemplar model is a function of the quality of the explanations relating them. This, in turn, depends on the quality of the inference chains relating the features of the case and the features of the exemplar, as well as on the relative importance of the features which are not matched. Protos's similarity function is a variant of the context model (Medin & Schaffer, 1978).

If the match between a new case and a recalled exemplar does not include some case features, Protos attempts to improve the match by examining difference links associated with the exemplar. Difference links from the exemplar are traversed in a hill-climbing procedure which attempts to locate a more similar exemplar.

Protos is not restricted to comparing a new case to only the most prototypical exemplar of a category. Rather, the strength of the combined reminding to a category indicates the degree to which that classification is worth pursuing. A strong combined reminding can lead Protos to consider several exemplars (in order of prototypicality), while a weaker one can lead it to consider only a single exemplar before moving on to another category. When an adequately explained match is found, the evidence for the classification of the new case is presented to the user.

C. THE PROTOS LEARNING PROCEDURES

Protos is a learning apprentice. It learns as a byproduct of attempting to perform classification under a teacher's guidance. The teacher presents a new case for classification. Protos attempts to classify the case and to explain its classification. If an error is made, the teacher is asked to supply additional knowledge to correct it.

The bulk of Protos's knowledge is the collection of cases, which are retained as exemplars of the categories learned by the system. Protos builds its knowledge base by selective retention of the cases presented to it by the teacher. It attempts to retain only the cases that are required to represent the significant variability that it has encountered in descriptions of category members. A new case becomes an exemplar only when Protos cannot classify it, or its similarity to an existing category member cannot be adequately explained (i.e., it has important unique features).

When a new exemplar is added to the category structure, Protos expects to be able to formulate an explanation of the relevance of each of its features to the category (i.e., classification). If its domain knowledge is inadequate to permit doing so, Protos requests an explanation (in its predefined explanation language) of why the presence of the feature increases the belief that the classification is correct. Explanations relating features to categories are heuristically analyzed to compile reminding links and to estimate the importance of the features to category membership. The validity of reminding links and importance ratings is continuously tested during classification. Whenever an incorrect classification occurs, the relevant remindings and importance are reassessed with respect to the current state of Protos's (incrementally changing) domain knowledge.

Protos's other indices are also learned. Censors are acquired directly from the teacher during the discussion of incorrect matches. Difference links are proposed by Protos as a result of "near-miss" matches and are confirmed by the teacher. Prototypicality ratings are heuristically estimated by crediting exemplars for strong, correct matches to new cases. (See Bareiss, 1989, for a detailed discussion of the mechanisms by which Protos learns and revises indices.)

D. EXPERIMENTAL EVALUATION OF PROTOS

Protos was designed to be a general-purpose knowledge acquisition and classification system for weak-theory domains. As a test of its effectiveness, it was applied to the task of acquiring knowledge for audiological diagnosis, which is representative of the classification tasks of interest (Bareiss, 1989; Porter, Bareiss, & Holte, 1990). Protos was trained directly by an expert audiologist without the intervention of a knowledge engineer. After a reasonable amount of training, the system classified hearing disorders as accurately as experienced human clinicians and substantially more accurately than knowledge bases constructed by a variety of machine learning techniques.

Although Protos learns and classifies quite well, the system possesses a significant designed-in limitation—it requires that all diagnostically significant features be part of the initial case presentation. In other words, Protos possesses no strategies for incremental data gathering and classification of cases. While this is not a handicap in performing a task like audiological diagnosis (in which the routine patient workup acquires most significant features), it is a limitation in more complex domains and is a clear divergence from the behavior of an expert human problem solver.

III. The ORCA System

Expert problem-solving involves more than routine data gathering followed by classification. It involves re-interpreting a complex problem situation in perhaps many ways as the expert's understanding grows. Experts intertwine data gathering and hypothesis formation. They explore alternative hypotheses and implement intermediate solutions. They gather further data and revise their assessments. This leads them to incrementally produce new and improved solutions to partially solved problems. To function at an expert level, an artificial problem-solver must be capable of this behavior in addition to being capable of correct classification given a full problem description.

The business task performed by a change management consultant, who helps organizations to deal with significant change, provides a good example of this type of expert problem solving. Beginning with only limited information, a change management consultant must assess the state of a company, determine its fundamental problems, assess its readiness for change, and support the implementation of changes in the company's structure or way of doing business. What the expert consultant brings to bear is the memory of similar experiences coupled with a weak theory of change management. Given the challenge of building an incremental problem-solver for this task, we distilled a set of design objectives for a knowledge-based assistant for interactive use by change management consultants. Such a system should:

1. encourage systematic exploration of a complex problem by asking relevant, context-sensitive questions
2. suggest necessary information to acquire from the client
3. propose multiple hypotheses about the client's problems when evidence of relevance is uncovered
4. present analogies to relevant past cases
5. recommend readings about general types of problem that the client may be facing
6. offer assistance in solving the client's problems by providing actions and outcomes associated with past cases and general prescriptive advice
7. manage information about the client over the course of a long consulting engagement
8. expand the system's memory by recording each completed consulting engagement as a new case

The result is the Organizational Change Advisor (ORCA), an interactive job aid and creativity tool for change management consultants which is being built for Andersen Consulting.

ORCA gathers information about a client's situation by posing a series of questions to the consultant (unlike Protos, which was given essentially complete information at the onset of problem-solving). The answers to these questions build up a featural description in ORCA's memory. Features, in turn, remind ORCA of additional questions to ask and of previous, similar cases. When ORCA chooses a story to tell the consultant, it is because that story matches the client's story in type of problem and general similarity. ORCA's cases, gathered both from interviewing experts and from searching professional journals, are intended to help the user consider realistic problem-solving alternatives and to familiarize the user with the cases in memory most closely related to their client's situation.

ORCA and Protos differ in significant ways other than data gathering and classification of problem situations. These differences result largely from the substantial gain of complexity in moving to a domain like organizational change. In contrast to a medical domain such as audiology, this business domain is much broader in terms of both the space of case features and possible categories of problems. Although both are "weak-theory" domains (as described earlier), the business domain encompasses virtually all of human organizational and economic behavior, which is much less understood than the audiology domain in which Protos was successfully applied. Furthermore, while Protos could classify the disease of an audiology patient accurately based on a handful of symptoms, ORCA is faced with analyzing the state of a "patient" that might have, with varying degrees of certainty and severity, dozens of symptoms and several simultaneous "diseases."

A.   THE ORCA KNOWLEDGE REPRESENTATION

ORCA is a case-based reasoning system that operates over a dynamic memory of cases represented as MOPS (Memory Organization Packets; Riesbeck & Schank, 1989; Schank, 1982). Unlike many case-based reasoners, however, cases are stories to be presented for use by a human user rather than fully represented entities for use in autonomous problem-solving. The sole representation of a case is indexical; that is, the only case features accessible to the system are those used in making retrieval decisions. The bulk of the case, including its problem-solving advice, is stored as a block of text (or, in some cases, video) that is opaque to the system. An example case is presented in Section VI, Appendix A: An Example ORCA Case.

Three types of attribute label cases in ORCA's memory: descriptive features of business situations and two separate systems of inferable abstract problem categories. The features are drawn from a vocabulary of descriptors of business situations that was developed by Andersen Consulting. These include direct observables, such as *a change in senior personnel has taken place,* and reasonably easy to make inferences, such as *friction exists between organizational units.*

1.   ORCA's Abstract Problem Categories

The abstract problem categories include a set of concepts taken from Andersen Consulting's change management methodology and another set of common sense categories borrowed from the study of conventional,

proverbial, wisdom. These categories provide an explicit way of organizing both the sets of problem-describing features and the cases which are
indexed by those features.

The abstract problem categories drawn from the change management
methodology are called *influence systems*. They are a set of 22 categories
with names like Vision, Image, and Planning. Each descriptor can take one
of three values: Weak, Neutral, or Strong. The formal methodology consists largely of discovering features of the client's situation and using them
to confirm the values of these influence systems.

The influence systems provide an abstract characterization of the state
of an organization, and the methodology associates general prescriptive
advice with each of the 66 possible influence system variable bindings. For
example, if the client has Weak Vision, the consultant is advised of the
client's need to "develop a comprehensive corporate mission statement."
The influence systems are, in essence, the foundation of a very formal
approach to problem-solving. An influence system value applies to an
organization if certain observable features are true of the organization, and
when these conditions are true, certain actions are appropriate. This turns
out to be both a strength and a weakness of the methodology. To make a
medical analogy, it is possible for the "patient" to be "somewhat
anemic," "very allergic," and "a little bit hyperactive," but there is no
recognition in the methodology that anemia and allergies might interact in
ways that could affect hyperactivity and therefore affect the patient's
course of treatment.

As a consequence of these somewhat artificial separations, the novice
consultant can cover a great deal of evaluative ground by simply asking
standard questions and operating on the basis of the results. However, the
influence system–based methodology suffers from a certain degree of
over-simplification due in large part to the orthogonality and discretization
built in to this system of description. This over-simplification can, in turn,
mislead the novice consultant with contradictory advice and possibly lead
to false starts in solving complex problems.

In an attempt to circumvent this systemic defect, ORCA incorporates
another scheme for abstract problem description based on an indexing
scheme that encodes a notion of common sense societal wisdom (Owens,
1990). For example, everyone knows that problems arise when an employee is made to report to more than a single boss: conflicting orders are
given, time is wasted negotiating priorities, and in the worst cases, the
bosses are dissatisfied and the employee is frustrated. Situations like this
are so well known that, over the centuries, society has developed and
preserved a shorthand system of aphorisms to describe them. In a case like
this, an impartial witness might observe, "No man can serve two mas-

ters," or, more picturesquely, "A pig with two masters will starve." In ORCA, proverbial expressions of this sort provide a framework of categories for organizing domain features and, hence, the corresponding influence systems. This higher-order organization groups the influence system values that are likely to co-occur, thus ameliorating the problem of artificial separation. Proverbs seldom, if ever, directly provide useful problem-solving advice. They are, however, useful as organizers of experience at a thematic level that enables cross-contextual remindings. These remindings associate stories together in a way that permits useful analogies to be drawn across varied domains. Proverbs also provide a common language for characterizing and discussing problems with ORCA's user.

Like Protos, ORCA represents its proverbial categories extensionally as sets of retained cases (i.e., exemplars). ORCA differs from Protos primarily in terms of the breadth of the knowledge base and the classification of cases within it. Rather than being exemplars of single abstract problem categories, ORCA's cases contain features relating to several different abstract problem categories. To repeat the medical analogy, each "patient" case typically has many "diseases." In addition to cases, each category has associated references to professional journal articles which are recommended reading on corresponding types of problem.

Unlike Protos, ORCA does not currently represent a body of general explanatory knowledge in its memory. As discussed earlier, the domain theory for organizational change is extremely broad and complex, in addition to being incomplete, uncertain, and contradictory. Consequently, representation in a simple language (like Protos's explanation language) to enable search-based inference is believed to be impractical. As a consequence, the knowledge engineering task for ORCA is more difficult. The knowledge engineers must take care to enter cases in a uniform featural language and relate features to categories (i.e., create reminding links) directly rather than counting on the program to infer them from domain knowledge as in Protos.

2. ORCA's Indices

The basic index in ORCA's memory is the reminding link. ORCA's reminding link is a generalization of Protos's in that a feature may remind ORCA of other features in addition to abstract problem categories and particular cases. Like Protos, ORCA also makes use of censors to suppress remindings.

The confirmatory link is a new index type that has been introduced to link abstract problem categories with features which tend to be confirmatory and hence, in general, worth pursuing when reminded of the category.

In other words, ORCA differs significantly from Protos in that featural representation is distributed between the categories and their exemplars. During problem-solving, determining the presence of a confirmatory feature in the client's situation suggests the relevance of presenting category instances to the user. In other words, confirmatory features are generally present in category instances and, hence, are reasonable to ask about when reminded of a category. No particular confirmatory feature is necessary to confirm the relevance of a category; however, one or more must be present.

Cases have prototypicality ratings with respect to both influence systems and proverbs. These qualitative ratings—strong, medium, and weak—partially order the cases as exemplars of the corresponding abstract problem categories. However, because of the extreme diversity of instances of an abstract problem category, ORCA differs from Protos in that prototypicality is not the sole determinant of the appropriateness of case retrieval during problem solving; a retrieved case must have a degree of surface similarity to the current situation as well (see Section III,B).

B.   THE ORCA PROBLEM-SOLVING PROCEDURE

When presented with a client situation, ORCA tries (1) to acquire a picture of the situation systematically by asking relevant questions; (2) to classify the situation repeatedly, as newly acquired information suggests relevant abstract problem types; and (3) to exemplify those problem types to the consultant (i.e., ORCA's user) by presenting similar past cases. The primary difficulty is that every situation that ORCA encounters will typically embody a multiplicity of problems. As a consequence, problem-solving involves reasoning from a multiplicity of partially matching cases. In doing so, ORCA makes the *noninteracting problem assumption*—the features of one problem will not mask the features of another. ORCA is faced with solving a Protos-like classification problem, but one in which the cases are much more complex, and the diagnostic assessment process is weak, subjective, inconsistent, and inconclusive.

Therefore, in ORCA, classification is an incremental process of forming and revising a set of active hypotheses as the user answers questions, providing additional data about the client's situation. At the beginning of an ORCA session, the user is asked to identify one or more significant business problems that the client is facing, chosen from a pre-enumerated list of problems (i.e., merger or restructuring). These are connected via reminding links to memory elements representing features, proverbs, and influence systems. Each element of which ORCA is reminded is placed on a "best-first" agenda, and questions to confirm each, ordered by importance, are added to a question agenda. At each step in the problem-solving process, ORCA asks the question at the head of the agenda.

Answering a question places its associated feature into a confirmation set, activates the associated remindings, and may cause all of ORCA's agendas to be re-evaluated. Generally, such a re-evaluation occurs as a result of a reminding link that associates the newly acquired feature with one or more abstract problem types. (As noted above, there can also be direct reminding links between features which correspond to follow-up questions to ask if a feature is observed.) For example, if the user confirms that "the company's R&D staff is small," ORCA will be reminded of an abstract problem characterized as "he who looks not ahead looks behind." This reminding will cause ORCA to seek a confirming feature, and the questions "Does the client neglect R&D in its planning and budgets?" and "Does the organization use outmoded equipment?" will be placed at the front of the question agenda. As the features, proverbs, and influence systems are confirmed, the cases (and article references), indexed by these elements, are placed on their own agenda. Cases that come to the front of the agenda may be presented to the user when a heuristic estimation of their relevance exceeds a predetermined threshold. Prototypicality ratings suggest the relevance of cases to abstract problem types, but because of the extreme diversity of instances of abstract problem types, they are not the sole determinant of which case is presented. When ORCA is reminded of a category, cases for consideration are selected on the joint basis of prototypicality and featural match to the client's situation. No matter how prototypical a case is, however, it will not be presented unless there is some degree of featural match. This requirement is imposed to suppress distant analogies that may not be of direct utility to a consultant. For example, a hot dog stand and a large commercial bank may both exhibit Weak Vision, but the featural differences between the two situations may overwhelm their abstract commonality.

After a case is presented, that is, its story is told, a follow-up dialog occurs in which the user is asked to compare the client's situation to the known features of the story. (Some of these elements are already known to be true of the client, of course, since the story was shown on this basis to begin with.) The follow-up dialog amounts to listing the additional descriptive features that are associated with the story and asking which of these are reasonably associated with the client case. This comparison affords the user the opportunity to think about the most relevant features of the client in the context of a previous case. On ORCA's side, newly acquired features elaborate its picture of the client's situation and produce remindings to additional problem categories.

Although classification is a crucial part of the overall problem-solving process, there is obviously more involved. Our research focuses on the classification aspect of complex problem-solving and relies on a human to handle other aspects of the task. ORCA's classifications, and the presentation of past cases, aid its user in determining the likelihood of various problems, give advice by analogy, and provide a tangible context for acquiring additional information about the client by prompting the user to provide explicit comparisons.

C. ADVICE GIVEN BY ORCA

ORCA gives four forms of advice: First, a report generated at the end of each session contains a list of the questions for the user to ask the client. These are the questions asked by ORCA that the user left unanswered or answered with "I don't know." Since these came to the front of the question agenda, ORCA judges them to be highly relevant with respect to the client situation. It is intended that the user will take the list into account in the next visit to the client. In this way, the user can return to subsequent ORCA sessions with further answers to enable ORCA to retrieve more cases and generate still more questions. A sample report is presented in Section VII, Appendix B: A Sample ORCA Report.

Second, each case retrieved for the user during a session represents a previous consulting experience. In addition to a description of the situation and problems of the previous client, each case can contain detailed descriptions of what remedies were attempted and how well they worked. Many cases also have associated information concerning lessons learned and things that should be done differently in future engagements.

Third, as discussed earlier, ORCA contains a representation of the associations between influence systems in the formal change management methodology and general prescriptive advice. As noted, these influence systems are treated as independent by the methodology; therefore, it is possible for the advice resulting from the confirmation of multiple influence systems to be conflicting.

Finally, to aid the user in interpreting the client's situation (and, potentially, in interpreting advice), ORCA compiles a list of articles from business journals. As features of the client's situation are confirmed, the articles in ORCA's memory, indexed by these features, are placed on their own agenda. Articles that exceed a certain reminding threshold are incorporated into a recommended reading list that is presented as part of the summary report at the end of an ORCA session. The articles on this reading list are likely to be relevant to the user because they too are indexed according to features, proverbs, and influence systems, and because they are assembled on the basis of answers given by the user.

As ORCA is consulted over the course of a consulting engagement, an increasingly refined picture emerges that characterizes the client, in general, as suffering from many types of problems. The picture may be incomplete, and problem types may be contradictory, as may the general problem-solving advice that ORCA presents. In the problem-solving process, the user plays the primary creative role—implementing a solution to the client's problems, based on the information presented by ORCA, as modified by human intuition and experience. The primary roles of ORCA in the problem-solving process are to serve as a creativity tool and to provide reliable access to a large corporate memory of experience.

D. THE ORCA LEARNING PROCEDURE

Like Protos, ORCA's learning is a byproduct of problem-solving. In the course of a consulting engagement, ORCA builds up an increasingly detailed representation of the user's client in terms of descriptive features, influence systems, and abstract problem types. All of these representational elements are drawn from a carefully hand-crafted core representation. Consequently, at the end of the engagement, it is straightforward to add the representation to ORCA's memory as a new case.

A three-step knowledge acquisition process is under development. First, the case representation, in terms of descriptive features, is presented for the user's approval. The user is given the opportunity to add and delete features. The addition and deletion of features may alter remindings to abstract problem categories, and this will cause the potentially relevant set to be recomputed.

Second, the abstract problem categories are presented to the user for final approval. Each category is presented, in turn, along with information about the reminding links and confirmatory features that suggest its relevance. If the user approves, the case is marked as an exemplar of the category, the user is asked to identify additional reminding and confirmatory links, and the process proceeds to the next category. If the user rejects the category, the opportunity is given to add censors or delete reminding links to suppress the reminding in future consultations in which a similar set of features occur. No attempt is currently made to enforce global consistency after local edits; this is a topic for future research.

Finally, after all potentially relevant classifications have been considered, the user is asked to type in a synopsis of the story in a standard format. The format includes such things as general client information, a description of the client's problems, any special methodologies employed, lessons learned, and things that should be done differently in future consulting engagements. As noted earlier, this portion of the case representation is opaque to ORCA; it is solely to inform a user who uses ORCA during a future engagement.

Currently ORCA's learning mechanisms are neither as varied nor as complex as those of Protos. In particular, no autonomous learning mechanisms have been contemplated. Learning is anticipated to be a primary focus of the next stage of ORCA research.

E.   AN EXAMPLE OF ORCA IN ACTION

The objective of an ORCA consultation is to provide advice by creating a *case* representing the client's situation and matching the case to previous experiences which may provide useful comparisons. This is an iterative picture that develops over days and weeks, as the consultant is able to gather information about the client. At first, the consultant is only expected to answer general or surface-level questions, and often the proper answer to a question is "I don't know." Over time, by following up on ORCA's suggestions, the consultant will find out the answers to specific questions that provide a detailed picture of the client's organization and its problems.

Imagine that a staff consultant is called into his manager's office, and she tells him only the following basic information:

> Bigbyte, a large software development company, plans the introduction of a computer-aided software engineering development environment. Software has been developed by autonomous teams that have been allowed to manage their own work in their own way. Management is under pressure from the stockholders and the board of directors, who are insisting that the new systems be installed as quickly as possible. They are afraid the upheaval will cause major disruption, and there have been indications that the programming staff will resist the new way of doing things.

The consultant begins his task by consulting ORCA. First, he enters the client's name and chooses one or more *change drivers* from a menu of eight (e.g., high-level problem types such as merger/acquisition, restructuring/reorganization, competitive threats, and so on).

> **ORCA:** ORCA (the Organizational Change Advisor) will assist you in analyzing a client's situation as you hear stories and answer questions. Is this a new client or an existing one?
> **USER:** New client.

ORCA: What is the client's name?
USER: The Bigbyte Software Company.
ORCA: Choose one or more change drivers and then press *continue* to answer questions on behalf of the client. ORCA will tell stories, ask follow-up questions, and give advice.
USER: Reorganization/restructuring and competitive threats. Continue.

Change drivers are initial entry points into ORCA's memory that are directly connected to some of its memory elements. Choosing a change driver reminds ORCA of certain features and abstract problem categories, causing confirming questions to be placed, best first, on the question agenda. ORCA then poses each of these to the user in turn. The change drivers "reorganization/restructuring" and "competitive threats" remind ORCA of a number of problem categories. The strongest reminding is to a category exemplified by the proverb "Who looks not before finds himself behind." ORCA puts several questions on the question agenda to attempt to confirm this problem.

ORCA: Now it is time to answer some questions about your client. You may answer the questions as they appear or scan the agenda to pick questions to answer.
Does the client neglect R&D in its plans and budgets?
USER: I don't know.
ORCA: Is the client's thinking behind current times?
USER: I don't know.
ORCA: Does the organization use obsolete or outmoded equipment?
USER: I don't know.
ORCA: Does the client seem to give little consideration to the future?
USER: No.

None of the user's answers confirm ORCA's hypothesis, so it goes on to its next best one—"You've got to spend money to make money."

ORCA: Is the organization willing to make investments that will pay off later?
USER: Yes.

The user's "yes" answer is insufficient to confirm ORCA's hypothesis, but it boosts another hypothesis—"If you don't invest in the short-term, there is no long-term"—to favored status. A confirming question is asked.

> **ORCA:** Does the organization exist in a highly competitive field?
> **USER:** Yes.

This hypothesis is confirmed. Based on prototypicality ratings within the problem category and features of the BigByte Case, ORCA is able to identify a case that the user might want to see. The case is presented at the request of the user.

> Story-9: "Caterpillar Strives for Quality in Factory 2000" (abridged)
> Caterpillar is on the road to building a "FACTORY 2000." They are moving towards creating a cutting edge work environment where quality and process control become king. In building the shop floor training program, video workstations have been developed where employees can check out what they're working on in more depth through the use of interactive video . . .

After the case is presented, the user is engaged in a contextually relevant follow-up dialog. ORCA goes through important case features and asks the user to consider whether these apply to the client or not. In each instance, the user is told the answer for the retrieved case (Caterpillar) and asked to compare it to his client's situation. For example, after the user reads Story-9, ORCA poses 20 questions, including:

> **ORCA:** Is the organization wandering without direction? (Caterpillar–No)
> **USER:** No.
> **ORCA:** Is the organization concerned with operational productivity? (Caterpillar–Maybe)
> **USER:** Yes.
> **ORCA:** Has the organization been examining processes for efficiency or because relationships between groups do not mesh as well as they could? (Caterpillar–Maybe)
> **USER:** Maybe.
> **ORCA:** Is the client introducing new processes that will demand

revised or wholly new standards and controls? (Caterpillar–
Probably)
USER: Yes.
ORCA: Is automation being introduced? (Caterpillar–Probably)
USER: Yes.
ORCA: Are people's responsibilities changing? (Caterpillar–
Probably)
USER: Yes.
ORCA: . . .

The features acquired during follow-up dialog enable ORCA to identify
another relevant case to present to the user. The case stays within the
proverbial category, "If you don't invest in the short-term, there is no
long-term," but has a higher degree of featural match to the client's
situation than the Caterpillar story. The relevance of this case is further
reinforced by the fact that it is also exemplary of another proverbial
category, "You've got to spend money to make money," which was also
confirmed during the follow-up dialog.

> Story-3: "Work groups streamline Blue Cross/Blue Shield"
>   (abridged)
> Change Management Services worked with Blue Cross/Blue
> Shield to organize interdependent work groups. These groups
> consist of various BC/BS reps with different expertise areas, who
> work together and "cross-train" as they go from case to case.
> They have proven a success. Some of the reasons given for their
> success include . . .

The ORCA consultation continues as long as the user believes it to be
worthwhile to answer questions and view cases. At the end of the session,
the user is given a report that includes a summary of all sessions to date
including a list of the features, influence systems, and proverbial categories that are confirmed for the client, a list of questions to ask the client
(i.e., questions that the user could not answer during the current session),
synopses of all cases presented, a list of article references, and general
advice associated with confirmed influence systems (see Section VII,
Appendix B: A Sample ORCA Report). Armed with this report, the user is
expected to gather further information and to use that information to
answer more of ORCA's questions in future sessions. At the end of the
consulting engagement, the new client case is added to ORCA's permanent

memory and becomes a part of the knowledge base that ORCA will use to reason about future clients.

IV.   Current Status of ORCA

ORCA is a work in progress. The current case base contains nearly 70 cases. Fifty-six of these are in text form. The cases came primarily from business journal articles. They were selected by Andersen staff people and were abridged by them for entry into the system. The other cases are in video form. These were acquired by interviewing partners and senior managers who served as instructors for Andersen's change management school. They are the beginning of a corporate memory of firsthand experience with Andersen's major clients. In addition to being longer and hence providing greater detail, many of these cases provide entry into an ASK network (Ferguson, Bareiss, Birnbaum, & Osgood, 1992) that permits a user to ask detailed follow-up questions about the particular case via a graphical interface.

As noted earlier, cases are classified in two ways. The first is Andersen's system of 22 influence systems. The second is 131 proverbial categories (see Section VI, Appendix A: An Example ORCA Case, for examples). We will soon evaluate the coverage and utility of these proverbial categories, and some changes in this aspect of the representation may result. In particular, we are considering the possibility that some categories are too vague and may need to be specialized to represent the corresponding business problems accurately. To represent these categories, ORCA has a vocabulary of over 200 features (see Section VII, Appendix 1: An Example ORCA Case, for examples).

After Andersen approves the design and functionality of the prototype, they will devote considerable content-expertise to the construction of the final system. In particular, they will assist us in amassing a large corpus of cases, refining the representational vocabulary, and indexing the cases in ORCA's memory. We anticipate that the size of the case base will have to increase by an order of magnitude to provide useful analogies across the breadth of the domain.

V.   Conclusion

The Protos approach is grounded in the cognitive science literature of the late 1970s and early 1980s. Despite this, however, we are reluctant to tout it as a cognitive model. Our theoretical goal was to formulate a set of principles that could guide the design of effective artificial problem-solvers, not to formulate a computational explanation of human problem-solving behavior. Although, in general, the Protos approach remains faithful to reliably observed psychological mechanisms, we have not hesitated to diverge from those mechanisms when improvement was clearly possible.

Given its demonstrated success, artificial intelligence researchers should take the Protos project as an object lesson in the utility of psychological research in the formulation of computational models. We believe this to be a key lesson in approaches to both AI research and the construction of practical knowledge-based systems.

The evolution of Protos into ORCA was motivated by a desire to extend the approach to apply to much more complex problems. Our work has taught us four general lessons about the design of AI problem-solvers: First, a problem-solver must possess a strategy for incremental data gathering and classification of problem situations. Second, complex problem-solving frequently involves multiply classifying a problem situation, perhaps by interpreting it with multiple models. Third, categories provide a focus for efficient problem-solving; remindings to categories restrict the space to be searched for matching exemplars. Fourth, knowledge representation should be distributed between categories and their exemplars to maximize the efficiency of search for relevant classifications.

We did not find psychological models of categorization to be sufficiently rich to give us the additional guidance we needed to build ORCA on the foundation of Protos. Consequently, our implementation decisions were based on the our analysis of the requirements of ORCA's task and on the general need for computational efficiency. Perhaps the approaches that arose from the lessons we learned will suggest corresponding psychological research to extend theories of categorization profitably.

VI. Appendix A: An Example ORCA Case

As discussed in Section III,A, ORCA stores cases as partially represented stories. Each story in memory is differentiated by the domain elements to which it is linked. There are three types of domain elements: (1) descriptive features either taken directly from the Andersen Consulting Change Management methodology or derived empirically from the stories themselves; (2) abstract problem descriptions, exemplified by aphorisms of societal or proverbial wisdom; and (3) influence systems, taken directly from the Andersen Consulting Change Management methodology.

The following story is adapted from Beer & Walton (1990).

A. STORY 41: JUST-IN-TIME CHANGE INTRODUCED CLUMSILY,
   UNDERMINING MANAGEMENT OBJECTIVES

A manufacturing plant renowned for its innovation encountered difficulty
in maintaining its culture when competitive pressure forced the introduction of a just-in-time manufacturing system. The plant originally was organized around semi-autonomous production teams, who had been previously allowed to manage their own work at their own individual rates.

Though some problems stemmed from the new system, most arose from
the style used by a new plant manager to introduce it. Under pressure from
corporate headquarters to use a system designed by an outside consulting
firm, he severely limited employee involvement in the process. Employees
received neither involvement in the design of the just-in-time system, nor
an explanation of the cost problem facing the plant.

The teams found their self-management and pacing undermined as the
just-in-time system eliminated the costly inventory which had allowed
each team to set its own pace. Disillusionment and cynicism concerning
the plant's commitment to the original vision of participative management
resulted.

B. THE FEATURES OF STORY-41

1. Very Important Features

Feature-6. A vision does not exist, is not understood, or is inconsistent
   with present practices or conditions.
Feature-25. Assessment tools indicate a high percentage of the work force
   is content with the status quo.
Feature-27. The organization exists in a highly competitive field.
Feature-48. Key managers or leaders are replaced.
Feature-53. New units are established. Old units are eliminated.
Feature-55. Processes are examined for efficiency or productivity.
Feature-59. A reorganization occurs, affecting at least some of the rela-
   tionships of individuals and/or work groups in the client's organization.
Feature-111. Traditional values are inappropriate for the new climate.
Feature-125. Change has been excessive, rapid, or reactive.
Feature-306. New processes are being planned or enacted.
Feature-314. The organization's leadership, work force, or ownership has
   significantly changed.

2. Moderately Important Features

Feature-3. Many confusing, overlapping programs are competing for the
   organization's attention and resources.

Feature-34. The organization is concerned about its culture.

Feature-44. The work force needs more knowledge concerning the plans and effects of a downsizing, merger, or reorganization.

Feature-86. A new vision, image, or style is planned.

Feature-91. Labor relations are of concern.

Feature-319. People's responsibilities are changing within the organization.

Feature-325. Restructuring is planned or taking place.

Feature-327. A major reorganization, merger, or downsizing is planned or occurring.

3. Slightly Important Features

Feature-58. Allocation systems are revised.

Feature-67. Changes in the organization's form or configuration causes a redefinition of roles.

Feature-312. Roles within the organization are being changed or revised.

Feature-326. A reconstruction or rebuilding is planned or taking place.

C. PROVERBS ASSOCIATED WITH STORY-41

1. Proverbs of Which Story-41 Is Strongly Prototypical

Proverb-41. Robin Hood would have failed if his men weren't merry.

Proverb-44. The tongue of experience has most truth.

Proverb-55. The road to hell is paved with good intentions.

Proverb-71. Do not throw out the baby with the bath water.

Proverb-72. A man convinced against his will is of the same opinion still.

Proverb-76. Penny wise, pound foolish.

2. Proverbs of Which Story-41 Is Moderately Prototypical

Proverb-22. Take time to be fast.

Proverb-31. Good and quickly seldom meet.

Proverb-73. One man's meat is another man's poison.

Proverb-78. All that glitters is not gold.

3. Proverbs of Which Story-41 Is Weakly Prototypical

Proverb-70. If it ain't broke don't fix it.

Proverb-89. There is nothing more difficult to carry out—nor more doubtful of success—nor more dangerous to handle—than to initiate a new order of things (Machiavelli).

Proverb-119. It is the feeling of powerlessness that corrupts most of all (Irwin Rubin & David Berlow).

D. INFLUENCE SYSTEMS ASSOCIATED WITH STORY-41

*1. Influence Systems of Which Story-41 Is
Strongly Prototypical*

Influence-system-5 (Neutral Image). Employees may not be proud to be
members of the organization.
Influence-system-22 (Strong Relationship). Employees believe that strong
relationships are a component of their jobs.
Influence-system-26 (Neutral Form). Employees are uncertain that the
structure is successful.

*2. Influence Systems of Which Story-41 Is
Moderately Prototypical*

Influence-system-15 (Weak Style). Employees do not believe that the
personality of the organization is appropriate and successful.
Influence-system-39 (Weak Communications). Employees believe that
poor communications exist within the organization.

*3. Influence Systems of Which Story-41 Is
Weakly Prototypical*

Influence-system-3 (Weak Vision). Employees believe that leadership has
not established what it wants to achieve in the future.
Influence-system-62 (Neutral Motivation). Not all employees gain a sense
of personal accomplishment from their work.
Influence-system-65 (Neutral Commitment). Employees may want to
leave the organization.

VII. Appendix B: A Sample ORCA Report

This report was automatically generated by ORCA at the conclusion of
an extended consultation regarding the example case, BigByte Software.

CONFIRMED ELEMENTS FOR BIGBYTE SOFTWARE

Change Drivers

Reorganization and/or Restructuring
Competitive Threats

The Features of BigByte Software

The organization exists in a highly competitive field. (Yes)

The organization's leadership, work force, or ownership has significantly changed. (Yes)

Restructuring is planned or taking place. (Yes)

A reconstruction or rebuilding is planned or taking place. (Yes)

A major reorganization, merger, or downsizing is planned or occurring. (Yes)

The client is concerned with operational productivity or efficiency. (Yes)

Productivity is a change driver. (Yes)

New processes are introduced that require new or revised standards and quality controls. (Yes)

Automation is introduced. (Yes)

People's responsibilities are changing within the organization. (Yes)

The organization is modifying its operations. (Yes)

The organization introduces new information systems that have direct impact upon its vital operations. (Yes)

New processes are being planned or enacted. (Yes)

New technology is introduced. (Yes)

Automation is being planned or introduced. (Yes)

A flexible work force is required. (Yes)

New information systems are being planned or introduced. (Yes)

Roles within the organization are being changed or revised. (Yes)

The nature of the work is heavily dependent on information. (Yes)

Changes in the organization's form or configuration causes a redefinition of roles. (Yes)

Any significant organizational change is to take place. (Probably)

A large project effort is planned. (Probably)

Job responsibilities are transferred or assumed elsewhere in the organization. (Probably)

The organization must improve the productivity, efficiency, or quality control of its operations. (Probably)

Relationships involving both individuals and work groups are examined for efficiency or productivity. (Maybe)

A new vision, image or style is planned. (Maybe)

The organization is wandering, without direction or exhibiting signs of chronic malaise. (No)

The organization is unwilling to risk undertaking a new system, process, or project. (No)

Two or more organizations are combined or collaborate upon the same work, and have to resolve conflicting managerial or work styles. (No)
A major reorganization causes changes in the organization's hierarchy or configuration. (No)

Influence Systems

Strong Innovation: Continue to communicate that innovation is possible in every area of the organization, not just in Research and Development, but also in accounting, human resources, marketing, and operations.

Questions to Ask the Client

Has the industry experienced major technological improvements in recent years?
Does new management come from a different nation or culture?
If new information or automation systems are planned, will the present educational level of employees be insufficient?
Are training and development primarily seen as helping employees to perform their present tasks better?
Do employees perceive resources as in place where the need usually arises?

Stories Seen

Caterpillar Strives for Quality in Factory 2000.   Caterpillar invests in the future with high-tech training for its factory employees, to put quality and process control at the top of its manufacturing agenda.

This story is strongly related to the feature "A new vision, image or style is planned" and strongly related to the influence system "Strong Innovation."

Work Groups Streamline Blue Cross/Blue Shield.   Blue Cross/ Blue Shield developed a work group style with Andersen's Change Management division. Success comes from BC/BS' particular way of handling salaries, organization, and insurance.

This story is somewhat related to the feature "A major reorganization causes changes in the organization's hierarchy or configuration," somewhat related to the feature "A new vision, image or style is planned," strongly related to the feature "The organization must improve the productivity, efficiency, or quality control of its operations," strongly related to the feature "Changes in the organization's form or configuration causes a redefinition of roles," and strongly related to the influence system "Strong Innovation."

StarKist Increases Labor Costs—Focuses On Efficiency versus Effectiveness. A large tuna canning company discovered that it can save money by adding workers and slowing down the production lines. This method prevents waste of fish from pushing too few workers too fast. In expanding the number of workers and producing more fish, the company saved ten million dollars.

This story is strongly related to the feature "The organization must improve the productivity, efficiency, or quality control of its operations" and strongly related to the influence system "Strong Innovation."

Recommended Readings

Henkoff, Ronald. Cost Cutting: How to Do It Right. *Fortune,* April 9, 1990, pg. 41 (cf. 90–9 pg. 23)
   This article is strongly related to the proverb "You've got to spend money to make money" and strongly related to the feature "The organization must improve the productivity, efficiency, or quality control of its operations."

Dumaine, Brian. What the Leaders of Tomorrow See. *Fortune,* July 3, 1989, pg. 49–57.
   This article is strongly related to the feature "A new vision, image or style is planned" and strongly related to the feature "Changes in the organization's form or configuration causes a redefinition of roles."

Hymowitz, Carol. When Firms Cut Out Middle Managers, Those at Top and Bottom Often Suffer. *Wall Street Journal,* April 5, 1990, pg. B1 (cf. 90–9 pg. 20).
   This article is strongly related to the feature "A major reorganization causes changes in the organization's hierarchy or configuration."

Barczak, Gloria; Charles Smith; & David Wilemon. Managing Large-Scale Organizational Change. *Organizational Dynamics,* 1986.

This article is strongly related to the feature "Changes in the organization's form or configuration causes a redefinition of roles."

Myers, Dale. Interactive Video: A Chance to Plug the Literacy Leak. *Industry Week* (no date given), pg. 92 (cf. 91–3 pg. 92).
This article is strongly related to the feature "Changes in the organization's form or configuration causes a redefinition of roles."

Main, Jeremy. How 21 Men Got Global in 35 Days. *Fortune*, Nov. 6, 1989, pg. 71 (cf. 90–5 pg. 44).
This article is strongly related to the feature "Changes in the organization's form or configuration causes a redefinition of roles."

Beer, Michael, & Elise Walton. Developing the Competitive Organization: Interventions and Strategies. *American Psychologist*, February 1990, pg. 154 (cf. 90–8 pg. 42).
This article is strongly related to the feature "A new vision, image, or style is planned" and strongly related to the feature "The organization must improve the productivity, efficiency, or quality control of its operations."

Council on Competitiveness. Building a Better Work Force. *Challenges*, Sept. 1989, pg. 3 (cf. 90–3 pg. 15).
This article is strongly related to the proverb "If you don't invest in the long term—there is no short term."

ACKNOWLEDGMENTS

The Protos approach was developed in collaboration with Bruce Porter and other colleagues at the University of Texas at Austin. The ideas were further refined through discussion with Susan Williams and other colleagues at Vanderbilt University. ORCA is being built at the Institute for the Learning Sciences by Mike Engber, Kerim Fidel, Jim McNaught, Tamar Offer-Yehoshua, and Josh Tsui, in collaboration with Beth Beyer, Marita Decker, Dan Halabe, and Maureen Zabloudil of Andersen Consulting. Roger Schank, Tom Hinrichs, and Chris Riesbeck have contributed valuable ideas throughout the process. Suggestions from Doug Medin, Glenn Nakamura, Dick Osgood, and Roman Taraban have greatly improved this paper. This research was supported in part by the Defense Advanced Research Projects Agency, monitored by the Air Force Office of Scientific Research under contract F49620-88-C-0058 and the Office of Naval Research under contract N00014-90-J-4117, by the Office of Naval Research under contract N00014-89-J-1987, and by the Air Force Office of Scientific Research under contract AFOSR-89-0493. The Institute for the Learning Sciences was established in 1989 with the support of Andersen Consulting. The Institute receives additional support from Ameritech and North West Water, Institute Partners, and from IBM.

REFERENCES

Bareiss, R. (1989). *Exemplar-based knowledge acquisition: A unified approach to concept representation, classification, and learning.* San Diego: Academic Press.

Bareiss, R., & Slator, B. M. (1992). From Protos to ORCA: Reflections on a Unified Approach to Knowledge Representation, Categorization, and Learning (ILS Tech Report 19). Evanston, IL: The Institute for the Learning Sciences.

Beer, M., & Walton, E. (1990). Developing the competitive organization: Interventions and strategies. *American Psychologist, 45,* 154.

Bylander, T., & Chandrasekaran, B. (1987). Generic tasks for knowledge-based reasoning: The right level of abstraction for knowledge acquisition. *International Journal of Man–Machine Studies, 26,* 231–243.

Ferguson, W., Bareiss, R., Birnbaum, L., & Osgood, R. (1992). ASK systems: An approach to the realization of story-based teachers. *The International Journal of the Learning Sciences, 2,* 95–134.

Langley, P., & Ohlsson, S. (1984). Automated cognitive modeling. *Proceedings of the National Conference on Artificial Intelligence* (pp. 193–197). Austin, TX: AAAI.

Medin, D. L. (1989). Concepts and conceptual structure. *American Psychologist, 44,* 1469–1481.

Medin, D. L., Altom, M. W., Edelson, S. M., & Freko, D. (1982). Correlated symptoms and simulated medical classification. *Journal of Experimental Psychology: Learning, Memory and Cognition, 8*(1), 37–50.

Medin, D. L., & Schaffer, M. M. (1978). Context theory of classification learning. *Psychological Review, 85,* 207–238.

Murphy, G. L., & Medin, D. L. (1985). The role of theories in conceptual coherence. *Psychological Review, 92,* 289–316.

Nii, H. P., Feigenbaum, E. A., Anton, J. J., & Rockmore, A. J. (1982 Spring). Signal-to-symbol transformation: HASP/SIAP case study. *The AI Magazine, 3,* 23–35.

Owens, C. (1990). *Indexing and retrieving abstract planning knowledge.* Doctoral dissertation, Yale University, New Haven, CT.

Porter, B. W., Bareiss, R., & Holte, R. C. (1990). Concept learning and heuristic classification in weak-theory domains. *Artificial Intelligence, 45,* 229–263.

Posner, M. I., & Keele, S. W. (1968). On the genesis of abstract ideas. *Journal of Experimental Psychology, 77,* 353–363.

Riesbeck, C., & Schank, R. C. (1989). *Inside case-based reasoning.* Hillsdale, NJ: Erlbaum.

Rosch, E. (1978). Principles of categorization. In E. Rosch & B. B. Lloyd (Ed.), *Cognition and Categorization* (pp. 28–49). Hillsdale, N.J: Lawrence Erlbaum Assoc.

Rosch, E., & Mervis, C. B. (1975). Family resemblance: Studies in the internal structure of categories. *Cognitive Psychology, 7,* 573–605.

Schank, R. C. (1982). *Dynamic memory: A theory of reminding and learning in computers and people.* New York: Cambridge University Press.

Slator, B. M., & Bareiss, R. (1992). Incremental reminding: the case-based elaboration and interpretation of complex problem situations. *Proceedings of the fourteenth annual cognitive science conference* (pp. 1122–1127). Bloomington, IN: Cognitive Science Society.

Smith, E. E., & Medin, D. L. (1981). *Categories and concepts*. Cambridge, MA: Harvard University Press.

Weiss, S. M., Casimir, A. K., & Amarel, S. (1978). A model-based method for computer-aided medical decision-making. *Artificial Intelligence, 11*, 145–172.

Winston, P. H. (1975). Learning structural descriptions from examples. In P. H. Winston (Ed.), *The Psychology of Computer Vision* (pp. 157–209). New York: McGraw-Hill.

Winston, P. H. (1986). Learning by augmenting rules and accumulating censors. In R. S. Michalski, J. G. Carbonell, & T. M. Mitchell (Eds.), *Machine learning: An artificial intelligence approach: Vol. 2* (pp. 45–62). San Mateo, CA: Morgan Kaufmann.

Wittgenstein, L. (1953). *Philosophical investigations*. New York: Macmillan.

PART II
DATA-DRIVEN AND THEORY-DRIVEN PROCESSING AND PROCESSING MODELS

INTEGRATING THEORY AND DATA IN CATEGORY LEARNING

Raymond J. Mooney

I. Introduction

Until recently, research in categorization in cognitive psychology and machine learning focused almost exclusively on empirical, data-driven models. The most frequently studied task was learning categories from simple examples represented as lists of features (Bruner, Goodnow, & Austin, 1956; Michalski & Chilausky, 1980; Quinlan, 1979; Smith & Medin, 1981). The role of background knowledge or domain theories on category learning was largely ignored. The focus was on understanding the basic process of induction from raw data.

In the past decade, researchers in both areas began to investigate knowledge-intensive concept learning. Several researchers in machine learning began developing systems that performed a detailed analysis of an individual example. Many of these systems could learn a new concept from a single example. These methods eventually became known as *explanation-based learning* (DeJong & Mooney, 1986; Mitchell, Keller, & Kedar-Cabelli, 1986). Meanwhile, cognitive psychologists were also turning their attention to the role of theories in categorization (Barsalou, 1983; Murphy & Medin, 1985; Nakamura, 1985). One important finding was that subjects, like explanation-based learning systems, could acquire a concept or schema from only a single example (Ahn, Mooney, Brewer, & DeJong, 1987).

THE PSYCHOLOGY OF LEARNING
AND MOTIVATION, VOL. 29

189

However, purely empirical (data-driven) and purely analytical (theory-driven) views of categorization are clearly end-points on a continuum. Most real category learning tasks involve an integration of background theory and empirical data. Recent research in both cognitive psychology and machine learning has begun to focus on the issue of integrating theory and data in concept learning (Ahn, Brewer, & Mooney, 1992; Birnbaum & Collins, 1991; Segre, 1989; Wisniewski & Medin, 1991). This research is attempting to unravel the complex interacting effects of theory and data on concept learning.

This article describes two recently developed machine learning systems that integrate theory and data, and discusses the extent to which these systems can model recent experimental results on human concept learning. Consequently, the article illustrates some of the interactions that are possible between machine learning and cognitive psychology. Ideas from machine learning can be experimentally tested to determine their psychological validity. The most direct approach involves giving subjects and programs the exact same task and comparing their results. On the other hand, ideas developed in psychology can be incorporated into machine learning systems. The work presented in this paper illustrates both of these types of interaction.

The remainder of the chapter is organized as follows. Section II briefly reviews standard empirical and explanation-based models of learning. Section III discusses various ways in which theory and data can interact in categorization. Section IV describes IOU, a computer program that uses a domain theory to bias category learning. Simulation results are also presented in Section IV, in which IOU is shown to model effects found when subjects in a standard learning-from-examples experiment are told the function of the underlying categories. Section V describes another machine learning system, EITHER, which modifies an existing domain theory based on empirical data. Section V also discusses how the methods used in EITHER could potentially model recent results on how human subjects use data to modify theories and theories to modify data. Section VI summarizes our results and presents some problems and ultimate goals for future research.

II. Review of Empirical and Explanation-based Learning

The majority of research in categorization within psychology and machine learning has concerned *empirical* or *similarity-based* methods. In these methods, categories are learned by examining similarities and differences between relatively large numbers of examples. In cognitive psychology, similarity-based methods are normally divided into *classical, probablistic,* and *exemplar* models (Smith & Medin, 1981). Classical or *rule-based* methods form abstract logical definitions of categories (Bruner et al.,1956; Medin, Wattenmaker, & Michalski, 1987; Quinlan, 1986). Probabilistic methods extract characteristic features that have associated weights or probabilities that are subsequently used to compute category membership (Fisher, 1987; Posner & Keele, 1968; Reed, 1972; Rosch, Mervis, Gray, Johnson, & Boyes-Braem, 1976; Rosenblatt, 1962). Exemplar models do not form abstractions but rather categorize examples based on similarity to specific stored instances (Aha, Kibler, & Albert, 1991; Bariess & Slator, this volume; Brooks, 1978; Estes, this volume; Kruschke, this volume; Medin & Schaffer, 1978; Nosofsky, 1984; Taraban and Palacios, this volume). Very little emphasis is given to the role of background knowledge in any of these models. Psychological experiments in this area generally use simple, artificial data so that subjects cannot employ their existing knowledge.

However, some recent work in both psychology and machine learning have emphasized the role of background knowledge and theories in category learning. In psychology, background knowledge and theories have been shown to have important effects in categorization (Brewer, this volume; Graesser, Langston, & Baggett, this volume; Mumma, this volume; Murphy, this volume; Murphy & Medin, 1985; Ward, this volume; Wattenmaker, Dewey, Murphy, & Medin, 1986). In machine learning, explanation-based learning methods have been developed that acquire a concept definition from a single example by using existing background knowledge to explain the example and thereby focus on its important features (DeJong, 1988). In the standard formalization (DeJong & Mooney, 1986; Mitchell et al., 1986), the *domain theory* is represented by a set of rules that allows the system to logically deduce that a concrete example satisfies an abstract definition of a given *goal concept*. Explanation-based generalization then consists of the following two steps:

1. Explain: Construct an explanation using the domain theory that proves that the training example satisfies the definition of the goal concept.
2. Generalize: Determine a set of sufficient conditions under which the explanation holds, stated in purely observable terms.

Machine learning systems have learned a number of concepts using this approach. For example, consider learning a structural definition of a cup from a functional definition and a single example (Winston, Binford, Katz,

& Lowry, 1983). Assume the example is described by the following observable features:

> owner = Fred, color = red, location = table, width = medium, has-bottom, flat-bottom, has-handle, lightweight, has-concavity, upward-pointing-concavity.

Assume one has the following functional definition of a cup:

> stable & liftable & open-vessel → cup

which states that anything that is stable, liftable, and an open-vessel is a cup. If the domain theory contains the following rules,

> has-bottom & flat-bottom → stable
> lightweight & graspable → liftable
> has-handle → graspable
> width = small & insulating → graspable
> has-concavity & upward-pointing-concavity → open-vessel

one can deduce that the example is a *cup* using the "explanation" or proof shown in Fig. 1. Note that by allowing multiple rules for inferring propositions such as *graspable,* a domain theory can represent disjunctive as well as conjunctive concepts. In most machine learning systems, such domain theories are interpreted in a strictly logical manner. There are no weights on features and there are no confidence values associated with conclusions. However, partial matching techniques can be used to incorporate feature weights and confidences (see Section IV,B,2).

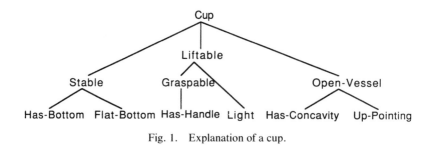

Fig. 1.   Explanation of a cup.

A definition of *cup* in purely observable terms can be obtained by compiling the explanation into a new rule. The root of the explanation forms the consequent of the new rule and the leaves form the antecedents. Below is the compiled rule for the cup example:

has-bottom & flat-bottom & has-handle & lightweight & has-concavity & upward-pointing-concavity → cup

Note that the generalization omits information about the color, owner, location, and width of the example, since these features are not used in the explanation. Once the rule has been compiled, instead of performing complicated inferencing, direct pattern matching can be used to classify examples as cups.

For a more psychologically motivated example of explanation-based learning, consider the following anecdote. Not long after moving to Texas, I encountered an example of an interesting device called a boot-jack. A rough sketch of a typical boot-jack is shown in Fig. 2. This device allows an urban cowboy to remove his boots easily and independently after a long, hard day at the office.

A boot-jack is used by stepping on the rear of the device with one foot, snugly inserting the heel of the other foot into the notch, and pulling one's leg upward to remove the boot. The first example of a boot-jack I encountered was made of brass and shaped like the head of a long-horn bull whose U-shaped horns formed the notch. After seeing this particular device used to remove a pair of boots, I immediately formed an accurate concept of a boot-jack. I knew that certain properties such as shape, size, and rigidity were important but that the long-horn image was superfluous and ornamental. I also immediately identified my acquisition of this concept as a

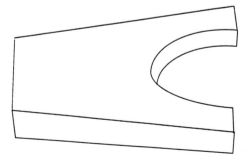

Fig. 2.   Sketch of a boot-jack.

type of explanation-based learning. Although the next example I encountered was very different, a simple piece of wood with the shape shown in Fig. 2, I was able to quickly and accurately classify it as an example of the same concept.

III. Combining Theory and Data

Empirical learning models have been criticized for ignoring the importance of existing knowledge, failing to account for the "coherence" of concepts, being susceptible to spurious correlations, and requiring too many training examples and intractable computational resources (Mitchell et al., 1986; Murphy & Medin, 1985; Schank, Collins, & Hunter, 1986). Explanation-based models have been criticized for requiring a complete, correct, and tractable domain theory, only learning deductive consequences of existing knowledge, and only increasing speed of processing rather than capability (Dietterich, 1986; Mitchell et al., 1986).

Addressing these problems usually entails integrating empirical and analytical methods. Consequently, there has been a growing interest in this subject in both machine learning and cognitive psychology. Dozens of machine learning systems that integrate theory and data have been developed over the last several years (Birnbaum & Collins, 1991; Michalski & Teccuci, 1991; Segre, 1989). There have also been a growing number of psychological experiments on the topic (Ahn & Brewer, 1988; Ahn et al., 1992; Pazzani, 1991; Wisniewski, 1989; Wisniewski & Medin, 1991).

Existing methods for integrating theory and data in learning can be divided into three broad, overlapping categories.

1. Theory as bias: The fundamental "problem of induction" is that there are multiple hypotheses consistent with any set of empirical data, where consistent means that they cover all of the positive examples while not covering any of the negative ones. Domain theories can be used to prefer certain hypotheses.
2. Theory revision: Empirical data can be used to revise domain theories that draw incorrect conclusions.
3. Theory for data interpretation: Theories can change or enhance the representation of data. For example, theories can derive abstract features from raw perceptual data.

A growing number of machine learning systems are attempting to integrate theory and data in one or more of these ways. Researchers have explored various ways of using domain theories to bias empirical learning (Cohen, 1990; Flann & Dietterich, 1989; Hirsh, 1990; Pazzani, 1991). Many of these systems employ an overly general theory that admits too many examples as members of a category, but is specific enough to constrain the hypotheses considered by induction. A number of other recent systems attempt to revise a domain theory to fit empirical data (Danyluk, 1991; Ginsberg, 1990; Rajamoney, 1990; Towell & Shavlik, 1991). However, all of these systems have important restrictions on the types of theory they can revise and the kinds of error they can correct. Finally, several systems have been developed that use theories to interpret data (Drastal, Czako, & Raatz, 1989; Michalski, 1983). These system generally use rules that derive additional features from the initial description of an example.

This article describes two recent systems and discusses their psychological relevance. Section IV discusses IOU, a system that uses a domain theory to bias induction. Section V discusses EITHER, a system that performs theory revision and uses theory for data interpretation.

IV. Induction over the Unexplained

This section describes a machine learning system that uses empirical and explanation-based methods to learn different parts of a concept definition. Many concepts have both explanatory and nonexplanatory aspects. For example, scripts for events such as a birthday party or a wedding have goal-directed as well as ritualistic actions. Concepts for artifacts such as a cup or a building have functionally important features as well as aesthetic or conventional ones. Animals have some attributes with clear survival value as well as more obscure features. Diseases have some symptoms that can be causally explained by current biological theory as well as others that are simply known to be correlated with the condition.

In IOU (Induction Over the Unexplained), explanation-based methods are used to learn the part of the concept definition that can be explained by an underlying domain theory. Empirical methods are used to learn the part of the concept definition consisting of unexplained regularities in the examples. First, IOU uses an existing domain theory to explain each example. It then extracts their explainable features as part of the concept definition. Explainable features are then removed from the examples and the reduced example descriptions are passed to a standard empirical learning system. This system finds additional commonalities which are added to the final concept definition. A test example must meet the requirements of the domain theory as well as the empirically learned definition in order to be considered a member of the concept. IOU uses its domain theory as a bias to prefer certain consistent concept definitions over others. In particular, the system prefers to include features that can be explained as relevant to the function or purpose of the concept. IOU can also be viewed as using theory to interpret and modify data, since it removes explained features and performs induction using only the unexplainable features of the examples.

A. IOU PROBLEM AND ALGORITHM

The general problem IOU addresses is *theory-based concept specialization* as defined by Flann & Dietterich (1989). The system is assumed to have a domain theory for a generalization of the concept to be learned. A definition of the specific problem addressed by IOU is as follows:

> Given:
> 1. A set of positive and negative examples of an intended concept, C_i
> 2. A propositional Horn-clause domain theory for an explainable concept C_e that is a generalization of the intended concept, i.e., $C_i \rightarrow C_e$
>
> Determine:
>
> A definition for the intended concept in terms of observable features that is consistent with the examples and a specialization of the explainable concept.

The current implementation of IOU employs a feature-based description language that includes binary, discrete, and real-valued attributes. A domain theory is restricted to a set of propositional Horn clauses. A propositional Horn clause is a rule of the form A_1 & A_2 & . . . $A_n \rightarrow C$, where all A_i and C are propositions. Propositions include feature value pairs (*color = red*), numerical thresholds (*length < 3*), and binary propositions (*has-handle*).

As an example of a problem suitable for IOU, consider a slight variation of the cup example introduced earlier. The standard functional definition is more accurately considered a definition of a drinking vessel rather than a cup since it cannot actually distinguish between cups, glasses, mugs, shot glasses, and so on. Therefore, assume that the overly general explainable concept is *drinking-vessel,* defined as:

> stable & liftable & open-vessel → drinking-vessel

Assume that the examples available are those shown in Fig. 3. The problem is to use the domain theory to learn the explainable features of a cup

	cup-1 (+)	cup-2 (+)	shot-glass-1 (-)	mug-1 (-)	can-1 (-)
has-bottom	true	true	true	true	true
flat-bottom	true	true	true	true	true
has-concavity	true	true	true	true	true
upward-pointing	true	true	true	true	true
lightweight	true	true	true	true	true
has-handle	true	false	false	true	false
width	small	small	small	medium	small
insulating	false	true	true	false	false
color	white	red	white	copper	silver
volume	small	small	tiny	large	small
shape	cylinder	cylinder	cylinder	cylinder	cylinder

Fig. 3. Examples for learning *cup*.

(*flat-bottom, has-concavity*, etc.) and to use empirical techniques to learn the nonexplanatory features (*volume = small*) that rule out shot glasses and mugs.

The basic IOU algorithm follows:

1. Using the domain theory, show that each of the positive examples is a member of the explainable concept and generalize them using explanation-based learning.
2. Disjunctively combine the resulting generalizations to form the explanatory part of the the definition, D_e.
3. Discard any negative examples that do not satisfy this explanatory component.
4. Remove the explainable features in D_e from the descriptions of the remaining examples.
5. Give the "reduced" set of examples to a standard empirical learning system to compute the unexplainable component of the definition, D_u.
6. Output: D_e & D_u as the final concept description.

Step 1 uses standard explanation-based techniques to generalize each of the positive examples. The explanation of *cup-1* is the same as that shown in Fig. 1, except the goal concept is *drinking-vessel* instead of *cup*. The explanation of *cup-2* differs only in how it is shown to be *graspable*. The resulting explanation-based generalizations are:

cup-1: has-bottom & flat-bottom & has-handle & lightweight & has-concavity & upward-pointing-concavity
cup-2: has-bottom & flat-bottom & width = small & insulating & lightweight & has-concavity & upward-pointing-concavity

Step 2 simply combines the explanation-based generalizations disjunctively and factors out common expressions. For the sample problem, this produces the following explanatory component:

D_e: has-bottom & flat-bottom & lightweight & has-concavity & upward-pointing-concavity & (width = small & insulating OR has-handle)

Step 3 discards negative examples that do not even satisfy the explanatory component. These negative examples are already eliminated as potential members of the intended concept and require no further consideration. In the sample problem, the negative example *can-1* can be discarded. Although it is a stable open-vessel, it is not graspable, because it is not insulating nor does it have a handle. Therefore it cannot function as a drinking vessel for hot and cold liquids.

Step 4 removes the explainable features of the remaining examples to allow the empirical component to focus on their unexplainable aspects. The resulting reduced set of data for the sample problem is shown in Fig. 4. In step 5, the unexplained data are given to a standard empirical system for learning from examples. We normally use a version of ID3 (Quinlan, 1986) as the empirical component. ID3 builds decision trees which IOU translates into a set of rules so that the final concept definition is in a uniform language. For the sample problem, ID3 generates the description *volume = small* for discriminating the cups from the shot glass and the mug. Like many rule-based induction systems, ID3 is biased toward simple, more-general descriptions, and this is the simplest description of the cups that excludes the non-cups.

However, ID3 is not a particularly good algorithm for modeling human empirical learning. Because it tries to construct a minimal discriminant description, it can fail to capture all the similarities among the positive examples. Therefore, a standard *most-specific-conjunctive* (MSC) learning algorithm (Haussler, 1988) can also be used as the empirical component of IOU. Early experiments by Bruner et al. (1956) indicated

	cup-1 (+)	cup-2 (+)	shot-glass-1 (-)	mug-1 (-)
color	white	red	white	copper
volume	small	small	tiny	large
shape	cylinder	cylinder	cylinder	cylinder

Fig. 4.   Reduced examples for learning *cup*.

that human subjects frequently use the MSC strategy (which they call *wholist*) when learning concepts from examples. This algorithm simply forms the conjunction of all feature-value pairs present in all of the positive examples. For the examples in Fig. 4, this method produces the description *volume = small* & *shape = cylinder*.

The final step of IOU simply combines the explanatory and nonexplanatory components into a final concept definition. This produces the following definition for *cup:*

> has-bottom & flat-bottom & lightweight & has-concavity & upward-pointing-concavity & (width = small & insulating OR has-handle) & volume = small & shape = cylinder → cup

IOU actually maintains the explanatory and nonexplanatory components separately in order to allow them to be treated differently during classification (see Section IV,B,2).

It is informative to compare IOU's results on this simple problem to those of purely empirical learning systems. When ID3 is run by itself on the data in Fig. 3, the extra example *can-1* causes *color* to be the most informative feature, and the system produces the following rule:

> color = red OR (color = white & has-handle) → cup

ID3 would clearly need many more examples to learn the correct concept. Applying the MSC algorithm to the examples in Fig. 3 generates the description:

> has-bottom & flat-bottom & lightweight & has-concavity & upward-pointing-concavity & width = small & volume = small & shape = cylinder → cup

This description is inconsistent with the training data since it still covers the negative example *can-1*. This is because the correct definition of the concept requires disjunction (i.e., there are no necessary and sufficient conditions). IOU uses the domain theory to learn the disjunctive portion of the concept, specifically, the two alternative ways to achieve graspability. Mooney (1993) presents additional theoretical and experimental evidence that IOU learns more accurate concepts from fewer examples than pure empirical learning methods.

In its current implementation, IOU is a *batch* learning system and processes all the training examples at once. However, the basic algorithm is easily made incremental if the empirical learner is itself incremental. The explanatory part of the definition can be assembled incrementally by disjunctively adding the explanation-based generalization of each new positive example. Also, each time a new example is encountered, it is either discarded as an unprovable negative example or its explainable features are removed and the remaining features are passed along to the empirical component, which incrementally forms the nonexplanatory part of the definition. For example, one could use an incremental version of ID3 (e.g. Utgoff's, 1989, ID5) or the MSC algorithm (which is naturally incremental).

B. Psychological Relevance of IOU

Although some of the ideas underlying IOU were derived from psychological results, it was not specifically designed as a model of human category learning. Nevertheless, there are two recent psychological studies that are relevant to viewing IOU as a cognitive model. First, there is an experiment by Ahn and Brewer (1988) that motivated the development of IOU by demonstrating that subjects learn explanatory and nonexplanatory aspects of a concept separately. Second, there is an experiment by Wisniewski (1989) demonstrating that subjects learn different concepts from the same examples depending on whether or not they are told the function of the categories.

1. Explanatory and Nonexplanatory Information

Some recent experiments by Ahn and Brewer (1988) were one of the original motivations behind the development of IOU. These experiments were designed to follow up previous experiments by Ahn, Mooney, Brewer, and DeJong (1987) that investigated subjects' ability to use explanation-based learning to acquire a plan schema from a single instance. The original experiments revealed that, like an explanation-based system, human subjects could acquire a general plan schema from a single specific instance described in a narrative. The follow-up experiments explored subjects' ability to learn event schemata that contain both explainable and unexplainable (conventional) aspects after receiving only a single example, and after receiving multiple examples. For instance, one of the schemata used in the experiments is the potlatch ceremony conducted by American Indian tribes of the Northwest. If one has the appropriate knowledge regarding the goals and customs of these Indians, many aspects of the potlatch ceremony can be explained in terms of a plan to increase the social status of the host. However, there are also a number of ritualistic features of the ceremony that cannot be explained in this manner.

The results of this experiment indicated that the explainable aspects of the potlatch ceremony were acquired after exposure to only a single instance, while the nonexplanatory aspects of the ceremony were only acquired after multiple instances were presented. This supports the view that people use different learning mechanisms to acquire these different aspects of a concept, as in the IOU method. Subjects were also asked to rate their confidence in their assertions that a component is a part of the general ceremony. The subjects' confidence ratings for explanatory components were significantly higher than for nonexplanatory ones after both one and two instances. Also, multiple examples increased subjects' confidence and accuracy with respect to nonexplanatory components but not with respect to explanatory ones. This suggests that, like IOU, people treat explanatory and nonexplanatory aspects of a concept differently.

2. Simulating the Effects of Functional Knowledge

This section demonstrates IOU's ability to model the specific results of some additional psychological experiments exploring the effect of background knowledge on concept learning (Wisniewski, 1989). It is important to note that IOU was not specifically designed to simulate these results, but rather the basic method was already developed when the author learned of the results of this experiment.

In Wisniewski's experiment, two groups of subjects performed a standard learning-from-examples task. Both groups received the same examples, but one group, the *function* group, was told the functions of the two categories to be discriminated and the other, the *discrimination* group, was not. For example, the function group was told that one category was used for killing bugs and the contrast category was used for wallpapering. Examples were described by a number of features. A particular feature value could be either *predictive* or *nonpredictive* of a particular category. In the training set containing 15 examples of each category, all examples containing a predictive feature value of a category were members of that category and 80% of the category members had the predictive feature value (the other 20% were missing a value for this feature). Nonpredictive feature values occurred equally often in both categories. A feature value was also *core* or *superficial*. A core feature value was relevant to a category's function, while a superficial one was not. For example, *contains poison* was a core feature value of the category whose function was *for killing bugs*, while *manufactured in Florida* was superficial. Each category contained three superficial feature values (two predictive and one nonpredictive) and two core feature values (one predictive the other nonpredictive). The superficial-nonpredictive feature value of a category was the core-nonpredictive feature value of its contrast category.

Figure 5 shows the different types of features for two contrasting categories used in the experiment. Each training example of a category contained 4 of the 5 characteristic features from this table. Each training example also had two additional features with random values. An example of a training example in the category *mornek* is:

> contains poison, contains a sticky substance, stored in a garage, manufactured in Florida, best if used in 1 year, comes in 16 oz. container

where the example is missing only one of the characteristic features of morneks (sprayed on plants) and the last two features have random values.

After learning the training data, subjects were given ten test examples of each category. Each of the ten examples of a category contained more predictive features of that category than the contrast category. *Superficial-core** test examples contained the two superficial-predictive feature values of the category and the two core feature values of the contrast category. *Core* examples contained just the core feature values of the category, while *superficial* examples contained just the superficial-predictive feature values. *Superficial-core* examples contained all of the core and superficial feature values. Each test example also had two extra random feature values. Sample test examples for the mornek category are shown in Fig. 6.

Subjects in both groups were asked to rate their confidence in the category of each test example on a scale of 1 to 7, where 1 was the most confident value for one category of the pair, and 7 was the most confident

Mornek	Plapel
Function: for killing bugs	Function: for wallpapering
sprayed on plants **C-P**	sprayed on walls **C-P**
contains poison **C-NP**	contains poison **S-NP**
contains a sticky substance **S-NP**	contains a sticky substance **C-NP**
stored in a garage **S-P**	stored in a basement **S-P**
manufactured in Florida **S-P**	manufactured in Ohio **S-P**

C-P: core predictive	**C-NP**: core non-predictive
S-P: superficial predictive	**S-NP**: superficial non-predictive

Fig. 5.   Different feature types for experimental categories.

superficial-core*	core
stored in a garage **S-P** manufactured in Florida **S-P** contains a sticky substance **C-NP*** sprayed on walls **C-P*** best if used within 1 year **R**	contains poison **C-NP** sprayed on plants **C-P** best if used within 5 years **R** came in a 32-ounce container **R**
superficial	**superficial-core**
stored in a garage **S-P** manufactured in Florida **S-P** best if used within 1 year **R** came in a 16-ounce container **R**	stored in a garage **S-P** manufactured in Florida **S-P** contains a sticky substance **S-NP** contains poison **C-NP** sprayed on plants **C-P** best if used within 1 year **R**

S-P: superficial predictive   S-NP: superficial non-predictive
C-P: core predictive   C-NP: core nonpredictive
C-P*: core predictive (of other class)   C-NP*: core nonpredictive (of other class)
R: random

Fig. 6.   Sample test items for mornek.

for the other. For example, subjects would give an example a score of 1 if they strongly believed it was a mornek, a score of 7 if they strongly believed it was a plapel, and an appropriate intermediate value if they were unsure. In general, the results demonstrated that subjects in the function group attributed more relevance to the core feature values while the discrimination group relied more heavily on superficial predictive features (see Table I). However, the function group also made some use of superficial-predictive features values, indicating they were using a combination of empirical and explanation-based techniques.

TABLE I

AVERAGE CONFIDENCE RATINGS FOR
TEST EXAMPLES

	Subjects		Simulation	
Item type	Function	Discrimination	IOU	MSC
Superficial-core*	4.00	5.02	3.79	4.60
Core	6.16	5.93	5.07	4.60
Superficial	6.04	6.36	4.86	5.20
Superficial-core	6.43	6.54	5.71	5.80

In the simulation, IOU was used to model the performance of the function group and a standard MSC empirical method was used to model the discrimination group. In both cases, the systems were given the same training and test examples as were given to the subjects. Simple intuitive domain theories were constructed for connecting core feature values to category membership. For example, IOU's overly-general theory for mornek is given below:

> contact-bugs & deadly → kills-bugs
> contains-poison → deadly
> electric-shock → deadly
> sprayed-on = plants → contact-bugs
> emits-light & location = outdoors → contact-bugs

The MSC method was also used as the empirical component of IOU. In order to accommodate missing feature values, only features that appear with different values in different positive examples are actually deleted from the MSC description. This has the same effect as replacing missing features with their most probable value given the class (Quinlan, 1986) before forming the MSC description.

Since all of the core and superficial features of a category shown in Fig. 5 are either present or missing a value in all of its examples, the MSC description of a category contains all of these characteristic features. Since the two remaining features ("best if used in" and "container size") have different random values, they are dropped from the MSC description. Since the two core features of each category are explained by the domain theory, they comprise the explanatory component of IOU's concept description. Since the superficial features of a category are either present or missing a value in all of its examples, they are all included in the MSC description of the unexplained features; however, the random features are dropped. Therefore, IOU's category descriptions also include all of the core and superficial features of the category. However, IOU separates them into explanatory and nonexplanatory components. For example, the concept description for morneks produced by both IOU and MSC is (explanatory features are capitalized):

SPRAYED-ON = PLANTS & CONTAINS-POISON & contains-sticky & stored-in = garage & manufactured-in = florida

The following equation was used to produce a confidence rating $(1 \leq C \leq 7)$ for the test examples:

$$C = 4 + 1.5 \, (M_1 - M_2)$$

M_1 and M_2 are match scores $(-1 \leq M_i \leq 1)$ for the two categories computed by examining each feature-value pair in the MSC description for the category and scoring as follows: 1 if the example had the same value, 0 if the feature was missing, and -1 if it had a conflicting value. The result was scaled by dividing by the maximum possible score. For IOU, explanatory (core) features were weighted more heavily by having them count twice as much (i.e., the match score was incremented or decremented by 2 instead of 1). This scoring technique is a simple method for obtaining a confidence rating between 0 and 7 based on the degree to which an example matches the MSC description of each of the two categories. Several other similar scoring mechanisms were tried without any significant effect on the qualitative results. The important factor is that the score is high when an example matches the description of the first category more than the second and low when an example matches the description of the second category more than the first. The qualitative results are also insensitive to the exact additional weighting assigned to the explanatory features (a weighting factor of 1.5 or 3 works as well as 2).

Table I shows both the original experimental results and the results of the simulation. Recall that each of the examples contained more predictive features of one category than the contrast category. In the table, the higher the rating, the more confident the subject or program was that a test example was a member of this more predictable category. Although the exact confidence values of the simulation do not match the subjects, all the important differences mentioned by Wisniewski (1989) are present. For the superficial-core* items, the IOU (function) scores are lower than the MSC (discrimination) scores. Although these items have the superficial features of the more predictable category, they have the core features of the contrast category, causing the function group (and IOU) to rate them lower. IOU (function group) scores the core items higher than the superficial items, while MSC (discrimination group) scores the superficial items higher than the core items. Finally, the IOU (function) scores are lower than the MSC (discrimination) scores for the superficial items but higher for the core items.

All of these correctly modeled effects stem from IOU's separation of concepts into explanatory and nonexplanatory components and its scoring procedure that weights the explanatory features more heavily. Since IOU is unique among current integrated machine learning systems in separating its concepts into explanatory and nonexplanatory components, it seems clear that other existing systems would be unable to model these results. However, the effects are not particularly dependent on the specific details of the IOU algorithm; and therefore other methods that include both explanatory and nonexplanatory features in their concepts and weight the former more heavily may also be able to model these results.

V. Theory Revision in EITHER

IOU uses a theory to bias induction but it cannot modify a theory to account for anomalous empirical data. EITHER (Explanation-based and Inductive THeory Extension and Revision) is a more recent system that can actually revise an existing domain theory to fit a set of data. As revealed by explanation-based learning, category knowledge is frequently best viewed as a complex set of interacting rules (a domain theory) rather than a simple set of features, conditional probabilities, or exemplars. Some of these rules may have been learned from direct instruction, and others may have been induced from examples of previously learned concepts. In any case, learning a new concept can involve using empirical data to revise an existing domain theory by modifying, adding, or deleting rules.

EITHER is a complicated system that has evolved over several years of research. In this article, I only have space to present an overview of the basic system. However, it should be noted that EITHER has already successfully revised two real-world rule-bases. One of these identifies biologically important DNA sequences called "promoters" and the other diagnoses diseased soybean plants. Interested readers are referred to Ourston and Mooney (1990) and Mooney and Ourston (1991b) for more details.

A. THE THEORY REVISION PROBLEM

EITHER combines explanation-based and empirical methods to provide a focused correction to an imperfect domain theory. The explanation-based part of the system identifies the failing parts of the theory and constrains the examples used for induction. The empirical part of the system determines specific corrections to failing rules that renders them consistent with the empirical data. The problem addressed by EITHER is more precisely defined as follows:

Given:
1. A set of positive and negative examples of a concept each described by a set of observable features
2. An imperfect propositional Horn-clause domain theory for the concept

Determine:

A minimally revised version of the domain theory that is consistent with the examples.

It is difficult to precisely define the term *minimal* used to characterize the revision to be produced. Since it is assumed that the original theory is approximately correct, the goal is to change it as little as possible. Syntactic measures such as the total number of symbols added or deleted are reasonable criteria. EITHER uses various heuristic methods to help insure that its revisions are minimal in this sense.

A domain theory can be incorrect in various ways. Figure 7 shows a taxonomy of incorrect theories. At the top level, theories can be incorrect because they are either overly general or overly specific. An overly general theory entails membership for some examples that are not members of a category. One way a theory can be overly general is when rules lack required antecedents, providing proofs for examples that should have been excluded. Another way a theory can be overly general is when a completely incorrect rule is present. By contrast, an overly specific theory fails to entail membership for some examples of a category. This can occur because the theory is missing a rule which is required in the proof of concept membership, or because existing rules have additional antecedents that exclude concept members. Consequently, incorrectly classi-

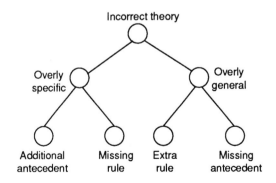

Fig. 7.   Taxonomy of incorrect theories.

fied examples can be of two types. A *failing positive* refers to an example that is not provable as a member of its own category. This indicates a need for generalizing the theory by adding rules or deleting antecedents. A *failing negative* refers to an example that is provable as a member of a category other than its own. This indicates a need to specialize a theory by adding antecedents or deleting rules.

As a concrete example, consider various errors that might occur in the theory for *cup* (*drinking-vessel*) introduced in Section II. Assume the set of training examples is shown in Fig. 8. These examples differ only in graspability. If the theory is missing the rule *has-handle* → *graspable*, then *cup-2* and *cup-3* can no longer be shown to be cups and are therefore failing positives, indicating that the theory needs to be generalized. If the theory is missing the antecedent *width = small* from the rule *width = small & insulating* → *graspable*, then *bowl-1* and *bowl-2* can be incorrectly shown to be cups and are therefore failing negatives, indicating that the theory needs to be specialized. If the theory has both of these faults, then *cup-2* is a failing positive and *bowl-1* and *bowl-2* are failing negatives. In this case, *cup-3* is no longer a failing positive since the overly general rule *insulating* → *graspable* can now be used to prove it is *graspable*. Given the examples in Fig. 8, EITHER can revise the theory to correct for either or both of these faults.

B. OVERVIEW OF THE THEORY REVISION ALGORITHM

This section reviews EITHER's basic revision method, which integrates deductive, abductive, and inductive reasoning, where abduction refers to the process of finding sets of assumptions that allow an observation to be explained (Charniak & McDermott, 1985). The system's top-level archi-

	cup-1 (+)	cup-2 (+)	cup-3 (+)	can-1 (-)	bowl-1 (-)	bowl-2 (-)
has-bottom	true	true	true	true	true	true
flat-bottom	true	true	true	true	true	true
has-concavity	true	true	true	true	true	true
upward-pointing	true	true	true	true	true	true
lightweight	true	true	true	true	true	true
has-handle	false	true	true	false	false	false
width	small	medium	medium	small	medium	medium
insulating	true	false	true	false	true	true
color	red	blue	tan	gray	red	blue
volume	small	small	small	small	small	large
shape	round	round	cylinder	cylinder	round	round

Fig. 8.   Examples for theory revision.

tecture is shown in Fig. 9. EITHER first attempts to fix failing positives by removing or generalizing antecedents and to fix failing negatives by removing rules or specializing antecedents, since these are simpler and less powerful operations. Only if these operations fail does the system resort to the more powerful technique of using induction to learn new rules to fix failing positives, and to learn new antecedents to add to existing rules to fix failing negatives.

EITHER initially uses deduction to identify failing positives and negatives among the training examples. It uses the proofs generated by deduction to find a near-minimal set of rule retractions that would correct all the failing negatives. During the course of the correction, deduction is also used to assess proposed changes to the theory as part of the generalization and specialization processes.

EITHER uses abduction to initially find the incorrect part of an overly-specific theory. In EITHER, abduction identifies sets of assumptions that allow a failing positive to become provable. These assumptions identify rule antecedents (called *conflicting antecedents*) that, if deleted, would properly generalize the theory and correct the failing positive. EITHER uses

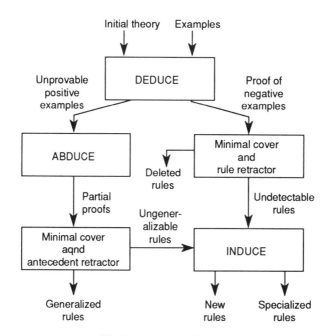

Fig. 9. EITHER architecture.

the output of abduction to find a near-minimum set of conflicting antecedents whose removal would correct all the failing positives.

If rule and antecedent retraction are insufficient, induction is used to learn new rules or to determine additional antecedents to add to existing rules. EITHER uses the output of abduction and deduction to determine an appropriately labeled subset of the training examples to pass to induction in order to form a consistent correction. EITHER currently uses a version of ID3 (Quinlan, 1986) as its inductive component. As in IOU, the decision trees returned by ID3 are translated into equivalent rules. The remaining components of the EITHER system constitute generalization and specialization control algorithms, which identify and specify the types of correction to be made to the theory.

As an example of the generalization process, consider missing the *has-handle* rule from the theory for cups. This results in *cup-2* and *cup-3* becoming failing positives. These examples are almost provable as cups except they cannot be shown to be *graspable*. Consequently, EITHER first focuses on the remaining rule for *graspable* and attempts to retract the antecedent *width = small* in order to make the failing positives provable. However, this over-generalizes and results in *bowl-1* and *bowl-2* becoming failing negatives. Consequently, the system uses *cup-2* and *cup-3* as positive examples and *bowl-1* and *bowl-2* as negative examples to induce a new rule for *graspable*. Since the single feature *has-handle* distinguishes these examples, ID3 induces the correct rule: *has-handle → graspable*.

As an example of the specialization process, consider missing the antecedent *width = small* from the rule *width = small & insulating → graspable*. EITHER first attempts to retract the resulting overly general rule: *insulating → graspable*, in order to remove the faulty proofs of the failing negatives, *bowl-1* and *bowl-2*. The system focuses on this rule because its removal eliminates the faulty proofs of the failing negatives while minimizing the number of failing positives created in the process. Since retracting this rule does create one failing positive (*cup-1*), the system decides it needs to specialize the rule by adding antecedents. Consequently, the system uses *cup-1* as a positive example and *bowl-1* and *bowl-2* as negative examples and passes them to ID3. Since the value of the single feature *width* distinguishes these examples, ID3 finds the correct missing antecedent *width = small* and adds it to the overly general rule for *graspable*.

C. Theory for Data Interpretation

EITHER also uses its theory to augment the representation of examples prior to passing them to induction. Using a process frequently referred to as *constructive induction* (Drastal et al., 1989; Michalski, 1983; Mooney &

Ourston, 1991a), the domain theory is used to deduce higher-level features from the observable features describing the examples. Specifically, when using induction to learn a new rule or to determine which antecedents to add to an existing rule, forward deduction is used to identify the truth values of all *intermediate concepts* for each of the failing examples. An intermediate concept is any term in a domain theory that is neither an observable feature used to describe examples nor a category into which examples are to be eventually classified.

Intermediate concepts that can be deduced are then fed to the inductive learner as additional features. If the truth value of an intermediate concept is highly correlated with the class of the failing examples, then it is likely to be used by the inductive learner. For example, assume that the cup theory is missing the rule for *liftable* but is otherwise correct. Performing forward deduction on the failing positives (all the cup examples in this case) will always add the feature *graspable*, since all cups are graspable. Therefore, the description of the positive examples is augmented with the higher-level feature *graspable* prior to being used for induction. In other words, the existing theory is used to interpret and redescribe the examples. Since the added *graspable* feature helps to discriminate between the positive and negative examples of *liftable*, it is very likely to be used by the empirical learner. Consequently, when the rule for *liftable* is removed from the theory, EITHER usually relearns the correct rule (*graspable* & *lightweight* → *liftable*) after 20 random training examples.

As another example of this process, assume the cup theory is missing the top-level rule: *stable* & *liftable* & *open-vessel* → *cup,* but is otherwise correct. In this case, forward deduction adds the features *stable, liftable,* and *open-vessel* to each of the positive examples. These high-level features can then be used by the inductive subsystem to help discriminate the positive and negative examples. Consequently, when the *cup* rule is removed from the theory, EITHER usually relearns the correct rule after about 30 random training examples. If the theory is not used to interpret the data, then 80 examples are usually required to learn the correct definition of CUP directly in terms of observable features.

D. PSYCHOLOGICAL RELEVANCE OF EITHER

Like IOU, EITHER was not specifically designed to model human category learning; however, many of its basic goals and methods have some psychological relevance. In particular, Wisniewski and Medin (1991) report some relevant psychological results on theory revision and data interpretation. Their experiments studied subjects learning to categorize children's drawings of a person. Some of the drawings used in the experiments are shown in Fig. 10. The methodology is a basic learning-from-examples paradigm, except that one group of subjects, the *standard* group, were given meaningless category names while subjects in the *theory* group were given meaningful names such as "drawings by high–IQ children" versus "drawings by low–IQ children" or "drawings by farm children" versus "drawings by city children." Subjects in both groups were asked to write down a rule for each category that someone else could use to accurately categorize the drawings.

One aspect of the subjects' rules that Wisniewski and Medin analyzed was the degree of abstraction. They divided rules into the following three types:

1. Concrete: Consisting of simple features that are easily observable, e.g., "buttons or stripes on their shirts and dark, thick hair."
2. Abstract: Consisting of features that are more complex, higher level, or less perceptual, e.g., "look more normal."
3. Linked: Consisting of connected abstract and concrete features, e.g., "added more detail such as teeth."

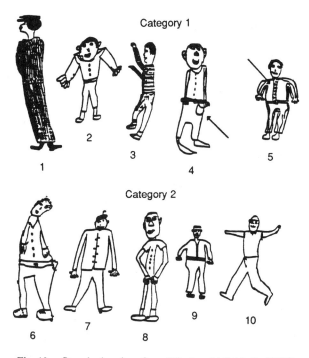

Fig. 10.   Sample drawings from Wisniewski & Medin (1991).

They found that subjects in the theory group produced more abstract and linked rules compared to the standard group. The specific results are shown in Table II. These results are nicely explained by the hypothesis that subjects in the theory group are using their background theories to interpret the data. Like EITHER adding *graspable* to its description of a cup, they are inferring abstract features and adding them to the data before inducing a rule. Linked rules occur because the subjects are also writing down the concrete features from which their abstract features were derived.

Wisniewski and Medin also note that subjects given different meaningful labels for categories extract different high-level features from the drawings. A subject told that the drawings in Category 1 of Fig. 10 were drawn by creative children interpreted the part of drawing 5 indicated by the arrow as "buttons." The subject mentioned this feature as evidence for detail, which implied creativity. On the other hand, a subject told that this figure was drawn by a city child interpreted it as a "tie." This subject mentioned the feature as evidence that the person was a business-person, implying it was drawn by a city person. This phenomenon is nicely explained by the hypothesis that different category labels "activate" different domain theories and therefore result in different abstract features being derived from the perceptual data.

Wisniewski and Medin also found evidence for theory revision in their results. Based on the data, subjects would sometimes change their definition of an abstract feature. In one particular case, a subject mentioned that a drawing depicted detailed clothing and therefore must have been drawn by a creative child. When told that the drawing was done by a noncreative child, they changed their definition for what counted as "detail." This is similar to EITHER altering its definition of *graspable* after misclassifying some examples or counter-examples of cups. In another case, a subject initially stated that a drawing was done by a city child because "it looks very detailed, has colored-in places." When told that it was actually drawn

TABLE II

FREQUENCY OF RULE TYPES

	Standard group (%)	Theory group (%)
Concrete rules	81	35
Abstract rules	16	37
Linked rules	3	28

by a farm child, the subject specialized his/her rule *detail* → *city-child* by adding a constraint induced from the data. Specifically, the person stated that "drawings with detail in specific clothing is more of a rule for city kids—not detail in body movement as this one had."

VI. Conclusions

Recent results in both machine learning and cognitive psychology demonstrate that effective category learning involves an integration of theory and data. Theories can bias induction and alter the representation of data, and conflicting data can result in theory revision. This paper has reviewed two recent machine learning systems that attempt to integrate theory and data. IOU uses a domain theory to acquire part of a concept definition and to focus induction on the unexplained aspects of the data. EITHER uses data to revise an imperfect theory and uses theory to add abstract features to the data. Recent psychological experiments reveal that subjects perform many of the same operations as these machine learning systems. Like IOU, people separate category definitions into explanatory and nonexplanatory components, acquire explanatory components earlier, and have more confidence in explanatory aspects. Like EITHER, people use background theories to derive abstract features from the data, and revise portions of their theories to account for conflicting data.

Nevertheless, in many ways, current machine learning systems are not nearly as adept as people at integrating theory and data in learning. Particular areas requiring further research concern revising probabilistic and relational theories. Most current integrated learning systems are restricted to theories expressed in propositional logic. Consequently, they are incapable of reasoning about their confidence in their theories and conclusions, and cannot handle complex, relational descriptions that require the expressive power of first-order predicate logic. These areas of machine learning are just beginning to be explored (Fu, 1989; Pazzani, Brunk & Silverstein, 1991; Richards & Mooney, 1991). In general, the interaction between theory and data in learning has just begun to be investigated.

From a machine-learning perspective, methods for integrating theory and data in learning can greatly improve the development of intelligent systems. Standard methods for building knowledge bases by interviewing experts are laborious and error-prone. Standard machine learning methods for learning from examples are also inadequate since one rarely has enough data to induce a complete and correct knowledge base from scratch. In addition, machine-induced knowledge fails to make use of existing human concepts and is therefore frequently unable to provide comprehensible explanations for the conclusions it warrants. Theory revision, on the other hand, allows a system to accept an incomplete, approximate knowledge base and refine it through experience. People acquire expertise through a combination of abstract instruction and experience with specific cases, and machine learning systems that integrate theory and data are trying to successfully emulate this approach.

From a psychological perspective, methods for integrating theory and data can hopefully improve our understanding of human category learning. Artificial learning problems that minimize the role of prior knowledge are not representative of the categorization problems that people confront every day. Machine learning algorithms that can simulate psychological data on the effect of prior knowledge on learning can provide valuable insight into how people learn in more natural settings. In turn, understanding the specific ways in which theory and data interact in human learning can hopefully lead to the development of more effective educational methods for combining the presentation of abstract rules and principles with concrete examples.

ACKNOWLEDGMENTS

I would like to thank the editors for their helpful comments on the initial draft of this article. This research was supported by the NASA Ames Research Center under grant NCC 2-629, by the National Science Foundation under grant IRI-9102926, and by a grant from the Texas Advanced Research Program.

REFERENCES

Aha, D. W., Kibler, D., & Albert, M. K. (1991). Instance-based learning algorithms. *Machine Learning, 6,* 37–66.

Ahn, W., & Brewer, W. F. (1988). Similarity-based and explanation-based learning of explanatory and nonexplanatory information. In *Proceedings of the tenth annual conference of the Cognitive Science Society* (pp. 524–530). Hillsdale, NJ: Erlbaum.

Ahn, W., Brewer, W. F., & Mooney, R. J. (1992). Schema acquisition from a single example. *Journal of Experimental Psychology: Learning, Memory, and Cognition, 18,* 391–412.

Ahn, W., Mooney, R. J., Brewer, W. F., & DeJong, G. F. (1987). Schema acquisition from one example: Psychological evidence for explanation-based learning. In *Proceedings of the ninth annual conference of the Cognitive Science Society* (pp. 50–57). Hillsdale, NJ: Erlbaum.

Barsalou, L. W. (1983). Ad hoc categories. *Memory and Cognition, 11,* 211–227.

Birnbaum, L. A., & Collins, G. C. (Eds.) (1991). Learning from theory and data. Section of *Proceedings of the eighth international workshop on machine learning* (pp. 475–573). San Mateo, CA: Morgan Kaufman.

Brooks, L. (1978). Nonanalytic concept formation and memory for instances. In E. Rosch & B. B. Loyd (Eds.), *Cognition and categorization* (pp. 169–211). Hillsdale, NJ: Erlbaum.

Bruner, J. S., Goodnow, J., & Austin, G. A. (1956). *A study in thinking*. New York: Wiley.

Cohen, W. W. (1990). Learning from textbook knowledge: A case study. In *Proceedings of the eighth national conference on artificial intelligence* (pp. 743–748). Cambridge, MA: MIT Press.

Charniak, E., & McDermott, D. (1985). *Introduction to artificial intelligence*. Reading, MA: Addison Wesley.

Danyluk, A. P. (1991). Gemini: An integration of explanation-based and empirical learning. In *Proceedings of the first international workshop on multistrategy learning* (pp. 191–206). Fairfax, VA: George Mason University.

DeJong, G. F. (1988). An introduction to explanation-based learning. In H. Shrobe (Ed.), *Exploring artificial intelligence* (pp. 45–81). San Mateo, CA: Morgan Kaufman.

DeJong, G. F., & Mooney, R. J. (1986). Explanation-based learning: An alternative view. *Machine Learning, 1*, 145–176.

Dietterich, T. (1986). Learning at the knowledge level. *Machine Learning, 1*, 287–316.

Drastal, G., Czako, G., & Raatz, S. (1989). Induction in an abstraction space: A form of constructive induction. In *Proceedings of the eleventh international joint conference on artificial intelligence* (pp. 708–712). San Mateo, CA: Morgan Kaufman.

Fisher, D. H. (1987). Knowledge acquisition via incremental conceptual clustering. *Machine Learning, 2*, 139–172.

Flann, N. S., & Dietterich, T. G. (1989). A study of explanation-based methods for inductive learning. *Machine Learning, 4*, 187–226.

Fu, L. (1989). Integration of neural heuristics into knowledge-based inference. *Connection Science, 1*, 325–339.

Ginsberg, A. (1990). Theory reduction, theory revision, and retranslation. In *Proceedings of the eighth national conference on artificial intelligence* (pp. 743–748). Cambridge, MA: MIT Press.

Haussler, D. (1988). Quantifying inductive bias: Artificial intelligence algorithms and Valiant's learning framework. *Artificial Intelligence, 36*, 177–221.

Hirsh, H. (1990). *Incremental version space merging: A general framework for concept learning*. Hingham, MA: Kluwer.

Medin, D. L., & Schaffer, M. M. (1978). Context theory of classification learning. *Psychological Review, 85*, 207–238.

Medin, D. L., Wattenmaker, W. D., & Michalski, R. S. (1987). Constraints and preferences in inductive learning: An experimental study of human and machine performance. *Cognitive Science, 11*, 299–239.

Michalski, R. S. (1983). A theory and methodology of inductive learning. In R. S. Michalski, J. G. Carbonell, & T. M. Mitchell (Eds.), *Machine learning: An artificial intelligence approach* (pp. 83–134). Palo Alto, CA: Tioga.

Michalski, R. S., & Chilausky, R. L. (1980). Learning by being told and learning from examples: An experimental comparison of the two methods of knowledge acquisition in the context of developing an expert system for soybean disease diagnosis. *Policy Analysis and Information Systems, 4*, 125–160.

Michalski, R. S., & Teccuci, G. (Eds.) (1991). In *Proceedings of the first international workshop on multistrategy learning*. Fairfax, VA: George Mason University.

Mitchell, T. M., Keller, R., & Kedar-Cabelli, S. (1986). Explanation-based generalization: A unifying view. *Machine Learning, 1*, 47–80.

Mooney, R. J. (1993). Induction over the unexplained: Using overly-general domain theories to aid concept learning. *Machine Learning, 10*, 79–110.

Mooney, R. J., & Ourston, D. (1991a). Constructive induction in theory refinement. In

Proceedings of the eighth international workshop on machine learning (pp. 178–182). San Mateo, CA: Morgan Kaufman.

Mooney, R. J., & Ourston, D. (1991b). A multi-strategy approach to theory refinement. In *Proceedings of the first international workshop on multistrategy learning* (pp. 115–130). Fairfax, VA: George Mason University.

Murphy, G. L., & Medin, D. L. (1985). The role of theories in conceptual coherence. *Psychological Review, 92,* 289–316.

Nakamura, G. V. (1985). Knowledge-based classification of ill-defined categories. *Memory and Cognition, 13,* 377–84.

Nosofsky, R. M. (1984). Choice, similarity, and the context theory of classification. *Journal of Experimental Psychology: Learning, Memory, and Cognition, 10,* 104–114.

Ourston, D., & Mooney, R. (1990). Changing the rules: A comprehensive approach to theory refinement. In *Proceedings of the eighth national conference on artificial intelligence* (pp. 815–820). Cambridge, MA: MIT Press.

Pazzani, M. J. (1991). Influence of prior knowledge on concept acquisition: Experimental and computational results. In *Journal of Experimental Psychology: Learning, Memory, and Cognition, 17,* 416–432.

Pazzani, M. J., Brunk, C., & Silverstein, G. (1991). A knowledge-intensive approach to learning relational concepts. In *Proceedings of the eighth international workshop on machine learning* (pp. 432–436). San Mateo, CA: Morgan Kaufman.

Posner, M. I., & Keele, S. W. (1968). On the genesis of abstract ideas. *Journal of Experimental Psychology, 77,* 353–363.

Quinlan, J. R. (1979). Discovering rules from large collections of examples: A case study. In D. Michie (Ed.), *Expert systems in the microelectronic age.* Edinburgh: Edinburgh University Press.

Quinlan, J. R. (1986). Induction of decision trees. *Machine Learning, 1,* 81–106.

Reed, S. K. (1972). Pattern recognition and categorization. *Cognitive Psychology, 3,* 382–407.

Rajamoney, S. A. (1990). A computational approach to theory revision. In J. Shrager and P. Langley (Eds.), *Computational models of scientific discovery and theory formation* (pp. 225–254). San Mateo, CA: Morgan Kaufman.

Richards, B. L., & Mooney, R. J. (1991). First order theory revision. In *Proceedings of the eighth international workshop on machine learning* (pp. 447–451). San Mateo, CA: Morgan Kaufman.

Rosch, E., Mervis, C. B., Gray, W. D., Johnson, D. M., & Boyes-Braem, P. (1976). Basic objects in natural categories. *Cognitive Psychology, 8,* 382–439.

Rosenblatt, F. (1962). *Principles of neurodynamics and the theory of brain mechanisms.* Washington, D.C.: Spartan Books.

Schank, R. C., Collins, G. C., & Hunter, L. E. (1986). Transcending inductive category formation in learning. *Behavioral and Brain Sciences, 9,* 639–686.

Segre, A. M. (Ed.) (1989). Combining empirical and explanation-based learning. Section of *Proceedings of the sixth international workshop on machine learning* (pp. 2–92). San Mateo, CA: Morgan Kaufman.

Smith, E. E., & Medin, D. L. (1981). *Categories and Concepts.* Cambridge, MA: Harvard University Press.

Towell, G. G., & Shavlik, J. W. (1991). Refining symbolic knowledge using neural networks. In *Proceedings of the first international workshop on multistrategy learning* (pp. 257–272). Fairfax, VA: George Mason University.

Utgoff, P. E. (1989). Incremental induction of decision trees. *Machine Learning, 4,* 161–186.

Wattenmaker, W. D., Dewey, G. I., Murphy, T. D., & Medin, D. L. (1986). Linear separability and concept learning: Context, relational properties, and concept naturalness. *Cognitive Psychology, 18,* 158–194.

Winston, P. H., Binford, T. O., Katz, B., & Lowry, M. (1983). Learning physical descriptions from functional definitions, examples, and precedents. *Proceedings of the third national conference on artificial intelligence* (pp. 433–439). San Mateo, CA: Morgan Kaufman.

Wisniewski, E. J. (1989). Learning from examples: The effect of different conceptual roles. In *Proceedings of the eleventh annual conference of the Cognitive Science Society* (pp. 980–986). Hillsdale, NJ: Earlbaum.

Wisniewski, E. J., & Medin, D. L. (1991). Harpoons and long sticks: The interaction of theory and similarity in rule induction. In D. H. Fisher, M. J. Pazzani, & P. Langley (Eds.), *Concept formation: Knowledge and experience in unsupervised learning* (pp. 237–278). San Mateo, CA: Morgan Kaufman.

CATEGORIZATION, CONCEPT LEARNING, AND PROBLEM-SOLVING: A UNIFYING VIEW

Douglas Fisher
Jungsoon Park Yoo

I. Introduction

Categorization and problem-solving are widely studied in psychology and artificial intelligence (AI), but these areas of research have been largely segregated. Several articles in this volume seek to rectify this situation by discussing relationships between categorization and problem-solving and the memory structures that support them (Brewer, this volume). We address these issues as well, albeit with considerable attention to learning issues as well. In particular, this chapter views categorization as an integral aspect of problem-solving: schemas are organized by well-known principles of category structure, problems are categorized in a manner that suggests schemas appropriate to their solution, and the transition from novice to expert problem-solving can be understood as largely a process of concept learning.

Our discussion draws from AI and cognitive psychology, which have followed parallel paths on a number of issues. Notably, both AI methods and psychological models of categorization and concept learning have explored the utility of probabilistic concept representations (Bareiss & Slator, this volume; Fisher & Pazaani, 1991; Malt, this volume; McDonald, this volume; Smith & Medin, 1981; Taraban & Palacios, this volume), and the relative roles of prior knowledge and observational data on concept learning and categorization (Mooney, this volume; Mumma, this volume; Murphy, this volume; Ward, this volume, Wisnewski & Medin, 1991). In general, psychology and AI have have much to say to one another. The common wisdom is that psychology provides a *specification* of intelligence, and AI provides tools for implementing this specification. However, the relationship should go beyond this loose coupling of disciplines. AI models of human intelligence should make predictions about currently unexplored or debated phenomena, thus suggesting areas for further psychological study. Without explicit attention to this feedback loop, the interaction between AI and psychology is of debatable utility.

This article illustrates the synergism between categorization and problem-solving, and between psychology and AI, using a computer model called EXOR (Yoo & Fisher, 1991a, 1991b). This system categorizes a problem using a *knowledge base* of previously experienced problems and their solutions. The solutions to problems found through categorization are reused in the solution to the new problem. Once solved, this new problem and its solution are added to the memory of experiences for future use. The principles underlying EXOR derive from a computer-implemented model of categorization called COBWEB (Fisher, 1987b), which traces its ancestry to EPAM (Feigenbaum, 1961) and other hierarchical categorization models (Kolodner, 1983). We begin by briefly describing COBWEB to better convey its principles as realized in EXOR and to highlight the commonality and differences between categorization models of object memory and problem-solving more generally.

II.   Concept Learning and Categorization

Concept learning is a major area of study in machine learning and cognitive psychology. The concept learning task requires a learner to discover concepts (i.e., rules) that adequately describe observations. For example, the learner may learn rules that distinguish patients with hypothyroid, hyperthyroid, and other thyroid conditions from patients that are healthy. This is an example of a *supervised* learning task, in which observations are labeled by category names; the learner's task is to characterize the commonalities between members of the same category and differences between contrast categories.

In contrast, an *unsupervised* task requires the learner to discover category structure in initially unclassified data. Experimental tasks like *sorting* are unsupervised in this sense, and a number of psychological models and computer implementations have been developed. EPAM (Feigenbaum, 1961; Richman, 1991) is an early computer-implemented cognitive model of unsupervised learning. It assumes that a hierarchical memory is gradually constructed by finding features that discriminate new observations from previous ones. EPAM is a learning model of human object *recognition,* that identifies objects that have been previously observed. However, this recognition process is mediated by generalized categories that are represented by nodes in an evolving categorization hierarchy. A more recent model of unsupervised learning has been developed by Anderson (Anderson, 1990; Anderson & Matessa, 1991), which attempts to discover the "most probable" categories in the data using a Bayesian probability approach.

EPAM and Anderson's approach differ in many ways, but both gradually construct categorization trees over a stream of unclassified observations. This process has been termed *concept formation,* and many other models in this paradigm have been developed (Fisher & Pazzani, 1991). This section describes one such system, COBWEB (Fisher, 1987b).

A. COBWEB: A CONCEPT LEARNING SYSTEM

Unsupervised tasks require the learner to find categories in data. However, there are a vast number of ways to group observations into contrast categories. Clearly, most of these possibilities are not informative to a learner. To ferret out the informative categorizations, an unsupervised system relies on a measure of category quality and a method of searching through the possibilities for the categorization that optimizes (or is satisfactory by) this measure. Corter and Gluck (1992) suggest that certain categories are preferred because they best facilitate predictions about observations in the environment. If observations are represented as sets of features V_j, then Corter and Gluck's measure of *category utility* (CU) can be partially described as a tradeoff between the *expected* number of features that can be correctly predicted about a member of a category C_k and the proportion of the environment $P(C_k)$ to which those predictions apply:

$$P(C_k)E(\text{no. of correctly predicted } V_j | C_k)$$

For example, little can be predicted about a highly general category like 'animals', but those features that can be predicted (e.g., 'animate') apply to a large population. In contrast, many features can be predicted with near certainty about highly specific categories like 'robins', but these predictions are true of a relatively small population. Intuitively, a category of intermediate generality such as 'birds' maximizes the tradeoff between the expected number of accurate predictions and the scope of their application.

The expectation can be further formalized by assuming that predictions will be generated by a *probability matching* strategy: one can predict a feature with probability $P(V_j|C_k)$, and this prediction will be correct with the same probability. Thus,

$$E(\text{no. of correctly predicted } V_j|C_k) = \sum_j P(V_j|C_k)^2$$

Gluck and Corter (1985) define CU as the *increase* in the expected number of features that can be correctly predicted, given knowledge of a category, over the expected number of correct predictions without such knowledge:

$$\text{CU}(C_k) = P(C_k)\left[\sum_j P(V_j|C_k)^2 - \sum_j P(V_j)^2\right]$$

Note that by moving the $P(C_k)$ term into the summation and applying Bayes rule

$$P(C_k)\sum_j P(V_j|C_k)^2 = \sum_j P(V_j)P(C_k|V_j)P(V_j|C_k)$$

Thus, $\text{CU}(C_k)$ is also a tradeoff between standard measures of cue validity $P(C_k|V_j)$ and category validity $P(V_j|C_k)$, weighted by the probability of V_j. As Medin (1983) notes, cue validity will tend to be higher for very general categories, since they have fewer contrasts. Inversely, category validity will tend to be higher for highly specific categories.

A concept formation system called COBWEB (Fisher, 1987b) uses CU to partition a set of observations into contrasting categories C_k so as to maximize the average utility of categories in the partition,

$$\frac{\sum_{k=1}^{n} \text{CU}(C_k)}{n}$$

where n is the number of categories in the partition. Because CU requires only information about individual feature distributions within each C_k, one can effectively represent a category with a probabilistic or independent cue representation (Smith & Medin, 1981), where each feature V_j is weighted by $P(V_j|C_k)$.

Figure 1 illustrates how COBWEB organizes categories at multiple levels of abstraction. In this example, observations correspond to animal descriptions. Each category is also weighted by the proportion of observations $P(C_k)$ classified under it.

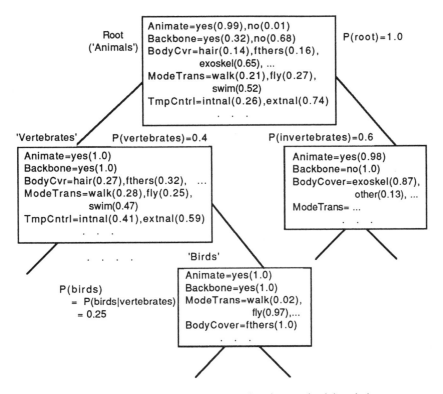

Fig. 1.   A probabilistic concept tree over imaginary animal descriptions.

The method that COBWEB uses to incorporate a new observation into an existing categorization tree is designed for simplicity and efficiency. COBWEB assimilates an observation by evaluating the partitions that result by adding the observation to each existing category, and the partition that results from creating a new singleton category. Intuitively, this latter action occurs if the observation is sufficiently dissimilar from each of the existing categories. It then evaluates each of these alternatives using CU and retains the best choice. Incorporating a new animal description into the tree of Fig. 1 would require three evaluations at the top level of the tree: adding the instance to the 'vertebrate' category, adding it to the 'invertebrate' category, and creating a new category that contained only the new instance. If the instance is incorporated into an existing category, then the observation is assimilated into the respective subtree by the same procedure. Anderson and Matessa (1991) describe an approach in which a Bayesian measure guides object assimilation in the same manner.

We noted that CU and COBWEB were motivated by a desire to facilitate inference—in this case, the prediction of features that are not directly observed in a new object. As with assimilation, COBWEB uses CU to guide object categorization: an observation is sorted down a path of *best matching* categories to a point where the unknown feature is best predicted. Some features may be best predicted at the leaves (specific, past instances) of the categorization tree, while others may be best predicted at categories of intermediate generality (Fisher, 1989).[1] For example, consider a zoological categorization that decomposes 'animals' into 'vertebrates' and 'invertebrates', and then further decomposes these categories into 'mammals', 'birds', and so on. If we observe that an observation has 'feathers', then the path of best matching categories will include 'animals', 'vertebrates', and 'birds'. During top-down categorization we may choose to predict that the object is probably 'animate' when categorization reaches the 'animal' category, that it has a 'backbone' when categorization reaches the 'vertebrate' category, and that it probably 'flies' at the 'bird' category. Thus, to the extent possible, inferences about an incomplete observation are accumulated as one descends the categorization hierarchy. This ability improves with learning. The exact nature of the learning curve and best point of prediction varies between features and is based on the degree that the features are intercorrelated with other features (Fisher & Langley, 1990).

B. A Psychological Perspective

The analysis above is primarily computational: COBWEB improves inference as learning proceeds, and it does so in a relatively efficient manner. However, these concerns with accuracy and efficiency are intricately linked to psychological concerns. For example, during top-down categorization COBWEB places an observation in one category at each level of the categorization tree; once made, it never reconsiders a categorization in light of subsequent data. This *localized* categorization policy is space and time efficient, but it also renders the system sensitive to the order of incoming data (Fisher, Xu, & Zard, 1992), which also characterizes aspects of human learning (Kline, 1983).

More generally, COBWEB's development is consistent with a *rational analysis* (Anderson, 1990): a reasonable starting point for modeling human processing is one that is optimal given the resource limitations under which humans operate. Gluck and Corter (1985) motivate CU in precisely this

---

[1] A feature's majority value at a node is used for prediction. This *probability-maximizing* strategy contrasts with the probability-matching assumption underlying *CU*. Nonetheless, *CU* favors categories that are better suited for prediction, even when predictions are actually generated by a probability-maximizing strategy (Fisher, 1987a).

way. Rationally, we wish to increase the expected number of correct inferences $P(V_j|C_k)^2 - P(V_j)^2$ that can be made about an observation, but this aspect of CU will be maximized for the most specific categories possible. Unfortunately, while a computer may easily memorize specific instances and treat them as singleton categories, humans often cannot do so. Thus, CU also rewards more general categories that represent some form of data compression through the $P(C_k)$ term. Consistent with a *bounded-rational* view of humans (Simon, 1969), CU trades off accuracy with space efficiency. As we noted, CU can be viewed as a tradeoff between cue and category validity, which also explains a preference for categories that are not overly general or specific as well (Medin, 1983).

1. Basic Level Effects

Psychological studies have shown that within hierarchical classification schemes there appears to be a *basic* level preferred by human subjects (Rosch, Mervis, Gray, Johnson, & Boyes-Braem, 1976; Lassaline, Wisniewski, & Medin, in 1992). For example, in a hierarchy containing {animal, vertebrate, mammal, dog, collie}, subject behavior may indicate that 'dog' lies at the basic level. Corter and Gluck developed CU as a predictor of these basic categories in humans.

Basic level studies by Murphy and Smith (1982) trained subjects to categorize artificial tools relative to hierarchically organized categories. After training, subjects affirmed that objects were members of their respective (intermediate) basic categories more quickly than they confirmed membership relative to superordinate or subordinate categories. Table I shows the predicted results of COBWEB's classification strategy on these data. The "True cases" measured subjects' response time to confirm that stimuli (observations) were members of a given superordinate, basic, or

TABLE I

HUMAN AND PREDICTED RESPONSE TIMES (MSEC) FOR
THE MURPHY AND SMITH (1982) DATA[a]

	True cases		False cases	
	Response time	Predicted time	Response time	Predicted time
Superordinate	879	869	882	879
Basic	678	646	714	738
Subordinate	723	764	691	669

[a] Adapted from Fisher and Langley (1990).

subordinate category. Predicted response times are computed through a linear regression ($r = -0.94$) over a CU-based measure of similarity between objects and learned categories (Fisher & Langley, 1990). Murphy and Smith also tested "False cases," which indicated that subjects were faster at recognizing that a stimulus was not a member of a basic category than at disconfirming membership relative to the other two levels. Three data points per case are too few for any conclusions about quantitative fit, but qualitatively the model ranks categories in the same order as response time ($r = -0.96$). This includes a predicted preference for subordinate over superordinate levels.

This account follows directly from CU's tradeoff between accuracy and space efficiency, which tends to favor categories at intermediate levels of abstraction. This result is not surprising since Corter and Gluck (1992) developed the measure as a predictor of basic levels, though we have extended their analysis to "False" cases.

2. *Typicality Effects*

In addition to basic levels, COBWEB has been applied to data on typicality effects from Rosch and Mervis (1975). For example, subjects will more quickly affirm that a 'robin' is a 'bird' than they will affirm that a 'chicken' is a 'bird'. The relative ranking of test items corresponds to a typicality ranking of category members.

Rosch and Mervis found that category members sharing features with many other members of the same category tend to be judged more typical. In addition, when a disjoint, contrasting category is involved, members that share few features with members of the contrasting category tend to be judged more typical. This sensitivity to intra-category and inter-category overlap of features is captured by the notion of it family resemblance. Rosch and Mervis trained subjects to recognize and distinguish nonsense strings from two contrast categories. In experiments testing the effect of intra-category similarity, members of one category were *JXPHM, QBLFS, XPHMQ, MQBLF, PHMQB,* and *HMQBL*. These strings shared no features (symbols) in common with members of the contrast category, but they varied in their intra-category overlap. For example, the symbols of *JXPHM* are present in an average of 2.0 other strings of Category A. This string is categorized slowly, and thus judged to have low typicality. In contrast, the symbols of *HMQBL* are present in an average of 3.2 other strings of Category A, yielding faster response and high typicality judgments. Similar experiments tested variability of inter-category overlap: response time increases and typicality decreases with greater inter-category overlap.

Actual response times and those predicted by the COBWEB model are shown in Table II. The good quantitative fits [$F(1, 4) = 114.1, p < 0.001$] are due to CU's tradeoff between cue validity and category validity, which accurately reflect differences in inter-category overlap and intra-category overlap, respectively.

3. Fan Effects

Finally, COBWEB's classification schemes fit data on fan effects by Anderson (1974), in which subjects were asked to recognize whether they had seen a test sentence or not during previous training (e.g., 'The teacher is in the bank', 'The fireman is in the park'). Each sentence contains a 'subject' (e.g., 'teacher', 'doctor') and a 'location' (e.g., 'church', 'bank'). Anderson's findings indicate that the greater the featural overlap of a test sentence with training sentences, then the longer the time required to confirm (True cases) or disconfirm (False cases) its presence in earlier training. Silber and Fisher (1989) and Fisher and Langley (1990) viewed COBWEB's account of these data as a special case of typicality. The task was to match a test sentence against a past sentence, which can be regarded as a singleton category. Because there is only one object per category, the intra-category overlap in training sentences is constant. Thus, differences in response time are due exclusively to inter-category overlap—the overlap between sentences. Actual response times and predicted response times for the "True" cases [$F(1, 7) = 36.3, p < 0.001$]

TABLE II

HUMAN AND PREDICTED RESPONSE TIMES (MSEC) FOR ROSCH AND MERVIS (1975) DATA[a]

	Response time	Predicted time
Intra-overlap		
High	560	535
Med	617	615
Low	692	713
Inter-overlap		
Low	909	968
Med	986	995
High	1125	1062

[a] Adapted from Fisher and Langley (1990).

and "False" cases $[F(1, 7) = 17.1, p < 0.004]$ are shown in Table III. Generally speaking, our analysis considers the memory process of recognition as a special case of categorization, whereas Anderson (1990), and psychological accounts generally, consider them distinct, though probably related.

In addition, this general view also speaks to the negative fan effect (Reder & Ross, 1983), which indicates that the more one knows about a particular observation relative to other observations, then the faster it will be recognized on average. In this case, we are increasing the intra-category similarity of one singleton category relative to others, since there are a greater number of facts known about it. Again, this is a degenerate case of typicality; a robust model of typicality appears sufficient to largely explain the phenomena.

C. Summary

This section has briefly described the COBWEB system, a model of categorization and concept learning. Inferences about unobserved dimensions of an object are accumulated during categorization, and learning improves the prediction accuracy of this process. The system has also been evaluated as a parameter-free model of human categorization. It is not a *process model* in the usual sense, since we do not suggest how the CU-based categorization procedure might be *implemented* by lower-level cognitive mechanisms. However, indexing schemes closer to the process level have been proposed (Fisher & Langley, 1990).

TABLE III

HUMAN AND PREDICTED (IN PARENTHESES) RESPONSE TIMES (MSEC) FOR ANDERSON'S (1974) FAN EFFECT DATA[a]

	Subject overlap					
	True cases			False cases		
Location overlap	1	2	3	1	2	3
1	1111	1174	1222	1197	1221	1264
	(1120)	(1157)	(1184)	(1168)	(1240)	(1306)
2	1167	1198	1222	1250	1356	1291
	(1157)	(1195)	(1259)	(1240)	(1312)	(1379)
3	1153	1233	1357	1262	1471	1465
	(1184)	(1259)	(1321)	(1306)	(1379)	(1444)

[a] Adapted from Fisher and Langley (1990).

The model accounts for basic level and typicality effects, as well as interactions between them (Jolicoeur, Gluck, & Kosslyn, 1984; Fisher & Langley, 1990). However, the model is particularly novel in its account of fan effects, which are not generally treated in a categorization mold (Anderson, 1990). This highlights an important principle of cognitive modeling: to be useful, a cognitive model should go beyond the known data, thus suggesting new conceptual frameworks and experimental directions.

COBWEB's approach to categorization and learning shapes our view of problem-solving, but inferences correspond to partial solutions that are accumulated into a complete solution as a problem is categorized relative to past experiences.

III. Categorization and Problem-solving

It is apparent that human problem-solving typically involves some form of categorization. For example, in chess (DeGroot, 1966), experts rapidly categorize board patterns and act on these categorizations during play. A classic study by Chi, Feltovich, and Glaser (1981) found that experts and novices alike classify physics problems, and (at least in the case of experts) these categorizations determine starting points for problem-solving. Production-system models (Anderson & Kline, 1979; Simon & Lea, 1979) make the "problem-solving as categorization" view explicit. Categorization leads to the application of *matching* operators, thus generating inferences or actual changes to the environment.

Given the apparent importance of categorization, it is natural to look to traditional models of the process, including hierarchical strategies like COBWEB. However, COBWEB's representation of concepts needs to be revised to handle problem-solving tasks.

A. THEORY AND DATA

Traditionally, research in both machine and human learning has focused on surface features as the basis for concept representations. Within psychology and machine learning there is growing dissatisfaction with this simple featural model (Medin, 1989; Porter, Bareiss, & Holte, 1990). In particular, *background knowledge*—what the learner already knows and which is not perceivable in the data—appears to play a vital role in category formation. For example, consider the task of teaching subjects about *straight* card hands in poker. Two sample straights include (5, clubs), (6, diamonds), (7, diamonds), (8, hearts), (9, clubs) and (7, spades), (8, spades), (9, clubs), (10, hearts), (Jack, diamonds). To correctly learn the concept requires knowledge that (3 succeeds 2), (4 succeeds 3), . . . (Jack succeeds 10), . . . (Ace succeeds King), which is not an explicit part of the observations but must be brought to the task from the learner's background knowledge (Vere, 1978).

In problem-solving the role of background knowledge is particularly important. In fact, all those aspects of a problem's solution that are not an explicit part of the problem statement are background knowledge. Studies by Chi et al. (1981) illustrated the importance of background knowledge to human categorization and problem-solving. They required subjects to sort physics problems into categories of their own design, thus revealing significant differences between the criteria used by "experts" (i.e., graduate students in physics) and "novices" (i.e., undergraduates) to create categories. Novices sorted based on surface features—those that were referred to in the problem statement (e.g., reference to an 'inclined plane', 'friction,' etc.), while experts formed categories of problems that required the application of similar solution strategies (e.g., application of 'Newton's second law'). In addition, experts generally required more time to produce an initial sort than novices. These findings indicate that expert subjects make an initial *qualitative analysis* of a problem prior to classification and derive abstract features from background knowledge (e.g., laws of physics).

Chi et al.'s (1981) study suggests that experts use abstract features, as opposed to surface features, to define categories in problem-solving contexts. However, in many cases, surface features more directly guide categorization, even in experts, when they are well correlated with the abstract features relevant to a problem's solution (Ross & Spalding, 1991). For example, observing 'boat' in the description of a simple algebra story problem will often cue the reader (perhaps incorrectly) that it is a motion problem that involves time, rate, and/or distance calculations.

These examples seem to offer two extreme views of categorization as being directed predominantly by abstract or surface features. However, as Ross and Spalding recognize, these extremes are oversimplified. For example, Wisniewski and Medin (1991) found that surface and background interact in subtle ways and continuously throughout categorization. Their studies looked at how adult subjects categorized childrens' drawings of people. When told that a drawing was by a mentally gifted child (which may or may not actually have been the case), subjects might postulate an abstract feature such as 'draws well'. The presence of 'buttons' (i.e., a surface feature) in the drawing might confirm 'detail' (i.e., an abstract feature) in the drawing, which then might be used to confirm the initially hypothesized characteristic of good drawing. Failure to find confirming surface features would cause some revision in the subject's hypothesis and interpretation of the drawing. In general, they argue that categorization iterates between reliance on surface and abstract features.

Despite the apparent interaction between surface and background knowledge in categorization and problem solving, COBWEB and other similarity-based categorization models typically make no distinction between these forms of knowledge and thus appear limited as models of categorization, particularly as it relates to problem-solving.

B. A COMPUTATIONAL PERSPECTIVE ON PROBLEM-SOLVING

This section describes a categorization model of problem-solving inspired by research on COBWEB but cognizant of background knowledge. We open with a view of problem-solving as a search-intensive process, then move to issues of learning that render the task more efficient.

1. Problem-solving as Search

Traditionally, much of the research on problem-solving in AI and cognitive psychology views it as a search task (Simon, 1969). Given a problem description, the task is to search background knowledge for a solution that satisfies all the constraints in the problem's description. As an illustrative example, consider an algebra story problem like those cataloged by Mayer (1981):

(1)   A train leaves a station and travels east at 72 km/hr. Three hours later a second train leaves and travels east at 120 km/hr. How long will it take to overtake the first train?

We assume that a (human or machine) problem-solver's background knowledge includes domain-specific knowledge about motion problems (e.g., $D = RT$) and general algebraic knowledge (e.g., $ab = c \rightarrow a = c/b$). Problem-solving requires a search of the possible ways to chain these background rules together in order to derive a complete solution. However, there are many factors that can complicate the process. In some cases the problem-solver's knowledge may be incorrect or incomplete, and the problem-solver may or may not have access to external assistance. For example, the problem-solver may realize that the time T_2 traveled by the second train equals the distance that it has traveled divided by its rate ($T_2 = D_2/120$), thus triggering an attempt to derive D_2 from the known facts: $D_2 = R_2T_2 = 120T_2$. However, this circularity leads to a dead end. Alternatively, the problem-solver might observe that the second train travels three hours less than the first train, or $T_2 = T_1 - 3$. Thus, solving T_1 provides a solution to T_2. In general, many paths may be tried before a solution is found. The line of reasoning above will be successful if the problem-solver observes that the distances traveled by the two trains to point of overtake are equal, $D_1 = D_2$. This additional constraint is necessary to solve the problem. If the problem-solver fails to encode this knowledge from the problem statement or lacks background knowledge to exploit it, then this line of reasoning will fail.

An alternative solution to the Overtake problem is abbreviated in Fig. 2a. The solution is expressed in a formal notation required by the computer, but intuitively it encodes that the time until overtake ($T = D/R$) is obtained from the distance that must be made up by the faster train, where D_1 is the distance traveled by the first train before the second train starts, and the relative rate of travel of the second train ($R = R_2 - R_1$). Again, if appropriate knowledge is lacking or incorrect, then this line of reasoning will fail as well.

The search for a correct solution to a problem will succeed if the neces-

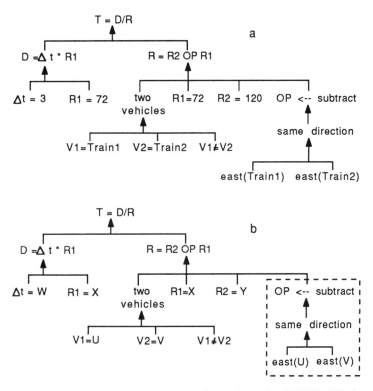

Fig. 2.   A specific solution and generalized schema for OVERTAKE.

sary constraints and facts are encoded from the problem statement and the required background knowledge is present. In cases where problem-solving is being learned, simultaneous fulfillment of these conditions is often not realizable. Rather, external coaching is required by an instructor. Nonetheless, the computer model that we will describe assumes that any problem presented to the system can be solved correctly and to completion. In this case, learning is exclusively concerned with speeding up problem-solving. Initially, even with complete and correct background knowledge, the problem-solver may search in a relatively unguided manner through many possible partial solutions, until happening upon a correct one. During this search, however, information about productive paths can be gleaned and reused to make future problem-solving more efficient. This speedup-learning focus is shared by Larkin's (1981) study of learning in *formal domains,* in which subjects know or are able to access (e.g., in textbooks) the requisite principles for problem-solving. Of course, assumptions of complete and consistent background knowledge limit the scope of predictions that can be made about human problem-solving, but we will argue later that the simplification nonetheless suggests a fruitful path for psychological study, and we believe that it is amenable to perturbations that relax the assumptions of completeness and consistency.

2. *Improving the Efficiency of Problem-solving*

Speedup learning improves problem-solving efficiency by reusing past experiences. The simplest form of reuse is to use a previous solution as is. Unfortunately, a particular solution trace like the one of Fig. 2a is tailored to only one problem—in this case, an overtake problems with two trains of 72 and 120 km/hr respectively, leaving three hours apart. However, we can generalize this solution trace by replacing constants (e.g., 72 km/hr) by variables, so that it matches problems other than the one for which it was first derived. This process of first deriving a solution to a particular problem by searching background knowledge, then generalizing it by appropriately replacing constants by variables, is known as *explanation-based generalization* (EBG; Mitchell, Keller, & Kedar-Cabelli, 1986), since a solution trace or proof is regarded as an ''explanation'' of the answer. A generalized solution or schema for overtake problems obtained by this process is shown in Fig. 2b. In the future, if the problem-solver notices that a problem involves 'two vehicles' moving in the 'same direction' at rates $R_1 = X$ and $R_2 = Y$, $Y > X$, then the overtake schema can be reused to solve it without searching background knowledge from scratch.

Unfortunately, even after variablization, the applicability of this schema will be highly limited. Consider a second, Opposite-direction problem:

(2)   Two trains leave the same station at the same time. One train travels 64 km/hr to the south and the other travels north at 104 km/hr. In how many hours will they be 1008 km apart?

This has a solution structure almost identical in form to the schema of Fig. 2b; it differs only in the structure of the boxed subtree: rates must be added, not subtracted, to obtain a relative rate in this latter case. Nonetheless, the earlier solution cannot be used as is to help solve the new problem. In addition, the overtake schema may be more than simply useless—it may actually slow future problem-solving. This happens because the solution to the new problem and the schema for the old problem share much in common. Most problem-solvers will require some time examining the old schema before abandoning it as a viable option. This adds to the time required to solve the new problem. More generally, if many schemas exist and differ in small ways, then considerable time can be spent searching unsuccessfully for the correct schema, if it exists at all.

In response, Flann and Dietterich (1989) suggest the utility of generalizing over several schemas of the type in Fig. 2b. Figure 3 illustrates the general process; schemas are superimposed, and subtree structure that is not shared by all the schemas is severed. Letters represent propositions, which must match across solutions as well. For example, generalizing the schemas for Opposite-direction and Overtake problems yield a tree structure with the boxed rightmost subtree of Fig. 2b severed.

The superimposition process results in schemas that can be reused in a

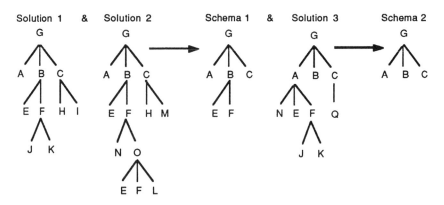

Fig. 3.   Acquiring generalized schemas by superimposing solutions.

wider variety of situations. Note that a generalized schema no longer provides the complete solution structure since some of this has been "severed," but it ideally provides a sizable chunk that can be completed by doing a small search of background knowledge. In this case a problem involving two vehicles with arbitrary rates would signify the relevance of the generalized schema; background knowledge would only be used to determine how the relative rate should be determined, based on whether actual directions of the vehicles implied that they were moving in the same or opposite directions.

It is apparent that something like this schema generalization process is required for effective reuse, but care must be taken in how the procedure is applied. For example, consider a Round-trip problem in which one vehicle goes from point to point at one rate and returns at another. In this case, relative rates are not applicable to computing trip time. Applying the superimposition method to a schema for Round-trip problems and a schema for either Overtake or Opposite-direction or both would result in a trivial schema: $T = D/R$. Little or no problem-solving advantage is gained by its derivation.

Our examples illustrate some important principles: overspecialized schemas can actually detract from problem-solving efficiency, since many distinct but similar schemas introduce redundancy into the search for past experiences that are relevant to new situations. In contrast, overgeneralization results in schemas that are underconstrained and provide little or no benefit. These principles correspond exactly to those of intra- and inter-category overlap. Neither overspecialization or underspecialization is desirable; in problem-solving, as in categorization, there appears to be an ideal level of abstraction for schemas and concepts. Roughly, these same principles were enumerated earlier by Gick and Holyoak (1983, pp. 8–9). In particular, they argued and experimentally supported the idea that analogical transfer to a new problem is best facilitated by a schema that captures the *optimal* commonality between *two* previous source problems. Reed (1989) stressed a corollary that the source problems may be such that any generalization will be an overgeneralization, thus providing no benefit; Reed posits that this was the case in his studies, thus explaining a lack of transfer due to schema abstraction on selected algebra story problems.

One methodological strategy for discovering abstract schemas for problem-solving is to define an analog measure to category utility for problem-solving. In fact, we turn to this task in Section IV,C, but initially we describe a method that stores schemas at many levels of abstraction and with experience discovers those that are most useful. In this way the system gradually converges on schemas that are optimal relative to the requirements of the environment.

C. EXOR: IMPROVING PROBLEM-SOLVING BY CONCEPT LEARNING

Yoo and Fisher (1991b) defined a system called EXOR (EXplanation ORga-nizer), which forms an abstraction hierarchy over a stream of problems and their solutions. For instance, in the domain of algebra story problems an abstraction hierarchy over 48 problems drawn from 12 problem types enumerated by Mayer (1981) is formed like the one shown in Fig. 4. Associated with each node is a generalized schema like those described previously. The schema at each node is shared by all the schemas stored below it; put another way, each schema extends its parent schema in a unique way.

1. An Example of Problem-solving by Categorization

The advantage of this abstraction hierarchy is that it constrains problem-solving search. Figure 5 illustrates how this process operates on a specific example. In step (1), a problem statement is presented along with a quan-tity that must be computed. The problem statement is compared against the schemas at the first level of the abstraction hierarchy. In this case, we want to solve for 'time', so a first-level node that solves this quantity is selected (as opposed to 'distance' or 'rate'). The general 'schema' that 'time' can be solved by dividing 'distance' by 'rate' is asserted as relevant to the current problem, and this becomes the current hypothesis. In step

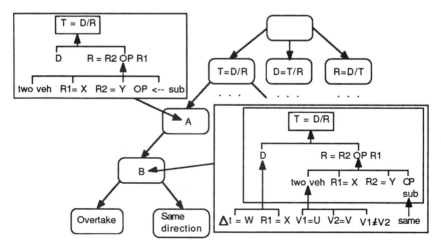

Fig. 4.   An abstraction hierarchy over problem schemas. Adapted from Yoo and Fisher (1991a, 1991 b).

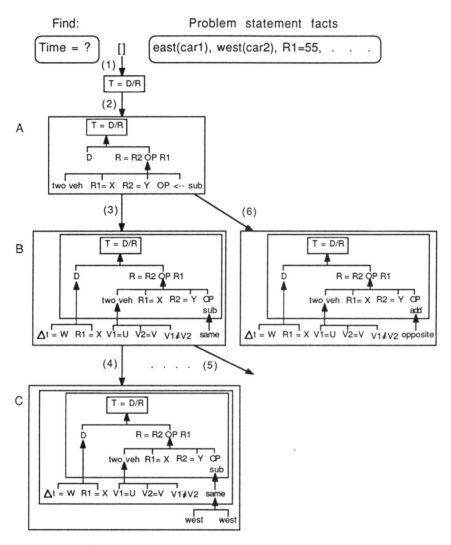

Fig. 5. An example of problem-solving by categorization.

(2) the schema is specialized further by categorizing the problem relative to one of the children of the current hypothesis. We will describe how a child is selected shortly, but suffice it to say that one is chosen, and its schema extends the current hypothesis. This extension to the current hypothesis becomes the new hypothesis. The specialization process continues in steps (3) and (4), but in step (4), a contradiction between the surface

features of the new problem and the surface features present in the highly specific schema is found. In particular, the new problem involves one car going 'east' and the other going 'west', whereas the specialized schema requires two cars going 'west'.

Thus, the new problem is incompatible with the hypothesis. This hypothesis is *retracted*, and one of its siblings is chosen as the current hypothesis in step (5). However, *no* extension of schema B will be applicable for this reason, though our problem-solver has no way of knowing this in advance of investigating all of B's specialized schemas. After all extensions of B are exhausted, a final attempt to complete B's schema using background knowledge is made, but this will not work for the reasons stated. Thus, attention returns to B's parent and a sibling of B is chosen as the next hypothesis in step (6). This hypothesis represents the class of problems with vehicles moving in opposite directions; one of its extensions, represented as an existing schema or found by a search through background knowledge if no appropriate extension has been previously encountered, will solve the current problem.

2. *Categorization and Learning*

Figure 6a generalizes our example; it illustrates that a new problem will be classified down an *appropriate* path of the hierarchy. At each node along the categorization path, the schema associated with the node is asserted as participating in the solution of the problem being classified. If at any point a condition known from the problem statement contradicts one of the conditions asserted at a node, then the partial schema of the node is retracted, and control returns to the node's parent where another child is investigated. If all children of a node fail to complete the node's partial schema, then an attempt is made to complete it by reverting to background knowledge (i.e., the dashed, triangular nodes of Fig. 6a). If this fails, then the node fails and control is returned to its parent as described before. The general categorization procedure is quite simple; as in COBWEB, inferences are accumulated as one descends the hierarchy, but unlike COBWEB each inference is a complex schema extension that can be retracted and redirected if necessary.

In describing the procedure above, we omitted two important points: how categorization is guided, and how new schemas are added to the categorization tree. To improve efficiency over a simple search of background knowledge, categorization must be well directed. An initial strategy guides a problem's classification using the conditions that are given in the problem statement. These correspond to surface features—such as the fact that a problem involves 'two' (versus 'one') 'cars' (versus

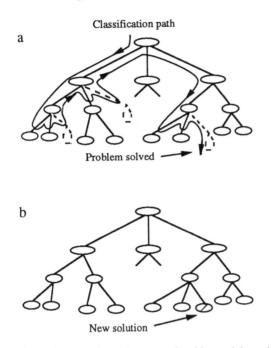

Fig. 6.   Categorization with and storage of problem-solving schemas.

'boats') going 'east' and 'west' (versus 'north' and 'south'). Section III.A pointed out that surface similarity is often correlated with problem types and solution strategies. In these cases, some gain in efficiency can be realized. In particular, EXOR computes category utility over the surface conditions, which provides a degree of match between a new problem and each node of the categorization hierarchy. The nodes of a level are ordered by this match score and investigated in order until a complete solution is found. Note that to compute this score we need to know the distribution of surface features among problems that are stored in the hierarchy. Thus, probability distributions over a subpopulation's surface features are stored at a node, in addition to background structure that is true of *all* of a node's descendants.

If a problem is solved by appealing to background knowledge at a particular node, then the solution is added as a new child (i.e., schema) to the tree at this point. If an existing schema solves the problem, then no change to the categorization structure is made, other than to update the probability distribution of surface features at nodes under which the problem was finally placed. In some cases the new solution is generalized with existing schemas as well, thus creating new schemas. In the tree of Fig. 6a, the solution to a new problem would be added as indicated in Fig. 6b. Thus, the system incrementally clusters problem-solving solutions and creates generalized schemas in the process.

3. Empirical Results

To test the merits of this problem-solving strategy, 32 training problems were incrementally added to the categorization hierarchy. At intermediate points in training, a separate set of 16 test problems was solved via categorization with the hierarchy. The average cost of solving these test problems was measured by the number of features that were instantiated (matched) during categorization. Roughly, this is the sum of the surface and background features in all the schemas successfully and unsuccessfully hypothesized in the course of solving a problem. This measure of cost is well correlated with the time required to solve the problem, but it does not depend so strongly on the efficiency characteristics of a particular computer implementation.

Figure 7 shows the learning curve averaged over 10 random orderings of the 32 training problems. The declining upper curve illustrates a decrease in the total cost of problem-solving; the darker, increasing curve represents the subset of instantiations performed just in matching features that are present in nodes of the hierarchy. The difference in the two curves is the number of instantiations performed using primitive background rules in an attempt to complete generalized schemas. Thus, total problem-

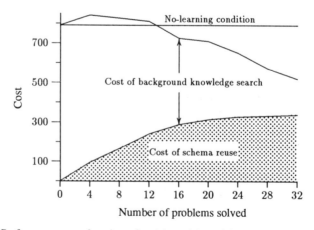

Fig. 7.   Performance as a function of training. Adapted from Yoo and Fisher (1991a, 1991b).

solving effort declines with training, but an increasing amount of that remaining effort is placed on the growing categorization hierarchy.

In sum, EXOR builds on the basic COBWEB strategy of top-down categorization and learning. Each node corresponds to a chunk or schema, which is a partial solution common to all category members. These problem-solving chunks are not used to guide categorization, but upon making a categorization they are asserted as applicable to a new problem. Rather, categorization relies on probabilistic distributions over the surface features.

4. Inferred Features and Pruning

The gains in EXOR's problem-solving performance can be improved in two ways. As we noted in Section III,B,2, overly specific schemas can detract from problem-solving efficiency. An example of this is illustrated by Schema C of Fig. 5. In this case it is not important that two vehicles are both moving 'west' (or both move 'east', 'north', or 'south'). It is only important that they are moving in the same direction. Likewise, for Opposite-direction problems it is only important that two vehicles are moving accordingly; the particular directions do not matter. Such schemas can differ in very small, but nonetheless significant ways from novel problems, thus "misleading" categorization for a large population of new problems. Therefore, each node of the categorization tree maintains two counts: a count of the number of times that the node was visited during problem-solving, and the number of problems successfully solved under the node. If the ratio of successful visits to total visits drops below a threshold (e.g., 0.5), then the node and its descendents are pruned from the categorization tree. Figure 8b illustrates the effect of this pruning. If all of a node's children are pruned, then an attempt to complete the node's schema appeals directly to background knowledge.

EXOR's problem-solving efficiency can be further improved by focusing on inferred features. EXOR categorizes problems based on facts presented in a problem statement, but recall that Chi et al. (1981) found that experts categorize problems based on principles that play an important role in a problem's solution (e.g., problems with solutions that depend on Newton's third law are categorized together).

As with surface features, useful inferred features are those that are discriminating of paths that should be followed during categorization. In general, these will be features, F_k with high cue validity $P(C_i|F_k)$ relative to a schema category C_i. Recall that cue validity is an important component of category utility. The more predictive a feature is of a particular path or small number of paths, the more efficiently search of the categorization

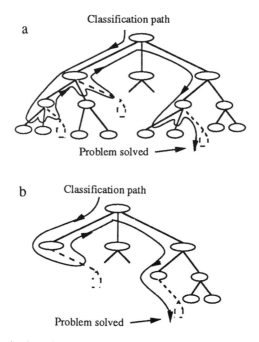

Fig. 8.   Categorization without and with pruning. Adapted from Yoo and Fisher (1991a, 1991b).

tree will be directed. For example, as we noted above, surface features indicating that one car is going 'east' and one car is going 'west' are of little predictive value, but an abstract feature that is highly predictive of a solution strategy is the fact that the two cars are moving in opposite directions. However, inference of a feature comes with a cost. Thus, we wish to weigh the predictiveness of a feature and cost savings in categorization due to its inference, against the cost that will be required to infer it.

We formalize this tradeoff in terms of the *expected number* of problem-solving steps (or features instantiated, or any of several other measures of *cost*) required to solve a problem with and without knowledge of a feature's truth. Let $EC(C_i)$ be the expected cost of solving an arbitrary problem beginning at node C_i of an EXOR categorization tree, $EC(C_i|F_k)$ the expected cost required to solve the problem if a (derived or surface) feature F_k is known, and $EC(\text{prove } F_k)$ the expected cost of proving (deriving) the feature. In the case of surface features, this latter cost is zero. Putting these quantities together, it is useful to verify a feature at a particular node C_i if

$$EC(C_i) > P(F_k|C_i)[EC(C_i|F_k) + EC(\text{prove } F_k)]$$
$$+ [1 - P(F_k|C_i)][EC(C_i|\neg F_k) + EC(\text{prove} \neg F_k)]$$

where $P(F_k|C_i)$ is the probability that we will be able to prove the truth of F_k (e.g., 'opposite-direction') and $1 - P(F_k|C_i)$ is the probability that its complement (e.g., 'same-direction') is true, which can also be predictive of a particular course of action. Intuitively, the more ways there are to infer a feature in background knowledge, the more possibilities that must be examined, and the greater the cost of inferring it.

EXOR identifies features that are good candidates for inference at each node in the categorization tree. Having made such identifications, statistics on these *cost-effective* background features are maintained and exploited in the CU calculation that was originally limited to surface features. Yoo and Fisher (1991b) report that the additional guidance provided by these inferred features, and the pruning method described above, collectively improves problem-solving efficiency by approximately 12% over the results of Fig. 7.

D. SUMMARY

COBWEB's approach to categorization and learning has shaped our view of problem-solving, but with some important caveats. Notably, inferences are still facilitated by categorization, but schemas composed of both surface and background features are inferred and accumulated into a complete solution as a problem is categorized relative to past experiences. EXOR's categorization appears consistent with the findings and ideas of Chi et al. (1991), Ross and Spalding (1991), and others: the system infers background features that guide categorization in problem-solving, but surface features are still used if they are predictive.

Furthermore, the evolutionary process underlying EXOR may also account for other data on the transition from novice to expert problem-solving. Larkin (1981) found that novices tended to reason backward from the goal, but that experts reasoned forward from the known facts. This forward-reasoning characteristic among experts was also found by Koedinger and Anderson (1990) in geometry problem-solving. However, expertise in other domains such as design and troubleshooting (or diagnosis) suggests a dominant backward-reasoning component (Perez, 1991). As Larkin suggests, EXOR begins as a backward reasoner: hypotheses are extended from the goal through categorization and/or background knowledge search until a solution consistent with the known facts is found. However, as cost-effective background features are identified, they are inferred at appropriate points in categorization by forward reasoning from the givens. We speculate that forward reasoning among experts is dominant in some domains because the top-level goals themselves are deemed cost-effective background features. This may help explain the variance of the forward versus background phenomena across domains and suggests that in many domains a combination of the two is most appropriate.

As a cognitive model EXOR is quite tentative, and we have noted that it is oversimplified in that it assumes complete and correct background knowledge, but it nonetheless suggests a line of research. While psychologists have uncovered plentiful evidence on the importance of inferred features in categorizing problem-solving experiences, we know of no work that identifies the criteria that humans use to select these features. Rather, a starting point in the search for these criteria is suggested on computational grounds: if humans are bounded-rational agents, then they may select inferred features that are *cost-effective*—relatively inexpensive to infer and effective at discriminating relevant past experience.

IV. General Discussion

This article argues that categorization guides inference in problem-solving, though the role, dominance, and form of categorization undoubtedly vary with domain (e.g., van Gelder, this volume). This section takes a step back, views our models within the larger literature on categorization and problem-solving, and speculates on what the unification of categorization and problem-solving buys us in terms of suggesting future exploration in both areas.

A. CATEGORIZATION AND INFERENCE

Smith and Medin (1981) point out the dual roles of categories and concepts: they allow data compression through categorization, and subsequent inferences about unobserved aspects of the individual. In COBWEB, probabilistic distributions over surface features are the sole basis of both categorization and inference. The tradeoff between categorization and inference is represented in category utility by cue validity, $P(C|V)$, which promotes identification of categories from features, and category validity $P(V|C)$, which promotes inference of features from categories. However, COBWEB is a degenerate case of more sophisticated categorization and inference schemes that distinguish both surface and background knowledge.

In Smith and Medin's analysis, a category's *identification procedure* (i.e., categorization) relies exclusively on surface features (or perceptual features in their terms), and a category's *core* contains those surface or abstract (i.e., background) features that are inferred after identification. In addition, the findings of Chi et al. (1981) and others indicate that some abstract features are inferred prior to and then guide categorization. Thus, identification too may well involve both surface and abstract features.

The dualism between identification and core is manifest in the representation and processing of schemas in EXOR. A probabilistic representation of surface features and cost-effective background features supports identification, but a logical conjunction of necessary and jointly sufficient features represents the core—those features that are inferred. Both psychological evidence and computational advantage speak for this dichotomy. Several studies on *goal-derived* (Barsalou, 1985) and *function-motivated* (Ahn, 1990) categories indicate that categories are formed around a common function, action, goal, and so on, but that principles of family resemblance often capture the surface structure of such categories. In fact, it is often not possible to conjunctively represent the various ways of satisfying a common goal; probabilistic representations of surface features allow flexibility representationally but provide more constraints than a logical *disjunctive* representation, thus better supporting discrimination between contrast categories (Fisher & Pazzani, 1991).

The debate between necessary and sufficient (or *classical*) and probabilistic representations is a long one (Smith & Medin, 1981). The most interesting aspect of current debate (Averill, this volume; Malt, this volume) is that the lines drawn between classical and alternative representations (e.g., probabilistic) seem closely, though not perfectly, aligned to the roles of surface and background knowledge in identification and inference. Some misalignment is implied by EXOR's probabilistic assessment of certain cost-effective background features, and other models allow probabilistic representations of background, as well as surface features (Pazzani, 1990). Thus, it is likely that the classical/core and probabilistic/surface dichotomy is oversimplified, but a natural generalization may be realistic: features increase in certainty, often but not necessarily to the point of logical certainty, as one moves from the surface to highly goal-oriented, background features.

B. LEARNING ISSUES

There are many aspects of learning to solve problems effectively. One aspect that we have not examined is improving the *accuracy* of problem-solving in the face of inconsistent and incomplete background knowledge; EXOR assumes that background knowledge is sufficient to *generate* complete and correct solutions. The utility of schemas constructed in this way is then empirically *tested* as new problems are solved, and low utility schemas are pruned. In a suitable extension to EXOR, this generate-and-test strategy can undoubtedly be adapted to prune incorrect schemas as well, provided that an external "teacher" identifies incorrect solutions. In addition, several researchers are addressing issues of incompleteness. For example, Mooney (this volume) uses a generate-and-test strategy like EXOR's to evaluate the merits of knowledge derived from background, but patterns discovered in observations are also used to fill gaps in background knowledge, thus extending the capabilities of the problem-solver. This general approach also appears in work on student modeling for intelligent tutoring (Sleeman, Hirsh, Ellery, & Kim, 1990): new (correct and "buggy") rules arise when a system (or human student) bridges a procedural gap in problem-solving knowledge. Similarly, research in knowledge acquisition (Bareiss & Slator, this volume) looks to human experts to fill the reasoning gaps of the automated system.

Work on EXOR has concentrated on two facets of speedup learning. One aspect is *chunk* acquisition; each schema is a composite of several inference rules, and as such it takes a relatively large step toward a solution. This aspect of speedup learning is related to considerable work on learning macro-operators (Iba, 1989) and knowledge *compilation* (Anderson, 1983; Laird, Rosenbloom, & Newell, 1986). However, to be helpful these chunks must be applied in appropriate circumstances. This second aspect of speedup learning improves the identification procedure (Langley, 1985). In particular, EXOR's probabilistic representation and CU-based categorization procedure search out reliable associations of surface and cost-effective features with the core features of the schema.

If reliable associations are not found, because the schema is retracted an inordinate number of times in the course of solving new problems, then the schema is pruned. This "forgetting" phenomenon relies on a *retrospective* analysis of a schema's utility, but psychological studies indicate that some categories may be *prospectively* pruned as well. Consider ad hoc concepts (Barsalou, 1983), which are goal-derived categories but which are nonetheless transient, in part because they lack an efficient identification procedure. For example, *things to remove from the house during a fire* might include 'family pictures', 'silverware', 'coin collections', and 'important documents'. These items are related by very abstract features such as 'high value', 'irreplaceable', and 'easy to remove', but they lack similarity 'close to' the surface level on which identification relies. EXOR does not model this prospective version of pruning, but undoubtedly forgetting in this case is desirable.

Unfortunately, the lack of a good identification procedure is often an unintentional consequence of nonoptimal training strategies. Bransford,

Sherwood, Hasselbring, Kinzer, & Williams (1990) describe the ubiquity of *inert* knowledge, which a subject possesses but which is not spontaneously accessed in relevant contexts. For example, a subject may know how to manipulate logarithms (i.e., core knowledge) but may not apply this knowledge when presented with large multiplication problems that would be considerably simplified by logarithms, apparently because they lack a suitable identification procedure. Thus, Bransford et al. advocate *anchoring* the instruction of problem solving knowledge to well-defined cases. This type of anchored or *case-based instruction* is central to EXOR's learning capabilities. Cases or problems are presented, solved, stored, and generalized as learning proceeds. While the cases that are used are impoverished compared to those advocated by Bransford et al., the requisite condition on them for effective learning remains the same: these problems must contain sufficient context so that the learner acquires an effective identification procedure.

The importance of improving the identification procedure is illustrated further by the *problem-solving fan effect,* which was identified by Shrager, Hogg, and Huberman (1988). They developed a formal, graph-theoretic model that learned chunks of problem-solving knowledge much like EXOR. Their basic finding was that if the identification procedure does not improve as the number of learned chunks increases, then overall performance degrades. In effect, learning increases the contrast set of schemas and the overall inter-category similarity between schemas, thus confusing a less than perfect identification procedure. This phenomenon is a different and refined view of the fan effect described by Anderson (1974): if the identification procedure does not improve in the presence of increasingly similar stimuli, then the most idiosyncratic stimuli will be recognized more quickly. It is not difficult to show that this behavior is nonoptimal. If our goal is to minimize problem-solving effort over a population of problems, then it is desirable to more efficiently handle problems with more common solution patterns.

C.   ABSTRACTION AND BASIC LEVELS OF PROBLEM-SOLVING

One way to mitigate fan effects is to explicitly modify the identification procedure as chunks are acquired, but an equivalent way reorganizes the knowledge on which the identification procedure is applied. By forming schemas from common portions of individual solutions, we remove redundancies in the search for relevant problem-solving experiences. Given a choice between contrast schemas, rational approaches will favor those that cover a larger proportion of the environment, as represented in category utility by the $P(C_k)$ term. That is, common patterns will be favored over idiosyncratic patterns, unless the idiosyncratic schemas allow for considerably larger steps to be taken toward a final solution. As we noted in Section III,B,2, problem-solving aspects of redundancy and step size correspond exactly to principles of intra- and inter- category overlap. Just as there is a basic level that optimizes a tradeoff between these concerns in object memory, there is an optimal level of abstraction in problem-solving.

Abstractions have long been recognized as important in guiding problem-solving (Korf, 1987),but there is little research on assessing ideal or optimal levels of abstraction in this context. Exceptions include Morris and Murphy (1990) and Rifkin (1985), each of whom found that subjects identify one level as basic in *event* hierarchies for reasons very similar to the principles that predict basic levels in object memory. Our own research suggests that basic levels enable an agent to minimize problem-solving (e.g., time, number of steps). For example, in communicating directions to a lost driver, a conscientious observer will attempt to minimize the expected effort of the driver by providing well-spaced landmarks between the current location and final destination. Too few landmarks increase the likelihood of a wrong turn, while too many may tax the driver's short-term memory, thus inviting mistakes as well.

This spatial example corresponds nicely to a graph-theoretic model of Shrager et al. (1988), where a schema is a set of selected states along one or more paths from an initial state to a goal state. A schema that lists all states along one path (i.e., a solution) directs problem-solving perfectly, but it is not applicable to other situations. Inversely, too few states may share many possible paths and thus be widely applicable but relatively unhelpful in constraining problem-solving. We define a basic level schema to optimize a suitable tradeoff between applicability and constraint, and propose CU as a tentative starting point in the search for a basic level predictor in problem-solving:

$$P(\text{schema})\sum_{j} [P(S_j|\text{schema})^2 - P(S_j)^2]$$

where S_j are states or subgoals that are indicated by the schema. This balances the applicability of a schema, which can be computed as the proportion of paths that pass through the schema's designated states, with the expected number of states that will be correctly predicted to lie on the final solution path. In the lost-driver example, this latter aspect corresponds to our ability to predict whether landmarks were passed or not by the driver, in addition to those supplied by the directions.

It may seem counterintuitive to adopt a measure of expected *accuracy* like CU to predict basic levels of problem-solving, which we define to minimize expected *cost*. In fact, an analog can be formalized that measures the expected cost of finding a correct solution (i.e., path). Intuitively, the categories (identified by category utility) that facilitate more accurate predictions with constant cost (i.e., one prediction per state), correspond closely to categories that insure a correct final solution (i.e., constant accuracy) with less expected cost.

In apparent contrast to our advocacy of basic levels, *case-based* reasoning models (Kolodner, 1987) superficially focus on how previous cases (i.e., instances, solutions) are best accessed and exploited in problem-solving. Case-based reasoning should not be confused with case-based instruction, since the vast majority of models in machine learning presume that learning advances by analyzing specific cases, though the role of cases is to form abstract schemas that are then used for problem-solving.

Moreover, despite the label, the vast majority of case-based systems form and exploit abstractions for categorization (e.g., through indexing) and inference. To do otherwise might invite fan effects. Thus, the distinction between case-based versus abstraction-based reasoning can distract analysis from more general insights into optimal levels of abstraction, cases or otherwise, as well as evaluation along other dimensions such as a system's ability to cope with incomplete background knowledge or an incomplete case library.

D. PRESCRIPTIONS FOR LEARNING AND TRAINING

From a speedup perspective, learning displaces fan effects by introducing abstractions. This displacement is illustrated in EXOR's learning curve of Fig. 7; initially, chunking diminishes performance until appropriate abstractions and a reliable identification procedure are formed. Ideally, a learner will evolve toward a basic level of description, which may, like EXOR and COBWEB, be further decomposed into more specialized concepts and schemas that are helpful in increasingly restricted contexts.

In general, we believe that our study of basic levels suggests a more fundamental analysis of *similarity* between problem schemas. Such an analysis may shed light on a number of phenomena. For example, it is well known that there is little or no transfer between isolated problem-solving experiences and similar, if not identical, new problems by novice subjects (Reed, Dempster, & Ettinger, 1985). EXOR predicts this, since an overly specific schema may be examined, but will not be transferred if it differs in the smallest way from a new problem. In fact, no meaningful transfer occurs until a contrast problem solution is examined and is generalized by superimposition with a previously cached solution. More generally, Gick and Holyoak (1983) argue that analogical transfer is greatly facilitated by a schema that is derived from at least two source analogs, since it abstracts out unimportant detail in each source, thus making the "similarity" between a new problem and the helpful aspects of the previous problems more apparent.

We can also use principles of similarity to prescribe training schedules. For example, EXOR and COBWEB (Fisher et al., 1992) master a domain most rapidly when problems of high contrast are presented repeatedly in sequence; learning is slowest when similar problems are presented back to back (i.e., as one might do when practicing a particular problem type before moving on to another type), though our computer model does not take into account short-term memory limits that might alter this preference. In addition to between-problem considerations, within-problem variations can promote effective learning as well. Notably, our lost-driver analogy argued that knowledge could be best communicated and reused by an appropriate spacing of landmarks, states, or subgoals (Ruby & Kibler, 1991). Simply presenting a student with a problem may cause a novice to flounder, thus requiring considerable effort to solve each problem. In contrast, presenting a student with complete solutions will not facilitate generalization to other problems, thus requiring more problems to master a domain. Thus, Julio Ortega (personal communication, March, 1991) suggests that presenting subjects with basic level schemas, which must then be completed by the student, will tend to minimize the overall effort required to master the domain, where effort is the product of the number of problems and the effort per problem required before a subject reaches a certain level of mastery.

In sum, the gradients implied by basic levels and similarity issues more generally suggest quantitative measures that can be used to assess, predict, and prescribe training schedules.

V. Concluding Remarks

This article argues the merits of a unified view of categorization, concept learning, and problem-solving. This view is advantageous to the extent that it suggests promising lines of research. Notably, we have argued that the transition from novice to expert problem-solving is mediated by principles of effective categorization, and that the early dominance of problem-solving fan effects is gradually displaced as one converges to basic levels of problem-solving. Metrics developed to assess category and schema quality can be used descriptively to track the course of learning, or prescriptively to direct it.

In closing, it is worth highlighting several methodological biases that stem from our view of cognitive modeling as a design task. Most prescriptions of design assume an initial specification of behavior, perhaps from several experimental studies, and the formulation of objective functions that specify desirable aspects of the input and output of the final product. Anderson's (1990) ideas of a rational analysis represent such a step, and in fact, Anderson traces these ideas to Marr (1982), who was influenced by design issues in the information-processing paradigm. The vital point is not that rational analyses per se are new to cognitive modeling, since others (e.g., Gluck & Corter, 1985) have adhered to these principles before, or that Anderson's specific (i.e., Bayesian) formulations are "correct," but that Anderson expounds a methodology that is rarely made explicit, even by those that use it: a reasonable starting point for cognitive modeling is a procedure that optimizes a suitable tradeoff between cost, correctness, and other aspects of bounded rationality.

The rational procedure offers several advantages, two of which we describe. The first recognizes that our ultimate goal is a process model, which commits to particular mechanisms. However, deficits of the process model can often be better understood and corrected by appealing to the higher level specification. For example, Richman (1991) describes a process model based on EPAM, which accounts for the same typicality data as presented in Section II,B,2, but CU suggests certain refinements to EPAM's attentional mechanisms, which might yield a better fit to the data. Second, for those at the interface of cognitive psychology and artificial intelligence, a rational procedure can be exploited in artificial (e.g., engineering) environments that enforce the same tradeoffs as the natural system that motivated the analysis. For example, COBWEB has been adapted as a clustering and data analysis tool for engineering applications (Fisher et al., 1991), as well as for cognitive modeling.

Finally, cognitive modeling is novel relative to other design applications in at least one very important respect. In many design applications, moving beyond the known data or specification is undesirable. In contrast, cognitive models are maximally helpful when they move beyond the data, thus pointing the way for further exploration. We have touched upon several ways in which COBWEB and EXOR do this, though in each case, but particularly with respect to EXOR, we have only tentatively embarked on the iterative process of refinement necessary for a robust understanding of categorization and problem-solving.

Acknowledgments

We thank the editors, Glenn Nakamura, Roman Taraban, and Doug Medin, for thorough and influential comments on earlier drafts. In addition, Laura Novick provided helpful comments and suggestions on correctness and style that went beyond the call of duty and that we have tried to accommodate. Discussion of the cognitive implications of COBWEB in

Section II is detailed in Fisher and Langley (1990). Discussion of EXOR, notably Section III,C, appears in expanded form in Yoo and Fisher (1991a, 1991b). This research was supported by NASA-Ames grant NCC 2-45.

REFERENCES

Ahn, W. (1990). Effects of background knowledge on family resemblance sorting. In *Proceedings of the twelfth annual conference of the Cognitive Science Society* (pp. 149–156). Cambridge, MA: Erlbaum.

Anderson, J. R. (1974). Retrieval of propositional information from long term memory. *Cognitive Psychology, 6,* 451–474.

Anderson, J. R. (1983). *The architecture of cognition.* Cambridge, MA: Harvard University Press.

Anderson, J. R. (1990). *The adaptive character of thought.* Hillsdale, NJ: Erlbaum.

Anderson, J. R., & Kline, P. J. (1979). A learning system and its psychological implications. In *Proceedings of the Sixth International Joint Conference on Artificial Intelligence* (pp. 16–21). Tokyo, Japan: Morgan Kaufmann.

Anderson, J. R., & Matessa, M. (1991). An incremental Bayesian algorithm for categorization. In D. Fisher, M. Pazzani, & P. Langley (Eds.), *Concept formation: Knowledge and experience in unsupervised learning* (pp. 45–70). San Mateo, CA: Morgan Kaufmann.

Barsalou, L. W. (1983). Ad hoc categories. *Memory & Cognition, 11,* 211–227.

Barsalou, L. W. (1985). Ideals, central tendency, and frequency of instantiation as determinants of graded structure in categories. *Journal of Experimental Psychology: Learning, Memory, and Cognition, 11,* 629–654.

Bransford, J. D., Sherwood, R. D., Hasselbring, T. S., Kinzer, C. K., & Williams, S. M. (1990). Anchored instruction: Why we need it and how technology can help. In D. Nix and R. Spiro (Ed.), *Cognition, education, multimedia: Exploring ideas in high technology* (pp. 115–141). Hillsdale, NJ: Erlbaum.

Chi, M., Feltovich, P., & Glaser, R. (1981). Categorization and representation of physics problems by experts and novices. *Cognitive Science, 5,* 121–152.

Corter, J. E., & Gluck, M. A. (1992). Explaining basic categories: feature predictability and information. *Psychological Bulletin, 111,* 291–303.

DeGroot, A. D. (1966). Perception and memory versus thought: Some ideas and recent findings. In B. Kleinmuntz (Ed.), *Problem solving: Research, methods, and theory* (pp. 19–50). New York: John Wiley.

Feigenbaum, E. (1961). The simulation of verbal learning behavior. In J. W. Shavlik and T. G. Dietterich (Eds.), *Readings in machine learning* (pp. 284–295), San Mateo, CA: Morgan Kaufmann, 1990. (Reprinted from *Proceedings of the western joint computer conference,* 1961, 121–132.)

Fisher, D. H. (1987a). *Knowledge acquisition via incremental conceptual clustering.* Doctoral dissertation, University of California, Irvine.

Fisher, D. H. (1987b). Knowledge acquisition via incremental conceptual clustering. *Machine Learning, 2,* 139–172.

Fisher, D. H. (1989). Noise-tolerant conceptual clustering. *Proceedings of the international joint conference on artificial intelligence* (pp. 825–830). Detroit, MI: Morgan Kaufmann.

Fisher, D., & Langley, P. (1990). The structure and formation of natural categories. In G. H. Bower (Ed.), *The Psychology of Learning and Motivation: Vol. 26* (p. 241–284). San Diego, CA: Academic Press.

Fisher, D., & Pazzani, M. (1991). Computational models of concept learning. In D. Fisher & M. Pazzani (Eds.), *Concept formation: Knowledge and experience in unsupervised learning* (pp. 3–43). San Mateo, CA: Morgan Kaufmann.

Fisher, D., Xu, L., Carnes, R., Reich, Y., Fenves, S., Chen, J., Shiavi, R., Biswas, G., & Weinberg, J. (1991). *Selected applications of an AI clustering technique to engineering tasks* (Technical Report CS-91-08). Nashville, TN: Vanderbilt University, Department of Computer Science.

Fisher, D., Xu, L., & Zard, N. (1992). Ordering effects in clustering. In *Proceedings of the ninth international conference on machine learning* (pp. 163–168). San Mateo, CA: Morgan Kaufmann.

Flann, N. S., & Dietterich, T. G. (1989). A study of explanation-based methods for inductive learning. *Machine Learning, 4,* 187–226.

Gick, M. L., & Holyoak, K. J. (1983). Schema induction and analogical transfer. *Cognitive Psychology, 15,* 1–38.

Gluck, M. A., & Corter, J. E. (1985). Information, uncertainty, and the utility of categories. *Proceedings of the seventh annual conference of the Cognitive Science Society* (pp. 283–287). Irvine, CA: Lawrence Erlbaum.

Iba, G. (1989). A heuristic approach to the discovery of macro-operators. *Machine Learning, 3,* 285–318.

Jolicoeur, P., Gluck, M., & Kosslyn, S., (1984). Pictures and names: Making the connection. *Cognitive Psychology, 16,* 243–275.

Kline, P. J. (1983). *Computing the similarity of structured objects by means of heuristic search for correspondences.* Doctoral dissertation, University of Michigan, Ann Arbor.

Koedinger, K. R., & Anderson, J. R. (1990). Abstract planning and perceptual chunks: Elements of expertise in geometry. *Cognitive Science, 14,* 511–550.

Kolodner, J. L. (1983). Reconstructive memory: A computer model. *Cognitive Science, 7,* 281–328.

Kolodner, J. L. (1987). Extending problem solver capabilities through case-based reasoning. *Proceedings of the fourth international workshop on machine learning* (pp. 167–178). Irvine, CA: Morgan Kaufmann.

Korf, R. E. (1987). Planning as search: A quantitative approach. *Artificial intelligence, 33,* 65–88.

Laird, J. E., Rosenbloom, P. S., & Newell, A. (1986). Chunking in Soar: The anatomy of a general learning mechanism. *Machine Learning, 1,* 11–46.

Langley, P. (1985). Learning to search: from weak methods to domain-specific heuristics. *Cognitive Science, 9,* 217–260.

Larkin, J. H. (1981). Enriching formal knowledge: A model for learning to solve textbook physics problems. In J. R. Anderson (Ed.), *Cognitive skills and their acquisition.* Hillsdale, NJ: Erlbaum.

Lassaline, M. E., Wisniewski, E. J., & Medin, D. L. (1992). Basic levels in artificial and natural categories: Are all basic levels created equal? In B. Burns (Ed.), *Percepts, concepts, and categories: The representation and processing of information* (pp. 327–378). Amsterdam: North Holland.

Marr, D. (1982). *Vision.* San Fransico: Freeman.

Mayer, R. (1981). Frequency norms and structural analysis of algebra story problems into families, categories, and templates. *Instructional Science, 10,* 135–175.

Medin, D. L. (1983). Structural principles of categorization. In T. Tighe & B. Shepp (Eds.), *Perception, cognition, and development.* Hillsdale, NJ: Erlbaum.

Medin, D. L. (1989). Concepts and conceptual structure. *American Psychologist, 44,* 1469–1481.

Mitchell, T., Keller, R., & Kedar-Cabelli, S. (1986). Explanation-based learning: a unifying view. *Machine Learning, 1,* 47–80.

Morris, M. W., & Murphy, G. L. (1990). Converging operations on a basic level in event taxonomies. *Memory & Cognition, 18,* 407–418.

Murphy, G., & Smith, E. (1982). Basic level superiority in picture categorization. *Journal of Verbal Learning and Verbal Behavior, 21,* 1–20.

Pazzani, M. (1990). *Creating a memory of causal relationships: An integration of empirical and explanation-based learning methods.* Hillsdale, NJ: Erlbaum.

Perez, R. S. (1991). A view from troubleshooting. In M. U. Smith (Ed.), *Toward a unified view of problem solving: Views from the content domains.* Hillsdale, NJ: Erlbaum.

Porter, B., Bareiss, R., & Holte, R. (1990). Concept learning and heuristic classification in weak-theory domains. *Artificial Intelligence, 45,* 229–263.

Reder, L. M., & Ross, B. H. (1983). Integrated knowledge in different tasks: The role of retrieval on fan effects. *Journal of Experimental Psychology: Learning, Memory, and Cognition, 9,* 55–72.

Reed, S. K. (1989). Constraints on the abstraction of solutions. *Journal of Educational Psychology, 81,* 532–540.

Reed, S. K., Dempster, A., & Ettinger, M. (1985). Usefulness of analogous solutions for solving algebra word problems. *Journal of Experimental Psychology: Learning, Memory, and Cognition, 11,* 106–125.

Richman, H. (1991). Discrimination net models of concept formation. In D. Fisher, M. Pazzani, & P. Langley (Eds.), *Concept formation: Knowledge and experience in unsupervised learning* (pp. 103–125). San Mateo, CA: Morgan Kaufmann.

Rifkin, A. (1985). Evidence for a basic level in event taxonomies. *Memory & Cognition, 13,* 538–556.

Rosch, E., & Mervis, C. (1975). Family resemblances: studies in the internal structure of categories. *Cognitive Psychology, 7,* 573–605.

Rosch, E., Mervis, C., Gray, W., Johnson, D., & Boyes-Braem, P. (1976). Basic objects in natural categories. *Cognitive Psychology, 18,* 382–439.

Ross, B. H., & Spalding, T. (1991). Some influences of instance comparisons on concept formation. In D. Fisher, M. Pazzani, & P. Langley (Eds.), *Concept formation: Knowledge and experience in unsupervised learning* (pp. 207–236). San Mateo, CA: Morgan Kaufmann.

Ruby, D., & Kibler, D. (1991). SteppingStone: An empirical and analytical evaluation. In *Proceedings of the ninth national conference on artificial intelligence* (pp. 527–532). Anaheim, CA: AAAI Press.

Shrager, J., Hogg, T., & Huberman, B. A. (1988). A graph-dynamic model of the power law of practice and the problem-solving fan effect. *Science, 242,* 414–416.

Silber, J., & Fisher, D. (1989). A model of natural category structure and its behavioral implications. *Proceedings of the eleventh annual conference of the Cognitive Science Society* (pp. 884–891). Ann Arbor, MI: Erlbaum.

Simon, H. A. (1969). *The sciences of the artificial.* Cambridge, MA: MIT Press.

Simon, H. A., & Lea, G. (1974). Problem solving and rule induction: A unified view. In L. W. Gregg (Ed.), *Knowledge and cognition.* Hillsdale, NJ: Erlbaum.

Sleeman, D., Hirsh, H., Ellery, I., & Kim, I. (1990). Extending domain theories: Two case studies in student modeling. *Machine Learning, 5,* 11–38.

Smith, E. E., & Medin, D. L. (1981). *Categories and concepts.* Cambridge, MA: Harvard University Press.

Vere, S. A. (1978). Inductive learning of relational productions. In D. A. Waterman & F.

Hayes-Roth (Eds.), *Pattern-directed inference systems* (pp. 281–295). New York: Academic Press.

Wisniewski, E., & Medin, D. L. (1991). Harpoons and long sticks: The interaction of theory and similarity in rule induction. In D. Fisher & M. Pazzani (Eds.), *Concept formation: Knowledge and experience in unsupervised learning* (pp. 237–278). San Mateo, CA: Morgan Kaufmann.

Yoo, J., & Fisher, D. (1991a). Concept formation over explanations and problem solving experience. In *Proceedings of the twelfth international joint conference on artificial intelligence* (pp. 630–636). Sydney, Australia: Morgan Kaufmann.

Yoo, J., & Fisher, D. (1991b). Concept formation over problem solving experience. In D. Fisher & M. Pazzani (Eds.), *Concept formation: Knowledge and experience in unsupervised learning* (pp. 279–303). San Mateo, CA: Morgan Kaufmann.

PROCESSING BIASES, KNOWLEDGE, AND CONTEXT IN CATEGORY FORMATION

Thomas B. Ward

I. Introduction

In contrast to many articles in this volume, the present work is concerned with early stages of category learning and decision-making. I mean early in the sense that the learners of most interest are preschool children. I also mean early in the sense that the focus is on how children make decisions about category membership after exposure to only one member of each novel category. Despite this focus on early stages, the themes addressed are general ones that surface in other articles in this volume (e.g., Malt, Mooney, Murphy) and that concern the relative contributions of stimulus properties and learner characteristics to the process of concept formation.

The starting point for this work is the idea that young children appear to be efficient category learners in the real world. Between the ages of 2 and 6 years, for example, children learn several thousand new words, many of which are nouns that refer to simple object categories. In addition, children in this same age range and earlier form many new concepts for which they do not yet have labels (Merriman, Schuster, & Hager, 1991; Nelson, 1973, 1974).

This observation of the young child's real-world success is often thought all the more remarkable because of some of the potential complications involved. One complication is that there are many possible ways to group any given set of objects. This is true even for sets of very simple geometric

257

forms. Consider, for example the items shown in Fig. 1. If a child focused on shape as the most important attribute, he or she might decide to put the two items on the left in one group and the two items on the right in another group. If the child focused on pattern, he or she would assign the items on the top to one group and the items on the bottom to another group. Note that these different possible groupings can be thought of in terms of the attributes that would be focused on in determining membership in the group. Further, the situation is even more complex for naturalistic items that vary in many more ways than these simple geometric forms.

Complicating the child's task even more is the fact that only some of the possible groupings are culturally valued or "correct." Thus, the child cannot just arbitrarily select any attribute from the possible set of available attributes and hope to achieve success in forming groups of objects. For example, some attributes may be highly perceptually salient, but uninformative with respect to category membership (e.g., color for the category of dogs).

In natural situations, young children must also learn the correct groupings for members of opposing categories even when there is a high level of between-category similarity. Particularly at subordinate levels of categorization (e.g., robin versus sparrow), members of opposing groups

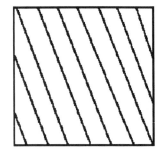
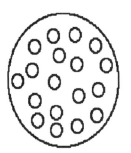

Fig. 1.   Geometric forms varying in shape and pattern.

share many salient perceptual attributes. In order to learn such groupings, children must come to focus on the differentiating rather than the shared attributes, even though the former may not always be as salient as the latter.

The basic result of these complications is that children's learning of real-world categories cannot be just purely stimulus-driven. This suggestion is, of course, consistent with ideas in the adult categorization and category learning literature concerning the limitations of similarity-based or empirically driven determinants of learning and category decision-making (see, e.g., Murphy & Medin, 1985; Wisniewski & Medin, 1991). It is also consistent with many contemporary views of conceptual development (e.g., Carey, 1985; Keil, 1989; Offenbach & Blumberg, 1985). Finally, it is consistent with suggestions regarding the limitations of purely inductive, machine learning systems (e.g., Mitchell, Keller, & Kedar-Cabelli, 1986; Mooney, this volume). The consensus appears to be that it is extremely difficult, if not impossible, for purely empirically driven inductive systems, be they human or machine, to master the task of dividing the world into useful categories.

The challenge, then, is to account for the child's real-world success given these sorts of complications. One approach is to postulate innate, early maturing or early acquired processing biases or constraints (see e.g., Behrend, 1990; Clark, 1983; Markman, 1989). These constraints would improve learning performance by helping the child to focus on what is most relevant in a given situation. Note that by postulating such constraints, one makes the suggestion that category learning is, at least partly, learner-driven. Again, this parallels suggestions in the adult, child, and machine learning literatures that categorization phenomena are best understood by examining knowledge-driven or theory-driven factors (e.g., Keil, 1989; Mitchell et al., 1986; Murphy & Medin, 1985; Wisniewski & Medin, 1991). The emerging consensus is that prior knowledge or theories determine which attributes will be selected, stored, and used in category learning and categorization.

The kinds of learner-driven constraints on children's category learning that have been suggested include whole object and taxonomic biases (Markman, 1989), and the shape bias (Landau, Smith, & Jones, 1988). These biases are most likely related to one another, and it is their combined effects that will be of most interest in the present chapter.

To appreciate the link between the whole object and shape biases note that, on hearing a novel label for a novel object, children appear to be particularly drawn to the shape of that object, and they use that property in extending the label to other entities (e.g., Landau et al., 1988). What this may mean is that children assume that the label refers to the object as a whole rather than to its parts or material substance, and as a member of a taxonomic category rather than as a participant in a thematic relation. Thus, children are drawn to an attribute that is often important in identifying objects, that is, their shape. For this reason, I refer to the combination of these constraints as an *object/shape bias.*

The object/shape bias is potentially valuable in the sense that shape may help to differentiate many object categories, particularly at the basic level (e.g., Rosch, 1978; Tversky & Hemenway, 1984). Thus, the bias may help to account for young children's early facility with basic-level categories (e.g., Horton & Markman, 1980; Mervis & Crisafi, 1982; Rosch, Mervis, Gray, Johnson, & Boyes-Braem, 1976; see however, Mandler & Bauer, 1988).

Much of this article is concerned with the extent to which this object/shape bias is flexible. The reasons for this concern are both practical and theoretical. From a practical standpoint, a rigid shape bias would be detrimental to learning about many categories for which shape is less central (e.g., substances). From a theoretical perspective, the question of flexibility is central to an understanding of the processing factors underlying the frequently observed object/shape bias.

To anticipate, I will suggest that the object/shape bias is actually a manifestation of a more general processing bias, that is, to selectively attend to *something* in making category decisions. We will see that what that something is depends on an interaction between perceptual properties of the stimuli and the learner's knowledge. Hence, I will argue that preschoolers' category learning is based on an interaction of stimulus-driven and knowledge-driven factors.

II. Evidence for an Object/Shape Bias

The findings of many studies are consistent with the existence of an object/shape bias (Baldwin, 1989; Landau et al., 1988; Taylor & Gelman, 1988; Ward, Becker, Hass, & Vela, 1989; Ward, Vela, Peery, Lewis, Bauer, & Klint, 1991). To set the stage for later studies, I will describe one example of such a result (Ward et al., 1991, Experiment 1). The subjects in this experiment were preschoolers whose mean age was 4 years, 7 months. In one condition, the children were shown drawings of two novel creatures and given a novel label for each creature. They were also told story about each one being a different type of animal living in a different cage at a zoo. Example prototypes are shown in Fig. 2.

With the drawings of the prototypes still in view, the children were then shown 16 possible variants one at a time and were asked to decide, for each

Fig. 2.   Creatures used by Ward et al. (1991).

variant, whether it was a member of one or the other or neither category. The variants were the possible combinations of two values on each of four attributes of size, number of legs, type of appendage at the end of the legs, and body shape. Children's responses were examined for patterns consistent with a focus on a particular single attribute or an attribute combination. Children who made 15 of 16 responses consistent with a given pattern were identified as having used that particular response rule.

The children tended to focus on single attributes in making decisions. More importantly, they showed a strong shape bias. Of the nine children who based their responses on a single attribute, eight selected shape as their preferred attribute.

III.   What Is the Nature of the Shape Bias?

The Ward et al. (1991) data that I have described to this point do not clarify the factors that underlie the shape bias. It is important to consider, for example, whether the bias could be based on perceptual preferences, knowledge of particular facts, naive theories, or some other characteristic of the learner. Is the shape bias based on some innate or early acquired preference for form as a perceptual attribute? If so, it should be observed when children make almost any type of classification decision. Is it based on prior knowledge that shape has been a useful attribute for making particular types of category discriminations? In this case, it should only be observed when the child has a reasonable expectation that these types of discriminations are called for.

It is unlikely that the shape bias observed by Ward et al. (1991) is simply based on the perceptual salience of the shape attribute for this one particular set of materials. Similarity scaling data collected in pilot studies reveals that the attributes are equally salient in a perceptual sense. In addition, it is clear that the shape bias is not limited to this one set of materials. Rather, it has been observed in several studies with several sets of two-dimensional and three-dimensional materials (e.g., Baldwin, 1989; Landau et al., 1988).

More importantly, Landau et al. (1988) presented data consistent with a knowledge-based explanation. In one condition of their third experiment they showed 2- and 3-year-olds a novel object and provided a novel label (e.g. *dax*) for the object. They then asked the children which of two test items was also a dax. Children's choices indicated a strong preference for a match on the attribute of shape in extending the novel label. However, when children of the same ages were given no labels, but were simply asked which of the test items went together with the sample item, they did not rely as heavily on shape in making their choices.

The failure to observe a shape bias in the absence of labels indicates that the bias is not simply a perceptual phenomenon that manifests itself any time children make decisions about how to group objects. Why then, is the bias observed when children are given labels for the objects? One way to interpret this phenomenon is that, through early language learning, children have come to know something about the usefulness of the attribute of shape. Children have learned many count nouns that refer to categories whose members share the same average shape. Thus, when they hear a novel term, they use that knowledge to determine the appropriate extension of the term (Landau et al., 1988). By this explanation, the shape bias is knowledge-driven rather than perceptually driven.

In a related way, Ward et al. (1991) presented data from a different condition that confirm Landau et al.'s basic conclusion that the shape bias is a consequence of prior learning. In that condition children received no labels and no story that the materials in Fig. 2 were animals. They were simply told that the items were pictures that had gotten out of order. These children showed no shape bias at all. Only 3 of 11 single attribute responders relied on shape in making their decisions. Again, the result is consistent with the idea that the shape bias is related to children having learned that shape is an informative attribute with respect to membership in certain categories. When the children receive no information (e.g., novel labels) that the objects are members of nonarbitrary categories, no shape bias is observed.

Data from two other conditions of the Ward et al. (1991) study help to complete the picture regarding the type of knowledge that underlies the shape bias. In one of these conditions, children received labels for the material shown in Fig. 2 but were not told any story about what kind of entities were being depicted. This comes closest to the label condition in the Landau et al. study. In the other condition, children were told a story about the example items being members of two different animal categories, but were given no novel labels for the different categories. Both of these conditions resulted in a strong shape bias, with 5 of 6 and 7 of 8 single attribute responders, respectively, basing their choices on the attribute of shape. Thus, labels are sufficient but not necessary for evoking a shape bias.

Note that there is a superficial discrepancy between the Ward et al. and Landau et al. results. In the last condition described above, Ward et al. (1991) found a strong shape bias without using labels. Landau et al. (1988) did not. How can we account for this discrepancy? One important difference is that, in the Landau et al. study, the no-label condition required the child to group together the items that, in the child's view, "went together." There was no indication to the child that a particular nonarbitrary grouping for the items might exist outside of the child's preferences. In contrast, in the Ward et al. study, conceptual information in the form of a story was used to convey to the child the idea that a new category existed to be learned. When children have no reasonable expectation that there is a new object category to be learned, they show no shape bias; when that expectation exists, they do show a shape bias.

Taken together, the results suggest that the shape bias is not a purely linguistic constraint having to do with the way in which children interpret novel labels. Rather, the fact that it can be elicited by way of a story about a new, unlabeled category suggests that the object/shape bias is a categorical constraint having to do with expectations about the properties that are relevant for determining membership in object categories, independently of whether those categories have labels. Put differently, the fact that labels can elicit a shape bias may be due, not to the fact that word learning is a unique phenomenon that evokes its own particular attentional bias, but to the fact that novel labels simply tell the child that there is a new category to be learned. Labels, stories, and other suggestions about the existence of categories to be learned are alternate paths to the same end: leading children to access and use knowledge about previously acquired categories to help direct their attention to attributes that have proven useful in the past. Thus, the shape bias is probably a knowledge-driven phenomenon, but that knowledge is likely the result of learning about categories rather than learning about words.

IV.   How Flexible Is the Shape Bias?

An important question that arises in considering any type of proposed constraint is how rigid the bias is presumed to be. We know from several studies that labels and other suggestions about nonarbitrary categories lead children to focus heavily on the attribute of shape. Is this bias applied in a mechanical fashion any time novel labels are used, even when it may be inappropriate or misleading? In contrast, is the shape bias sensibly flexible, as might be expected from the fact that it appears to be knowledge-driven? The answers to these questions have implications for the exact way in which the bias would be expected to facilitate children's real-world category learning. A rigid bias would greatly facilitate learning about object categories at the basic level, but would inhibit learning about other types of categories such as substances, for which shape is largely irrelevant. In contrast, a flexible bias might confer less of an advantage on basic object categories, but would also present less of a disadvantage for other types.

There are many questions that could be asked about the flexibility of the shape bias. One version of what it means for the bias to be sensibly flexible has to do with the evident consequences of changes in the posture of animate objects. Animate objects can change the superficial appearance of their shape by changing their posture. Snakes, for example, look different when they are curled than when they are stretched out straight. A tendency to reject a curled snake after observing and learning about a single straight exemplar of the category would be detrimental to the child's learning about snakes and other animate creatures that change posture.

In addition to the practical question about children's ability to discount superficial changes in shape, there is a deeper theoretical reason for considering the issue of posture changes: the data can provide information about the specific type of knowledge on which the shape bias is based. Is it based on knowledge of the simple fact that items in the same category have the same shape, or the more elaborate idea that some shape differences make a difference and some do not? In the latter case, the knowledge would come closer to what might be called a naive theory because decisions would be based not just on the fact of a similarity or difference in apparent shape, but on the basis of explanations about why some differences matter and others do not. Theories, after all, should contain explanations not just facts.

In an earlier study, we found a hint that preschoolers do not use shape rigidly even when they hear labels and stories that imply membership in particular types of categories (Ward et al., 1989). In that study, we tested preschoolers (mean age 4;7), second-graders, and college students. In addition to the materials shown in Fig. 2, subjects made judgments regarding three other sets of materials, the most important of which is depicted in Fig. 3. Note that these materials varied in size, number of wings, type of wings and body shape (wavy versus straight). As described previously, subjects were given novel labels and were told a story about the items being animals. Subjects then made decisions about the category membership of the possible variants. The most important result is that, although the preschool children showed a bias toward shape for the materials depicted in Fig. 2, they did not show a shape bias for the materials depicted in Fig. 3. That is, only two of nine children who reliably focused on a single attribute in making their decisions used shape and assigned all wavy creatures to one group and all straight creatures to the other group.

Why should preschoolers rely on shape in classifying the materials depicted in Fig. 2 but not those depicted in Fig. 3? One speculative account is that the children do not believe that the shape differences between the items in Fig. 3 are relevant to category membership. For example, they may have knowledge about the properties of movement, acceleration, deceleration, or change of direction that impact on the superficial shape of animate creatures. That knowledge serves as an explanation

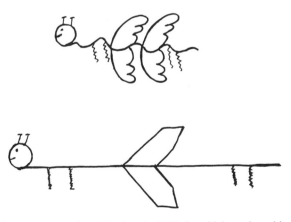

Fig. 3.   Animate creatures from Ward et al. (1989) for which no shape bias was found.

of why the depicted shape differences do not make a difference to category membership. If it is true that preschoolers use their knowledge to provide explanations for the importance or lack of importance of particular types of shape differences, then even young children's category decisions seem to be not just knowledge- or fact-driven but rather theory-driven.

The Ward et al. (1989) study was not designed specifically to examine whether young children judge some types of shape differences to be more important to category membership than others. Thus, this interpretation of their results must be viewed as quite speculative. Becker and Ward (1991b), however, studied the issue more systematically with a new set of materials depicted in Fig. 4.

Note that these materials varied in their pattern, type of eyes, presence versus absence of arms, and shape [flat (a), curled (b) and (d), and snail-

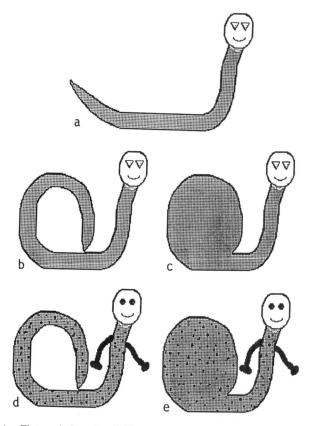

Fig. 4.   Flat, curled, and snail-like creatures from Becker and Ward (1991b).

like (c) and (e)]. All possible combinations of the attributes were used, with the result that there were eight flat, eight curled, and eight snail-like creatures in the entire set. Note also that the curled creatures have the same outline shape as the snail-like creatures and that both differ considerably from the flat creatures in outline shape. Despite these similarities and differences in outline shapes, the sensible interpretation that most adults make is that the curled creatures are actually flat ones in a different posture and that the snail-like creatures are a different kind of thing entirely.

Subjects were shown just one prototype rather than two prototypes as in previous studies. They were given a novel label for that creature and told that it was a type of pet that a particular child wanted. The prototype was always one of the flat creatures (e.g., the item in Fig. 4a). With the prototype still in view, the children then saw each of the 24 possible variants one at a time and decided whether or not each was a member of the same category as the labelled prototype.

Data from younger (3;5–4;5) and older (4;5–5;5) preschoolers and adult college students are shown separately in Fig. 5. The figure shows the number of acceptances (i.e., labeling a creature the same as the flat prototype) out of a possible 8 for each type of shape item (flat, curled, snail-like). The flat creatures tend to be accepted more often than the other types, but the most important result is that the curled creatures are accepted as members of category much more often than snail-like creatures by all age groups. Consistent with the speculative account of the Ward et al. (1989) results, it appears that knowledge of animate movement influ-

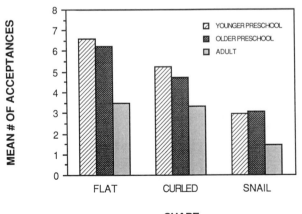

Fig. 5.   Mean number of acceptances of flat, curled, and snail-like test items from Becker and Ward (1991b).

ences even preschoolers' interpretations of shape differences. Knowledge about possible posture changes in animate creatures provides an explanation for the apparent difference in shape between the flat and curled creatures.

It is important to note that the children were basing their judgments about test stimuli on experience with a single presentation of a static exemplar. Thus, even with no direct experience of the different postures the exemplar was capable of, they were apparently able to use more general knowledge about movement to project what shapes the exemplar could assume.

Although it is not central to the present discussion, I should also note what is evident in Fig. 5: Adults accepted fewer creatures overall than the children. This was because they tended to require a match on more than just shape (e.g., arms and eyes also) whereas children relied more exclusively on the single attribute of shape (Becker & Ward, 1991b).

The explanation-based interpretation of children's responding is consistent with the spirit of other views of the child's conceptual functioning as being theory-driven (e.g., Keil, 1989). Keil, for example, has conducted an elegant series of studies concerned with the types of transformation that will lead children to conclude that the category membership of a given object has been changed. As an example of one such transformation, children were told that some doctors had dyed a racoon black, bleached a white stripe down the middle of its back, and implanted a sac of "super smelly, yucky stuff." Children were then asked whether the resulting entity was a racoon or a skunk. A particularly important result that emerges across these transformation studies is that young children's willingness to state that the transformation had changed the category membership of the item (e.g., that the racoon was now a skunk) depended on the degree to which the transformation was temporary or permanent. The more temporary the transformation was, the more likely children were to indicate that the transformation had not changed the category membership of the entity. For example, when the appearance of an organism was changed simply by putting a costume on it, even kindergartners were unlikely to say that the category membership of the entity had changed.

Postural changes represent an extremely temporary type of transformation. Thus, the curled creatures in the Becker and Ward (1991b) study can be thought of as depicting a very simple temporary transformation of the flat prototype. The results, then, are consistent with Keil's suggestion that even preschoolers' knowledge is developed enough to allow them to disregard some types of temporary transformations when judging category membership.

V.   Additional Evidence for the Flexibility of the Shape Bias

The evidence presented in the previous section documents one way in which the shape bias exhibited by preschoolers is flexible: children are able to use knowledge about animate movement to overlook certain types of superficial differences in outline shape. This flexibility would be expected to facilitate their learning about animate entities.

Interestingly, the children in Becker and Ward's study did not overlook shape entirely. They still focused on shape, but simply decided that some types of shape differences were more important than others. There are other category learning tasks in which it would be beneficial for children to be flexible enough to give up a reliance on shape entirely. Specifically, shape is irrelevant and texture and color are much more important in learning about substances (e.g., mashed potatoes, wood). A rigid tendency to focus on shape to the exclusion of other attributes would inhibit children's learning about substances.

Are children able to shift attention to other attributes in learning about substances? The answer appears to be yes, at least for nonsolid substances. For example, Soja, Carey, and Spelke (1991) showed preschoolers unfamiliar solids (e.g., a copper plumbing fixture) or nonsolid substances (e.g., setting gel). The researchers provided labels for the presented exemplars and asked the children to choose which of two test items should also receive the same label. The pairs of test items were designed to allow the investigators to know whether children had interpreted the labels as referring to the shape of the labeled entity as a whole or to the material of which it was made. Using the labeled copper plumbing fixture as an example, one member of the pair of test items varied from the labeled exemplar in shape and number but maintained the same material type (e.g., three irregularly shaped chunks of copper) and the other varied in material or substance but maintained the same shape or object type (e.g., a white plastic plumbing fixture of the same type as the labeled copper one). Using the nonsolid setting gel as an example, the test items would be three irregular blobs of setting gel, and one blob of hand cream mixed with gravel formed into the same shape as the originally labeled pile of setting gel. Note that the second test item in each of these pairs differed from the labeled entity in the observable attributes of color and texture. The labels were presented using either neutral syntax (e.g., *my blicket*) or informative syntax (e.g, *a blicket* for the solids and *some blicket* for the nonsolids).

Soja et al. found that even two-year-olds attended primarily to color and texture rather than to shape in making decisions about the nonsolids. That is, for stimuli such as the setting gel, children were highly likely to choose the three irregular piles of setting gel as the test item deserving of the label rather than the other substance in the same shape as the original pile of gel. This was true even when the syntax used in presenting the nonsolids was neutral. Dickinson (1988) has reported the same phenomenon for three-to-five-year-olds. These results mean that even young preschoolers are not so rigid in adhering to a shape bias that they focus on that attribute when it would be plainly inappropriate to do so (i.e., when they are learning about substances that appear to have no characteristic shape). This flexibility indicates that the shape bias that preschoolers have been found to exhibit in other situations is not so rigid that it would put them at a disadvantage in learning about nonsolid substances.

One interpretation of the Soja et al. and Dickinson results is that children have already learned by the age of two that some types of materials can be readily deformed into almost any shape whereas others cannot. One particularly prevalent situation in which this type of learning would take place is mealtime; foods, particularly those typically handled by two-year-olds, can be mashed into a limitless variety of shapes. Children's knowledge about readily deformable materials would tell them that shape was not a relevant attribute for making category decisions about those materials. The same learning experiences would tell them that other attributes such as color and texture do consistently differentiate nonsolid substances from one another. As a result of this previously acquired knowledge, their attention would be diverted away from shape and toward color and texture, at least for materials that have directly observable perceptual properties that indicate deformability. Again, knowledge drives attention toward or away from particular attributes.

Although preschoolers relinquish their shape bias in dealing with nonsolids, they apparently adhere to it when they learn about solids. That is, consistent with previous reports of a shape bias, Soja et al. found that, with neutral syntax or syntax that implied the entity was an object, children as young as 2 years of age relied heavily on shape in making category decisions about the solids that were presented. Furthermore, Dickinson (1988) found that three-to-five-year-olds relied heavily on the shape of the objects to make category decisions even when the objects were presented with a mass noun syntax that implied the entity being labeled was a substance (e.g., *some trag*). Although the mass syntax did shift children away from the near total reliance on shape that occurred in a neutral syntax condition, there was still a strong shape bias. For example, even when solid objects such as the copper plumbing fixture were referred to as *some trag*, 78% of the five-year-olds' responses were for the same shaped object made of a different material.

Does the shape bias for solids mean that young children will be at a disadvantage in learning about solid substances such as copper and wood, which have the solid (non-deformable) characteristic of objects? If the typical learning situation includes no information other than the single entity to be learned about and syntactic cues, then the answer would be yes. However, my belief is that learning situations are often richer than this. Children learn in rich contexts that provide much more information about what kind of entity is being labeled. For example, they learn about new animals in the context of picture books containing other novel and familiar animals or in the context of a visit to a zoo; they learn about new foods in the context of picture books about food or at meals. I will refer to this situational information as the *conceptual context* in which learning occurs, and I believe that it is an essential factor that helps children to apply their processing biases sensibly rather than rigidly. Like the perceptual information about the deformability of the nonsolid substances available to children in the Soja et al. and Dickinson studies, this conceptual context might provide children with the information needed to overcome a shape bias. However, that context might provide the needed information even when children are learning about more solid appearing substances for which perceptual information about deformability is lacking.

A rich conceptual context is often missing in studies of children's extension of novel labels, partly because the focus in these studies is on the idea that children can and do learn in ambiguous circumstances. Thus, because the studies present the child with an ambiguous task, they provide critical information on how children are able to make the best of a sometimes difficult learning task. However, because children do learn in richer, more informative contexts, it is important to determine the extent to which they make use of available clarifying information.

Becker and Ward (1991a) examined the role of the conceptual context in influencing the shape bias in preschoolers' category decisions. Four-, five-, and six-year-olds made categorization decisions for one of two types of material: three-dimensional structures that varied in their overall shape (bimodal versus unimodal) and texture/material composition (blue glitter versus bluish chunks of styrofoam), and black and white drawings that also varied in shape (bimodal or unimodal) and texture/pattern (granular or lumpy). For each set, four stimuli were created from the possible combinations of the levels of each attribute. The three-dimensional structures and the drawings were created to allow a plausible interpretation of the materials as either objects or substances. Examples of the drawings are shown in Fig. 6.

For both sets of materials, subjects were tested in one of two instructional conditions that were designed to provide different conceptual contexts. In either of the instructional conditions they saw a single prototype (e.g., the item in Fig. 6a), heard a novel label for it, and made judgments about the appropriate extension of that label to each of the four variants. In the Zoo instructional condition they were told that the prototype stimulus was a *diffle*, and that a diffle is a kind of animal that lives in a cage at the zoo with other diffles. In the Food instructional condition, they were told that the prototype stimulus was *a pile of diffle*, and that diffle is a kind of food that a particular creature likes to eat.

It is important to emphasize that subjects in the Zoo and Food conditions judged the exact same stimulus materials. The most salient difference across these instructional conditions was the nature of the conceptual context provided by the experimenter. In one case, the context indicated that the labeled stimulus was a kind of animal. In the other, it indicated that the stimulus was a type of food. To obtain an intuitive sense of what might be sensible responses in these two conditions, consider which of the items in Fig. 6b and 6c belongs in the same category with the item in Fig. 6a. If the item in Fig. 6a is an animal called a *diffle*, then the item in Fig. 6b would also be a diffle. If the item in Fig. 6a is a pile of a food called *diffle*, the item in Fig. 6c would be a more likely candidate to also be a pile of diffle.

If the shape bias is rigid and uninfluenced by the conceptual context, then children would be expected to make their decisions on the basis of shape in both conditions. Again using the items in Fig. 6, children would be more likely to assign the item in Fig. 6b to the category *diffle* regardless of whether they were in the Zoo or the Food condition. On the other hand, if

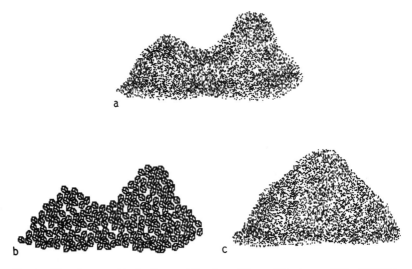

Fig. 6.   Drawings used in the Zoo and Food conditions of Becker and Ward (1991a).

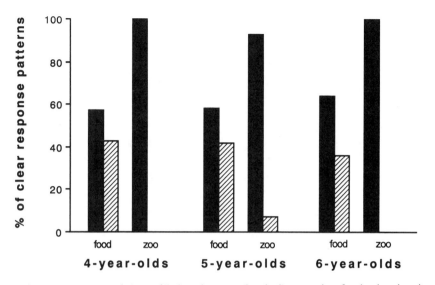

Fig. 7. Percentage of shape (filled) and texture (hatched) responders for the drawings in the Zoo and Food conditions of Becker and Ward (1991a).

children are capable of using the conceptual context to override the shape bias, then they would be expected to attend to shape in the Zoo condition but to texture in the Food condition.

The data for black-and-white drawings are shown in Fig. 7 and those for the three-dimensional materials are shown in Fig. 8. The figures show the number of children in each group who consistently relied on shape or texture in making their category decisions.[1] As can be seen in Fig. 7, all age groups showed a greater reliance on shape in the Zoo than in the Food condition for the drawings. As shown in Fig. 8, a similar effect occurred for the three-dimensional structures. In fact all age groups showed a reversal from a predominance of shape in the Zoo condition to a predominance of texture in the Food condition.

The implication of these findings is that the conceptual context matters a great deal. Even four-year-olds were able to overcome the shape bias

---

[1] Children were categorized as shape responders if they focused exclusively on shape or if they used a combination of shape and texture. They were categorized as texture responders only if they focused exclusively on texture and not shape. The rationale for dividing response patterns in this way is that rejecting a pile of food on the basis of its shape would represent an "error" in the Food condition (e.g., spinach is spinach regardless of the shape of the pile), whereas considering texture differences is not necessarily an error in the Zoo condition (e.g., cats and armadillos differ as much in texture as they do in shape).

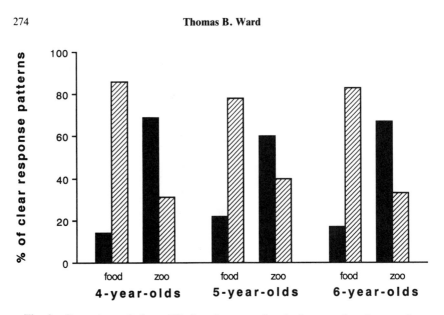

Fig. 8.   Percentage of shape (filled) and texture (hatched) responders for ...e three-dimensional materials in the Zoo and Food conditions of Becker and Ward (1991a).

when conceptual information is provided that might help the child determine the relative importance of shape and texture.

VI. Functional Parts and the Object/Shape Bias

There are other examples of preschool age children failing to show a shape bias in extending novel words. For example, Ward et al. (1989) also presented children with the materials shown in Fig. 9 and identified them as toys that particular children wanted to play with. The subjects did not have a strong tendency to group by way of the attribute of shape. In fact, a reanalysis of the data (see Ward, 1990) indicated that the most common response among five-year-olds was to extend labels on the basis of the type of wheels (cogged versus smooth) depicted on the prototypes and test items. Six of twelve children who focused on a single attribute made their decisions on the basis of the type of wheels. One way to interpret this finding is that the children judged the wheels to be a significant functional part of the toy. For example, the different types of wheels might impact on the movement characteristics of the toy. What this means is that, when parts that have obvious functional significance are present, children may give up a reliance on shape in favor of a reliance on those parts to make

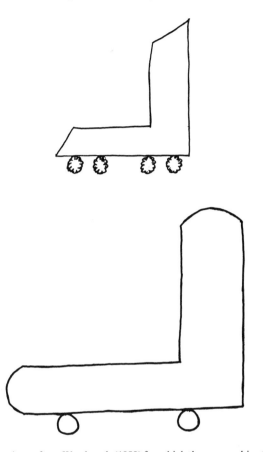

Fig. 9.   Inanimate items from Ward et al. (1989) for which there was a bias toward the type of wheel (cogged versus smooth).

category decisions. Again, this highlights how much the child's selection of attributes appears to be knowledge-driven.

In a more recent study we have also examined children's extensions of labels for materials that varied in the presence versus absence of particular functional parts (legs, wings, and plumes) and the shape of the central body (Ward et al., 1991). Two results are of interest. First, central body shape was not important in most five-year-olds' choices. Second, many children used a combination of attributes (e.g., legs, wings, and plumes) in making their decisions. This last result is in strong contrast to the typical finding in which children rely heavily on a single attribute. Again, the results point to the important role functional parts play in children's category decision-making.

The results described in the previous paragraph also serve to highlight some of the complexities involved in defining shape. In addition to the central body of a creature, the presence versus absence of parts in a particular configuration is a way to characterize shape (see, e.g., Biederman, 1987; Tversky & Hemenway, 1984). In the present case, children's reliance on legs, wings, and plumes is consistent with Tversky & Hemenway's contention that the often observed importance of shape may be based on its link to a configuration of functional parts.

VII. Attribute Availability

An organizing framework for interpreting the results described in this chapter is the *attribute availability* model of children's category learning (Ward, 1990; Ward et al., 1991). The model describes young children's category learning as an interaction between stimulus-driven and learner-driven factors. It states that children's category learning is facilitated by an interaction between the stimulus factor of natural category structures that provide informative attributes and the learner-driven factor of processing tendencies that lead to selective attention to those attributes.

Considering stimulus factors first, natural and artifact categories of the type that young children are learning about are described as having family-resemblance structures (see, e.g., Rosch & Mervis, 1975). That is, rather than possessing defining attributes that are necessary and sufficient for determining category membership, members of real-world categories share characteristic attributes each of which may be true of many, but not all category members. In other words, real-world categories tend to have several partially predictive attributes rather than one or more absolutely predictive attributes. Different members possess different numbers and different specific combinations of the characteristic attributes. Given this type of attribute structure, a young child who randomly chose some attribute to attend to might achieve some measure of success in making category decisions. That is, by chance, the child might happen upon an attribute that is at least partially predictive of category membership.

Although a random selection of an attribute to attend to might help some children with some categories, it is clear that some attributes are more informative than others with respect to category membership. Shape, for example, is more informative than color and texture with respect to membership in simple object categories. In contrast, color and texture are more informative than shape with respect to membership in substance categories. Thus, in addition to providing many partially informative attributes, real-world category structures provide some highly informative attributes. A child whose attention was selectively drawn to those informative attributes would be at a great advantage in learning about those categories. To return to the notion of availability, informative attributes are available in the stimuli to be learned about.

The second aspect of the attribute availability model is a learner-driven or processing component. The model states that category learning situations lead even very young children to selectively attend to some attributes more than others in making category decisions. The idea that selective attribute processing by preschoolers is characteristic of category learning situations deserves further comment. The model does not imply that young children will always or even often process information in this analytic, selective fashion. Indeed, there are data that indicate that young children process information holistically rather than analytically when they perform simple classification tasks (see, e.g., Shepp, Burns, & McDonough, 1980; Smith & Kemler, 1977; Ward, 1980). Furthermore, although there have been questions about exactly how "holistic" older preschoolers are in these tasks, even sophisticated analyses involving stimuli with a wide range of dimensional variation indicate that three-year-olds may give truly holistic responses (Smith, 1989). However, the difference between category learning situations and these simple classification tasks is that the latter convey to the child the idea that there are no right or wrong groupings; classification is presented as being a matter of the child's preference. Under such a condition, there is no particular reason for the child to seek out an attribute to help in making a "correct" classification decision.

In contrast, when a child hears a new word, this can provide a clue to the child that a new category exists to be learned. Thus, rather than processing in a simple holistic manner, the child is led to selectively seek out the attributes of the labelled entity that may be informative in the sense of helping him or her to recognize other members of the category in the future.

As noted earlier, a new word may not be the only aspect of category learning situation that can evoke this type of selective processing. For example, a suggestion that an entity is some yet unlabeled type of animal appears to be enough to evoke selective attention to the attribute of shape (Ward et al., 1991). More generally, any suggestion that a nonarbitrary category grouping exists to be learned would be expected to bring about selective attribute processing.

Finally, the model implies that the selection of attributes in obvious category learning situations is not random. Rather, it is driven by the child's developing knowledge base. Among other things, by two years of age that knowledge base appears to contain the idea that shape is an important attribute for making basic object category discriminations (e.g., Landau et al., 1988). It also appears to contain the idea that color and texture are more important for some types of discriminations, at least when perceptual cues about deformability are directly available, as in the case of nonsolids (Soja et al., 1991). By four years of age children are able to use knowledge about the importance of color and texture for some types of contrasts even when no perceptual cues about deformability are present (Becker & Ward, 1991a).

Many aspects of the learning context can influence which portions of the child's developing knowledge base are brought to bear on the task. This can include linguistic factors such as mass versus count syntax which might activate information relevant to substances versus objects. It can also include conceptual information which might differentially activate knowledge about broad domains (e.g., Becker & Ward, 1991a).

Within the attribute availability model, then, the shape bias that has been observed in many situations is viewed as a specific version of a more general processing bias. That bias is to selectively attend to "something" when it is clear to the processor that there is a new category to be learned. Which attribute is selected for special treatment is determined by a variety of factors including the child's knowledge of the importance of different attributes for different broad domains. One implication of this view is that, in addition to any basic level categories the young child may be forming, he or she must also be rapidly evolving broad domains of knowledge that help to guide attention to attributes of potential members of those domains. Recent work in other laboratories indicates that broad domains may indeed be forming in children as young as two years of age and possibly younger (Massey & Gelman, 1988; Mandler & Bauer, 1988; Soja et al., 1991).

VIII. Conclusions

Theoretical positions holding that children operate according to specific constraints as they learn new categories (e.g., a shape bias) have been extremely valuable in showing what children can do with limited input. Because children do sometimes learn under impoverished input conditions in the real world, it is important to know how they might be able to learn so quickly despite the ambiguous nature of the task. However, it is equally clear that children do not always operate in ambiguous environments and it is important to know the limits that may exist on any observed constraints. In this article, I have considered the limits on one specific type of constraint, the shape bias.

It is clear that children do not rigidly apply the shape bias. Preschoolers' use of shape is influenced by their knowledge about animate movement, which appears to provide them with an *explanation* of why some types of shape differences are unimportant to category membership decisions. Their reliance on shape is also influenced by conceptual information about whether the entity being labeled is an animal, for which shape would matter, or a type of food, for which color and texture are more important. Children's reliance on shape also appears to be modified by their knowledge about the significance of particular types of functional parts such as wheels, legs, and wings.

Although children's category learning may sometimes occur under ambiguous circumstances, it also occurs in rich interactive contexts characterized by much disambiguating information. There is linguistic information that may be provided by adults, such as the presence versus absence of articles (e.g., Taylor & Gelman, 1988). In addition, there is information directly available in the labeled entity about what kind of thing it is. This can include something as small as the presence versus absence of eyes to indicate an animate versus inanimate entity (e.g., Jones, Smith, & Landau, 1991). It can also include perceptual clues as to the deformability of the entity (Soja et al., 1991).

In addition to linguistic and entity information, learning situations often provide a conceptual context within which to interpret a new entity. Parents, for example, might clarify that a new entity is an animal, a pet, a type of food, and so on. Even without such direct statements, there may be implicit suggestions about the broader domain from which a new entity comes. For example, new animals are often encountered in the context of known animals at the zoo or in picture books. New foods are encountered in the context of old foods and in familiar settings such as at regular mealtimes. These explicit and implicit suggestions about the relevant domain can lead to the activation of particular knowledge structures and in turn to the selective processing of attributes that are particularly relevant for those domains.

In highly ambiguous situations with no linguistic or entity information and no clarifying conceptual context, default biases may come into play. The shape bias that has been observed to date may be just such a bias. The exact way in which default biases, linguistic cues, entity information, and conceptual context interact to determine children's interpretations of new entities must be the focus of future research. Much remains to be done, including a documentation of the ages at which children first exhibit sensitivity to each of these factors and the relative contribution of each factor throughout development.

Although the exact pattern of interactions at different ages is not clear, what is clear is that "early" category learning and decision-making appear to involve interactions among stimulus, situational, and learner (knowledge) characteristics. Thus, the present work is highly consistent with adult work described by Wattenmaker, Nakamura, and Medin (1987), Wisniewski and Medin (1991), and others who have shown that adult category formation involves these types of interactions. It appears to be a very general human tendency to learn categories via an interaction of stimulus-driven and knowledge- or theory-driven factors. Further, the explanation-based approach to machine learning indicates that "theories" are needed for machines to learn efficiently from experience with exemplars (see e.g., Mooney, this volume). Thus, these interactions may not be limited to humans, but rather may typify inductive systems in general.

The easy work is over. We have acknowledged and demonstrated the importance of existing knowledge systems in driving inductions that are made from experiences with category exemplars. The much harder task of explaining how those knowledge systems evolve from experiences with exemplars remains.

Acknowledgments

The research reported in this chapter was supported by grant MH-43356 from the National Institute of Mental Health.

References

Baldwin, D. A. (1989). Priorities in children's expectations about object label reference: Form over color. *Child Development, 60,* 1291–1306.

Becker, A. H., & Ward, T. B. (1991a, April). *Children's use of shape and texture with objects and substances.* Paper presented at the meeting of the Society for Research in Child Development, Seattle, WA.

Becker, A. H., & Ward, T. B. (1991b). Children's use of shape in extending novel labels to animate objects: Identity versus postural change. *Cognitive Development, 6,* 3–16.

Behrend, D. A. (1990). Constraints and development: A reply to Nelson (1988). *Cognitive Development, 5,* 313–330.

Biederman, I. (1987). Recognition-by-components: A theory of human image understanding. *Psychological Review, 94,* 115–147.

Carey, S. (1985). *Conceptual change in childhood.* Cambridge, MA: MIT Press.

Clark, E. V. (1983). Meanings and concepts. In J. H. Flavell & E. M. Markman (Eds.),

Handbook of child psychology: Vol. 3. Cognitive development (pp. 787–840). New York: Wiley.

Dickinson, D. K. (1988). Learning names for materials: Factors constraining and limiting hypotheses about word meaning. *Cognitive Development, 3,* 15–35.

Horton, M. S., & Markman, E. M. (1980). Developmental differences in the acquisition of basic and superordinate level categories. *Child Development, 51,* 708–719.

Jones, S. S., Smith, L. B., & Landau, B. (1991). Object properties and knowledge in early lexical learning. *Child Development, 62,* 499–516.

Keil, F. C. (1989). *Concepts, kinds, and cognitive development.* Cambridge, MA: MIT Press.

Landau, B., Smith, L. B., & Jones, S. S. (1988). The importance of shape in early lexical learning. *Cognitive Development, 3,* 299–321.

Mandler, J. M., & Bauer, P. J. (1988). The cradle of categorization: Is the basic level basic? *Cognitive Development, 3,* 247–264.

Markman, E. M. (1989). *Categorization and naming in children.* Cambridge, MA: MIT Press.

Massey, C. M., & Gelman, R. (1988). Preschooler's ability to decide whether a photographed unfamiliar object can move itself. *Developmental Psychology, 24,* 307–317.

Merriman, W. E., Schuster, J. M., & Hager, L. B. (1991). Are names ever mapped onto existing categories? *Journal of Experimental Psychology: General, 120,* 288–300.

Mervis, C. B., & Crisafi, M. A. (1982). Order of acquisition of subordinate-, basic-, and superordinate level categories. *Child Development, 53,* 258–266.

Mitchell, T. M., Keller, R., & Kedar-Cabelli, S. (1986). Explanation-based generalization: A unifying view. *Machine Learning, 1,* 47–80.

Murphy, G. L., & Medin, D. L. (1985). The role of theories in conceptual coherence. *Psychological Review, 92,* 289–316.

Nelson, K. (1973). Structure and strategy in learning to talk. *Monographs of the Society for Research in Child Development, 38* (Whole No. 149).

Nelson, K. (1974). Concept, word, and sentence: Interrelations in acquisition and development. *Psychological Review, 81,* 267–285.

Offenbach, S. I., & Blumberg, F. C. (1985). The concept of dimensions in developmental research. In H. W. Reese (Ed.), *Advances in child development and behavior: Vol. 19* (pp 83–112). New York: Academic Press.

Rosch, E. (1978). Principles of categorization. In E. Rosch & B. Lloyd (Eds.), *Cognition and categorization* (pp. 28–46). Hillsdale, NJ: Erlbaum.

Rosch, E., & Mervis, C. B. (1975). Family resemblances: Studies in the internal structure of categories. *Cognitive Psychology, 7,* 573–605.

Rosch, E., Mervis, C. B., Gray, W. D., Johnson, D. M., & Boyes-Braem (1976). Basic objects in natural categories. *Cognitive Psychology, 8,* 382–439.

Shepp, B. E., Burns, B., & McDonough, D. (1980). The relation of stimulus structure to perceptual and cognitive development: Further tests of a separability hypothesis. In F. Wilkening, J. Becker, & T. Trabasso (Eds.), *Information integration by children* (pp. 113–145). Hillsdale, NJ: Erlbaum.

Smith, L. B. (1989). A model of perceptual classification in children and adults. *Psychological Review, 96,* 125–144.

Smith, L. B., & Kemler, D. G. (1977). Developmental trends in free classification: Evidence for a new conceptualization of perceptual development. *Journal of Experimental Child Psychology, 24,* 279–298.

Soja, N. S., Carey, S., and Spelke, E. (1991). Ontological categories guide young children's inductions of word meaning: Object terms and substance terms. *Cognition, 38,* 179–211.

Taylor, M., & Gelman, S. A. (1988). Adjectives and nouns: Children's strategies for learning new words. *Child Development, 59,* 411–419.

Tversky, B., & Hemenway, K. (1984). Objects, parts, and categories. *Journal of Experimental Psychology: General, 113,* 169–193.

Ward, T. B. (1980). Separable and integral responding by children and adults to the dimensions of length and density. *Child Development, 51,* 676–684.

Ward, T. B. (1990). The role of labels in directing children's attention. In J. T. Enns (Ed.), *The development of attention: Research and theory* (pp. 321–342). Amsterdam: Elsevier Science Publishers.

Ward, T. B., Becker, A. H., Hass, S. D., & Vela, E. (1991). Attribute availability and the shape bias in children's category generalization. *Cognitive Development, 6,* 143–167.

Ward, T. B., Vela, E., Peery, M. L., Lewis, S., Bauer, N. K., & Klint, K. (1989). What makes a vibble a vibble: A developmental study of category generalization. *Child Development, 60,* 214–224.

Wattenmaker, W. D., Nakamura, G. V., & Medin, D. L. (1987). Relationships between similarity-based and explanation-based categorization. In D. Hilton (Ed.), *Contemporary science and natural explanation: Common sense conception of causality.* Sussex: Harvester Press.

Wisniewski, E. J., & Medin, D. L. (1991). Harpoons and long sticks: The interaction of theory and similarity in rule induction. In D. Fisher & M. Pazzani (Eds.), *Computational approaches to concept formation* (pp. 237–278). San Mateo, CA: Morgan Kaufmann.

CATEGORIZATION AND RULE INDUCTION IN CLINICAL DIAGNOSIS AND ASSESSMENT

Gregory H. Mumma

I. Overview

Clinical decision making encompasses the range of judgments, choices, and diagnostic decisions made by the psychologist in the process of providing clinical services to a patient. These decisions range from dispositional recommendations and the development of a treatment plan to particular therapeutic responses to the patient within a psychotherapy session. In the process of making these decisions, the cognitive activity of the clinician involves repeated instances of categorization and rule induction inherent to both clinical diagnosis and assessment (Korchin, 1976; Millon, 1991; Sundberg & Tyler, 1962).

Clinical diagnosis is a classification task which uses features or dimensions of relevance across individuals (e.g., the patient's mood) to categorize aspects of the patient's functioning into one or more of a finite set of diagnostic disorders, such as those in the DSM-III-R (American Psychiatric Association, 1987; Millon, 1991). In contrast, clinical assessment involves developing an individualized "theory of the person situation," an integrated and coherent description of the intrapsychic and interpersonal functioning of the patient including the circumstances or conditions under which psychological distress or dysfunction occur (Korchin, 1976; Persons, 1989; Sundberg & Tyler, 1962).[1] During the past decade, certain principles about the nature of categories which were developed in models of similarity-based categorization of natural object categories have been found to apply to clinical diagnostic categories. However, this research has focused almost exclusively on issues of categorization of psychiatric disorders, an understandable and convenient focus because certain characteristics of disorder-level categorization make it particularly amenable to study via the methods developed in experimental investigations of categorization in cognitive laboratories.

In contrast, researchers have paid relatively little attention to aspects of categorization which occur prior to the diagnosis of the disorder in the sequence of information processing in diagnosis occurring in clinical settings. Categorization and rule induction in the clinical assessment process has received even less attention.

This article examines the role of categorization and rule induction in clinical evaluation. First, general characteristics of categorization and rule induction processes in clinical evaluation are examined and compared to those of laboratory categorization experiments. The implications of these differences are discussed in terms of the nature of the models which need to be developed to understand categorization in clinical evaluation. Following a summary of the major characteristics and purposes of diagnosis, recent advances in understanding clinicians' mental representations of psychiatric disorders are reviewed. *Lower-level* categorization in clinical diagnosis is then examined. This is categorization which occurs prior to the disorder classification and involves decisions about the diagnostic criteria of a diagnostic disorder. Issues which are addressed include (1) the decomposition, context embeddedness, and multidetermination of features in clinical categorization; (2) the contribution of the clinician's domain knowledge (including both formal clinical theory and informal theory) to successful categorization; and (3) mechanisms whereby both clinical theory and previous exemplar and category-label information can interfere with successful diagnosis. These issues are formalized in a preliminary model of lower-level categorization in clinical diagnosis.

In the final section of the article, clinical assessment is differentiated from clinical diagnosis in terms of the nature of the categorization goal and process. A framework for the study of categorization and rule induction in clinical assessment is developed based on recent work in (1) information

---

[1] Since both diagnosis and assessment use the clinical interview as the primary source of data (features) about the patient, I refer to both as *clinical evaluation*—thereby indicating the general activity of evaluating, interpreting, or understanding a patient's present and past functioning based primarily upon interview data. These activities differ from personality assessment, which uses data primarily from psychometric tests to develop an understanding of the patient.

processing investigations of scientific discovery and medical decision-making, (2) explanation-based learning, and (3) recent conceptualizations of the essential structure of the case formulation in clinical assessment. The article concludes by suggesting several mechanisms which clinicians may use to generate the core rules in clinical assessment. The emphasis throughout the article is on reviewing and discussing a selective sample of the clinical and categorization literature in the context of a conceptual analysis of the interplay of theory-driven and data-driven processes in clinical evaluation.

The overlap between problem solving and categorization embodied in the model of lower-level categorization in clinical diagnosis and the clinical assessment framework developed in this article has also been discussed by Simon and Lea (1974), Medin (1989), and Fisher and Yoo (this volume). The clinician's search for clinically significant behaviors (findings) within the complex and virtually boundless array of patient behaviors, a search which is guided by the goal of inducing the core rules in the case formulation, is related to the notion of deep-structural or deep-causal information search discussed by Graesser, Langston, and Baggett (this volume). Notions that the utility of categorization involves more than featural prediction are central to both clinical diagnosis and assessment and are related to issues discussed by Murphy (this volume). Recent developments in single-instance category learning within explanation-based models of categorization (see Ahn, Brewer, & Mooney, 1992; Mooney, this volume) provide a basis for the study of this historically respected inference process within clinical assessment. Finally, a major theme of this article reflects an issue which Brewer (this volume) raises on a more general level: limits to the applicability and generalizability of categorization models which have been developed using simplified, artificial, and primarily perceptual stimuli. The model of clinical diagnostic categorization and the framework for studying clinical assessment developed in this article suggest that some models of categorization in complex, context-dependent, and theoretically rich domains may need to have a very different nature and structure from those developed in simplified, theoretically impoverished domains.

II. Requirements for Models of Categorization in Clinical Evaluation

To maximize their potential applicability to and utility for clinical diagnosis and assessment, models of categorization and rule induction need to take into account several basic characteristics of the clinical evaluation task. First, under certain circumstances, prescriptive models (or when available, normative models) of categorization or rule induction should be developed and juxtaposed to descriptive models of task processing (Baron, 1988). The former incorporate strategies which should increase the probability of an accurate decision or inference, while the latter describe actual task performance. This approach has yielded important results concerning the impact of human information processing limitations and heuristic biases in clinical judgment (see Arkes, 1981; Faust, 1986; Turk & Salovey, 1985; Wedding & Faust, 1989, for reviews). However, most studies to date have use simplified diagnostic or judgment tasks (Dawes & Corrigan, 1974; Goldberg, 1970; Meehl, 1954, 1986; Sawyer, 1966), which have been criticized for their low ecological validity (e.g., Holt, 1978, 1988; Korchin, 1976; Rock, Bransford, & Maisto, 1987; Sarbin, 1986; Sundberg & Tyler, 1962).

A second requirement for models of categorization and rule induction in clinical evaluation is that they must account for information processing over time occurring within the context of the patient–clinician interaction. The clinician is actively searching for and acquiring information, and obtaining feedback about his/her hypotheses from additional patient data (Persons, 1993; Rock et al., 1987; cf. Einhorn & Hogarth, 1981; Hogarth, 1981). This context differs substantially from a reception paradigm in which the subject receives the information (e.g., Bruner, Goodnow, & Austin, 1956, chap. 5; Nosofsky, Clark, & Shin, 1989; Wisniewski & Medin, 1991). The importance of examining pre-decisional behavior, particularly task performance during information acquisition, has been a basic principle of decision-making research for over a decade (e.g., Einhorn & Hogarth, 1981; Jacoby, Chestnut, Weigl, & Fisher, 1976; Payne, Braunstein, & Carroll, 1978; Ford, Schmitt, Schectman, Hults, & Doherty, 1989) and has been used in many studies of rule induction or concept attainment (e.g., Bruner et al., 1956, chap. 4; Wason & Johnson-Laird, 1972; Mynatt, Doherty, & Tweney, 1977, 1978; Klahr & Dunbar, 1988).

In the traditional laboratory category-learning or rule-induction task, the subject receives feedback from the experimenter concerning whether each exemplar is or is not an instance of the target concept, rule, or category (e.g., Bruner et al., 1956, chap. 4; Gorman, 1986; Nosofsky et al., 1989; Wason & Johnson-Laird, 1972). Such veridical feedback is absent in the clinical evaluation context. However, performance in rule-induction tasks in which the subject must self-evaluate the meaning of the feedback obtained from an information search has been successfully modeled in some recent laboratory investigations and simulations (Holland, Holyoak, Nisbett, & Thagard, 1986; Klahr & Dunbar, 1988; Kulkarni & Simon, 1988; Mynatt et al., 1977, 1978; cf. also Graesser et al., this volume). Such models would seem particularly relevant to categorization and rule induction in clinical evaluation.

Finally, models of categorization and rule induction in clinical evaluation need to accommodate stimuli, the behavior of the patient, which involve a rich bundle of complex featural information. In contrast, in typical laboratory experiments, the experimenter uses relatively simple stimuli involving a fixed set of features or dimensions that take on a fixed number or a well defined range of values (Ahn et al., 1992).

III. Categorization in Clinical Diagnosis

A. CHARACTERISTICS AND FUNCTIONS OF DIAGNOSIS IN CLINICAL EVALUATION

This section provides a brief overview of the nature and functions of psychiatric taxa and diagnosis. Its purpose is to provide a common framework for the discussion of clinical categorization.

One of the key characteristics of psychiatric taxa and of the *DSM-III-R* classification system [American Psychiatric Association (APA), 1987] is that it is a classification of behavioral syndromes, each of which is an interrelated set of behavioral features. Aside from general notions of organic versus functional (psychogenic) etiology and certain specific organic mental syndromes, the classification system does not include underlying cause or etiology as a feature or component of the classification system. This situation is unlike the diagnostic ideal in medicine, whereby a configuration of symptom features suggests one or more plausible causal agents, which, once confirmed, results in the diagnosis cum cause (e.g., a particular viral infection; Clancey, 1988).

Unlike earlier versions of the *Diagnostic and Statistical Manual,* the *DSM-III* was developed with the intent to minimize the impact of and adherence to any one theoretical framework (APA, 1987). The diagnostic criteria (core features and identification properties) are generally stated in descriptive language, with inferences and concepts peculiar to any one theoretical system avoided. That is, theories of etiology and psychopathology for a disorder are not part of the formal classification system itself. This approach was adopted by the developers of the *DSM-III* to increase the acceptance and use of the manual by clinicians utilizing different theoretical orientations (APA, 1987). Thus, despite differences in etiological theories of the causes, say, of depression, clinicians are able to achieve relatively high inter-rater agreement on diagnoses (Matarazzo, 1983) and to communicate with other professionals using a common language.

Psychiatric diagnostic categories are designed to be relatively homogeneous taxa with explicit sets of core and identifying features. These two types of features correspond to defining and characteristic features in the cognitive literature (e.g., Rosch, 1975; Rosch & Mervis, 1975; Smith, Shoben, & Rips, 1974). Both types of features are used as diagnostic criteria. For instance, Table I lists the diagnostic criteria for Major Depressive Episode. The essential or core features are either depressed mood or diminished interest or pleasure. For the diagnosis of Major Depressive Episode, a total of five symptoms must be present for a certain length of time, including one or both of the two core features. Certain other criteria (B to D) relating to the absence of an organic etiology, psychotic symptoms, and various psychotic disorders must also be satisfied for the Major Depressive Episode diagnosis. The classification rule for Major Depressive Episode is a conjunctive-disjunctive rule.

Diagnosis occurs on each of five axes, of which Axis I is most relevant for the present discussion. For Axis I disorders, a configuration of behavior is diagnosed, not a person (Millon, 1991). That is, the instance to be categorized is a configuration of behavior along relevant dimensions, which may comprise only a subset of the patient's symptoms.[2] This implies, of course, that an individual may have multiple Axis I diagnoses. That is, the categories are not mutually exclusive. For each disorder, the symptoms are the features or attributes of the diagnostic category which are formalized as the diagnostic criteria.

Diagnostic categories are hierarchically organized. For example, Major Depressive Episode may be part of Major Depressive Disorder, or of one of two types of bipolar disorders. Each of these disorders is subsumed under either a Depressive Disorder or a Bipolar Disorder, which together form the super-category of Mood Disorders. This hierarchical organization permits generalization across different lower-level categories, even those with seemingly disparate features such as depression and mania (cf., Wisniewski & Medin, 1991).

Diagnostic categorization serves several functions which make it useful for the clinician. Diagnosis provides predictive utility, involving both concurrent and prospective prediction. Concurrent prediction involves accessing features which are associated with a disorder but are not part of the core or identifying features of the disorder itself. For Major Depressive Episode, for example, co-occurring behaviors might include social withdrawal and difficulty completing work activities. Concurrent prediction also includes co-morbidity—additional mental disorders which are likely to co-occur with the diagnosis (e.g., alcohol abuse or personality disorders: Farmer & Nelson-Gray, 1990; Rohde, Lewinshon, & Seeley, 1991). Prospective prediction includes predictions about the course of the disor-

---

[2] The term *symptom* or *finding* is used generally to describe a clinically significant behavior which manifests itself as either distress or dysfunction.

TABLE I

DIAGNOSTIC CRITERIA FOR MAJOR DEPRESSIVE EPISODE[a]

A. At least five of the following symptoms are present during the same two-week period and represent a change from previous functioning; at least one of the symptoms is either depressed mood or diminished interest. (With the exception of (9), the symptom must be present nearly every day.)
  1. Depressed mood
  2. Markedly diminished interest or pleasure in all, or almost all, activities
  3. Significant weight loss or gain, or decrease in appetite
  4. Insomnia or hypersomnia
  5. Psychomotor agitation or retardation
  6. Fatigue or energy loss
  7. Feelings of worthlessness or excessive or inappropriate guilt
  8. Diminished ability to think or concentrate, or indecisiveness
  9. Recurrent thoughts of death, suicidal ideation, attempt, or plan
B. 1. An organic factor did not initiate or maintain the disturbance
  2. The disturbance is not a normal reaction to the death of a loved one
C. Delusions, if present, accompanied by prominent mood symptoms
D. Not superimposed on schizophrenia, schizophreniform disorder, delusional disorder, or other psychotic disorders

[a] Adapted, with permission, from American Psychiatric Association, *Diagnostic and Statistical Manual of Mental Disorders, Third Edition, Revised.* Washington, DC, American Psychiatric Association, 1987.

der and probable response to certain treatments (Blashfield & Draguns, 1976; Bellack & Hersen, 1990). Prediction is a well-recognized function of categorization in general (see Anderson, 1990, 1991; Murphy, this volume).

Finally, by defining a relatively homogeneous population, diagnosis permits the development of theories of etiology and maintenance of the disorder. These theories, which may be biological or psychological in nature, can be useful in treatment planning for the patient (e.g., Beck, Rush, Shaw, & Emery, 1979; Segal, 1988).

Several properties or characteristics of the diagnostic categorization process and of the predictive and etiological functions of diagnosis warrant further discussion. First, categorization for an (Axis I) diagnostic category involves a filtering-out process—the to-be-classified instance is only a portion of the patient's functioning. Other symptoms of clinical import that are not subsumed by the diagnostic category may be present and may require clinical evaluation. For instance, consider Mary, who presents with symptoms including a two-month history of depressed mood, insomnia, weight loss, guilt, and feelings of worthlessness as well as a tendency to feel that she is flawed and to berate herself under certain circumstances.

The latter two symptoms are not included as diagnostic criteria for depression, but may have substantial clinical significance.[3]

Second, the web of clinical concepts and theory accessed via the diagnostic category involves probabilistic (stochastic) relationships. The probabilistic nature of these relationships has two interrelated components. First, the predictive and etiological relationships are probabilistic. For example, although cognitive-behavior therapy may decrease depression in a certain proportion of patients diagnosed with Major Depressive Episode (Freeman, 1990), there is no guarantee it will work for a particular patient with the diagnosis. The second component is a function of the typicality of the case. Presumably, the statistical relationships (e.g., of treatment utility) hold most strongly for those cases most characteristic of the category rather than borderline cases, even assuming the latter are diagnosed reliably.

B. CLINICIANS' REPRESENTATIONS OF CATEGORIES FOR DIAGNOSTIC DISORDERS

A distinction must be made between the psychiatric taxa as summarized in the *DSM-III-R* and described above, and the clinician's mental representation and use of this system (Morey & McNamara, 1987). The structure of the taxa (classical vs. prototypical; categorical, dimensional, class-quantitative) needs to be determined via experimental investigation of the relevant clinical populations (Blashfield, 1984; Blashfield & Draguns, 1976; Millon, 1991). This structure may then be compared to the clinician's mental representation of the categories.

Studies of these mental representations by Cantor, Smith, French, & Mezzich (1980), Horowitz and colleagues (Horowitz, Post, French, Wallis, & Siegelman, 1981; Horowitz, Wright, Lowenstein, & Parad, 1981), Blashfield and colleagues (Blashfield, Sprock, Haymaker, & Hodgin, 1989; Blashfield, Sprock, Pinkston, & Hodgin, 1985), and Clarkin, Widiger, Frances, Hurt, & Gilmore (1983) have indicated that probabilistic similarity-based models—specifically prototype models—of clinicians' mental representations of diagnostic categories explain issues such as diagnostic reliability and confidence more adequately than classical (nec-

---

[3] The notion of *clinical significance* is important in both applied clinical evaluation and clinical research. In the latter context, it refers to a degree of change which involves a meaningful improvement (hopefully) over the pre-intervention functioning of the patient (see, e.g., Jacobsen & Traux, 1991). In clinical evaluation, the term applies to a behavior which is diagnostic or otherwise noteworthy or potentially meaningful, and in need of further exploration and/or interpretation. Thus, it is analogous to the concept of a "finding" in medical decision-making (Elstein, 1988; Elstein, Shulman, & Sprafka, 1978).

essary and sufficient features) approaches to categorization. For instance, the typicality effect found in natural kind categories (Rosch, 1975; Rosch & Mervis, 1975), whereby instances of a category that share a number of features in common (family resemblance) with other category instances are rated as more typical of the category, has been found for a variety of psychiatric disorders. Clinicians diagnose typical exemplars more quickly and reliably than less typical exemplars and are more confident in their diagnosis for typical instances (Blashfield et al., 1985, 1989; Cantor et al., 1980; Clarkin et al., 1983; Genero & Cantor, 1987; Horowitz, Post, French, Wallis, & Siegelman, 1981). Clinicians' mental representations of disorders are hierarchically organized, so that features common to higher-order categories are present in lower-order categories (Cantor et al., 1980), a characteristic which fairly accurately reflects the taxonomic structure of the disorders. The superordinate, basic, and subordinate levels (e.g., mood disorder, major depressive episode, major depressive episode melancholic type) are also found in natural object categories (Rosch, Mervis, Gray, Johnson, & Boyes-Braem, 1976).

Several studies have examined how the clinician's organization of the mental representation of disorders varies as a function of level of training. Genero & Cantor (1987) investigated category representation as a function of level of training in undergraduates and graduate students. Pre-novices appeared to benefit most from information presented as a prototype, while the novices (trainees) appeared to benefit most from information presented as multiple exemplars. Murphy and Wright (1984) investigated clinicians' conceptual structure of children's disorders as a function of level of training/experience. As expected, they found that conceptions of more highly trained and experienced clinicians were richer in number of features and contained more highly consensual features. Interestingly, the categories of more experienced clinicians also contained more non-distinctive features, more features which overlapped between categories. This result, however, is consistent with the literature on the nature of children's psychopathology, where substantial overlap in symptoms (features) across disorders is found (see, e.g., Pope, Bierman, & Mumma, 1991, where the correlations across factor-analysis derived dimensions of childhood psychopathology ranged from .49 to .64.)

C.   Lower-Level Categorization in Clinical Diagnosis

In contrast to the attention given to clinicians' representations of diagnostic categories at the level of disorders, relatively little attention has been focused on issues pertinent to the lower-level categorization involved in determining if each of the diagnostic criteria for a particular disorder has been met. In terms of our patient Mary, for example, previous research has focused on issues pertinent to how many of the diagnostic criteria for Major Depressive Episode are present in a narrative description of her functioning (e.g., depressed mood, insomnia, weight loss). What has not been investigated is how clinicians use the behavioral information obtained from the patient (e.g., 90 minutes average sleep-initiation latency, intermittent use of anxiolytics at bedtime, a recent history of caffeinism) to categorize Mary's functioning as either "depression-relevant insomnia" or "within-normal-limits sleep" (or some other category such as "insomnia related to a known organic factor" or "primary insomnia": APA, 1987).

Problems inherent to lower-level clinical categorization are of two major types: (1) issues pertinent to any particular diagnostic criterion for a disorder, and (2) the interrelations of the diagnostic criteria within the disorder and their relationship to clinical theory and prior information. This section describes some of the former issues. The latter issues are discussed in Section IV,B. Table II compares the nature and structure of the categories and the clinician's categorization task at the disorder level and the diagnostic criterion level.

The first problem is that for a particular diagnostic criterion, the *DSM-III-R* provides only a general definition of the core features. For example, for the diagnostic criterion "insomnia or hypersomnia nearly every day" (Table I), the definition of insomnia is "Difficulty falling or staying asleep," while the essential features include the following: "Initial insomnia is difficulty in falling asleep. Middle insomnia involves an awakening, followed by difficulty returning to sleep, but eventually doing so. Terminal insomnia is awakening at least two hours before one's usual waking time and being unable to return to sleep" (APA, 1987, p. 400). Thus, although essential features and definitions are available, a set of invariant attributes to be used for comparing the target instance to the stored prototype or exemplars is not prescribed and is unlikely to be agreed upon across clinicians. Returning to the patient Mary, one clinician may use average latency to sleep onset and use of sleep aids as features, while another may use proportion of nights during past month with sleep-onset difficulties and typical (premorbid) proportion as features.

Another problem is that while a normative decision rule for categorization exists at the disorder level which specifies how the features are to be combined, such rules are typically lacking at the diagnostic criterion level. While structured diagnostic interviews have provided some explication and elaboration of identification properties and decision rules for categorization (e.g., Spitzer, Williams, Gibbon, & First, 1990), these instruments are primarily designed to elicit a standardized set of initial

TABLE II

CHARACTERISTICS OF DISORDER- AND DIAGNOSTIC CRITERION-LEVEL CATEGORIES AND CATEGORIZATION IN CLINICAL DIAGNOSIS

Characteristic	Disorder level	Diagnostic criterion level
1. Core features and identification properties	Both specified via normative model	General definitions only: Clinician determines specific features
2. Normative decision rules for categorization	Present	Absent
Type of decision rule	Non-compensatory: Conjunctive and/or disjunctive	Varies with diagnostic criterion and/or clinician: Compensatory and non-compensatory
3. Degree of theory embeddedness	Atheoretical: Serves to organize and access theoretical knowledge	Several components are theory-embedded
4. Context of feature	Each feature evaluated independently of others. Context resolved at diagnostic criterion level	Each feature is context-dependent and multidetermined
5. Feature value coding	Dichotomous: Present vs. absent	May vary across features or within features across clinicians or patients
6. Dependability of feature information	Depends, partly, on dependability of diagnostic criterion-level information	Multiple potential sources of inconsistency

patient data. Most diagnostic interviews also recognize the need (1) for follow-up questions to provide a more detailed feature list for certain patients, and (2) flexibility in how this information should be combined to make a diagnostic criterion categorization (Spitzer et al., 1990).

One result of the indeterminacy in featural explication for diagnostic criterion–level categorization is that the clinician's theoretical orientation may influence which features are considered relevant for categorization. For example, features relevant to the "feelings of worthlessness" diagnostic criterion may include a context of longstanding and deep sense of inferiority for an Adlerian-oriented clinician, whereas the features relevant for a cognitive-behavioral clinician may be verbalization of more circumscribed self-referent speech involving synonyms for the term *worthlessness*.

One solution for the above problems would be to establish a standardized explicit set of identification properties and an associated categorization rule. However, such a solution would be difficult if not impossible to implement for two reasons. First, clinicians would not have the time to investigate an exhaustive set of standardized features for all patients seen, and in many cases it would be unnecessary (cf., Genero & Cantor, 1987). Second, the determination of which attributes are relevant for the categorization of a particular instance, as well as the level or value of the patient's functioning on each attribute, is highly context-dependent. For example, Mary's two-month history of 90-minute sleep initiation insomnia means something very different if she characteristically falls asleep immediately versus typically takes 40 to 50 minutes to fall asleep. Although this type of context dependency could be readily handled by difference scores, it is also likely that Mary's pre-morbid sleep initiation difficulties also covaried with situational or (interpersonal) environmental factors such as job stress or degree of tension/dissatisfaction with her spouse, or may have been caused by a physiological condition (e.g., caffeinism). That is, other intrapsychic, interpersonal, situational, or physiological factors unrelated to the diagnosis (or its predictive or etiological theories) may be contributing to the development and maintenance of the symptoms. In other words, the symptoms are multiply determined. Thus, a model of clinical diagnostic criterion categorization must be able to accommodate this fourth problem—the high degree of environmental, situational, and intrapersonal contextual-embeddedness of the category-relevant features and the probable multidetermination of each feature—without exceeding human information processing capacities (Simon, 1990).

A fifth problem is variability in how information is encoded for each attribute. For a particular diagnostic criterion, relevant features are likely to involve information which must be encoded differently. For instance, attributes relevant to insomnia could include both qualitative information (such as use of sleeping pills: coded yes/no) and quantitative information (such as average latency to sleep onset; see Smith & Medin, 1981, chap. 2). Even for a particular feature, variability in encoding probably exists across different clinicians, target instances (patients), or situational contexts. For example, one clinician might encode information about Mary's latency to sleep onset using a continuous quantitative scale such as average number of minutes, while another might encode this information using an ordinal qualitative scale such as mild, moderate, or severe (Elstein, 1988).

Finally, there may be problems with the dependability of featural information. Numerous sources of potential unreliability in the information can be identified and, if present, must be resolved by the clinician in the process of determining the value of each attribute. These sources include (1) differences across occasions, (2) variation in response as a function of the wording of the clinician's probe, (3) cross-modal incongruities in the patient's presentation (Mary may deny difficulties in concentrating, but these may be observed during the interview), (4) discrepant reports from different individuals (Mary says it takes her 90 minutes to fall asleep but her husband says it's only 40 minutes).

IV. A Model of Lower-Level Categorization in Clinical Diagnosis

The previous section summarized difficulties in categorization inherent to any particular diagnostic criterion for a disorder. The research on disorder-level categorization (see Section III,B) has generally circumvented these difficulties by using brief written case summaries as the stimulus materials. These difficulties are also not present in laboratory investigations of categorization or category learning which use stimulus materials differentiated via clear-cut perceptual features. In such situations, the core properties also serve as the identification properties (Smith & Medin, 1981). One implication of the issues described in the previous section is that in order to determine the correct diagnostic criterion categorization, the clinician must engage in substantial further processing of information in addition to the similarity comparisons which form the basis of similarity-based categorization models. Thus, the categorization process will share some characteristics with problem-solving processes (see Fisher & Yoo, this volume; Medin, 1989; Simon & Lea, 1974).

This section describes a preliminary model of categorization for the diagnostic criteria comprising a disorder. This model incorporates the requirements for clinically relevant categorization models suggested in Section II while addressing the issues raised in Section III,C (see Table II). This preliminary model consists of two major parts. The prescriptive part is a model of how task and domain knowledge and general heuristics might be used to approximate an ideal categorization (a categorization which, at minimum, incorporates those few normative guidelines provided by formalized diagnostic systems and procedures such as the *DSM-III-R* and structured diagnostic interviews). The second major part of the model consists of departures from the prescriptive model due to the influence of clinical theory or previous information.

A. Prescriptive Components of the Model

The prescriptive part of the model can be divided into four major components: (1) feature-slot generation and information acquisition, (2) determining the feature value and ruling out other causes, (3) prototype or exemplar retrieval, (4) and similarity judgments via an adjusted categorization rule. See Fig. 1.

1. Feature Slot Generation/Retrieval and Information Acquisition

The above described problem of the indeterminacy of the set of features for a diagnostic criterion category can be partly resolved via hypothesizing a consistent and comprehensive set of feature slots for a particular diagnostic criterion which may be filled to varying degrees by the clinician for a particular patient (Component 1A). (See Clancey, 1988; Klahr & Dunbar, 1988; Minsky, 1975; and Smith & Medin, 1981, p. 87, for discussions of the notion of feature slots in medical decision making, scientific discovery, knowledge representation, and similarity-based categorization respectively.) For example, relevant feature slots for initial insomnia might include average latency to sleep onset at present, premorbid average latency, variability in present latency, duration of present symptoms, use of sleep-inducing drugs (e.g., anxiolytics, alcohol), name and amount of drugs used, response to sleep aids, and so on. These slots are determined prescriptively through elaboration of definitions and essential features within the *DSM-III* via domain theory to develop clinically relevant identification properties.

Thus, domain theory functions to constrain the potentially infinite number of features available in the feature-rich stimuli presented by the patient to those features slots which are diagnostic. Presumably, the mechanism for feature-slot generation involves use of causal explanatory models involving relational properties both between the category and the feature, and among the features. For example, feature slots for both "average latency to sleep onset at present" and for "use of sleep-inducing medications" are generated because (1) the former is a core feature related to the definition of the sleep-onset insomnia category, (2) the latter is diagnostic of this type of insomnia (the probability of use of sleep aids for persons correctly categorized to the sleep-onset insomnia category is greater than the probability for persons in the "normal sleep" category), and (3) domain knowledge specifies a relation between these two features such that the use of a sleep-inducing drug generally reduces sleep latency because of the sedating effects of the drug on the central nervous system. Note that this relation is of an explanatory, cause–effect nature (cf. Medin, 1989;

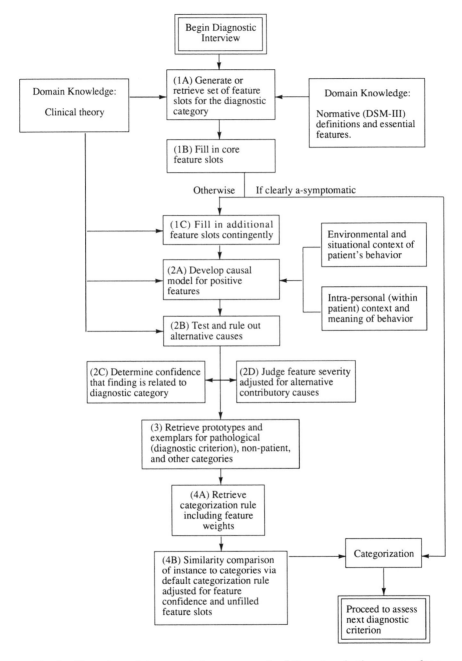

Fig. 1. Flow chart of the prescriptive components of the categorization process for a diagnostic criterion.

Murphy & Medin, 1985; Wattenmaker, Nakamura, & Medin, 1988) and should reduce the possibility of a false negative classification which might occur if the clinician obtained data for the "average latency to sleep-onset at present" feature slot but not the "sleep-inducing medications" feature slot. In other words, Mary could report a "within normal limits" sleep onset latency but still have "depression-related insomnia" because she is using a central-nervous-system depressant medication to treat the symptom. Once the clinician initially generates a set of feature slots for a given diagnostic criterion, these slots may be retrieved directly from long-term memory when diagnosing patients in the future.

The feature slots are filled via a two-stage process of information acquisition (see, e.g., Spitzer et al., 1990). Initial questioning of the patient focuses on core feature slots such as "average latency to sleep onset at present" (Component 1B). If the patient is clearly asymptomatic (e.g., no difficulty falling asleep, no use of sleep aids), a categorization of "within normal limits sleep" is made, further information search is not pursued, and the clinician proceeds to evaluate the next diagnostic criterion for the disorder. If there are indications of problems, the extent of contingent information search and the resulting level of detail of information obtained for the feature slots proceeds so as to minimize effort for clear-cut positive or negative cases, but provide detailed information for borderline cases (Component 1C; cf. Arkes, 1991; Genero & Cantor, 1987). Presumably, rules for contingent information search are coded in a production-like form (Anderson, 1983; Smith, 1984) indicating the conditions for which further search is necessary.

2. Determining the Feature Value and Ruling Out Alternative Causes

If the value for the core feature slot(s) is positive (Mary's 90-minute "average latency to sleep onset at present"), the clinician must determine if this finding is related to the targeted diagnostic disorder. The problem is that a given finding may have multiple causes as a result of the multidetermination of behavior and the complexity of the patient/environment system. Mary's insomnia may have other physiological, psychological, or environmental causes in addition to the depression.

To address this issue, the clinician uses both formal and informal theory to generate a set of plausible rival causes for the finding, that is, a causal mental model (Component 2A; cf. Einhorn, 1988; Einhorn & Hogarth, 1986; see also Clancey, 1988; Elstein, Shulman, & Sprafka, 1978; and Gauron & Dickinson, 1966, for analogous processes in medical and psychiatric diagnostic decision-making). The clinician then systematically tests each cause to determine if it can be ruled out as a cause for the finding (Component 2B). For example, formal theories are used to generate plausible conditions which may cause or contribute to Mary's sleep-initiation insomnia (e.g., hyperthyroidism, caffeinism, marital difficulties, conditioning from earlier physically caused insomnia). Using information obtained from the patient (or additional sources such as medical records) and knowledge of the base rate probability of each of the alternative causes, the clinician rules out one or more of these causes.[4] Based upon the extent to which the alternative causes have been ruled out, the clinician then determines how confident s/he is that the findings are related to the diagnostic criterion category (Component 2C). Presumably the clinician's weighting of that feature in the categorization rule (see below) is determined, in part, via a monotonic function of this confidence rating.

Once the contribution of plausible alternative causes to the finding has been made, a final (posterior) judgment of the feature value is made after adjusting for those alternative causes (i.e., those causes unrelated to the target disorder) which were not ruled out (Component 2D). For example, if Mary's 90-minute average sleep initiation insomnia is partly an exacerbation of a long-standing 50-minute sleep-initiation problem related to caffeinism, the feature severity judgment might be changed from moderate (before considering other causes) to mild.

This process of ruling out alternative causes for a finding and the consequent (1) adjustment of the initial feature value and (2) determination of the confidence in this feature value are the primary mechanisms whereby the issues of context dependency and multidetermination of behavior are addressed in the categorization process. Thus, contrary to the typical situation in laboratory classification tasks, determining feature values in clinical diagnostic criterion categorization involves dual-space search within the context of generating and testing hypotheses to form a causal

---

[4] For some disorders, the alternative causes for a diagnostic criterion are ruled out as part of the prescriptive decision process formalized in the *DSM-III*. For example, symptoms of hallucinations or delusions relevant to the diagnosis of schizophrenia must not be attributable to an organic cause such as alcohol withdrawal or psychoactive substance intoxication. This situation differs from the situation just described in that the validity of the symptom (hallucination) as an indicator of the category "psychotic state" has already been established. The question of etiology is at the disorder (syndrome) level (e.g., what caused the psychotic episode or state?). In the insomnia example in the text, alternative causal hypotheses must be ruled out at the featural level (e.g., "average latency to sleep onset at present") prior to the behavior being established as a valid feature relevant to the diagnostic criterion category of insomnia. That is, the insomnia diagnostic criterion for major depressive episode implicitly assumes that the insomnia is not being caused by an agent other than the depression and that the clinician has ruled out such alternative causes.

model (cf. Einhorn, 1988; Klahr & Dunbar, 1988; Kulkarni & Simon, 1988).

3. Retrieval of Prototypes or Exemplars

Either stored prototypes or exemplars, or both, of patient symptom configurations relevant to that particular diagnostic criterion are retrieved from long-term memory. Also, exemplars or prototypes of the feature configuration of (1) non-patients on the relevant features for that diagnostic criterion and (2) other "pathological" categories related to the diagnostic criterion (e.g., "primary insomnia" or "insomnia related to a known organic factor": APA, 1987) should be retrieved. Similarity of the target configuration to both depressive, non-patient, and other "pathological" prototypes and exemplars can then be ascertained, and the target instance categorized to the appropriate category.

The probability of an accurate categorization should increase if the clinician uses two prescriptive information-retrieval heuristics. First, if the clinician is considering a patient with a symptom configuration which is near the threshold for categorization on that particular diagnostic criterion, exemplars with symptom severity close to, but both above and below the threshold, should be differentially retrieved to provide a relatively high resolution context for such difficult judgments (cf. Arkes, 1991). This strategy is formalized in certain psychometric tests calling for clinical judgment on the scoring of item responses, whereby examples of responses just above and below the threshold are given (e.g., Wechsler, 1981). A second prescriptive heuristic is that the exemplars retrieved are those most relevant to that particular diagnostic criterion, even if this constitutes a different set of exemplars from those needed for another diagnostic criterion within the disorder.

4. Similarity Judgments via an Adjusted Categorization Rule

Once the value for each of the relevant features has been determined and the prototypes and/or exemplars for relevant categories retrieved, a decision rule for the categorization similarity comparison also needs to be retrieved (Component 4A). Categorization rules may be either compensatory (e.g., an additive linear model involving weighting of features) or non-compensatory (e.g., a disjunctive or conjunctive rule). Certain diagnostic criteria may require a combination of these two types of decision rules. For example, the sleep disturbance diagnostic criterion for Major Depressive Episode is a disjunctive rule involving the presence of either hypersomnia or insomnia (see Table I), while the latter itself involves a disjunction of initiation, middle, or terminal insomnia, each of which may involve different categorization rules. The categorization rule needs to provide a balance between uniformity (or standardization) and flexibility. The former maximizes consistency in the application of the rule, whereas the latter involves adjustments to the decision rule related to issues of context dependency, multidetermination, and a probable incomplete feature matrix due to contingent information search.

Prescriptive adjustments to the feature weights in the default categorization rule are related to the clinician's confidence in the feature weight for that particular patient. As described above (Component 2C), these adjustments are a function of the extent to which other potentially contributory causes have been ruled out.

Once these modifications have been made, the similarity judgment used for the categorization decision could use the types of rules described in similarity-based categorization models such Medin and Schaffer's (1978) context model or Anderson's (1990, 1991) Bayesian-based model (Component 4B). In the latter model, for instance, the posterior probability of membership in one of the categories (e.g., symptom positive or negative) is a function of the ratio of the base rates (prior probabilities) of the two categories and the likelihood ratio. (See Finn, 1982; Meehl & Rosen, 1955; Morey & McNamara, 1987, for discussion of the importance of base rate information in clinical categorization.)

5. *Summary*

Two of the four components of this preliminary prescriptive model of diagnostic criterion categorization in clinical evaluation rely heavily on domain theory: Component 1, to generate and constrain the feature slots and determine if further contingent information search is necessary, and Component 2, to rule out alternative causes for clinically significant feature values (e.g., 90-minute sleep initiation insomnia). The clinician is in a position to apply categorization or decision rules only after completing this substantial pre-processing. This context is in contrast to that in which similarity-based categorization models were developed: laboratory experiments using simplified, non-meaningful stimuli, constructed so as to prevent subjects from using domain knowledge. The shortcomings of similarity-based models of categorization have been discussed by Ahn et al. (1992); Fisher & Yoo (this volume); Medin (1989); Mooney (this volume); Murphy & Medin (1985); and Wattenmaker et al. (1988). Interestingly, the traditional and predominant paradigm in clinical decision-making research has also investigated one small component of clinical evaluation—how clinicians combine and integrate information—using information which is decontextualized (from the patient's history, environment, and situation) and presented within a non-interactive, non-dynamic environment. (See Holt, 1978, 1988; Korchin, 1976; Rock et al., 1987, for a discussion of these limitations in clinical decision-making research.) Thus, the generalizability and applicability of research results from such simplified environments involving a high degree of experimenter-imposed task constraints to more ecologically valid task environments in which the subject imposes task-processing constraints via domain theory has been challenged within both the categorization and clinical-inference literature. The preliminary model described above suggests that the information processing involved in ecologically valid categorization of diagnostic criteria in clinical diagnosis is a potentially rich area for investigating theory-embedded categorization processes.

B. Departures from the Prescriptive Model

So far, the model of diagnostic criterion categorization within clinical evaluation has focused on four prescriptive components of information processing. The following section briefly describes certain ways in which domain theory and previous experience can lead to departures from this model. These departures or information processing biases are summarized in Table III. For each bias, the component(s) of the prescriptive model most likely affected is listed.

1. Anchoring Effects and the Organization and Prior Activation of Exemplars in Long-Term Memory

Anchoring effects have been studied in a wide variety of decision-making tasks, including clinical judgment (e.g., Bieri, Orcutt, & Leaman, 1963; Friedlander & Stockman, 1983; Richards & Wierzbicki, 1990). However, the mechanism whereby these effects are generated in clinical decision-making is poorly understood. Anchoring effects in lower-level clinical diagnosis may be the result of a breakdown in the prescriptive model (Fig. 1) at Components 1C and 3. The essential problem is the retrieval of exemplars which were activated in response to earlier encountered information, as during the categorization of a previous diagnostic criterion for the disorder. Two aspects of this process could be problematic: (1) the exemplars retrieved may not be the most appropriate for the categorization of the target diagnostic criterion, and (2) the exemplars may be retrieved and used too early in the categorization process and may influence the depth or thoroughness of information search during Component 1C.

For instance, if Mary reports strong feelings of worthlessness early in the interview, the clinician may judge her sleep disturbance as more severe

TABLE III

Departures from the Prescriptive Model of Lower-Level Categorization in Clinical Diagnosis

Effect	Definition	Component	Probable mechanism and result
Anchoring	Undue influence of early information	3	Retrieval of primed, non-optimal exemplars Possible case-wise organization of exemplars in long-term memory
		1C	Inadequate information search related to early retrieval of above
Base-rate effects	Influence of previously encountered exemplars	3	Exemplars retrieved may not be most relevant for categorization of target patient in present setting
Halo	General impression or theory-based expectations	1C	Insufficient information search based on salience of concurrent feature information
		2A,B	Inadequate generation or testing of alternative causes
		4A,B	Retrieval or use of categorization rule with improper weighting of non-diagnostic information for that diagnostic criterion
Illusory correlation	Theory-based distortion of feature-category correlation	1A	Generation and/or retrieval of non-diagnostic slots based on inaccurate theoretical expectations (beliefs)
		2A,B	Inadequate generation or testing of alternative causes
		4A	Improper decision rule retrieved
Labeling or suggestion	Suggested category influences categorization	1A-C	Retrieval of feature slots and consequent information search for incorrect category
		2A,B	Plausible alternative categories not considered
		3	Prototype or exemplars for non-suggested category not retrieved

than if this information were encountered later in the interview (an anchoring effect). The early-encountered, relatively extreme information may lead to retrieval of relatively pathological exemplars from long-term memory (LTM) for the sleep disturbance categorization also. For example, during the clinical interview with Mary, early discussion of her relatively severe symptoms relevant to the "worthlessness" diagnostic criterion may trigger retrieval of a previously stored exemplar for John, who was moderately to severely depressed, during Component 3 (Fig. 1). However, due to its increased availability as a function of this earlier activation, the John exemplar is also likely to be retrieved during Component 3 of the insomnia diagnostic criterion categorization. This availability effect is likely to be particularly pronounced if the organization of exemplar information in LTM is on a case-wise rather than a symptomwise (diagnostic criterion) basis. If the pathological exemplar is retrieved and used relatively early in the categorization process (e.g., at the same time the feature slots for the sleep disturbance category are retrieved: Component 1A), then the clinician may engage in an abbreviated information search, allowing some of the sleep disturbance feature slots to be filled in via extrapolation from the pathological exemplar (John), a departure from Component 1C, possibly resulting in a false positive.

Although I am not aware of a study which directly tests the above model of anchoring effects, there is indirect evidence concerning the role of extent of information processing in reducing such biases in that further processing of already-acquired information has been shown to decrease cognitive biases such as hindsight and anchoring effects (Arkes, Faust, Guilmette, & Hart, 1988; Mumma & Wilson, 1991). The critical components of the hypothesized departures from the prescriptive model (early retrieval of primed exemplars, case-wise organization of exemplar information in LTM, abbreviated information search) are all amenable to empirical testing.

2. Experiential Base-Rate Effects

The similarity judgment described in Component 4B of the prescriptive model includes information relevant to the base rate of the category. Although earlier research on the use of base-rate information in human judgment suggested that such information was ignored (see review in Fischhoff & Beyth-Marom, 1983), this bias occurs primarily when the base-rate information is presented as a statistical summary as opposed to experientially (e.g., Christensen-Szalanski & Beach, 1982; Christensen-Szalanski & Bushyhead, 1981; cf. Barsalou, 1985). However, Medin and Edelson (1988) have reported results indicating that the use of experientially learned base-rate information may be quite complex and related to principles involving competition between features from various categories and the context in which the subject is asked to use this information. To what extent are a clinician's judgments miscalibrated when changing settings (e.g., private practice to inpatient state psychiatric facility) or as the result of recent experiences with particularly salient exemplars? Questions such as these need to be addressed in the context of real-world clinical categorization.

3. Halo, Illusory Correlation, and Suggestion Effects

Expectancy effects (halo, illusory correlation, suggestion) can influence diagnostic criterion categorization via either (1) information received prior to the interview; (2) information encountered earlier in, or concurrent with, the categorization decision during the interview; or (3) through theory-based expectations. Most of the clinically oriented research investigating these effects has focused on the disorder level of categorization. The ubiquity and resilience of many of these effects suggests that they are also probably relevant to diagnostic criterion categorization.

Two perspectives on what *halo effects* are and how they occur have been suggested (Jacobs & Kozlowski, 1985). Cooper (1981) defined halo effects as occurring when a general impression or salient feature(s) of a person's behavior or presentation unduly influences other judgments. The second perspective considers halo effects as primarily theory-based— created by the perceiver's theories, beliefs, or assumptions about covariation amongst features and/or rating dimensions (Murphy & Medin, 1985; Nisbett & Wilson, 1977). In either case, halo effects occur when the magnitude of the perceived or rated correlations between attributes exceeds the true intercorrelations (Cooper, 1981). The direction of the correlation is unimportant.

A halo effect occurs when the categorization of the instance suggests a relationship between one or more features and the category which is not consistent with the diagnosticity of the feature(s). Diagnosticity is given by the likelihood ratio (Fischhoff & Beyth-Marom, 1983), which is $P(F|C_1)/P(F|C_2)$ where $P(F|C_1)$ is the probability of the feature given Category 1, and C_2 is Category 2. (Diagnosticity, of course, must be determined empirically and independently of the process of categorization of the instance.) For example, if Mary's non-verbal behavior is indicative of depressed mood rather than "normal" mood (e.g., little eye contact, flat affect, slowed speech), the clinician may judge features relevant to insomnia (e.g., 90-minute sleep initiation latency) as more severe than if Mary had reported the same information about insomnia but with less pathological metacommunication. Thus, the correlation between the judged severity of the "depressed mood" and "insomnia" diagnostic criteria (Table I) is higher than if the two judgments were made independently. Mechanisms which may contribute to a departure from prescriptive diagnostic criteria categorization are suggested in Table III. For example, Mary's strong concomitant non-verbal behavior may lead to reduced generation and testing of alternative plausible causes for insomnia (Component 2A, 2B), resulting in an increased probability of a positive (symptomatic) categorization when compared to non-pathological concomitant behavior.

Illusory correlation is a related phenomenon in which the clinician believes there is a stronger (or different) correlation between the feature and the category than empirically exists (Chapman & Chapman, 1967; Shweder, 1977; Starr & Katkin, 1969). As in halo effects, the breakdown is in the believed versus empirically present diagnosticity of the feature. (Illusory correlation effects can be conceptually differentiated from halo effects in that the latter involves the influence of prior or concurrent information about the patient, whereas illusory correlation can be demonstrated without reference to other information about the instance.) Illusory correlation effects have proved generally quite resistant to debiasing, suggesting that the clinician's strong prior beliefs or theories override learning new concepts based upon veridical feature covariance (Chapman & Chapman, 1967; Golding & Rorer, 1972; Kayne & Alloy, 1988; Kurtz & Garfield, 1978). As suggested in Table III, the nature of the departure from the model of prescriptive categorization may be quite similar for halo effects and illusory correlation.

Suggestion effects are related phenomena which can occur in clinical diagnosis when a previously encountered or suggested label (e.g., diagnosis) influences the perception and diagnosis of, and possibly also the clinician's attitude and behavior toward, the patient. Labeling effects were first demonstrated by Temerlin (1968) for prestige suggestion and have been replicated and extended by other investigators (Gjerde, Sand, & Kleiven, 1979; Sushinsky & Wener, 1975). Recent investigations have also indicated that, for instance, labeling or expectancy effects may influence the clinician's general attitude toward the client as well as the nature of the approach to treatment recommendations, even when the source of the suggestion is not prestigious (Lange, Beurs, Hanewald, & Koppelaar, 1991). The nature and direction of influence appears to be related to the theoretical orientation of the clinician and the congruence between the theoretical orientation of the clinician and that of the source of the information (Langer & Abelson, 1974; Lange et al., 1991). If the latter is congruent, for instance, the expectancy effects are in the predicted direction, but if incongruent, the clinicians' judgments are influenced in a direction opposite to the information given (Lange et al., 1991). That is, when the theoretical orientations of the clinician and the source of prior information differ, the clinicians' judgments are influenced in a direction opposite to the information given.

Table III suggests several points at which departures from the prescriptive categorization model may result in suggestion or labeling effects on categorization. In addition to these departures, the clinician appears to be responding to the implications of the suggested diagnosis in terms of its meaning within (1) theories of psychological treatment, (2) informal theories or schemas (e.g., stereotypes) which influence attitudes toward others, and (3) the social-psychological and/or professional identity implications of the congruence between the theoretical orientation of the source of the suggestion and the clinician.

Such departures from prescriptive information processing during categorization are not capable of being incorporated into similarity-based models of categorization. Expectancy effects influence categorization in ways, and at points in time, which necessitate a categorization model incorporating components involving information acquisition over time, dynamic feedback and interactive influence, and the potentially powerful influence of domain knowledge to the exclusion, at times, of diagnosticity and covariation information within the data.

4. Departures Due to Information-processing Limitations

The relationship between task complexity and task-processing strategy has been well established in decision making. As task complexity increases, decision-making strategy changes from compensatory strategies involving consideration of all the information for each alternative, to non-compensatory strategies such as elimination by aspects (Ford et al., 1989; Paquette & Kida, 1988; Tversky, 1972). Furthermore, in complex, informationally rich environments, even such simplified rational mechanisms may break down, and non-rational mechanisms of information extraction and compilation may be used (Agnew & Brown, 1986). Larichev and Moshkovich (1988), for instance, have demonstrated clear limits to the reliability of diagnostic categorization as the number of diagnostic categories, category features, and feature gradations increase. In the complex and informationally rich environment provided by patient data, the clinician's judgments about a particular diagnostic criterion may not be particularly reliable, unless substantial simplifying strategies are employed. Further research is needed as to the impact of using simplifying heuristics on feature slot generation and information acquisition (Fig. 1, Component

1A–C), and on the generation and testing of plausible alternative causes for findings (Component 2A, 2B). (See Curley, Yates, & Young, 1990; Elstein et al., 1986, 1978; and Kern & Doherty, 1982, for related empirical work pertinent to medical diagnosis.)

V. Rule Induction in Clinical Assessment

A. Clinical Diagnosis and Assessment Compared

Clinical diagnosis and assessment are complementary activities. Many clinicians may engage in both tasks during the patient interview, and there may be some overlap in the data which are used for the diagnosis and the assessment. Both can provide useful information for predicting future behavior and for treatment planning, although the level of detail of the predictions, treatment plans, and goals differs. Despite these interconnections, diagnosis and assessment differ in many fundamental ways. These differences are summarized in Table IV, and certain points are discussed below.

Diagnosis is a nomothetic activity, using features or dimensions of relevance across individuals (e.g., presence of depressed mood, insomnia) to place entities into one or more diagnostic categories selected from a large, but finite and predetermined, set of potential diagnoses. Clinical diagnosis is a bounded and relatively well structured categorization task.

Clinical assessment involves developing an individualized model or theory of the patient which interrelates his/her symptoms into a coherent case formulation, explains the origins and meaning of the symptoms, and is useful for predicting future behavior and for treatment planning (Korchin, 1976; Persons, 1989, 1993; Sundberg & Tyler, 1962). Clinical assessment is an idiographic or morphological activity. It involves determining the pattern, structure, or organizing themes in the life of a particular individual, and uses the narrative mode of inference (Allport, 1962; Runyan, 1983; Sarbin, 1986; Zukier, 1986).

One of the characteristics of clinical assessment which has greatly complicated its in vivo empirical study is that it is an ill-structured task. Ill-structured problems are characterized by several features (Reitman, 1965; Simon, 1973; Voss & Post, 1988): (1) a large number of initial open constraints on the task which are closed as the problem representation is developed; (2) relevant constraints are generally provided by the background (domain) theory used by the subject; (3) since the constraints are theory-bound, there may be disagreement among problem solvers about what constraints are needed to achieve the task goals, as well as about the structure and content of the task solution; and (4) an absence of clear-cut stopping rules indicating task completion. Table IV indicates that all four of these characteristics of an ill-structured problem apply to clinical assessment.

Although clinical assessment has long been conceptualized as a problem-solving process involving both hypothesis generation and testing (Crosson, 1990; Korchin, 1976; Persons, 1991, 1993; Sundberg & Tyler, 1962; Wolpe & Turkat, 1985), the relevance of categorization and rule induction to this process has not been directly addressed. There has also been longstanding concern about the adequacy of the methods historically used to investigate clinical decision making to provide a suitable framework for understanding the process of clinical assessment (Holt, 1978, 1988; Korchin, 1976; Rock et al., 1987; Sarbin, 1986; Sundberg & Tyler, 1962). In this section, I suggest that recent developments in three areas can be brought to bear on clinical assessment to provide a fruitful framework for the scientific study of this important aspect of clinical evaluation. These areas are: (1) theories of explanation-based learning in unsupervised learning environments (see Ahn et al., 1992; Fisher & Yoo, this volume; Mooney, this volume) and emerging notions of psychological essentialism (Medin, 1989; Wattenmaker et al., 1988), (2) recent developments in the application of heuristics-level information processing analyses to medical decision-making and ill-structured scientific discovery tasks (e.g., Clancey, 1988; Klahr & Dunbar, 1988; Kulkarni & Simon, 1988; Qin & Simon, 1990), and (3) conceptualizations of the core structure of the clinical case formulation. We turn to the latter development next.

B. A FRAMEWORK FOR THE STUDY OF CATEGORIZATION IN CLINICAL ASSESSMENT

1. The Core Formulation: Psychological Essentialism in the Clinical Case Formulation

During the past 5 to 10 years, several theoretically diverse approaches to clinical psychopathology and psychotherapy have independently developed the concept that the most essential information relevant to a patient's psychopathology can be summarized in one or a few relatively brief core themes, processes, or conflicts. The summary theme or issue serves as the essence or core of the clinician's idiographic formulation of the patient, the clinician's "theory of the person situation," and is called the *core rule* or *core formulation*. The core formulation is the clinician's representation of the underlying core-organizing principle(s) or core-ordering process(es) of the patient (Mahoney, 1990, 1991, chap. 8; Meichenbaum & Gilmore, 1984). The underlying or deep structural rule explains the patient's func-

TABLE IV

Comparison of Categorization in Clinical Diagnosis (Disorder Level) and Clinical Assessment

Dimension	Clinical diagnosis (disorder level)	Clinical assessment
Basic goal	Classification: Subsumption of instance into one or more diagnostic categories	Case formulation: Induction of explanatory core rule and construction of associated mini-theory of patient functioning
Nature of evaluation	Nomothetic: Features (e.g., depressed mood) and categories relevant across individuals	Idiographic: Features and core rules pertinent to a particular individual
Nature of instance	Configuration of behavior within patient	A single behavior or pattern of behavior within patient
Nature of end-point	Taxonomic category	Core rule: An ad-hoc goal-derived category (Goal: Explain symptoms and develop treatment goals and plan)
Degree of task structure: Initial open constraints	*Few:* Finite number of pre-determined taxonomic categories (Bounded task)	*Many:* Infinite number of case formulations or core rules (Boundless task)
Constraints provided by domain theory	*None:* Clinician's theoretical orientation should not influence diagnosis (disorder level)	*Substantial:* Clinician's theoretical orientation has strong impact on content and structure of case formulation
Disagreement about task goal structure and content (inter-clinician reliability)	*Low:* Task goal structure and content is prescribed. Moderate to high inter-clinician reliability, average = .78 (Matarazzo, 1983)	*High:* Inter-clinician reliability probably moderate to low (cf., Barsalou, 1987)

	Present	Absent
Clear-cut stopping rules	*Present:* Stop categorization when diagnosis made	*Absent:* Core rule may be revised repeatedly in response to new information
Probable mental representation	Prototype and/or multiple exemplars (see Section III.B) Set of correlated features Set of abstract rules (Associated explanatory theories of psychopathology and etiology not used in disorder-level diagnosis)	No prior explicit representation for a particular patient Types of core rules may be stored as abstract knowledge within a theoretical framework or as prototypes or exemplars after encountering repeated instances of similar core rules (cf. Persons, 1989)
Stability of graded structure (of instances)	Explicit diagnostic criteria and decision rules used to increase stability of graded structure and reliability of classification Ideally, is context and theory free	Stability of graded structure varies with: Intra-patient context of symptoms Patient's environmental (socioeconomic, interpersonal) context (cf. Barsalou, 1987) Clinician theoretical framework
Criteria for accuracy	Equated with diagnostic reliability since independent validating criteria do not exist	Subsumption of symptoms, especially consilience Internal consistency/integrity of the mini-theory
Criteria for utility	Aggregate level (sample of patients with the diagnosis): Typical course of the disorder (Blashfield & Draguns, 1976) Potential for diagnosis-based prescriptive treatment (Reid, 1989; Bellack & Hersen, 1990)	Individual level (a particular patient): Context-dependent predictions Treatment utility of the assessment (Hayes, Nelson, & Jarrett, 1987; Persons, 1991)

Continues

TABLE IV *continued*

Dimension	Clinical diagnosis (disorder level)	Clinical assessment
Prescriptive components	Explicit set of features (diagnostic criteria) Standardized diagnostic interviews	Varies with theoretical framework; e.g., cognitive-behavioral: Comprehensive problem list (Persons, 1989) Make predictions and test against new patient data (Persons, 1989; Turkat & Maisto, 1985)
Role of clinical theory	None (on disorder level; for diagnostic criterion level; see Section IV)	Provides concepts, particularly hypothetical constructs Determination of clinical significance Defines internal structure: Explanatory relations amongst features (symptoms) and between features and core rule Role in single-instance inference
Source of category/conceptual coherence (Murphy & Medin, 1985)	Prototype with essential features and identification properties (see Section III,B) Correlated features (true halo: Cooper, 1981)	Explanatory: Provided by clinical theory (see Role of clinical theory)
External structure (Murphy & Medin, 1985)	Hierarchical structure of diagnostic categories (Section III.A) Etiological and psychopathological theories associated with disorders	Consistency of inter-feature and core rule-feature relational structure with clinical theory

tioning and should be useful in establishing individualized treatment goals and interventions (Luborsky, 1984; Persons, 1989, 1991, 1993; Safran, Vallis, Segal, & Shaw, 1986; Teyber, 1992; Wolpe & Turkat, 1985). These rules are inferred by the clinician.

Although much of the following analysis would also apply (at least structurally) to Luborsky's (1984) psychoanalytic conceptions of the core conflictual relationship theme, I will focus on cognitive–behavioral approaches to clinical assessment which incorporate the notion of the core formulation. This focus is adopted in order to constrain the issues concerning the structure and process of arriving at the core rule. It should be noted that many approaches to clinical assessment do not utilize the concept of the core formulation (principle, theme, process, issue). The core formulation approach, however, is receiving considerable attention within certain clinical perspectives (cognitive behavioral, psychoanalytic) and is highly useful in terms of its relevance to categorization issues.

The concept of the core formulation has been described in most detail by Persons (1989, 1991; 1993), by Safran and Segal and colleagues (Safran et al., 1986; Safran, Segal, Hill, & Whiffen, 1990; Segal & Kendall, 1990), and by Turkat and colleagues (Turkat & Maisto, 1985; Wolpe & Turkat, 1985). Persons (1989, 1993) suggests that the core formulation is a working hypothesis which generally describes a basic underlying irrational belief which may have an if . . . then . . . format, such as "If I experience a negative life event, then it means I am imperfect and deserve punishment." Other core formulations represent the patient's basic beliefs about the self, others, or the world, such as "I am unworthy" (Persons, 1993). Such basic irrational beliefs are seen as causal/generative mechanisms, perhaps trait-like in their consistency throughout the patient's life (Beck, Emery, & Greenberg, 1985), and from which automatic thoughts and other cognitions directly accessible to the patient are derived.

As the essence of the mini-theory of the patient situation, the core formulation has two major purposes. First, regarding the patient's present and past functioning, (1) it interrelates the various symptoms and dysfunction experienced by the patient, including seemingly disparate behaviors, via a deep-structural rule or underlying principle or theme; (2) it specifies the conditions or situational determinants under which the symptoms occur; and (3) together with relevant domain theory, explains their development, psychological meaning, and significance. Second, regarding future functioning, (1) it can be used to predict the patient's behavior in context specific conditions and (2) it can be used in individualized treatment planning, including specifying treatment goals, selecting appropriate intervention strategies, and guiding the therapist in making specific micro-process interventions during a therapy session.

Core rule induction is a theory-laden activity involving ascertaining essential or deep structural rules about the patient's functioning. Clinical theory is used to link the core rules to the surface behavior to develop the "mini-theory of the patient situation." The surface behavior, however, varies in centrality vis-à-vis the core rule. The core formulation is a mental model which is analogous to an ad hoc goal-derived category (Barsalou, 1983, 1987) in that it (1) is developed to achieve the clinician's goal (of being able to explain, predict, and plan for the treatment of that particular patient), (2) possesses graded structure (variations in centrality) which is context sensitive, and (3) is probably not well established in memory (although it can become so following repeated exposure to the target patient).

The core rule (which for our Mary example is, "If I experience a negative life event, then it means I am imperfect and deserve punishment") is a formalization of the notion of psychological essentialism. It is the essence of the category which incorporates that particular patient's dysfunctional behavior. Since the features of this category are idiographic (vary from patient to patient), so is the core rule. Together with associated clinical theory, the core rule can be used to generate additional features or predictions which will themselves vary in centrality (cf. Medin, 1989). For example, separating from one's spouse is an instance of a "negative life event" which is relatively high in centrality. Using Mary's core rule, we can predict a high probability of self-punishing behaviors following this event (e.g., self-critical thoughts, ineffective functioning at work leading to criticism from her supervisor).

The core rule has the advantage of substantial cognitive economy in the clinician's mental representation of the patient (cf. Genero & Cantor, 1987; Murphy, this volume; Rosch et al., 1976). It is probably best understood as a useful heuristic for summarizing clinically meaningful aspects of the patient's functioning including, and especially, those aspects unique to a particular individual. Is it a correct approach to clinical assessment? The question of whether it accurately represents underlying reality is an issue beyond the scope of this article. The correctness of a particular core formulation is a matter of its accuracy in predicting patient functioning (above base-line predictions such as those provided by the patient's diagnosis) and its utility in treatment planning (Persons, 1993; cf. Hayes, Nelson, & Jarrett, 1987), both of which can be determined empirically. On a more general level, the utility of the core formulation approach to clinical assessment is also a matter for empirical research (Persons, 1991).

2. Induction of Explanatory Rules in Scientific Discovery and Clinical Assessment

The second perspective which contributes to a framework for understanding categorization in clinical assessment involves the application and extension of heuristics-level information processing approaches to ill-structured tasks including (1) certain scientific discovery tasks (e.g., Klahr & Dunbar, 1988; Kulkarni & Simon, 1988; Qin & Simon, 1990) and (2) medical decision-making tasks in which the physician is constructing a model of how and why the patient's symptoms developed in a particular sequence (Clancey, 1988). I focus here on certain parallels between scientific discovery tasks and clinical assessment. This analogy applies both to the structure of the task endpoint (development of a scientific theory vs. the core formulation of the patient) and to the basic characteristics of the information processing required for both tasks. This analysis rests largely on the framework for induction developed by Holland et al. (1986).

The goal of both scientific discovery and clinical assessment is to ascertain deep structural rules about phenomena (cf. Mahoney, 1980). Within the Holland et al. (1986) framework, these rules have a condition–action (*if . . . then . . .*) structure and are of two types: synchronic rules, which are used to categorize and make available associational material, and diachronic rules, which are used to describe relations or outcomes over time. Theories in both scientific discovery and clinical assessment relate seemingly disparate phenomena by using hypothetical constructs (e.g., gravity, anxiety) as the action component of synchronic rules. These constructs then serve as the condition of a diachronic rule. Returning to our example of Mary, if she gets a flat tire, fails to meet a deadline, and has an argument with her spouse, the clinician may categorize all of these events as instances of a "negative life event." That is, each of these instances serves as the condition part of a synchronic rule for which the action part is the construct "a negative life event." If following such events, Mary typically engages in self-critical behavior and berates herself for deficiencies, then the induced core rule involves the diachronic relation between the "negative life event" and the "imperfect and deserve punishment" constructs as follows: "If I experience a negative life event, then it means I am imperfect and deserve punishment." Thus, this framework provides a cognitive basis for the *if . . . then . . .* structure of the underlying assumption in Persons' (1989; 1993) conceptualization of the core formulation. In addition to the above function, synchronic core rules can also function as associative or interpretative rules involving blanket underlying beliefs about the self, others, or the world in general, e.g., "I am inadequate" (Beck et al., 1979; Ellis, 1962; Persons, 1993).

Consider the above in light of the nature of observable phenomena to induced scientific laws and theories as described by Holland et al. (1986).

> Scientific laws are general rules. Scientific ideas are concepts that organize laws and other rules into useful bundles. Scientific theories are complexes of rules that function together computationally by virtue of the concepts that connect them. (p. 322)

> Theories are distinguished from sets of laws by several important characteristics. First, whereas an observational law is expected to give an account of a set of observations, theories are often used to explain sets of laws, not merely particular observations. . . . Second, theories are intended not merely to apply to phenomena in one domain but to unify phenomena in different domains. . . . Third, theories generally achieve their great unifications by postulating non-observable entities. (pp. 325–326)

Thus, the core rule is analogous to a scientific theory in that both use synchronic and diachronic relations (rules) involving abstractions or hypothetical constructs to explain disparate phenomena and predict future behavior.[5] Both also use background domain theories to provide constraints on the structure and content of permissible concepts and relationships.

In addition to the similarity of task end-point structure, scientific discovery and clinical assessment are similar in the general nature of the information processing required. Both are ill-structured tasks. Both are hypothesis generation and testing tasks requiring a dual-space search of the hypothesis space (domain knowledge such as cognitive–behavioral theory) and the instance space (patient data for clinical assessment). Once a hypothesis (a rule) is generated, its validity is evaluated using criteria of (1) subsumption and consilience (the ability to explain all the data including seemingly disparate data), and (2) accuracy of prediction (Holland et al., 1986; Klahr & Dunbar, 1988; Persons, 1989).

3.   Single-Instance Inference and Explanation-based Learning

Recent research in explanation-based learning of concepts has indicated that, under certain circumstances, both humans and machines can learn concepts from a single instance (Ahn et al., 1992; Mooney, this volume). This ability has long been considered an important characteristic of clinical expertise (Korchin, 1976), and is illustrated by the following excerpt of a clinical inference occurring in the context of a psychotherapy session:

---

[5] This may be contrasted to clinical diagnosis. On both the disorder and the diagnostic criterion level, the categories are collections of behaviors (e.g., symptoms). While these categories are predictive of future behavior, they are not explanatory. Explanation is provided by ancillary psychological theory, which is external to the categorization per se (Morey, 1991).

One session at this time took the following course. After a few sentences about the uneventful day, the patient fell into a long silence. She assured me that nothing was in her thoughts. Silence from me. After many minutes she complained about a toothache. She told me that she had been to the dentist yesterday. He had given her an injection and then had pulled a wisdom tooth. The spot was hurting again. New and longer silence. She pointed to my bookcase in the corner and said, "There's a book standing on its head." Without the slightest hesitation and in a reproachful voice I said, "But why did you not tell me that you had an abortion?" (Reik, 1948, p. 263)

It is clear from this example that this inference (which, by the way, was correct) could be made only with the extensive use of well-developed domain theory (cf., Ahn et al., 1992). Of course, such inferences must be regarded as hypotheses to be tested (Korchin, 1976; Persons, 1989).

C. MECHANISMS OF CORE RULE GENERATION

Three mechanisms which the clinician may use to generate or retrieve a core formulation will be suggested. First, however, it is necessary to put the process of core rule generation in the context of other information processing occurring during the clinical assessment: Core rule generation occurs after the clinician has already obtained some information about the patient's functioning and has determined which information is clinically significant (i.e., what behaviors are "findings"). After the clinician generates a plausible core formulation via one of the three mechanisms suggested below, this hypothesis must then be tested against additional patient data to determine its accuracy (Persons, 1989, 1993; Safran et al., 1986; Turkat & Maisto, 1985).

The three hypothesized mechanisms of core rule generation differ in that one relies primarily on retrieval of previously stored exemplar (or perhaps prototype) information, a second is a data-driven method involving searching for patterns of relationships in the patient's behavior, while the third involves single-instance hypothesis generation drawing heavily on domain theory.

1. Forward Reasoning and Direct Exemplar Retrieval

A search of the hypothesis space (in LTM) may be made in an attempt to retrieve previous exemplar-level information which can serve as a starting point for the core rule for the present patient. This retrieval may be accomplished via either of two hypothesized mechanisms: Forward reasoning involves the activation of a knowledge structure from which a stored core formulation prototype or exemplar is retrieved (cf. Patel & Groen, 1991). The knowledge structure may be a diagnostic category which has certain types of associated core rules (e.g., core formulations

for depression: Beck et al., 1979; Persons, 1989). A second process of
hypothesis space search involves direct retrieval of a core formulation
exemplar from LTM due to featural overlap of the present patient with this
exemplar (e.g., Mary reminds the clinician of Joe, who had a similar
configuration of symptoms, resulting in direct retrieval of Joe's core formulation.) Once the core rule is retrieved, the clinician checks the consistency of this rule with patient data already acquired (cf. Fisher, 1987), and,
if within tolerable limits, the core formulation is retained for hypothesis
testing. If not, the hypothesis is abandoned, and a search of the instance
space (patient data) or hypothesis space within that or another frame is
undertaken to generate another core formulation.

2. Data-driven Hypothesis Generation

This process consists of recognition of patterns of consistent behavior
based on multiple instances of similar behavior occurring across settings
or occasions. For example, the clinician may note that when Mary is late
for an appointment she typically says, "I keep thinking about what I did
wrong to make me late." The clinician forms a relatively non-inferential
descriptive generalization based on these data (Korchin, 1976). Background (domain) psychological theory is then used to categorize seemingly
disparate descriptive generalizations into one or more unified concepts
involving hypothetical constructs such as "negative life event" (Korchin,
1976; Sundberg & Tyler, 1962; cf. Holland et al., 1986). These hypothetical
constructs, which are activated via synchronic rules, permit the use and
accessing of quite general diachronic rules which have constructs as their
conditions, as described above. The result is an empirically induced core
formulation hypothesis (e.g., "If I experience a negative life event, then it
means I am imperfect and deserve punishment").

Certain aspects of this process resemble similarity-based category
learning. However, given the complex and potentially boundless domain
of behaviors on which the clinician could focus, it is clear that domain
theory must provide substantial constraints to focus the clinician on certain aspects of the patient's functioning in searching for patterns across
occasions or settings. Furthermore, domain theory is used to provide
explanations for the relations (1) among various patient behaviors, and
(2) between these behaviors (features) and the core rule.

3. Single-Instance Rule Generation

A third mechanism for generation of core rules lies between the above two
and involves concept and rule induction from a single instance (cf. Ahn et
al., 1992; Mooney, this volume). This method differs from data-driven
hypothesis generation in that a search for consistent patterns across situa-

tions, contexts, or occasions is not pursued. It differs from hypothesis generation via forward reasoning or direct exemplar retrieval in that the rule is constructed specifically for that particular patient and is highly theory-laden (see earlier example). Presumably when a core rule hypothesis is generated via this process, a process of consistency checking with already acquired data is also pursued.

VI. Summary

A preliminary model of categorization in clinical diagnosis and a framework for understanding categorization within clinical assessment were developed in this chapter. The model of categorization in clinical diagnosis focused on categorization of diagnostic criteria (within a disorder), a lower-level categorization process which occurs prior to assignment of the patient to a diagnostic disorder category. Unlike disorder-level categorization, there are few normative guidelines (e.g., identification properties, explicit decision rules) for categorization at this level. A number of important characteristics which differentiate this categorization task and the typical laboratory categorization task were delineated and incorporated into the model. The model consisted of prescriptive and descriptive components. Use of domain theory (to develop a constrained set of feature slots and a mental model of alternative causes for a finding) and the ability to obtain information within a dynamic, interactive framework are key components which must take place prior to a similarity-based comparison to the diagnostic criterion and other relevant categories. Empirically observed and theoretically probable departures from prescriptive processing in lower-level clinical diagnostic categorization were discussed and, for each, the probable location of the departure from the prescriptive model was suggested. Some of these information processing biases (e.g., illusory correlation) highlight the extent to which clinical categorization occurs within the context of the background knowledge, including clinical theory, which the clinician brings to bear on the clinical categorization process.

In contrast to the nomothetic, relatively well structured task of diagnostic categorization, the goal of clinical assessment is to develop an individualized mini-theory of the patient/situation to be used for explaining the patient's symptoms, and for the individualized prediction of future behavior and treatment planning. Some recent conceptualizations of this idiographic, ill-structured task suggest that the clinician should develop one or more core rules which are representations of underlying mechanisms, such as core ordering or deep structural principles. The core formulation can be viewed as a prototype for the application of psychological essentialism in professional inference and is analogous to an ad hoc, goal-driven category, with context-dependent graded structure present in the patient's symptoms. Similarities between the structure of the clinical assessment task and rule induction in scientific discovery were also used to develop a framework for understanding the core formulation. The core formulation consists of abstract synchronic and diachronic rules which are linked to specific patient behaviors (features) via explanatory relational theory. These relationships are explicated in the "theory of the person situation" for that patient. Three mechanisms for the generation of core rules were suggested and include single-instance category learning (a type of inference highly valued in clinical evaluation and requiring explanation-based models of categorization), forward reasoning, and a data-driven search for patterns in the patient's behavior. It is hoped that the casting of clinical assessment within this framework will foster the ecologically valid scientific investigation of this important aspect of clinical evaluation.

ACKNOWLEDGMENTS

I would like to thank Glenn Nakamura, Douglas Medin, Jacqueline Persons, and Steve Wilson for helpful comments on earlier drafts. Preparation of this manuscript was supported in part by a grant from the Research Enhancement Fund, College of Arts and Sciences, Texas Tech University, and by National Institute of Mental Health Grant MSM-1-1-RO3-MH49095-01 to the author.

REFERENCES

Agnew, N. M., & Brown, J. L. (1986). Bounded rationality: Fallible decisions in unbounded decision space. *Behavioral Science, 31*, 148–161.

Ahn, W., Brewer, W. F., & Mooney, R. J. (1992). Schema acquistion from a single example. *Journal of Experimental Psychology: Learning, Memory, and Cognition, 18*, 391–412.

Allport, G. W. (1962). The general and the unique in psychological science. *Journal of Personality, 30*, 405–422.

American Psychiatric Association (1987). *Diagnostic and statistical manual of mental disorders* (3rd ed., revised). Washington, DC: Author.

Anderson, J. R. (1983). *The architecture of cognition.* Cambridge, MA: Harvard University Press.

Anderson, J. R. (1990). *The adaptive character of thought.* Hillsdale, NJ: Erlbaum.

Anderson, J. R. (1991). The adaptive character of human categorization. *Psychological Review, 98*, 409–429.

Arkes, H. R. (1981). Impediments to accurate clinical judgment and possible ways to minimize their impact. *Journal of Consulting and Clinical Psychology, 49*, 323–330.

Arkes, H. R. (1991). Costs and benefits of judgment errors: Implications for debiasing. *Psychological Bulletin, 110*, 486–498.

Arkes, H. R., Faust, D., Guilmette, T. J., & Hart, K. (1988). Eliminating the hindsight bias. *Journal of Applied Psychology, 73*, 305–307.

Baron, J. (1988). *Thinking and deciding.* New York: Cambridge University Press.

Barsalou, L. W. (1983). Ad hoc categories. *Memory and Cognition, 11*, 211–227.

Barsalou, L. W. (1985). Ideals, central tendency, and frequency of instantiation as determinants of graded structure in categories. *Journal of Experimental Psychology, 11,* 629–654.

Barsalou, L. W. (1987). The instability of graded structure: Implications for the nature of concepts. In U. Neissar (Ed.), *Concepts and conceptual development: Ecological and intellectual factors in categorization* (pp. 101–140). New York: Cambridge University Press.

Beck, A. T., Emery, G., & Greenberg, R. L. (1985). *Anxiety disorders and phobias.* New York: Basic Books.

Beck, A. T., Rush, A. J., Shaw, B. F., & Emery, G. (1979). *Cognitive therapy of depression.* New York: Guilford.

Bellack, A., & Hersen, M. (1990). *Handbook of comparative treatments for adult disorders.* New York: Wiley.

Bieri, J., Orcutt, B., & Leaman, R. (1963). Anchoring effects in sequential clinical judgments. *Journal of Abnormal and Social Psychology, 67,* 616–623.

Blashfield, R. K. (1984). *The classification of psychopathology: Neo-Kraepelinian and quantitative approaches.* New York: Plenum Press.

Blashfield, R. K., & Draguns, J. (1976). Evaluation criteria for psychiatric classification. *Journal of Abnormal Psychology, 85,* 140–150.

Blashfield, R. K., Sprock, J., Haymaker, M. A., & Hodgin, J. (1989). The family resemblance hypothesis applied to psychiatric classification. *The Journal of Nervous and Mental Disease, 177,* 492–497.

Blashfield, R. K., Sprock, J., Pinkston, K., & Hodgin, J. (1985). Exemplar prototypes of personality disorder diagnoses. *Comprehensive Psychiatry, 26,* 11–21.

Bruner, J., Goodnow, J., & Austin, G. (1956). *A study of thinking.* New York: Wiley.

Cantor, N., Smith, E., French, R., & Mezzich, J. (1980). Psychiatric diagnosis as prototype categorization. *Journal of Abnormal Psychology, 89,* 181–193.

Chapman, L., & Chapman, J. (1967). Genesis of popular but erroneous psychodiagnostic observations. *Journal of Abnormal Psychology, 72,* 193–204.

Christensen-Szalanski, J. J., & Beach, L. R. (1982). Experience and the base-rate fallacy. *Organizational Behavior and Human Performance, 29,* 270–278.

Christensen-Szalanski, J. J., & Bushyhead, J. B. (1981). Physicians' use of probabilistic information in a real clinical setting. *Journal of Experimental Psychology: Human Perception and Performance, 7,* 928–935.

Clancey, W. (1988). Acquiring, representing, and evaluating a competency model of diagnostic strategy. In M. Chi, R. Glaser, & M. Farr (Eds.), *The nature of expertise* (pp. 343–418). Hillsdale, NJ: Erlbaum.

Clarkin, J. F., Widiger, T. A., Frances, A., Hurt, S. W., & Gilmore, M. (1983). Prototypic typology and the borderline personality disorder. *Journal of Abnormal Psychology, 92,* 263–275.

Cooper, W. (1981). Ubiquitous halo. *Psychological Bulletin, 90,* 218–244.

Crosson, B. (1990, January). Group 3A: Professional practice—didactic component. In C. D. Belar & N. W. Perry (Eds.), *Proceedings of the national conference on scientist-practitioner education and training for the professional practice of psychology* (pp. 19–59). Sarasota, FL: Professional Resource Press.

Curley, S. P., Yates, J. F., & Young, M. J. (1990). Seeking and applying diagnostic information in a health care setting. *Acta Psychologica, 73,* 211–223.

Dawes, R. & Corrigan, B. (1974). Linear models in decision making. *Psychological Bulletin, 81,* 95–106.

Einhorn, H. J. (1988). Diagnosis and causality in clinical and statistical prediction. In D. C. Turk & P. Salovey (Eds.), *Reasoning, inference, and judgment in clinical psychology* (pp. 51–72). New York: Free Press.

Einhorn, H. J., & Hogarth, R. M. (1981). Behavioral decision theory: Processes of judgment and choice. *Annual Review of Psychology, 32,* 53–88.

Einhorn, H. J., & Hogarth, R. M. (1986). Judging probable cause. *Psychological Bulletin, 99,* 3–19.

Ellis, A. (1962). *Reason and emotion in psychotherapy.* New York: Lyle Stuart.

Elstein, A. S. (1988). Cognitive processes in clinical inference and decision making. In D. C. Turk & P. Salovey (Eds.), *Reasoning, inference, and judgment in clinical psychology* (pp. 17–50). New York: Free Press.

Elstein, A. S., Holzman, M. D., Ravitch, M. M., Metheny, W. W., Holmes, M. M., Hoppe, R. B., Rothert, M. L., & Rovner, M. D. (1986). Comparison of physicians' decisions regarding estrogen replacement therapy for menopausal women and decisions derived from a decision analytic model. *American Journal of Medicine, 80,* 248–258.

Elstein, A., Shulman, L., & Sprafka, S. (1978). *Medical problem solving: An analysis of clinical reasoning.* Cambridge, MA: Harvard University Press.

Farmer, R., & Nelson-Gray, R. O. (1990). Personality disorders and depression: Hypothetical relations, empirical findings, and methodological considerations. *Clinical Psychology Review, 10,* 453–476.

Faust, D. (1986). Research on human judgment and its application to clinical practice. *Professional Psychology: Research and Practice, 17,* 420–430.

Finn, S. E. (1982). Base rates, utilities, and DSM-III: Shortcomings of fixed-rule systems of psychodiagnosis. *Journal of Abnormal Psychology, 91,* 294–302.

Fischhoff, B., & Beyth-Marom, R. (1983). Hypothesis evaluation from a Bayesian perspective. *Psychological Review, 90,* 239–260.

Fisher, S. D. (1987). Cue selection in hypothesis generation: Reading habits, consistency checking, and diagnostic scanning. *Organizational Behavior and Human Decision Processes, 40,* 170–192.

Ford, J. K., Schmitt, N., Schechtman, S., Hults, B., & Doherty, M. B. (1989). Process tracing methods: Contributions, problems, and neglected research questions. *Organizational Behavior and Human Decision Processes, 43,* 75–117.

Freeman, A. (1990). Cognitive therapy. In A. S. Bellack & M. Hersen (Eds.), *Handbook of comparative treatments for adult disorders* (pp. 64–87). New York: Wiley.

Friedlander, M., & Stockman, S. (1983). Anchoring and publicity effects in clinical judgment. *Journal of Clinical Psychology, 39,* 637–643.

Gauron, E., & Dickinson, J. (1966). Diagnostic decision making in psychiatry: II. Diagnostic styles. *Archives of General Psychiatry, 14,* 233–237.

Genero, N., & Cantor, N. (1987). Exemplar prototypes and clinical diagnosis: Toward a cognitive economy. *Journal of Social and Clinical Psychology, 5,* 59–78.

Gjerde, P., Sand, R., & Kleiven, J. (1979). An experimental investigation of the labelling effect of psychiatric diagnosis. *Scandanavian Journal of Psychology, 20,* 187–192.

Goldberg, L. R. (1970). Man versus model of man: A rationale, plus some evidence, for a method of improving on clinical inferences. *Psychological Bulletin, 73,* 422–432.

Golding, S. L., & Rorer, L. G. (1972). Illusory correlation and subjective judgment. *Journal of Abnormal Psychology, 80,* 249–260.

Gorman, M. E. (1986). How the possibility of error affects falsification on a task that models scientific problem solving. *British Journal of Psychology, 77,* 85–96.

Hayes, S. C., Nelson, R. O., & Jarrett, R. B. (1987). The treatment utility of assessment: A functional approach to evaluating assessment quality. *American Psychologist, 42,* 963–974.

Hogarth, R. M. (1981). Beyond discrete biases: Functional and dysfunctional aspects of judgmental heuristics. *Psychological Review, 90,* 197–217.

Holland, J. H., Holyoak, K. F., Nisbett, R. E., & Thagard, P. R. (1986). *Induction: Processes of inference, learning, and discovery.* Cambridge, MA: MIT Press.

Holt, R. R. (1978). *Methods in clinical psychology, Vol. 2: Prediction and research.* New York: Plenum.

Holt, R. R. (1988). Judgment, inference, and reasoning in clinical perspective. In D. C. Turk & P. Salovey (Eds.), *Reasoning, inference, and judgment in clinical psychology* (pp. 233–250). New York: Free Press.

Horowitz, L., Post, D., French, R., Wallis, K. D., & Siegelman, E. (1981). The prototype as a construct in abnormal psychology: 2. Clarifying disagreement in psychiatric judgments. *Journal of Abnormal Psychology, 90,* 575–585.

Horowitz, L., Wright, J., Lowenstein, E., & Parad, H. (1981). The prototype as a construct in abnormal psychology: 1. A method for deriving prototypes. *Journal of Abnormal Psychology, 90,* 568–574.

Jacobs, R., & Kozlowski, S. (1985). A closer look at halo error in performance ratings. *Academy of Management Journal, 28,* 201–212.

Jacobsen, N. S. & Traux, P. (1991). Clinical significance: A statistical approach to defining meaningful change in psychotherapy research. *Journal of Consulting and Clinical Psychology, 59,* 12–19.

Jacoby, J., Chestnut, R. W., Weigl, K. C., Fisher, W. (1976). Pre-purchase information acquisition: Description of a process methodology, research paradigm, and pilot investigation. In B. Anderson (Ed.), *Advances in consumer research: Vol. III* (pp. 306–314). Urbana, IL: Association for Consumer Research.

Kayne, N., & Alloy, L. (1988). Clinician and patient as aberrant actuaries: Expectation-based distortions in assessment of covariation. In L. Abramson (Ed.), *Social cognition and clinical psychology: A synthesis* (pp. 295–364). New York: Guilford.

Kern, L., & Doherty, M. E. (1982). ''Pseudodiagnosticity'' in an idealized medical problem-solving environment. *Journal of Medical Education, 57,* 100–104.

Klahr, D., & Dunbar, K. (1988). Dual space search during scientific reasoning. *Cognitive Science, 12,* 1–48.

Korchin, S. (1976). *Modern clinical psychology.* New York: Basic.

Kulkarni, D. & Simon, H. A. (1988). The processes of scientific discovery: The strategy of experimentation. *Cognitive Science, 12,* 139–175.

Kurtz, R. M. & Garfield, S. L. (1978). Illusory correlation: A further exploration of Chapman's paradigm. *Journal of Consulting and Clinical Psychology, 46,* 1009–1015.

Lange, A., Beurs, E. D., Hanewald, G. & Koppelaar, L. (1991). The influence of prior information about clients on evaluations and responses of clinicians during family therapy. *Journal of Social and Clinical Psychology, 10,* 21–36.

Langer, E. & Abelson, R. (1974). A patient by any other name . . .: Clinician group differences and labeling bias. *Journal of Consulting and Clinical Psychology, 42,* 4–9.

Larichev, O. I. & Moshkovich, H. M. (1988). Limits to decision-making ability in direct multiattribute alternative evaluation. *Organizational Behavior and Human Decision Processes, 42,* 217–233.

Luborsky, L. (1984). *Principles of psychoanalytic psychotherapy.* New York: Basic.

Mahoney, M. J. (1980). Psychotherapy and the structure of personal revolutions. In M. J. Mahoney (Ed.), *Psychotherapy process: Current issues and future directions* (pp. 157–180). NY: Plenum.

Mahoney, M. J. (1990). Representations of self in cognitive psychotherapies. *Cognitive Therapy and Research, 14,* 229–240.

Mahoney, M. J. (1991). *Human change processes: The scientific foundations of psychotherapy.* New York: Basic.

Matarazzo, J. (1983). The reliability of psychiatric and psychological diagnosis. *Clinical Psychology Review, 3,* 103–145.

Medin, D. (1989). Concepts and conceptual structure. *American Psychologist, 44,* 1469–1481.

Medin, D. L., & Edelson, S. M. (1988). Problem structure and the use of base-rate information from experience. *Journal of Experimental Psychology: General, 117,* 68–85.

Medin, D. L., & Schaffer, M. M. (1978). Context theory of classification learning. *Psychological Review, 85,* 207–238.

Meehl, P. (1954). *Clinical versus statistical prediction.* Minneapolis: University of Minnesota Press.

Meehl, P. E. (1986). Causes and effects of my disturbing little book. *Journal of Personality Assessment, 50,* 370–375.

Meehl, P. E., & Rosen, A. (1955). Antecedent probability and the efficiency of psychometric signs, patterns, or cutting scores. *Psychological Bulletin, 52,* 194–216.

Meichenbaum, D., & Gilmore, B. (1984). The nature of unconscious processes: A cognitive-behavioral perspective. In K. S. Bowers & D. Meichenbaum (Eds.), *The unconscious reconsidered* (pp. 273–298). New York: Wiley.

Millon, T. (1991). Classification in psychopathology: Rationale, alternatives, and standards. *Journal of Abnormal Psychology, 100,* 245–261.

Minsky, M. (1975). A framework for representing knowledge. In P. H. Winston (Ed.), *The psychology of computer vision* (pp. 211–280). New York: McGraw-Hill.

Morey, L. C. (1991). Classification of mental disorder as a collection of hypothetical constructs. *Journal of Abnormal Psychology, 100,* 289–293.

Morey, L. C., & McNamara, T. P. (1987). On definitions, diagnosis, and DSM-III. *Journal of Abnormal Psychology, 95,* 283–385.

Mumma, G. H., & Wilson, S. (1991, August). *Procedural debiasing of anchoring effects in social judgment.* Paper presented at the 1991 Annual Convention of the American Psychological Association, San Francisco, CA.

Murphy, G. L., & Medin, D. L. (1985). The role of theories in conceptual coherence. *Psychological Review, 92,* 289–316.

Murphy, G. L., & Wright, J. C. (1984). Changes in conceptual structure with expertise: Differences between real-world experts and novices. *Journal of Experimental Psychology: Learning, Memory, and Cognition, 10,* 144–155.

Mynatt, C., Doherty, M., & Tweney, R. (1977). Confirmation bias in a simulated research environment: An experimental study of scientific inference. *Quarterly Journal of Experimental Psychology, 29,* 85–95.

Mynatt, C., Doherty, M., & Tweney, R. (1978). Consequences of confirmation and disconfirmation in a simulated research environment. *Quarterly Journal of Experimental Psychology, 30,* 395–406.

Nisbett, R., & Wilson, T. (1977). The halo effect: Evidence for unconscious alteration of judgments. *Journal of Personality and Social Psychology, 35,* 250–256.

Nosofsky, R. M., Clark, S. E., & Shin, H. J. (1989). Rules and exemplars in categorization, identification, and recognition. *Journal of Experimental Psychology: Learning, Memory, and Cognition, 15,* 282–304.

Patel, V. L., & Groen, G. J. (1991). The general and specific nature of medical expertise: A critical look. In K. A. Ericsson & J. Smith (Eds.), *Toward a general theory of expertise: Prospects and limits* (pp. 93–125). New York: Cambridge University Press.

Paquette, L. & Kida, T. (1988). The effect of decision strategy and task complexity on decision performance. *Organizational Behavior and Human Performance, 41,* 128–142.

Payne, J., Braunstein, M., & Carroll, J. (1978). Exploring predecisional behavior: An alternative approach to decision research. *Organizational Behavior and Human Performance, 22,* 17–44.

Persons, J. B. (1991). Psychotherapy outcome studies do not accurately represent current models of psychotherapy: A proposed remedy. *American Psychologist, 46,* 99–106.

Persons, J. B. (1989). *Cognitive therapy in practice: A case formulation approach.* New York: Norton.

Persons, J. B. (1993). Case conceptualization in cognitive-behavior therapy. In K. T. Kuehlwein & H. Rosen (Eds.), *Cognitive therapy in action: Evolving innovative practice* (pp. 33–53). San Francisco: Jossey-Bass.

Pope, A. W., Bierman, K., & Mumma, G. H. (1991). Aggression, hyperactivity, and inattention-immaturity: Behavior dimensions associated with peer rejection in elementary school boys. *Developmental Psychology, 27,* 663–671.

Qin, Y., & Simon, H. A. (1990). Laboratory replication of scientific discovery processes. *Cognitive Science, 14,* 281–312.

Reid, W. (1989). *The treatment of psychiatric disorders.* New York: Bruner Mazel.

Reik, T. (1948). *Listening with the third ear.* New York: Farrar, Strauss.

Reitman, W. R. (1965). *Cognition and thought: An information processing approach.* New York: Wiley.

Richards, M. S., & Wierzbicki, M. (1990). Anchoring errors in clinical-like judgments. *Journal of Clinical Psychology, 46,* 358–365.

Rohde, P., Lewinsohn, P. M., & Seeley, J. R. (1991). Comorbidity of unipolar depression: II. Comorbidity with other mental disorders in adolescents and adults. *Journal of Abnormal Psychology, 100,* 214–222.

Rock, D. L., Bransford, J. D., & Maisto, S. A. (1987). The study of clinical judgment: An ecological approach. *Clinical Psychology Review, 7,* 645–661.

Rosch, E. (1975). Cognitive representations of semantic categories. *Journal of Experimental Psychology: General, 104,* 192–233.

Rosch, E., & Mervis, C. B. (1975). Family resemblances: Studies in the internal structure of categories. *Cognitive Psychology, 7,* 573–603.

Rosch, E., Mervis, C. B., Gray, W. D., Johnson, D. M., & Boyes-Braem, P. (1976). Basic objects in natural categories. *Cognitive Psychology, 8,* 382–439.

Runyan, W. M. (1983). Idiographic goals and methods in the study of lives. *Journal of Personality, 51,* 413–437.

Safran, J. D., Segal, Z. V., Hill, C., & Whiffen, V. (1990). Refining strategies for research on self-representations in emotional disorders. *Cognitive Therapy and Research, 14,* 143–160.

Safran, J. D., Vallis, T. M., Segal, Z. V., & Shaw, B. F. (1986). Assessment of core cognitive processes in cognitive therapy. *Cognitive Therapy and Research, 10,* 509–526.

Sarbin, T. R. (1986). Prediction and clinical inference: Forty years later. *Journal of Personality Assessment, 50,* 362–369.

Sawyer, J. (1966). Measurement *and* prediction, clinical *and* statistical. *Psychological Bulletin, 66,* 178–200.

Segal, Z. V. (1988). Appraisal of the self-schema construct in cognitive models of depression. *Psychological Bulletin, 103,* 147–162.

Segal, Z. V., & Kendall, P. C. (1990). Selfhood processes and emotional disorders. *Cognitive Therapy and Research, 14,* 111–112.

Shweder, R. A. (1977). Illusory correlation and the MMPI controversy. *Journal of Consulting and Clinical Psychology, 45,* 917–924.

Simon, H. A. (1973). The structure of ill structured problems. *Artificial Intelligence, 4,* 181–201.

Simon, H. A. (1990). Invariants of human behavior. *Annual Review of Psychology, 41,* 1–19.

Simon, H. A., & Lea, G. (1974). Problem solving and rule induction. In L. V. Gregg (Ed.), *Knowledge and cognition* (pp. 329–346). Hillsdale, NJ: Erlbaum.

Smith, E., & Medin, D. (1981). *Categories and concepts.* Cambridge, MA: Harvard University Press.

Smith, E. E., Shoben, E. J., & Rips, L. J. (1974). Structure and process in semantic memory: A featural model for semantic decisions. *Psychological Review, 81,* 214–241.

Smith, E. R. (1984). Model of social inference process. *Psychological Review, 91,* 392–413.

Spitzer, R., Williams, J., Gibbon, M., & First, M. (1990). *Structured clinical interview for DSM-III-R—Patient Edition* (SCID-P, Version 1.0). Washington, DC: American Psychiatric Press.

Starr, B. J., & Katkin, E. S. (1969). The clinician as aberrant actuary: Illusory correlation and the incomplete sentence blank. *Journal of Abnormal Psychology, 74,* 670–673.

Sundberg, N., & Tyler, L. (1962). *Clinical psychology: An introduction to research and practice.* New York: Appleton-Century-Crofts.

Sushinsky, L. W., & Wener, R. (1975). Distorting judgments of mental health: Generality of the labeling bias effect. *Journal of Nervous and Mental Disease, 161,* 82–89.

Temerlin, M. (1968). Suggestion effects in psychiatric diagnosis. *Journal of Nervous and Mental Disease, 147,* 349–353.

Teyber, E. (1992). *Interpersonal process in psychotherapy.* (2nd ed.). Pacific Grove, CA: Brooks/Cole.

Turk, D. C., & Salovey, P. (1985). Cognitive structures, cognitive processes, and cognitive-behavior modification: II. Judgments and inferences of the clinician. *Cognitive Therapy and Research, 9,* 19–33.

Turkat, I. D., & Maisto, S. A. (1985). Personality disorders: Application of the experimental method to the formulation and modification of personality disorders. In D. H. Barlow (Ed.), *Clinical handbook of psychological disorders* (pp. 502–570). New York: Guilford.

Tversky, A. (1972). Elimination by aspects: A theory of choice. *Psychological Review, 79,* 281–299.

Voss, J. F., & Post, T. A. (1988). On the solving of ill-structured problems. In M. Chi, R. Glaser, & M. Farr (Eds.), *The nature of expertise* (pp. 261–285). Hillsdale, NJ: Erlbaum.

Wason, P. C., & Johnson-Laird, P. N. (1972). *Psychology of reasoning: Structure and content.* London: Batsford.

Wattenmaker, W. D., Nakamura, G. V., & Medin, D. L. (1988). Relationships between similarity-based and explanation-based categorization. In D. Hilton (Ed.), *Contemporary science and natural explanation: Commonsense conceptions of causality* (pp. 205–241). Brighton, England: Harvester Press.

Wechsler, D. (1981). *WAIS-R Manual.* New York: The Psychological Corporation.

Wedding, D., & Faust, D. (1989). Clinical judgment and decision making in neuropsychology. *Archives of Clinical Neuropsychology, 4,* 233–266.

Wisniewski, E. J., & Medin, D. L. (1991). Harpoons and long sticks: The interaction of theory and similarity in rule induction. In D. Fisher & M. Pazzani (Eds.) *Computational approaches to concept formation* (pp. 237–278). San Mateo, CA: Morgan Kaufmann.

Wolpe, J., & Turkat, I. D. (1985). Behavioral formulation of clinical cases. In I. D. Turkat (Ed.), *Behavioral case formulation* (pp. 5–36). New York: Plenum.

Zukier, H. (1986). The paradigmatic and narrative modes in goal-guided inference. In R. Sorrentino & E. T. Higgins (Eds.), *Handbook of motivation and cognition* (pp. 465–502). New York: Wiley.

A RATIONAL THEORY OF CONCEPTS

Gregory L. Murphy

I. Introduction

Research on human concepts can be divided into two general categories. One class includes formal models of categorization, in which the goal is to discover the learning algorithm and representational format for concepts. This work addresses the empirical aspects of learning concepts, in which a learner is exposed to a certain number of examples and must induce concept representations for the examples' categories. Such work is formal, because it typically attempts to provide a mathematical rule that relates the distribution of features in the learning set to the learned representation. The articles in this volume by Estes, Kruschke, and Taraban and Palacios are good examples of this type. The other class is the "knowledge-based" approach, in which the influence of general knowledge structures on concepts is investigated. Here, the issue is how one's "theories" about a domain or one's expectations influence the information learned about concepts and how that information is organized in memory. Because there is no well-developed mathematical analysis of knowledge structures and their effects, this work typically does not result in formal models. The articles on explanation-based learning, conceptual combination, and essentialist approaches to concepts by Bareiss and Slator, Malt, and Mooney are all examples.

This distinction represents a serious rift in the psychology of concepts, one that can be found throughout the literature and that surfaces whenever

327

psychologists interested in concepts talk. I think that researchers working on concepts find it difficult to understand the import of work from the approach that they do not follow. And, indeed, it is difficult to bridge this gap. What does research on whether natural kinds have an essence (a knowledge-based issue) tell us about whether exemplars or prototypes are the basis for category learning (a more formal issue)? And conversely, what does the comparison of different formal learning rules tell us about concepts that are formed without viewing any examples, as during language comprehension (such as conceptual combination) or problem-solving?

This chasm between formal modeling approaches and knowledge-oriented approaches can lead researchers in one camp to deny the utility or relevance of the other camp's work. Although such claims are rare in print, they are not at all rare in conversations at conferences, in reviews of articles submitted to journals, and in other informal arenas. This kind of exclusionism is not scientifically defensible, in my opinion. The influence of knowledge on concepts has been documented by much empirical evidence (reviewed by Murphy, 1993). In fact, it is difficult to see how one could learn concepts without a knowledge base to direct hypothesis testing (Keil, 1989; Murphy & Medin, 1985). But by the same token, empirically based approaches to concept formation must have some validity if only because we tend to form the categories that are actually in the world, rather than the ones we believe or wish were in the world—that is, we actually do learn from examples. Given that people must acquire evidence in some order, represent it in some manner, and use a decision rule to categorize objects, the formal approach has its place in the psychology of concepts as well. Nonetheless, there is a kind of incommensurability in these two approaches, because neither one seems to address the problems that the other seeks to answer. A major problem for research on concepts is how to bridge this gap, in order to address both kinds of issues in a single theory.

One possible solution to this problem might be found in John Anderson's (1991a) *rational model* of categorization, which is based on his adaptive theory of cognition. Anderson attempts to motivate a formal category learning model through an ecological analysis of the concept formation task, implicitly drawing on the theory of evolution to justify its assumptions. By using real-world constraints to derive a formal rule, his work could provide a connection between the "neat" formal model and the "scruffy" real-world learner. However, Anderson adopts the exclusionary attitude mentioned above, arguing that effects of knowledge on categorization are not in fact part of concept learning as it is traditionally defined, and so he does not include any "theories" or knowledge base in the model. Instead, his model is purely formal. The success of his model could well be taken as evidence against the knowledge-based approach.

Because the rational model is an interesting mix of ecological considerations and formal modeling, and because it bears directly on the importance of knowledge-based processes in concept use, it is a suitable topic for an in-depth analysis and critique. Thus, describing and evaluating this model is the main goal of this chapter, with the more general goal of exploring the relation between formal and knowledge-based approaches. My major source for the rational model is Anderson (1991a), which focuses on the categorization component of the rational model, though Anderson (1990) is useful in describing his general motivation and overall framework. A peer commentary review of Anderson's overall approach appeared after this article was begun (Anderson, 1991b). I make no effort to exhaustively list the points of agreement and disagreement between my views and the commentaries there; the categorization model formed only one part of its discussion.

The structure of this article largely follows that of Anderson (1991a). It begins with a discussion of the main components of the rational analysis of categorization. A brief description of the details of Anderson's model follows. Then I discuss Anderson's treatment of the theory approach and his defense of a purely empirical approach. Finally, I consider whether evolutionary considerations can provide feasible constraints on cognitive theories.

II. The Steps in a Rational Analysis

Anderson's presupposition is that cognition as a whole is formed through adaptation to the environment. Our minds have developed so as to be generally accurate and optimal for the jobs they do. If they were inaccurate or irrational, then humans would not be very successful at surviving. Our success (so far), therefore argues that the human mind is a rational, generally optimal system (though see the discussion of evolutionary reasoning below).

Anderson (1991a) describes a number of steps that one must go through in order to provide a rational analysis of the mind. The most important ones are to: (1) specify what the mind is trying to optimize, (2) discover or make assumptions about the structure of the environment to which the mind is adapted, (3) calculate the costs associated with different processes that the mind might carry out, and (4) use the first three steps to derive *optimal behavioral functions* that should describe human behavior. Anderson's assumption is that the structure of the environment (step 2) must be an especially strong determinant of our conceptual structure. This assumption seems to be that to the degree that our concepts mirror reality, the more accurate and adaptive our behaviors based on these concepts will be.

Anderson's model of concepts is not a detailed process model of the sort familiar to cognitive psychologists and described elsewhere in this volume (e.g., by Estes, Kruschke, or Taraban). Instead, it is a functional approach that combines hypotheses about the goal of the conceptual system with an optimality assumption to say what the system *should* do. However, the analysis has no way of specifying *how* the system carries out this goal in detail. Thus, the specific equations and representations that Anderson describes are not meant to imply that people calculate those exact equations or store those exact representations. Rather, the relevant part of the analysis is the relation between inputs (objects) and outputs (categorization decisions or feature predictions)—not a processing algorithm. This distinction will be relevant when we discuss the computational constraints on the system.

At this stage, I want to emphasize that I think that this general approach could well be a very useful one. In particular, I believe that it is essential to look at the animal in its normal environment in order to derive constraints on theories of its behavior—the ecological approaches that Anderson cites, such as those of Gibson, Marr, and Shepard, could be very useful to the psychology of concepts. However, it will become apparent that I do not agree that Anderson in fact takes this approach in forming his theory of concepts. Furthermore, I will argue that it is just the ecological considerations that he ignores that lead one to understand the importance of a knowledge base in concept learning. The next sections describe the steps in the rational analysis Anderson proposes for categorization.

A. THE GOAL OF CATEGORIZATION

Anderson's first step in a rational model requires him to identify the function or goal of the system, which will later be used to specify its optimal level of performance. In general, this function is said to be the prediction of features.[1] Simply put, "if one can establish that an object is in

---

[1] In Anderson (1991a), this discussion (pp. 410–411) is rather obscure. He first describes three answers to the question "Why do people form categories (assuming that they do)?" but none of them is in fact an answer to this question. One explanation is based on language: "A linguistic label provides a cue that a category exists, and people proceed to learn to identify it. This is the view at least implicit in most experimental research on categorization" (p. 410). Obviously, this does not describe a goal of categorization. It might be that Anderson is implying that communication is a primary goal of categorization, but this is explicitly denied later (p. 425). The next proposed goal is titled "Feature overlap," and it describes that when

a category, one is in a position to predict a lot about that object'' (p. 411). Unfortunately, this proposal is not justified at any length.

Anderson is clearly correct in arguing that concepts are useful for prediction. If you know that something is a dog, you can predict many of its behaviors and attributes, without having any more information about it. Its specific identity (Fido, Sandy's dog) is not necessary for making many reliable predictions about the object. Thus, categorization aids in our making predictions about the environment. However, it is not so clear that this is the only function of categorization. For example, the influential work of Rosch (1978; Rosch, Mervis, Gray, Johnson, & Boyes-Braem, 1976) has emphasized the benefits of concepts for memory representation, through her principle of cognitive economy. She argues that without concepts, our memories would become swamped with details of particulars. Furthermore, Rosch has argued that the phenomena of prototypes and basic level concepts demonstrate that particularly efficient representations are used. Thus, cognitive economy may be another goal of concept formation. If prediction were the only goal of categorization, then one would expect that the most predictive concepts would be formed and favored. However, the most predictive concepts are always the most specific (Medin, 1983; Murphy, 1982), with representations of individual objects being the most predictive of all. But, of course, considerable research shows that concepts at an intermediate stage of specificity are favored (Mervis & Pani, 1980; Murphy & Brownell, 1985; Murphy & Smith, 1982; Rosch et al., 1976, among others). Thus, prediction may not be the only goal of concept formation.

Other functions of concepts may be discovered if we consider a wider range of cognitive activities, beyond traditional categorization tasks (see Barsalou, 1991): One's concepts of a domain are (in part) the inputs to problem solving, planning, language comprehension, memory retrieval, and learning. For example, one's concepts of dogs could be crucial in order to plan what to do with a dog during a vacation, in understanding or recalling a story about a dog, or in deciding how to approach a strange barking dog. It is not obvious that these uses of concepts can be reduced to the goal of "prediction." At least, without more detail, it is not clear what the function of prediction includes and rules out.

---

exemplars overlap in their properties, they are often included in the same category. This appears to be a purely structural description of categories—why people form concepts is not described here either. Finally, Anderson says that "similar function" can be the basis of categorization of objects, which also does not answer why people form categories. It is only after these three answers that the final answer is given that Anderson uses throughout the rest of the article, feature prediction. Other writings (Anderson, 1991b) confirm that this is the intended function.

Readers may wonder whether I am asking too much of the rational model. After all, it is not surprising if a psychological theory does not cover every phenomenon in a domain. Perhaps the rational model explains categorization from the perspective of feature prediction and not from other perspectives. Although this response is quite reasonable, it is important to understand that the project that Anderson (1990, 1991a) has taken on requires him to identify *the* goal of categorization, in order to derive its optimal function. A system with two goals may have a very different optimal function from one with only one of those goals. Thus, it is surprising that Anderson does not provide a more complete discussion of the goals of categorization, since the derivation of his entire model rests on this foundation.

B. The Structure of the Environment

The next step in the rational analysis is to describe the structure of the environment that gave rise to the behavior under discussion. Anderson (1990) emphasizes that environmental structure rather than cognitive rules may be largely responsible for the structure of our concepts. Thus, this proposal is very much in the spirit of the work of ecological psychologists in perception (see Gibson, 1979; Michaels & Carello, 1981). One would expect, then, a rather detailed discussion of the environment in which people normally live and behave. And, in fact, this is a standard part of ecological analyses in the perceptual domain (e.g., Gibson, 1979, chaps. 1–3).

However, this expectation is not fulfilled, as the description of the structure of the environment in Anderson (1991a) is quite brief (three paragraphs). This description makes three main points:

1. Categories form a nearly disjoint partitioning of objects in the world;
2. Features are probabilistically associated with categories; and
3. Features within a category are largely independently distributed.

Anderson cites biological species as his model for category structure. Clearly, species have ecological validity, in that the human conceptual system developed in an environment in which different species were found and probably had to be distinguished. Species are essentially disjoint (point 1), species members vary in most attributes (point 2), and Anderson argues that the features within a species are usually independently displayed (point 3). One problem with these assumptions is that most theorists say that *category membership* is also probabilistic (see Smith & Medin, 1981), which may not be true of species membership, and which

Anderson does not list as part of the structure to be modeled. This issue would seem to require more serious discussion.[2]

In Anderson's view, using species as the model for concepts makes use of "the aid science and biology gives in objectively specifying the organization of these objects" (p. 410). However, there are serious problems with this proposal. A major aspect of the human conceptual system which has been intensively studied is its hierarchical structure. Concepts of varying degrees of specificity can usually be organized in an inclusion hierarchy. Thus, a single object can be a desk chair, a chair, a piece of furniture, an artifact, and a thing; another object can be a wire terrier, a terrier, a dog, a canine, a mammal, a vertebrate, an animal, and a living creature. Some writers have argued that the development of this hierarchical system of concepts is a major attainment of human intelligence (see Markman & Callanan, 1984). However, hierarchies are by definition not disjoint: the *same* object is a wire terrier, mammal, animal, etc. Thus, Anderson's claim about the structure of the environment is at odds with one of the major facts about the conceptual system.

Furthermore, the reference to biology is a surprising one, because a whole subspecialty of biology, *taxonomy,* is devoted to discovering the nested categories that describe the same organisms. Bitter debates have arisen over whether some species are in the same or different genus or class or family. The categories of *arthropod, primate, mammal, endosperms* or *maple* exist just as much as species do, and work in biology has been devoted to discovering these classes and using them to predict evolutionary relations. Biology also uses other category terms that cross-cut the taxonomic terms, and which are therefore not disjoint. For example, categories related to environment and behavior are important and common in biological discourse: Categories like *leafy* or *insect-pollinated plants* and *carnivorous, aquatic, quadruped, diurnal,* or *migrating animals* form important biological classes. There are properties typical to insect-pollinated plants that distinguish them from air-pollinated plants, even though these cross-cut species categories; the same is true of the distinction between carnivores and herbivores. Thus, there seems to be little in the nature of biological categories that supports the assumption that categories are disjoint. And at higher levels of categorization than the species, features are not independent: Mammals bear live young, have

[2] In a personal communication (February, 1992), Anderson explained that the model assumes that the categories are not probabilistic in the world, but that people's confidence in their categorizations does admit of degrees, thereby meeting some of the requirements of a probabilistic theory. Although this "classical view" of categories might be true for species, it seems debatable for other common categories, such as artifacts or social categories.

hair, nurse their young, and so on, whereas birds have none of these properties. So at a higher taxonomic level, there may be important feature correlations in the environment. Whether people's concepts represent such feature correlations is a matter of some controversy, with most authors arguing that they do, contrary to the rational model's assumption (e.g., Malt & Smith, 1984; Medin, Altom, Edelson, & Freko, 1982; but see Murphy & Wisniewski, 1989).

In addition, it must be mentioned that human categorization as practiced by most Americans is not focused on the level of the species. The preferred level of biological categorization has been found to be quite a bit higher than that of the species (Dougherty, 1978; Rosch et al., 1976). Rosch et al. had hypothesized that subjects would prefer to use categories like *trout, oak,* and *robin,* which are at the genus level or higher. However, the categories that their subjects actually preferred were considerably higher, at the level of *fish, tree,* and *bird.* In biological domains that we are not experts in, we are often not sure which level is the species. For example, *maple* is not a species of tree, but a family, which is largely found in one genus. There are in fact about 125 species of maples, with 13 species native to North America (Little, 1980). So, if your expertise in trees is like mine, your preferred concept is not at the species (e.g., *black maple*), nor at the genus (*maple*), but at a much higher level, in which *tree* is separated from other plants. Thus, even if species were the main "objective" biological categories, they should not be proposed as the prototypical human concepts.

An additional point of interest is Malt's (1991) observation that some very common names for biological entities do not in fact refer to any category in standard biological taxonomies. She points out *fruit, tree,* and *fish* as examples that do not refer to any standard category, although people seem to believe that they do. Other very useful and common concepts like *weed, vegetable, herb,* and *flower* "refer to groups of biologically diverse plants that have certain commonalities in size, shape, taste . . ." that are salient to us, but which lack biological significance (Malt, 1991, p. 46). Apparently, the connection between our concepts and the "objective" classification of the world by biology is not very strong. Furthermore, because the preferred level of categorization changes with cultural expertise and interest (Dougherty, 1978; Berlin, Breedlove, & Raven, 1973; Rosch et al., 1976), it is apparent that the "objective" categories as defined by biology cannot determine conceptual structure.

The upshot of this discussion is that the rational model's assumptions about the structure of the environment do not seem to be supported. And again, it is rather puzzling that a more in-depth and complete analysis of this very difficult question was not attempted. If one really believes that the structure of the environment determines a cognitive ability, then perhaps *most* of the description of the theory should be devoted to arguing for a particular analysis of the environment, rather than a brief sketch. Lacking such a discussion, it is hard to see how a theory can ignore the existence of hierarchical organization and cross-cutting categories like *carnivore*. Anderson's response to some of these criticisms is considered below.

C. COMPUTATIONAL CONSTRAINTS AND THE OPTIMAL BEHAVIORAL FUNCTION

The next step of a rational model is specifying the constraints that might limit cognitive processes. Clearly, if we had infinite memories and infinite processing capacity, we could all be optimal actors. But with limitations on human thought in general, the conceptual system can only be expected to be optimal to a degree. Anderson (1991a) does not consider general constraints on the cognitive system—rather, he proposes a particular "optimal" categorization rule and then modifies it so that it is more computationally tractable.

The rational model assumes that if probabilistic feature prediction is the goal of categorization, Bayes' theorem is the optimal rule by which one could accomplish this (p. 410). (Gigerenzer, in Anderson, 1991b, provides an interesting critique of this assumption.) However, the task under consideration is not just category *learning*, but category *formation*. That is, the rational model does not assume that the category learner is getting feedback concerning the accuracy of categorization, nor that the learner has a knowledge base to start with. Instead, the learner is exposed to an unorganized set of exemplars one at a time and has to group them together into whatever categories seem appropriate. The two constraints that Anderson puts on this system are that it not allow "backtracking" (i.e., once an object is categorized, it is stuck in that category), and that the system commit to an analysis after each object is seen (so, the learner cannot hold all the exemplars in working memory before making a decision). The objects are encountered in a specific order, and the most recent category structure is updated after each object is seen. There is no explicit memory representation of a concept in this system: The category is simply the grouping of objects that have been seen in the past.

In order to discuss computational constraints more completely, it is necessary to describe the model's proposed "optimal behavioral function" that will fulfill the goal of the system, based on environmental structure, keeping within the computational constraints. The rational model consists of two separate components. The first uses a Bayesian rule in order to classify a new object. The rule calculates whether the object should be grouped with an existing class or whether it should begin its own category. The second component also employs a Bayesian rule, to predict unknown features of an object, given the objects already observed. The bulk of the description of the rational model is a derivation of the probability theory necessary to perform the clustering into categories and then the feature predictions that arise from them. Anderson (1991a) improves on the earlier description of the model (Anderson, 1990) by allowing for the representation of continuous dimensions (instead of only discrete features).

The description here cannot do justice to Anderson's derivation. (Actually, the derivation is not what is at issue. If one accepts the premises of this theory, then the derivation seems fairly uncontroversial. But it is those premises that are being questioned.) One important point that should be mentioned, however, is the nature of the model's prediction rule. Once the categories are formed, and the model is presented with an object O, how should it decide whether the object has feature j? One might plausibly expect the model to place O into a category and then to use the prevalence of j in the category as the prediction. However, the model instead calculates the probability of O being in *each* of its categories (by examining feature overlap of O and the category members) multiplied by the probability of each category having feature j. The sum of these joint probabilities over all categories is taken as the overall probability of O having j. But note that this rule results in the category structure having little effect on the prediction of feature j. In essence, the model is comparing O to all the objects it has seen, and if it is similar to objects that have j, then it will predict a high probability of having j. Whether the objects are in one category or another has little influence on the final result (for example, see the following discussion of the model's simulation of Medin & Schaffer's, 1978, data, in which its categories are very different from Medin & Schaffer's, but it predicts features very well).

Anderson notes that his algorithm is more accurate than one that first categorizes the object and then uses that category as the basis for prediction (p. 412). But this seems to contradict the earlier claim that categorization improves prediction, since the model is not using the object's most likely category as the basis for prediction. If one retains access to all the exemplars seen in the past, then it is hard to see how grouping them into categories will improve prediction. There may be a subtle benefit from category formation in this system (perhaps especially when few exemplars have been seen), but it is not clear from the description what it would be.

The computational constraints in the rational model do not seem to have the serious problems that made the other parts of the rational analysis problematic. (Clearly, the prohibition against changing one's mind about the category of an object is too strong. But it may be reasonable for short time frames such as a single experimental session.) However, there is again a noticeable lack of detail in this discussion. Surely, no one will argue that a totally unconstrained application of Bayes' theorem is psychologically plausible or that the constraints Anderson places on his system do not simplify it. But are these constraints sufficient? Is the model still too complex for the human processor to carry out? Are the bounds of working memory being stretched by the necessary computations? These questions are not addressed.

Anderson (1991a, p. 414) is not claiming that people calculate Bayesian probabilities on the fly. As mentioned earlier, his is a functional analysis, in which it is claimed that the processes people actually carry out will have a result similar to the output of the rational model. Unfortunately, by staying at this more abstract level, Anderson makes the discussion of computational constraints much less tractable. One can imagine different algorithms that would carry out the behavior of this model to varying degrees of approximation. The problem is that different instantiations require very different computational constraints. For example, if our theory were that people actually attempt to compute Bayesian probabilities, then constraints on working memory and on the accuracy of mental arithmetic would be relevant. But suppose that our theory was that people form long-term memory descriptions of each category, and then categorize objects by comparing them to the most salient and similar representations. Now, the constraints on mental arithmetic would be totally irrelevant, and constraints on long-term memory would be needed. Without more concrete claims about the actual processes that people go through, it is hard to know how computational constraints can be specified. The constraints that Anderson mentions (pp. 411–412) are relevant to the Bayesian equations, but since he is not claiming that people actually compute the Bayesian formulas, it is uncertain whether these constraints are even relevant. I believe that the main function of these constraints is to simplify the computational requirements of the rational model so that it may be efficiently simulated. There is nothing wrong with doing this, but it should not be confused with true psychological constraints.

In summary, the constraints Anderson suggests might well be reasonable ones. But I have argued that it is very difficult to specify constraints, as the rational analysis requires, without a fairly concrete process model, since different models of the same task can require very different constraints. Therefore, it is not clear whether the constraints embodied in the rational model are in fact sufficient.

III. Empirical Results

Given that a central tenet of the rational model is to use the structure of the environment as a major determinant of categorization, with a broader ecological goal of explaining how intelligent behavior developed in that environment, it is a bit surprising that all the empirical discussion in Anderson (1991a) centers around artificial category learning experiments. The reason is probably because these are the studies that provide quantitative data that can be tested against the mathematical realization of the model. However, the drawback is obviously that these experiments, and especially their stimulus structures, may or may not mirror the kinds of concepts normally found in the environment. And if they do not, then subjects' behavior in those experiments may reflect a stimulus-specific strategy that is not typical of normal concept learning. (Indeed, Anderson, 1991b, argues that studies on reasoning are not realistic enough to tell whether people's behavior in natural situations is optimal.) In fact, the rational model's categories did not always match the categories claimed by the authors of the experiments it simulated. For example, its best simulation of Medin and Schaffer's (1978) stimuli resulted in every stimulus forming its own category (instead of two categories), and its simulation of Nosofsky (1988) resulted in two, three, or four categories, depending on the order of stimulus presentation. Apparently, it is not unusual for the model to split the experimenters' categories into subclasses.[3]

Such apparent disconfirmation of the model (though see footnote 3)

---

[3] The rational model assigns each object to its own category, whereas Medin and Schaffer (1978) only had two categories. Yet, the model's classification accuracy is reported as high: a .87 correlation with Medin and Schaffer's results. How is this possible? The term *category* is ambiguous here. On the one hand, the clusters output by the program seem to be its categories. But on the other hand, the category representation includes a feature for the category name (as assigned by Medin and Schaffer), so items with the same names form a different "category." The clusters that the model forms are completely independent of the category names (in this case), which seems to be suggesting two different ideas of what a category is—not distinguished by Anderson (1991a). I am treating the model's clusters as the "real" categories, in part because treating the category name as just another feature is contradicted by empirical data on word learning to be discussed later (and see Murphy, 1991a). However, it should be understood that the .87 correlation of the name feature with the subjects' naming is taken by Anderson as revealing a nearly correct category structure (where category = name), in spite of the fact that each object is in its own category (where category = model cluster). Whether this ambiguity is harmless or indicates some problem is not fully clear to me.

could be rebutted by the claim that the categories constructed by Medin and Schaffer and the other experimenters are not quite natural: the model's goal is to pick up the "real" structure, not the one imposed by the experimenters. Although this sounds reasonable, the rational model has no way of specifying in advance what a natural category structure is— Anderson's (1991a) analysis of the environment did not describe in enough detail how real categories are structured. The work of others on concept naturalness or coherence (e.g., Keil, 1981, 1989; Murphy & Medin, 1985; Rosch, 1978) has not been incorporated in the model. Also, if the experimenters' classes can be rejected as being unnatural, then it would seem most appropriate to test the model on real categories, which are not subject to this criticism, by definition. Nonetheless, it should be noted that the rational model is able to simulate the results of a number of artificial category experiments, a fact which should be accounted for. I discuss its successes later.

IV.   The Nature of Category

In the section "The Nature of Category," Anderson (1991a) responds to criticisms that the model does not include knowledge-based phenomena and that its goals are too limited. As a general strategy, he takes the position that the model is "tied to the goal of prediction and to the phenomena of species in living things" (p. 424) and that complaints about its inability to do other tasks are not truly part of the (same) psychology of categorization. I will discuss each of the issues he raises, as his positions here would have important consequences for much current work on concepts, if they were accepted.

A.   CROSS-CATEGORIZATION

Anderson recognizes that there is some cross-categorization, contrary to his assumption of disjoint partitioning. Here is his discussion of this issue (p. 424):

> A common example is to point out that a creature is both a dog and a pet. Clearly, the rational algorithm would choose the biological category, dog, as the true category and note that dogs are found in homes, are faithful (with a certain probability), and have the labels dog and pet. Perhaps there are certain predictions associated with the social phenomenon of pets that this model could not make, but it is a mistake to think all inference is a matter of categorical generalization.

(He goes on to distinguish causal inference as a separate kind of inference.)

Anderson's example only mentions the categories *dog* and *pet,* and not the many other categories that this object falls into, including different category levels (e.g., *german shepherd, mammal, vertebrate*) as well as true cross-cutting categories (e.g., *carnivore, female, quadruped, land-dweller, guard dog,* etc.). Thus, the model is missing many possible categories—not just one. This would be understandable if it were correct that *dog* is the "true category," as stated, but it is hard to make sense of this remark. There is nothing "false" about *pet, mammal,* and so on that makes them inappropriate categories. And, of course, people normally do use multiple categorization. It would not be surprising if the rational model (or any model) did not include all such categories—but the problem here is that the rational model does not allow *any* of them, except for *dog.*

The most important element of this argument is its claim that not all "inference is a matter of categorical generalization." Although this may be true, it does not seem to have any bearing on the question of *dog* and *pet.* Clearly, *pet* is a real category, one represented by a single lexical item in English, known to children and adults and having a set of associated attributes, like other category names. Most people know that pets typically live in the home, are cuddly, are friendly, are not dangerous, are fed and taken care of by their owners, form emotional attachments with their owners, and so on. Like the other features in the rational model, these are not necessary and sufficient; not all pets have every feature. Nonetheless, people make inferences from knowing that I own a pet, such as inferring that I feed it regularly.

Anderson's argument seems to assume that there is a contradiction between biological and other kinds of categories, but this is not the case. An animal can be both a pet and a dog, without us having to decide which is the "true category," just as a person can be both a woman and a lawyer or a father and a husband. Perhaps he is assuming that the species concept has primacy because of its scientific standing. However, such an argument is difficult to accept, as most of our everyday concepts are not biological or determined by some scientific taxonomy (and as pointed out earlier, our preferred biological categories are generally not species). The most prominent counterexamples are our concepts of artifacts (which is a very rich domain in American society) such as furniture, clothing, tools, weapons, vehicles, computing devices, manufacturing machinery, buildings, transportation systems, prepared foods, home appliances, electronic entertainment devices, and so on. We encounter nonscientific categories outside the realm of objects as well, including personality and social relations (Cantor & Mischel, 1979), legal and political categories, most events (Rifkin, 1985), scenes (Tversky & Hemenway, 1983), games and sports, music, literature, and art. If all these domains are eliminated as appropriate subjects for the psychology of concepts, then the remaining domains will be a small minority of our everyday concepts. Furthermore, cross-categorization seems to be the rule in many of these other areas as well, in that hierarchical structure has been observed for a number of them (Cantor & Mischel, 1979; Rifkin, 1985; Tversky & Hemenway, 1983). In the particular domains of events and personality categories, it has been argued that the relational nature of these categories makes them very open to multiple categorization even within a taxonomic level (see Cantor & Mischel, 1979; Morris & Murphy, 1990; Vallecher & Wegner, 1987). Clearly, individual people fit a very large number of social categories simultaneously.

In short, this defense of the inability of the rational model to allow cross-classification does not hold up to scrutiny. In a later discussion, Anderson (1991a) specifically addresses the issue of higher-level categorization found in taxonomies (pp. 425–426). He points out that more general categories don't help one to predict the features of an object more than the basic-level category does: "We are much better off predicting the cat-chasing propensity of Fido knowing that he is a dog than knowing he is a mammal" (p. 425), seeming to suggest that it is not necessary to have higher levels of analysis in order to make inferences. This is true, so long as one always has the information that Fido is a dog. But if one is not sure that Fido is a dog (perhaps only having seen rustling in the underbrush to identify him), then it might be quite useful to have higher-level categories such as *animal*. Indeed, Osherson, Smith, Wilkie, Lopez, and Shafir (1990) have shown that higher level categories like *mammal* and *bird* are used in feature induction tasks (such as predicting whether larks have some feature, given that sparrows have it), and this is clearly a matter of categorical prediction. Furthermore, when taken to its extreme, Anderson's argument entails that *dog* is too general a category as well. For if we know that Fido was a doberman pinscher or a chihuahua, we could predict his cat-chasing propensity with even more accuracy than just knowing that he is a dog. In fact, as mentioned earlier, the greatest predictive power comes from the most specific categories (Corter & Gluck, 1992; Medin, 1983; Murphy, 1982), and so something besides predictive power is needed to explain why categories are formed above this level.

In this section, Anderson mentions some Bayesian techniques that can be used to develop hierarchies, but he has not incorporated them into his model. One might wonder why he does not simply modify the model to form multiple categories. I think that the basic problem here is that *the rational model has no concept representation.* That is, the model is a clustering algorithm that groups together objects in a way similar to what people might do. But it does not describe a memory representation of concepts. If the model had a description of *dogs*, say, then it could also

form a description of *mammals,* and perhaps form an appropriate link
between them. But because the model is clustering objects, and each
object can go into only one cluster, there is no way to form different
conceptual representations that apply to a single object. This shortcoming
is not a problem from the point of view of a category formation model, but
it does seem to prevent the model from addressing other psychological
issues that have been central in the study of concepts, such as how the
concept is represented and used in reasoning. Thus, it is not that Anderson
has arbitrarily decided to ignore hierarchical structure and cross-
classification—these sorts of issues cannot be addressed within the rational model, because of its lack of representation.[4]

B. THEORY-BASED APPROACHES

Anderson seems to believe that his model is not consistent with
knowledge- or theory-based approaches to concepts. However, it is not
clear whether this is really the case, or whether it is only due to a miscon-
ception about what those approaches are. As he describes it,

> "Some people (e.g., Murphy & Medin, 1985) have questioned the extent to which
> similarity-based categories exist and have argued that most categories are theory based.
> They point out that people display rich rules for reasoning about objects. . . . Most
> cited cases of such theory-based categories involve levels of aggregation much higher
> than would be produced by the rational model." (p. 425)

The conflict between similarity and theory is not one of mutually exclusive alternatives, as this quotation suggests. In fact, the paper cited (Murphy & Medin, 1985) contains numerous statements that members of
categories are usually quite similar and that similarity is not an incorrect or
misleading determinant of category membership (e.g., "We emphasize
[that similarity is] *insufficient* here because we do not want to imply that
this approach is completely wrong or misleading. It is clear that category
members are similar to one another, but we have argued that similarity is
too flexible to give any specific, natural explanation of conceptual coher-

---

[4] Anderson and Mantessa (1991) do present a hierarchical algorithm based on the rational
model, but I must confess that I do not fully understand it. In particular, their paper does not
describe how the categories at different levels are used in predicting features, and so it is not
clear whether the higher level classes serve the functions attributed to natural category
classes. Anderson and Mantessa report that using the hierarchy seems to provide greater
stability to their results but does not improve its feature prediction dramatically. However,
the data they used to test the model were not based on hierarchically organized stimuli (e.g.,
the Medin & Schaffer, 1978, data), so the import of this finding is not very clear.

ence," p. 297). The argument made by Murphy and Medin was that similarity is insufficient to explain category membership, because there is no objective similarity metric that can predict it. Rather, similarity must always be taken with respect to certain dimensions. For example, in deciding whether something is a *dog,* similarity with respect to genetic structure and parentage are central; but in deciding whether the same thing is a *pet,* parentage is less relevant, and behaviors are central. One's theory of these domains is needed to select these respects (see Rips, 1989). (Murphy & Medin also argued that theories would be helpful in organizing concepts in memory, but as noted above, the rational model does not address memory organization.)

One might argue that the empirical success of the rational model is a counterexample to this claim, because it apparently does not include any general knowledge or theories. Murphy (1993) recently discussed computer models of categorization and data-analytic techniques of category formation (such as clustering analyses) and concluded that these models used theories to make them work, just as people do. However, here the theory is in the mind of the programmer, who carefully selects the input for the system so that it is relevant and useful. This task seems to be ignored as an uninteresting part of the "front end" of the category model, but this is where a considerable part of category formation really occurs: in culling out the features so that only a small number of nonredundant, especially useful ones are considered. In a real-world encounter with an object, there is a huge number of features available, and a major aspect of concept acquisition is figuring out which ones are relevant (e.g., the time of day an object is observed is a relevant feature in learning about *bats* but not *trees*). If *all* the features that one could encode for each object were to be input to a program, no computer would be large enough to run the simulation. (In fact, Murphy & Medin, 1985, argued that most objects have an infinite number of predicates in common, so that a "pure" similarity metric that does not select relevant features could not work.) This selective function of theories has been empirically demonstrated by Pazzani (1991) and Wisniewski and Medin (1991).

The rational model is no exception. It was not given raw sensory inputs as the data for its category formation. Instead, Anderson himself identified the relevant features (usually based on the original experimenters' designs) and gave them to the system. Furthermore, all the studies Anderson (1991a) simulates use very simple artificial stimuli. For example, they never include inferential features, such as "dangerous" or "useful." By using such stimuli and performing the encoding for the model, Anderson avoids the main problems that "theories" were intended to solve. Thus, its successes do not provide a test of similarity versus knowledge-based approaches. To avoid any misunderstanding, I want to emphasize that I am not criticizing the use of artificial stimuli, which I have often used in my own research (e.g., Murphy, 1991b; Murphy & Smith, 1982). My point is that such stimuli and models based on them cannot possibly be used as evidence that general knowledge structures are not needed to explain concept formation in the real world.

Anderson's defense of pure similarity does not mention the now considerable empirical evidence that neutral similarity judgments do not predict categorization. For example, Carey (1985) provides numerous such examples, with both adults and children, using common biological categories. Gelman and Markman (1986) showed that children's feature predictions were often controlled by two objects sharing a category name, even when overall similarity suggested a different prediction. This result depends in a very reasonable way on the type of categories and features tested. For example, children think that two birds have the same basic biological functions but perhaps not the same weight or location. The rational model does not allow such content effects or domain specificity. Rips (1989) discusses a number of dissociations, again with common categories, in which an object is rated as more similar to one of two categories but is judged as a member of the other category (see also Smith, Jones, & Landau, 1992). Research on similarity is now showing just how complex a relation it is. For example, a number of recent papers have shown that not only feature overlap but *relations* between features are important in similarity judgments (Markman & Gentner, 1990), and that decisions about similarity and dissimilarity are differentially affected by such relations (Medin, Goldstone, & Gentner, 1990). The rational model is not sensitive to relations. "Similarity" is not one basic, objective relation that can be computed independently of knowing about the task, the domain of objects being considered, and so on.

Thus, the point is not that similarity is incorrect, or that similarity-based categories don't exist, but that similarity needs constraints and direction in order to work, and this is what the theories help do. Because Anderson (1991a) does not address the evidence that has been cited in support of this approach, the conclusions against theory-based views have little force. (In a personal communication, February, 1992, Anderson suggests that theories might be integrated into the rational model by influencing the prior probabilities in the Bayesian equations. This is an interesting suggestion, though it would not account for all theory effects, such as those on feature encoding. But if this adjustment of prior probabilities used complex reasoning in knowledge-rich domains, it would clearly require a significant elaboration of the rational model.)

C. LINGUISTIC CATEGORIES

The rational model treats category names simply as another feature of the category (Anderson, 1991a, p. 425). Once again, it might have been thought that this claim would be subjected to an empirical investigation, since there is considerable evidence on how the exposure to category names affects learning, especially in children (Au & Glusman, 1990; Callanan, 1985a; Markman, 1989; Markman & Hutchinson, 1984; Mervis, 1987; Ward, this volume; Waxman & Kosowski, 1990). Contrary to the assumption of the rational model, these studies give considerable evidence that providing a category name during learning qualitatively changes the nature of the learning process.

The main result has been that when children are asked to cluster categories with no constraints on them (as the rational model does), they predominantly choose thematically related objects, like a dog and bone, a spoon and bowl, or a pail and sand. But when they are told that one of the objects is a *dax* (or other unfamiliar name), then they tend to choose taxonomically, putting together a dog and cat, a spoon and knife, or a pail and shovel (see Waxman, Shipley, & Shepperson, 1991, for additional results). Markman (1989) explains such results by arguing that children start out with constraints on their word-learning such that they consider different hypotheses when learning names for objects than they do in other categorization situations. A recent study by Smith et al. (1992) reveals that children pay attention to different features of objects when they are labeled by nouns versus adjectives and that naming an object could drastically change categorization over an unnamed condition. In short, giving an object a name may qualitatively change the nature of category formation, perhaps through constraints on word-learning of the sort discussed by Markman (1989).

This is a somewhat ironic situation, because one can easily imagine how such constraints would be highly adaptive for a young creature faced with numerous possible groupings and many possible features to consider, especially considering the computational limitations on a young child. Thus, it is not clear why Anderson ignores such constraints in his theory. He admits that

> It is legitimate to try to study and understand these phenomena surrounding these linguistic categories. However, I question what they have to do with the sense of category that is the topic of this article. The categories of this article are potentially nonverbal, nonconscious, and need only be implicit in prediction behavior. (1991a, p. 425)

This response appears to contradict the spirit of the rational model. Given the broad scope of the model, with its claim that the human conceptual system (and, indeed, cognition in general) is optimally adapted to the environment, it is hard to see why linguistic concepts in particular should not fit the theory. But more to the point, this remark is apparently an attempt to exclude phenomena that might disconfirm the theory, without adequate justification. The argument that the categories under discussion are potentially nonverbal and unconscious is misleading, since almost all the data simulated by the rational model are from categories with names, which subjects study consciously and intently for some time. In fact, rather than being implicitly learned and used, it is not unusual in these studies for a fair proportion of subjects never to reach the learning criterion, even with small numbers of exemplars and multiple learning trials (e.g., Medin & Schwanenflugel, 1981; Nosofsky, Clark, & Shin, 1989; both cited in Anderson, 1991a). In contrast, children learn the vocabulary of their native language, mapping appropriate concepts onto the new words, with as little experience as a single exposure (Carey & Bartlett, 1978), without explicit study, and with a remarkably high success rate. Thus, if any data are suspect, it would seem to be our psychological experiments, rather than evidence from language learning.

In a somewhat different context, Anderson criticizes the study of goal-derived categories (Barsalou, 1983) such as *things to carry from a burning house*. He argues that this represents a confusion of linguistic labeling and categories (p. 425), presumably meaning that such things are linguistic descriptions that do not correspond to real categories. If this criticism is correct, then it is a problem for other areas in the psychology of concepts, such as conceptual combination (see Murphy, 1988, 1990; Smith, Osherson, Rips, & Keane, 1988; Shoben, this volume, since these are also linguistically defined categories. Yet conceptual combination has been shown to be subject to the normal processes of categorization, such as typicality (Hampton, 1988; Smith et al., 1988), and Gerrig and Murphy (1992) provide evidence that when combinations occur in discourse, they are understood through concept formation. Again, this criticism is difficult to understand from the ecological perspective that underlies the rational model. Goal-derived categories arise out of planning processes that occur in everyday life, in which people must select alternatives that fit certain descriptions in order to complete their goals. As Barsalou (1991) describes in detail, categories such as *places to go on vacation when you don't have much money* or *people to eat lunch with* are likely to arise not in an experiment, but in the decisions that people have to make in their normal lives. Barsalou's elegant work on this topic seems eminently related to an ecologically valid model of category formation.

V.   What Is the Rational Model, Really?

I have been depressingly consistent in my evaluation of the rational model so far: I have found serious problems with each of its major assumptions. However, I do not think that the model is unworthy of interest by any means; in fact, it has a number of strengths. But in order to evaluate the model properly, it is necessary to separate what it actually does from what it has been claimed to do. With a different perspective on what could reasonably be expected from this model, I think that one could give a more positive evaluation than I have so far.

My discussion of the first sections of Anderson (1991a) have, I believe, made it clear that the rational model in its current version is not truly an ecologically based theory. It does not seem to take into account the environment as experienced by human and animal categorizers, and its inclusion of computational limitations and the goals of categorization is minimal. But nonetheless, the model is quite good at capturing the results of a class of experiments, those involving the learning of artificial categories, in which prior knowledge has little if any role. Why is the model so successful in this domain, if it falls short in its theoretical underpinnings, as I have argued?

I think that the appropriate perspective with which to view the rational model is as a formal model of category learning of the sort described at the beginning of the article (see Estes, 1991, for a review). The studies of Medin and Schaffer (1978), Nosofsky (1986, 1988), Gluck and Bower (1988), Estes (1986), and Kruschke (1992) are other prominent examples. In fact, Nosofsky (1991) has shown that the rational model is very similar to the seminal context model of Medin and Schaffer (1978). These models operate under the assumption that there are learning processes common to many different domains of concept acquisition, and that by elucidating these principles in a well-controlled set of stimuli, one may be able to generalize to a wide range of concept learning. Thus, these researchers are attempting to discover the principles of category learning independently of the knowledge-based influences. From this perspective, a number of aspects of the rational model are novel and interesting, including its emphasis on category formation (rather than teacher-based learning) and its feature prediction rule.

One could argue whether the formal approach is likely to be successful and, in particular, whether the learning of dot patterns or schematic faces is likely to be much like word learning by children, learning of physics concepts by college students, learning of social stereotypes, and so on. However, as I stated at the beginning of the article, it seems clear that top-down processes cannot account for concept formation in and of themselves. There must be some means by which examples are encoded, stored, and used in forming a concept. Although this argument does not entail that there is a domain-general method by which this is done, it does seem to imply that work on these learning rules will be a necessary and important part of the total picture of concept acquisition. But by the same token, it also seems clear that these domain-general rules of learning cannot provide a complete explanation of categorization, because of their inability to access knowledge that will influence the input into those rules and that will interpret their output. And as mentioned earlier, there are a number of empirical results that a purely formal approach cannot account for (e.g., Nakamura, 1985; Pazzani, 1991; Rips, 1989; Wattenmaker, Dewey, T. Murphy, & Medin, 1986).

The rational model falls squarely into the formal approach, because it attempts to provide a mathematically specified (i.e., formal) rule for categorization that applies across every domain of categorization. It is beyond the scope of this chapter to compare it in detail to other such models and to evaluate their relative effectiveness. However, the rational model differs from the others, in that Anderson has claimed (1) that it is based on ecological principles and (2) that other aspects of categorization that it cannot account for are not part of the realm of categorization. I have already addressed both these issues: I argued that the model is not in fact based on ecological principles (and see below) and that Anderson provides no actual arguments for excluding the data that the model cannot handle.

I think that rather than claiming some special ecological and rational basis for this model, it would have been appropriate to propose this model as an account of the data-driven aspects of categorization. Its apparent empirical successes suggest that it may be a good account of this component of the categorization process. However, the model doesn't seem to say anything one way or another about knowledge-based processing, and this matter could have been left for another theory to address, rather than attempting to dismiss all this work. A more constructive approach might be a "separate but equal" policy, in which researchers who prefer to focus on one aspect of the psychology of concepts do not downplay or dismiss the existence or utility of other aspects. The success of one learning rule in explaining artificial category learning does not mean that there is no influence of knowledge; and the pervasiveness of theory-based processing does not imply that there is no learning or data-driven processing. However, this separate but equal policy ignores the issue of how the two kinds of processes will be incorporated into one model. Wisniewski and Medin (1991) have recently suggested that these two aspects are highly interactive, and if correct, this would mean that we cannot indefinitely continue to study the two separately. Ultimately, an integrated explanation will probably be necessary. But before such an explanation can be arrived at, it is necessary for researchers on both sides to acknowledge the necessity of the component that they do not themselves study.

VI. Optimality and Rationality

A final issue that I would like to raise concerns the possibility of an analysis based on ecological considerations. I believe that an ecological perspective could be very helpful in limiting the kinds of explanations that psychologists generate. Attention to the real-world plausibility of psychological mechanisms might filter out some of the theories that would seem to work only within the confines of an experimental situation. Also, attention to the successes and difficulties of conceptual tasks that people normally go through (e.g., word learning, learning of scientific concepts or inference in comprehension) might expand our horizons beyond those of the traditional concept acquisition task popular since Bruner, Goodnow, and Austin (1956).

However, the rational model goes beyond this use of ecological constraints to the claim that the concept formation mechanism is optimal. The model has the escape clause of computational limits, so its prediction of optimality is somewhat weakened. That is, lack of optimality can always be attributed to the computational limits of the mind that prevent it from fully implementing an optimal function. Even so, it seems to me that optimality is far too strong a claim to make, and that it is not in fact licensed by evolutionary theory.

A. EVOLUTIONARY JUSTIFICATIONS OF OPTIMALITY

Before beginning this discussion, I must make a digression. After reading Anderson (1991a), I was convinced that he intended an evolutionary justification for the optimality claim, based on references to cognition being "adapted to the environment" and his comment that "perhaps such models are ultimately to be justified in terms of maximizing some evolutionary criterion like number of surviving offspring" (p. 409). However, Anderson (1991b) explicitly denies any such evolutionary justification. I discuss this reasoning nonetheless, because I believe that it is a very natural motivation for a claim of optimality—in fact, I will later argue that an optimal model is somewhat rootless without it. However, it should be emphasized that the rational model does not explicitly claim an evolutionary basis for the position that concepts are optimally adapted to the environment.

To begin the discussion, it is important to understand that organisms evolve within an environmental niche—not to be optimal in some general sense. The niche is an important part of the argument, because without it, optimality would be obviously false. For example, consider this argument: my eyesight is better than a bat's, therefore the bat must be suboptimal, and therefore the optimality assumption is false. But, an optimality proponent would answer, the bat does not really need very good eyesight—in its niche, echolocation is a much more useful skill, which it has and you do not. Now, I could argue that the bat would be better off still if it also had excellent eyesight, and that I would be better off if I also had echolocation skills, and therefore optimality is still incorrect. But these additional skills would come at a cost (in genetic encoding, in space taken up in the nervous system, in metabolic energy required to implement them, and so on), and for all we know, the cost may be greater than the gain. Thus, optimality can be maintained, because of the costs attributed with each ability and the possible low gain within an animal's niche. In short, the concept of the ecological niche is central to this theory's explanation of how optimality can be true while organisms differ widely in their behavioral abilities.

But now, the search to prove optimality has become a circular endeavor: We are defining an animal's niche by its behaviors and abilities, and then we are saying that its abilities are optimal within the niche. For example, we assumed that the niche of a bat includes flying at night as a major part; therefore, we can argue that excellent eyesight is not a very useful skill, and so its poor eyesight is not a counterexample of optimality. But note that we defined the niche by virtue of the bat's abilities and then used the niche to determine what abilities it "should" have (since only skills useful within the niche are considered; e.g., we discounted good eyesight as an useful attribute). So this argument essentially used the animal's current abilities to determine whether its abilities are optional. Thus, I would argue that the claim of optimality is largely empty.

Another important point is that evolution does not generally result in perfection. In fact, Mayr (1982, p. 489) says that the belief of early naturalists that nature was a perfect mechanism was one reason that they rejected the notion of natural selection, which could only take place if some organisms were less successful than others. Mayr points out Darwin's belief that "There is room for improvement in all species" (p. 490). Any gene that is even slightly more adaptive than its competition will rather quickly become the predominant one, as mathematical analyses have shown (see Dawkins, 1987)—thus, perfection is not required. Mayr (1982, p. 589) summarizes this point nicely:

> Selection cannot produce perfection, for in the competition for reproductive success among members of a population, it is sufficient to be superior and not at all necessary to

be perfect. Furthermore, every genotype is a compromise between various selection pressures, some of which may be opposed to each other, as for instance, sexual selection and crypsis, or predator protection. . . . After each shift into a new adaptive zone [i.e., niche], certain adaptations to the previous zone become liabilities.

As Mayr's last sentence points out, the historical nature of evolution also provides constraints on what kinds of adaptation can occur, limiting the chances of real optimality.

Gould (1990) points out that many people believe that evolution results in continuous progress (often additionally assuming that human beings are the endpoint of evolution, because they are so obviously the pinnacle of progress). Although complex organisms do arise through evolution,

the modal organism on Earth, the most common organism on Earth, remains a simple prokaryotic cell, a bacterial level of organization. That has never changed in the history of life on Earth. . . . There are more *E. coli* bacteria in the digestive tract of every one in this room than there have ever been human beings on Earth. And those bacteria are going to outlive us [humanity]. (Gould, 1990, pp. 10–11)

Clearly, most animals are quite successful without the higher mental processes that humans have, suggesting that optimal cognitive functioning is not a necessary ability. Furthermore, although organisms are of course well adapted to their environments, not every feature is the result of selection. Some of them are neutral, or else arose as a side effect, as a result of some other adaptation (Gould & Lewontin, 1984; Mayr, 1982, p. 590). It is difficult to prove that any one attribute of an organism is the result of an adaptive advantage. Careful argumentation and even experimentation is necessary for each such proposed feature.

I believe that a similar argument can be made regarding rationality. Ever since the seminal work of Simon (1969) and of Tversky and Kahneman (see Kahneman, Slovic, & Tversky, 1982, or Nisbett & Ross, 1981), it has been widely observed that people's decisions do not follow the normative rules that have been developed for decision-making. In some cases, these rules can be shown to be optimal by relatively uncontroversial criteria (e.g., following them would maximize the amount of money one makes, in a situation in which one wants to make money). In other cases, the normative criteria come from well-accepted theories or the laws of probability. Simon (1969) has pointed out that normative optimality is not necessarily a reasonable goal. That is, he argued that an animal does not need to find the maximum amount of food, does not need to remember things exactly, does not need to be perfect in its decisions—rather, it needs to be good enough to get by. He points out that the costs associated with being perfect are considerable: vast computing power is needed, considerable time is necessary to make decisions, large amounts of information are required, and so on. Ultimately, perfection is impossible for finite beings. So, all of our cognitive mechanisms are a tradeoff between the need for reasonably good decision-making and the costs associated with those processes. This is analogous to the observation that a single attribute of an organism is not selected for, but that the organism as a whole is selected for. One might be able to make perfect probability judgments, but at a resulting cost (say, in time spent or in the amount of nervous tissue devoted to this task) that could outweigh any gain. Simon's conclusion is that normative models of reasoning (e.g., Bayes' theorem) should not be our models of thought processes.

The point of this discussion is that starting with an assumption of true rationality does not seem warranted. It seems unlikely that evolution would bring humans (or any other animal) to a level of perfect performance suggested by normative rules, given the costs associated with such performance. Furthermore, defining rationality in a more limited way, such as performance that is "good enough" for the animal to survive, raises the specter of circularity.

As remarked earlier, Anderson (1991b) explicitly denies the link between evolutionary theory and optimality. Unfortunately, it is not so easy simply to disclaim this justification, because without it there is no clear motivation for the assumption of optimal adaptation to the environment (Godfrey-Smith, in Anderson 1991b, makes the same argument). It is certainly unbelievable that the cognitive system *just by chance* developed into a system that is optimally adapted to our environment. Keep in mind that the rational model does not just claim that people's concepts happen to be veridical, but that the concept formation and prediction *mechanisms* are such that they will form veridical concepts in our environment. There clearly must be some causal connection between the environment and our cognitive structures that led to such a close relationship. In the absence of any compelling explanation of how optimality would come about, given its evolutionary implausibility, I would argue that we should turn our attention to different ecological constraints, described in the next section.

B.   AN ALTERNATIVE ECOLOGICAL APPROACH

One could follow the ecological considerations that Anderson mentions in a different direction, namely to study people's actual concept learning in the real world. Thus, rather than starting from normative assumptions, one could use situated behavior as the source of theories about the structure of the conceptual system (see Barsalou, 1991). In this approach, one uses people's everyday activities to (1) discover new conceptual processes, (2) discover the constraints necessary to explain concept learning in these situations, and (3) collect data to evaluate theories developed in artificial category paradigms.

This is an increasingly popular approach in developmental psychology, where it is of great interest to discover the exact input that the child receives and to plot the child's acquisition of concepts as a result of that input (Callanan, 1985b; Mervis, 1987). By discovering the nature of the input, the rate of acquisition and the pattern of errors that children make, we may discover constraints on the learning process that might not be evident from experiments on category learning.

In adults, a similar technique can be used in studying the acquisition of expertise. By sampling concepts over the course of learning some complex domain, one can simultaneously discover details of the initial and final concepts in the domain and the learning process itself. In many such studies, the emphasis has been on problem-solving or learning, with little attention paid to the conceptual organization of the domain, but in other cases, the concepts formed have been investigated (e.g., Barsalou & Hale, 1991; Chi, Feltovich, & Glaser, 1981; Chi, Hutchinson & Robin, 1989; Murphy & Wright, 1984; Tanaka & Taylor, 1991).

A different domain of naturally generated concepts that could be a source of informative data is communication. Research on conceptual combination has often addressed the comprehension and generation of noun phrases that combine a number of category terms, like *apartment dog*. Clearly, such concepts are an ecologically valid result of a normal process, even though they may be formed without direct experience of the category members. Finally, as mentioned earlier, planning and problem-solving can lead to the formation of new concepts (e.g., Barsalou, 1983, 1991; Ross, 1989), which then are available to form new plans or solve new problems. This is another natural case of concept formation that may not be found in the traditional paradigms.

I am citing these examples, albeit very briefly, to show that a different kind of ecological orientation may be very useful in concept formation. Rather than relying on familiar paradigms or on normative assumptions, this approach studies concept formation in the wild. Although I do not think that this research method will supplant more familiar laboratory experimentation, I believe that it is an important means of studying concepts which fulfills some of the goals that motivated Anderson's adaptive model of cognition.

I argued earlier that the theory view is especially consistent with this ecological approach. Much of its motivation comes about through trying to understand how a young child learns a language and discovers the structure of its environment (see Carey, 1985; Keil, 1989; Markman, 1989; Murphy & Medin, 1985). Theories are said to provide one necessary filter that allows the child to make reasonable hypotheses about the world, to constrain what would otherwise be an impossible learning situation (Quine, 1960). Experiments such as the ones simulated by the rational model avoid much of this problem by greatly simplifying the situation and concept to be learned. Such experiments can give a misleading view of the utility of knowledge to define the relevant features and choose a likely rule, but an ecological approach, which looks at the real problems of concept learning in the everyday world, seems to support the necessity of such theoretical structures.

VII. Conclusions

In Section I, I rashly promised that this article would illuminate some issues beyond the rational model in particular. I will therefore end by pointing out what I think some of the morals of this story are. First, it seems clear that an ecologically based model of categorization will have to involve an in-depth empirical study of the environment in which concepts are learned, rather than an armchair-derived set of assumptions. Fortunately, there are data available to begin to address this question, from developmental research and studies of knowledge acquisition. Second, I argued that a consideration of concept formation in the real world would likely lead to support for the role of knowledge and theories in concept formation. Given the amount of information in a real-world stimulus and the amount of information to be organized in our memories, knowledge may be even more necessary there than in laboratory experiments.

Although I cannot give a strong argument for the third conclusion, the uncertain status of the theory of evolution in the rational model suggests that such uses of evolutionary theory are premature. When biologists argue for an evolutionary explanation of some attribute, they must do so with a detailed knowledge of the organism's niche, and they must rule out numerous alternative explanations (e.g., that the attribute is a side effect of some other selected feature). The simple argument that "animal X would be better adapted if it had feature F than if it didn't" is not a sufficient evolutionary argument. And given our still rather sketchy knowledge of the mind, it is not possible to justify such arguments in a more detailed way, showing how such a cognitive capacity would fit into the rest of the mind. Thus, until demonstrated otherwise, I would argue that such evolutionary arguments are beyond the scope of our current knowledge.

Another conclusion that I argued for was that both knowledge-based and data-driven approaches to concepts will be necessary to form a complete picture of concept formation. Anderson's dismissal of theory-based approaches, linguistic categories, and ad-hoc categorization is an excellent example of the chasm between the two approaches to concepts that I described at the beginning of this article. But no matter how convincing one's arguments might be for dismissing one of these approaches, neither one by itself is likely to explain concept formation in full. However, *saying* that the two approaches are both necessary is not the same as integrating the two, and this is where much of the future work in this field needs to be focussed.

ACKNOWLEDGMENTS

This research was supported by NIMH grant MH41704. I am very grateful to Larry Barsalou, Stephanie Doane, Barbara Malt, Kevin Miller, and Brian Ross for their comments on an earlier version of this article. None of my opinions should be attributed to them, however. Also, I would like to thank John Anderson for graciously reading a draft of the chapter and providing helpful comments.

REFERENCES

Anderson, J. R. (1990). *The adaptive character of thought*. Hillsdale, NJ: Erlbaum.

Anderson, J. R. (1991a). The adaptive nature of human categorization. *Psychological Review, 98,* 409–429.

Anderson, J. R. (1991b). Is human cognition adaptive? *Behavioral and Brain Sciences, 14,* 471–517.

Anderson, J. R., & Mantessa, M. (1991). An incremental Bayesian algorithm for categorization. In D. H. Fisher, Jr., M. J. Pazzani, & P. Langley (Eds.), *Concept formation: Knowledge and experience in unsupervised learning* (pp. 45–70). San Mateo, CA: Morgan Kaufmann.

Au, T. K., & Glusman, M. (1990). The principle of mutual exclusivity in word learning: To honor or not to honor? *Child Development, 61,* 1474–1490.

Barsalou, L. W. (1983). Ad hoc categories. *Memory & Cognition, 11,* 211–227.

Barsalou, L. W. (1991). Deriving categories to achieve goals. In G. H. Bower (Ed.), *The psychology of learning and motivation: Vol. 27* (pp. 1–64). New York: Academic Press.

Barsalou, L. W., & Hale, C. R. (1991, November). *System topography as an explanatory constraint on category learning.* Paper presented at the 31st Annual Meeting of the Psychonomic Society, New Orleans.

Berlin, B., Breedlove, D. E., & Raven, P. H. (1973). General principles of classification and nomenclature in folk biology. *American Anthropologist, 75,* 214–242.

Bruner, J. S., Goodnow, J., & Austin, G. (1956). *A study of thinking.* New York: Wiley.

Callanan, M. A. (1985a). Development of object categories and inclusion relations: Preschoolers' hypotheses about word meaning. *Developmental Psychology, 25,* 207–216.

Callanan, M. A. (1985b). How parents label objects for young children: The role of input in the acquisition of category hierarchies. *Child Development, 56,* 508–523.

Cantor, N., & Mischel, W. (1979). Prototypes in person perception. In L. Berkowitz (Ed.), *Advances in experimental social psychology: Vol. 12* (pp. 3–52). New York: Academic Press.

Carey, S. (1985). *Conceptual change in childhood*. Cambridge, MA: MIT Press.

Carey, S., & Bartlett, E. (1978). Acquiring a single new word. *Papers and Reports on Child Language Development, 15*, 17–29.

Chi, M. T., Feltovich, P. J., & Glaser, R. (1981). Categorization and representation of physics problems by experts and novices. *Cognitive Science, 5*, 121–152.

Chi, M. T. H., Hutchinson, J. E., & Robin, A. F. (1989). How inferences about novel domain-related concepts can be constrained by structured knowledge. *Merrill-Palmer Quarterly, 35*, 27–62.

Corter, J. E., & Gluck, M. A. (1992). Explaining basic categories: Feature predictability and information. *Psychological Bulletin, 111*, 291–303.

Dawkins, R. (1987). *The blind watchmaker*. New York: W. W. Norton.

Dougherty, J. W. D. (1978). Salience and relativity in classification. *American Ethnologist, 5*, 66–80.

Estes, W. K. (1986). Memory storage and retrieval processes in category learning. *Journal of Experimental Psychology: General, 115*, 155–174.

Estes, W. K. (1991). Cognitive architectures from the standpoint of an experimental psychologist. *Annual Review of Psychology, 42*, 1–28.

Gelman, S. A., & Markman, E. M. (1986). Categories and induction in children. *Cognition, 23*, 183–208.

Gerrig, R. J., & Murphy, G. L. (1992). Contextual influences on the comprehension of complex concepts. *Language and Cognitive Processes, 7*, 205–230.

Gibson, J. J. (1979). *The ecological approach to visual perception*. Boston: Houghton Mifflin.

Gluck, M. A., & Bower, G. H. (1988). Evaluating an adaptive network model of human learning. *Journal of Memory and Language, 27*, 166–195.

Gould, S. J. (1990). *The individual in Darwin's world*. Edinburgh: Edinburgh University Press.

Gould, S. J., & Lewontin, R. C. (1984). The spandrels of San Marco and the Panglossian Paradigm: A critique of the adaptationist programme. In E. Sober (Ed.), *Conceptual issues in evolutionary biology: An anthology* (pp. 252–270). Cambridge, MA: MIT Press.

Hampton, J. A. (1988). Overextension of conjunctive concepts: Evidence for a unitary model of concept typicality and class inclusion. *Journal of Experimental Psychology: Learning, Memory, and Cognition, 14*, 12–32.

Kahneman, D., Slovic, P., & Tversky, A. (1982). *Judgment under uncertainty: Heuristics and biases*. Cambridge: Cambridge University Press.

Keil, F. C. (1981). Constraints on knowledge and cognitive development. *Psychological Review, 88*, 197–227.

Keil, F. C. (1989). *Concepts, kinds and cognitive development*. Cambridge, MA: MIT Press.

Kruschke, J. K. (1992). ALCOVE: An exemplar-based connectionist model of category learning. *Psychological Review, 99*, 22–44.

Little, E. L. (1980). *The Audubon Society field guide to North American trees*. New York: Knopf.

Malt, B. C. (1991). Word meaning and word use. In P. J. Schwanenflugel (Ed.), *The psychology of word meanings* (pp. 37–70). Hillsdale, NJ: Erlbaum.

Malt, B. C., & Smith, E. E. (1984). Correlated properties in natural categories. *Journal of Verbal Learning and Verbal Behavior, 23*, 250–269.

Markman, A. B., & Gentner, D. (1990). Analogical mapping during similarity judgments. In *Proceedings of the twelfth annual conference of the Cognitive Science Society* (pp. 38–44). Hillsdale, NJ: Erlbaum.

Markman, E. M. (1989). *Categorization and naming in children: Problems of induction*. Cambridge, MA: MIT Press.

Markman, E. M., & Callanan, M. A. (1984). An analysis of hierarchical classification. In R. Sternberg (Ed.), *Advances in the psychology of human intelligence: Vol. 2* (pp. 325–365). Hillsdale, NJ: Erlbaum.

Markman, E. M., & Hutchinson, J. E. (1984). Children's sensitivity to constraints on word meaning: Taxonomic vs thematic relations. *Cognitive Psychology, 16,* 1–27.

Mayr, E. (1982). *The growth of biological thought: Diversity, evolution, and inheritance.* Cambridge, MA: Harvard University Press.

Medin, D. L. (1983). Structural principles of categorization. In T. Tighe & B. Shepp (Eds.), *Perception, cognition, and development: Interactional analyses* (pp. 203–230). Hillsdale, NJ: Erlbaum.

Medin, D. L., Altom, M. W., Edelson, S. M., & Freko, D. (1982). Correlated symptoms and simulated medical classification. *Journal of Experimental Psychology: Learning, Memory, and Cognition, 8,* 37–50.

Medin, D. L., Goldstone, R. L., & Gentner, D. (1990). Similarity involving attributes and relations: Judgments of similarity and difference are not inverses. *Psychological Science, 1,* 64–69.

Medin, D. L., & Schaffer, M. M. (1978). Context theory of classification learning. *Psychological Review, 85,* 207–238.

Medin, D. L., & Schwanenflugel, P. J. (1981). Linear separability in classification learning. *Journal of Experimental Psychology: Human Learning and Memory, 7,* 355–368.

Mervis, C. B. (1987). Child-basic object categories and early lexical development. In U. Neisser (Ed.), *Concepts and conceptual development: Ecological and intellectual factors in categorization* (pp. 201–233). Cambridge: Cambridge University Press.

Mervis, C. B., & Pani, J. R. (1980). Acquisition of basic object categories. *Cognitive Psychology, 12,* 496–522.

Michaels, C. F., & Carello, C. (1981). *Direct perception.* Englewood Cliffs, NJ: Prentice-Hall.

Morris, M. W., & Murphy, G. L. (1990). Converging operations on a basic level in event taxonomies. *Memory & Cognition, 18,* 407–418.

Murphy, G. L. (1982). Cue validity and levels of categorization. *Psychological Bulletin, 91,* 174–177.

Murphy, G. L. (1988). Comprehending complex concepts. *Cognitive Science, 12,* 529–562.

Murphy, G. L. (1990). Noun phrase interpretation and conceptual combination. *Journal of Memory and Language, 29,* 259–288.

Murphy, G. L. (1991a). Meaning and concepts. In P. Schwanenflugel (Ed.), *The psychology of word meaning* (pp. 11–35). Hillsdale, NJ: Erlbaum.

Murphy, G. L. (1991b). Parts in object concepts: Experiments with artificial categories. *Memory & Cognition, 19,* 423–448.

Murphy, G. L. (1993). Theories and concept formation. In I. Van Mechelen, J. Hampton, R. Michalski, & P. Theuns (Eds.), *Categories and concepts: Theoretical views and inductive data analysis* (pp. 173–200). London: Academic Press.

Murphy, G. L., & Brownell, H. H. (1985). Category differentiation in object recognition: Typicality constraints on the basic category advantage. *Journal of Experimental Psychology: Learning, Memory, and Cognition, 11,* 70–84.

Murphy, G. L., & Medin, D. L. (1985). The role of theories in conceptual coherence. *Psychological Review, 92,* 289–316.

Murphy, G. L., & Smith, E. E. (1982). Basic level superiority in picture categorization. *Journal of Verbal learning and Verbal Behavior, 21,* 1–20.

Murphy, G. L., & Wisniewski, E. J. (1989). Feature correlations in conceptual representations. In G. Tiberghien (Ed.), *Advances in cognitive science: Vol. 2. Theory and applications* (pp. 23–45). Chichester: Ellis Horwood.

Murphy, G. L., & Wright, J. C. (1984). Changes in conceptual structure with expertise: Differences between real-world experts and novices. *Journal of Experimental Psychology: Learning, Memory, and Cognition, 10,* 144–155.

Nakamura, G. V. (1985). Knowledge-based classification of ill-defined categories. *Memory & Cognition, 13,* 377–384.

Nisbett, R., & Ross, L. (1981). *Human inference: Strategies and shortcomings of social judgment.* Englewood Cliffs, NJ: Prentice-Hall.

Nosofsky, R. M. (1988). Similarity, frequency, and category representations. *Journal of Experimental Psychology: Learning, Memory, and Cognition, 14,* 54–65.

Nosofsky, R. M. (1991). Relation between the rational model and the context model of categorization. *Psychological Science, 2,* 416–421.

Nosofsky, R. M., Clark, S. E., & Shin, H. J. (1989). Rules and exemplars in categorization, identification, and recognition. *Journal of Experimental Psychology: Learning, Memory, and Cognition, 15,* 282–304.

Osherson, D. N., Smith, E. E., Wilkie, O., Lopez, A., & Shafir, E. (1990). Category-based induction. *Psychological Review, 97,* 185–200.

Pazzani, M. J. (1991). Influence of prior knowledge on concept acquisition: Experimental and computational results. *Journal of Experimental Psychology: Learning, Memory, and Cognition, 17,* 416–432.

Quine, W. V. O. (1960). *Word and object.* Cambridge, MA: MIT Press.

Rifkin, A. (1985). Evidence for a basic level in event taxonomies. *Memory & Cognition, 13,* 538–556.

Rips, L. J. (1989). Similarity, typicality, and categorization. In S. Vosniadou & A. Ortony (Eds.), *Similarity and analogical reasoning* (pp. 21–59). Cambridge: Cambridge University Press.

Rosch, E. (1978). Principles of categorization. In E. Rosch & B. B. Lloyd (Eds.), *Cognition and categorization* (pp. 27–48). Hillsdale, NJ: Erlbaum.

Rosch, E., Mervis, C. B., Gray, W. D., Johnson, D. M., & Boyes-Braem, P. (1976). Basic objects in natural categories. *Cognitive Psychology, 8,* 382–439.

Ross, B. H. (1989). Remindings in learning and instruction. In S. Vosniadou & A. Ortony (Eds.), *Similarity and analogical reasoning* (pp. 438–469). Cambridge: Cambridge University Press.

Simon, H. A. (1969). *The sciences of the artificial.* Cambridge, MA: MIT Press.

Smith, E. E., & Medin, D. L. (1981). *Categories and concepts.* Cambridge, MA: Harvard University Press.

Smith, E. E., Osherson, D. N., Rips, L. J., & Keane, M. (1988). Combining prototypes: A modification model. *Cognitive Science, 12,* 485–527.

Smith, L. B., Jones, S. S., & Landau, B. (1992). Count nouns, adjectives, and perceptual properties in children's novel word interpretation. *Developmental Psychology, 28,* 273–286.

Tanaka, J. W., & Taylor, M. E. (1991). Categorization and expertise: Is the basic level in the eye of the beholder? *Cognitive Psychology, 23,* 457–482.

Tversky, B., & Hemenway, K. (1983). Categories of environmental scenes. *Cognitive Psychology, 15,* 121–149.

Vallecher, R. R., & Wegner, D. M. (1987). What do people think they're doing? Action identification and human behavior. *Psychological Review, 94,* 3–15.

Wattenmaker, W. D., Dewey, G. I., Murphy, T. D., & Medin, D. L. (1986). Linear separability and concept learning: Context, relational properties, and concept naturalness. *Cognitive Psychology, 18,* 158–194.

Waxman, S. R., & Kosowski, T. D. (1990). Nouns mark category relations: Toddlers' and pre-schoolers' word-learning biases. *Child Development, 61,* 1461–1473.

Waxman, S. R., Shipley, E. F., & Shepperson, B. (1991). Establishing new subcategories: The role of category labels and existing knowledge. *Child Development, 62,* 127–138.

Wisniewski, E. J., & Medin, D. L. (1991). Harpoons and long sticks: The interaction of theory and similarity in rule induction. In D. H. Fisher, M. J. Pazzani & P. Langley (Eds.), *Concept formation: Knowledge and experience in unsupervised learning* (pp. 237–278). San Mateo, CA: Morgan Kaufman.

PART III

CONCEPTS, CATEGORY BOUNDARIES, AND CONCEPTUAL COMBINATION

CONCEPT STRUCTURE AND CATEGORY BOUNDARIES

Barbara C. Malt

I. Introduction

Why do we call one furry, four-legged creature a cat but another furry, four-legged one a dog? Why do we call one wooden piece of furniture that is used for sitting on a chair, and another wooden piece of furniture that is used for sitting on a stool? Clearly, the concepts *dog* and *cat,* and the concepts *stool* and *chair,* although sharing some content, must also differ from each other, and the differences are critical in determining how objects that are similar to one another in many respects will be categorized. The goals for a theory of concepts have thus been to specify (1) what the contents of concepts consist of; and (2) how the contents constrain the categorization of objects in the world.

Theories of categorization during the mid-1970s to mid-1980s proposed a relatively loose concept structure consisting of features associated with a category with some less than perfect probability (e.g., Rosch & Mervis, 1975; see Smith & Medin, 1981). For instance, the property "barks" might be associated with the dog category with a .90 probability, and the property "long fur" might be associated with a .50 probability. Under this view, concepts differ from one another in the particular set of properties they contain and the strength of association of each property with the category. Categorization is then accomplished simply by comparing the properties of an object to those contained in different concepts: an animal will be considered a dog if some threshold number of its properties overlap with properties associated with dogs, and it will be considered a cat if its properties overlap with those associated with cats.

Recently, though, there has been concern that this type of proposal is too unconstrained in at least two senses. First, the sorts of properties that count as relevant in deciding if an object belongs in a category are not well specified; there is no principled way of deciding that "barks" should be relevant for "dog" but "bigger than a breadbox" should not be (Murphy & Medin, 1985). Second, partly as a consequence of this fact, models based on the approach do not sufficiently constrain what entities they predict will be considered to belong to a category. If categories like "chair" and "dog" are so fuzzy, what prevents all sorts of things that have many of the features associated with a category from being considered members of the category? If a beanbag chair, which lacks many of the properties strongly associated with chairs (e.g., legs, arms, being made of wood or metal), can be considered a chair, why can't stools be considered chairs? If a tiny chihuahua that never barks can be considered a dog, why can't some large, ferocious cats be considered dogs? Apparently, the presence or absence of characteristic features is not enough to fully determine category membership.

These problems suggest that theories of concepts need to consider more explicitly both what sort of information is relevant to determining category membership for objects, and how this information might be used to constrain category membership in ways that are consistent with empirical facts about category membership judgments. The earlier failure of the necessary-and-sufficient-features view of concepts (see Smith & Medin, 1981) suggests that there will not be any obvious physical features (e.g., "barks" for *dog* or "has four legs" for *chair*) represented in concepts that can be identified as the key to separating category members from nonmembers. Recently, though, other sorts of candidates have been proposed for providing the necessary constraints on category membership.

An important possibility is that although people may not know defining features in the sense of obvious physical features, each concept may contain a different, less obvious, piece of information that is central to category membership (cf. Fisher & Yoo, this volume). For artifact concepts such as *boat* or *chair,* the function associated with the concept may be critical to determining what things belong to the category (e.g., Keil, 1989; Rosch, Mervis, Gray, Johnson, & Boyes-Braem, 1976; Schwartz, 1978). For instance, although a particular shape or a particular form of propulsion may not be necessary in order for something to be a boat, perhaps the function of being used to carry things across water is. For natural kind concepts such as *dog* or *gold,* people may not know exactly what sort of property is critical, but they may have a *belief* in the existence of some property or properties shared by all the things that belong to the category (e.g., Carey, 1985; Keil, 1989; Malt, 1990; Medin & Ortony, 1989). Keil (1989), for instance, found that when subjects were given a description of a raccoon that had surgery to make it look and act just like a skunk, they still considered the animal to be a raccoon. The subjects appealed to a raccoon "essence"; they believed there was something hidden and internal that made the raccoon stay a raccoon, even though they didn't know exactly what that essence consisted of. So, for natural kind concepts, a possibility is that beliefs like these are the important piece of information that constrains what things are considered to be members of a given category: something will be accepted as a category member only if it is believed to share the relevant essence.

I have recently carried out several studies investigating the nature of concept structure and category boundaries. I have found that, in contrast to the possibility that there is one central kind of property or belief that heavily constrains category membership, there seem to be a variety of factors that influence whether something will be accepted as a category member or not. The results that I discuss here argue for retaining a view of concepts as relatively fuzzy in the sense of not having one central type of information that is most central to category membership. However, assuming concept fuzziness of this sort does not mean that category membership is not constrained in important ways. The results that I present go beyond earlier "fuzzy category" formulations in providing more specific suggestions about what sorts of information are included in concept representations, and about what sorts of constraints determine whether an object will be accepted as a member of a category.

I first discuss studies on the nature of artifact concepts like *chair* and *boat*. Later, I discuss one particular natural kind concept, *water*, which has been widely used as an example in arguments for the importance of a belief in an essence, and I present some evidence relevant to assessing the role of such beliefs in constraining category membership. I then suggest some conclusions from all the studies taken together about how concepts are structured and how category membership is determined.

II. What Constrains Artifact Category Membership?

A. Laboratory Studies of Artifacts

Although function has often been cited as central to artifact category membership, there has been little systematic exploration of its exact role in determining membership. Eric Johnson and I therefore carried out a series of studies to test more thoroughly the role of function in determining membership in artifact categories. Our studies (Malt & Johnson, 1992) explored two very simple predictions that can be made if the function associated with a concept like *boat* or *chair* is truly the main factor that determines membership in the associated categories: first, objects that do have this function should be considered category members; and second, objects that do not have this function should not be considered category members.

To test whether these predictions are right, we first needed to find out what functions are normally associated with a variety of common artifact categories. We asked subjects to list the functions of 12 artifact categories (e.g., "boat," "boot," "couch," "desk"). We made sure that the functions they listed were specific to the target category by asking subjects to differentiate the target category from other similar ones. For instance, we asked them to describe the function of boats specifically enough to distinguish them from rafts and submarines, and the function of sweaters specifically enough to distinguish them from jackets, shirts, and sweatshirts.

We ended up with functions such as, for "boat": "to carry one or more people over a body of water for purposes of work or recreation"; and for "ruler": "to measure distances of up to 1 foot, and to draw lines of a specific length (up to 1 foot)." We then double-checked the functions by asking a new group of subjects what artifact each belonged to, and we found that the dominant answer for each one was the category we intended.

As a final step, we generated descriptions of the normal physical features of the target objects ourselves, and we double-checked these descriptions by asking a new group of subjects to read them and name the category they thought each one belonged to. The target category was the most frequent response for each.

To test our predictions, we then made up descriptions of new objects that either had the normal function but had unusual physical features, or had normal physical features but an unusual function. We asked another group of subjects to judge whether each was an example of the category, and we contrasted their responses to responses to descriptions with normal functions and normal physical features.

An example of the version with a normal function and unusual physical features for "boat" is as follows: "This thing is spherical and made of rubber, is hitched to a team of dolphins, and has a large suction cup that can keep it in one place. This thing is manufactured and sold to to carry one or more people over a body of water for purposes of work or recreation. Is this thing a BOAT?"

For the stimuli with unusual functions and normal physical features, we designed three versions for each category so that we could examine the effect of different variations from the normal function. In the first version, *related function,* the function overlapped somewhat with the normal function but also differed from it in some noticeable way. For instance, the version of "boat" with normal physical features and related function was: "This thing is wedge-shaped, with a sail, an anchor, and wooden sides. This thing is manufactured and sold as a holding area for dangerous criminals or persons in exile by detaining them a certain distance offshore. Is this thing a BOAT?" In this case, the function is related to the original function in that it involves holding people over water, but it also differs noticeably from the normal function as derived in our pretest.

In the second, *bizarre function* version, the function was more distant from the normal function. For "boat," it consisted of providing shelter for marine animals. In the third or *denial function* version, the function explicitly mentioned that the object could not be used to satisfy the standard function of the target category. For "boat," it consisted of providing a sterile collection station for marine samples in which no people were ever allowed.

If function is really central to artifact category membership, the objects with the normal functions should be accepted as category members even though their appearance is unusual, and the objects with the unusual functions should be rejected even though they physically resemble ordinary category members. However, the results were in clear contrast to these predictions. We found that many objects with normal functions but unusual physical features were excluded from category membership: 9 out of 12 stimuli, or 75%, received predominantly "no" responses to the category membership question. In contrast, the control stimuli with the normal functions and normal physical features were uniformly accepted as category members; all received "yes" responses from virtually all subjects.

We also found that many objects with unusual functions but normal physical features were accepted. There were 36 stimuli of this sort (created by combining the 12 target categories with each of the three unusual function versions). Twenty-one of them, or 58%, received predominantly "yes" answers to the category membership question. Strikingly, the tendency to accept items with unusual functions was as true for those with the most unusual functions as for those with the least unusual: 8 out of 12 of the related items, 5 out of 12 of the bizarre items, and 8 out of 12 of the denial items received predominantly "yes" answers. Thus, even when the normal function is explicitly denied, many of the items were still found to be acceptable category members.

These results indicate that the appearance of an object plays an important role in determining category membership as well as the function: if physical features are normal, an object may be accepted despite a strange function, whereas if the object is physically odd, even the normal function may not ensure category membership. In a follow-up experiment, we found that physical features, not function, actually seemed to be the dominant influence on category decisions. In this experiment, subjects gave category membership ratings instead of making yes–no decisions. Some subjects rated the same physical feature/function combinations that the previous subjects had seen, and others rated either functions presented by themselves or physical features presented by themselves. Ratings were made on a 7-point scale, with 1 indicating that the description definitely belonged to the category and 7 that it definitely did not. We found that category ratings for the physical feature/function combinations were close to ratings of the physical features alone and were more distant from ratings of the functions alone. Specifically, the mean rating for the unusual physical features alone was 3.66, and for the normal functions alone was 5.95; the mean rating for stimuli with the combined unusual physical features and normal functions was 3.77. Similarly, the mean rating for the normal physical features alone was 5.79, and for the unusual functions alone was 2.78; the mean rating for the stimuli with the combined normal physical features and unusual functions was 4.90. These numbers show that objects with unusual physical features and normal functions received ratings that were low and close to the rating for the physical component alone, while objects with normal physical features and unusual functions received ratings that were higher and again close to the ratings for the physical component alone. In other words, the ratings indicate that physical features had a greater influence on perception of category membership than function did.

Together, these studies do not support the idea that there is one central type of information, function, that strongly constrains what objects will be considered members of an artifact category. One might be tempted to argue that this conclusion applies mainly to basic level categories such as "boat" and "ruler," and not to superordinates such as "furniture" or "vehicle." Property lists for the latter have shown a higher proportion of functions relative to physical features (Rosch et al., 1976). There is an important distinction to note, though, that undermines this argument. Although subjects may find it difficult to think of physical features shared by different types of furniture, the functions they produce are not any more adequate in accounting for what entities are category members. For instance, typical functions listed for "furniture" are "used in houses and other buildings" and "used for eating, sleeping, etc." These functions apply to many non-furniture items as well as to many types of furniture, and they also do not explain why some objects such as a lamp (which is not necessarily used for eating or sleeping) and lawn furniture (which is not used in a house or other building) are considered to belong to the category. Although we have not explicitly tested superordinate level categories, the conclusions of our studies with basic level artifact categories seem equally likely to apply to superordinate level ones.

B. THE STRUCTURE OF REAL-WORLD ARTIFACT CATEGORIES

Exploring categorization by using artificial stimuli presented under laboratory conditions has the usual advantages of laboratory experimentation. At the same time, though, category decisions are not usually made so consciously, nor are they made on the basis of written descriptions of objects presented in isolation from any context. I have recently been using another approach to explore how categories are structured that involves looking in depth at categories that exist in the world. By looking at what sorts of objects are considered to belong to a given category, we can gain information about the constraints that operate in determining category membership under natural circumstances.

The strategy I have used is to collect large sets of examples of objects that are called by a common category name, such as "bottle," "box," "juice," or "water." Later on, I will discuss data from the natural kind category, "water." Here, though, I want to focus on two artifact categories that we have studied, "bottle," and "tape." Data from these two categories directly address the issue of the relative roles of function and appearance in constraining membership in artifact categories.

To collect examples of different types of objects that are called by a particular category name, we used several different sources: (1) Observation of the use of the category name in everyday conversations, newspapers, television, and so on. My students and I simply noted different examples of things called "bottle," "tape," "juice," and so on, as we have observed them. (2) A computer search through the Brown text corpus (source of the Kucera & Francis, 1967, word frequency counts) to find all the different things that get labeled by the target name in the samples of text. We determined what sort of object was being referred to by either the presence of an adjective attached to the noun (e.g., "beer bottle") or by other information in the context (e.g., the mention of beer spilling from the bottle). (3) A laboratory task asking subjects to generate examples of the target nouns, including not just the most obvious ones, but also ones that would be hard for someone else to think of. For instance, they might be asked to generate examples of types of bottles other than Coke and beer bottles. From these three sources, we compiled 19 examples of objects commonly called "tape" and 37 examples of objects commonly called "bottle."

The next step was to ask a group of 26 subjects to rate each of these for how typical they were as examples of the named categories; this provides us with information about which category members are most central to the concept. From these we can also draw hypotheses about what sorts of properties are central to the concept. Table I provides the typicality ratings for the 19 tape examples and for the 20 bottle examples that I will discuss further. (The bottle examples eliminated from the original 37 consist of some that are unfamiliar to many people and others that are highly similar in shape and use to the beverage bottles on the list.)

The final step in our analysis was to collect similarity ratings between pairs of examples for each category and obtain a scaling solution of the similarity data. The clusters that emerge in the scaling solution provide additional information about the properties or dimensions that are salient within the categories. They also provide information about the way in which other members of each category are related to the most typical ones.

TABLE I

EXAMPLES OF "BOTTLE" AND "TAPE" AND MEAN TYPICALITY RATINGS

Bottle example	Typicality	Tape example	Typicality
Soda (plastic)	6.19	Adhesive	6.54
Coke	6.15	Masking	6.54
Beer	6.00	Duct	5.81
Wine	5.88	Electrical	5.65
Water	5.54	Audio cassette	5.62
Baby's (plastic)	5.23	Packaging	5.46
Juice	5.19	First-aid	5.31
Milk	5.15	Video cassette	5.19
Catsup (squeeze)	5.04	Wrapping	5.00
Catsup (glass)	4.96	Double-sticking	4.73
Baby's (glass)	4.81	Ankle	4.35
Medicine	4.81	Carpenter's	4.23
Shampoo	4.65	Reel-to-reel audio	4.04
Aspirin	4.42	Vinyl	3.52
Detergent (plastic)	3.62	Magnetic (computer)	3.25
Bleach	3.42	Cash register	3.15
Hamster's water	3.35	Magic	3.13
Hot water	3.31	Ticker	2.84
Hand lotion (pump)	3.23	Police	2.36
Ink	3.00		

The ratings were collected by presenting 20 subjects for each category with each of the 190 possible pairs of examples (one additional type of tape, hem tape, was added to the tape list to make 20 examples). Subjects simply rated the similarity of the members of each pair on a scale of 1 to 9. The scaling technique used was an extended tree analysis (Corter & Tversky, 1986), which provides information about both nested and non-nested relationships among stimuli. Figures 1 and 2 present the tree structures obtained. Segments marked by letters indicate features shared by non-adjacent stimuli.

1. Bottle

As Table I shows, for the "bottle" category, beer, Coke, and plastic soda bottles received the highest typicality ratings. These three were at or above 6.00 on the 7-point scale. These bottles share both the familiar graduated bottle shape and the function of containing familiar beverages. Other bottles that are rated high share these same properties to a large extent. The topmost cluster in the scaling solution is consistent with the typicality ratings in containing the three most typical examples and also several of the next most typical: milk, juice, and wine bottles. Thus the particular properties of graduated shape and holding drinkable liquids appear to be salient ones that are central to the bottle concept. The important question, then, is to what extent the other bottle examples share these particular properties. Does either the shape or the function constrain what sorts of containers are commonly referred to as bottles?

The second cluster from the top of the diagram contains bottles that are also used for holding drinkable liquids, but that vary somewhat from the most typical in both their exact use and their shape. Baby's bottles and hamster's water bottles diverge somewhat from the typical graduated bottle shape, especially in the nature of their neck and opening. Water bottles (e.g., as taken hiking or camping) are usually cylindrical, not graduated like the typical beverage bottles. Hot water bottles, likewise, contain a drinkable liquid (although not meant to be drunk in this case), but they are flatter than most beverage containers. Each of these types of bottle is used in somewhat different circumstances than general beverage bottles (for caring for babies and pets; for storing and transporting water on trips; for treating aches and pains). Thus this second group seems to overlap somewhat with typical bottles in both appearance and use, but also to diverge somewhat on both dimensions.

The next major cluster of bottles in the scaling solution contains hand lotion, shampoo, detergent, and bleach bottles. Linked to those are ink, medicine, and aspirin bottles. Noteworthy about the first group is the fact

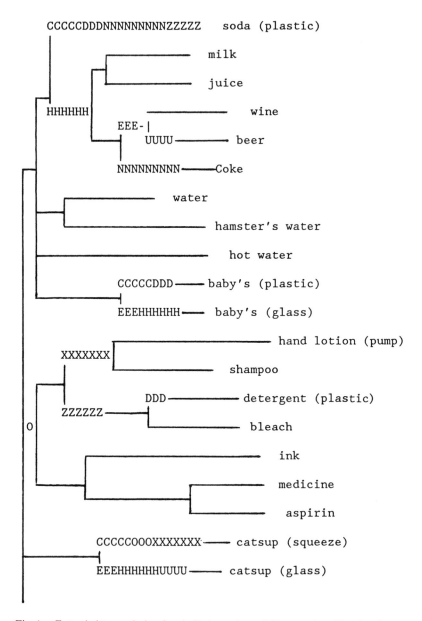

Fig. 1.   Extended tree solution for similarity ratings of 20 examples of bottles. Segments marked by letters indicate features shared by non-adjacent nodes.

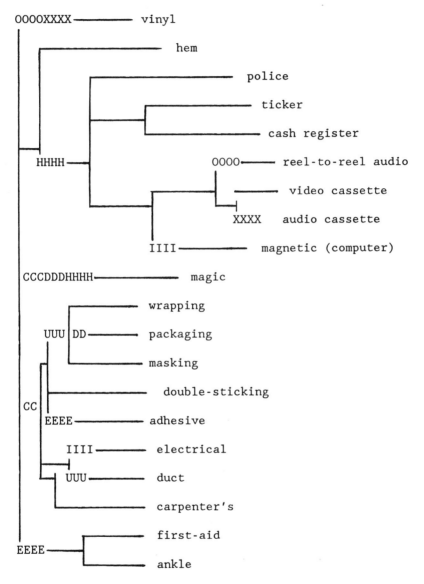

Fig. 2. Extended tree solution for similarity ratings of 20 examples of tape. Segments marked by letters indicate features shared by non-adjacent nodes.

that none of them holds a drinkable liquid. Shampoo and hand lotion can be fairly thick, and neither they nor bleach and detergent are drinkable. Noteworthy about the second group is that they likewise do not hold drinkable liquids. Most strikingly, aspirin is not a liquid or even a mass substance (e.g., a powder) at all, but instead is dry and in the form of individual tablets. Thus these bottles diverge to a large extent from the function of the most typical bottles. In addition, they, like the previous cluster, are in shapes that can roughly be thought of as graduated, but that are much more marginal on this dimension than the more typical ones. The variation here is so large, in fact, that it is not clear whether the objects would necessarily be seen as sharing a common shape if they did not share a common label. For instance, some ink bottles are square except for a short, narrow neck at the top just big enough for the cap to screw onto, and some hand lotion bottles are also square or rectangular except for the pump on top.

Finally, the last major cluster consists of the two catsup bottles (plastic and glass). These are fairly similar to the typical bottles in having a graduated shape, but they contain a substance that is thick and is not drunk. Again, these two overlap somewhat with the most typical examples, but they diverge quite a bit as well, especially on function.

If there is any overall commonality among the properties of these examples that I have highlighted, it seems to be in their shape. They all might be considered at least roughly graduated cylinders. However, the great amount of variation suggests that shape does not provide a strong constraint on what containers are considered to be bottles. In fact, some containers that are called jars (e.g., of mustard and jelly) are graduated cylinders that fall with the range of variation of the bottles. As for function, the fact that some bottles are used for holding thick substances like catsup, others for holding non-liquids like aspirin, and others for non-consumables like bleach and shampoo, means that the only sort of storage function common to all of them would be one that is extremely broad, such as "contains stuff." Since this sort of function obviously would also apply to other containers such as cans, jars, and boxes, it could not serve as a strong constraint on what sorts of objects are considered to be bottles. An alternative might be to think of the function as being something more like "to pour restricted amounts of the contents at a time," in contrast to, say, cans, where the contents tend to be dumped out in a less measured fashion. However, inspection of the examples again suggests the same sort of problem as with the idea that bottles are used to contain a particular type of substance. Some of the bottles are not really used to pour from (such as the hamster and baby water bottles, the hot water bottle, and the hand lotion bottle with the pump top). If the proposed function were broadened to be "to provide restricted amount of contents at a time," this would also encompass many non-bottles such as aerosol cans, cans of Ajax with shaker tops, tubs of margarine, and jars of jam or mustard. Again, it seems there is no single way to formulate the function of even the 20 bottles we have considered here so that it provides a strong constraint on what sorts of objects will be accepted as bottles.

2. Tape

For the "tape" category, two exemplars, masking tape and adhesive tape, were above 6.00 in rated typicality. These two have the properties of coming in a roll of long, narrow product, being sticky, and being used to wrap or secure something. The next most typical tapes are duct tape, electrical tape, and audio cassette tape. Although there is a fairly substantial gap in typicality between the top-rated group and these, and more diversity among them than there is for the bottles, the second group does share the properties of the most typical ones to a large extent. Duct and electrical tape are also sticky coils of long, narrow material; audio cassette tapes are long, narrow, and coiled, although not sticky. The two most typical tapes appear in the scaling solution with other tapes that share these properties; thus these properties appear to be ones central to the tape concept. Again, we can now ask how other things that are considered to be types of tape are related to these particular properties.

There are two major clusters within the scaling solution. The topmost one is composed of tapes that are long and thin but that lack the sticky quality and are not used for wrapping or securing things. Within this cluster, the lower group (reel-to-reel audio, video cassette, audio cassette, and magnetic computer tapes) share the properties of being magnetic and found coiled within a case or cassette of some sort. The upper group (hem, police, ticker, and cash register tapes) are made of paper, plastic, or cloth, and may be stored coiled but are probably more often encountered in an uncurled state. The uses of these tapes are quite diverse, including storage of information in both magnetic and printed form, restraining people from entering an area (police tape), and finishing hems (hem tape). As with the bottles, then, there appears to be some overlap of the physical properties of these examples with the most typical ones, but also some divergence on this dimension, and at the same time, substantial deviation from the most typical ones in function.

The second major cluster consists of tapes including the two most typical and others that are also kept coiled, are sticky, and are used for wrapping and securing. (The only anomaly is carpenter's tape, which subjects may have interpreted as referring to a type of sticky tape instead of as a measuring device.) The upper group in this cluster (wrapping, packaging, masking, double-sticking, and adhesive tapes) are general-purpose household tapes, while the lower group (electrical, duct, and carpenter's tapes) are tapes used by professionals and other people in more specialized contexts.

In addition to the two larger clusters, there is a small cluster at the bottom of the scaling solution consisting of two tapes that are used for treating injuries (first-aid and ankle tape). The first of these is sticky, while the second is stretchy fabric and not sticky. Ankle tape overlaps with typical tapes in being kept coiled and in being used for wrapping, but the wrapping is generally to apply pressure or provide support, rather than to secure something in place. These, like the others, thus show some overlap with typical tapes but also some divergence of both physical and functional properties.

The tape examples, like the bottle examples, together highlight the difficulty of finding any function that could be common to members of the category in question. To an even greater extent than for bottles, it appears impossible to identify any function that could encompass objects as diverse as masking tape, police tape, audio cassette tape, and ankle tape. At the same time, though, to a greater extent than the bottle examples, it appears that there may be some commonality of form that holds the various tape examples together as members of a category (the fact of being long and narrow and stored in coiled form). Thus they, like the bottle examples, argue against the possibility that function is the central factor that constrains membership in artifact categories.

I have called these examples all members of a single category, "tape," but the question may arise whether the major clusters of tapes here represent two (or more) senses of the word "tape" that refer to different categories. If so, perhaps it is wrong to use the entire set of examples to conclude that members of one category may be linked by form when there are no commonalities of function. However, I think that restricting the analysis to one of the major clusters also leads to the conclusion that function is not necessarily what is causing them all to be placed in one category. If we restrict the analysis to the lower major cluster of relatively typical tapes, we see that all the members of this cluster share the physical properties of being long and narrow, sticky, and kept coiled, as well as sharing their general function of sealing things. Thus there is no particular reason to think that it is function that provides the basis for category membership. If we restrict analysis to the upper cluster, similarity of form actually appears to be greater than similarity of function, since a police tape, for instance, has no obvious common function with ticker tapes or cash register tapes. We could, of course, go a step further and consider there to be many separate senses of "tape," one corresponding to ticker-tape-type tapes and one corresponding to cash-register-type tapes, etc., with each labeling a separate category. However, this move ignores the fact that ticker tape and cash register tape are rated as highly similar to one another, and it completely begs the question of why a variety of objects that do, in fact, overlap on some salient properties are all called by a common name, "tape."

In sum, the results from these studies of two artifact categories in the real world are consistent with the laboratory studies of artifacts in suggesting that function may not be as central to artifact category membership as some researchers have suggested. They also suggest that at least two different dimensions, both function and physical properties, contribute to determining category membership for artifacts. (And, in fact, both sets of artifact experiments suggest that physical properties may contribute as much or more than function does to category membership.)

C. HISTORICAL CONNECTIONS

In another study on artifacts, I am exploring one additional factor that may influence what objects are considered to be examples of an artifact concept. This is the historical relationship of an object to a category. It seems likely that some objects belong to a category mainly because of a historical connection to the category. For instance, consider automobiles as they were produced at the turn of the century. These vehicles had open-air bodies similar to horse-drawn buggies, had to be cranked to be started, and ran quite slowly. In other words, they didn't look very much like modern cars, they weren't constructed very much like modern cars, and they didn't function to carry people nearly as fast or as efficiently as modern cars. In terms of physical and functional similarity, they are probably closer to a dune buggy or current versions of horse-drawn carriages than to a modern car. But we consider them to be cars because of their historical relationship to modern cars; they are an earlier version of the modern vehicle that we call "car." In fact, in our collection of examples of category members from the study I described above, we found several objects that seem to have this sort of relationship to their category. Frozen orange juice cans are now made of cardboard, and we found virtually no other examples of cans that were cardboard. However, frozen orange juice cans were formerly made of metal like more typical cans, and it is probable that the current version is considered to be a can mainly because it is the modern version of something that had always been called a can. Similarly, one manufacturer of shampoo, L'Oreal, now sells shampoo in a rectangular plastic container with a small flip-top opening. We have informally asked many people to name the object, and most have called this a bottle of shampoo. Again, although the container itself is quite different from other containers called "bottle," it is a modern version of more traditional shampoo bottles, and probably for that reason is still accepted into the category.[1]

In order to test the possible role of historical links more systematically, I am currently carrying out an experiment in which the historical relationship of an object to current category members is manipulated. In this experiment, we are giving subjects descriptions of objects that differ somewhat in appearance and use from familiar objects, and we are varying whether we tell subjects the object exists currently or will exist at some time in the future. Since the earlier artifact studies had indicated that subjects were inclined to find a wide range of variations on either appearance or function as acceptable for category membership, especially if one varied and the other was normal, these stimuli were designed to vary heavily on appearance and to also vary somewhat in function from the typical current version of the object. Changes of this nature should provide enough room for doubt about category membership to see any effect of the historical relationship. For instance, here is the current version for the category "couch":

> A manufacturer of household goods has added a new product to its usual line of products. This object consists of a double row of air jets set into the living room floor, which when turned on, produce flows of air strong enough to support the weight of humans. The first row forms a seat wide enough for two or three people to sit on, while the back row provides back support. This product is being sold to households for relaxing, reading, and watching TV, and soothing young children to sleep. Is this object a COUCH?

Here is the contrasting version, in which the same object is described as something that will appear in the future. Note that whereas the current version described the object as one being added to a manufacturer's line of

---

[1]Note that although this line of argument might seem to suggest that it is having a common function that provides the link, and thus that function is the central factor in determining membership, this suggestion is contradicted by another example. Supermarkets are now beginning to carry frozen orange juice in a reduced-waste package that is a rectangular cardboard container. The package label itself, as well as all the people I have informally asked, call the object an orange juice box. Apparently, the discrepancy in form prevents it from being considered a can, despite the common function. Some overlap in both form and function may be necessary in order for the historical link to maintain category membership.

products, and so would presumably contrast with other products, the future version indicates that the object will supersede, not contrast with, an object currently in production.

> A manufacturer of household goods is developing a new product to eventually replace something in its current line of products. This object consists of a double row of air jets set into the living room floor, which when turned on, produce flows of air strong enough to support the weight of humans. The first row forms a seat wide enough for two or three people to sit on, while the back row provides back support. This product will be sold in the society of the future to households for relaxing, reading, and watching TV, and soothing young children to sleep. Is this object a COUCH?

We anticipate that people will consider unusual objects to be acceptable members of a familiar category if they can imagine an evolutionary relationship between the unusual object and current category members. In contrast, they may refuse to consider the unusual object a member of a familiar category if it exists at the same time as other category members that it does not resemble very much. In this case, they may consider that the object should be named to contrast with the other category, as "dune buggy" does with "car." If this prediction is right, we will have identified another factor that influences whether something is considered to be an example of a concept. Preliminary data indicate a trend in the predicted direction.

D. SUMMARY OF THE ARTIFACT STUDIES

These studies of artifact concepts suggest that the nature of the concepts, and the boundaries of the associated categories, cannot be captured by appealing to any one central type of information. Both physical qualities and function appear to be involved in determining category membership for artifacts, and historical relationships among exemplars may also be important. Before drawing more general conclusions, I describe a study on one natural kind concept, the concept of *water*.

III. Water: A Case Study of a Natural Kind Concept

The concept *water* has been widely cited in discussions of the "essence" possibility, which, as I described earlier, is the idea that people know about, or at least believe in, some hidden essence that makes a thing a member of a plant, animal, or other natural kind category. The example I discussed earlier was of a belief in a raccoon essence that makes a raccoon still considered to be a raccoon even if it has been altered to look like a skunk.

With respect to water, most people are familiar with the idea that compounds such as water have a particular chemical composition, and they are also aware that water itself is considered to be H_2O. So the assumption has been that the liquids people will accept as examples of the concept *water* will be heavily determined by a belief that they have the particular chemical composition H_2O. The philosopher Hilary Putnam, from whose work the psychological version of essences derives in large part, argued that use of the word "water" will be restricted to liquids that people believe have the appropriate essence (Putnam, 1975). This argument leads to a clear prediction about actual category membership judgments: If someone believes a liquid is H_2O, then he or she will consider it to be water; if the person believes it is not H_2O, he or she will not consider it to be water.

Despite the simplicity of the prediction, there has been little empirical evidence testing its correctness. The evidence supporting the idea has consisted mainly of intuitions that H_2O must be critical to something being water, and arguments such as that if a liquid called "water" were discovered to be made of some completely different chemical compound, then people would probably stop calling it water (Putnam, 1975). To test the prediction of the essence idea more fully, I collected examples of liquids that are normally considered to be water, and examples of liquids that are similar in one way or another to them, but that are not normally considered to be water. If the essence prediction is correct, people's beliefs about the composition of these liquids should distinguish between those that they consider to be water and those that they do not.

Our sets of examples of liquids considered to be water came from the same three sources that we used in collecting the bottle and tape examples I discussed earlier: (1) observation of the use of the word "water" in everyday conversations, newspapers, television, and so on; (2) computer search through the Brown corpus to find all the different things labeled "water" in the samples of text; and (3) a laboratory task asking subjects to generate examples of water including not just the most obvious ones, but also ones that would be hard for someone else to think of.

Our sets of examples of liquids that are not considered to be water came from two sources: (1) observation in grocery and drug stores and elsewhere of liquids that are somewhat similar to water but that are called by other names; and (2) a laboratory task similar to the one we used to obtain examples of water. In this version, subjects were asked to try to generate examples of liquids that are similar to water but are not called "water." Some of the examples of waters and non-waters that we collected are given in Table II.

We had subjects rate the proportion of H_2O they felt was contained in each instance of water, and we had another group of subjects rate the proportion of H_2O they felt was contained in each instance of non-water. (Separate groups of subjects were necessary so that they did not simply base their ratings on whether the word "water" appeared in the name.) The average percentage of H_2O estimated for each liquid is given in Table II along with the examples.

There are two critical observations about the results that contradict the essence prediction. First, although the overall percentage of judged H_2O was higher for waters than for non-waters, the dominant substance in both

TABLE II

SOME WATER AND NON-WATER EXAMPLES AND MEAN JUDGED PERCENTAGE OF H_2O

Water example	Mean judged percentage of H_2O	Non-water example	Mean judged percentage of H_2O
Pure water	98.1	Tea (cup of)	91.0
Purified water	94.8	Saliva	89.3
Natural spring water	92.6	Coffee (cup of)	89.1
Bottled water	92.3	Tears	88.6
Rain water	90.9	Sweat	87.3
Ice water	90.4	Lemonade	86.9
Soft tap water	89.9	Chicken broth	81.3
Drinking water	89.4	Saline solution for	
Fresh water	89.1	contact lens	80.1
Water fountain water	88.8	.	.
.	.	.	.
.	.	.	.
.	.	Transmission fluid	54.2
Pond water	78.8	Corn syrup	52.8
Ocean water	78.7	Aftershave lotion	52.6
Chlorinated water	78.1	Bleach	51.3
Dish water	77.1	Creme rinse (hair	
Polluted water	70.6	conditioner)	50.7
Muddy water	70.3	Vodka	48.5
Unpurified water	69.2	Tree sap	48.2
Swamp water	68.8	Nail polish remover	46.8
Radiator water	67.3	Lighter fluid	42.3
Sewer water	67.0	Cool Whip	41.8

water and non-water, according to our subjects, is H_2O. The average for non-waters was 67%, and the average for waters was 83%. This means that people do not necessarily call a liquid "water" whenever they believe the main ingredient is H_2O.

Second, although the average is higher for waters than non-waters, there is noticeable overlap between individual liquids called "water" and ones not called "water." Some non-waters were actually rated higher in H_2O than some waters. Most strikingly, some waters are judged to be as low as 67% H_2O, while some non-waters are judged to be as high as 91% H_2O. Swamp water, for instance, is judged to be lower in H_2O than many familiar beverages such as coffee and tea. This means that there is no dividing line; people do not call a liquid "water" just because they believe it has more H_2O than things they call by other names.

So, these two results together lead to the conclusion that apparently, the set of things that are considered to belong to the category "water" is not determined only by what people believe about the presence of H_2O in the liquid.

We also collected typicality ratings for the examples of water from another group of subjects, and these data suggested the same thing. The example of water rated the best example was drinking water, and tap and rain water were next in line. The H_2O judgments show that people do not believe any of these to be pure H_2O. The waters that were judged closest to pure H_2O—pure, purified, and natural spring water—are only 8th, 5th, and 15th in typicality, respectively. This ordering suggests that waters that are particularly familiar and useful to people may be the most typical, whereas waters that are less common are less central, even if they are purer. So, the typicality ratings also suggest that dimensions other than chemical composition are critical to the concept of water. The ratings along with the other results together contradict the idea that a belief in a hidden essence is the key to understanding the natural kind concept *water,* and that this sort of belief fully constrains the boundaries of the associated category.

One possible issue this conclusion raises is whether "water" might, in fact, have two senses and therefore name two different sorts of categories. One of the senses may correspond to the essence view of its meaning, while the other refers to a mixture of H_2O with other ingredients. This possibility is a reasonable one. In scientific contexts, for instance, the term "water" may well be used to refer only to the pure compound H_2O, and there may also be some everyday contexts in which non-scientists adopt this restricted usage. However, this observation does not undermine any of the arguments that I have been making. Since our list of waters encompassed all the common forms of water that we and our subjects could think of, and since the data indicate that subjects did not view any of them as consisting of pure H_2O, it would seem that the dominant sense of the word is not the more restricted one. Clearly, a complete theory of concept structure should be able to account for the common use of the term "water" as well as any more restricted use.

A second issue that might be raised is whether the data really indicate that the term "water" is applied to mixtures at all. The liquids that were judged to contain less than 100% H_2O were never actually labeled "water" alone for the subjects; they were labeled "salt water," "swimming pool water," and so on. Under this account, if someone uses the label "water" by itself in reference to any of the liquids in our sample, the person does not intend to refer to the mixture as a whole, but only to the H_2O part of the mixture. For instance, someone gesturing toward the liquid in the ocean while talking about "water" would only mean to label the H_2O part; the liquid as a whole would be viewed as water plus salt and other ingredients (Averill, this volume).

It is certainly true that the data I have presented do not directly test whether someone calling the liquid in the ocean "water" means to pick out the mixture as a whole or only the part of the mixture that is H_2O. However, there are at least two reasons to think that the account I have just described is not the correct one. First, about half the examples that we used came from the laboratory task in which subjects listed examples of water. These examples were then verified by another group of subjects who evaluated whether each was truly an example of water. If either group of subjects felt that the mixtures were not examples of water, they need not have included them as water in their responses. Second, many everyday sentences using the term "water" by itself clearly do refer to the mixture, not only to the H_2O component. Someone who has been swimming in the ocean and says "I got water in my ear" or "I swallowed a mouthful of water" is not likely to be referring to only the H_2O molecules, since it was the entire mixture that went into the ear or mouth. In some cases, use of the term "water" to refer to a mixture is quite explicit, as in the statement in a traveler's guide to East Africa, "Water in East Africa simply has different minerals than you are used to drinking" (Voyagers International, 1988). Thus it seems that the mixtures we studied are regarded as types of water by our subjects, and the term "water" itself is used to refer to mixtures in everyday language.

In sum, the water data are consistent with the results of the artifact experiments in arguing that there may not be a central piece of information, whether an observable property or a more hidden essence, that serves as the core of a concept and determines category boundaries.

IV. Discussion

A. RELATIONSHIP TO DATA ON BELIEFS IN AN ESSENCE

I have argued throughout this chapter that, contrary to recent suggestions, neither a single specifiable property nor belief in a more hidden essence provides the key to understanding category structure. The argument against essentialist beliefs as central may seem to contradict both my own earlier data (Malt, 1990) and those of Keil (1989) that I cited earlier in introducing the essence point of view. Both of these sets of data supported the idea that people believe in the existence of some sort of essential property or properties underlying category membership for natural kinds. In addition, classification judgments made by Keil's subjects (about, for instance, the raccoon that was altered to look like a skunk) supported the idea that people actually use their beliefs about essences in making category judgments. Before drawing further implications from the data I have just presented, I want to address this apparent contradiction and argue that the observations are not, in fact, inconsistent with each other.

A first point to note is that people often hold beliefs that are not correct. In this case, they may hold beliefs about how categories are constrained, and about how they themselves make classification judgments, that do not accurately reflect the actual constraints or judgment processes. Many factors may give rise to erroneous naive beliefs about categorization, including incomplete introspective access to the relevant representations and processes, and the tendency to retrieve mainly prototypes and clear-cut cases of category members when thinking about category membership. Thus there is no real inconsistency between observations that people hold certain essentialist beliefs about concept structure and observations suggesting that essentialist beliefs are not the deciding factor in classification.

The second issue is how to reconcile the actual classification judgments made by Keil's subjects with the sorts of data I have presented in this article. Several factors may have influenced Keil's subjects to make judgments consistent with a belief in an underlying essence, even though this belief may not be the primary constraint on classification under other circumstances. One factor is that Keil's stimuli always incorporated features of two different existing categories of animal (e.g., the raccoon insides with the external appearance altered to resemble a skunk), and the classification decision required choosing between these two existing categories. The internal parts were the original parts of the animal, whereas the external parts were created through manipulations that are not likely to fully mimic the natural external properties of the other category (e.g., a "smelly sack" was sewn into the raccoon). As a result, subjects may have felt that the animal better matched the original classification, regardless of the nature of the properties involved. In general, subjects are aware that people are not the creators of animals, so manipulations involving human intervention may not seem very convincing.

A second factor is that in a forced-choice situation where they are asked to verbalize their reasoning, people may tend to focus on cues that match their naive beliefs about how categories do get formed. However, in other circumstances, such cues may be less salient and may not dominate classification. For instance, people do not necessarily refer to, or think of, a fertilized human egg as a human being, even though the complete genetic endowment is present as soon as sperm and egg join. In this case, the lack of other properties such as neural development or the presence of consciousness is salient enough to preclude inclusion in the same category as an adult or a more fully developed infant, despite recognition of the continuity between them. Similarly, we distinguish between tadpoles and frogs, and between caterpillars and butterflies. Most people know that the earlier form changes into the later form, so they recognize that the genetic endowment of the two forms are the same. Nevertheless, in everyday English there is no single category label that encompasses both forms; they are put into separate categories on the basis of the highly salient differences in their forms. Again, the recognition of some common "essence" appears to play less of a role here than other sorts of properties in creation of the categories. Thus, Keil's task may have led people to produce answers consistent with a belief in an essence, but that fact does not necessarily indicate that they would behave in accordance with the belief under all classification circumstances.

In short, I think that any contradictions between earlier data and the sort of data that I have presented in this chapter are more apparent than real. I do not mean to imply that discussions and data about beliefs in an essence are unimportant for understanding concepts. If the beliefs exist, their very existence means that they are part of the mental representation of a category and should be included in discussions of concept structure. However, the existence of these beliefs does not necessarily dictate that the key to understanding classification lies with them.

B.   What Is in a Concept, and How Do We Categorize?

I opened this article by noting that theories of concepts have been aimed at answering two questions: (1) What sort of information is contained within concepts? and (2) How do the contents of concepts constrain the categorization of objects in the world? I start by discussing what the experiments reported here suggest about the content of concepts. I then argue that the content of concepts per se does not fully constrain categorization, and that the second question should, in fact, be expanded to examine how category membership is influenced by factors external to the concepts themselves. This theme has recently been sounded by other authors as well, most notably Murphy and Medin (1985). However, I will suggest influences on categorization that are somewhat different in nature from those proposed by Murphy and Medin.

1. What Sort of Information Is Contained in Concepts?

I think it is fairly indisputable at this point that concepts must contain at least three kinds of information: (1) properties associated with the categories, (2) knowledge of what exemplars or properties are most typical of a category, and (3) beliefs about how categories are structured. The studies I have presented have little to add about the content of naive beliefs or how typical properties or instances are computed. The studies do make one central point about the status of the properties and beliefs associated with categories. The artifact data argue against either function or physical properties providing the "core" information for membership in artifact categories, and the water data likewise argue against beliefs about composition as fully constraining what liquids will be considered to be water. This point is not to say that all information contained in a concept is weighted equally; for instance, if all the properties associated with a category could be compared, some would certainly be more important than others to category membership. However, the studies I presented have tested the most likely candidates for special status as the core of the concepts, and the data indicate that none of these candidates does have that status. Taken together, the studies suggest it is unlikely that cores in the sense of a single dominant type of information will be found for many common concepts.

2. How Does the Information in Concepts Constrain Categorization?

I have just argued that neither beliefs about the basis for categorization, nor any one property such as a function or a physical characteristic, constitute concept "cores." This argument might seem to suggest a return to a prototype view, where entities are considered members of a category as long as they have sufficient overlap with the category prototype. However, this move would only resurrect the original problem with this sort of view: If category membership requires just having some threshold degree of overall similarity to a prototype, why can't lemonade be categorized as a type of water, if sewer water is? Why can't a graduated mustard jar be considered a bottle, if a square ink container is? and so on. Again, we have to conclude that overlap with a prototype does not fully explain category membership.

An alternative approach to explaining the relatively loose structure of the categories is via Lakoff's (1987) suggestion that categories may show a radial structure (in which extensions from the prototype can occur along different dimensions) and chaining (in which an exemplar may join a category because of a connection to some other member of the category, rather than through direct overlap with a prototype). For instance, it might argued that the "bottle" category shows a radial structure: some things might be considered bottles because they are related to prototypical bottles on the dimension of having a graduated shape despite dissimilarity in contents (e.g., aspirin bottles), while others might be considered bottles because they are related to prototypical bottles on the dimension of holding drinkable liquids despite dissimilarity in shape (e.g., cylindrical water bottles). Similarly, chaining may account for some of the stranger objects that are considered to be bottles: square ink bottles or rectangular hand lotion bottles with a pump top might be considered to be bottles not because they share a threshold amount of overlap with prototypical bottles that are graduated in shape and hold drinkable liquids, but because they form a chain with ink bottles and hand lotion bottles that have the more usual bottle shape.

The radial structure/chaining approach has the advantage of being flexible enough to account for a wide range of category members. At the same time, though, this flexibility has the disadvantage that it does not give a full account of what entities will end up being members of a category and what ones will not; it is more a description of category structure than a prediction of category membership. Since the principles of chaining and radial structure do not themselves fully constrain what entities will become members of a category, we need to look further for additional factors that will influence whether a particular entity becomes a member of a given category. Although there may a variety of factors at work, I would like to suggest three constraints or factors in particular. These are: (1) historical relationships among exemplars, (2) proximity of other concepts, and (3) labeling by manufacturers or other sources that establish convention.

a. Historical Relationships. As I discussed earlier, historical relationships between entities may influence whether or not they are considered to be members of the same category. An old-fashioned car and a modern car may both be part of the same category despite many dissimilarities in appearance and functioning, because they are linked by the evolutionary path from one to the other. In contrast, a motorcycle and a moped may share about as many physical and functional features as the old and modern car, but they are named differently. I would argue that it is because they exist at the same time, and the differences between them (in size, power, price, etc.) are more important to capture in categorizing them than the similarity.

   b.   *Proximity of Other Concepts.*   The data and examples I have presented also indirectly suggest another factor that influences category membership: the existence of other, related concepts. For example, although a range of different shapes and sizes seem to be acceptable as members of the category "bottle," certain variations were not among the bottle examples that we collected. In particular, objects that share other characteristics with bottles but have wide mouths were not included in the category; no doubt these are generally considered to be jars instead. The existence of the jar concept apparently will pre-empt membership in the bottle category for containers with this particular variation on the prototypical bottle shape. Similarly, I noted (see footnote 1) that cardboard frozen orange juice containers seem to be considered cans by virtue of a historical link to the older metal containers, but, on the other hand, the new rectangular cardboard juice containers are considered to be boxes instead of cans. Here, existence of the "box" category, for which square or rectangular shape is a salient feature, seems to preclude inclusion of the new version in the can category, despite the historical link. Finally, it is clear that liquids with a wide range of substances in addition to H_2O are accepted into the water category. What precludes some with a large amount of H_2O, such as lemonade or tea, from being accepted? The domain of beverages is an important and highly differentiated one in American culture, with the result that liquids that are drunk are placed in this category and given names that contrast them with plain old water. I suggest that if beverages did not exist as such an important concept, we might consider liquids such as water with lemon and sugar added, or water with tea leaves in it, to be two more types of water.

   c.   *Labeling by Manufacturers, and Other Sources of Convention.*   A third factor that may influence categorization is convention: a category label may be given to an object by a manufacturer or other source, and that label may then affect the way that people think of the object. For instance, club soda and soda water may have the same contents, but a drink labeled by the manufacturer as "soda water" may be more likely to be thought of as a type of water than a drink labeled as "club soda." A cylindrical glass container that fancy jam comes in may be called a jam jar because jams are generally considered to come in jars, but exactly the same shape container that holds olives may be considered to be either a jar of olives or a bottle of olives because, for whatever reasons, the convention for naming olive containers is less rigid. We have found explicit appeals to this sort of role of convention in a study in progress focusing on boxes and cartons. Subjects can verbalize some properties that correspond to their classification decisions about cartons versus boxes. However, when asked to explain certain classifications, such as why they consider Chinese food take-out containers to be cartons, they often appeal to convention: "That's just what they're called."

C. Conclusion

So, should we conclude from the data and discussion that concepts are simply fuzzy, as Rosch and others originally proposed? I believe that the data and examples I have presented in this article argue that category boundaries are not fixed by any single particular type or source of information, and in that sense, that categories are indeed fuzzy. This conclusion applies to at least some natural kind categories as well as to artifact categories. However, "fuzzy" may be a less appropriate way of describing the nature of categories and the concepts on which they are based than "flexible." The concept may contain certain information that is itself relatively clear-cut, such as a category prototype and knowledge of relevant dimensions of variation. The application of this information to categorizing objects in the world, however, appears to be a flexible process that may be influenced by a variety of factors external to the contents of the concept itself.

Acknowledgments

The work reported here and preparation of this article were supported by NSF grant BNS-8909360 to B. C. Malt. I thank James Corter for carrying out the scaling solutions for "bottle" and "tape." I also thank Bethann Schultz, Christopher Santi, and especially Yongming Gao for assistance in carrying out the studies reported here. Douglas Medin, Glenn Nakamura, and Roman Taraban provided helpful comments on an earlier draft.

References

Carey, S. (1985). *Conceptual change in childhood.* Cambridge, MA: MIT Press.
Corter, J. E. & Tversky, A. (1986). Extended similarity trees. *Psychometrika, 51,* 429–451.
Keil, F. C. (1989). *Concepts, kinds, and cognitive development.* Cambridge, MA: MIT Press.
Kucera, N., & Francis, W. N. (1967). *A computational analysis of present-day American English.* Providence, RI: Brown University Press.

Lakoff, G. (1987). *Women, fire, and dangerous things: What categories reveal about the mind*. Chicago: University of Chicago Press.

Malt, B. C. (1990). Features and beliefs in the mental representation of categories. *Journal of Memory and Language, 29*, 289–315.

Malt, B. C., & Johnson, E. C. (1992). Do artifact concepts have cores? *Journal of Memory and Language, 31*, 195–217.

Medin, D. L., & Ortony, A. (1989). Psychological essentialism. In S. Vosniadou and A. Ortony (Eds.), *Similarity and analogical reasoning* (pp. 179–195). New York: Cambridge University Press.

Murphy, G. L., & Medin, D. L. (1985). The role of theories in conceptual coherence. *Psychological Review, 92*, 289–316.

Putnam, H. (1975). The meaning of "meaning." In H. Putnam, *Mind, language, and reality: Philosophical papers: Vol. 2*. Cambridge, England: Cambridge University Press.

Rosch, E., & Mervis, C. B. (1975). Family resemblances: Studies in the internal structure of categories. *Cognitive Psychology, 7*, 573-605.

Rosch, E., Mervis, C. B., Gray, W. D., Johnson, D. M., & Boyes-Braem, P. (1976). Basic objects in natural categories. *Cognitive Psychology, 8*, 382–439.

Schwartz, S. P. (1978). Putnam on artifacts. *The Philosophical Review, 97*, 566–574.

Smith, E. E. & Medin, D. L. (1981). *Categories and concepts*. Cambridge, MA: Harvard University Press.

Voyagers International (1988). *Voyagers safari guide: Travel tips & information for East Africa*. Author: Ithaca, NY.

NON-PREDICATING CONCEPTUAL COMBINATIONS

Edward J. Shoben

I. Introduction

Research on the psychology of concepts has proceeded at a rapid pace during the past decade. From its beginnings as an investigation of semantic memory in the 1970s (Collins & Quillian, 1972; Smith, Shoben, & Rips, 1974), work on categorization has progressed to the point where we now have highly sophisticated models of how objects are classified (see Medin, 1989; Nosofsky, 1991; Kruschke, 1992; and this volume).

At the same time, comparatively little attention has been focused on how these concepts are combined. Although we now have at least plausible accounts of how people may categorize chairs as furniture, we have far less understanding of how people comprehend combinations such as lawn furniture, kid furniture, or red furniture.

Research on conceptual combinations is important for at least two classes of reasons. First, the area is important in its own right as we often partition the world into categories that are qualified in some way. For example, describing an emu as a bird is not terribly informative. One may think it is a typical bird; describing it as a large, flightless bird that resembles an ostrich is much more helpful and that requires us to understand both "large bird" and "flightless bird."

Second, an understanding of conceptual combinations is likely to advance our understanding of concepts. One of the crucial questions is what kind of information must we possess about concepts in order to combine them correctly? If, for example, it turns out that we need a great deal of world knowledge in order to understand what is meant by "milk money" in the context of "The president of the dairy farmers association admitted that milk money had provided the funds for the candidacy of the corrupt politician," then it would add a great deal of credence to the claims of people like Murphy & Medin (1983) that a great deal of world knowledge is stored with individual concepts.

A. TYPES OF CONCEPTUAL COMBINATIONS

At least at first blush, there are two types of conceptual combinations. *Predicating combinations,* such as "red furniture," can be paraphrased as "furniture that is red." In contrast to these straightforward combinations, attempts to paraphrase "lawn furniture" or "kid furniture" in the same way result in nonsensical statements: "furniture that is lawn" or "furniture that is kid."

The last two examples are *non-predicating combinations* that cannot be paraphrased the way red furniture can be. Instead, "lawn furniture" means "furniture that is used on the lawn" and "kid furniture" means "furniture that is used by kids." The first relation is locative and the second indicates the agent.

Although there are some models of how we comprehend predicating adjective phrases such as "red furniture" (Smith & Osherson, 1987), there are no formal models for comprehending non-predicating combinations. Moreover, the approach that has been taken for predicating adjectives will clearly not work with non-predicating ones.

It is also argued here that predicating combinations are straightforward only at a surface level. One might be tempted to think that an Adj-N is an N that is Adj, and that otherwise the N is the same as before. For example, this analysis is quite plausible in the context of "yellow apple." It is an apple that is yellow but that in all other respects is just like an apple. One formal model that takes this approach is the modification model.

According to the modification model (Smith & Osherson, 1987; Smith, Osherson, Rips, & Keene, 1988), each concept is composed of a set of dimensions, each of which has a number of votes. Thus, for example, "apple" has a number of dimensions, one of which is color. This dimension has a number of values, such as red and yellow, and red presumably has more votes than yellow because red apples are more common than yellow ones. The model then assumes that a combination like "red apple" is like "apple" except that its votes on the color dimension are now all red.

In addition, the model also assumes that the diagnosticity of the color dimension has increased.

Matching in the model is done by comparing votes for each dimension. This mechanism allows the model to make typicality judgments. If subjects are shown a picture of a red apple and one group is asked to what degree this picture is of an apple, the subjects will compare all the values on each of the dimensions of the picture with all the values on the concept. In this example, picture and concept will presumably match for most dimensions (such as shape and texture) except color, where most of the votes will match (because most apples are red) but some will not (because some votes for the color dimension will be yellow and green, which do not match with the picture of the red apple). Thus, the picture of the red apple will be judged as a very good, although not perfect example of the concept apple.

A second group of subjects judged how good an example the same picture was of the concept "red apple." Now, picture and concept match on virtually all votes on all dimensions (including color). Thus the model predicts that this picture of a red apple will be judged a better example of the concept "red apple" than of "apple."

This prediction was confirmed. Moreover, this result is important because it disconfirms an account of the process that has considerable appeal. One might think that for an object to be both *A* and *B,* then its goodness of example would be limited by the degree to which it was a poor example of either *A* or *B.* Thus for example, "A Jaguar is an expensive car" is an acceptable sentence because Jaguars are certainly cars and they certainly are expensive, whereas "A Toyota is an expensive car" is less acceptable not because Toyotas are any less cars than are Jaguars, but because Toyotas are less expensive.

Thus, one accomplishment of the modification model is its ability to predict reversals of this *min* effect where the goodness of the combination can turn out to be greater than the goodness of its least acceptable part. "Pet fish" is the near classic example: A guppy is a poor example of a pet and a poor example of a fish, but it is an excellent example of a pet fish.

Despite this accomplishment, there are good reasons to question the adequacy of the modification model as a theory of predicating combinations. As Medin and Shoben (1988) noted, a critical problem is that the model assumes that only the votes on the relevant dimension are the ones that change. For "apple," only color changes. Although such an assumption is plausible here, it is clearly false in most other circumstances.

Consider the concept "spoon." If we imagine the attributes of "spoon," we have certain intuitions about its size, what it is made of, what it is used for, and so on. The question is, If we specify one of the values on these dimensions, are other values unchanged, as the modification model would predict? Put another way, if we change from "spoon" to "wooden spoon," is one's estimate of the size of the spoon unchanged? Medin and Shoben (1988) showed that people felt that a wooden spoon was likely to be larger than a spoon.

It is also the case that these kinds of correlations cannot invariably be predicted from knowledge of the individual components. For example, although "wooden spoon" is larger than "spoon," there is no doubt that "wooden soldier" is smaller than "soldier." Thus, it is not clear whether a wooden N is larger or smaller than an N.

Whatever the merits of the modification model as a theory of predicating adjectives, it is clear that this approach will not work for non-predicating combinations. There is no obvious dimension of money, lamp, or pills that will enable us to understand non-predicating combinations such as "oil money," "picture lamp," or "headache pills." One might be tempted to argue that pills for instance, have the dimension of "what they cure." Although such an analysis would work for headache pills, it would not work for fertility pills.

Given that a dimensional analysis will not work, what kind of approach may prove fruitful? One possibility is that conceptual combinations are not combinations at all, but are simply multi-word concepts. Thus, for example, it is plausible to believe that such combinations as "honey bee," "tax law," and "mountain range" are all lexicalized and that we simply represent them as we do their individual components.

Although such an approach appears reasonable for these examples, there are several reasons to question its viability as a general model. First, it precludes the kind of generative possibilities that conceptual combinations permit. For example, in addition to "mountain range," we can have "mountain home," "mountain shoe," "mountain car," "mountain motel," and "mountain magazine." It is difficult to believe that we have separate lexical entries for all of these terms, yet all are readily comprehensible. Moreover, if we claim that all combinations have separate lexical entries, then the computational explosion that results is extreme. If we make the very conservative estimate that each potential adjective can combine with 20 nouns and each noun can combine with only 20 adjectives (consider nouns like *law, treatment,* and *money* to see how conservative this estimate is), then our storage requirements in memory have expanded by a factor of 400.

This discussion is not to say that there are no multi-word concepts. There undoubtedly are some. The claim here is that the argument that all non-predicating combinations are lexicalized is not viable.

II.   Thematic Roles

A more promising avenue is to consider the importance of *thematic roles*. By thematic roles, we mean the kinds of relations that non-predicating combinations can assume. For example, consideration of the roles that the adjective *mountain* can assume makes it clear that most of the time, a mountain X is an X that is located in the mountains. "Mountain stream," "mountain tree," "mountain vehicle" are examples. However, there are clearly exceptions. A mountain range is a range composed of mountains and a mountain magazine is a magazine about the mountains. Consequently, a prerequisite to an analysis of thematic roles is that we delineate just what kind of roles can be specified by non-predicating combinations.

Douglas Medin and I began our investigation of this question by looking at some work in linguistics. Gleitman and Gleitman (1970) did some early work on this question, and the most extensive work that we found was done by Levi (1978). In addition to providing a detailed taxonomy, she also provided a derivational account based on the then current generative theory. Our primary concern was with the taxonomy she offered.

A.   TAXONOMY OF NON-PREDICATING ADJECTIVES

We ended up with fourteen categories, of which ten (A–J) were taken directly from Levi. These categories along with an example are depicted in Table I. We refer to the adjective and noun in the combination as Adj and N, respectively.

The first two categories, A and B, are causals, where N causes Adj or Adj causes N. Examples of this category are "blinding light" and "electric shock." Categories C and D are possessives that can be paraphrased as "N has Adj" or "Adj has N," respectively. Examples here are "picture book" and "lemon peel." Categories E and F deal with a "make" relation, although the symmetry between these two classifications is far less than that in the first two pairs. "Honey bee" is a bee that makes honey, and a chocolate bar is a bar made of chocolate. Category G can be paraphrased as an "N that is an Adj," as in "servant girl." Category H denotes the "use" relation: an N that uses Adj, as in "wood stove." The locative relation is captured in category I, an N in location Adj, as in "urban store." Category J can be paraphrased as "an N for Adj," as in "nose drops."

In addition to these ten categories, Medin and I also found it desirable to create four new ones. Category K denotes the "about" relation: N about Adj. "Tax law" is an example. Our remaining three categories can all be thought of as inverses of prior ones. Thus, Category F' is an N that is made

TABLE I

Types of Non-predicating Adjectives

	Type	Example
A.	N causes Adj	Flu virus
B.	Adj causes N	Heat rash
C.	N has Adj	Picture book
D.	Adj has N	Lemon peel
E.	N makes Adj	Honey bee
F.	N made of Adj	Sugar cube
F′.	N derived from Adj	Oil money
G.	Adj is N	Servant girl
H.	N uses Adj	Gas stove
H′.	N used by Adj	Finger toy
I.	N located by Adj	Urban riots
I′.	Adj located N	Murder town
J.	N for Adj	Nose drops
K.	N about Adj	Tax law

from Adj. "Oil money" is an example, as in "Oil money built the sky-scrapers of downtown Houston." Category I′ is an inverse locative, an Adj located in N. "Murder town" is an example. Finally, Category H′ is an inverse of the use relation. "Finger toy" is an example in which the N is used by the Adj.

It is probably the case that our taxonomy is not exhaustive; there are probably some meaningful combinations that cannot be easily classified according to our system. At the same time, it does appear that these fourteen categories do cover the vast majority of these non-predicating combinations, and thus our taxonomy is at least plausible.

1. The Function of Thematic Roles

We must now specify how these thematic roles affect the comprehension of non-predicating combinations. Our first task was to examine a corpus to see how these roles were distributed. What we did was to select ten examples from each of Levi's ten categories. These were selected on the basis that we felt that they were good and relatively unambiguous examples of a particular thematic role. We then constructed a matrix by pairing each adjective in the examples with each noun. This 100 × 100 matrix was reduced by repetitions to a 93 × 96 matrix.

Subsequently, three people judged whether the combination in each cell of the matrix had an acceptable (and non-metaphorical) meaning. If two of the judges found an acceptable meaning, we then attempted to classify the combination according to the taxonomy given above. Disputes were resolved by discussion.

Although an extended characterization of this huge matrix is clearly beyond the scope of this article, there were several findings that are worthy of mention. First, not all of our categories were equally represented. Causals were relatively rare, as were the "have" relations, Categories C and D, and the "make" relation, Category E. The "made out of" relation, Category F, was relatively common, as were Categories I, J, and K. With the exception of Category F', all of our inverse relations were relatively rare.

Second, some concepts exhibited a propensity to enter into certain categories of combinations, whereas others did not. For example, "chocolate" almost always combines to form a Category F combination (chocolate bar, chocolate bunny, chocolate bee) and "mountain" usually combines to form a locative or Category I relation (mountain stream, mountain cabin, mountain tree). Other concepts formed many different types of combinations. For example, a wood stove is a stove that uses wood, a wood polish is a polish for wood, a wood desk is a desk made of wood, and a wood report is a report about wood. It should be made clear that it is not the case that some adjectives always combine to form a single relation (note the exceptions mountain range, a range made out of mountains, and chocolate treatment, a treatment using chocolate), but that these terms do differ in the degree to which they tend to be used in a particular relation. Similar observations can be made for our nouns.

One conclusion from this cursory analysis is that there is no clean set of correspondence rules between various concepts and the roles that they can assume in combination. The data do not warrant some nice conclusion, such as certain terms enter into relations F, H, and K, whereas others enter into causal relations. Although there are certainly some concepts with tendencies, there do not appear to be universals. One possibility that Douglas Medin and I explored experimentally was that some relations were inherently more complex than others. For example, it seemed to us that the causal relations (Categories A and B) were inherently more complex than the possessives (Categories C and D), just because causality is more complex than possession. In addition, Categories I and J are marked by case endings in some languages. One could argue in addition that Category K relations resemble ablatives in Latin. Thus, the complexity hypothesis predicts that causals will be more difficult than other types of non-predicating combinations.

Consequently, Medin and I performed a simple experiment in which we measured the time it took subjects to read various non-predicating combinations. Each trial began with a sentence frame, such as "The appliance repair man was fearful of." When subjects had read the frame, they pressed the spacebar on the console and then saw the combination "electric shock." When they read it, they pressed the spacebar again and then had to decide whether "The appliance man knew electricity was dangerous" was true or false. We included this question as a check of comprehension. Our primary interest was in the time it took to read the conceptual combination.

The materials in this study consisted of eight exemplars from each of ten categories of conceptual combinations, A through K. For each, we selected the materials such that all were unambiguous (at least to the authors) in their categorization and all were clearly sensible. Although none was truly novel, the combinations varied in frequency from those that were arguably lexicalized, such as "mountain range," "electric shock," and "financial report," to those that appeared to be much less common, such as "municipal property," "tire rim," and "student committee."

Contrary to expectations, the results offered no support for the complexity hypothesis. Although there was an overall effect of category of combination, the differences among groups were not what we expected. The overall mean reading time for the combinations was 1201 msec. However, the causals were very close to this average, with a mean of 1209 msec for Category A (flu virus) and 1190 msec for Category B (heat rash). The possessives, which we expected to be comprehended relatively quickly, were in fact among the slowest in the experiment. Category C combinations (picture book) were read quite quickly (1164 msec), but Category D combinations (lemon peel) were among the slowest in the experiment (1295 msec).

Overall, some combinations were faster than average and some were slower. Unfortunately, it does not appear that there is anything principled about this results. The "make" relations, Categories E and F, and the "is" relation, Category G, were somewhat faster than the mean, whereas Categories H, I, J, and K (use, location, "for," and about) were somewhat slower than average.

2. Thematic Roles as Schemata

Before dismissing this experiment as an abject failure, however, it may be profitable to examine our results a bit more closely. One alternative is to consider the possibility that our thematic roles are schemata. As such they take on default values, and comprehension difficulty may reflect the degree to which each individual combination matches the ideal.

For example, let us consider the comprehension times for the "made out of" relations, Category F:

Floral wreath	1167
Mountain range	1343
Chocolate bar	1124
Sugar cube	1015
Paper money	1223
Student committee	1134
Cable network	1101
Plastic toy	1142
Mean	1156

As the tabulation indicates, these items were among the most rapidly comprehended in the study. However, let us consider what the schema is for this type of combination. Category F items can be paraphrased as "an N made out of Adj." Note that most of these items fit this paraphrase quite well; "student committee" is paraphrased better as a "committee made up of students," but it is close to the original paraphrase. However, there is one clear case where the paraphrase fits relatively poorly. "Mountain range" is not "a range made out of mountains"; this combination fits this schema only very loosely. "Mountain range" is the slowest item in this group; it is 187 msec slower than the mean, and over 100 msec slower than any other item. Moreover, arguments about frequency or lexicality will not provide an explanation of the slow reading time for "mountain range," as this item is clearly a relatively common combination.

An examination of several others categories is useful in our consideration of whether regarding thematic roles as schemata is a viable approach. Let us turn next to category D, which can be paraphrased as "Adj has N":

Student power	1187
Lemon peel	1068
Tire rim	1317
Municipal property	1454
Party members	1350
Family antiques	1389
Maternal instincts	1232
National resources	1365
Mean	1295

As the tabulation indicates, these combinations were among the slowest in the study. At the same time, note that "lemon peel" is comprehended very rapidly. One possibility is that the schematic representation for the possessives is not just "has N" or "has Adj" (in the case of Category C), but also incorporates the notion "as physical part." Physical parts play an important role in other aspects of categorization (Tversky & Hemenway, 1984) and may be important here as well. At first blush, there are two items among the eight for which this "has as physical part" is an appropriate paraphrase: "lemon peel" and "tire rim." These two are comprehended on average more than 130 msec faster than the other six items in the study. Even this comparison may understate the difference, as "tire rim" may engender some confusion over whether it is referring to the edge of the tire or the rim of the wheel on which the tire rests.

In contrast to our analysis for Category F, there is unfortunately a clear possible confound: word length is a problem, as "lemon peel" and "tire rim" are two of the shortest combinations in this category. Nevertheless, these results are at least consistent with the idea that thematic roles are a kind of schema.

The results for Category G are as follows:

Winter season	1015
Cash basis	1103
Murder charge	1128
Cactus plant	1159
Star shape	1126
Finger lakes	1509
Pine tree	1075
Servant girl	1170
Mean	1161

These combinations are all comprehended uniformly rapidly with one exception: "finger lakes." This combination requires 350 msec more time than any other combination. With this exception, all the items in this category can be paraphrased as "An N that is Adj." For "finger lakes," the "is" is replaced by "is shaped like." Thus, "finger lakes" does not fit the schema very well and is comprehended more slowly.

Finally, let us consider the results from Category K. This combination can be paraphrased as "N about Adj." The comprehension times are as follows:

Tax law	1214
Financial report	1260
Adventure story	1125
Sports magazine	1164
Sex scandal	1119
Oil crisis	1146
Historical drama	1510
Ideological debate	1751
Mean	1286

Although these items, considered en masse, are among the longest in the experiment, note that the comprehension times for the first six average 1171 msec, much faster than the overall mean. However, two of the items, "historical drama" and "ideological debate," are among the slowest in the experiment. As with Category D, one wonders how much to attribute to phrase length, as these two items are among the longest. Nevertheless, they do not fit the paraphrase very well. A historical drama is not really about history itself; it is about some aspect of history. Similarly, an ideological debate is not about ideology itself, but is instead about some aspect of ideology or is a debate that employs ideology.

This entire analysis is admittedly post hoc. As we have seen, how well the examples fit their schema is not always uncorrelated with other potentially confounding variables such as word length and the like. At the same time, this analysis does suggest that thinking of thematic roles as schemata may prove fruitful.

B.   PROCESSING ACCOUNTS

To this point, little has been said about how people process these non-predicating combinations. Given that an Adj–N combination can be interpreted in many different ways, we must determine whether one considers each of the possibilities serially or all at once. A third possibility is that there is some means by which selection can be guided so that the number of alternatives is greatly reduced. I consider this last possibility later. I consider here the possibility of the straightforward serial or parallel interpretations.

The results of the previous experiment suggest that a serial explanation is not very likely. Unless the order in which each of the thematic roles is considered random, one would expect that some combinations would generally take longer than others. Although one might argue that the reliable effect of conceptual category is consistent with such a notion, there are three reasons to doubt this idea. First, there was no principled order to the relations; seemingly complex and intuitively less frequent relations were often comprehended more rapidly than others. Second, similar relations (such as Categories C and D) were often comprehended with rapidly varying ease. Third, if the comparison were serial, we would assume that a predicating interpretation would be near or at the top of the list, and this makes the prediction that predicating combinations should always be more readily comprehended than non-predicating ones.

Murphy (1990) has provided some evidence that bears on this question. He compared typical predicating adjectives, atypical predicating adjectives, and non-predicating adjectives. Subjects decided whether the combinations were sensible or not. Murphy found that the typical predicating adjectives were comprehended faster than either of the other two classes, whose comprehension rates did not differ from each other. Thus, although predicating adjectives were overall faster than non-predicating ones, it does not appear that this result is universally true.

A parallel account also seems improbable. First, it seems like a waste of processing resources for the system to attempt to compute more than a dozen interpretations of every combination. Second, according to most parallel models, some of the comparisons would be faster than others, and thus the same objection made above to the serial account would apply here as well.

C. RELATION SELECTION

If we object to both a parallel and a serial account, then we must argue for some selection operation that points the system toward a particular interpretation. More specifically, something orders the relations so that the appropriate relation is among the first to be considered. There are several possibilities as to how this selection could occur.

1. Selection by Knowledge of the Combining Concepts

We have already noted that some concepts tend to enter into certain relations. For example, a chocolate N is usually an N made out of chocolate. Chocolate most commonly enters into this category F type of relation. It does not, for example, commonly enter into causals (although "chocolate rash" is clearly an exception). Thus, one's knowledge of the concept "chocolate" may point one in the direction of a Category F relation, and thus people may try to work out this interpretation before they go on, if necessary, to try others. A similar, though less striking, account can be made for nouns. People know that an Adj law is a law about Adj, as in "tax law," "divorce law," and "labor law." At the same time, "mountain law" and "ghetto law" clearly do not admit this interpretation. Nevertheless, if one were to minimize effort, then one should try (ignoring the aspects of the adjective) to fit "Adj law" into Category K.

According to this account, knowledge of the individual concepts leads one to a particular interpretation. It is premature to speculate on the relative contributions of adjective and noun, but based on English word order, it would be surprising if the noun contributed more than the adjective.

2. Selection by Analogy

The preceding view is abstractionist in the sense that it assumes that people have abstracted from their experience the relative likelihood that a particular concept will combine in a particular way. In this sense, it is a kind of prototype model that discards particular information and retains only the summary.

The analogy view is just the opposite, in the sense that it retains no summary information. Although one can have an analogy to a prototype or other summary representation, *analogy* is used here as a kind of single exemplar model that bases its best guess on a known exemplar that is presumably retrieved by similarity. For example, if one were asked what a chocolate dog was, one might check first to see that there was no entry for this combination and then retrieve "chocolate bunny." Assuming one knew that a chocolate bunny was a bunny made out of chocolate, one could then make the analogy that "chocolate dog" had the same kind of interpretation as "chocolate bunny."

III. An Experimental Strategy

At present, we clearly have no basis upon which to select among these possibilities. We do not even have empirical evidence by which we can reject the serial or parallel proposals discussed earlier. However, we can begin to attack this problem by asking how flexible the system is. In other words, if there is a fixed order by which potential meanings are considered, then changing the context should have no effect on how these combinations are interpreted.

A. CONTEXT EFFECTS

Our strategy here was to come up with non-predicating combinations that were ambiguous. For example, is a horse rash a rash on a horse, or is it a rash caused by contact with a horse? Clearly, both interpretations are plausible, as people have no difficulty reading sentences as "John was distressed to learn he had a horse rash again," or "The jockey was distressed to learn his prize mount had a horse rash."

We tried to influence what definition people would give to "horse rash" by having them read one of two sentences previously. Half the subjects read "The child was disappointed to learn that she had a cat rash." The remaining subjects read "The kid was sorry to hear his pet had a hamster rash." The critical question was whether reading the prior sentence would influence the interpretation subjects would later give to the phrase "horse rash."

More specifically, subjects saw a sequence of trials. They first read eight sentences and were told to study them for a memory test. After 2 minutes, they were given a recognition memory test in which they were presented with 32 words, half of which had appeared in the prior set of sentences. The words were selected in the following manner. Two words were chosen from each sentence, the adjective from the conceptual combination and an unrelated noun. To go back to the "rash" example, the words "child" and "cat" were presented from the sentence "The child was disappointed to learn she had a cat rash," and "kid" and "hamster" were selected from "The kid was sorry to hear his pet had a hamster rash." For subjects who received the former sentence, "child" and "cat" were targets and "kid" and "hamster" were foils. For subjects who received the latter sentence, foils and targets were reversed. Thus, all subjects received the same set of recognition items.

Following the recognition test, subjects were given 2 minutes to provide definitions for nine non-predicating combinations. The first item was a filler and was not analyzed. The remaining eight items repeated the noun from the combination included in the eight study sentences. After completing the definition task, the cycle repeated with a new set of study sentences.

The results of primary interest are the definitions. Before presenting the general findings, it is instructive to examine the findings for our example, "horse rash":

	Cause	Locative
Cat rash	7	8
Hamster rash	2	13

Here, the question is how many subjects interpret this combination as a causal or a locative depending on the sentence they had studied. When subjects had studied a sentence containing "rash" used in combination as a causal (cat rash), they interpreted "horse rash" as a locative about half the time. In contrast, when they studied a sentence containing "rash" used as a locative (hamster rash), 13 out of 15 subjects interpreted "horse rash" as a locative. Overall, there was clearly a tendency to interpret "horse rash" as a locative, but this tendency was affected rather strongly by how the noun in the combination was used in the studied sentence.

Collapsed across items, the results show the same pattern. Several combinations were excluded either because subjects saw no ambiguity in them or because they interpreted them in idiosyncratic ways. For example, we did not include the results for "coal lamp" because no one interpreted this combination as a lamp made out of coal; all considered it a lamp that used coal for fuel. Similarly, we excluded "sugar chicken" because the diversity of interpretations provided suggested that "sugar chicken" was likely an anomalous phrase. Finally, we also excluded "silver bee" because virtually all subjects interpreted this combination as a predicating combination. They felt that a silver bee was a bee that is silver, not a bee that makes silver or a bee made of silver. I return to this last observation in the discussion.

The overall results are as follows, where one can see that the general predictions were upheld.

	Interpretation favored by S1	Interpretation favored by S2
Subjects saw S1	122	103
Subjects saw S2	90	141

When subjects studied a sentence that used a noun in a particular way, they tended to ascribe the same interpretation when given the same noun with a new adjective. To give a new example, when asked to interpret "sickness drops," subjects defined the phrase as "drops that cause sickness" more often when they had studied "death drops" earlier. Conversely, subjects more often interpreted "sickness drops" as "drops for sickness" when they had earlier studied "infection drops."

B. FLEXIBILITY IN ROLE SELECTION

These results suggest that the determination of the appropriate relation between two concepts used in combination is a flexible process. It is not the case that there is some canonical order in which all these relations are evaluated. This experiment demonstrates that prior context will affect the relation that is chosen.

It remains to be shown how this selection might occur. One possibility is that thematic roles may be activated by their prior exposure. Thus, for example, "The child was disappointed to hear she had a cat rash" may activate the causal role for "rash." It is important to note that we must assume that these activations are concept-specific, given the results of our experiment. There were too many priming sentences for it to be otherwise.

The fact that the causal role is active for "rash" will lead people to interpret "horse rash" in a similar manner. In some sense, this interpretation is a variant of encoding specificity theory (Tulving & Thomson, 1973; Light & Carter-Sobell, 1975) in that it picks out a particular sense of the meaning.[1] Just as studying "river bank" selects one sense of "bank," studying "cat rash" selects one role for "rash."

There are admittedly other interpretations. One could look upon these roles as schemata of a particular concept. One could also provide an interpretation in terms of semantic features. Roth and Shoben (1983) explore these explanations for how context may have its effect.

At present, we regard this experiment as a kind of priming study in which activation of a particular thematic role for a noun tends to make that role a more likely interpretation in a subsequent determination. From these preliminary results, it is not clear how this activation occurs or even whether activation is the proper metaphor to use. In any case, it does appear that particular thematic roles can indeed be primed. It is not clear just how far one can extend this analogy to priming as, for example, whether the cost–benefit strategy (Posner & Snyder, 1975) will prove fruitful.

IV.   Computation of Roles

I began this discussion with how one might determine the appropriate role. So far, I have shown that this determination is flexible and that an analogy strategy is viable. In some sense, this last experiment has provided subjects with an analogy for interpreting the critical combination. Thus, in determining the meaning of "horse rash," our subjects were given an analogy, either "cat rash" or "hamster rash." Our results certainly do not argue that people retrieve another combination in every case, but our findings do demonstrate that people can make use of such analogies.

My claim that people can use analogies does not necessarily mean that

---

[1] I thank Glenn Nakamura for pointing out this similarity to me.

people do not use abstract knowledge of the combining concepts. In the absence of an experimentally provided analogy, people may rely on their knowledge of particular terms. For example, people may know that a "horse N" is usually either a possessive (horse hair), a "for" relation (horse hay), or a locative (horse insect). Similarly they may know that "rash" is usually either a locative (leg rash) or a causal (heat rash) and thus may try the locative relation first. Christina Gagne and I are currently investigating this possibility.

V. Comprehension of Conceptual Combinations

Whether by analogy or by abstract knowledge of the components of the combination, people come up with a possible interpretation of the compound. Based on the post-hoc analysis of our first study, people then judge how well the interpretation fits the thematic role.

This account is far from a complete theory of how people comprehend non-predicating combinations. The empirical support for it is weak, and important questions remain unresolved. We must determine whether people can use abstract knowledge of the kinds of combinations concepts can enter into. Do the adjective and the noun exert equivalent levels of influence? Preliminary evidence that Gagne and I have collected suggest that the adjective has a disproportionate influence, although this conclusion should be considered speculative at present. We need far better evidence concerning the role of analogies in determining the roles to be selected. Are analogies used only when they are experimentally present, or are they also retrieved "on the fly" in the comprehension of everyday discourse? Finally, is it true that there is a comparison process in which people evaluate the interpretation against a default schematic representation of the role?

Finally, we should consider non-predicating combinations and predicating ones together and ask whether they should be considered separately or together. Given the relative complexity of non-predicating combinations, one might be tempted to think that in such cases comprehension will be quite different from the comprehension of predicating combinations. Recall that "silver bee" was universally interpreted by our subjects as "a bee that is silver" and not as "a bee that uses/makes silver." Although such a conclusion is tempting, there are several good reasons not to succumb to this temptation.

First, if we postulate a fundamental difference between the two types of combination, then we must introduce a mechanism by which one first determines which type of combination is present. One might first try a predicating interpretation and then search for a non-predicating one only if that fails. Such a mechanism seems an unlikely prerequisite to comprehension. It is certainly not intuitively obvious that one must reject the interpretation of "criminal laywer" as "a lawyer who is criminal" before arriving at the correct interpretation. Second, similar models of psychological processes have not fared too well. The comprehension of indirect requests, for example, was originally thought to require a determination of the implausibility of the literal meaning (Clark & Lucy, 1975). Subsequent work by Gibbs and his colleagues (Gibbs, 1984; Gibbs & Nayak, 1989) has shown that many indirect interpretations are reached as rapidly as literal ones.

Thus, it seems that a separation strategy is not a particularly good one. Instead, it may be useful to think of predicating combinations as just another kind of thematic role, an N that has attribute Adj. A thorough understanding of all these types of combinations will be a useful advance in our study of concepts and their use.

ACKNOWLEDGMENTS

Preparation of this article was supported in part by Grant BNS86-08215 from the National Science Foundation. I would like to give special thanks to Douglas Medin, with whom I collaborated on much of the research reported here. I am also grateful to Douglas Medin, Glenn Nakamura, and Roman Taraban for their comments on earlier drafts. Finally, I would like to thank Greg Murphy for much helpful discussion.

REFERENCES

Clark, H. H., & Lucy, P. (1975). Understanding what is meant from what is said: A study in conversationally conveyed requests. *Journal of Verbal Learning and Verbal Behavior, 14,* 56–72.

Collins, A., & Quillian, M. R. (1972). Experiments on semantic memory and language comprehension. In L. W. Gregg (Ed.), *Cognition and learning.* New York: Wiley.

Gibbs, R. (1984). Literal meaning and psychological theory. *Cognitive Science, 8,* 275–304.

Gibbs, R., & Nayak, N. (1989). Psycholinguistic studies on the syntactic behavior of idioms. *Cognitive Psychology, 21,* 100–138.

Gleitman, L. R., & Gleitman, H. (1970). *Phrase and paraphrase.* New York: Norton.

Kruschke, J. K. (1992). ALCOVE: An exemplar-based connectionist model of category learning. *Psychological Review, 99,* 22–44.

Levi, J. N. (1978). *The syntax and semantics of complex nominals.* New York: Academic Press.

Light, L. L., & Carter-Sobell, L. (1970). Effects of changed semantic context on recognition memory. *Journal of Verbal Learning and Verbal Behavior, 9,* 1–11.

Medin, D. L. (1989). Concepts and conceptual structure. *American Psychologist, 44,* 1469–1481.

Medin, D. L., & Shoben, E. J. (1988). Context and structure in conceptual combination. *Cognitive Psychology, 20,* 158–190.

Murphy, G. L. (1990). Noun phrase interpretation and conceptual combination. *Journal of Memory and Language, 29,* 259–288.

Murphy, G. L., & Medin, D. L. (1985). The role of theories in conceptual coherence. *Psychological Review, 92,* 289–316.

Nosofsky, R. (1991). Exemplars, prototypes, and similarity rules In A. Healy, S. Kosslyn, & R. Shiffrin (Eds.), *Essays in honor of W. K. Estes.* Hillsdale, NJ: Erlbaum.

Posner, M. I., & Snyder, C. R. R. (1975). Attention and cognitive control. In. R. L. Solso (Ed.), *Information processing and cognition: The Loyola symposium.* (pp. 55–85) Hillsdale, NJ: Lawrence Erlbaum Associates.

Roth, E. M., & Shoben, E. J. (1983). The effect of context on the structure of categories. *Cognitive Psychology, 15,* 346–378.

Smith, E. E., & Osherson, D. N. (1987). Compositionality and typicality. In S. Schifter & S. Steele (Eds.), *The second Arizona colloquium on cognitive science* (pp. 37–52). Tucson: University of Arizona Press.

Smith, E. E., Osherson, D., Rips, L. J., & Keane, M. (1988). Combining prototypes: A selective modification model. *Cognitive Science, 12,* 485–527.

Smith, E. E., Shoben, E. J., & Rips, L. J. (1974). Structure and process in semantic memory: A featural model for semantic decisions. *Psychological Review, 81,* 214–241.

Tulving, E., & Thomson, D. (1973). Encoding specificity and retrieval processes in episodic memory. *Psychological Review, 80,* 352–373.

Tversky, B., & Hemenway, K. (1984). Objects, parts, and categories. *Journal of Experimental Psychology: General, 113,* 169–193.

EXPLORING INFORMATION ABOUT CONCEPTS BY ASKING QUESTIONS

Arthur C. Graesser
Mark C. Langston
William B. Baggett

I. Introduction

Some of our knowledge about particular concepts is acquired by active inquiry in the form of question asking and answering. For example, suppose that a group of adults were having a conversation about music and someone mentioned the term *oboe*. Adults unacquainted with the concept of oboe might ask a series of questions in order to fill gaps in their knowledge base. They might begin by asking, "What does *oboe* mean?" "What does an oboe look like?" or "What does an oboe sound like?" The more knowledgeable adults might ask esoteric questions, such as "What causes an oboe to have such a nasal sound?" or "How can an oboe player prevent the sound from going flat?" The content and representation of a particular concept presumably is to some extent determined by active inquiry.

Active inquiry is manifested in a variety of behavioral and cognitive activities. The most obvious form of active inquiry consists of verbal question asking and answering. Search behavior is another obvious manifestation of active inquiry. When a person searches a house for a set of lost keys, for example, the underlying question that motivates the person's actions is, "Where are the keys?" The process of problem-solving may be construed as a form of inquiry in the sense that the problem-solver implic-

411

itly asks, "How do I accomplish a particular goal?" and attempts to answer such a question. Decision-making involves such questions as "Should I select *A* or *B*?" and "Should I do *A* or not do *A*?" Eye movements may be directed by such implicit questions as "What is located in region *R*?" and "Is *X* located at region *R*?" Although active inquiry has a variety of manifestations, our present concern is with the most obvious case, namely verbal question asking and answering.

The primary purpose of this article is to investigate the process of exploring information about concepts by asking questions and comprehending answers to the questions. We report a study in which college students used a hypertext computer environment to explore information about woodwind instruments. The software contained a "Point and Query" (P&Q) interface in which the student (1) points to a particular word or picture element on each computer screen, (2) points to a question on a menu of questions that are relevant to the element, and (3) reads the answer to the question (Graesser, Langston, & Lang, 1992). Thus, the student learned entirely by asking questions and interpreting answers. The questions on the question menu tapped different types of knowledge: taxonomic, definitional, sensory, spatial, procedural, and causal, as is discussed in the next section. We analyzed the types of questions and knowledge that the students selected when they explored the knowledge base. Their selection of questions was expected to vary systematically as a function of their purpose in acquiring information about woodwinds, their prior knowledge about music, and their exposure to the woodwind software. By examining their selection of questions, we could investigate the evolution of their knowledge about woodwinds.

The questions available to the students on the question menu critically depended on the focus element (i.e., the word or picture element on the screen that the subject pointed to) and those knowledge structures that underlie the focus element. For example, the focus element *embouchure* is embedded in a causal structure in addition to other types of structures; when the embouchure tightens on a reeded woodwind, the mouthpiece opening becomes smaller and the sound becomes more sharp (higher in pitch, as opposed to flat). The questions that are particularly important for causal structures are why, how, and what-if questions. Our working assumption was that questions and answers are intimately related to the particular types of knowledge structures associated with concepts. The questions that are central in one type of knowledge structure (e.g., causal) may not be particularly central in another type of knowledge structure (e.g., taxonomic or spatial knowledge). More generally, both questions and answers are systematically related to the content and organization of the knowledge structures underlying concepts.

The remainder of this article is organized into two major sections. Section II selectively reviews literature on the organization of knowledge and concepts. Section II also identifies how particular categories of question map systematically onto particular types of knowledge. Section III reports an empirical study of concept exploration with the P&Q software.

II.   Organization of Concepts, Knowledge, and Questions

Early theories of concepts and categories frequently attempted to explain how word concepts within a semantic field are interrelated (Collins & Quillian, 1969; Keil, 1981; Miller & Johnson-Laird, 1976; Norman & Rumelhart, 1975; Rosch, Mervis, Gray, Johnson, & Boyes-Braem, 1976; Smith, Shoben, & Rips, 1974). A semantic field is a cluster of word concepts that are highly related. For example, there is a semantic field for musical instruments, which are expressed as nouns (e.g., *saxophone*) or noun phrases (*alto saxophone*). Musical instruments are organized in a hierarchical taxonomic structure, with abstract musical instrument categories at the superordinate level (i.e., brass, woodwinds, strings, percussion), subclasses of instruments at the basic levels (saxophone, clarinet, oboe, flute, etc.), and particular types of instruments at the subordinate levels (Bower, 1972; Collins & Quillian, 1969; Graesser & Mandler, 1978; Mandler, 1967; Rosch et al., 1976). There is a semantic field for motion concepts, which are normally expressed as verbs (*flow*) or propositions (*the air flowed through the saxophone*). Motion concepts are probably not interrelated in a hierarchical fashion (Graesser, Hopkinson, & Schmid, 1987; Huttenlocher & Lui, 1979; Miller & Johnson-Laird, 1976). The concepts in many if not most semantic fields are probably not organized in a strict hierarchy, with sets of concepts at one level being a subset of concepts at superordinate levels. This is because a semantic field will drift from a strict hierarchy to the extent that the set of word concepts can be organized along multiple, uncorrelated dimensions, frames, and perspectives (Barsalou, 1992; Graesser & Clark, 1985; Norman & Rumelhart, 1975).

It is possibly a hopeless objective to arrive at an elegant explanation of how word concepts in a semantic field are organized. Humans are not in the practice of actively organizing word concepts per se, unless they are lexicographers, anthropologists, linguists, or investigators of concepts and categories. It is widely recognized that many concepts are not labeled with lexical items in a particular language and that the knowledge associated with a concept is best construed as being alinguistic. It is more appropriate to consider the organization of "conceptual fields" than linguistically based "semantic fields" in investigations of concepts and categories. The pressing theoretical issues focus on the representation and organization of concepts in a conceptual field.

Theorists have offered several proposals on how concepts in conceptual fields are packaged and organized in the cognitive system. According to a schema-theoretic view, humans are in the practice of comprehending the actions of agents, the events in the physical world, and the setting which provides a background for these experiences (Brewer & Nakamura, 1984; Bruner, 1986; Graesser & Nakamura, 1982; Mandler, 1984; Schank, 1986; Schank & Abelson, 1977). Bruner (1986) claims that humans are better equipped to handle this experiential "narrative" thought than to handle "paradigmatic" thought, that is, logic and formal semantic systems. A RESTAURANT schema, for example, would help organize thousands of experiences that an individual has had eating at a restaurant. The RESTAURANT schema contains a hodgepodge of information about the spatial setting, objects, props, character roles, goals, actions, norms, obligations, and so on. This RESTAURANT schema would functionally organize the following set of concepts: cook, plate, tip, eat, check, menu, customer, order, and egg. It should be noted that this ensemble of words would never be included in a single semantic field in traditional theories of semantics. Barsalou (1992) has recently proposed that "frames" provide the fundamental representation of knowledge in human cognition. Unlike previous frame-based theories which assume that frames are rigid configurations of independent attributes (e.g., Minsky, 1975), Barsalou proposes that frames are dynamic relational structures whose form is flexible and context-dependent.

Perhaps it is not essential that a theory of concepts and categories explain how concepts in a conceptual field are interrelated. Instead, a theory might concentrate entirely on the internal representation of particular concepts rather than on meaningful relationships between concepts. For example, it has been proposed that a concept is represented as a set of necessary and jointly sufficient features (i.e., the classical definition of a concept), as a set of typical features (Estes, 1991; Smith et al., 1974), as a large set of particular exemplars (Medin & Schaffer, 1978; Smith & Medin, 1981), as one or a small set of prototypes (Posner & Keele, 1968; Rosch et al., 1976), or as a set of weights in a connectionist network (Kruschke, 1991; Rumelhart, Hinton, & Williams, 1986). Nevertheless, there is either a direct or an indirect concern with relations between concepts as soon as one aspires to explain how concepts are learned, what features a concept possesses, how features are correlated, or why an exemplar is a member of one concept rather than another (Barsalou, 1992; Fisher, Pazzani, & Langley, 1991; Murphy & Medin, 1985). For example, when we say that a bass saxophone is large, we are saying that bass saxophones are larger than a contrast set of saxophones. When we say that the feature "X is large" is correlated with the feature "X has a low pitch," we compare four sets of actual or potential concepts: large instruments with low pitch, large instruments with high pitch, small instruments with low pitch, and small instruments with high pitch. Alternatively, there is a "theory" (i.e., an organized conceptual structure) which explains the causal relationship between instrument size and pitch (Medin & Ortony, 1989; Mooney, 1990; Murphy & Medin, 1985; Wiesniewski & Medin, 1991). An adequate account of concept representation must at some point address meaningful relationships between concepts.

All theories of concepts and categories accept the incontrovertible claim that the knowledge is multifacited. For the purposes of this article, we assume that concepts, categories, and schemata are all amalgamations of the following types of knowledge, or what some have called "viewpoints" (Graesser & Clark, 1985; Souther, Acker, Lester, & Porter, 1989; Stevens, Collins, & Goldin, 1982).

1. *Taxonomic knowledge.* This includes taxonomic hierarchies and definitions of concepts.
2. *Spatial composition.* This is the spatial layout of objects, parts, and features of parts.
3. *Sensory information.* This includes visual, auditory, kinesthetic, and other modalities.
4. *Procedural knowledge.* This embodies the actions, plans, and goal structures of agents.
5. *Causal knowledge.* This embodies causal networks of events and states in technological, biological, and physical systems.

These types of knowledge are tightly integrated with each other in the sense that they mutually constrain each other and that there are mappings between the elements/features of the different types of knowledge.

Traditional research in the concept and category literature has normally emphasized taxonomic knowledge rather than the other types of knowledge. The idea of including more knowledge in concepts has frequently been discussed (Barsalou, 1992; Graesser & Clark, 1985; Malt & Smith, 1984; Smith & Medin, 1981) but has stimulated comparatively little empirical work. We adopt the theoretical perspective that a concept is a rich, multifaceted knowledge structure. Moreover, a subset of this knowledge is acquired through question asking, question answering, and other forms of active inquiry. In order to illustrate the five types of knowledge, consider the semantic field of woodwind instruments in Fig. 1. There is a hierarchical taxonomic structure that contrasts air reed and mechanical reed instru-

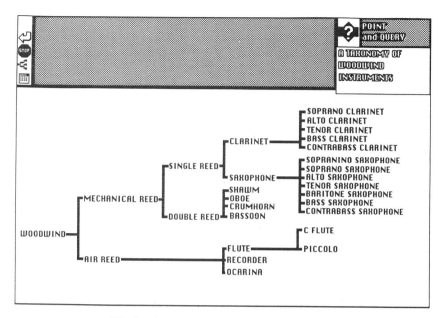

Fig. 1.   A taxonomy of woodwind instruments.

ments at the highest, most abstract level; the terminal concepts are at the lowest level in the hierarchy, such as alto, tenor, and baritone saxophones. The taxomonic knowledge also includes the definitions of terms that are associated with woodwind instruments, such as *reed, scale, key, embouchure,* and *vibrato.* Spatial composition specifies that a particular component contains subcomponents (e.g., a mouthpiece contains a reed and a ligature), that a component is connected to another component (the ligature is clamped to the reed), and that there are spatial relations between parts of an instrument (e.g., the neck is between the mouthpiece and the tube). Sensory information includes the sound characteristics of each instrument and its visual attributes. For example, a flute has a pure sound that is comparatively high in pitch. Procedural knowledge specifies how a person assembles, holds, and plays the instrument. Causal knowledge specifies how air flows through the player's mouth and embouchure, continues through the instrument, gets modified by the size of the chamber and the holes, and produces a sound with a particular pitch, intensity, quality, and duration.

There are systematic relationships between these five types of knowledge. For example, Tversky and Hemenway (1984) have discussed how the spatial composition of the parts of objects are systematically related to concepts in an object taxonomy. Specifically, the basic level objects in a taxonomy are at the highest level of abstraction such that the entities share common parts (e.g., flutes have common parts whereas woodwinds do not). Similarly, there are systematic relationships between other types of knowledge. The size of the instrument (spatial or visual information) constrains how it is played (procedural knowledge); a soprano saxophone is held by the player with two hands whereas a bass saxophone rests on a stand. A flute has a pure sound (sensory information) which is caused by the acoustics of the mouthpiece on air reeds (causal knowledge). It would be impossible to have a large woodwind instrument produce a high-pitched sound.

When people learn a new conceptual field, such as that of woodwind instruments, they sample and integrate the information from these viewpoints. We believe that the representation and organization of concepts are to some extent a product of exploratory processes during learning. The active exploratory processes may be manifested in several ways, including question asking and answering, experimentation by manipulating the world, and observational analyses. If our assumption is correct, then some serious effort should be devoted to investigating the process of exploring knowledge within a conceptual field. For example, if adults never explore the causal knowledge that explains the operation of instruments, then we would not expect them to correlate features of the mouthpiece and properties of the sound (e.g., air reeds are correlated with pure sounds).

Graesser, Person, and Huber (1992) developed a system of classifying questions on the basis of the content of the information sought and the type of knowledge under consideration. They identified 18 categories of questions. Some of these question categories elicit short answers. For example, an appropriate answer to a *verification* question is "yes," "no," or "maybe" (e.g., Is a saxophone made of silver?). *Concept completion* questions inquire about the referent of a noun-phrase (e.g., Who? What? Where? When?). *Feature specification* questions inquire about the attributes of an entity (e.g., What are the properties of X?).

Some question categories invite lengthy answers of a sentence or paragraph. For example, a *causal antecedent* question requires an answer that traces the causal chain of events and enabling states that produce the queried event. Answers to a *causal consequence* question trace the causal chain of events that unfold into the future. Answers to *instrumental-procedural* questions specify the instrument, resource, or plan that allows an agent to accomplish a goal (i.e., How does an agent perform action A?); in contrast, a *goal orientation* question elicits the motives behind an agent's action (i.e., Why does an agent perform action A?). Answers to *definitional* questions have a genus-differentiae frame, which is adopted in most dictionaries. This includes (1) the superclass of the concept defined and (2) properties that distinguish the concept from its contrast concepts.

The question categories in the Graesser, Person, and Huber scheme map systematically onto the five types of knowledge that were discussed earlier (taxonomic, spatial, sensory, procedural, and causal). Instead of presenting the complete set of mapping rules, this chapter focuses on ten questions that were asked in the P&Q study on woodwind instruments, which is reported in Section III. Table I presents these ten questions. For each question, we identify the theoretical question category in the Graesser-Person-Huber scheme and the type of knowledge structure(s) involved.

It is important to acknowledge that the mappings between question categories and types of knowledge should be viewed as probabilistic approximations rather than discrete mappings. Given that the types of knowledge are tightly integrated, as discussed above, an answer to a particular question can tap more types of knowledge than are specified in Table I. When asked ''What does *reed* mean?'' for example, the answer is supposed to include taxonomic and definitional knowledge according to Table I. However, the answer might refer to actions, events, and attributes that are part of procedural, causal, spatial, and sensory knowledge as well. Although the primary answer content is compatible with the mapping rules in Table I, there sometimes are indirect links to other types of knowledge.

TABLE I

Questions Associated with Types of Knowledge

Question	Theoretical question category	Type of knowledge
What does X mean?	Definition	Taxonomic hierarchy and definitions
What are the properties of X?	Feature specification	Taxonomic hierarchy
What are the types of X?	Concept completion	Taxonomic hierarchy
What does X look like?	Feature specification	Spatial composition, sensory
What does X sound like?	Feature specification	Sensory information
How does a person use/ play X?	Instrumental/procedural	Procedural knowledge
How does X affect sound?	Causal consequence	Causal
How can a person create X?	Causal antecedent	Causal
What causes X?	Causal antecedent	Causal
What are consequences of X?	Causal consequence	Causal

III.   An Exploratory Study of Concept Exploration

A.   OVERVIEW OF STUDY AND PREDICTIONS

This section reports a study that traced the exploratory patterns of college students when they learned about the woodwind instruments shown in Fig. 1.[1] The students learned entirely by asking questions and reading answers to questions displayed by the computer. The computer software was written in a hypertext environment with a P&Q interface (Graesser, Langston, & Lang, 1992). The computer recorded the questions that the students asked and the order of the questions. We also manipulated the goals of the learner and compared students with high versus low knowledge about music.

Several predictions may be made about the sampling of information when college students explore woodwind instruments. There is no empirical research that has investigated knowledge exploration for taxonomic-definitional, spatial, sensory, procedural, and causal knowledge in a rich domain such as woodwind instruments. Therefore, our predictions are motivated by theoretical considerations rather than an established body of empirical research.

One central prediction addressed the sampling of deep causal knowledge versus the comparatively superficial knowledge, that is, the taxonomic-definitional, sensory, spatial, and procedural knowledge. A "theory-based" approach to learning and categorization (Murphy & Medin, 1985) emphasizes the important role of the learner's prior knowledge in the processing of concepts and categories, unlike the more traditional similarity-based approaches (Estes, 1991; Rosch et al., 1976; Smith et al., 1974). Therefore, the amount of prior knowledge about a topic would be expected to influence the sampling of causal versus superficial knowledge. More specifically, the sampling of causal knowledge was predicted to increase as a function of the amount of prior knowledge about music. According to research in developmental psychology (Bransford, Arbitman-Smith, Stein, & Vye, 1985; Piaget, 1952) and the acquisition of knowledge about devices (Kieras & Bovair, 1984), the construction of deep mental models of causal systems occurs after the learner acquires the superficial knowledge involving taxonomies, the perceptual surfaces of objects, and the procedures for manipulating objects. According to some theories of expertise, there is a shift from surface features to more abstract, implicit principles as expertise develops (Chi, Feltovich, & Glaser, 1981; Chi, Glaser, & Farr, 1988). Abstract principles and mechanisms are part of any causal explanation that relates physical properties of an instrument to properties

---

[1] A more succinct version of this study was also reported in Langston and Graesser (1992).

of sound. Given our working assumption that question preferences will reflect the underlying process of knowledge acquisition, then we would predict that causal questions will increase with expertise on woodwind instruments and also with the time course of exploring knowledge about woodwinds during the learning session.

A second central prediction addressed the goals of the learner. We manipulated the goals of the learner in an effort to vary the extent to which the students asked questions about causal knowledge versus superficial knowledge. The learners' goals in a *Design Instrument* condition encouraged subjects to sample deep causal knowledge, whereas this causal knowledge was not needed in an *Assemble Band* condition. The details of these conditions are discussed later. If the goals of the learner have a substantial impact on exploratory processes, then subjects should explore more causal knowledge in the Design Instrument condition than in the Assemble Band condition; the opposite should be the case for the superficial knowledge. It should be noted that the goal of a learner can be construed as a higher level question. In the Design Instrument condition, the implicit question was, "How do I design an instrument that satisfies a particular set of constraints?"; in the Assemble Band condition, the question was, "How do I assemble a band that satisfies a particular set of constraints?"

There are several theories in the concept and category literature that have emphasized the importance of top-down, goal-directed processing (Barsalou, 1985, 1992; Wattenmaker, Dewey, Murphy, & Medin, 1986). Barsalou (1985) investigated the differences between common taxonomic categories (e.g., food, animals, sports) and goal-directed categories that are constructed top-down in a particular context (e.g., food to eat on a diet). The typicality of an exemplar for a category was quite different in the case of common taxonomic categories versus goal-directed categories. The typical exemplars for a goal-directed category satisfied an ideal constraint or dimension (e.g., 0 calories) that was associated with the goal (e.g., lose weight), but did match the central tendency of the category, (i.e., the prototypical food). In contrast, the typical exemplars of a common taxonomic category tended to match the central tendency prototype (and also the ideals associated with the category). These findings underscore the importance of goals and people's dynamic ability to construct concepts. Therefore, we would expect that the learners' goals would have a substantial impact on what information is sampled and what questions are asked when our subjects explored woodwind instruments.

We are uncertain about the impact of the goals of the learner on the time-course of exploring causal versus superficial knowledge within a learning session. There is some foundation for expecting a fixed order of knowledge that gets explored, such that the superficial knowledge precedes deep causal knowledge (Chi et al., 1981, 1988; Dillon, 1984; Kieras & Bovair, 1984). Dillon (1984) reviewed some theories that propose a canonical ordering of ideal research questions. Specifically, questions about the existence of a concept and the properties of a concept should precede questions about the correlation between properties or between events; after establishing a correlation between properties or between events, one can inquire whether there is a causal relationship. On a more intuitive level, we would expect a person to become familiar with the meaning of the terms and the physical features of a system before embarking on causal mechanisms that explain the operation of the system. That is, a person would identify the physical components of a device and would learn how to operate its controls before figuring out how the device worked. If there is a canonical ordering of knowledge exploration, then one would expect the superficial, taxonomic-definitional information to be sampled before causal information, regardless of the goals of the learner. On the other hand, there may be a more flexible ordering of knowledge exploration that directly corresponds to the learner's goals.

B. METHOD

1. Subjects

The subjects were 32 undergraduate students at Memphis State University who participated to fulfill a psychology course requirement. We screened the subjects so that half the subjects had low knowledge of music and half had comparatively high knowledge. Those with high knowledge rated themselves as having moderate to high knowledge on a 6-point scale and also played an instrument. Those with low knowledge did not play any instrument and rated themselves as having low knowledge.

2. Computer Software and P&Q Interface

The computer software on woodwind instruments consisted of a hypertext system with a P&Q interface. The computer was a Macintosh II microcomputer. There were approximately 500 "cards" (i.e., screen displays) in the hypertext system. These cards included a woodwind taxonomy card (see Fig. 1), an air flow diagram card (Fig. 2), and answers to questions that could potentially be asked by the subjects. Thus, the organization of the database centered around answers to questions and was seeded by the two pivotal cards shown in Figs. 1 and 2.

There were four major windows on each screen display, as illustrated in Fig. 3. These windows included a content window, a question window, a

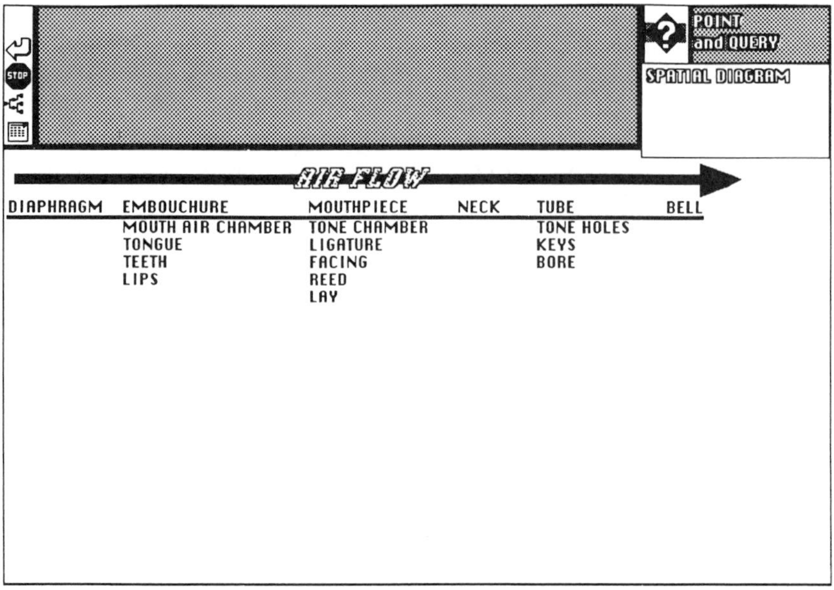

Fig. 2.   An air flow diagram that traces sound production in woodwind instruments.

function window, and a context window. The *content window* was the bottom 80% of the screen and displayed either the answer to a question, the woodwind taxonomy, or the air flow diagram. The subject pointed to an element in the content window in order to declare which word or picture element was to be queried. The subject physically pointed with a mouse; that is, the subject moved the cursor on the screen by mechanically moving the mouse on the mouse pad and declared the element by clicking the mouse. Any word in capital letters could be queried. The computer did not respond when the user pointed to a word in small letters. In the Fig. 3 example, the subject was curious about the word REED so he pointed to this word element.

The *question window* was a menu of questions presented at the top center of the screen display. The questions were presented in two columns and included the ten types of questions presented in Table I. The order and spatial layout of the ten types of questions was always the same across screen displays. The computer varied the subset of questions displayed on the menu according to the queried content element. For example, three questions were relevant to the word REED: "What does X mean?" "How does X affect sound?" and "What does X look like?" The set of questions presented in the question menu was based on theoretical considerations,

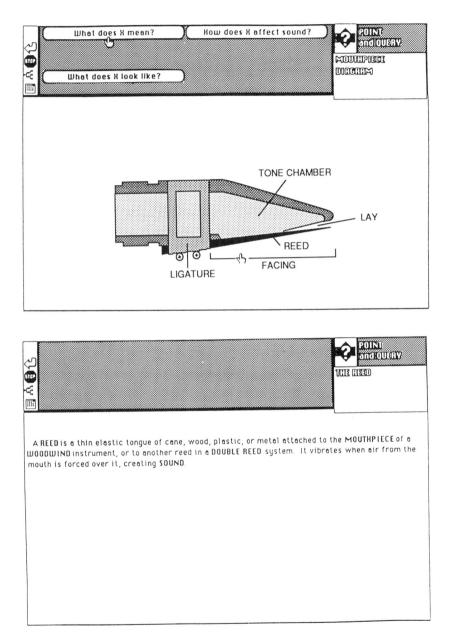

Fig. 3.   Computer displays that illustrate the Point and Query (P&Q) interface.

which are discussed later. In the example in Fig. 3, the subject pointed to the question "What does X mean?" by manipulating the mouse. The answer to the question "What does *reed* mean?" was presented in the content window of the subsequent display.

The *function window* displayed five symbols that referred to special-purpose functions. These included: (1) getting help; (2) backing up one display, which could be applied recursively; (3) stopping the session; (4) jumping to the woodwind taxonomy (see Fig. 1); and (5) jumping to the air flow diagram (see Fig. 2). The subjects were instructed how to use these functions at the beginning of the session.

The *context window* identified the P&Q software and presented a description that referred to the current card. This was the least informative window from the subject's point of view.

The success of the P&Q interface obviously depends on both the answers to the questions and the questions presented in the question window. The question options and the answers to the questions were formulated on the basis of a psychological theory of question answering, called QUEST (Graesser & Franklin, 1990; Graesser & Hemphill, 1991; Graesser, Lang, & Roberts, 1991). This theory has similarities to previous symbolic models of question answering in artificial intelligence (Allen, 1983; Lehnert, 1978; Schank & Abelson, 1977; Souther et al., 1989). Notably, these models assume that text and world knowledge are organized in the form of structured databases containing informational nodes and associative, labeled links between nodes. Question answering procedures access these information sources and search through the structures systematically by traversing some paths of nodes and links, but not others. Unlike the models of question answering in artificial intelligence, however, the question answering procedures of QUEST have been tested on human subjects and validated to some extent.

QUEST handles a broad diversity of questions in the context of taxonomic, spatial, causal, and procedural knowledge. Good questions vary among these types of knowledge structures (see Table I). For example, why, how, what-if, and consequence questions are natural questions in the context of causal and procedural knowledge but comparatively uninformative questions in the context of taxonomic, spatial, and sensory knowledge. In contrast, the good questions for taxonomic structures are "What does X mean?" "What are the types of X?" and "What are the properties of X?" The question options in the question window depended on the type of knowledge structure (or structures) associated with the queried content element, as shown in Table I. Suppose that the learner pointed to content element X and there was informative causal and procedural knowledge associated with X; then the question categories associated with causal and procedural knowledge would be presented in the question window (i.e., question categories 6–10 in Table I). If an answer to a question was trivial or uninformative, then the question option was not displayed. In summary, the questions in the question window were based on (1) the QUEST model of question answering; (2) informative types of knowledge structures associated with the queried content element; (3) the good questions that are associated with the type of knowledge structure, as declared in Table I; and (d) the extent to which there would be an informative answer to a question.

It is important to acknowledge that there are some inherent limitations with the P&Q software that we developed. One limitation is that the menu of question options could not handle all the questions that individuals might ask while learning about woodwind instruments. A learner might ask a question about the history of woodwind instruments, yet history was outside the scope of the content covered. A learner might pose a question in a question category that was not on the menu, such as a comparison question (e.g., How is an oboe different from a clarinet?). Our hope was that our version of the P&Q software in the present study would handle most of the questions that learners would ask, but it is an empirical question exactly what percentage of the learners' questions was available on the question menus. In principle, the P&Q software could be augmented to handle an increasing percentage of learner questions. A second limitation with the P&Q software is that it involves the *selection* of a question from a set of question options rather than the *generation* of a question without external prompts. We are uncertain about the extent to which the process of question selection is similar to the process of question generation. Our working assumption is that there is some overlap between these two processes.

The answers to most of the questions were formulated according to QUEST's strategies of answering questions. There is a unique strategy for each question category that operates on knowledge structures. Consider definitional questions in the context of taxonomic hierarchies, namely, "What does X mean?" An answer is produced by a "genus-differentiae" strategy which includes (1) the superclass of X and (2) properties of X that distinguish X from its contrast concepts, that is, the concepts that have the same superclass as X. For example, the definition for an alto saxophone is "a saxophone of medium size that is in the key of E-flat." In this case, the superclass is "saxophone," whereas the conjoint features of [medium size, key of E-flat] uniquely distinguish the alto saxophone from other types of saxophones.

The question answering strategies of other question categories are quite different from that of definitional questions. The question answering strategy for causal antecedent questions taps causal networks and produce antecedent events and enabling states that explain a queried event. When asked "What causes vibrato to occur in a saxophone?" an appropriate answer would be, "As air flows through the mouthpiece, the player alternates between having a tight and loose embouchure." Answers to question categories 7 and 10 in Table I tap causal consequences of an action or event. The answers to instrumental/procedural questions include (1) the plan that an agent executes while performing an intentional action and (2) an object, part, or resource that is needed to execute a plan. The question answering strategies for some types of questions were not handled by the original QUEST model but are quite obvious. For example, the answer to "What does X look like?" is a picture of X. The answer to "What does X sound like?" is a 10-second digitized recording of the actual instrument playing a scale.

3. Goals of Learner

We manipulated the goals of the learner so that half the subjects were expected to acquire deep causal knowledge of woodwind instruments and the other half could get by with superficial knowledge. The Design Instrument condition required deep causal knowledge, whereas the Assemble Band condition did not. In the Design Instrument condition the subjects were told their goal was to design a new instrument that had a deep, pure tone. A solution to this problem required them to know that large instruments produce deep tones (notes with low pitch or frequency), and that pure tones are produced by woodwinds with air reeds rather than single or double reeds. An ideal instrument would perhaps be a large flute, although it might be difficult for an average diaphragm to sustain an air flow in such an instrument. In any event, a solution to this problem required the subject to have knowledge about the causal relationships between physical features of instruments and the features of the sounds produced by instruments. The air flow diagram in Fig. 2 traces the flow of air as it begins in the player's diaphragm, passes through the embouchure and mouthpiece, continues through the instrument, and exits the bell. The sound gets modified systematically at each step in this process.

The subjects in the Assemble Band condition were instructed that they would be assembling a six-piece band with woodwinds that would play at a New Year's Eve party for 40-year-old yuppies. The subjects did not need a deep causal knowledge of woodwind instruments and sound characteristics in order to solve this problem. It would be satisfactory to have a superficial knowledge of what the instruments looked like, what they sounded like, and what their names were.

Half the 16 subjects with high music knowledge were randomly assigned to the Design Instrument condition and half to the Assemble Band condition. Similarly, 8 of the subjects with low music knowledge were in the Design Instrument condition and 8 were in the Assemble Band condition. Therefore, there was an orthogonal variation of prior music knowledge and learner goals.

4. Procedure

The subjects first completed a questionnaire that assessed their knowledge of music and computers. On the basis of this questionnaire, subjects were segregated into those subjects with high versus low music knowledge, as defined earlier. The experimenter described the goals of their task (i.e., Design Instrument vs. Assemble Band) and then gave a 5-minute demonstration of how to use the P&Q interface. They were instructed how to ask a question by pointing to a content element in the content window and then to a question in the question window. They were also instructed and shown how to use the five functions, help, back up one screen, stop session, jump to taxonomic structure, and jump to air flow diagram.

The subjects had 30 minutes to explore the database on woodwind instruments. They were told they could ask as many questions as they wanted, in whatever order the questions came to mind. The computer recorded the cards that the subject explored and the questions that were asked, in the order that the subject asked them. After the 30-minute learning session, the subjects completed the tasks that were assigned to them. That is, they wrote down a design of a new instrument or a band that was to be assembled for a party. They completed this task at their own pace. For the purposes of the present article, we were interested only in the questions that subjects asked during the 30-minute learning session.

C. Results and Discussion

In an initial analysis, we assessed the incidence of question asking behavior by simply computing the mean number of questions asked by the subjects during the 30-minute learning session. The subjects asked a mean of 75.6 questions per session in the Design Instrument condition and 59.9 questions in the Assemble Band condition. Therefore, the rate of asking questions in this P&Q interface was 135 questions per hour. This rate is about 7 times the rate of question asking during normal tutoring (Graesser, Person, & Huber, 1992) and 800 times the rate of student questions in a classroom setting. The high rate of question asking on the P&Q software is perhaps not surprising, because the only way a student could learn was to ask questions and interpret answers. Nevertheless, the P&Q software clearly has some promise in facilitating curiosity and question asking behavior during learning. The P&Q interface and other question-menu interfaces (Schank, Ferguson, Birnbaum, Barger, & Greising, 1991; Sebrechts & Swartz, 1991) remove many of the barriers of information exploration compared to the traditional methods of posing questions on computer.

In order to trace the evolution of knowledge throughout the course of exploration, we segregated the session into time blocks and the questions into knowledge categories. Each 30-minute session was segregated into three 10-minute time blocks, yielding time blocks 1, 2, and 3. We clustered the 10 question categories in Table I into four categories that tapped the following types of knowledge: taxonomic-definitional (question categories 1, 2, and 3 in Table I), sensory-spatial (categories 4 and 5), procedural (category 6), and causal (categories 7, 8, 9, and 10). It should be noted that we combined sensory and spatial knowledge because the question "What does X look like?" addressed both of these types of knowledge. We computed the base rate percentage of questions in these four knowledge categories when considering all possible cards, content elements, and unique questions in the P&Q system. These proportions were 35%, 9%, 1%, and 55% for taxonomic-definitional, sensory-spatial, procedural, and causal knowledge, respectively.

An ANOVA was performed on the frequencies of questions asked, using a mixed design with four independent variables: condition (Design Instrument vs. Assemble Band), prior experience (high vs. low music knowledge), time block (1, 2, or 3), and knowledge type (taxonomic-definitional, sensory-spatial, procedural, or causal). Condition and prior experience were between-subject variables, whereas time block and knowledge type involved repeated measure variables.

We were surprised to learn that prior experience had absolutely no impact on the exploration of knowledge. Prior experience did not have a significant main effect on question frequency and was not part of any significant statistical interaction. This outcome could be explained in a number of ways. Perhaps there was not a sensitive variation of music expertise. A sample of experienced woodwind players would presumably differ radically from the two groups of students in this study. Perhaps the knowledge about woodwind instruments in this software was too specialized to be covered by a college student with relatively high music knowledge. Perhaps the constraints of learner goals are extremely robust, to the extent of masking any effects of prior knowledge. For whatever reason, prior music knowledge had no impact on knowledge exploration. This outcome is incompatible with previous research on expertise (Chi et al., 1981, 1988) and our intuition that low-knowledge subjects would show a comparatively high frequency of taxonomic-definitional questions. Once again, however, the results might have been quite different if we had included a group of accomplished woodwind players.

Two of the three remaining main effects were statistically significant. The frequency of questions did not significantly vary as a function of time blocks, with means of 22.8, 23.4, and 21.2 questions in time blocks 1, 2, and 3, respectively. Therefore, the absolute volume of questions was approximately constant across the three 10-minute segments. More questions were asked in the Design Instrument Condition than in the Assemble Band condition, $F(1, 28) = 5.00$, $p < .05$. The number of questions per time block significantly differed among the four knowledge types, with means of 8.8, 5.3, 1.1, and 7.3 for taxonomic-definitional, sensory-spatial, procedural, and causal knowledge, respectively, $F(3, 84)$ ^{0}56 27.62, $p < .05$. However, this outcome is not particularly informative because the base rates were quite different among these four knowledge types. The empirical percentages were 39%, 24%, 5%, and 32%, whereas the base rates were 35%, 9%, 1%, and 55% for the four respective types of knowledge. Compared to the base rates, the subjects undersampled causal knowledge and oversampled the other three knowledge types (particularly the questions in the sensory category).

The most informative results involved interactions among condition, time block, and knowledge type. There was a significant three-way interaction among these three variables, $F(6, 168) = 2.89$, $p < .05$. The three two-way interactions were also statistically significant. Figure 4 plots the cell means that expose the three-way interaction. The figure and follow-up statistical analyses were compatible with the trends discussed below.

1. Taxonomic-Definitional Knowledge

The frequency of the taxonomic-definitional questions started out the same (i.e., block 1) in both the Design Instrument condition and the Assemble Band condition. Exploration of this knowledge subsequently decreased over time in the Design Instrument Condition but remained constant in the Assemble Band condition. It appears that taxonomic knowledge and definitions of terms needed to be established before learners could branch out into regions of knowledge that more directly addressed their goals. This outcome is compatible with the notion that there is a canonical order of asking questions during knowledge exploration: questions about taxonomic-definitional information precede questions about causal information. As discussed earlier, Dillon (1984) reviewed a number of theories that would predict this canonical ordering of questions

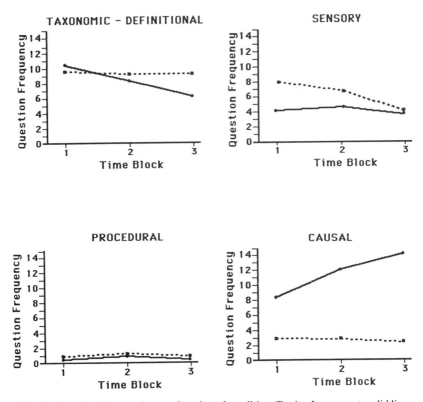

Fig. 4. Question frequencies as a function of condition (Design Instrument, solid line vs. Assemble Band, broken line), time block, and type of knowledge.

in the context of scientific research. This ordering is also compatible with some theories of the knowledge development and expertise (Chi et al., 1981; Kieras & Bovair, 1984).

2. Causal Knowledge

The frequency of causal questions was extremely high and increased over time in the Design Instrument condition. In contrast, the frequency was extremely low and constant in the Assemble Band condition. Therefore, the goals of the learner had a robust impact on the sampling of causal information. When deep causal knowledge was needed, as in the Design Instrument condition, then the learner explored causal information. This emphasis on causal knowledge was often at the expense of the taxonomic-definition, sensory-spatial, and procedural knowledge. On the other hand, if learners could rely on superficial knowledge in solving their problem, as in the Assemble Band condition, then exploration continued after block 1 by seeking additional taxonomic-definitional knowledge. Causal knowledge was indeed not explored very much unless the learner was forced to seek this knowledge in pursuit of a goal. It should be noted that the causal information was technical, so it is unlikely that a typical learner had already known this information.

The finding that deep causal knowledge was rarely sampled, unless the learner had a goal to sample such knowledge, has nontrivial implications for theories of concepts. Specifically, it would appear that there is a natural tendency for learners to rely on superficial knowledge during concept acquisition rather than constructing deep mental models of causal systems (see also Bransford et al., 1985; Brown et al., 1983; Graesser & Clark, 1985; Kieras & Bovair, 1984). This superficial knowledge includes the definitions of concepts, the perceptual surfaces of objects, and the procedures for manipulating objects. We found additional support for this claim when we collected data in a condition where learners were not given any specific goals prior to using the P&Q software; their data were perfectly consistent with the Assemble Band condition rather than the Design Instrument condition. These findings are compatible with the notion that deep causal explanations in biology, physical science, and technology are difficult for the cognitive system to assimilate, compared to explanations that appeal to the goals, plans, and activities of agents (see also Graesser & Hemphill, 1991). If this claim proves to be general, it would impose some constraints on the types of explanations that should be included in explanation-based theories of concept representation that have been proposed in the fields of machine learning, artificial intelligence, and cognitive science (Chi, Bassok, Lewis, Reimann, & Glaser, 1989; Mitchell, Kellar, & Kedar-Cabelli, 1986; Mooney, 1990; Schank, 1986).

3. Sensory-Spatial Knowledge

Once again, the goals of the learner influenced the information sampled during the session. The frequency of sensory and spatial questions was comparatively low and constant in the Design Instrument condition. In contrast, the frequency was high in the Assemble Band condition but decreased over time. The students in the Assemble Band condition wanted to find out what the instruments looked like and sounded like early in their exploration. This superficial visual and auditory information was important to the subjects who were trying to assemble a band, whereas deep causal knowledge was unimportant.

4. *Procedural Knowledge*

There was a floor effect in sampling this type of knowledge, so it was difficult to decipher trends. Subjects in the Assemble Band condition asked approximately twice as many questions in this category, as did subjects in the Design Instrument condition. No doubt, procedural knowledge plays a more prominent role in other tasks and knowledge domains, such as computer programming (Sebrechts & Swartz, 1991) and cooking (Norman & Rumelhart, 1975).

IV. Summary and Conclusions

This article has documented how individuals explore knowledge when they learn about woodwind instruments. The knowledge embodied in this conceptual field, as well as other conceptual fields, is extremely rich and multifaceted. The knowledge is an amalgamation of taxonomic, definitional, spatial, sensory, causal, and procedural information. We believe that an adequate theory of concepts and categories would need to capture this degree of richness and complexity. Knowledge exploration was measured by observing the questions that college students asked about woodwind instruments when they used the Point and Query interface.

The results of our study must be treated with some caution because we examined only one conceptual field (i.e., woodwind instruments) and we collected data with a new methodology (i.e., question asking with the P&Q software). Nevertheless, the results uncovered a number of thought-provoking findings. We found that exploration patterns were unaffected by the college students' prior knowledge of music. In contrast, there were dramatic changes in exploration as a function of the their goals and the time course of the learning session. We found that the learners initially sampled taxonomic knowledge and definitions of terms; this tendency prevailed even when the goals of the learner varied. In contrast, subsequent exploration patterns in the 30-minute session were substantially affected by the learners' goals. Specifically, deep causal knowledge was sampled extensively if the learners' task was to solve a deep causal problem; otherwise, the learner resorted to asking questions about the comparatively superficial knowledge: taxonomic, definitional, sensory, spatial, and procedural information. Once again, however, we would need to investigate a more diverse set of topics before we could be confident in the generality of these trends.

This article has demonstrated the value of the P&Q software and other "question menu" interfaces in investigating the process of exploring knowledge. It is extremely easy for the user to ask questions on these systems, unlike previous query-based interfaces on computers. The user simply points to an element on the computer screen and then to a question on the question menu. There are minimal technological and social barriers between an individual's curiosity and the posing of a question, at least compared to conventional computer interfaces, classroom settings, and tutoring settings. The P&Q software therefore has the potential to rekindle curiosity in even the passive learners.

ACKNOWLEDGMENTS

This research was funded by grants awarded to the first author by the Office of Naval Research (N00014-88-K-0110 and N00014-90-J-1492).

REFERENCES

Allen, J. (1983). Recognizing intentions from natural language utterances. In M. Brady & R. C. Berwick (Eds.), *Computational models of discourse* (pp.107–166). Cambridge, MA: MIT Press.

Barsalou, L. W. (1985). Ideals, central tendency, and frequency of instantiation as determinants of graded structure in categories. *Journal of Experimental Psychology: Learning, Memory, and Cognition, 11*, 629–654.

Barsalou, L. W. (1992). Frames, concepts, and conceptual fields. In E. Kittay & A. Lehrer (Eds.), *Frames, fields, and contrasts: New essays in semantic and lexical organization* (pp. 21–75). Hillsdale, NJ: Erlbaum.

Bower, G. H. (1972). A selective review of organizational factors in memory. In E. Tulving & W. Donaldson (Eds.), *Organization of memory* (pp. 93–137). New York: Academic Press.

Bransford, J. D., Arbitman-Smith, R., Stein., B. S. & Vye, N. J. (1985). Analysis— Improving thinking and learning skills: An analysis of three approaches. In S. F. Chipman, J. W. Segal, & R. Glaser (Eds.), *Thinking and learning skills: Vol. 1.* (pp. 133–206) Hillsdale, NJ: Erlbaum.

Brewer, W. F., & Nakamura, G. V. (1984). The nature and function of schemas. In R. S. Wyer and T. K. Srull (Eds.), *Handbook of social cognition* (pp. 119–160). Hillsdale, NJ: Erlbaum.

Brown, A. L. (1990). Domain-specific principles affect learning and transfer in children. *Cognitive Science, 14*, 107–133.

Brown, A. L., Bransford, J. D., Ferrara, R. A., & Campione, J. C. (1983). Learning, remembering, and understanding. In J. H. Flavell & E. M. Markman (Eds.), *Handbook of child psychology* (4th ed., vol. 3, *Cognitive development*, pp. 77–166). New York: Wiley.

Bruner, J. (1986). *Actual minds, possible worlds*. Cambridge, MA: Harvard University Press.

Chi, M., Bassok, M., Lewis, M., Reimann, P., & Glaser, R. (1989). Self-explanations: How students study and use examples in learning to solve problems. *Cognitive Science, 13*, 145–182.

Chi, M., Feltovich, P., & Glaser, R. (1981). Categorization and representation of physics problems by experts and novices. *Cognitive Science, 5*, 121–52.

Chi, M., Glaser, R., & Farr, M. (1988). *The nature of expertise*. Hillsdale, NJ: Erlbaum.

Collins, A. M., & Quillian, M. R. (1969). Retrieval from semantic memory. *Journal of Verbal Learning and Verbal Behavior, 8,* 240–247.

Dillon, J. T. (1984). The classification of research questions. *Review of Educational Research, 54,* 327–361.

Dillon, J. T. (1988). *Questioning and teaching: A manual of practice.* New York: Teachers College Press.

Estes, W. (1991). Cognitive architectures from the standpoint of an experimental psychologist. *Annual Review of Psychology, 42,* 196–212.

Fisher, D., Pazzani M., & Langley, P. (1991). *Computational approaches to concept formation.* San Mateo, CA: Morgan Kaufmann.

Graesser, A. C., & Clark, L. C. (1985). *Structures and procedures of implicit knowledge.* Norwood, NJ: Ablex.

Graesser, A. C., & Franklin, S. P. (1990). QUEST: A cognitive model of question answering. *Discourse Processes, 13,* 279–303.

Graesser, A. C. & Hemphill, D. (1991). Question answering in the context of scientific mechanisms. *Journal of Memory and Language, 30,* 186–209.

Graesser, A. C., Hopkinson, P., & Schmid, C. (1987). Differences in interconcept organization between nouns and verbs. *Journal of Memory and Language, 26,* 242–253.

Graesser, A. C., Lang, K. L., & Roberts, R. M. (1991). Question answering in the context of stories. *Journal of Experimental Psychology: General, 120,* 254–277.

Graesser, A. C., Langston, M., & Lang, K. L. (1992). Designing educnational software around questioning. *Journal of Artificial Intelligence in Education, 3,* 235–241.

Graesser, A. C., & Mandler, G. (1978). Limited processing capacity constrains the storage of unrelated sets of words and retrieval from natural categories. *Journal of Experimental Psychology: Human Learning and Memory, 4,* 86–100.

Graesser, A. C., & Nakamura, G. V. (1982). The impact of schemas on comprehension and memory. In G. H. Bower (Ed.), *The psychology of learning and motivation: Vol. 16,* pp. 60–109). New York: Academic Press.

Graesser, A. C., Person, N., & Huber, J. (1992). Mechanisms that generate questions. In T. Lauer, E. Peacock, & A. Graesser (Eds.), *Questions and information systems* (pp. 167–187). Hillsdale, NJ: Erlbaum.

Graesser, A. C., Person, N., & Huber, J. (1992). Question asking during tutoring and in the design of educational software. In M. Rabinowitz (Ed.), *Advances in cognition and instruction* (p. 229–252). Hillsdale, NJ: Erlbaum.

Huttenlocher, J., & Lui, F. (1979). The semantic organization of some simple nouns and verbs. *Journal of Verbal Learning and Verbal Behavior, 18,* 141–162.

Keil, F. C. (1981). Constraints on knowledge and cognitive development. *Psychological Review, 88,* 197–227.

Keil, F. C. (1989). *Concepts, kinds, and cognitive development.* Cambridge: MIT Press.

Kieras, D. E., & Bovair, S. (1984). The role of a mental model in learning to operate a device. *Cognitive Science, 8,* 255–274.

Kruschke, J. K. (1991). Dimensional attention learning in models of human categorization. *Proceedings of the Thirteenth Annual Conference of the Cognitive Science Society* (pp. 281–286). Hillsdale, NJ: Erlbaum.

Langston, M. C., & Graesser, A. C. (1992). Question asking during learning with a Point and Query interface. *Proceedings of the fourteenth annual conference of the Cognitive Science Society* (pp. 921–926). Hillsdale, NJ: Erlbaum.

Lehnert, W. G. (1978). *The process of question answering.* Hillsdale, NJ: Erlbaum.

Malt, B. C., & Smith, E. E. (1984). Reconstructive recall of linguistic style. *Journal of Verbal Learning and Verbal Behavior, 23,* 250–269.

Mandler, G. (1967). Organization and memory. In K. W. Spence and J. A. Spence (Eds.), *The psychology of learning and motivation: Vol. 1*, (pp. 327–372). New York: Academic Press.

Mandler, J. M. (1984). *Stories, scripts, and scenes: Aspects of schema theory.* Hillsdale, NJ: Erlbaum.

Medin, D. L., & Ortony, A. (1989). Psychological essentialism. In S. Vosniadou and A. Ortony (Eds.), *Similarity and analogical reasoning* (pp. 179–195). Cambridge, MA: Cambridge University Press.

Medin, D. L., & Schaeffer, M. M. (1978). Context theory of classification learning. *Psychological Review, 85*, 207–238.

Miller, G. A., & Johnson-Laird, P. N. (1976). *Language and perception.* Cambridge, MA: Harvard Univ. Press.

Minsky, M. (1975). A framework for representing knowledge. In P. H. Winston (Ed.), *The psychology of computer vision* (pp. 211–277). New York: McGraw-Hill.

Mitchell, T. M., Keller, R. M., & Kedar-Cabelli, S. T. (1986). Explanation-based generalization: A unifying view. *Machine Learning, 1*, 47–80.

Miyake, N., & Norman, D. A. (1979). To ask a question, one must know enough to know what is not known. *Journal of Verbal Learning and Verbal Behavior, 18*, 357–364.

Mooney, R. J. (1990). *A general explanation-based learning mechanism and its application to narrative understanding.* San Mateo, CA: Morgan Kaufman.

Murphy, G. L., & Medin, D. L. (1985). The role of theories in conceptual coherence. *Psychological Review, 92*, 289–316.

Nakamura, G. V., Graesser, A. C., Zimmerman, J. A., and Riha, J. (1985). Script processing in a natural situation. *Memory and Cognition, 13*, 140–144.

Nelson, K. (1986). Event knowledge and cognitive development. In K. Nelson (Ed.), *Event knowledge: Structure and function in development* (pp. 1–19). Hillsdale, NJ: Erlbaum.

Norman, D. A., & Rumelhart, D. E. (1975). *Explorations in cognition.* San Francisco: Freeman.

Piaget, J. (1952). *The origins of intelligence.* New York: International University Press.

Posner, M. I., & Keele, S. W. (1968). On the genesis of abstract ideas. *Journal of Experimental Psychology, 77*, 353–363.

Reisbeck, C. K. (1988). Are questions just functions calls? *Questioning Exchange, 2*, 17–24.

Rosch, E., & Mervis, C. (1975). Family resemblances: Studies in the internal structure of categories. *Cognitive Psychology, 7*, 573–605.

Rosch, E., & Mervis, C. (1978). Family resemblances: Studies in the internal structure of categories. *Cognitive Psychology, 7*, 573–605.

Rosch, E., Mervis, C., Gray W., Johnson, D., & Boyes-Braem, P. (1976). Basic objects in natural categories. *Cognitive Psychology, 8*, 382–439.

Rumelhart D. E., Hinton G. E., & Williams, R. J. (1986). Learning internal representations by error propagation. In D. E. Rumelhart & J. L. McClelland (Eds.), *Parallel distributed processing* (Vol. 1 *Foundatoins*, pp. 318–362). Cambridge, MA: MIT Press.

Rumelhart, D. E., & Ortony, A. (1977). The representation of knowledge in memory. In R. C. Anderson, R. J. Spiro, & W. E. Montague (Eds.) *Schooling and the acquisition of knowledge* (pp. 99–135). Hillsdale, NJ: Erlbaum.

Schank, R. C. (1986). *Explanations patterns: Understanding mechanically and creatively.* Hillsdale, NJ: Erlbaum.

Schank, R. C., & Abelson, R. (1977). *Scripts, plans, goals and understanding: An inquiry into human Knowledge structures.* Hillsdale, NJ: Erlbaum.

Schank, R., Ferguson, W., Birnbaum, L., Barger, J., & Greising, M. (1991). ASK TOM: an experimental interface for video case libraries. In the *Proceedings of the thirteenth annual conference of the Cognitive Science Society* (pp. 570–575). Hillsdale, NJ: Erlbaum.

Sebrechts, M. M., & Swartz, M. L. (1991). Question asking as a tool for novice computer skill acquisition. In S. Robertson (Ed.), *Proceedings of international conference on computer–human interaction* (pp. 293–297).

Smith, E. E., & Medin, D. L. (1981). *Categories and concepts.* Cambridge, MA: Harvard University Press.

Smith, E. E., Shoben, E. J., & Rips L. J. (1974). Structure and process in semantic memory: A feature model for semantic decisions. *Psychological Review, 81,* 214–241.

Souther, A., Acker, L., Lester, J., & Porter, B. (1989). Using view types to generate explanations in intelligent tutoring systems. *Proceedings of the eleventh annual conference of the Cognitive Science Society* (pp. 123–130). Hillsdale, NJ: Erlbaum.

Stevens, A., Collins, A., & Goldin, S. E. (1982). Misconceptions in students' understanding. In D. Sleeman & J. S. Brown (Eds.), *Intelligent tutoring systems* (pp. 13–24). New York: Academic Press.

Tversky, B., & Hemenway, K. (1984). Objects, parts, and categories. *Journal of Experimental Psychology: General, 113,* 169–193.

Wattenmaker, W. D., Dewey, G. I., Murphy, T. D., & Medin D. L. (1986). Linear separability and concept learning: Context, relational properties, and concept naturalness. *Cognitive Psychology, 18,* 158–194.

Wiesniewski, E. J., & Medin, D. L. (1991). Harpoons and long sticks: The interaction of theory and similarity in rule induction. In D. Fisher, M. Pazzani, & P. Langley. (1991) *Computational approaches to concept formation* (pp. 237–278). San Mateo, CA: Morgan Kaufmann.

HIDDEN KIND CLASSIFICATIONS

Edward Wilson Averill

I. Introduction

Science has much to say about the nature of many of the objects ordinary people think about, which raises a question about some everyday classifications. Suppose, regarding some ring, Sally says or thinks that the ring is gold. But a dispute arises over whether or not the ring is made of gold or fool's gold. So Sally, who has no gold expertise, takes the ring to an expert chemist. Either the expert uses the word "gold" to refer to whatever it is that Sally uses the word "gold" to refer to, or there is no point in Sally taking the ring to an expert because what Sally wants to know (whether or not the ring is gold in her sense of the word "gold") is not what the expert will tell her. So, since the expert uses the word "gold" to refer to stuff that has the atomic number of 79, Sally uses the word "gold" to refer to stuff that has the atomic number of 79. But Sally knows nothing about atomic theory. So how did she use the word "gold" to refer to stuff that has the atomic number of 79 when she first said or thought that the ring is gold?

Consider how the Sally Problem plays out on some traditional exemplar accounts of mental representation. Suppose Sally's thought is that the ring is like some exemplars of gold, where Sally grasps or understands the nature of this likeness. (The latter point is what makes this account traditional.) If rings made of fool's gold are like exemplars of gold, then there is no point in Sally taking the ring to an expert because the expert and Sally do not use the word "gold" to refer to the same sort of stuff. Such an

437

account of Sally's thought is implausible because it does not explain how Sally draws the distinction between gold and fool's gold. If rings made of fool's gold are not like exemplars of gold, because to be like an exemplar is to have the atomic structure of the exemplar, then Sally's thought is that the ring is like some exemplars of gold in atomic structure and the Sally Problem persists. A solution to the Sally Problem in terms of a traditional exemplar theory would say how rings made out of fool's gold are not like exemplars of gold, where being like an exemplar is something that Sally understands (and so it is not a matter of having a similar atomic structure). I doubt that a plausible solution exists along these lines.

More generally the following seems to hold: if the propositional content of mental representations must be constituted by concepts the representor grasps or understands (as it is in a traditional exemplar theory), then the Sally Problem is unsolvable. This will drive some to argue that the Sally Problem is not a genuine problem. My main contention is that the Sally Problem is genuine and has a solution, which rests on the work of Saul Kripke (1970) and Hilary Putnam (1970/1979a, 1975/1979b). However, if the Sally Problem has a solution, then given the above, the propositional content of one's own mental representations is not always constituted, or determined, by concepts one grasps! What else could the propositional content of one's thought be constituted by? This question is not hard just because it is difficult to distinguish true from false answers. It is also hard because, like many philosophical problems, it is difficult to distinguish intelligible answers from unintelligible ones. In this article, I do not cite experimental results to defend my version of the Kripke-Putnam solution to the Sally Problem. I try to clearly and coherently articulate the problem, its generalization, and the solution; and I mention ways in which the views set out here are related to empirical investigations and to other psychological theories. However, to get further into the Kripke-Putnam solution to the Sally Problem the problem needs to be sharpened.

II.   Sharpening the Sally Problem

Many terms, call them "general terms," can be truly predicated of some things, falsely predicated of other things, and (because of vagueness) can be neither truly nor falsely predicated of still other things. Examples of general terms include "gold," "red," "fox," "river," "heart," "atomic number of 8." (All kind terms are general terms, but not conversely. See Section III.) By definition, the things that a general term can be truly predicated of form the *reference class* of the term. Although there are two ways of specifying classes, by enumeration and by setting out necessary and sufficient conditions for class membership, it is not possible to specify the reference class of most general terms by enumeration. So, by definition, *the specification-condition of a general term* is the necessary and sufficient condition that an object must meet to be a member of the term's reference class. If the specification-condition for a term is not determinate for every object, the term is vague. For example, the specification-condition for the term "atomic number of 8" is having the atomic number of 8. Nitrogen, with the atomic number 7, can be transmuted into oxygen, which has the atomic number 8. When this transmutation takes place, there is a transition period during which the bombarded substance neither clearly has the atomic number of 8 nor clearly has the atomic number of 7. So the term "atomic number of 8" is, to some extent, vague. (Sober, 1980, p. 356.) Note also that many terms are ambiguous, because they are used in different contexts with different specification-conditions to pick out different reference classes. In some contexts "gold" is used to refer to a metal and in others to refer to a color. (The specification-condition of the term "yellow" is, of course, being yellow, but this does not spell out the specification-condition for "yellow" in a clarifying way.)

Here are some examples of the distinction between the specification-condition of a term and the reference class of a term. The reference class of the word "dog" changes from day to day as new dogs are born and old dogs die, but the specification-condition for "dog" does not change. If the specification-condition for "dog" changed, it would change because the use of the word "dog" in English changed. The reference class of a term will, in general, be different in different possible worlds. The reference class of the term "yellow" in the actual world includes my dog Fido. In possible worlds where Fido does not exist, Fido is not part of the reference class of "yellow"; and in possible worlds where Fido is black, Fido is not part of the reference class of "yellow." In these examples the reference class of "yellow" is different in different possible worlds (because what "yellow" can be truly predicated of changes), but the specification-condition of "yellow" does not change in these possible worlds. In short, the specification-condition of "yellow" (however that is to be spelled out) generates different reference classes in different possible worlds.

Any statement, whose propositional content is that some specific object is a *G,* where "*G*" is a general term, is true if and only if the object meets the *G* specification-condition. This connection between truth and specification-conditions can be extended from general terms to concepts, and from statements to thoughts. The concepts considered here are specification-conditions that could be, but need not be, the specification-condition of a general term. Necessarily, two general terms express the same concept if and only if their specification-condition is the same (making, in each possible world, their reference class identical). Presumably the term "dog," as it is used in English, and "chien," as it is used in French, express the same concept. (Note that "red" is primarily used as an adjective, "gold" as a mass noun, and "fox" as a count noun. So neither the concept nor the reference class associated with a general term determines the entire use of the term; see Averill, 1980.) If a person can sort Xs from non-Xs, then that person has (grasps, understands) the X concept (and thus the X specification-condition); but this classifier may not know a term that expresses the X concept or be able to explicate the specification-condition of the X concept. Here is the point. With thoughts, as with statements, there is a logical connection between specification-conditions, or concepts, and truth: a thought, whose propositional content is that some specific object instantiates some specific concept, is true if and only if the object instantiates the specification-condition of the concept.[1]

Before returning to the Sally Problem, I consider how this account of concepts is related to some accounts of concepts to be found in the literature. Smith and Medin (1981, pp. 1–2) say that the *classical* view of concepts "held that all instances of a concept shared common properties, and that these common properties were necessary and sufficient to define the concept." Perhaps the classical view can be interpreted as a metaphysical claim about a connection between an abstract world, which includes concepts and properties, and the concrete world of the things we perceive. Here, however, the classical view is interpreted as a claim about some of our common beliefs concerning the connection between our language (or thought) and the world. As such the classical view is an empirical thesis. In the account of general terms developed above I appealed to the reader's intuitions concerning the connection between language and the world, which makes sense on the second interpretation but not on the first.

Clearly, different versions of the classical view can be generated by adding to the Smith and Medin definition stipulations on what counts as a property. The notion of specification-condition used above is such a version of the classical view, but to get to this version two stipulations on properties will have to be added to the Smith and Medin definition. First, the conditions an object must meet to be an instance of a specification-condition can include much that might not be considered the having of a property. So "property" in the Smith and Medin definition must be understood very broadly to include, for example, disjunctive properties, dispositional properties, and participation in events or facts. The second qualification is much more subtle, and to bring out this point I begin by

---

[1] Quine (1960, p. 145) distinguishes opaque from transparent thoughts. Here all thoughts are construed opaquely.

qualifying the Smith and Medin definition in a way that generates a version of the classical view, call it the *classical-I view,* which I do not accept.

To get the classical-I view of concepts, add to the Smith and Medin definition the following metaphysical thesis (or, more accurately, think of the following as a commonly held metaphysical belief): for any property, and for any object, the object either has or fails to have the property. Let the *classical-II view* of concepts be the negative claim that this metaphysical thesis is false. Five paragraphs back, the concept having-the-atomic-number-of-8 was used to illustrate vagueness. On the classical-I view, a substance either meets this specification-condition or it does not. Suppose that scientists cannot tell if a particular substance undergoing transmutation really has the atomic number of 8. On the classical-I view, the concept having-the-atomic-number-of-8 cannot be applied here, and so one who holds the classical-I view can claim that the concept having-the-atomic-number-of-8 is vague. Here vagueness comes in at the level of the application of the concept, and not at the level of the concept itself. By contrast with the classical-I view, in the example presented five paragraphs ago the specification-condition for having-the-atomic-number-of-8 is not vague because it cannot be applied; it is vague because the specification-condition itself is vague. The difference is this: on the classical-I view, at all times the object undergoing transmutation either has or fails to have the atomic number of 8, even if scientists cannot tell at every instance when this is the case; on the classical-II view, there are times when there is no fact that makes it either true or false that the object undergoing transmutation has the atomic number of 8. Switch the example to tadpoles becoming frogs, and consider an animal that has many of the features of a frog as well as many of the features of a tadpole. Is the animal a frog? (Or, to take a case that does not involve transmutation, consider whether a clock is a piece of furniture.) On the classical-I view this question has a yes-or-no answer (either the animal has the property of being a frog or it fails to have this property, either the clock is or is not a piece of furniture), even if we cannot determine the answer. I think that the classical-I view is very implausible as an account of what we commonly believe, because it implies that we commonly believe that the frog–tadpole distinction (or the furniture–nonfurniture distinction) is in some cases hidden, not only from us but from any imaginable investigation by any being. On the classical-II view supported here, the specification-condition for being a frog, insofar as it distinguishes frogs from tadpoles, is itself vague. Consequently, there is no fact about the world that determines whether or not the animal undergoing a transmutation is a frog. Those who adopt the classical-I view will feel that the classical-II view of specification-conditions is not really an account of the conditions needed to specify the reference classes of general terms, because the reference classes on the classical-II view are not well defined in the mathematical sense of "class" or "set" and therefore not really classes at all. Again, given the classical-I view, the problem with the classical-II view is that the specification-conditions for a specific concept do not determine for every object whether or not it is or is not in the reference class of the concept. (The driving intuition behind the classical-I view is this: the reference classes of concepts are classes in the mathematical sense of "class.") However, for the reason just stated about the hiddenness of the frog–tadpole distinction, I do not accept the metaphysical claim of the classical-I view concerning the connection between objects and properties. But what do I replace it with? What is a property (i.e., what is our common conception of a property), if it is not something that every object either has or fails to have? What is an indeterminate property? Is vagueness a matter of the way the world is, and not just a matter of the way our language is about the world? I do not have answers to these questions, and as far as I know there is no satisfactory account of properties and the connection between properties and objects. (These problems will drive some to give up an account of concepts in terms of necessary and sufficient conditions, and try for a probabilistic or an exemplar account of concepts. Some of the problems with such moves have been set out in Medin, 1989.) In summary, the view supported here is a classical-II version of the Smith and Medin definition of the classical view, but to fully develop this classical-II view more needs to be said (by others) about the notion of indeterminate specification-conditions.

The classical-II view supported here does not rule out an exemplar account of a concept. Given some exemplars of Xs, and an account of what it means to be similar to an X, the specification-condition for being an X can be set out. In Section IV, thesis (2) sets out the specification-condition for being gold in terms of exemplars. In practice it is usually very difficult to spell out an appropriate similarity relation on an exemplar account of a concept. (For more on how necessary and sufficient conditions can be set out in terms of exemplars, see Quine, 1969; Putnam, 1970/1979a, 1975/1979b; and Averill, 1992.)

Medin (1989, p. 1476) defines *psychological essentialism* as follows: "People act as if things (e.g. objects) have essences or underlying natures that make them the thing they are." Medin is careful to say that it is no part of psychological essentialism that a person must know, or indeed that anyone must know, the hidden essence of a thing for it to have an essence. I think that this view is correct and that it is the basis of the Sally Problem. If psychological essentialism is correct, then this problem arises: How can we refer to, think about, or mentally represent a hidden essence that we do not understand? The Sally Problem arises when some people, experts, understand a hidden essence but others do not. (The case where nobody understands a hidden essence is, in part, the problem of explaining how science gets off the ground, and is taken up in Section IV,A.) As I see things, the Sally Problem assumes psychological essentialism, and so this article can be regarded as a way of supporting psychological essentialism by showing how—in terms compatible with psychological essentialism—the Sally Problem can be solved. But I am getting ahead of myself.

The Sally Problem can be restated in the following way. Suppose Sally, and the expert she takes her ring to, use different specification-conditions for "gold," so they use the word "gold" to refer to different sorts of stuff. In this case what Sally wants to know about the ring is not the same as what the expert will find out about the ring, which is absurd. So Sally and the expert use the same specification-condition for "gold." The specification-condition the expert uses with "gold" is having the atomic number of 79. So Sally uses "gold" with this specification-condition. The problem is to show how it possible for Sally to think that the ring is gold, if she does not grasp the concept of gold. Again, the problem is to explain how, and in what sense, Sally can believe that the ring is gold, but not have any clear understanding of the conditions that would have to hold to make it true that the ring is gold.

If one assumes that both Sally and the expert use the word "gold" as a general term, the Sally Problem is hard to avoid. One might try holding that Sally uses "gold" as a meta-term, and not as a general term, to refer to whatever it is that experts, who use "gold" as a general term, call "gold." This implies that it is possible for experts to be wrong about what gold is (perhaps they think that copper is a form of gold), while Sally is right about what gold is. I do not think that such a view has much initial plausibility, but perhaps such an account of what "gold" refers to could be worked out. However, in this paper the Sally Problem is assumed to be a genuine problem.

Perhaps the following remarks give the flavor of the theory to be worked out here. A person can think that a ring is gold, even if the person only grasps (understands, knows) this much: the ring is gold, whatever kind that is. In one sense the thinker mentally represents the ring as gold, because that is the propositional content of her thought; but in another sense she does not mentally represent the ring as gold, because she does not fully grasp the propositional content of her own thought. But how can a thinker who does not know what gold is think about gold? This question is answered in Section IV,B. One implication for psychology is this: if partial graspings of concepts really occur, then this is a phenomenon that can be investigated by cognitive psychology.

The purpose of this article is to spell out how the Sally Problem should be generalized (e.g., why does the Sally Problem arise for gold things and not for yellow things?), as well as the Kripke-Putnam solution to that problem. Here it is maintained that the Sally problem arises with respect to certain classifications, hidden kind classifications. Section III sets out the nature of kinds and hidden kinds. The reason for developing the complex machinery of Section III—about kinds, hidden kinds, and easily observable properties—is to bring out the general features of the Sally Problem, so that we can see how and why similar problems arise in other situations. Sections IV–VI take up different sorts of hidden kinds. Section IV develops the solution to the Sally Problem and how the solution generalizes to physical kinds other than gold. More specifically, Section IV breaks down as follows: since an account of partial graspings of the concept of gold cannot be developed without an account of the full concept of gold, the concept of gold is developed in Section IV.A (the complex machinery of this section is due to the fact that gold is a hidden kind); Section IV.B takes up mental representations of gold, when the concept of gold is only partially grasped; Section IV.C shows that gold is a hidden kind; and the logical role of fool's gold in the Sally Problem is set out Section IV.D.

The position set out in Section IV is generalized to biological kinds in Section V, and to functional kinds in Section VI. One criticism of Kripke-Putnam (Dupré, 1981; Keil, 1989) holds that, if biological theory identifies biological kinds, they are not the sorts of kinds the Kripke-Putnam theory needs. Section V is an answer to this objection. Section VII takes up another sort of criticism of Kripke and Putnam that has to do with the role of impure kinds, and in that context develops the relation between subject and predicate reference in classifications. Unfortunately, there is not space enough to consider several other criticisms that have been made of the Kripke-Putnam theory (Smith & Medin, 1981).

III.   Kinds

A *kind* is a categorization of objects in terms of a causal role. Usually the causal role is set out in a scientific theory. (In the case of some functional kinds the causal role has to do with human intentions, so the causal role of such kinds does not involve much, if any, scientific theory.) In any case a kind concept presupposes that certain sorts of causal relations exist, and they will in general be different for different kinds. So in a possible world where the causal relations presupposed by a specific kind term do not hold, or only partially hold, the specification-condition of the kind term may not generate a reference class.

To get at the notion of a hidden kind consider the type–token distinction. This distinction is often applied to words: "cat" and "cat" count as two tokens of one word type. When applied to properties, a yellow sweater and a yellow car count as two tokens, or instances, of the property-type yellowness.[2] For many properties there is a distinction between easily observable tokens of the property and tokens of the property that are not easily observable. (Philosophers often distinguish between *determinable* properties—having a mass, having a shape, having a color—and *determinate* properties—having a mass of 3 grams, being square, being a specific shade of red; e.g., Bennett, 1972, p. 90. Here "property" always refers to determinate properties.) Easily observable tokens of a property are instances of a property that are easily observable to some ordinary humans under some ordinary conditions without the use of sophisticated tools.[3] The yellowness of my car is an easily observable instance of yellowness, but a yellow rock on a far-away planet is not an easily observable token of yellowness. If four atoms in an atomic lattice of an object are arranged in a square, then this particular token of squareness is not an easily observable token of squareness. By definition, a property-type is *easily observable* if and only if some of the tokens of the property-type are easily observable. So yellowness and squareness are easily observable properties; having a square atomic lattice and having the atomic number of 12 are not easily observable properties; and the definition of "easily observable property" is too vague to determine whether being a 64th of an inch in length is an easily observable property. By definition, the specification-condition of a hidden kind concept does not, by itself, logically or causally determine any of the easily observable properties of the members of its reference class; and the specification-condition of a hidden kind concept is not logically or causally determined by any combination of easily observable properties. It follows that *neither necessary nor sufficient conditions for being a hidden kind can be stated in terms of easily observable properties*. Both "yellow" and "square" are general terms, but neither expresses a hidden kind concept. Of course nothing said here is inconsistent with claims of this form: objects with such-and-such easily observable properties are likely to belong to such-and-such a hidden kind. Medin (1989, p. 1476) writes, "One of the things that theories do is to embody or provide causal linkages from

---

[2] In Averill (1992) it is argued that "*x* is red" expresses a three-way relation: *x* is red for such-and-such a population living in such-and-such an environment. In most contexts it is tacitly assumed that the population term is filled in with "the human population of the actual world" and the environmental term is filled with "the environment of the actual world." So in most contexts "red" functions as a property term.

[3] Here "human" and "condition" rigidly designate humans and conditions on earth as they now occur.

deeper properties to more superficial or surface properties." This point is not in doubt here. Eventually I want to consider the propositional content of Sally's thought that the ring is gold. Given the point italicized above (and that gold is a hidden kind), it is no part of this content that the ring is yellow. (Note that fool's gold is yellow and Sally is distinguishing between gold and fool's gold.) But Medin is also right to insist that being yellow is not just an arbitrary fact about gold. (More on the connection between yellowness and gold in Section IV.C–D.)

What is being proposed in the following pages is an account of how classification works with certain concepts, hidden kind concepts, that play a role in both ordinary language and in causal explanations. So this is not a complete account of classification. It is the hiddenness of hidden kinds, together with their role in complex causal explanations, that tends to put them beyond the conceptual reach of most people. Thus classifying an object as a member of a hidden kind by a nonexpert will raise a Sally-like problem.

IV. Physical Kinds

A. THE CONCEPT OF GOLD

Physical kinds are defined in terms of a metaphysical view about the composition of the objects we perceive about us. These objects have a microstructure. Let a microscopic property be any property that it is physically possible for a microscopic bit of microstructure to have, and which makes it physically possible, in virtue of having this property, for a microstructure with this property to causally interact with another microstructure. Given modern science, having a square atomic lattice is a microscopic property. Although "being square or having mass" is a property, a disjunctive property, it is not a microscopic property, because microstructures do not causally interact in virtue of disjunctive properties. Although being 6 feet tall is a property that some microstructures have, it is not a property that a microscopic bit of microstructure can have.

(1) A physical kind is defined in terms of a microscopic property: for a given microscopic property P, all and only the members of the P physical kind have a microstructure that instantiates P; and, if any member of the P kind is divided into parts by processes that only involve physical changes, then after the division both parts are members of the P kind.

Physical changes, unlike chemical or atomic changes, are changes that objects undergo that do not create or destroy physical kinds. So "physical kind'' and ''physical change'' are defined in terms of each other. This metaphysics has no empirical guts to it until experts decide that certain specific changes are physical changes and that certain specific objects compose a specific physical kind.

Objects made of H_2O form a physical kind; some are solids, others are liquids, and still others are gases. All microstructures containing a hydrogen atom form the hydrogen physical kind. Hydrogen gas, hydrogen sulfide, and H_2O are examples of this physical kind. The division condition of (1) does not allow a member of a physical kind to be a simple mixture of microstructures, such as air or muddy water. (More on impure physical kinds in Section VII.)

Given the metaphysical assumption that there are physical kinds, as set out in (1), how should investigators go about identifying them? If a set of objects have many of the same easily observable properties, and if they interact with many other objects in more or less the same way, then it is reasonable to conclude that the objects have a common underlying microstructure.[4] For example, there are many yellow, shiny, and malleable objects. Using these as paradigm cases, the investigators might take a stab at identifying a physical kind by defining the word ''gold'' as follows:

(2) Gold is a physical kind that all paradigm instances of gold instantiate but none of the paradigm instances of nongold instantiate. (So a necessary and sufficient condition for an object to be gold is that the object be a member of a certain physical kind, the physical kind common to all the paradigm instances of gold, but not to any of the paradigm instances of nongold.)

Thesis (2) presupposes that there is a physical kind, and thus a microscopic property, that is common to all the paradigm instances of gold but not to any paradigm instance of nongold. Here is the important point: if this presupposition is true, *even if no one knows whether or not this presupposition is true*, then (2) establishes by definition a specification-condition for ''gold.''

Experts try to pick the paradigm cases of (2) so that the presupposition of (2) holds. Hence the definition may be revised in the light of new findings by changing the paradigms. For example, not all instances of yellow, shiny, and malleable objects have the same melting point. This situation raises a question for the investigators: Does the difference in melting point show that, among the objects that are being taken as paradigm examples of gold, there are really two different physical kinds (gold and iron pyrites are

---

[4] Medin (1989, p. 1477) writes, ''Surface characteristics that are perceptually obvious or are readily produced on feature listing tasks may not so much constitute a core of a concept as point toward it.'' I am making a very similar point.

different physical kinds); or does the difference in melting point among the objects that are being taken as paradigm examples of gold only show that there are subkinds of the kind being investigated (gold has different isotopes)? In answering this question the investigators may change the definition of "gold" [i.e., (2)] by changing what counts as a paradigm instance of gold. Of course experts will sometimes disagree with each other on such issues.[5] [Putnam says, 1975/1979b, p. 250, that pure gold is almost white; copper gives gold its distinctive yellowish color. Since the paradigm instances of gold are yellow, how can the paradigm instances of (2) be paradigm instances of gold? This question is put off until Section VII, where impurities are considered.] Experts on physical kinds now think that the microscopic property that distinguishes gold is a type of atomic structure characterized by the atomic number of 79. [Assuming today's science, it follows that gold is stuff that has the atomic number of 79; but new science may show that today's science on this point is wrong. Perhaps the atomic theory is all wrong. In any case, (2) does not imply that gold is stuff that has the atomic number of 79. See Averill, 1982.] This amounts to the following identity claim:

(3)   The specification-condition for "gold," set out in (2), is identical to having the atomic number of 79.

Claim (3) implies that in any possible world the specification-condition set out in (2) and the specification-condition has-the-atomic-number-of-79 are equally well defined, and to the extent that they are defined, they sort things in the same way. So in any possible world, where physical kinds (of the sorts that occur in the actual world) enter into explanations of causal interactions (of the sorts that occur in the actual world), the reference class of "gold" is identical to the reference class of "has the atomic number of 79."[6] (Given the explanatory nature of physical kinds—see Section III—

---

[5] Paradigm examples of gold are metallic, solid at room temperature, yellow, malleable, and shiny. The last three are easily observable properties. Perhaps metal is a physical kind, and gold is a paradigm example of a metal. In this case it follows from the definition of "metal," but not from (2), that gold is a metal; and so there is not, and could not be, nonmetallic gold.

[6] When considering what "gold" refers to across physically possible worlds, we who speak English interpret (3) as follows: the word "gold" refers to the physical kind that all paradigm instances of gold (as they occur in the actual world) instantiate, but none of the paradigm instances of non-gold (as they occur in the actual world) instantiate. The people on Twin Earth (as described in Section IV,B), who do not speak English, have a different interpretation of (3). They substitute, for the above parenthetical expressions, expressions that have the force of "(as they occur on Twin Earth)."

there may not be a possible world where gold placed in *aqua regia* does not react with the *aqua regia*.)

The assumption that experts have established (3) implies the following:

(4)   A necessary and sufficient condition for stuff to be gold is that the stuff have the atomic number of 79.

To see the force of (4), suppose someone were to claim that they had found some green gold. (Pure gold can be a solid, liquid, or gas. There are different isotopes of gold. Since the atomic number of a lump of pure gold does not determine all the properties of the lump, the claim that there is green gold cannot be dismissed out of hand.) Clearly experts would want to know whether or not tests showed that this stuff had the atomic number of 79, because this would determine whether or not the stuff was gold. Given (4), this is because having the atomic number of 79 is sufficient for being gold. Similarly suppose someone found some object that was yellow, malleable, and shiny, and in any other way you wish had the easily observable properties of gold; and they found that the object did not have the atomic number of 79. Surely experts would say that the object was not gold, but fool's gold. Given (4), this is because having the atomic number is necessary for being gold. [Section VII takes up an objection to the necessary condition in (4).]

B.   Mentally Representing Gold

Regarding a particular ring, what does a person need to grasp about the concept of gold to classify the ring as gold? The classifications of three sorts of people will be considered; A-experts, who know (2), (3), and (4); B-experts, who know (2), but neither (3) nor (4); and nonexperts. Let each of these people think of a particular ring that it is gold. Given (2), (3), and (4), the propositional content of this thought, which is that the ring is gold, is true if and only if the ring is made of stuff that has the atomic number of 79. (See footnote 1, p. 440.)

An A-expert knows (grasps, understands) the specification-condition for gold. So the A-expert fully grasps the conditions that would make her thought, which is that the ring is gold, true.[7] Given (3), when an A-expert and a B-expert each think of a particular ring that it is gold, they are not using different conceptions of gold. If the difference between the A-

---

[7] Like the A-expert making gold classifications, we grasp the specification-condition of our yellow classifications; unlike the A-expert making gold classifications, most of us cannot explicate the specification-condition we use in making yellow classifications. See Averill (1992).

expert's and the B-expert's thought about the ring does not lie in the concepts they use, where does it lie? It lies in the extent to which they grasp the specification-condition, or concept, of gold. A B-expert does not fully grasp the specification-condition for gold, because, unlike A-experts, she does not know what it is about the microstructure of the paradigm examples of gold that distinguishes them from other physical kinds. Hence, when a B-expert thinks that some ring is gold, the B-expert does not fully grasp the conditions that would make the propositional content of her thought true; and this distinguishes the B-expert's thought from the A-expert's thought about the ring. Putnam's (1975/1979b) Twin Earth argument is a dramatic way of making this point.

Let Twin Earth be exactly similar to Earth, except that wherever gold occurs on Earth another physical kind, call it "tw-gold," occurs on Twin Earth that does not have the atomic number of 79 but has the xyz microstructure. (I am changing Putnam's example from water to gold.) Suppose further that tw-gold has all the easily observable properties of gold, and that tw-gold reacts, in many simple reactions, in the same way gold reacts. Finally suppose that the experts on Earth have only gotten as far as (2) in identifying gold, and so the experts on Twin Earth have only gotten as far as (2) in identifying tw-gold. The context in which the experts use "gold" is different on Earth and Twin Earth [because the paradigm cases of (2) are paradigms of gold on Earth and tw-gold on Twin Earth], and this difference affects what experts refer to by using the word "gold." On Earth B-experts use the word "gold" to refer to gold. So, when these Earth experts say of a particular ring "this is gold," the condition that would make their thought true is for the ring to be made of stuff that has the atomic number of 79. On Twin Earth the twins of Earth's B-experts use the word "gold" to refer to tw-gold. So, when these Twin Earth experts say of a particular ring "this is gold," the condition that would make their thought true is for the ring to be made of stuff that has the xyz microstructure. By hypothesis the internal states of the experts, including all brain states and all dispositions to behave, are exactly the same on Earth and Twin Earth. Here is the point: since what the experts on Earth and Twin Earth refer to by using "gold" is different (i.e., they are using "gold" with different specification-conditions), but their internal states are the same, their internal states do not include a full understanding of what they are using the word "gold" to refer to. So their internal states do not include a full grasp of the conditions that would make their thoughts true. Thus we again reach the conclusion reached in the previous paragraph: a B-expert does not fully grasp the conditions that would make the propositional content of her gold classifications true.

When a B-expert thinks of some ring that the ring is gold, then the condition that would make the propositional content of her thought true is that the ring is made of stuff that has the atomic number of 79. What a B-expert grasps of the propositional content of her own thought is something like this: this ring is gold, which is a physical kind common to the paradigm examples of gold but not to the paradigm examples of nongold (however that physical kind should be spelled out in terms of microstructure). Here the parentheses do not indicate a qualified conception of gold, but indicate the extent to which the concept of gold is grasped. The propositional content of the B-expert's thought that the ring is gold is not constituted by concepts that the B-expert fully grasps. The propositional content of this thought is constituted by a concept of gold, but which concept is that? The answer depends in part on how the presupposition of (2) is fulfilled; in the actual world the physical kind picked out by (2) is stuff with the atomic number of 79 rather than, say, *xyz*. The propositional content of the B-expert's thought that the ring is gold is constituted by a concept, whose specification-condition is having the atomic number of 79, that the B-expert does not fully grasp but that is still part of the B-expert's thought because of the way (2) determines the specification-condition of "gold." A cognitive psychologist investigating a B-expert with respect to the propositional content of the thought that the B-expert expresses by saying "the ring is gold" cannot fully determine the specification-condition of "gold" (the gold concept) that the B-expert is using by investigating the B-expert, because the B-expert does not fully grasp this concept. The B-expert does not fully grasp her own thought.

A similar account of how the thought of nonexperts can be about gold does not work, since nonexperts do not know what atomic theory is about [and so they do not understand (4)] and they do not know what counts as a paradigm case of gold [and so they do not understand (2)]. So what determines the concept that the nonexpert uses when she uses the word "gold"? Suppose the following: *After experts have identified gold, along the lines of either (2) or (4), knowledge of the identification spreads from experts to nonexperts, where this knowledge amounts to knowing the following: experts have identified some kind or other, which they call "gold."* This spread comes about because the experts talk about gold to their nonexpert friends. Based on this knowledge, nonexperts as well as experts come to believe that ascribing gold to an object entails that the object belongs to a kind. *If the above supposition holds for some nonexperts, then an ascription of gold to an object by such a nonexpert is true if and only if the object is made of stuff that has the atomic number of 79; and these nonexperts use "gold" with the same specification-condition that experts use with "gold."* (This is modified from Kripke, 1970, p. 91 and pp. 127–134, but all that is interesting about this suggestion comes from

Kripke.) The italicized sentences say that a sufficient condition for a nonexpert to use the word "gold" with the same specification-condition as the expert use of "gold" depends on two factors: a certain use of "gold" by nonexperts (this is captured in the entailment mentioned above), and a symbol-to-kind-connection (the use of the word "gold" to stand for a specific kind has spread from expert use to nonexpert use). Nonexperts believe that experts have identified some kind or other, which the experts call "gold"; but nonexperts may not know who the experts are, or how their nonexpert use of "gold" is dependent on the expert use of "gold" through the spread of knowledge.

Here are some consequences of the above claim. If a nonexpert thinks (in terms of the word "gold") that this ring is gold, and the above supposition holds, then the propositional content of this thought is that the ring is gold, and is true if and only if the ring is made of stuff that has the atomic number of 79. The content of the classification that is grasped by the nonexpert is this: this ring is gold (whatever kind that is). Again the parentheses are used to indicate, not a qualified conception of gold, but the extent to which the concept of gold is grasped. Like the B-expert's, the content of the nonexpert's classification is not fully grasped by the classifier. The combination of what the nonexpert grasps and the connection of her use of "gold" to gold determine the concepts that go to make up the propositional content of the nonexpert's thought. So the propositional content of the nonexpert's thought that the ring is gold is partly constituted by a concept that the nonexpert does not fully grasp, but which is part of the nonexpert's thought given that the supposition described in the preceding paragraph holds. A cognitive psychologist, investigating a nonexpert with respect to the propositional content of the thought that the nonexpert expresses by saying "the ring is gold," cannot fully determine the specification-condition of "gold" (the gold concept) that the nonexpert is using by investigating the nonexpert, because the nonexpert does not fully grasp this concept. The nonexpert does not fully grasp her own thought.

Smith and Medin (1981, p. 5) ask, "Do people have a mental representation that corresponds to a classical-view definition of the concept?" This question is much like the following: when nonexperts think about gold, do they have a mental representation of gold that corresponds to the concept of gold set out in (4)? There are two answers. Since the propositional content of the thought of the nonexpert is about gold, that is, stuff that has the atomic number of 79, there is a sense in which the nonexpert has a mental representation of gold that corresponds to the concept of gold set out in (4); the nonexpert's thought that a ring is gold is true if and only if the ring is made of stuff that has the atomic number of 79. However, since the propositional content of the thought of the nonexpert about gold is not fully grasped by the nonexpert, there is also a sense in which the nonexpert does not have a mental representation of gold that corresponds to the concept of gold set out in (4). Mental representations can be individuated by what they represent (or by their truth conditions)—in this sense all experts and nonexperts have the same mental representation when they think of a particular ring that it is gold (see footnote 1, p. 440). But mental representations can be individuated more finely by considering the extent of a subject's grasp of what her mental representations represent—in this sense the A-experts, the B-experts, and the nonexperts have different mental representations when they think about the ring. So the Smith and Medin question is really two different questions that have two different answers.

What about the nonexpert's evidence for the classification? A nonexpert may learn various facts about gold—gold objects are often yellow, shiny, and malleable, and gold is often used in jewelry—that she may use in identifying objects as gold. If the nonexpert is thinking that this ring is gold because a jeweler or her mother told her it was gold, then her evidence is an authority. In this case the nonexpert is not so much making a classification as repeating a classification made by someone else. If the nonexpert infers that the ring is gold, then, presumably, she does so because she thinks it is like examples of gold she has been shown (perhaps the ring is shiny and yellow) or that it has features that are commonly associated with gold (she saw it in a jewelry store). To make this point more clearly, switch the example to gallium. If a nonexpert has never seen any examples of gallium and knows no common features of gallium, like myself, then that person cannot have a basis for classifying an object as gallium. However, such a nonexpert can use the word "gallium" to refer to gallium in thought and speech. Indeed, I have just done so. The word "gallium" stands in a [baptismal, (2)-like] relation to gallium and in a certain (not purely cognitive) relation to myself. In virtue of these relations I can refer to gallium by using the word "gallium." But I cannot have evidence for the classification of an object as gallium without more knowledge about features associated with gallium. (Maybe I cannot even make an unjustified inference, if that inference is to be more than a wild guess, that an object is gallium without more knowledge about features associated with gallium. One would like to see more clearly what counts as an inference here.) In any case, the nonexpert's evidence for making a classification, the epistemology of (or inference to) the classification, is distinct from the propositional content of the classification.

As noted earlier, the account of mental representation set out here seems to have implications for cognitive psychology. For example, the task of representing a hidden kind is divided between a symbol-to-kind-connection (a connection between the symbol a person uses to mentally represent a hidden kind and the kind itself), and the aspect of the kind concept the person grasps. This division is weighted differently in the case of the B-expert and the nonexpert. Maybe such weights can be operationally defined and investigated. Indeed, a finer analysis than is given here would distinguish between the different extents to which nonexperts grasp atomic theory and thus the concept of gold.

C.   WHY IS GOLD A HIDDEN KIND?

If gold is a hidden kind, then the easily observable properties of gold (being yellow, malleable, and shiny) are not causally, or logically, determined by gold's specification-condition alone. Consider malleability first. Suppose that, due to food pollution, all humans became very weak. Surely this is a physically possible world that contains water, cats, and gold. The gold in this world is the stuff that has the atomic number of 79. However, in this possible world gold is not malleable because it cannot be easily hammered into different shapes. So malleability is not determined by (4) alone.

Consider yellowness. Suppose that radiation has effected human DNA in a way that has changed the vitreous humor (i.e., the liquid in the eyeball between the lens and the retina) of human beings. This fluid now absorbs all and only light in the lower part of the yellow frequencies of the spectrum—light between 587 nm and 590 nm is absorbed. After this change, light from this very narrow band of the spectrum no longer reaches the human retina. For many objects, including many yellow objects, light from the lower yellow frequencies is such a small percentage of the light that they reflect under normal lighting conditions that the change would not effect their apparent color. Objects that only reflect light from the lower yellow frequencies look black after the change; and objects that only reflect light from the lower yellow frequencies and the red part of the spectrum look red to normal observers under optimal viewing conditions after the change. Surely water, cats, and gold continue to exist after the change. But gold only reflects light from the lower yellow frequencies and the red part of the spectrum, so gold looks red after the change.[8] Is gold red

---

[8] The change described above has not made normal observers colorblind, or at least they are no more colorblind after the change than they are before the change. To see this, suppose that on two canvases a figure is painted with paint that only reflects light from the lower yellow frequencies of the spectrum. On one canvas the background is filled in with paint that is a metamer of the paint used for the figure. On the second canvas the background is painted black. Before the change, under normal lighting conditions, the first canvas appears to be a solid yellow but the second one clearly contains a yellow figure on a black background. After the change, the first canvas appears to contain a black figure against a yellow background, but the second canvas appears solid black. For more on these points see Averill (1985, 1992).

or yellow after the change? Color plays a very important role in our identification of things in everyday situations. Indeed the identification of objects by their color is so important to us that it would be preserved after the change in our eyes. But to preserve this common sense method of identification we would, after the change, have to think of gold as being red. So after the change gold would be red, and not yellow. Since we are the people imagined in this argument, and since we use the same language as the people imagined in this possible world, to be consistent we ought to say (now, in the actual world) that in the possible world being imagined gold is red. So red gold is possible.

These considerations show that gold's specification-condition (i.e., having the atomic number of 79) does not, by itself, causally, or logically, determine any of the easily observable properties of the members of gold's reference class. It has just been shown that gold's yellowness and malleability are not determined by the atomic number of gold. Although the (determinate) shape properties of solid hunks of gold are among the easily observable properties of those hunks, they are not determined by the specification-condition of gold. Of course gold's specification-condition does not determine whether or not an instance of gold is a solid, liquid, or gas.[9] So gold's atomic number does not, by itself, determine either logically or causally the easily observable properties of the instances of gold.

Yellowness and malleability are sometimes called "secondary qualities," or properties that do not depend entirely on the nature of the object perceived but also depend on the nature of the perceiver. The secondary qualities of an object are not determined by the object's microstructure, since changes in us can change the secondary qualities of objects. The physical kinds an object belongs to have more to do with the way the object is governed by natural laws than the secondary qualities of the object. Secondary qualities are often the easily observable properties of objects *because* they depend on the nature of the perceiver's perceptual mechanisms. Thus secondary qualities of objects figure strongly in our everyday identifications (but not in expert identifications) of objects, and physical kind properties figure strongly in accounts of how objects interact.

So far it has been shown that gold's specification-condition does not determine, by itself, the easily observable properties of gold. To show that gold is a hidden kind it must also be shown that gold's easily observable properties do not determine gold's specification-condition. The existence of fool's gold is enough to establish this point. Thus it is shown that gold is a hidden kind.

[9] The solid, liquid, gas properties are not easily observable properties. Window glass turns out to be a liquid, which flows very slowly; and the distinction between an aerosol and a gas is not easily observable.

D. FOOL'S Xs

If the observers of gold are held fixed (e.g., no changes in their eyes, as imagined above) and if the environment of gold is held fixed (e.g., if, instead of the eyes of the observers changing, the atmosphere had changed so that it absorbed light in the lower yellow frequencies, gold would look red to all of us), then the easily observable properties of gold are causally determined by their microstructure. Both iron pyrites and gold have many of the same easily observable properties, even though they have different microstructures. The reason for this is that different causes can have the same effect.

From here on the following is assumed: for any combination of easily observable properties that objects have, in our environment and for human observers as they are at present, more than one microstructure can cause either this combination or a very similar combination. This assumption has the following implication: *If a term "X" refers to a hidden physical kind, then it is possible for there to be another hidden physical kind whose objects (call them "fool's Xs") have the same easily observable properties as some Xs (although they are not Xs).* (Since Xs and fools's Xs really have the same easily observable properties, nothing is a fool's X by virtue of looking as though it has the easily observable properties of an X but really not having such easily observable properties.) No object could have the easily observable properties of being a plane figure with four equal sides and four equal angles and not be a square. So there are not, and cannot be, any "fool's squares." This shows that squares are not hidden physical kinds. (Of course, something can look square and not be square, but this is the point that there are conditions under which we are mistaken about the easily observable properties of objects. That iron pyrites looks like gold is not due to a optical illusion about the easily observable properties of iron pyrites, but due to the fact that solid hunks of iron pyrites really do have many of the easily observable properties of solid hunks of gold.) Again, "yellow" is not a hidden physical kind term, because something cannot have the property of looking yellow under normal conditions, and not be yellow. There is not, and cannot be, any "fool's yellow".[10] (This fits nicely with the point made in Section III that "yellow" is not a hidden kind term.) On the other hand it seems that there can be a liquid that looks like water, feels like water, and tastes like water, but is not water. If so, this shows that "water" passes the necessary condition for referring to a

---

[10] Care is needed here. It does not follow from the fact that "red" does not refer to a physical kind that "red" does not refer to a disjunctive property. "Red" might refer to a disjunctive property, where the components of the disjunct were physical kinds. Many philosophers hold, mistakenly, I believe, this latter view. See Averill (1985, 1992).

hidden physical kind. (Even if many of us could not tell silver from plutonium, this does not make plutonium fool's silver. This is a case of ignorance about the easily observable properties that can be used to distinguish one physical kind from another. It is not a case where one physical kind has the same easily observable properties as another physical kind.)

V. Biological Kinds

The nature of biological kinds is quite controversial: Do biologist really appeal to kinds? Is there more than one type of biological kind? If there are biological kinds, can the theory set out in Section IV be extended to these kinds? If there are biological kinds, how are common words like "horse," "tree," and "bug" related to these kinds? Here I maintain that there are biological kinds, that there is a horse kind that biologists refer to (so this use of "horse" is defined in terms of a causal role), and that at least one use of the ordinary term "horse" refers to this biological kind. This will be enough to extend the Kripke-Putnam theory of Section IV to some biological kinds. Presumably some ordinary uses of the term "horse" are purely taxonomic (and thus nonexplanatory). Note: The theory proposed in this section only applies to classifications where the category involved meets two conditions: there is a general term in ordinary language for this category, *and* the category is a kind because it plays a causal role in biological explanations. The Kripke-Putnam theory cannot be extended to purely taxonomic categories of plants and animals, because such taxonomic categories are not kinds. (Why not? Since the members of such a taxonomic category could have evolved from many different origins, and could inhabit different ecological niches in different environments, biological theory does not ascribe a distinctive evolutionary role—or any other distinctive causal role that I know of—to such a category.)

All sides agree that there are DNA kinds. So one way of extending the Kripke-Putnam account of physical kinds to biological kinds is to assume that, like physical kinds, biological kinds are defined by a common DNA structure. This position does not work very well. If a fox had all its DNA molecules destroyed by (say) radiation of some sort, the animal would not cease to be a fox any more than a fox which lost a leg would cease to be a fox.[11] (At least this is my intuition, but intuitions can differ here.) So having a certain DNA structure is not necessary to be a fox. If a fox had all its DNA molecules changed by (say) radiation of some sort, so that its

---

[11] I owe this point to my friend and colleague from the biology department, Kent Rylander.

DNA was exactly like that of some chicken, the animal would not become a chicken in virtue of this change. The animal would be a fox with a very unusual sort of DNA. So having a certain sort of DNA is not sufficient to make an animal a chicken. (Note how this is unlike the case where a piece of gold had its atomic number changed by radiation.) These considerations show that the above extension of the Kripke-Putnam account of physical kinds to DNA kinds is not very plausible.

To get an appropriate biological kind, note that the phylogenetic tree can be divided into parts, along the following lines, to get ancestral kinds.

(1′)   A biological kind is defined in terms of a set of biological entities (call it the ancestral set of the kind): for a given set of entities S, the S biological kind are all and only those objects that have every member of S as an ancestor. (So S is the ancestral set of the S biological kind.)

Mammals are warm-blooded and, in general, the females have milk-producing glands (although mutant females may not have such glands). This is not true by virtue of the definition of "mammal" but is to be explained (in part) in terms of a common ancestry. Presumably, differences between mammalian subkinds are due to differences in evolutionary forces on the mammalian subkinds. The reason for thinking that (1′) does set out a biological kind is this: a common ancestry is explanatory—biological entities having a common ancestry often have common traits that are explainable in terms of that common ancestry. (Given this definition of biological kinds, tadpoles and frogs are the same kind. This just shows that, in so far as being a frog is different from being a tadpole, more than ancestry is involved.)

Definition (1′) cannot be directly applied in many cases because biological kinds are historically defined and the historical record is not well known. Suppose, however, that a set of biological entities have many of the same easily observable properties and that they interact with their environment in the same way (e.g., feed on the same things, scatter their seeds by the same mechanisms, have common enemies). Since a common ancestry could account for these common properties, it is reasonable to assume, as a hypothesis, that this set of biological entities form the living members of a biological kind. For example:

(2′)   Horses form a biological kind that all paradigm instances of horses instantiate but none of the paradigm instances of a nonhorse instantiate. (So a necessary and sufficient condition for an object to be a horse is that the object be a member of a certain biological kind, the biological kind common to all the paradigm instances of horses, but not to any of the paradigm instances of a nonhorse.)

Within the horse kind there are other subkinds (e.g., the various breeds of horses), just as within the gold kind there are various isotopes of gold. In fact, biologists have found typical examples of the ancestral set of horses. They call these animals, which lived about 50,000 years ago, *"Equus caballus."* The ancestral set of horses is a subset of *E. caballus,* although, of course, not enough is known to say exactly which subset of *E. caballus* is the ancestor set of horses.

(3') The horse kind, as specified in (2'), is identical to a biological kind whose ancestral set is a subset of *E. caballus.*

(4') A necessary and sufficient condition for object *O* to be a horse is that every member of the horse ancestral set, some subset of *E. caballus,* be an ancestor of *O*.

Of course the horse kind has an explanatory role: the properties that modern horses generally have in common are due to a common ancestry. And the specification-condition for being a horse, (2') or (4'), is not enough to determine the easily observable properties of a horse, since there are, for example, three-legged horses due to mutation and due to accidents. So the horse kind is a hidden kind.

Does (4') really set out a necessary condition? If there were animals that looked like horses, and had internal organs like horses, but were descended from a different ancestral set, would they be horses? Since we do not say that zebras and donkeys are horses, it seems reasonable to think that the imagined creatures are not real horses but fool's horses. I am inclined to think that the imagined animals would not be horses even if they could mate with horses. Fool's horses might come about through co-evolution—or the case where different ancestral kinds develop similar traits because they are subject to similar evolutionary forces. Shrews are fool's mice. (In Section IV,D, "fool's *X*s" is defined for physical kinds. Of course, "physical kind" must be replace with "biological kind" before applying this definition to horses.) Note that if "horse" is used in a purely taxonomic way, then fool's horses are impossible. (If I am right, then the extent to which "horse" is used to refer to an ancestral kind and the extent to which it is used to refer to a taxonomic category is an empirical question.)

Does (4') really set out a sufficient condition? All sorts of mutants are born to horses and we say that these are deformed horses. And horses deformed by accidents or surgery are still horses. Given (4'), such animals are horses because they meet a sufficient condition (an ancestral condition) for being a horse. (If "horse" were always used in a purely taxonomic way, there could not be horses that did not have the taxonomy of normal horses, i.e., there could not be deformed horses. So "horse" is not always used in a purely taxonomic way.) But this is not all there is to (4') as a sufficient condition for being a horse.

Consider the following objection to (4') as a sufficient condition. Suppose that, through a fantastic mutation, a horse gave birth to a being that looked like, acted like, had the internal organs of, and even DNA like that of a chicken. Would such a being be a horse? In Section III it was claimed that a kind categorizes objects in terms of a causal role. The biological point of the ancestral relation is that some traits can be causally explained because they are passed down. Trying to imagine the "chicken horse" is trying to imagine how biological kinds are instantiated under conditions where these concepts have lost their causal role. This is like trying to imagine a lump of gold that does not chemically react with *aqua regia*. Such examples are cases where the reference class of a kind concept cannot be determined, because the presuppositions about the world on which the concepts are built do not hold. (See the first paragraph of Section III for more on this point.) Of course in the purely taxonomic concept of chicken, the "chicken horse" is a real chicken. (The "chicken horse" is similar to Dupré's, 1981, p. 88 example of chicken that lays walnuts.)

Although biological taxa purport to define biological kinds, along the lines of either (2') or (4'), biological taxa do not exhaust the biological kinds as set out in (1'). If a child dies without producing any children, then the child is a biological kind (whose ancestral set is its parents), although an uninteresting kind. Similarly there are many unnamed physical kinds. (For more examples of biological kinds that do not appear in the lexicon of biological theory see Dupré, 1981, p. 74, on prickly pears and lilies. I agree with Ereshefsky, 1991, that, although species are an important biological kind, they are not the only biological kind.)

For nonexperts to make horse classifications, their use of "horse" (in the ancestral, nontaxonomic sense of "horse") must have the correct sort of connection to the expert use of "horse" so that their use of "horse" is about horses. Most nonexperts will only know that a horse is a kind and be able to correctly recognize a few clear-cut examples as horses. So a nonexpert is likely to classify a donkey or a zebra as a horse. Similarly, the nonexpert is likely to classify penguins and ostriches as nonbirds and bamboo as nongrass. This is like the nonexpert who classifies iron pyrites as gold, or window glass as a solid.

Nonexperts may also be mistaken about whole kinds. Perhaps many of us think that trees form an ancestral kind, but we may be mistaken (Dupré, 1981, p. 80). The similarity among trees may have nothing to do with a common ancestry but a lot to do with coevolution. Similarly, people at one time thought that air was a physical kind (along with earth, fire, and water), but they were mistaken.

Note that it is no part of the theory being proposed here that every ordinary term that refers to biological entities purports to pick out an ancestral kind; perhaps "vegetable" and "bug" are not biological kinds, just as "mud" is not a physical kind. There are no fool's bugs, and there is no fool's mud. What is being proposed here is an account of how classification works in cases where kind terms from biological theory are part of ordinary language, and not an account of all classifications we commonly make with respect to biological entities. (Here Dupré and I disagree as to what the Kripke-Putnam theory is about; See Dupré, 1981, p. 74).

VI. Functional Kinds

By definition, objects of the X sort have function F if and only if: (1) when a well-formed and undamaged X occurs in circumstance C, F is a consequence (or result) of the occurrence of the X in C; (2) the causal account of why Xs are produced depends on the fact that Condition 1 is the case.[12] An object that meets Condition 1 but not Condition 2 can function as an F in C; but this is not its function. A suitcase can function as a doorstop, but this is not its function. An X may be unable to do F in circumstance C because it is damaged (at one time X was able to do F in C) or malformed (something went wrong in the production process). Condition 2 can be met in either of two ways: if Xs are biological organs, then Xs are produced through the process of natural selection; if Xs are artifacts, then Xs are produced by fabrication. Perhaps some objects, such as nests, are produced by both fabrication and natural selection. Some objects, such as planets, are not produced in either way, and so do not have a function. The circumstances C may not be usual circumstances; thus, the function of a fire alarm is to make a warning signal in cases of fire, even if no fire ever occurs, and the function of white blood cells is to attack invading cells even if this rarely occurs.

Functional kinds are analogous to physical kinds:

(1″) A functional kind is defined in terms of some function F: the members of the functional kind are all and only those objects that have the F function.

Condition (2) for being a function guarantees that functional kinds have a causal role, and so they meet the condition set out in Section III for being a kind.

---

[12] I believe that this is a restatement of Wright's (1973, p. 161) definition of "function," but I shall not stop to argue the point.

(2'')   Hearts form a functional kind that all paradigm instances of hearts instantiate but none of the paradigm instances of a nonheart instantiate. (So a necessary and sufficient condition for an object to be a heart is that the object be a member of a certain functional kind, the functional kind common to all the paradigm instances of heart but not to any of the paradigm instances of a nonheart.)

(3'')   The heart specification-condition, set out in (2''), is identical to the functional kind whose members pump blood, in circumstances where they are hitched up to a body so that the blood moves to lungs or gills and then to the rest of the body without damaging the blood.

(4'')   A necessary and sufficient condition for a thing to be a heart is that it pump blood in the way set out in (3'').

A pump that was inserted in a leg vein would pump blood, but it would not be a heart. Of course it is the ability of well-formed and undamaged natural hearts to pump blood that explains why biological hearts are produced through natural selection; and it is the ability of well-formed and un-damaged artificial hearts to pump blood that explains why artificial hearts are produced in laboratories. Hearts are able to make a throbbing noise as well as pump blood, and the ability to make a throbbing noise is very useful in diagnosing heart problems. However, the ability to make a throbbing noise is not part of the function of a heart, because making a throbbing noise, unlike pumping blood, does not explain why hearts are produced. Given the many different possible natural and artificial hearts, it is clear that the specification-condition for being a heart [i.e., (2'') or (4'')] does not determine the easily observable properties of hearts, and so hearts form a hidden kind.

Statement (3'') assumes that "heart" is defined functionally and not anatomically. Consider an anatomical description of a healthy human heart. Such a description describes a set of objects independent of their blood pumping function. Although most such objects do in fact have a blood pumping function, they do not have it in virtue of meeting the anatomical description. To see this, note that tissue meeting the ana-tomical description could conceivably be cobbled together by accident (and so fail to be produced to pump blood); or, if the world had been quite different, tissue meeting the anatomical description might have been pro-duced through natural selection to make a thump-thump sound (because such a sound scares away certain poisonous insects), and they make this sound by pumping water round and round from a reservoir in the chest cavity. (The first biological organs that pumped blood were not hearts, since they were produced by mutation and not because they pumped blood. Of course these organs functioned as hearts, or as hearts do. The first hearts were not produced by mutations, but by natural selection from mutations that pumped blood.)

"Carburetor" is defined functionally: by definition, a carburetor is an artifact whose function is to mix fuel and air in the appropriate circumstances. Some nonexperts who do not know much about cars may only know that a carburetor is a kind of some sort or other. However, when they say, think, or believe that the engines in cars have carburetors, their thought refers to carburetors if their use of "carburetor" is connected in the right sort of way to expert use of the term. Also note that there could be "fool's carburetors." Perhaps these devices sit right under the air filter, and they use the air coming through to make a honking sound when a button is pushed.

The heart and carburetor examples are analogous to physical and biological kinds, because in these cases it makes sense to appeal to a difference between expert and nonexpert knowledge of the function. But how about cases where the function of a functional kind is common knowledge? For example, the function of a second hand is to make the time, down to the second, easy to read; the function of a fire alarm is to warn people that a fire has started. In these cases virtually everyone is an expert, and no Sally-like problems arise.

VII. Identifying the Classified

Classification statements involve more than predicate reference, they also involves subject reference. To see how subject reference and predicate reference work together, consider the following criticism of the necessary condition of (4), when (4) is generalized to water. We often call stuff "water," the criticism assumes, which we know contains substances other than H_2O. Examples include tap water, chlorinated water, salt water, dish water, and fresh water. Since people who believe of some mixture that it is a mixture of salt and water sometimes say of such a mixture that it is water, the reference class of "water" includes examples that are not pure H_2O. So water is not necessarily H_2O.

Classifications have two parts: the picking out of an object and the typing of the object as a so-and-so. For example, some classifications are of the form "This is a such-and-such" (said while pointing), and others are of the form "The so-and-so is a such-and-such." Classifications are more or less informative, depending on how the picking out of the object is related to its classification. If the object to be classified is picked out independently of its classification, then the classification is fully informative. In most contexts, "My doorknob is an antique" is fully informative. If the picking out of an object to be classified depends entirely on how it is classified, then the classification is circular and completely uninformative. In other words, a classification of the form "The C is C" (e.g., My dog is a dog) is uninformative. If the object to be classified is partially but not entirely picked out by its classification, then the classification is partially informative. So classifications are more or less informative, and thus it is a mistake to assume that all classification is fully informative.

Statements of the form "This is a so-and-so" accompanied by pointing are partially informative classifications. To see this note that, although we can point toward things, pointing is often ambiguous. Suppose, for example, someone holds up a glass of water in his left hand and points toward it with a finger of his right hand. The person could be pointing at a hand holding a glass, or at a glass, or at a glass of water, or at water. For another example, think of the difference between pointing to a table, to a table's color, to a table's surface, and to a table's shape. Or consider pointing out President Clinton. One cannot tell just from the pointing whether the object pointed to is wearing clothes or the clothes are part of the object pointed out. (One of Wittgenstein's most enduring lessons was that pointing does not determine reference.) Our pointing conventions are not entirely uninformative, since what is being pointed at is in the direction of the pointed finger. However, since pointing is ambiguous, classification is often used to disambiguate the object pointed at. For example, if a person holds up a glass and says "This is a glass" (accompanied with pointing), the listener uses the predicate "glass" to disambiguate the object pointed at. So the statement "This is a glass" (accompanied with pointing) is only a partially informative classification. Of course similar remarks hold for "Here is a glass" and "There is a glass."

Presumably, if in some circumstances person P would point toward a glass and say, "That is salt water," then there are other circumstances in which P would point toward the same glass and say, "That is water." Given the physical kind account of "water," in these two circumstances P points in the same direction but at different things. In the first case P points at the entire contents of the glass; in the second case P points at the water (i.e., the H_2O molecules) in the glass. The criticism made above tacitly assumes that these two cases of pointing are cases of pointing at the same thing, which (I claim) is false. (Could empirical research into our use of "water" show whether "water" always refers to pure H_2O or sometimes refers to impure H_2O? What "that" refers to in sentences of the form "that is _____ ,'' accompanied by pointing, can only be determined after the blank is filled in. So an account of what "water" refers to is needed *prior to* grasping what "that" refers to in sentences of the form "that is water," accompanied by pointing. Hence sentences of this form cannot be used to show what we use "water" to refer to.)

The above points can be generalized. Presumably, if in some circumstances person P would say

(5)   The liquid in this glass is salt water.

then there are other circumstances in which P would say of the same glass

(6)   The liquid in this glass is water.

Note that in the first circumstance P could also say either (5′) or (5″).

(5′)   The liquid in this glass is a solution of salt and water.

(5″)   The liquid in this glass is water with salt dissolved in it.

Both of these latter classifications are partially informative. In (5′) "the liquid in this glass" refers to a mixture that contains Na^+ ions, Cl^- ions, and H_2O molecules. In (5″), "the liquid in this glass" refers to the H_2O molecules in the glass, and the statement goes on to say that these H_2O molecules are mixed with Na^+ ions and Cl^- ions. The difference between (5′) and (5″) is that in (5′), but not in (5″), "the liquid in the glass" refers to the mixture as a whole and not to just the water part of it. Thus the phrase "the liquid in the glass" in (5) does not by itself pick out a unique object. So it is quite plausible that it is used to pick out different objects in (5) and (6), as the physical kind account of "water" requires. However, the argument set out in the opening paragraph of this section (which reaches the conclusion that "water" is used to refer to stuff that is not pure H_2O) tacitly assumes that in both circumstances the phrase "the liquid in this glass" is used to pick out exactly the same stuff. Of course it is this very assumption that is in dispute.

These points make it clearer how the paradigm examples of (2) work. One points and says "this stuff is gold," where "this stuff" refers to the gold physical kind and not to the impurities in it. Indeed one can even say "this yellow stuff is gold" (recall that pure gold is almost white) if what one means is "this stuff, which looks yellow (due, perhaps, to impurities mixed in with the stuff), is gold." If the argument that opens this section were right, it would not just undermine (4); it would undermine the idea behind (2) that physical kinds can be defined by paradigm examples, thus making it hard to understand how physical theory can get started.

It may be objected that on the physical kind account "water" and "pure water" should mean the same thing, but surely they do not mean the same thing. On the view argued for here, they *refer* to the same thing, but they do not *mean* the same thing because they are used differently. (Reference does not determine use, as parenthetically remarked in Section II.) If one pointed to a glass of water and said either "That is impure water" or "That is pure water," then clearly the entire content of the glass is being referred to. So to explain the difference between saying "That is water" and "That is pure water," is to disambiguate the reference of "that." The first sentence can be used when the speaker believes that the glass contains a mixture of salt and water, but not the second. "Water" and "pure water" both refer to H_2O, but they are used differently.

The mistake in the opening argument of this section can be brought out by applying the reasoning of the argument to another kind of case. Some dictionaries define "jacket" as a waist-length coat with sleeves. Presumably, people who know that a certain waist-length coat with sleeves has a handkerchief in one of its pockets will point toward the coat and say, "This is a jacket." Such pointing shows that the word "jacket" in this context refers to something that is more than simply a waist-length coat with sleeves. (Similar pointing shows that "water" refers to stuff that is more than H_2O molecules.) The absurd conclusion follows that the dictionary definition of "jacket" is wrong because it implies that a necessary condition for an object to be a jacket is that it be nothing more than a waist-length coat with sleeves. Even if the dictionary definition is wrong (perhaps there are short-sleeve jackets), it is not wrong for this reason. Clearly, the problem with this reasoning is the tacit assumption that statements like "This is a jacket" are fully informative.

VIII.   Conclusion

Sections III–VII constitute an argument for the claim that a large part of our classifications are hidden kind classifications. Furthermore, for any hidden kind classification that a nonexpert makes, there is a distinction between the propositional content of the nonexpert's classification and what the nonexpert grasps about the propositional content of that classification. Since this distinction is important for many classifications, perhaps it is also important in other areas of mental representation. Does it occur when one person mentally represents another person by using a proper name (Kripke, 1970)? Does it occur in visual representation (Burge, 1986)?

REFERENCES

Averill, E. W. (1980). Why are colour terms primarily used as adjectives? *The Philosophical Quarterly, 30*, 19–33.

Averill, E. W. (1982). Essence and scientific discovery in Kripke and Putnam. *Philosophy and Phenomenological Research, 43*, 253–257.

Averill, E. W. (1985). Color and the anthropocentric problem. *The Journal of Philosophy, 82*, 281–304.

Averill, E. W. (1992). The relational nature of color. *The Philosophical Review, 101*, 551–588.

Bennett, J. (1972). *Locke, Berkeley, Hume: Central themes*. Oxford: Clarendon.

Burge, T. (1986). Individualism and psychology. *The Philosophical Review, 95*, 3–46.

Dupré, J. (1981). Biological taxa as natural kinds. *The Philosophical Review, 90*, 66–90.

Ereshefsky, M. (1991). Species, higher taxa, and the units of evolution. *The Philosophy of Science, 58*, 84–101.

Keil, F. C. (1989). *Concepts, kinds, and cognitive development*. Cambridge, MA: MIT Press.

Kripke, S. (1970). *Naming and necessity*. Cambridge, MA: Harvard University Press.

Medin, D. L. (1989). Concepts and conceptual structure. *American Psychologist, 44*, 1469–1481.

Putnam, H. (1979a). Is semantics possible? In H. Putnam, *Mind, language and reality*, (pp. 139–152). Cambridge, England: Cambridge University Press. (Original work published 1970)

Putnam, H. (1979b). The meaning of "Meaning." In H. Putnam, *Mind, language and reality* (pp. 215–271). Cambridge, England: Cambridge University Press. (Original work published 1975)

Quine, W. V. (1960). *Word and object*. Cambridge, MA: MIT Press.

Quine, W. V. (1969). Natural kinds. In W. V. Quine, *Ontological relativity and other essays* (pp. 114–138). New York: Columbia University Press.

Smith, E. E., & Medin, D. L. (1981). *Categories and concepts*. Cambridge, MA: Harvard University Press.

Sober, E. (1980). Evolution, population thinking, and essentialism. *Philosophy of Science, 47*, 350–383.

Wright, L. (1973). Functions. *The Philosophical Review, 82*, 139–168.

IS COGNITION CATEGORIZATION?

Timothy J. van Gelder

I. Introduction

Categorization is surely a major component of human cognition. George Lakoff was probably guilty only of mild hyperbole when he wrote:

> There is nothing more basic than categorization to our thought, perception, action, and speech. . . . Without the ability to categorize, we could not function at all, either in the physical world or in our social and intellectual lives. An understanding of how we categorize is central to any understanding of how we think and how we function, and therefore central to an understanding of what makes us human. (Lakoff, 1987, pp. 5–6).

But might it be more than this? Could all cognizing be a matter of categorizing? Is cognition a kind of categorization, rather than categorization a kind of cognition? In recent years, there has been a certain drift in this direction in high-level theorizing about cognition. A number of people have proposed perspectives on the nature of cognition that elevate something like categorization from its usual status as a critical component to the essence of cognitive processing.[1] A position like this is also implicit in the practice of many others in the contemporary counterculture of alternatives to mainstream computational cognitive science. This article briefly lays out, and argues against, a prototypical version of this position. Along the way, it makes a few points about what a process must be like in order to

[1] Note that Lakoff himself does not subscribe to this stronger position; see, e.g., Lakoff (1987, pp. 6ff.).

THE PSYCHOLOGY OF LEARNING
AND MOTIVATION, VOL. 29
469

count as one of categorizing and discusses one domain in which categorization might be the essence of cognition and two in which it clearly is not. The upshot is that, important as categorization is, it is fundamentally the wrong kind of category in terms of which to think about cognition in general.

II.   Extracting the Prototype

A sense for this view might best be achieved by means of exposure to a series of exemplars which more or less approximate it. Probably the most uninhibited view in the vicinity is that developed by Howard Margolis. In his 1987 book *Patterns, Thinking, and Cognition* he straightforwardly proposed that "Pattern recognition is all there is to cognition" (p.3). William Bechtel, a philosopher increasingly well known in cognitive science circles for his discussions of connectionism, is a little more cautious than Margolis but entertains no less bold a thesis; he has suggested that cognition is essentially a matter of pattern recognition, a cognitive function naturally implemented with a connectionist network (Bechtel, 1991; Bechtel & Abrahamsen, 1991). Perhaps the most prominent exemplars, however, are the views of two leading philosophers of cognitive science, Hubert Dreyfus and Paul Churchland.

A.   THE DREYFUS POSITION: HOLISTIC ASSOCIATION AND DISCRIMINATION

For many years, most notably in his controversial book *What Computers Can't Do* (1979), Dreyfus has maintained a vigorous wholesale critique of that dominant part of artificial intelligence (AI) that takes intelligence, and human action in general, to be the product of the operation of a digital computer—or, more precisely, the product of rule-governed manipulation of discrete, context-free symbolic representations. Probably the most basic charge that Dreyfus levels against AI is that, following a long tradition of mainstream philosophical theorizing, it assumes that *practice* is explained by *theory;* that, in other words, AI takes our ability to be able to *do* anything intelligent to be dependent on, and hence explicable in terms of, our knowing and using facts and rules about the task and its domain. For example, AI considers our ability to understand simple stories, as evidenced in our ability to answer questions about them, to be a matter of constructing an appropriate symbolic representation of the events in the story and using that representation and stored general knowledge to infer the answers to the questions. Against this general approach, Dreyfus marshals numerous arguments to a common conclusion: that it is impossible, in principle, effectively to formalize in terms of symbolically represented facts, rules, and procedures all the background knowledge that would be needed for this approach to be successful. Dreyfus takes the great difficulties that fields of AI such as natural language understanding have encountered to be technological confirmation of the misguidedness of the traditional endeavor of trying to account for thought in terms of "rule-governed operations on situation-free discrete elements" (1979, p. 304).

Dreyfus does more than criticize; with his brother Stuart, he sketches an alternative to the symbolic information processing model of human cognition (Dreyfus & Dreyfus, 1986). They claim that intelligent human behavior is based on a range of basic abilities, founded on embodiment and acculturation, to deal skillfully with the specifically human world. Deliberately reversing the traditional assumption that practice is explained by possession and utilization of theory, they are arguing that knowing how to skillfully cope with the world, in a specifically human sense, is more basic than any kind of articulatable knowledge. More recently they have elaborated on the basic notion of skill which lies at the heart of this alternative conception. Skillful behavior is expert behavior, and we are each of us expert at myriad everyday activities, such as recognizing faces, driving, talking, and walking. Expert behavior is based on a vast amount of accumulated experience, and in particular on the ability to holistically recognize the current situation as similar to one which we have experienced before and for which we have already learnt an appropriate response. As they put it,

> The expert has experienced a great number of concrete situations and as a result his brain can discriminate classes of such situations. A new situation falls into one such discriminable class and the brain of the expert has learned from experience to associate an action, decision, or plan as well as various expectations with each class of discriminable situations. (p. 91)

Their general term for this basic capacity to classify situations and produce appropriate responses is "holistic discrimination and association"; in basic structure, it is clearly a form of categorization. Thus, the ability to categorize, broadly construed, is basic to the Dreyfuses' account of intelligent behavior, from bodily skills such as walking at one end to traditionally "cognitive" activities such as language use at the other.

B. CHURCHLAND: PROTOTYPE ACTIVATION

Paul Churchland has followed an intellectual trajectory that is surprisingly similar in broad outline, though different in important details. In his first book, *Scientific Realism and the Plasticity of Mind* (1979), Churchland presented a powerful critique of both (1) sentential epistemology—the position that sentences are the basic units of knowledge and rationality—and (2) 'Language of Thought' models in cognitive science, which take sentence-like units to be the basic units of cognitive operation. Making such a critique, of course, led naturally to the demand for an alternative overall account of the nature of cognitive activity. Churchland has more recently been constructing just such an account, drawing heavily upon theories, models, and insights emerging from neuroscience and connectionist modeling. On this new view, "Knowledge acquisition is primarily a process of learning *how*: how to recognize a wide variety of complex situations and how to respond to them appropriately" (1988, p. 298). The parallel with Dreyfus at this point is obvious. Churchland goes on to give some details of an account of the neural implementation of such pattern-recognition–based *knowledge how:* "The basic kinematics of cognitive creatures is a kinematics not of sentences but of high-dimensional activation vectors being transformed into other such vectors by passing through large arrays of synaptic connections" (1988, p. xvi).

The specific kind of vector-transformation that underpins this pattern-recognition–based conception of cognition is that of *prototype-activation.* Activation vectors in one network state-space belong to distinct categories (such as *mine* or *rock*, to mention one of Churchland's favorite examples), and the basic operation of the neural networks carrying out these transformations is to map vectors from a given category onto, or as close as possible to, a canonical vector in another space which functions as the prototypical representation of that category. This prototypical representation is in turn easily mapped by a network to an appropriate response. As Churchland puts it, "The picture I am trying to evoke, of the cognitive lives of simple creatures, ascribes to them an organized 'library' of internal representations of various prototypical perceptual situations, situations to which prototypical *behaviors* are the computed output of the well-trained network" (1988, p. 207). This picture does not apply only to the perceptual-motor activities of simple creatures; Churchland takes it as the model for an account of all of human cognitive processing, including functions as sophisticated as scientific reasoning and moral judgment. If prototype activation is correctly classified as a form of categorization, then Churchland, like Dreyfus, is placing categorization at the very heart of human cognition.

The prototype that concerns me is probably now clearly emerging. Margolis and Bechtel describe cognition in terms of pattern recognition, the Dreyfuses in terms of holistic discrimination and association, and Churchland in terms of prototype activation; nevertheless, despite numerous differences in terminology and details, there is enough generic similarity between the views to warrant abstracting out an apparent core element for independent consideration. It is the view that, roughly, all cognitive operations are just categorizing operations. It is this simplified, core element that I will argue is misguided; my points will tell against particular renditions only insofar as they do indeed approximate that prototypical position. Quotes and examples are drawn from work of these various authors primarily for illustrative purposes.

Note that the general view under attack here is quite independent of connectionism, even though a number of its supporters have been inspired by connectionist approaches. Connectionist models are capable of many other kinds of processing than just categorizing, and adherents to the "cognition is categorization" thesis need not be connectionists; there are many other ways of implementing categorizing processes.

It might be claimed that in attacking a simplified, core view I am only attacking a straw man. So be it; straw men often exert a powerful effect on the way issues are framed, and if my criticisms are successful, at least we will have one less straw man to deal with. Moreover, attacking the straw man in the vicinity will help clarify exactly what mistakes a less vulnerable position must be avoiding.

III. Categorizing Categorization

A. WHAT CATEGORIZATION IS

What exactly is categorization, anyway? If the doctrine that categorization is the heart of cognition is to present a serious empirical issue, we must be able to settle on some understanding of what categorization actually is that is sharp enough to allow serious evaluation, though not so narrow as to render the thesis trivially refutable. According to one authority, Edward Smith, a category is "a class of objects that we believe belong together," and categorization is "the process by which people assign objects to categories" (Smith, 1990, p. 33). In many categories, the objects are believed to belong together because of some overt *similarity*, such as presenting similar visual appearances. In other cases, overt similarities matter less than some deeper, perhaps theoretically specified, commonality; thus, a bird which suffered an accident making it look overtly similar to an insect, but which nevertheless produces offspring normally with another bird, is usually categorized as a bird rather than an insect (Rips, 1989). Consideration of these kinds of cases has led to alternative accounts of categorizing known loosely as theory- or explanation-based accounts. For current purposes, however, the difference between traditional similarity-based categorization on one hand and theory- or explanation-based categorization on the other is not crucial; in both cases, there has to be *some* kind of commonality between objects, on the basis of which they are believed to belong together. From this very general perspective, then, categorization is the process of recognizing objects as belonging together in virtue of some relevant commonality, and treating those objects in some unified and appropriate way.

In order to give plenty of room for the doctrine to be true if it can, we need to understand the various terms of this characterization in a suitably broad fashion. Thus, the "objects" recognized as belonging together can be pretty much anything we like: everyday objects, visual stimuli, social situations, linguistic patterns, temporally extended objects, artifacts, and so on. Likewise, the unified and appropriate treatment of the objects so recognized can take many forms—simple labeling, judgments of similarity, motor responses, and so on. And we should be entirely open-minded about the kinds of commonalities on the basis of which categorization is performed. Perhaps the objects are visually similar; or bound together only by some theory; perhaps the commonality is cuturally conditioned rather than a matter of physical structure; perhaps it is best described in terms of the objects' relationship to a prototype; and so forth. From this point of view, categorization and pattern recognition are generically the same kind of function; the difference between them is partly a matter of theoretical focus, and partly just a matter of boundaries between academic disciplines. Categorization tends to be the real human capacity that the psychologists or psycholinguists study in the laboratory, while pattern recognition tends to be what computer scientists or neurobiologists study when trying to work out how anything could have any such capacity. Both domains involve the treating of objects that belong together in a unified way; categorization researchers tend to focus on human classifying of random dot patterns or birds, while pattern recognition folks tend to focus on machine classifying of digitized images of faces or of nuts and bolts.

B.   WHAT CATEGORIZATION IS NOT

We cannot afford to be *too* generous with the concept of categorization, however. In order for the thesis to have some real content, there have to be some reasonable restrictions on it. If the thesis is not going to end up being true trivially, then there must be kinds of processes which are *not* ones of categorizing.

In order to settle on some such restrictions, it is important to reflect on the concept of categorization as it is characterized by Smith and deployed (though not under the same name) by the various theorists described in Section II. The key components are (1) a *category*—a class of objects that belong together—and (2) a process of categorizing, which involves recognizing that a given object belongs in that class by virtue of its relationship to other members and producing for it the single response that is appropriate for any member of that class. If this is right, then it follows that categories must always have multiple members, and that a process will only count as one of categorizing if it involves treating an object as belonging to some multiply-membered set. Another way to put this is that a process is not one of categorizing, for current purposes, if it involves producing a unique appropriate response for every distinct object. Mathematically speaking, there is such a thing as a class of one, and recognizing an object as belonging to the class to which only it belongs might be called "categorizing" if you wish. But this is the limiting and trivializing case. There is no recognizing objects as similar, no assimilation of the current instance to other instances of the category, no treating an object as a member of a class of objects which are believed to belong together, at least in any sense which anyone with practical concerns in categorization would care for. To allow one-membered categories would only be to render the claim that categorization is the heart of cognition empty in advance.[2]

Second, it seems essential that the process of categorization produce an identifiable, discrete response to a whole object or situation. One thing ruled out by this condition is cases in which a process produces a continually changing response that is evolving at the same time as a continually changing input.[3] Think, for example, of a radio receiver transforming electromagnetic wave forms into sound patterns. This process is fascinating and complex, but, whatever else it is, it is not categorization. One

[2] It is sometimes suggested that one-membered categories are legitimate, in the context of the issues being discussed in this paper, if one has repeated experiences with the category. Thus, we can allow a Dan Quayle-category, with only one member in it, as long as Dan Quayle is repeatedly confronted. It is, however, crucial to keep separate two subtly different categories. The first is the category of Dan Quayles, which has only one member. The second is the category of Dan Quayle appearances or presentations. This category has a vast number of members. Whenever one confronts Dan Quayle, or a picture of him, one has to, in effect, categorize the presentation as belonging to the class of Dan Quayle appearances, and thereby identify the object before one, or pictured, as Dan Quayle. *For the purposes of the current arguments*, the former process is one of categorization, and the category of Dan Quayle appearances is a legitimate category. The latter process is not one of categorization, and the set with only Dan Quayle in it is not a category.

[3] In formulating this second condition I am *not* concerned with what are known as *continuous stimulus–response relations*, that is, situations where the input item and the appropriate response are drawn from continuous sets (see, e.g., Koh & Meyer, 1991).

reason is that there is no treating of a whole set of cases in the same way because they belong to the same category—that is, it fails the previous condition. Just as importantly, however, there is no sense in which there is a naturally identifiable input "object" which is classified one way or another. The receiver does not wait around until some portion of the signal has accumulated in some buffer; there is no segmentation of the input into discrete objects, no segmentation of the output into discrete responses, and consequently no way to produce appropriate responses to all members of the same category.[4]

IV.   Refining the Thesis

What would it be for a kind of process to be the essence of cognition? Again, if the general issue is to be decidable at all, we need an understanding of what this means that is precise and strong enough to render the doctrine a live empirical issue, but not so extreme as to make refuting it trivial. Surely, for example, we would be doing the doctrine an injustice if we took it to require that *every* aspect of cognition be a matter of categorizing. Even the most enthusiastic proponents of categorization typically suppose that categories must be *learnt*, and this process cannot—on pain of regress—be one of categorization. On the other hand, the view that processes of categorization are a major *component* of human cognition is entirely unobjectionable. What, more exactly, is the interesting and contestable position between these extremes?

A sense for this position can be gained by examining one domain in which cognition might well be a matter of categorizing. To the relatively

---

[4] I am *not* ruling out the possibility that the internal processing involved in producing an eventual categorizing response as output might be a matter of continual development in response to changing input; nor am I ruling out the possibility that there be a series of particular categorizing responses. All that I am requiring is that there be some naturally identifiable input that is assigned to some category by virtue of a recognizable, standardized response. Roman Taraban (personal communication, January, 1992) has suggested for comparison the on-line computing of the thematic role of the initial noun phrase in a sentence. "After reading *The_____* (input), the category Agent is partly active; after reading *The crook_____*, the category is probably fairly active; after *The crook was_____*, the activation probably changed somewhat, and perhaps the category Patient is also partially activated; after *The crook was robbed,* activation for the category Agent dropped substantially; Patient is fully active." In this case, there is a discrete, identifiable object to be categorized (i.e., the initial noun phrase); and at any given time there is an identifiable categorizing response— Agent, or Patient, or some mix. The key point is that, although the particular category to which the system assigns the noun phrase may well be continually changing, the continually changing output is not itself a categorizing response; it is an extended series of categorizing responses.

inexperienced, the game of chess seems to be a matter of search: exploring the various possible combinations of moves, responses, and so on that one might make at any given point and selecting the strongest one. Computers designed to play chess basically work in this way: they investigate a wide range of moves as far ahead as possible and select the best one from the vast range of considered sequences. Since the number of possible move sequences grows exponentially the "deeper" the search goes, the search process must have some finite limit; in order to find the best move under such conditions, programs build in various strategies, rules of thumb, and so on known as *heuristics*. Thus, both untutored intuition and AI suggest that the basic structure of the kind of cognitive processing underlying chess is heuristic search. On this picture, the expert chess player would presumably be the one who can search the range of possible moves most deeply, quickly, or in the most organized fashion.

The Dreyfuses, however, have been promoting a plausible alternative account of skilled chess play (Dreyfus & Dreyfus, 1986), an account that originated in work by de Groot (1965), Chase & Simon (1973), and others. Their claim is that good chess players operate by recognizing whole chess positions as belonging to a familiar kind of position to which an appropriate response has already been learnt. In their account, the expert chess player has the ability to swiftly recognize some 50,000 kinds of positions with associated responses. They have actually performed experiments on expert chess players which appear to confirm their claims about the kind of cognizing underlying expert chess performance. The key point here is that the processing underlying chess play has been thoroughly recast in its basic structure. The kind of "thought" that produces good chess moves is not a matter of searching through a range of possibilities, but one of swift recognition and response. The Dreyfuses have taken a domain of cognitive operation and argued persuasively that, in effect, processing in that domain fits the logical structure of categorization.

Chess is usually regarded as game requiring a great deal of thought and intelligence. The fact that the cognition underlying expert chess appears to be a matter of categorization prompts one to ask how many other kinds of cognition might be properly construed this way as well. Perhaps it is the case that *all* domains of cognitive operation fit this bill; this at least is the position that I will be considering. It is the claim that all active, ongoing cognitive processes—processes that are involved in handling some particular situation or problem that the cognizing system is currently faced with—are, in their basic structure, processes of categorization. As in the case of expert chess play, there must be no higher organizational principles such that processes of categorization are subordinate to those principles.

Taking this approach, then, we can proceed to the real issue: is something like categorization (so understood) really the essence of cognition (so understood)? This is still a pretty vague question, and definitive answers to vague questions are rarely forthcoming. Nevertheless, there is a strong case for a negative answer. There are numerous broad areas of active cognition such that categorization, even on a construal as broad as that given above, simply has the wrong kind of basic structure to describe processing in that area. I will discuss just two, from extreme ends of the spectrum of cognitive functioning: sensorimotor control and language comprehension. Note that not all the theorists I have discussed have claimed explicitly or otherwise that cognitive functioning is essentially just categorization in these two areas in particular, and so what I say in each area cannot automatically be taken as directly criticizing their specific position. As already stressed, my primary concern is with the prototype that is obtained by generalizing away from their positions.

V.   Sensorimotor Control

A.   CATEGORIZATION, CONTROL, AND CRABS

The claim that categorization is the essence of cognition is often bundled together with claims to the effect that "high-level" cognition has much more in common with "low-level" cognition than the mainstream computational paradigm would suggest, or that the same evolutionarily basic neural mechanisms that account for low-level cognition such as perception and motor control may also be able to account for other more recently acquired cognitive functions. As a bundle, then, these claims imply that basic capacities like motor activity can be thought of as a matter of categorizing. Judging by their passing references, it seems that some kind of position along these lines is held by a number of the theorists cited above. At various points the Dreyfuses talk about their "holistic discrimination and association" conception of cognitive functioning as applying to bodily skills such as walking and riding a bicycle; even a sensorimotor control problem as complex as boxing is apparently a matter of categorizing visual situations: "A boxer seems to begin an attack, not by combining by rule various facts about his body position and that of his opponent, but when the whole visual scene in front of him and sensations within him trigger behavior which was successful in an earlier similar situation"

(1986, p. 28).[5] The idea that sensorimotor control may be explicable in terms of something like pattern recognition was reinforced by some early connectionist-style models of control. In particular, in 1986 Paul Churchland published what was in many ways a visionary and influential article sketching a radical new neuroscientifically inspired conception of cognition. This article included a popularization for philosophers of work by Pellionisz and Llinas on the cerebellum and sensorimotor control. That article introduced "Roger the Crab," a highly schematic illustration of the problem, and a framework within which to discuss the neural machinery for solving that problem (Fig. 1).

The control problem for Roger is to be able to grasp an edible food object once visually located, and to solve this problem he must be able to compute where to move his arm on the basis of the visual information available. More specifically, this problem is taken to be that of computing the two joint angles of the desired arm configuration given the two angles of the eyes when fixated upon the target. Churchland discusses various possible ingenious neurocomputational solutions to this problem, including the notions of phase-space "sandwiches" and neural matrices for high-dimensional coordinate transformation.

It can be tempting to say of this framework that it proposes solving eye–arm control via a process of recognition of the current visual input and automatic generation of an appropriate response—that is, that the problem of eye–hand control has been reduced to a matter of pattern recognition. Generalizing this account, we might be inclined to say that sensorimotor control is a matter of recognizing the current sensory input and producing, in response to that input, an appropriate motor command by means of these kinds of seemingly sophisticated neurocomputational mechanisms. This in turn suggests that the kind of informal claims Bechtel and Dreyfus are making might really be supported by the details of the basic neurocomputational implementation.

Yet all this would be highly misleading. For one thing, if Roger is going

[5] For another example, consider Bechtel's claim that

focusing on pattern recognition or categorization as a basic cognitive activity has the virtue of readily placing the study of cognition in an evolutionary framework. Most self-initiated motor activity of animals is initiated by the animal recognizing a situation in its environment and responding to it. An animal must recognize a food source and also recognize what action is needed to acquire the food. It must also recognize predators and ways to avoid them. . . . There are major parts of our lives which do depend primarily on recognizing and categorizing external stimuli and responding accordingly. A major part of our life involves navigating in an environment, recognizing and avoiding obstacles, identifying objects that are useful to us, etc. (1991, p. 14)

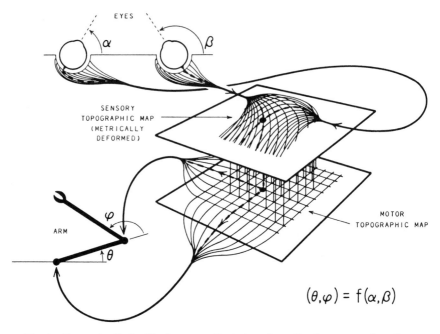

Fig. 1.   Roger the Crab effecting a coordinate transformation by means of contiguous, metrically deformed, vertically connected topographic maps. Reproduced, by permission of MIT Press, from Churchland (1988, p. 89). This diagram first appeared in *Mind* (1986), *95*, 279–309.

to catch his dinner successfully, he must produce a distinct arm position for every distinct position of an edible target. In other words, the kind of mapping between input and output required here must fail the first of the key conditions described above for a function to count as categorizing. There is no recognizing of members of a whole class of visual stimuli as belonging to one category so that there can be one standardized response for every member of that class of inputs. If Roger's control system actually operated by grouping food item positions into categories, to which a single kind of arm-movement response was appropriate, his arm would move only into the rough vicinity of most food items; he would end up pretty hungry.

For this reason, sensorimotor control would not properly be construed as a matter of categorization even if the above general conception of such control were entirely correct. But it is not; and when the general framework is elaborated sufficiently that it might begin to approach the true problems of sensorimotor control, it becomes even more obvious that such control could not be a matter of mere categorization.

First, the real control problem even in such a schematic case as Roger the Crab is not merely that of specifying the *target* arm position given the visual input; rather, the problem is to specify how to *move* the arm from where it is to that target position. What is needed as output is not a target position but rather a movement with the target as its end point. The Roger the Crab framework only seems plausible if we assume that the "body" or "motor system" can somehow itself generate such a movement on the basis of a specification of the target position. In his original discussion, Churchland explicitly made exactly that supposition: "Suppose that this intersecting pair of orthogonal motor fibers, when jointly activated, induces the arm to assume the position that is *appropriate* to the specific motor coordinate intersection where this motor signal originates" (1988, p. 88). He is supposing, in other words, that there are some further unspecified mechanisms which can take a target position command and figure out how to move the arm to that position. But this is itself virtually the whole problem of motor control—what commands does one give to get the arm to assume such a position? How is a specification of where your arm should be translated into an arm movement that actually gets your arm there?

A suggestion within the spirit of Churchland's overall perspective on these matters is that the actual output of processing should be not a specification of the target alone, but rather a specification of *trajectory* through motor space—that is, through the space of arm positions from the current arm position to the target. Trajectories of this kind apparently can be generated by recurrent neural networks, in which iterated processing generates a succession of state space positions. If the current visual stimulation is the input to such a network, it might "kick" the network into a processing sequence such that an appropriate trajectory is output.

Even this approach, however, seriously misconceives the nature of the problem. Ultimately what is needed is not a trajectory in the space of actual arm positions; this too is at best only a specification of the top-level *problem* of sensorimotor control. That is, suppose you know that your arm has to move through a certain trajectory in real, physical space. How do you coordinate the various muscles to actually get your arm to move through that trajectory? How do you get from a specification of the movement that the arm must perform to a specification of the muscle actions that would generate that movement?

B.   REAL SENSORIMOTOR CONTROL

At this stage it is worth taking at least a bare glimpse at the number and complexity of the factors involved in actually moving a limb. In the human arm there are basically twenty-six major muscles controlling a limb with four joints and a total of seven degrees of freedom (Turvey, Fitch, & Tuller, 1982). Coordinated movement is produced by controlling the contraction of these muscles. This is a daunting task. Individual muscles are highly complex, each one comprising between hundreds and thousands of more basic motor units. The force generated in contraction depends on the particular kind of fiber layout of the muscle, its length (i.e., how much it is extended), and direction and rate of length change (Bingham, 1988). Muscle contraction is dependent on blood flow (itself dependent on muscular activity) and fatigue level. Muscles are joined to limbs by means of tendons with their own length-dependent tension characteristics. All these complexities are present even before contextual variabilities are taken into account. Basically, the effect that a given muscular contraction actually has depends crucially on the current state of the arm. The same contraction can have very different effects on movement of the limb depending on the position that the limb is already in. The various torques, inertial properties, and external forces (e.g., gravity) that the muscle must act either against or in conjunction with also depend on the position of the arm. The context of forces in which movement takes place can be radically changed by already-existing movement of the limb or by contingent forces which arise from the nature of the task (e.g., the resistance of a bicycle pump). Finally, to add insult to injury, non-linearity pervades every aspect of the system; the properties of the whole cannot be ascertained simply by studying the properties of the various components.

In short, the idea that motor control is a matter of issuing to the arm a command specifying where it should be, or even what spatial trajectory it should follow, does not really begin to scratch the surface of the complexities involved in actual motor control.

The point, however, is not merely that the Roger the Crab model of sensorimotor control is an oversimplification. It conceptualizes the problem the wrong way from the ground up. It envisions sensorimotor control as a sequential, open loop process. Its sequential character is obvious: at time t_1, there is perceptual input from environment; at t_2, neural computation; at t_3, a motor command is issued. It is "open loop," in the sense traditional in discussions of motor control. A motor command is issued to the arm and is supposed achieve the desired result directly; there is no provision for feedback to allow the system to control the movement and take into account changing conditions. It is these features, with their structural similarity to the categorization process, which make it superficially plausible to suppose that sensorimotor control might be construed as some kind of categorization. Real problems of sensorimotor control, however, are very different in their basic structure. First, there is typically continuous, ongoing sensory input (visual, proprioceptive, etc.), both before and during the coordinated action. The Roger the Crab picture suggests that the sensory input is a kind of static prior presentation, to which the sensorimotor control machinery responds as a whole. Second, movement is temporally extended, and so motor control must itself be an ongoing process—not just a matter of a one-time issuing of a command to a limb. Third, there is ongoing, computationally relevant nervous activity in both sensory and motor areas. (Indeed, sensory and motor areas may not be neatly separable or independent at all; there is evidence that motor activity involves activity in sensory areas and vice versa.) Fourth, the coordinated action produces external effects which are themselves part of the sensory situation to which motor control must be responsive. There is no neat separation of the sensory situation and the motor response, as is suggested by the Roger the Crab picture.

In its generic structure, then, sensorimotor control is more like the radio receiver than it is like categorization (except that in the case of the radio receiver, the electromagnetic input is quite independent of the sound output). In other words, it would be better to begin thinking of the sensorimotor control system as dynamically transforming sensory input into motor output, rather than as performing a sequential mapping of whole sensory input situations to appropriate motor responses—that is, as also inherently violating the second of the key conditions for a process to count as categorizing. Thus, I am not arguing that sensorimotor control is such an awesomely difficult problem that it is implausible that it might be solved by categorization-like processes; rather, I am arguing that we already know enough about sensorimotor control to be able to establish that it cannot possibly be a matter of categorization, since it has a fundamentally different structure. The impressive neurocomputational feats of Roger the Crab are no evidence that sensorimotor control might be some form of categorization, since Roger the Crab is simply not operating in the vicinity of serious problems of sensorimotor control. And more generally, the generic notion of categorization has fundamentally the wrong kind of structure to be applicable to basic sensorimotor control, notwithstanding the superficial plausibility of casual, high-level redescriptions of human action in such terms.[6]

VI. Language Understanding

Perhaps it is inappropriate to attempt to extend the doctrine that categorization is the heart of cognition to low-level functions like motor control. Perhaps the real strength of the position will be revealed in how it can

[6] For a fascinating presentation of some related criticisms, see Skarda (1986).

account for relatively high-level cognitive phenomena such as our linguistic capacities.

A. Categorizing Linguistic Capacities

Bechtel, Dreyfus, and Churchland seem to be in basic agreement at this level: (1) Our ability to understand language is not a matter of the rule-governed processing of symbolic or propositional representations—rather, it is to be accounted for in terms of more basic skillful capacities, or *knowing how;* and (2) This *knowing how* is in turn to be accounted for in terms of some form of pattern-recognition (Bechtel), "experience-based, holistic, similarity recognition" (Dreyfus), or prototype activation (Churchland). None of them explain in any significant detail how linguistic capacities are supposed to be carried out by processes of categorization; they offer at best pointers in the direction of a kind of account of language use. The Dreyfuses for example consider everyday language use to be a matter of skilled performance, at which we all usually perform at expert level. The general account of expert performance is described in the following passage:

> We usually do not make conscious (or, as far as anyone can tell, unconscious) decisions when we talk, ride a bicycle, drive, make turkey sandwiches, or carry on most social activities. . . . With enough experience with a variety of situations, all seen from the same perspective or with the same goal in mind, but requiring different tactical decisions, the mind of the proficient performer seems gradually to decompose this class of situations into subclasses, each member of which shares not only the same goal or perspective, but also the same decision, action, or tactic. At this point, a situation, when seen as similar to members of this class, is not only thereby understood but simultaneously the associated decision, action, or tactic presents itself. (1987, p. 102)

The idea is that with enough experience with linguistic situations, we gradually learn to "decompose this class of situations into subclasses" for which an appropriate response ("decision, action, or tactic") has already been learned. At the bottom of this process is "experience-based, holistic similarity recognition." Presumably, what this means is that we recognize the current linguistic situation—a particular utterance in a particular kind of situation—as similar to situations we have previously encountered and for which we have learnt an appropriate response.[7]

---

[7] Bechtel intimates a very similar approach:

> What is central is that the child learns to recognize a pattern encompassing the situation in which an utterance is made, the utterance, and the consequences, and that the child learns how to reinstate this pattern when the circumstances are appropriate and the consequences are desired. (1991, p. 26)

Churchland offers no specific account of how his general conception of cognitive activity is supposed to apply to language, but it is not difficult to see in outline how his account would have to go, at least for perception and comprehension: perception of an utterance would be a matter of activation of a prototypical activity vector for utterances of that kind, which could in turn presumably be transformed, along with contextual information, into a semantic prototype corresponding to the meaning of that utterance. Both kinds of prototypical representation would result from the networks in the relevant parts of the brain having been shaped by previous exposure to similar utterances. This extrapolation of Churchland's position is supported by the fact that one of his favorite examples of cognitive activity is the famous NETtalk, a PDP network which produces "speech," or rather "phonemes" from written text. This network functions by generating, in a hidden layer, a prototypical activity vector corresponding to the appropriate letter-to-phoneme transformation for the current input.

Apparently, then, we need to assess the general view, common to these various perspectives, that language comprehension is a matter of recognizing the current utterance in its context as similar to previously experienced situations and producing the response that was previously learned to be appropriate. Rephrased, the generic view is that perception and comprehension of language is basically a matter of correctly categorizing the utterance with which one is currently confronted.

B.   WHY UNDERSTANDING IS NOT CATEGORIZING

As in the case of sensorimotor control, however, this kind of approach seriously misconceives the domain from the outset. This follows almost immediately from a commonplace observation about language, namely that it is productive; because sentences are by their very nature systematically built up out of regular parts, there is a practical infinity of linguistic forms in the language that we can handle easily and quickly. This truism creates two deep structural problems for the proposal that comprehension of utterances is a matter of categorization, however that account might be spelled out. First, by and large, distinct linguistic forms have distinct meanings and demand different treatment. One might put this point by saying that sentences typically belong in their own uni-membered categories. Consequently, processing a sentence cannot count as categorizing it in any significant sense; there is here no treating distinct objects as belonging to the same type and treating them in a uniform way for objects of that kind. Indeed, to do that would be disastrous. When you understand a sentence such as Haugeland's "Mongolian lizards avoid strong cheese," you are not recognizing it as belonging to a whole class of utterance types for which one has a standardized response. You are not treating it as an instance of type T to which response R is appropriate; in order to handle this sentence correctly, you have to treat it as an instance of the category *Mongolian lizards avoid strong cheese.*, of which sentence category there is only one instance.[8] Consequently, comprehension of an utterance cannot be, at the highest level, a matter of categorization; it violates the first basic condition for a process to count as categorization.

Note that it *is* the case that, for any given sentence type, there is a large range of acoustic events that can count as an utterance of that type; thus the process of *perceiving* the utterance—that is, determining its type—might on this basis be regarded as a process of categorizing utterance-tokens into sentence types. However, even this process cannot in fact be one of categorization, for it also succumbs to the second major objection based on the productivity of language. Given productivity, a vast proportion of the utterances we encounter are novel in type and consequently in acoustic form. It is, however, in principle impossible to treat a sentence as a member of a given type in virtue of what it has in common with other members of that type if one has never before encountered other members of that type. Consequently, the processes involved in perceiving and understanding an utterance cannot be *just* categorizing processes, as defined above; they must involve constructive operations based on general and systematic knowledge gained from exposure to other *different* utterances.

This is not to deny that categorization is very important to language; indeed, as Lakoff for one has stressed, language use depends on categorization in all kinds of ways. It is just to deny that language understanding *is* a matter of categorization, at the level at which some proponents of the categorization thesis superficially appear to be maintaining it.

C.   UNDERSTANDING IS CATEGORIZING AT LOWER LEVELS?

At this point, defenders of categorization might be tempted to concede that the *overall* process of sentence comprehension cannot be regarded as merely categorization, but nevertheless insist that categorization or pattern recognition of some kind is the primary cognitive operation at underlying levels. There are many distinct stages in the overall speech comprehension process; according to this response, some process of

---

[8] It might be objected that this sentence actually belongs to a class of variants which also includes, for example, the sentence "*Strong cheese is avoided by Mongolian lizards,*" and for all of which there is a common appropriate response. However, this kind of move cannot overcome the productivity problem, for there is still a practical infinity of such classes.

categorization is the dominant operation at each stage. To illustrate this point, in a way that directly confronts the objections from productivity, it might be pointed out that our ability to recognize and understand a novel sentence is grounded in more basic abilities to directly recognize and process sub-patterns such as words and phrases.

There are at least two drawbacks with this kind of response, however. First, far from being a surprising and interesting *alternative* to mainstream views, the claim that categorization is the essence of cognition construed this way now seems to be entirely compatible with what certain traditional cognitive psychologists have been saying all along. Thus, John Anderson and others have been developing an overall account of the process of parsing (translating from a word-level representation to a meaning representation) utilizing productions whose task it is to scan the word-level representation looking for particular patterns that typically have certain kinds of meanings. As Anderson puts it:

> Pattern-recognizing production systems are a means of implementing the idea that people have a set of strategies and rules for dividing a sentence up into constituents, identifying the character of each constituent, and applying a semantic interpretation to each constituent. (1990, p. 365)

In view of this, to claim that some kind of pattern recognition is crucial to language processing at *some* lower organizational level is not to present any kind of *alternative* to mainstream computational perspectives; rather, it is to fall in line with them. This is certainly not what the enthusiasts of categorization have typically intended to do. In fact, they do very often have deep disagreements with standard computational theorists such as Anderson. They would claim, for example, that there is no straightforward symbolic encoding of the sentence, its meaning, or the productions responsible for the pattern recognition; that it would be impossible to produce any adequate set of explicit productions; that the process of recognizing particular patterns within a sentence could not be done independently of some sense of the sentence as a whole; and so forth. These are interesting and important points. My point here is that such differences are not adequately summarized by insisting that language processing involves categorizing at some lower levels.

The second drawback is even more serious. If one retreats to the claim that categorization is dominant at lower levels of organization, it becomes considerably less clear why anyone should grant the major claim, that cognitive processes are a matter of categorizing. A kind of process can completely dominate at a suitably low level without the resulting cognitive operations taking on the character of those low-level processes. For an extreme analogy, most people agree that spiking activity in neurons is the medium of cognition when considered at a neurochemical level, yet nobody supposes that cognitive processes are spiking processes. Not all low-level neural spiking amounts to cognition, and that which does only does so by virtue of some higher-level organizational principles, which are themselves what makes a process truly cognitive. For another and more directly pertinent example, consider the following claim by Pylyshyn:

> An atomic symbol is a formal entity whose only property is that it is discrete and can be unambiguously "recognized" when it occurs again—that is, from the standpoint of the system as a whole, all copies (tokens) of a particular symbol are indistinguishable from one another yet distinguishable from tokens of every other symbol. Thus the operation of comparing two symbol tokens and taking action which is contingent on whether they are tokens of the same symbol is a primitive operation in all computational systems. (1987, p. 302)

In a minimal sense, it seems, something like categorizing is a primitive operation even in standard symbol-manipulation–based information processing systems. Again, however, nobody is tempted on this basis to claim that cognitive operations are categorizing operations. The general point is this: the top-level structure of cognitive processes is simply not dictated by the structure of lower-level operations which underlie or implement those higher processes.

What the proponents of the categorization thesis would need, in order to substantiate this line of defense (i.e., to defend the main thesis by pointing to categorizing processes at lower levels), is an overall account of the cognitive processes involved in language processing in which categorization figures, but in such a way as to avoid two equally serious pitfalls. One is claiming that language processing *is* a matter of categorization at the highest level; we already know that must be wrong. The other is assigning categorization a lowly role that makes it subordinate to higher-level organizational principles to the extent that it is no longer plausible to claim that cognitive operations are, in their general structure, ones of categorizing. Suffice to say for the moment that no such account of the processes underlying language use has been proposed by any of those maintaining that cognizing is something like categorizing.

VII. Conclusion

A. Dethroning Categorization

In at least these two very broad areas, then, it appears that categorization is entirely the wrong concept in terms of which to attempt to frame one's most general claims about cognition. This is not to downplay the real importance or prevalence of processes of categorization *within* cognition, but simply to reject the idea that categorization is a suitable conceptual tool for developing speculative or philosophical generalizations about the nature of cognition as a whole. It simply has the wrong kind of structure to be what cognition *is*.

There are at least three crucial structural features possessed by many cognitive processes that conflict with the basic format of categorization. The first is a kind of flexibility or adaptability. In a wide variety of cognitive domains, every new problem or situation we confront demands a response tailored to its particular character. Though the current situation may be rather like situations we have encountered previously and learned how to respond to, there is no single response which is always the right way to deal with all those alike situations. In his work on analogy-making, for example, Douglas Hofstadter has stressed that although the current situation may be in some deep ways similar to some previously experienced situation, there are often crucial differences as well, and so the previously learned response must be adapted (or, as he puts it, ''slipped'') to meet the particular details of the current situation (see, e.g., Hofstadter & Mitchell, 1992). The extra cognitive effort involved in adapting the response marks the difference between interesting cases of analogical reasoning on the one hand and mere categorization as defined above on the other. More generally, the remarkable fact about our cognitive capacities in many domains is their ability, on the basis of previous experience, to produce the *right* response, not the *same* response.

Second, and related, some cognitive domains are such that we are constantly confronting and dealing successfully with entirely novel kinds of situation. This is particularly true in *productive* domains such as language. As stressed previously, dealing with such situations simply cannot be, in general, a matter of categorizing them. The key to our being able to deal with them, of course, is that they are in some way systematically constructed from familiar parts, and we have an ability to systematically handle complex wholes on the basis of their parts. When responding to such situations we are not merely recognizing them as being relevantly like previously experienced situations and producing the one response learnt to be appropriate to situations of that kind; we are systematically *constructing* an entirely *novel* response to the whole situation on the basis of quite general knowledge of the significance of the familar parts.

The third deep structural feature has a rather different flavor; it is that many kinds of cognition have an essentially dynamic or temporal aspect. The most obvious examples, of course, are perception and motor control. These kinds of cognition are intimately interlocked with the environment and must happen in real time. Moreover, they are structured so that there are no temporal disparities between input, cognitive processing, and output; rather, all are ongoing and cotemporaneous. Categorization, thought of as a matter of generating a response to an input, has fundamentally the wrong kind of temporal structure to account for these kinds of cognition— even though, of course, some *other* kinds of cognition are categorizing.

The fact that categorizing is a kind of function that standard connectionist networks seem to implement particularly well might lead one to suppose that I am arguing that cognition is not, in general, "connectionist" in character. But this is not so; the stance taken here is quite independent of any verdict on the validity of connectionism as a research paradigm in cognitive science. For one thing, it may turn out that the right kind of connectionist network will provide the best models of categorization, and hence the best accounts of those kinds of cognition that are best construed in such terms. Further, connectionist networks are by no means limited to operations of categorization, and so may be able to account for those kinds of cognition which are *not* a matter of categorizing. Thus, for example, recurrent networks seem to be well suited to providing the sort of continuous control needed in sensorimotor control. I remain agnostic about these particular issues here; the point is simply that my arguments leave plenty of room for connectionism, broadly construed, to be the most appropriate framework in which to develop models of cognition.

B.   CATEGORIZATION: WHAT'S THE APPEAL?

Why might the prototypical position have seemed so superficially appealing? One tendency that may partly explain the powerful influence it seems to be exerting is an over-readiness to generalize from examples of cognitive phenomena, or models of such, which are indeed plausibly construed as a matter of categorization. Thus, as noted, the Dreyfuses promote a revealing and plausible categorization-based account of how expert chess is played. In their accounts of other skills, the chess example looms large; it appears to be the basic blueprint when constructing an account of skilled performance in general. Churchland and Bechtel, by contrast, have nourished their thinking about the nature of cognition by paying particular attention to early connectionist networks, and in particular three-layer back propagation networks. These networks often can be regarded as performing some form of categorization. Churchland for one has openly maintained that his view that cognition is essentially prototype activation is an extrapolation from careful study of the behavior and properties of these network models. These kinds of case studies and computational models are certainly powerful and appealing. The trouble is, if one focuses attention on them for too long, they are apt to exert undue prior influence on the way one thinks about other phenomena that, on more careful reflection, turn out to be really very different.

Reflection on the nature of cognition that is already dominated by certain kinds of examples has a tendency to find itself reinforced by casual analogies. Having found that some isolated cognitive activities are plausibly accounted for—in a reasonably detailed and sophisticated way—in terms of pattern recognition, it is easy to find and draw comfort from intuitive, high–level descriptions of other phenomena in pattern-recognition terms. Consider the following passage from Churchland:

> Children learn to recognize certain prototypical kinds of social situations, and they learn to produce or avoid the behaviors prototypically required or prohibited in each. Young children learn to recognize a distribution of scarce resources such as cookies or candies as a *fair* or *unfair distribution*. . . . They learn to discriminate unprovoked cruelty, and to demand or expect punishment for the transgressor and comfort for the victim. . . . They learn to recognize these and a hundred other prototypical social/moral situations, and the ways in which the embedding society generally reacts to those situations and expects them to act. (1988, p. 299)

What we have here is a redescription of certain everyday phenomena in terms of categorization. It is certainly not an unnatural redescription, but it is important to see that it is metaphorical, in the sense that it is taking a particular technical vocabulary and transplanting it into a wholly new domain. Similarly, the Dreyfuses' writings are replete with natural-sounding extensions of the theoretical vocabulary of the psychology of categorization into everyday domains; for example,

> By playing with all sorts of liquids and solids every day for several years, a child may simply learn to discriminate prototypical cases of solids, liquids, and so on and learn typical skilled responses to their typical behavior in typical circumstances. (1988, p. 33)

Now, generating such redescriptions is relatively easy, natural, and often illuminating. There is nothing wrong in such speculative extensions of one's theoretical tools; indeed, that's just the kind of thing philosophers are expected to do, and it may be the first step in some genuine scientific progress. There are, however, at least two dangers. The first is that one might suppose that one has actually said something helpful about the nature of the cognitive mechanisms *responsible* for the redescribed phenomena. A child may come to recognize unfair distributions, but merely describing what the child does this way does not in itself provide any real evidence that this process is a matter of, say, prototype activation. The cognitive mechanisms underlying the ability to recognize a fair distribution might turn out to involve substituting into a complex set of rules and exceptions, and we might equally well informally describe the child as learning, if implicitly, some general rules of fair distribution.

The second danger is that one will take the casual redescriptions and regard them as further evidence for the general theory that cognition is categorization. A historical parallel may make these points more clear. Behaviorists undoubtedly had all kinds of real successes in training rats and pigeons to exhibit conditioned behavior. Notoriously, certain behaviorists such as Skinner, inspired by such successes, went on to redescribe everyday phenomena in behaviorist vocabulary. Thus, he regarded my uttering "Dutch" when confronted with an old painting as merely my exhibiting the behavior that, in the past, I found reinforcing in such circumstances. Again, the redescription is not wholly ridiculous, but the same two problems are present. First, we have come to realize that to redescribe my utterance this way has little scientific utility, no matter how useful behaviorist tools may be in describing the behavior of rats. Skinner, impressed with the fact that this redescription was *possible* and indeed made a certain sense, made the mistake of thinking that some scientific progress had *already* been made in understanding my utterance. Second, Skinner made the even more grievous error of taking the phenomena redescribed this way to be yet further *evidence* for the very behaviorist approach on which the metaphorical redescription itself was based.

In his devastating attack on Skinner, Chomsky criticized this tendency of Skinner to draw evidential comfort from metaphorical extensions of his theoretical tools:

> Skinner . . . utilizes the experimental results as evidence for the scientific character of his system of behavior, and analogic guesses (formulated in terms of a metaphoric extension of the technical vocabulary) as evidence for its scope. This creates the illusion of a rigorous scientific theory with a very broad scope, although in fact the terms used in the description of real-life and of laboratory behavior may be mere homonyms, with at most a vague similarity of meaning. (1959/1980, p. 51)

It is possible that a similar process is operating when it seems plausible that categorization is the essence of cognition. Those specific cases in which cognitive phenomena can, with reasonable strictness and accuracy, be accounted for in terms of categorization lend scientific reputability to the general doctrine, while additional casual redescriptions of everyday activities as recognizing patterns or situations or whatever lend it the appearance of wide scope.

A third tendency that may be partly responsible for the seductiveness of the idea that cognition might be reduced to categorization is a classic philosophical trap, that of assuming or hoping that big questions have short answers. The mistake of supposing that categorization is the essence of cognition is probably an instance of a wider mistake of supposing that *anything* is the essence of cognition—of supposing that, in other words, there is any *one* proper deep characterization of cognitive operations.

When in a philosophical mood there is always a temptation to say something both succinct and general about the domain one is studying. Others were inclined to say things like that intelligent behavior is a matter of conditioned response, or that cognition is symbol manipulation; given that both of these are wrong when taken in their full generality, one feels tempted to substitute for the erroneous views: to say what cognition *is*, given that it is not *those* things. But cognition, like a national economy, is more likely to be the sum of many *different* kinds of phenomena and processes and structures. There is likely to be just no short, unified answer to the question: What is cognition?

ACKNOWLEDGMENTS

This article has benefited from advice and comments from Roman Taraban, Glenn Nakamura, Doug Medin, Doug Hofstadter, Anil Gupta, and Stuart Dreyfus. Special thanks to Geoff Bingham for patient coaching on the topic of sensorimotor coordination.

REFERENCES

Anderson, J. R. (1990). *Cognitive psychology and its implications* (3rd ed.). New York: W. H. Freeman.

Bechtel, W. (1991, April). *Breaking the link between mentality and language: A connectionist perspective*. Paper presented at the American Philosophical Association Central Division meeting, Chicago.

Bechtel, W., & Abrahamsen, A. A. (1991). *Connectionism and the mind*. Cambridge, MA: Blackwell.

Bingham, G. P. (1988). Task-specific devices and the perceptual bottleneck. *Human Movement Science, 7*, 225–264.

Chase, W. G., & Simon, H. A. (1973) The mind's eye in chess. In W. G. Chase (Ed.), *Visual information Processing*. New York: Academic Press.

Chomsky, N. (1980). [Review of B. F. Skinner, *Verbal behavior*]. In N. Block (Ed.), *Readings in philosophy of psychology: Vol. 1* (pp.48–63). Cambridge, MA: Harvard University Press. (Reprinted from *Language*, 1959, *35*, 26–58)

Churchland, P. M. (1979). *Scientific realism and the plasticity of mind*. Cambridge: Cambridge University Press.

Churchland, P. M. (1986) Some reductive strategies in cognitive neurobiology. *Mind, 95*, 279–309.

Churchland, P. M. (1988). *A neurocomputational perspective*. Cambridge, MA: MIT Press.

de Groot, A. D. (1965) *Thought and choice in chess*. The Hague: Mouton.

Dreyfus, H. L. (1979). *What computers can't do: The limits of artificial intelligence* (Revised ed.). New York: Harper.

Dreyfus, H. L., & Dreyfus, S. E. (1986). *Mind over machine: The power of human intuition and expertise in the era of the computer*. New York: The Free Press.

Dreyfus, H. L., & Dreyfus, S. E. (1987). How to stop worrying about the frame problem even though its computationally insoluble. In Z. W. Pylyshyn (Ed.), *The robot's dilemma: The frame problem in artificial intelligence* (pp.95–111). Norwood, NJ: Ablex.

Dreyfus, H. L., & Dreyfus, S. E. (1988). Making a mind versus modeling the brain: Artificial intelligence back at a branchpoint. *Daedalus, 117*, 15–44.

Hofstadter, D. R., & Mitchell, M. (1992). An overview of the copycat project. In K. J. Holyoak & J. Barnden (Eds.), *Connectionist approaches to analogy, metaphor, and case-based reasoning*. Norwood, NJ: Ablex.

Koh, K., & Meyer, D. E. (1991). Function learning: Induction of continuous stimulus–response relations. *Journal of Experimental Psychology: Learning, Memory and Cognition, 17*, 811–836.

Lakoff, G. (1987). *Women, fire and dangerous things*. Chicago: University of Chicago Press.

Margolis, H. (1987). *Patterns, thinking, and cognition: A theory of judgment*. Chicago: University of Chicago Press.

Pylyshyn, Z. W. (1987). Cognitive science and the study of cognition and language. In E. C. Schwab & H. C. Nusbaum (Eds.), *Pattern recognition by humans and machines* (pp. 295–314). Orlando, FL: Academic Press.

Rips, L. J. (1989). Similarity, typicality, and categorization. In S. Voisniadou and A. Ortony (Eds.), *Similarity, analogy, and thought*. New York: Cambridge University Press.

Skarda, C. A. (1986). Explaining behavior: Bringing the brain back in. *Inquiry, 29*, 187–202.

Smith, E. E. (1990). Categorization. In D. N. Osherson & E. E. Smith (Eds.), *An invitation to cognitive science: Vol. 3. Thinking* (pp.33–53). Cambridge, MA: MIT Press.

Turvey, M. T., Fitch, H. L., & Tuller, B. (1982). The Bernstein perspective: 1. The problems of degrees of freedom and context-conditioned variability. In J. A. S. Kelso, (Ed.), *Human motor behavior: An introduction* (pp.239–252). Hillsdale, NJ: Erlbaum.

WHAT ARE CONCEPTS? ISSUES OF
REPRESENTATION AND ONTOLOGY

William F. Brewer

I. Introduction

In this article I analyze a number of central questions about the nature of concepts. In particular I attempt to provide answers to the questions *What are concepts?* and *How are concepts represented?* The article is designed to provide a framework that organizes theories of concepts in the fields of philosophy, biology, and psychology, with a focus on understanding psychological theories of concepts. It focuses on (1) assumptions about ontology and (2) assumptions about representation. The analysis of ontology (i.e., hypotheses about what exists) has not been a traditional topic for discussion in this area. However, I hope to show that implicit ontological assumptions have played a major role in directing theory and experimentation in the investigation of concepts. The analysis of representation has always been a major issue in the psychological study of concepts. This article continues that concern and relates it to relevant issues in philosophy and biology.

A. CONCEPTS VERSUS MORE MOLAR FORMS
OF REPRESENTATION

Until about 1975 the great majority of researchers in human cognition assumed that most, if not all, human knowledge could be captured by concepts and their associations. However, in the mid-1970s a series of papers by Minsky (1975), Rumelhart (1975), and others proposed that additional forms of representation are needed to deal with more molar cognitive phenomena (see Brewer & Nakamura, 1984, for a discussion of this issue).

It seems to me that the core distinction here is a difference in the types of phenomena that are studied by investigators interested in concepts and those studied by investigators interested in schemata and theories. The phenomena studied by those interested in concepts are typically *objects*, taken loosely to refer to (1) biological organisms such as cats, (2) natural objects such as water, (3) human artifacts such as cars, and (4) human social entities such as vice presidents.

The phenomena studied by those interested in schemata and theories are the more molar phenomena that occur when objects are related to other objects by time (scripts), by intentions (plans), by space (mental maps), and by explanations (theories). Thus, for me, the distinction between concepts and schemata or theories is partly derived from a difference in the domain of phenomena that each class of theories is attempting to capture.

B. MAJOR ISSUES

1. *Ontology*

One major issue that divides theories of concepts is the ontological issue of the existence of structure in the physical world. Some theorists believe that the physical world consists of unique entities and that concepts are mental constructs imposed by humans on the individual entities. Other theorists believe that the physical world is itself structured and that some of the entities in the world are organized into category clusters. In discussing the issue of the nature of biological species, the biologist Dobzhansky formulated the question as: "Is, then, the species a part of the 'order of nature,' or a part of the order-loving mind?" (1935, p. 345).

Within the theories that assume some type of structure in the world there is a wide range of positions. Some theories make the minimal assumption that some entities are more similar to each other than they are to other entities. Other theories make slightly stronger assumptions about the nature of the similarity relations (e.g., that there is graded structure). Finally, there are theories that postulate very explicit forms of structure (e.g., natural kinds) and argue that the similarity relations derive from this structure.

2. Representation

The other major issue that distinguishes theories of concepts is the particular representation that is used to account for the phenomena related to concepts and categorization (cf. Brewer & Pani, 1983, for discussion of some of these issues). Some of the theorists in this area make explicit proposals about some form of mental representation (e.g., words, individual images, generic images, conscious ideas, unconscious ideas). However, for many of the constructs used to discuss concepts (e.g., physical similarity, defining features, basic level, graded structure, family resemblance), the researchers are not explicit about the nature of these forms of representation. It seems to me that these proposals could be viewed as: (1) formal devices that can be used to predict the data with no implication about the actual underlying psychological/physiological processes; (2) proposals about the structure of the representation at a relatively general and abstract level of analysis; and (3) actual proposals about the mental representation of concepts. It is probably the case that these theorists differ on these issues and that there are some who would choose each of these options. In general, I have tried to use the most specific form of proposal that has been provided, even though this means that the different proposals for the representation of concepts are not always at the same level of analysis.

C. CLASSIFICATION OF THEORIES

The core of this article is an attempt to organize theories of concepts in terms of their ontological assumptions and the types of theoretical entities developed to represent concepts.

1. Ontology

I classify concept theories into nine major groups in terms of their ontological assumptions and discuss them in terms of the richness of their assumptions about the structure of the physical world, from those that assume the least amount of structure to those that assume the most. Many concept theorists simply assume a particular ontology without ever overtly discussing it, so I have often had to use my judgment in classifying a particular theory. The nine ontological positions are as follows:

1. Only instances in the world
2. Instances in the world contain common physical elements
3. Instances in the world show similarity
4. Graded structure in the world

5. Family resemblance in the world
6. Concepts as parts of a single instance
7. Unspecified structure in the world
8. Natural kinds in the world
9. Rich ontology

2. Representation

Within each group of theories defined in terms of ontological assumptions, I further subdivide them in terms of the form of representation postulated (e.g., images, words, etc.). The major forms of mental representation covered are as follows:

1. Individual images
2. Words
3. Generic images
4. Abstract ideas
5. Theories

In addition to these forms of mental representation, I also discuss a number of other forms of representation:

1. Common physical elements
2. Exemplars
3. Overall physical similarity
4. Aristotelian concepts
5. Family resemblance
6. Graded structure
7. Basic level
8. Formal objects

3. Disciplines

My overall goal is to understand psychological theories of concepts; in order to meet this goal, however, I review the relevant literature from three disciplines: philosophy, biology, and psychology. I discuss the literature from philosophy because for over 2,400 years the problem of concepts has been a core issue in philosophy, and most current theories of concepts derive directly or indirectly from the work in philosophy. I have also chosen to discuss the literature on the "species problem" from biology. Species is a core construct in biology, and there is a large literature in biology on the nature of the species concept. I decided to examine this literature because I thought it would give perspective to the study of concepts in psychology to see how scientists in a separate discipline have approached the problem of concepts. Within each category defined in terms of ontology and representation I first discuss theories from philosophy, then biology, and finally those from psychology.

This classification scheme does appear to reveal the "ecological niches" for possible theories of concepts, and in some cases I found exemplars of a particular category from each of the three disciplines. However, for some categories I was only able to identify examples from one or two of the disciplines. In these cases it is not clear whether the gaps indicate that the members of that discipline, for one reason or another, never proposed that type of concept theory, or whether I simply was not able to locate an appropriate example.

A number of the biological theories and some of the philosophical and psychological theories do not deal with the issue of representation. In cases where the theory does not postulate a specific form of representation, the discussion is restricted to issues of ontology.

4. Concept Phenomena

One of the core phenomena that theories of concepts have traditionally attempted to explain is the ability of individuals to make inductive generalizations on the basis of previously experienced individual instances to new instances (often treated in philosophy as the problem of "universals"). It is this important aspect of concepts that I focus on in this article.

II. Only Instances in the World

In this section I review theories that assume that there are only instances in the world and that these instances have no intrinsic structure. Theorists who adopt the position that the physical world consists only of arbitrary instances frequently postulate some form of psychological structure or formal structure to account for the apparent occurrence of categories of objects in the physical world.

A. INDIVIDUAL IMAGES

In the long history of thought about the representation of concepts, the theory that concepts are represented in terms of some form of mental image has probably had the longest run.

Philosophy

The British philosopher Berkeley held a strong form of the view that concepts can be explained in terms of individual mental images. In discussing the concept *man* Berkeley stated, "the idea of man that I frame to myself must be either of . . . a crooked, a tall, or a low, or a middle-sized man" (1710/1965, p. 8). He continued this argument in his classic attack on John Locke's discussion of the concept of *triangle*. Berkeley noted,

> If any man has the faculty of framing in his mind such an idea of a triangle as is here described, it is in vain to pretend to dispute him out of it, nor would I go about it. All I desire is that the reader would fully and certainly inform himself whether he has such an idea or no. And this methinks, can be no hard task for anyone to perform. What more easy than for anyone to look a little into his own thoughts, and there try whether he has, or can attain to have, an idea that shall correspond with [Locke's description] of the general idea of a triangle, which is "neither oblique nor rectangle, equilateral, equicrural nor scalenon, but all and none of these at once"? (1710/1965, pp. 12–13)

Berkeley is assuming that when you try to form a mental image of a triangle it will be a specific triangle, and thus your introspective data will show that Locke is incorrect.

Berkeley argued that it is possible to derive generality from concrete instances. He states that in reasoning about triangles one cannot use an abstract idea of triangle (since there are no such things), but instead one uses a particular image of a triangle that "does equally stand for and represent all rectilinear triangles whatsoever, and is in that sense *universal*" (1710/1965, p. 14).

Berkeley's theory suffers from a number of problems—some that Berkeley himself noted in later years. For example, if someone asked Berkeley to verify the statement "all triangles have a right angle" and he happened to image a right triangle, he should give the wrong answer. Aaron (1967, pp. 62–63) has noted that it is not clear how one can appropriately use a single instance to serve for the general class without smuggling in some form of abstraction. A second problem for Berkeley's theory is how to represent abstract concepts such as *soul* or *truth*. Since Berkeley was committed to using specific images to represent everything, there was no easy way for him to deal with abstract concepts. And, in fact, in the 1734 edition of the *Principles* Berkeley conceded this point and introduced an additional form of representation ("notions") to deal with abstract concepts.

B.   WORDS

Another solution to the problem of universals is to attempt to derive the generality from the words that are used to describe the unique instances in the world. This position has traditionally been referred to as *nominalism*.

1. Biology

A number of biologists have taken the position that there are no natural breaks across organisms as they occur over the historical course of evolution (i.e., in the evolutionary chain each individual is of the same species as its parent with no qualitative breaks). Several theorists have then argued that the categories that appear to exist in the world are produced by linguistic usage. This is an extremely pure form of nominalism. For example, Haldane (1956, p. 95) states, "A species in my opinion is a name given to a group of organisms for convenience." He goes on to say, "A dispute as to the validity of a specific distinction [in biological classification] is primarily a linguistic rather than a biological dispute" (p. 96).

It seems to me that this position suffers from a variety of crucial defects. For example, it is not clear how it would account for the ability of human beings to recognize new instances of a category or to make inductive generalizations. In other words, if one learns to apply the name "cat" for cat instances 1 through 3, how does one know to apply the word "cat" to the next new instance that comes along? In addition, it is hard to see how this position can account for the fact that one can make successful predictions about the internal structure of the new instance (e.g., it will have a heart) or the behavior of this new instance (e.g., it will stalk birds).

2. Psychology

During the behaviorist era a number of psychologists also adopted an extreme form of nominalism. For example, Archer (1964) defined concepts as "meaningful words which label classes of otherwise dissimilar stimuli" (p. 238). This view is, of course, subject to all of the objections that have just been outlined in the criticisms of the extreme nominalist view above.

C. FAMILY RESEMBLANCE

Psychology

In 1956, Bruner, Goodnow, and Austin carried out a classic series of experiments on concept learning. This work is frequently discussed as an example of a psychological theory of concepts that assumes concepts have a single defining feature (an issue discussed in a later section). The present discussion focuses on another less noted aspect of the work of Bruner et al. They appear to have adopted the position that the world consists of arbitrary instances. For example, they state,

> The categories in terms of which we group the events of the world around us are constructions or inventions. The class of prime numbers, animal species, ... squares

and circles: all of these are inventions and not "discoveries." They do not "exist" in the environment. (1956, p. 232)

They also state that their view is consistent with the "contemporary nominalism" (p. 7). The stimuli in their experiments were consistent with their stated ontology—they were designed so that all the attributes (number, color, shape) could be crossed and thus the stimulus set was a set of arbitrary instances. In their monograph they report an innovative series of experiments on the learning of disjunctive concepts (e.g., a concept that consisted of one red square *or* one black square *or* two black circles). In retrospect one can see this subset of experiments as studies of family resemblance. The term "family resemblance" comes from Wittgenstein's *Philosophical Investigations* (1958), where he made a classic critique of theories that defined a concept in terms of a necessary feature or a prototype. He used the concept *game* to argue that many concepts were characterized as showing family resemblances where the instances had no one feature in common. Thus, the experiments on disjunction in Bruner et al. can be thought of as an example of a study of a Wittgensteinian family resemblance concept with arbitrary instances.

The philosopher Bambrough (1961) has pointed out the poverty of applying Wittgenstein's family resemblance theory to arbitrary instances. He notes that concepts of this type are "closed" and cannot be learned in the same way as natural concepts can. After having mastered this type of arbitrary concept one cannot make an inferential projection to new instances as one can with natural family resemblance concepts (e.g., in the example from Bruner et al., one cannot know if three red circles is an instance of the concept). It is interesting to note that in Bruner's autobiography (1983) he makes a similar attack on the approach he used in the experiments he had carried out 27 years earlier (pp. 118–120, 127–128).

D. ABSTRACT IDEAS

Another solution to the representation of concepts is to postulate that they are represented in terms of a nonlinguistic, nonimage form of mental representation. This view has traditionally been known as *conceptualism*. Clearly, the English language is somewhat biased in favor of this form of representation since the term often used for this form of representation is "concept." However, to avoid linguistic confusion I use the term "abstract idea" for this specific form of representation and retain the term "concept" as the theory-neutral term for the general topic we are investigating.

Biology

In biology, an example of this position can be found in the work of Bessey (1908). He stated that "Nature produces individuals, and nothing more. . . . So species have no actual existence in nature. They are mental concepts, and nothing more" (p. 218). He suggested that the species concept is used to reduce the demands on memory that would result from having a unique representation for each instance!

Davidson (1954) stated that the concept of the biological species has the same scientific status in biology as phlogiston does in current chemistry. He provides only a sketchy account of the psychological component of the species concept. He states, "We mentally group the similar individuals together into a single unit, despite the fact that the only units present are the individual plants" (p. 249). In other places he refers to the psychological process as one of "mental aggregation" or as "mental perception." These particular applications of abstract ideas as a form of representation face the same problems as the word theory described earlier.

E.   Unspecified Artificial Constructs

Some theorists have adopted the view that there are only instances in the world without proposing any specific representation to provide an account of the apparent existence of the categories of ordinary experience.

Biology

As mentioned earlier, a number of biologists have thought that the Darwinian revolution required one to give up the idea that species were natural kinds that existed in the world. The argument is that if species change in a gradual way over time there can be no fixed species categories in the world. It appears that Darwin himself drew this conclusion from his work. He stated, "we shall have to treat species in the same manner as those naturalists treat genera, who admit that genera are merely artificial combinations made for convenience" (1859/1952, p. 242).

Mayr (1982) notes that Darwin's theory and practice may not have been in agreement. Mayr states, "When one glances over the statements about species made by Darwin in the *Origin*, one might get the impression that he considered species as something purely arbitrary and invented merely for the convenience of taxonomists. Some of his comments remind one of Lamarck's statement that species do not exist, only individuals. And yet, in their taxonomic work both men treated species in a perfectly orthodox manner . . . as if they were so many independent creations" (pp. 268–269). This tradition has continued in biology so that Burma (1949) gave a working definition of species and then concluded that "a species . . . is a fiction, a mental construct without objective existence" (p. 369).

F. FORMAL OBJECTS

Another solution to the problem of concepts has been to deny that concepts are to be given mental representation and to postulate that they exist in a nonphysical, nonmental world. This position is one that is frequently held by theorists concerned with the existence of numbers and other abstract objects. It has traditionally been referred to as a variety of *Platonism*.

Biology

Gregg (1950) has used modern set theory to deal with the species problem. He argued that it was a mistake to claim that species are "real" and to attempt to use biological evidence such as inbreeding relations to defend this position. Instead he argued that species were formal objects. For example Gregg (1950) stated that species are classes and "all classes of objects . . . are abstract, non-spatiotemporal entities" (p. 426).

Burma (1954) argued that a purely formal approach to categories was not appropriate for biology. He stated, "If 'exist' of the propositions 'All species exist' and 'Some species exist' is of the type of logical existence only, then the discussion of these topics is *purely* theoretical . . . [and of no] particular interest to biologists as biologists, whose concern is also with real, not logical existences" (p. 197). Buck and Hull (1966) point out that with Gregg's application of set theory there would be no more reason to add a new instance of a dog to the taxon *Canis familiaris* than there would be to add a new instance of a cockroach.

III. Instances in the World Contain Common Physical Elements

One interesting solution to the problem of universals is to postulate that categories consist of instances in the world that share a common physical element.

A. ARISTOTELIAN CONCEPTS

Philosophy

Aristotle had a complex view of concepts that included the belief that each entity in a category shares an essential property with all other members of that category. The issue of "essences" is discussed below in the section on natural kinds. Of interest for the present section is Aristotle's view on the definition of concepts. In summarizing Aristotle's position, Ross (1964) notes that Aristotle "distinguishes a certain set of fundamental attributes which is necessary and sufficient to mark [some concept] B off from everything else. . . . To know that [some instance] C is B it is enough to know that it has the essential attributes of B—the genus and the differentiae" (pp. 37–38).

B. COMMON PHYSICAL ELEMENTS

Psychology

Many psychologists have interpreted Aristotle's view to mean that members of a concept share a common *physical* element. This interpretation avoids the need to postulate some underlying abstract entity to account for universals and, to some extent, even avoids the need for a construct of similarity. This ontological assumption has been very pervasive. Most of the early experimental studies of concept formation explicitly adopted this view and, in fact, many experimental studies in the current literature implicitly adopt this position. Historically it is interesting to note that this assumption was shared by both introspective psychologists (e.g., Fisher, 1916) and behaviorists (e.g., Hull, 1920). The very influential experiment of Hull (1920) is a good example of this position. Hull gave as his archetype example of how one learns concepts the example of a child being exposed to a number of instances of dogs and coming to develop the concept *dog*. He states that this concept is "a characteristic more or less common to all dogs and not common to cats" (p. 6). The stimuli Hull used in his experiments were designed so that each concept (Chinese characters) contained a common physical element (a radical). In the figure showing the stimuli he labels the common physical element as the "concept."

Hull made no suggestions about representation; however, Fisher (1916) made the interesting proposal that in the early stages of learning, concepts were represented as visual images, but that with practice the image is replaced by other forms of representation.

The hypothesis of common physical elements has come under severe attack. The basic line of argument has been to deny the basic ontological assumption. Thus, Smoke (1932) notes, "Life situations simply do not present 'common elements' in stimulus patterns. No learner of 'dog' ever found a 'common element' running throughout the stimulus patterns through which he learned" (p. 5). Osgood (1953) made similar arguments: "What perceptual commonness exists among mittens, hats, and neckties (they are all 'clothing')? Among crawl, swim, and fly (they are all 'loco-motions')? Among France, Japan, and Russia (they are all 'nations')?" (p. 668).

IV. Instances in the World Show Similarity

In this section I discuss concept theories that postulate a somewhat richer ontological structure in the world. The theories described in this section assume that there are instances in the world and make the minimal as-sumption that some of the instances are more similar to each other than they are to other instances. Thus, these theories assume that particular cats are more similar to each other than they are to elephants. However, these theories do not provide any specific hypotheses about the structure of the similarity. For example, one of the positions discussed in a later section postulates that cats are natural kinds and that they have an under-lying essence (roughly, their DNA) that accounts for the naturally occur-ring groupings of animals and allows one to predict that the next new instance of a cat will have a heart but may be a different color. The theories in the present section postulate that some objects are more similar than others but make no distinction between the similarity of natural kinds (two cats) and the similarity of artificial kinds (two nonsense drawings).

Many theorists use the similarity construct without an explicit discus-sion of their ontological position. Therefore, as a practical matter, I have made an arbitrary decision to place in this section all theorists who men-tion the use of similarity in the formation of concepts and provide no additional specification of the nature of similarity or the origin of the similarity. This means that I am conflating two different types of theories: (1) those that assume that there are similarities in the world and that hu-man beings are able to respond psychologically to these similarities; and (2) those that assume that the world is totally arbitrary, but that humans can form consistent similarity patterns from the arbitrary world. Those theories that adopt the second position, if they could be explicitly iden-tified, would actually belong with the theories discussed earlier that as-sume that the world consists only of unique instances.

A. INDIVIDUAL IMAGES AND WORDS

Philosophy

The British philosopher Hobbes postulated that images were "decaying perceptions"; therefore, mental representations had to be the images of specific things. For example, he stated, "Whatsoever we image is *finite*. Therefore there is no idea or conception of anything we call *infinite*" (1651/1952, p. 54), and "a man can have no thought representing anything not subject to sense. No man therefore can conceive anything, but he must conceive it in some place; and endued with some determinate magnitude" (p. 54). Hobbes then argued that the power to generalize beyond the individual instances derived from the use of words (nominalism). He stated that there was "nothing in the world universal but names; for the things named are every one of them individual and singular. One universal name is imposed on many things for their *similitude* [emphasis added] in some quality, or other accident" (p. 55). Hobbes took this psychological position quite seriously. For example, he argued that if a "deaf and dumb" person (i.e., someone without language) were to look at a particular triangle and work out that the sum of the angles added up to 180 degrees, this individual would have to work it out all over again for each new triangle they came across because they would have no words to carry the generalization (pp. 55–56).

Hobbes' selection of language as the sole construct used to provide inductive generalizations seems untenable. It suffers from the problems pointed out in the earlier discussion of nominalist views and, in addition, it is now known that nonlinguistic organisms such as pigeons can correctly classify new instances of a natural concept such as *fish* (Herrnstein & de Villiers, 1980).

B. WORDS

During the behaviorist period some psychological theorists adopted Hobbes' general position but simply omitted the forbidden mental images.

Psychology

In a revision of an earlier pure nominalist position, Archer (1966) proposed that concepts are "the *label* of a set of things that have something in common" (p. 37). This attempt to obtain generality through verbal labels of instances suffers from the problem discussed above that nonverbal animals show (in the behaviorist's language) "conceptual behavior."

C. Individual Images

Philosophy

David Hume (1739/1978) also adopted the position that the mind only deals with specific images and used a similarity construct ("resemblance"). However, he had a different procedure for trying to obtain generality from the instances. He stated that sometimes ideas

> are not really and in fact present to the mind, but only in power; nor do we draw them all out distinctly in the imagination, but keep ourselves in a readiness to survey any of them, as we may be prompted by a present design or necessity. (p. 20)

Hume then used this proposal to argue that if one happens to have the incorrect specific image when trying to verify a general statement, the appropriate specific images "immediately crowd in upon us, and make us perceive the falshood of this proposition" (p. 21). Hume thus apparently proposed that one searches stored (unconscious?) images until one finds the appropriate instance. This was an ingenious proposal for the time, but clearly he needed to provide a mechanism that selects the "appropriate" specific image, and it is not obvious how he could have done this within his theory.

D. Exemplars

Psychology

In current experimental psychology a class of theories has been proposed (e.g., Medin & Schaffer, 1978) that bear a family resemblance to Hume's theory. These exemplar theories assume that categorization is carried out on the basis of stored instances. In Medin and Schaffer's theory, category judgments are based on the similarity of a given instance to all stored examples. These theories can predict a wide variety of experimental findings and, in fact, Barsalou (1990) has recently argued that it may be difficult or impossible to distinguish theories of this type from theories that assume some form of abstraction. Medin and Schaffer do not suggest how the stored "exemplars" might be represented.

One problem with an instance theory that makes only a minimal similarity assumption about the structure of the instances is that it has no motivated way to account for the origin of the similarity relations between instances (cf. Murphy & Medin, 1985).

E. Generic Images

Another form of representation for concepts that has been proposed is the *nonspecific* mental image. This position has attempted to derive generality through the abstraction of the information in the specific instances in the world into a generic mental image.

1. Philosophy

It is clear that I ought to discuss the work of the British philosopher John Locke, but his thinking is complex both on the issue of ontology and on the issue of representation. On the issue of ontology, Locke (1690/1959) draws a distinction between "real essences," roughly the structure of the physical world, and "nominal essences," psychological structure imposed on the world. Many secondary sources (e.g., Aaron, 1967; Dupré, 1981) suggest that Locke thought we could not have knowledge of real essences, so that in my terms he should be classified as a theorist who holds that the world is composed of unique instances. However, on the basis of the following quote, I think Locke can be seen as postulating that similarity relations exist in the physical world. Locke stated,

> I would not here be thought to forget, much less to deny, that Nature, in the production of things, makes several of them alike: there is nothing more obvious, especially in the races of animals, and all things propagated by seed. But yet I think we may say, the sorting of them under names is the workmanship of the understanding, taking occasion, from the *similitude* [emphasis added] it observes amongst them, to make abstract general ideas. (1690/1959, vol. 2, p. 23)

The terms "general idea" and "abstract idea" play a major role in Locke's theorizing, and it is clear that Berkeley took Locke to mean a generic mental image by these terms. I agree that *sometimes* Locke did use these terms to mean a generic mental image; however, I also believe that Locke frequently used the term to mean an abstract idea (see the discussion in a later section for more detail). An example of a typically ambiguous section in Locke that suggests the construct of a generic mental image is: "For, since all things that exist are only particulars, how come we by general terms . . . ? Words become general by being made the signs of general ideas: and ideas become general, by separating from them the circumstances of time and place" (1690/1959, vol. 2, pp. 16–17).

Now, I think there is good evidence for the existence of generic mental images (Brewer, 1986, p. 38); however, they must be based on surface visual similarity, so they cannot be a general solution to the problem of concepts. For example, how could they represent concepts such as *furniture, truth,* or *triangle?* In addition, the generic image hypothesis suffers because it tends to discard low frequency information and so will lead to incorrect inferences. For example, if one's generic image of the inside of a car has the steering wheel on the left, then one will give the incorrect truth value to the statement "all cars have their steering wheel on the left."

2. Biology

The biologists have not explicitly proposed that species are represented in terms of generic mental images. However, occasionally one runs across suggestive passages such as, "The taxonomist bases his decision on a mental image of these species that is the result of past experience with the stated species" (Mayr, 1957, p. 12). Another example occurs in a discussion by Burma (1954) of the ability of nonscientists to successfully classify organisms. He states, "when the native Papuan . . . recognized a given individual bird as a fantail, he compares this individual with a composite mental image of all fantails of his experience [and] checks to see that the individual in question conforms in essential characters" (pp. 199–200).

3. Psychology

In psychology the study of generic images was taken up by the English scientist Sir Francis Galton. Galton carried out some experiments in which he made generic photographs by taking multiple exposures of different instances of a class such as faces or coins. He noted that "The word generic presupposes a genus, that is to say, a collection of individuals who have much in common and among whom medium characteristics are very much more frequent than extreme ones" (1879, p. 162). He then argued that "the generic images that arise before the mind's eye . . . are the analogues of these composite pictures" (p. 166).

However, it should be noted that Galton appears to have realized that there are strong restrictions on the type of instances that can be accounted for by a theory of generic mental images. He stated,

> No statistician dreams of combining objects into the same generic group that do not cluster towards a common centre, no more can we compose generic portraits out of heterogeneous elements, for if the attempt be made to do so the result is monstrous and meaningless. (1879, pp. 162–163)

The image approach to concepts was banished in the field of psychology in the United States for about 50 years during the behaviorist period, but then came back in full form in the work of Allan Paivio in the late 1960s. Paivio (1971) argued that visual images were the form of representation for concrete words.

This tradition continued in the work of Eleanor Rosch and her co-workers. In summarizing their work on basic level categories they stated, "Basic objects are shown to be the most inclusive categories for which a concrete image of the category as a whole can be formed" (Rosch, Mervis, Gray, Johnson, & Boyes-Braem, 1976, p. 382). However, in Rosch's work the image is just one strand of a much more complex theory.

Although there is some limited evidence that generic visual images play a role in concept tasks, they cannot be a general solution since they can only capture surface visual similarity and so cannot deal with concepts such as *furniture* or *vacations*.

F. UNINTELLIGIBLE THEORIES

While there are many problems with the particular theories reviewed in this article, they all seem directed at giving an explanatory account of the traditional philosophical problem of universals. However, during the behaviorist period in psychology, theorists were faced with the difficulty that most obvious solutions to the problem of universals involve the postulation of entities that behaviorists wanted to exclude from the science of psychology. Faced with this bind they produced a number of theories that do not seem to be in the same conceptual universe as the other theories in this article. One brief example follows: Kendler (1964) states that concepts "are associations, they function as cues (stimuli), and they are responses" (p. 226).

G. OVERALL PHYSICAL SIMILARITY

A large number of theories have used overall physical similarity as a way to classify instances into categories. Many of these theories do not take a stance on exactly how the overall similarity might be represented, but since this is an important issue it will be discussed here.

1. Philosophy

A number of philosophers have made use of a construct of overall physical similarity. Quine is a particularly interesting example. Quine argues that any behaviorist/empiricist theory of learning must, at a minimum, incorporate an innate similarity space. He states that the learner

> must, so to speak, sense more resemblance between some stimulations than between others. Otherwise a dozen reinforcements of his response "Red", on occasions where red things were presented, would no more encourage the same response to a thirteenth red thing than to a blue one. . . . In effect therefore we must credit the child with a sort of prelinguistic quality space. (1960, p. 83)

In his later writing Quine (1969) goes on to argue that the initial innate similarity metric evolves into a theory-based similarity metric.

Quine makes clear that he does not believe that the innate similarity metric is imposed on an arbitrary world. He asks,

Why does our innate subjective spacing of qualities accord so well with the functionally
relevant groupings in nature as to make our inductions tend to come out right? Why
should our subjective spacing of qualities have a special purchase on nature and a lien
on the future? (1969, p. 13)

He answers that evolution will select for those similarity metrics that are
associated with survival in the physical world. The problem with theories
based purely on physical similarity is discussed below.

2. Biology

A group of biologists known as numerical taxonomists or pheneticists have
taken a very positivist/empiricist approach to the species concept (e.g.,
Sokal & Sneath, 1963). The members of this school argue that species
should be defined in terms of overall physical similarity. They attacked
Aristotelian approaches to species (see below) on two counts. They state
that the Aristotelian's use of single logical divisions frequently does not
work in practice (i.e., does not give "natural" groups). The pheneticists
proposed to replace the Aristotelian logical analysis with a family resemblance approach to species. They also argued that, in practice, Aristotelian
approaches were based on "intuitive" overall similarity. The pheneticists
proposed to measure physical similarity by an "objective" unweighted
index of the physical characteristics of the organism being classified. The
pheneticists also attacked the theory-embedded approach to classification
that has often been adopted by those biologists using a "biospecies"
definition of species. The pheneticists argued that for most practical decisions about how to classify an organism, the use of evolutionary phyletic
criteria (e.g., the occurrence of interbreeding) was often purely speculative and therefore one was better off using a "theory-neutral" unweighted
set of physical characteristics.

Hull (1970/1976) mounted a powerful theory-based attack on the pheneticists' attempt to use unweighted similarity to classify species. He argued
that observation is always theory-laden, so that claims that one is using
theory-neutral characteristics are an illusion. Thus, the decision to use a
particular "physical attribute" such as dorsal nerve cords as a one of the
characteristics of a species reflects a long theoretical tradition in biology.
Nor would a pheneticist who found a insect specimen with a broken
antenna choose that particular physical attribute for purposes of classification. In practice the pheneticists are not able to adopt a theory-neutral
approach to species. For example, the pheneticists' decisions to classify
male and female peacocks as members of the same species is based on an
implicit biological theory and not on physical similarity.

3. *Psychology*

Many psychologists have also adopted a theory of concepts based on the assumption that concepts are formed on the basis of overall (physical?) similarity. For example, Smith (1981) states that "overall similarity is the dominant relation by which complex objects are segregated into categories" (p. 811). Recently, similarity-based approaches in psychology have come under strong criticism (Murphy & Medin, 1985; Vosniadou & Ortony, 1989). The basic line of attack has been to argue that similarity-based models just assume similarity exists in the world and do not provide an account of the origin of the similarity. In addition, these approaches do not have a motived way to distinguish between artificial and natural ("coherent") categories.

V.   Graded Structure in the World

The theories in this section are similar to the similarity-based theories just discussed, but they postulate somewhat more specific structure in the world. The theories in this section assume that entities in the world have a graded structure, with a core and instances that show decreasing amounts of similarity as they diverge from the core.

GRADED STRUCTURE

1. *Philosophy*

The natural philosopher William Whewell suggested that the traditional Aristotelian techniques of classification and definition do not apply well to biological natural kinds. He proposed that concepts have a graded structure, which he said was "so contrary to many of the received opinions respecting the use of definitions and the nature of scientific propositions, they they will probably appear to many persons highly illogical and unphilosophical" (1847/1967, vol. 1, p. 493). He stated that for biological concepts, "The class is steadily fixed, though not precisely limited; it is given, though not circumscribed; it is determined, not by a boundary line without, but by a central point within; not by what it strictly excludes, but by what it eminently includes; by an example, not by a precept" (p. 494). This approach avoids the problem of defining concepts in terms of necessary and sufficient features and appears to capture one interesting aspect of the structure of human categories. However, a simple graded structure does not seem to provide enough structure. For example, the graded structure might locate both hummingbirds and penguins as fairly nonfocal birds, but would not give an account of our understanding about the very different reasons that they are nonfocal. It seems likely that it is other forms of knowledge that *produce* the graded structure.

2. *Psychology*

Eleanor Rosch has made arguments for graded structure in the field of psychology. In an important article Rosch (1973) broke the long tradition in experimental psychology of using artificial instances generated by rules and proposed that categories have internal structure. She stated that this structure included "a 'core meaning' which consists of the 'clearest cases' (best examples) of the category, 'surrounded' by the other category members of decreasing similarity to that core meaning" (p. 112). With this type of assumption, new instances can be categorized by checking to see how similar they are to the prototypes (best examples) of the category. Rosch did not give an explicit account of how graded structure might be represented. In fact, in Rosch (1978, p. 40) she explicitly stated that the construct of a prototype is not a theory of representation.

In the 1973 article Rosch did not actually state whether she believes the graded structure is a property of the world or a property of the human categorizer. If she believed that the graded structure is imposed on a world of arbitrary individuals, then her position would actually belong with the ontological instance positions discussed earlier.

The hypothesis that the world has graded structure and that human concepts can map this structure can predict a wide range of data (cf. Mervis & Rosch, 1981). However, using an overall metric of similarity to place *clock* and *bookcase* fairly far from the center of the furniture category seems to ignore much qualitative knowledge that individuals have about these members of the furniture category.

VI. Family Resemblance in the World

The theories in this section postulate that many (or perhaps all) entities in the world are structured in overlapping similarity patterns in the way that the faces of the members of a human biological family are structured. The entities in a cluster share overlapping sets of features but do not all have any one particular feature in common. Note that the family resemblance view contains an ontological assumption about the world that is somewhat more specific than the minimal similarity view discussed earlier. The similarity view does not have to imply a family resemblance structure. One could postulate that instances in the world have necessary properties and nonnecessary properties and that category similarity is based on some combination of these features (a nonfamily resemblance position).

FAMILY RESEMBLANCE

1. Philosophy

As discussed earlier, Wittgenstein (1958) introduced the family resemblance construct to deal with concepts in which the instances lacked a single common feature. However, while he rejects the idea that all the instances have a common feature, it is clear that Wittgenstein thought family resemblance concepts reflected *some* type of structure in the world. He noted, "we see a complicated network of similarities overlapping and criss-crossing: sometimes overall similarities, sometimes similarities of detail" (p. 32). While Wittgenstein's analysis provides a powerful critique of theories that postulate that concepts have a common necessary feature, he does not provide much help in explaining the basis of one's ability to make inferential projections of a family resemblance concept.

2. Biology

Hull (1965a, 1965b) made a powerful attack on biologists who were using the Aristotelian technique of necessary and sufficient features. He argued that the fact that in modern evolutionary theory species change gradually over time shows that the species cannot be defined in the traditional Aristotelian fashion, and he goes on to suggest that species are better thought of as "cluster concepts," as argued by Wittgenstein.

Ruse (1988) has also discussed application of family resemblance concepts in biology. He notes that "Species can thus be given 'polythetic' or 'polytypic' definitions, whereby membership is determined by possession of some from a set of attributes, no one of which is necessary but a number of which is sufficient" (p. 54). However, Ruse goes on to make the important qualification that "This, of course, still leaves open the question of why one should think that species are natural or objective" (p. 54).

3. Psychology

In a very influential paper, Rosch and Mervis (1975) attacked the view that the natural concepts used by humans are logical categories possessing a common feature. They referred to Wittgenstein's arguments and carried out a series of experiments which they interpreted as showing that some natural categories as used by humans are structured in terms of family resemblances. They are not explicit on the ontological issue but do suggest in one place that certain types of categories occur because that is where "cuts in the world may be made" (p. 575). They are ambivalent about how family resemblance might actually be represented in the mind. They suggest that it might be represented by "images," or "ideas," or an "abstract representation," or by the comparison of new instances to certain category instances (p. 575).

It is clear that human beings *can* form family resemblance categories for even arbitrary instances (cf. the earlier discussion of the work of Bruner et al., 1956). However, the position leaves open the issue of where the observed family resemblances in natural concepts comes from.

VII.   Concepts as Parts of a Single Instance

In recent years many biologists have attempted to solve the species problem by asserting that species are not a class but a single individual delimited in time and space. Thus, this position postulates considerable structure in the world—but, structure of a fundamentally different kind than that postulated by all the other positions in this article. For this position the basic structural relation in the world is that of an instance as part of a whole.

Biology

The biologists adopting this approach certainly appear to have carved out a completely original solution to the problem of concepts, but not one that I think recommends itself to other disciplines. This approach was initially proposed by Ghiselin (1974), elaborated by Hull (1976, 1978), and has been recommended to the cognitive science community (Ghiselin, 1981). Ghiselin (1977) states that his original article was an overt attempt to cause a Kuhnian paradigm shift in the way that biologists deal with species. There are several concerns that appear to motivate this ontological shift. One factor is that in evolutionary theory species are dynamic and change over time. A second factor is the concern that species occur at a fixed time and place in evolutionary history and thus are not timeless universals. The solution is to argue that a species is a single individual and that individual specimens are *part* of this single "superorganism." For example Hull (1976) states that under this new view, "Organisms remain individuals, but they are no longer members of their species. Instead an organism is part of a more inclusive individual, its species" (pp. 174–175). The obvious problem that the individual organisms that make up the parts of a species do not seem as spatio-temporally compact as the parts of traditional individuals is dealt with by making an analogy between a species and a corporation, which can be thought of as a individual, yet is not a spatio-temporally compact entity.

Even though this view is apparently the currently preferred view of the species concept among philosophically sophisticated biologists, it seems to me to be fatally flawed. Clearly, one crucial function that a concept of species plays, both for naive use and for scientific use, is that it supports inductions. For example, in a discussion of the purposes of biological classifications, Platnick and Nelson (1981) note,

> What taxonomists do is to hypothesize, generally on the basis of a very small sample of characters, that nature is ordered in a certain specifiable pattern, and that no matter what other characters of a group we might choose to examine in the future, we will find the same pattern again and again. (p. 117)

Yet, it is not clear how the theory of the species as an individual can serve this role. For example, Hull (1978) states, "Organisms are not included in the same species *because* they are similar to . . . each other but *because* they are part of the same chunk of the genealogical nexus" (p. 353). The problem is that the relation *part of* does not seem to support the correct form of induction. Thus, one is not able to make strong inferences from an individual's fingernail to knowledge about their liver or about the headlights of a car from knowledge of its carburetor; whereas, for both the ordinary and the scientific concept of *cat,* one can make powerful inferences about the characteristics of a new instance of a cat based on a previous instance of a cat.

VIII. Unspecified Structure in the World

In this section I discuss theories of concepts that assume the existence of a physical world that has some degree of structure, but the nature of the structure is relatively unspecified. Once again it is sometimes difficult to be sure of a given theorist's views on this ontological issue, and so some of the theories I discuss in this section might actually belong in one of the earlier sections.

ABSTRACT IDEAS

1. Philosophy

One of the first people to attempt to break away from the image view of concepts was St. Augustine, some 600 years after Aristotle. Augustine believed that most concepts were represented in terms of images, but he argued that certain types of information such as those learned in the "liberal sciences" were not represented in image form. He noted that after he had been taught some subject matter in Greek he might have images of the words as he heard them but that "the things are neither Greek, nor Latin, nor any other language" (Augustine, 1952, p. 76). However, Augustine remained a strong imagist and so did not actually adopt the abstract idea approach for this type of information. Instead, he took the somewhat counter-intuitive approach that whereas objects were represented as images, the information from the liberal arts were stored as "the things themselves" (p. 75).

One of the first clear statements of the abstract idea position was that of the French philosopher Descartes. He made a clean distinction between images and ideas. He stated, "by 'ideas' I do not just mean the images depicted in the imagination. . . . Instead, by the term 'idea' I mean in general everything which is in our mind when we conceive something, no matter how we conceive it" (Descartes, 1641/1970, p. 105). Descartes noted that if he thought about a "chiliagon" (a thousand-sided polygon), "I certainly conceive truly that it is a figure composed of a thousand sides . . . but I cannot in any way [image] the thousand sides of a chiliagon" (Descartes, 1642/1931, vol. 1, pp. 185–186). Descartes is, of course, assuming that one's visual mental image of a chiliagon would be indistinguishable from one's mental image of a circle.

Earlier, in discussing the English philosopher John Locke, I argued that he used the term "abstract idea" to include both generic mental images and abstract ideas; therefore, he belongs in this section in addition to the previous one. Locke stated,

> The mind makes the particular ideas received from particular objects to become general; which is done by considering them as they are in the mind such appearances,—separate from all other existences, and the circumstances of real existence, as time, place, or any other concomitant ideas. This is called ABSTRACTION, whereby ideas taken from particular beings become general representatives of all of the same kind. (1690/1959, vol. 1, pp. 206–207)

This passage can be read to mean generic images or abstract ideas, but Locke's discussion of the chiliagon case (ibid., p. 493) and his discussion of abstract concepts such as *murder* make clear that he intends the terms "general idea" and "abstract idea" to be much more abstract than the construct of a generic image (cf. Aaron, 1955, pp. 201–202; Aaron, 1967, pp. 28–33).

The evidence for the placement of this class of theories is weak. These theorists have rarely been explicit about their views on the structure of the world, and they may actually be better thought of as examples of a similarity ontology. However, I have resisted classifying them in that section because the examples they give when trying to distinguish their view from an image view (e.g., chiliagon, murder) suggest that they think of the abstract ideas as having considerable structure.

The theory that the world contains structure and that concepts are abstract, nonlinguistic, psychological entities that represent that structure can deal with many of the phenomena associated with concepts; however, the approach has achieved sufficiency by giving up the constraints imposed by forms of representation such as specific or generic mental images. Thus, this approach has become so unconstrained that it provides little structure for detailed theories of concepts.

2. *Biology*

Reig (1982) has argued that taxonomic species are best treated within a conceptualist epistemology. He formulates the position as follows: "The taxa are concepts which refer to groups or organisms existing in the realm of reality" (p. 484). In another place he states, "The relationships between taxa and the organisms which belong to them, are relationships between concepts and things" (p. 485).

3. *Psychology*

One possible early example of the abstract idea approach in cognitive psychology is Posner's investigations of subjects' learning to classify sets of dot patterns generated from a single underlying base form. This work was explicitly titled, "On the Genesis of Abstract Ideas." However, a careful reading of Posner and Keele (1968) and Posner (1969) shows that their view of representation was inconsistent (much like Locke's). For example, in Posner and Keele (1968) they state that after learning a series of dot patterns, the "Ss might have an image or mental picture of the individual instances or of the abstracted central tendency. Or perhaps the material is in the form of verbal description" (p. 362). However, the discussion of the form of representation in Posner (1969) stated,

> The description that S stores about the dot patterns is a description of his *visual* experience, and it can be used to recognize visual information. However, this does not mean that the information is stored in terms of a visual image, that S could see or visualize the sets of dots that represent the central tendency of the pattern, or that the formation of the abstract representation was free from verbalization. (p. 73)

One psychologist who does belong in this section is a younger version of myself. In 1975 I carried out a series of memory experiments showing that subjects recalling sentences that contained an English synonym (i.e., a concept with two lexical instantiations, such as "difficult" and "hard") often gave the wrong lexical item in recall (e.g., given "difficult" they would recall "hard"). I concluded that the memory for those concepts was stored "in terms of nonlinguistic, nonimage, abstract representations (ideas)" (Brewer, 1975, p. 458). However, in the conclusion of the article I argued that the construct of *idea* as used in the article did not provide enough structure to give a satisfying account of the phenomena (p. 464).

IX.   Natural Kinds in the World

In this section I discuss theories of concepts that postulate that entities in the world are organized into natural groups (e.g., cats, gold). These naturally occurring groups have traditionally been called *natural kinds*. It is assumed that these natural kinds exist independently of human minds. Theorists who hold this view typically postulate that there is some underlying property (an "essence") that causes different instances of a natural kind, such as gold, to be alike and to be qualitatively different from other natural kinds, such as sulfur. And, in fact, modern chemistry can be thought of as the success story that resulted from the assumption that natural substances have essences.

A.   ARISTOTELIAN CONCEPTS

Aristotle proposed a particular form of representation for natural kinds. He argued that each natural kind could be defined in terms of a set of necessary and sufficient features.

1.   Philosophy

Aaron (1967) summarizes Aristotle's view on natural kinds as

> Each species has its specific form, although the form does not exist separated. On the contrary, each object belonging to the species possesses this form as its essence, since it is shared in common by all objects pertaining to that species. For instance, there is the specific form of man which all men have in common, the real essence which makes them men rather than horses or apes. (p. 24)

It is not completely clear what type of psychological representation Aristotle adopted; however, most translators assume he believed in some form of image theory. For example, a section of *De Anima* is translated as, "To the thinking soul images serve as if they were the contents of perception. . . . That is why the soul never thinks without an image" (1952, p. 663).

However, it is not this aspect of Aristotle's theory of concepts that has major consequences for later theories of natural kinds. The important aspect of his theory is his hypothesis that species can be defined in terms of a set of necessary and sufficient features. Some of the difficulties with this position are discussed below.

2. Biology

One of the early approaches to taxonomic analysis in biology was the work of Linnaeus, which was based on the earlier work of Aristotle. Linnaeus assumed that each species had an essence and that the task of the biologist was to define each species in the Aristotelian logical form. For each organism the biologist was to give its Genus, the aspect of its essence which is predicable of other organisms, and its Differentia, that aspect of its essence which is uniquely predictable of the organism being defined (cf. Cain, 1958). The particular Aristotelian assumption that these essences were "pure" changeless underlying forms that could be captured by a single essential feature has received severe criticism (Hull, 1965a, 1965b). The basic line of attack has been to argue that species conceptualized in terms of population genetics must be much less rigid than the Aristotelian view.

B. THEORIES

1. Philosophy

Putnam (1970) has adopted the view that natural kinds are classes of things that appear to be held together or explained by underlying mechanisms. He has suggested that these concepts may be represented in terms of theories. He states, "A natural kind term is simply a term that plays a certain kind of role in scientific or pre-scientific theory: the role, roughly, of pointing to common 'essential features' or 'mechanism' beyond and below the obvious 'distinguishing characteristics'" (p. 52).

2. Biology

A number of biologists have taken the recent discussions of natural kinds in philosophy and applied them to the species concept. Kitts and Kitts (1979) were among the first to make this argument. They state that "a biological species is . . . a kind whose members share an essence" (p. 614). They appear to believe that essences are grounded in scientific theories. They state, "What determines whether an organism belongs to some species is the possession of an *underlying trait* which is recognized not in immediate observation but in the course of scientific investigation" (p. 614).

Somewhat earlier, Dobzhansky (1937) had made a point that can be interpreted as support for the natural kind position. He noted that, in actual practice, the classification of organisms did not change dramatically after Darwin even though the theory of what a species was did change. Dobzhansky concluded that "the only inference that can be drawn from [this fact] is that the classification now adopted is not an arbitrary but a natural one, reflecting the objective state of things" (p. 305).

X. Rich Ontology

In this section I discuss concept theories that assume a very rich ontology. These theories are similar to those that postulate natural kinds, but they adopt an even stronger realist position and assume that the natural groupings in the world also include such things as human artifacts (e.g., cars, computers), social kinds (extroverts, professors), and psychological kinds (e.g., fears, intentions). One way to see the distinction is to consider what kinds of entities would be in the world if human beings did not exist. Presumably the natural kinds that were discussed in the previous section would exist regardless of whether humans were around or not. The ontological position in this section assumes, in addition to natural kinds, the existence of objects made by people, human mental states, and socially defined entities. None of these entities would exist if there were no humans. Some of these entities are clearly completely conventional (e.g., there is no requirement that there be a sport of baseball). However, once these entities come into being, they provide structure in somewhat the same way as natural kinds.

A. BASIC LEVEL CONCEPTS

Psychology

Rosch et al. (1976) made a strong attack on the ontological assumptions of earlier psychological theories of concepts that (implicitly) assumed that the instances in the world are arbitrary. They state that "it is an empirical fact 'out there' that wings co-occur with feathers more than with fur" (p. 429). They carried out an impressive series of experiments that seem to show that certain types of categories ("basic categories") are psychologically "privileged" across a wide variety of psychological tasks. They argued that the basic categories occur because "the perceived world is not an unstructured total set of equiprobable co-occuring attributes. Unlike the artificial stimulus arrays typically used in concept identification research, the material objects of the world possess high correlational structure" (p. 428). They went on to suggest a very rich ontology in which the categories might be structured in terms of things such as common attributes, common function, and common shapes. These authors provide no explicit theory of representation though they give some hints, such as the suggestion that subjects "were thinking of prototypical category members when making the judgments" (p. 433). This ontological position avoids many of the criticisms that have been leveled at other theories, but, as a psychological theory, this approach has not yet been well articulated.

B. THEORY-EMBEDDED CONCEPTS

1. Philosophy

The view that concepts derive their meaning from being embedded in theories has been a common thread running through many different views on the philosophy of the science. For example, Hempel (1966) makes the general point that "concepts of science are the knots in a network of systematic interrelationships in which laws and theoretical principles form the threads" (p. 94). Suppe (1977) discusses a more radical position in which it is argued that "all the principles of the theory contribute to the meanings of the terms occurring in them; hence any change in theory alters the meanings of all the terms in the theory" (p. 199). While this more extreme position has run into difficulties, the general position that scientific concepts are embedded in theories seems to be a core characteristic of science. The question for the issues discussed here is, Does this analysis apply to the broader class of ordinary nonscientific concepts? In the section on psychology below we will see that some researchers do think this approach applies to ordinary concepts.

2. Biology

In a very important article in the literature on the biological concept of the species, Ruse (1969) made some general proposals about the relationship of theories and concepts. He applied these ideas to biology and suggested that the appropriate concept of species for biologists was one that was embedded in a network of laws. He argued that, for science, what it means for something to be real was for it to enter into a network of laws (p. 107). He then argued that one particular definition of species, the biospecies definition, was real. (A biospecies approach defines species as an actual or potentially interbreeding population.) He noted that definitions of species based purely on physical similarity were arbitrary and thus not "real" except insofar as they happened to reflect some underlying nonarbitrary theoretical construct.

3. *Psychology*

In an important article, Murphy and Medin (1985) argue that previous psychological theories of concepts are inadequate and that treating categories as embedded in theories resolves many of the difficulties. They focus on the issue of what makes some categories coherent and others not. They argue that most psychological theories of concepts treat concepts as prototypes or as collections of attributes and so cannot provide enough structure to account for category coherence, because every pair of objects has many features in common and so high or low similarity can be arbitrarily achieved by selecting an appropriate subset of features. They propose that human beings have naive theories of the world and that it is these theories that select appropriate features and give coherence to categories (e.g., subjects will tend to think that birds have light bones because of beliefs they have about animals and flying objects). It is the theories that allow one to make inductive projections from one instance of a category to new instances.

Murphy and Medin do not take an overt position on the issue of structure in the world; however, if they do not assume that the naive theories are reflecting the structure of the natural world, then it is difficult to see how the theories lead to successful inferences about these objects. The theory-based approach with a rich ontology can deal with most of the objections that have been raised with earlier theories of concepts. However, it lacks specificity. What does it actually mean to say that something is represented in terms of a theory? Much of the force of this view comes from our implicit views on the role of theories in science, and clearly the proposal that ordinary, everyday concepts can be represented as theories or as embedded in theories needs to be made more explicit.

XI.   Conclusions

So, gentle reader, now that we have waded through this enormous range of theories—what *are* concepts? and how *are* they to be represented?

A.   STRUCTURED WORLD

It seems to me that this review shows that theories of concepts that adopt a view that there is no structure in the physical world consistently run into one fundamental difficulty—they have no way to account for the structure of concepts that motivates the whole endeavor. For example, proponents of an unstructured world have severe trouble in explaining why one can project the properties of one instance of a natural kind such as gold to the next instance of gold one encounters. To put it bluntly, I think theorists who believe that the structure of the natural world is totally imposed by human cognition would have some real explaining to do to a male robin who hears about this theory and attempts to mate with a female sparrow!

B. RICH ONTOLOGY

In developing psychological theories of concepts, it seems to me that we must adopt a very rich ontology of entities that humans can think about. It appears that human beings can form concepts of: (1) natural kinds such as gold and cats, (2) nonexistent natural kinds such as ghosts and phlogiston, (3) human artifacts such as cars and furniture, (4) social entities such as aunts and librarians, (5) psychological entities such as pleasure and mental images, and (6) abstract entities such as prime numbers and truth. Thus, any theory of concepts that is striving to be observationally adequate must be able to represent these types of entities.

The review of theories of concepts in this article shows that many theorists think that that there is no structure to the physical world and that the apparent structure that we see is imposed by us on the world. Other theorists implicitly draw a line between entities in the physical world and other types of entities and assume that there is structure in the physical world, but that all other entities are arbitrary. The analysis of these issues presented in this chapter suggests that one must adopt a very rich ontology in which there are many different types of ontological entities (e.g., natural kinds, human artifacts, psychological entities, social entities, abstract entities) and that all of them impose structure on human concepts. The degree of constraint may differ for the different ontological categories, but there is considerable structure nonetheless.

For example, consider the classification of theoretical positions in this article—certainly a very confusing and flexible set of entities! The classification of concept theories in this article is quite different from other recent attempts (e.g., Medin & Smith, 1984), yet, once one accepts the premise that it is fruitful to classify concept theories in terms of ontology and representation, then there is structure in the theories that provides strong constraints on their classification. Thus, Berkeley's theory does not belong with Rosch's family resemblance view, but Aristotle's and Linnaeus's theories do belong together. Additional evidence that it is not "anything goes" for the various types of nonphysical entities is that the readers of earlier drafts of this article convinced me that I was simply wrong in the way I had classified certain positions. If the classification scheme developed in this paper is a completely arbitrary system imposed by me on these theoretical positions, then how could I have been convinced that I should change the classification of a number of the theories?

Note, however, that there appears to be more constraint on some classes of entities than others. It seems that one has more flexibility in classifying entities such as these theories than one does in classifying natural kinds. It is presumably this difference that has caused some theorists to assume that there is a qualitative distinction to be made between concepts of natural kinds and concepts of other types of entities. However, I am proposing that there is structure across all types of ontological categories.

C. CONCEPTS REFLECT STRUCTURE IN THE WORLD

The above argument provide considerable support for the position that psychological concepts are based on the structure provided by physical, social, and psychological entities. In a weak moment I might for a brief instance agree with the idealists that I can't be *absolutely* certain about the structure of the world. But, basically, I think that our concepts are strongly driven by the structure in the world and that this is, in fact, what underlies our ability to make successful inductions from one instance of a category to a new instance.

The argument I am making for theories of concepts is analogous to one that Johnson-Laird has used to criticize other forms of representations (e.g., Johnson-Laird, Herrmann, & Chaffin, 1984). In an earlier article, Johnson-Laird (1980) had proposed mental models as a form of representation. In that article he stated,

> A model *represents* a state of affairs and accordingly its structure is not arbitrary like that of a propositional representation, but plays a direct representational or analogical role. Its structure mirrors the relevant aspects of the corresponding state of affairs in the world. (p. 98)

The position advocated in the present article is that the world is richly structured and that concepts represent that structure.

XII. Implications

A. IMPORTANCE OF ONTOLOGY

Psychologists rarely make their ontological positions explicit and rarely discuss the positions of other theorists. Yet, the analysis in this article shows that a concept theorist's theories and experiments are often dramatically determined by underlying ontological assumptions. If one does not believe that there are natural kinds, then it makes perfect sense to use arbitrary stimuli in concept experiments and to think that the findings of these experiments will generalize to natural world concepts.

If one believes that instances of concepts in the world contain a common physical property (e.g., Hull, 1920), then it makes sense to use Chinese characters in which the concepts are defined in terms of a common physical feature. In retrospect, one may find the problems with Hull's view obvious; however, most theorists are not aware of the ontological assumptions they are making. For example, in the openings pages of Hull's article he states that "For the results of a psychological experiment to be taken as characteristic of any actual life-process, it is obvious that the experiment must duplicate all of the conditions essential to that process" (p. 3).

The analysis of the ontology of concept theories is also revealing in other ways. For example, it appears that the excitement generated by Rosch's work on concepts was largely the result of her ontological positions, not her views on representation, since in these papers she rarely made specific proposals about representation.

B. ARBITRARY STIMULI

In this review it has become evident that psychologists who have chosen to use well-controlled artificial experimental materials have run into trouble. This observation about the use of simple well-controlled materials seems to fly in the face of the success that the physical sciences have achieved through the use of highly simplified experimental situations. However, one has to take into account the ontological issues. The simplification strategy only works if the simple model of the phenomena captures the essence of what the researcher was intending to study. If there is an important distinction between artificial and natural kinds and the simplification ignores this, it can run into real trouble. If there is richer structure in the world than just physical similarity, then experimenters who restrict their stimuli so that the categories are based only on physical similarity may find their findings of limited theoretical scope. In general, the use of arbitrary stimuli reduces, or eliminates, the ability of the subject to use relevant old knowledge, so, in that way, it does not model the typical case in the natural world.

C. AD HOC CONCEPTS

Barsalou (1983) published an interesting article investigating "ad hoc categories." He showed that humans can form categories such as "things to take from one's home during a fire" (children, stereo, blanket) that have properties similar to classic taxonomic object categories. This study had a large impact on the psychological study of concepts because ad hoc concepts violated the assumption of many researchers that categories are derived from overall physical similarity. Note, however, if one adopts the view that there is a rich ontology that includes such things as human intentions and that concepts reflect this structure, then one would predict the existence of structures such as Barsalou's ad hoc categories.

D. STRUCTURE-BASED UNIVERSALS

If one adopts the strong realist view I have argued for, then there are a number of interesting consequences. For example, if one assumes that concepts are reflecting a richly structured world, then, for individuals with similar sensory systems, there ought to be some strong similarities in their conceptual categories. Cross-cultural research comparing folk taxonomies with Western scientific taxonomies provides strong support for this hypothesis. Anthropologists and biologists (Berlin, 1973; Diamond, 1966; Atran, 1987) have found that there is remarkable agreement in the way biological organisms are classified across many diverse cultures.

One can probably even stretch the natural kinds argument to include our biological cousins. For example, Lorenz (1951) made the interesting observation that in studying the imprinting of young birds "we [have] never yet found the subject's responses irreversibly fixated on the individual that had induced the imprinting process, but only on the species of that individual" (p. 169). This, of course, suggests that biological species are a natural kind for both humans *and* birds.

E. PHYSICAL SIMILARITY AND THEORY-BASED CONCEPTS

Ruse (1971) argues that in the case of the biological species concept, physical similarity is embedded in a theory-based concept. He states, "These clear cut morphologically delimited groups correspond to reproductively delimited groups" (p. 370). He uses a psychological argument to back up his position and states,

> The reason why I feel justified in resting my case on the existence of such groups is simply that biologists and laymen alike do seem to have the ability to delimit the same groups of organisms on the basis of morphological characters. (p. 370)

Reed (1979) has made a somewhat similar argument. He states that the human sensory system has evolved to categorize other organisms and then states, "The reason why static, intuitive notions of similarity do work in systematics is that they approximate to the natural, evolutionary criteria" (p. 76). Caplan (1980) has also supported this view. He states, "The hidden 'essences' of species taxa are the genotypes and environments which produce the similarities of traits we observe among organisms" (p. 76).

Medin and Ortony (1989) also point out that surface similarity characteristics of instances are frequently useful guides to underlying properties.
However, they propose that this relationship is based on *psychological*
essentialism, not metaphysical essentialism. By "psychological essentialism" they mean that people operate *as if* objects have essences. However,
by placing the essences in psychology instead of in the world, they are in
the awkward position of not having a way to account for why essences
seem to work (e.g., why *is* it that one sample of the yellow metal gold melts
at about the same temperature as the next?).

F. CONSTRUCTIVISM AND A STRUCTURED ONTOLOGY

While one of the major themes of this article has been the impact of the
structure of the world on the structure of concepts, it is clear that one does
not want to think of concepts as simply mirroring the physical world. As
human beings acquire the enormous amount of knowledge that makes up
adult culture, concepts may be reorganized by being embedded in layer
after layer of new theory. For example, in the Greek language there are
two words for the star-like objects in the sky. One set of objects is called
"fixed stars" and another set is called "wandering stars." The fixed stars
are what we now call stars and the wandering stars are what we now call
planets. I think it is clear that these lexical items reflect an initial categorization of the star-like objects into those that appear to move with respect
to the others and those that do not. However, with the development of
Ptolemaic astronomy, these initial concepts were embedded in a theory of
epicycles; then later with the Copernican revolution they were embedded
in a different theory which even involved reclassifying the earth itself as an
instance of a "wandering star" or planet. Note that in each of these
frameworks the concept of *star* is relatively constrained. It appears that
constructivism's strong wedge is in the choice of the initial assumptions,
and after that there are numerous constraints on concepts.

G. THEORIES OF CONCEPT REPRESENTATION

The arguments for a rich ontology and the ability of humans to form
concepts for a wide range of entities appears to rule out many classes of
theories of concept representation. The review and analysis of the proposals presented earlier in this article strongly suggest that the following
types of proposals for the representation of concepts cannot be sufficient:
individual images, generic images, words, common physical elements,
formal objects, concepts as a single individual, Aristotelian concepts, and
all theories based on physical similarity alone. However, there may be
domains where some of these proposals play a role in an overall theory of

concepts. Proposals that attempt to capture family resemblance and natural kinds in terms of abstract ideas or theories seem more promising but
currently lack specification.

ACKNOWLEDGMENTS

I would like to thank the students in Psychology 493, Knowledge Representation, in
the Fall of 1991 for commenting on an very early version of this article. I also would like to
thank Ellen Brewer, Don Dulany, Doug Medin, Clark Chinn, Gregory Murphy, and Glenn
Nakamura for very helpful comments on a later version of this article (in fact, the last three
folk must not have seen me coming in time to run, and actually were forced to read two
different drafts).

REFERENCES

Aaron, R. I. (1955). *John Locke* (2nd ed.). Oxford: Clarendon.
Aaron, R. I. (1967). *The theory of universals* (2nd ed.). Oxford: Clarendon.
Archer, E. J. (1964). On verbalizations and concepts. In A. W. Melton (Ed.), *Categories of human learning* (pp. 237–241). New York: Academic Press.
Archer, E. J. (1966). The psychological nature of concepts. In H. J. Klausmeier & C. W. Harris (Eds.), *Analyses of concept learning* (pp. 37–49). New York: Academic Press.
Aristotle. (1952). *The works of Aristotle* (Vol. 1) (Great books of the Western world, Vol. 8). Chicago: Encyclopaedia Britannica.
Atran, S. (1987). Ordinary constraints on the semantics of living kinds: A commonsense alternative to recent treatments of natural-object terms. *Mind and Language, 2,* 27–63.
Augustine. (1952). *The confessions.* (Great books of the Western world, Vol. 18). Chicago: Encyclopaedia Britannica.
Bambrough, R. (1961). Universals and family resemblances. *Proceedings of the Aristotelian Society, 61,* 207–222.
Barsalou, L. W. (1983). Ad hoc categories. *Memory & Cognition, 11,* 211–227.
Barsalou, L. W. (1990). On the indistinguishability of exemplar memory and abstraction in category representation. In T. K. Srull & R. S. Wyer, Jr. (Eds.), *Advances in social cognition: Vol. 3. Content and process specificity in the effects of prior experiences* (pp. 61–88). Hillsdale, NJ: Erlbaum.
Berkeley, G. (1965). A treatise concerning the principles of human knowledge. In C. M. Turbayne (Ed.), *Principles, dialogues, and philosophical correspondence* (pp. 1–101). Indianapolis, IN: Bobbs-Merrill. (Original work published 1710)
Berlin, B. (1973). Folk systematics in relation to biological classification and nomenclature. *Annual Review of Ecology and Systematics, 4,* 259–271.
Bessey, C. E. (1908). The taxonomic aspect of the species question. *American Naturalist, 42,* 218–224.
Brewer, W. F. (1975). Memory for ideas: Synonym substitution. *Memory & Cognition, 3,* 458–464.
Brewer, W. F. (1986). What is autobiographical memory? In D. C. Rubin (Ed.), *Autobiographical memory* (pp. 25–49). Cambridge: Cambridge University Press.
Brewer, W. F., & Nakamura, G. V. (1984). The nature and functions of schemas. In R. S. Wyer, Jr. & T. K. Srull (Eds.), *Handbook of social cognition* (Vol. 1, pp. 119–160). Hillsdale, NJ: Erlbaum.

Brewer, W. F., & Pani, J. R. (1983). The structure of human memory. In G. H. Bower (Ed.), *The psychology of learning and motivation: Vol. 17* (pp. 1–38). New York: Academic Press.

Bruner, J. (1983). *In search of mind: Essays in autobiography.* New York: Harper & Row.

Bruner, J. S., Goodnow, J. J., & Austin, G. A. (1956). *A study of thinking.* New York: Wiley.

Buck, R. C., & Hull, D. L. (1966). The logical structure of the Linnaean hierarchy. *Systematic Zoology, 15,* 97–111.

Burma, B. H. (1949). The species concept: A semantic review. *Evolution, 3,* 369–370.

Burma, B. H. (1954). Reality, existence, and classification: A discussion of the species problem. *Madroño, 12,* 193–209.

Cain, A. J. (1958). Logic and memory in Linnaeus's system of taxonomy. *Proceedings of the Linnean Society of London, 169,* 144–163.

Caplan, A. L. (1980). Have species become déclassé? In P. D. Asquith & R. N. Giere (Eds.), *PSA 1980: Vol. 1* (pp. 71–82). East Lansing, MI: Philosophy of Science Association.

Darwin, C. (1952). *The origin of species by means of natural selection* (Great books of the Western world, Vol. 49). Chicago: Encyclopaedia Britannica. (Original work published 1859)

Davidson, J. F. (1954). A dephlogisticated species concept. *Madroño, 12,* 246–251.

Descartes, R. (1931). Meditations. In E. S. Haldane & G. R. T. Ross (Eds.), *The philosophical works of Descartes* (2 Vols.) (vol. 1, pp. 131–199). Cambridge: Cambridge University Press. (Original work published 1642)

Descartes, R. (1970). *Descartes: Philosophical letters.* Oxford: Clarendon. (Original work published 1641)

Diamond, J. M. (1966). Zoological classification system of a primitive people. *Science, 151,* 1102–1104.

Dobzhansky, T. (1935). A critique of the species concept in biology. *Philosophy of Science, 2,* 344–355.

Dobzhansky, T. (1937). *Genetics and the origin of species.* New York: Columbia University Press.

Dupré, J. (1981). Natural kinds and biological taxa. *Philosophical Review, 90,* 66–90.

Fisher, S. C. (1916). The process of generalizing abstraction; and its product, the general concept. *Psychological Monographs, 21*(2, Whole No. 90).

Galton, F. (1879, April 25). Generic images. *Proceedings of the Royal Institution of Great Britain, 9,* 161–170.

Ghiselin, M. T. (1974). A radical solution to the species problem. *Systematic Zoology, 23,* 536–544.

Ghiselin, M. T. (1977). On paradigms and the hypermodern species concept. *Systematic Zoology, 26,* 437–438.

Ghiselin, M. T. (1981). Categories, life, and thinking. *Behavioral and Brain Sciences, 4,* 269–283.

Gregg, J. R. (1950). Taxonomy, language and reality. *American Naturalist, 84,* 419–435.

Haldane, J. B. S. (1956). Can a species concept be justified? In P. C. Sylvester-Bradley (Ed.), *The species concept in palaeontology* (pp. 95–96). London: The Systematics Association.

Hempel, C. G. (1966). *Philosophy of natural science.* Englewood Cliffs, NJ: Prentice-Hall.

Herrnstein, R. J., & de Villiers, P. A. (1980). Fish as a natural category for people and pigeons. In G. H. Bower (Ed.), *The psychology of learning and motivation: Vol. 14* (pp. 59–95). New York: Academic Press.

Hobbes, T. (1952). *Leviathan.* (Great books of the Western world, Vol. 23). Chicago: Encyclopaedia Britannica. (Original work published 1651)

Hull, C. L. (1920). Quantitative aspects of the evolution of concepts. *Psychological Monographs, 28*(1, Whole No. 123).

Hull, D. L. (1965a). The effect of essentialism on taxonomy—Two thousand years of stasis: I. *British Journal for the Philosophy of Science, 15*, 314–326.

Hull, D. L. (1965b). The effect of essentialism on taxonomy—Two thousand years of stasis: II. *British Journal for the Philosophy of Science, 16*, 1–18.

Hull, D. L. (1970). Contemporary systematic philosophies. *Annual Review of Ecology and Systematics, 1*, 19–53. (Reprinted in M. Grene & E. Mendelsohn, Eds., 1976, *Topics in the philosophy of biology*, pp. 396–440, Dordrecht, Holland: D. Reidel)

Hull, D. L. (1976). Are species really individuals? *Systematic Zoology, 25*, 174–191.

Hull, D. L. (1978). A matter of individuality. *Philosophy of Science, 45*, 335–360.

Hume, D. (1978). *A treatise of human nature* (2nd ed.). Oxford: Clarendon. (Original work published 1739)

Johnson-Laird, P. N. (1980). Mental models in cognitive science. *Cognitive Science, 4*, 71–115.

Johnson-Laird, P. N., Herrmann, D. J., & Chaffin, R. (1984). Only connections: A critique of semantic networks. *Psychological Bulletin, 96*, 292–315.

Kendler, H. H. (1964). The concept of the concept. In A. W. Melton (Ed.), *Categories of human learning* (pp. 211–236). New York: Academic Press.

Kitts, D. B., & Kitts, D. J. (1979). Biological species as natural kinds. *Philosophy of Science, 46*, 613–622.

Locke, J. (1959). *An essay concerning human understanding* (2 Vols.). New York: Dover. (Original work published 1690)

Lorenz, K. Z. (1951). The role of Gestalt perception in animal and human behaviour. In L. L. Whyte (Ed.), *Aspects of form* (pp. 157–178). New York: Pellegrini & Cudahy.

Mayr, E. (1957). Species concepts and definitions. In E. Mayr (Ed.), *The species problem* (pp. 1–22). Washington, DC: American Association for the Advancement of Science.

Mayr, E. (1982). *The growth of biological thought*. Cambridge: Harvard University Press.

Medin, D., & Ortony, A. (1989). Psychological essentialism. In S. Vosniadou & A. Ortony (Eds.), *Similarity and analogical reasoning* (pp. 179–195). Cambridge: Cambridge University Press.

Medin, D. L., & Schaffer, M. M. (1978). Context theory of classification learning. *Psychological Review, 85*, 207–238.

Medin, D. L., & Smith, E. E. (1984). Concepts and concept formation. *Annual Review of Psychology, 35*, 113–138.

Mervis, C. B., & Rosch, E. (1981). Categorization of natural objects. *Annual Review of Psychology, 32.* 89–115.

Minsky, M. (1975). A framework for representing knowledge. In P. H. Winston (Ed.), *The psychology of computer vision* (pp. 211–277). New York: McGraw-Hill.

Murphy, G. L., & Medin, D. L. (1985). The role of theories in conceptual coherence. *Psychological Review, 92*, 289–316.

Osgood, C. E. (1953). *Method and theory in experimental psychology*. New York: Oxford University Press.

Paivio, A. (1971). *Imagery and verbal processes*. New York: Holt, Rinehart and Winston.

Platnick, N. I., & Nelson, G. (1981). The purposes of biological classification. In P. D. Asquith & I. Hacking (Eds.), *PSA 1978: Vol. 2* (pp. 117–129). East Lansing, MI: Philosophy of Science Association.

Posner, M. I. (1969). Abstraction and the process of recognition. In G. H. Bower & J. T. Spence (Eds.), *The psychology of learning and motivation: Vol. 3* (pp. 43–100). New York: Academic Press.

Posner, M. I., & Keele, S. W. (1968). On the genesis of abstract ideas. *Journal of Experimental Psychology, 77,* 353–363.

Putnam, H. (1970). Is semantics possible? In H. E. Kiefer & M. K. Munitz (Eds.), *Language, belief, and metaphysics* (pp. 50–63). Albany, NY: State University of New York Press.

Quine, W. V. O. (1960). *Word and object.* New York: Wiley.

Quine, W. V. (1969). Natural kinds. In N. Rescher (Ed.), *Essays in honor of Carl G. Hempel* (pp. 5–23). Dordrecht, Holland: D. Reidel.

Reed, E. S. (1979). The role of symmetry in Ghiselin's "Radical solution to the species problem." *Systematic Zoology, 28,* 71–78.

Reig, O. A. (1982). The reality of biological species: A conceptualist and a systemic approach. In L. J. Cohen, J. Los, H. Pfeiffer, & K.-P. Podewski (Eds.), *Logic, methodology and philosophy of science VI* (pp. 479–499). Amsterdam: North-Holland.

Rosch, E. H. (1973). On the internal structure of perceptual and semantic categories. In T. E. Moore (Ed.), *Cognitive development and the acquisition of language* (pp. 111–144). New York: Academic Press.

Rosch, E. (1978). Principles of categorization. In E. Rosch & B. B. Lloyd (Eds.), *Cognition and categorization* (pp. 27–48). Hillsdale, NJ: Erlbaum.

Rosch, E., & Mervis, C. B. (1975). Family resemblances: Studies in the internal structure of categories. *Cognitive Psychology, 7,* 573–605.

Rosch, E., Mervis, C. B., Gray, W. D., Johnson, D. M., & Boyes-Braem, P. (1976). Basic objects in natural categories. *Cognitive Psychology, 8,* 382–439.

Ross, D. (1964). *Aristotle.* London: Methuen.

Rumelhart, D. E. (1975). Notes on a schema for stories. In D. G. Bobrow & A. Collins (Eds.), *Representation and understanding* (pp. 211–236). New York: Academic Press.

Ruse, M. (1969). Definitions of species in biology. *British Journal for the Philosophy of Science, 20,* 97–119.

Ruse, M. (1971). The species problem: A reply to Hull. *British Journal for the Philosophy of Science, 22,* 369–371.

Ruse, M. (1988). *Philosophy of biology today.* Albany, NY: State University of New York Press.

Smith, L. B. (1981). Importance of the overall similarity of objects for adults' and children's classifications. *Journal of Experimental Psychology: Human Perception and Performance, 7,* 811–824.

Smoke, K. L. (1932). An objective study of concept formation. *Psychological Monographs, 42*(4, Whole No. 191).

Sokal, R. R., & Sneath, P. H. A. (1963). *Principles of numerical taxonomy.* San Francisco: W. H. Freeman.

Suppe, F. (Ed.). (1977). *The structure of scientific theories* (2nd ed.). Urbana, IL: University of Illinois Press.

Vosniadou, S., & Ortony, A. (Eds.). (1989). *Similarity and analogical reasoning.* Cambridge: Cambridge University Press.

Whewell, W. (1967). *The philosophy of the inductive sciences* (2 vols.). New York: Johnson Reprint. (Original work published 1847)

Wittgenstein, L. (1958). *Philosophical investigations* (G. E. M. Anscombe, Trans.) (2nd ed.). Oxford: Blackwell.

INDEX

CONTENTS OF RECENT VOLUMES

ISBN 0-12-543329-8

90040